The
Pocket
Commentary
of the Bible

THE BOOK OF
GENESIS

The
Pocket
Commentary
of the Bible

by

BASIL F. C. ATKINSON
M.A., Ph.D.

*Under Librarian of Cambridge
University*

THE BOOK OF
GENESIS

MOODY PRESS
820 NORTH LASALLE STREET
CHICAGO, 10. ILL.

This Commentary
is dedicated
to Members of the
Cambridge Inter-Collegiate Christian Union
past and present

FOREWORD

THE idea of this Commentary began in 1950 when discussing with the President of the Cambridge Inter-Collegiate Christian Union the need for exposition of the Scriptures and deeper knowledge of the Bible among students and teachers. The purpose of the Commentary is both Theological and Devotional, for I believe true theology and true devotion to be inextricably intertwined. The Commentary is designed to bring out the message of the Bible for Christians of today in the light of the Gospel. Its aim is not only to enable preachers and teachers to expound the Word, but to open the rich treasury of the Holy Scriptures to every reader.

As its title indicates, it is issued in parts that are easily handled and carried, and it is believed that these features will commend it to a very large number of people. Probably few readers recognize to the full, the wealth and profit to be obtained from a thorough understanding of the Scriptures, and this Commentary is issued in the hope that it may inspire a love of the deeper study of the Word.

I pray for wisdom, understanding and skill, as well as for life and health, that I may be able to carry out, as God designs, the work to which I have set my hand; and that the Commentary may be a blessing to all into whose hands it may come, the world over. I would like to thank interested friends for their encouragement and advice, also my Publisher, whose unbounded energy, and ingenious plans for the production of the work which he has sympathetically made his own, will I hope make the business side a success.

I thank the Heavenly Father with all my heart for entrusting me with this work, and ask the prayers of all readers, especially members of the C.I.C.C.U., that I may not fail in carrying out any purpose of blessing that God may have, through the Commentary.

BASIL F. C. ATKINSON.

Cambridge, January, 1954.

GOOD COMMENTARIES ON THE ENGLISH BIBLE

1560.   Geneva Bible, with most profitable annotations on all the hard places.

1649.   Authorised Version, with most profitable annotations upon all the hard places.

1651.   Annotations upon all the Books of the Old and New Testament. Good.

1700.   Poole (Matthew): Annotations upon the Holy Bible.

1761.   Henry (Matthew): Exposition on the Old and New Testament.

1770.   Dodd (William): Commentary.

1814.   Brown (John): Self-Interpreting Bible.

1815.   Royal Standard Devotional Family Bible.

1817.   Brown (John): Self-Interpreting Bible, revised by Thomas Raffles.

1817.   D'Oyly (G.) and Mant (R.): Bible with Notes.

1817.   Kershaw (J.): Bible with Notes selected from the Commentary of Matthew Henry.

1823.   Scott (T.): Bible with Notes. Good.

1824.   Boothroyd (B.): New Family Bible.

1825-7.   Williams (T.): Cottage Bible and Family Expositor.

1828.   Alexander (W.): Bible Illustrated with Notes.

1837.   Cobbin (I.): Condensed Commentary and Family Exposition of the Bible.

184-.   Benson (J.): Bible with Notes. Good.

1842.   Girdlestone (C.): Bible with Commentary arranged in Lectures. Good.

1842.   Hawker (R.): Commentary on the Bible. Very good.

1844.   Patrick, Lowth, Arnold, Whitby and Lowman: Critical Commentary and Paraphrase of Old and New Testament.

1846.   Cobbin (I.): Portable Commentary.

1853.   Shittler (R.): Domestic Commentary.

1857.   Campbell (J.): Bible with Notes.

1859.   Commentary wholly Biblical.

1861.   Jamieson (R.) and Bickersteth (E. H.): Devotional and Practical Commentary.

1866-70.   Jamieson (R.), Fausset (A. R.) and Brown (D.): Commentary.

1867.   Lee (J.): Bible Illustrations.

1868-80.   Lange (J. P.): Commentary, translated by P. Schaff.

1868.   Annotated Paragraph Bible.

1871-81.   Cook (F. C.): Speaker's Commentary.

1874.   Clarke (A.): Commentary, condensed by R. N. Young.

1875.   Wordsworth (C.): Bible with Notes and Introductions.

1878-82.   Blunt (J. H.): Annotated Bible.

1879-87.   Fuller (J. M.): Students' Commentary.

1880-96.   Spence (H. D. M.) and Exell (J. S.): Pulpit Commentary.

1885.   Ellicott (C. J.): Bp. of Gloucester: Commentary for Schools.

1887-1905.   Nicoll (W. R.): Expositor's Bible.

1901.   Parker (J.): Pulpit Bible.

1953.   New Bible Commentary (I.V.F.).

GOOD COMMENTARIES ON THE OLD TESTAMENT

1788-91.	Orton (J.): Exposition of the O.T., edited by R. Gentleman.
1810.	Gill (J.): Exposition of the O.T. Very good indeed.
1864.	Wordsworth (C.): Bible with Notes.
1875-92.	Preacher's Homiletical Commentary.
1876.	O.T. with Commentary.
1879-84.	Wordsworth (C.): Bible with Notes. New Edition.
1882-4.	Ellicott (C. J.): Bp. of Gloucester: O.T. Commentary. Good.

GOOD COMMENTARIES ON PART OF THE OLD TESTAMENT

1627.	Ainsworth (H.): Annotations on the Five Books of Moses. Very good.
1843.	Ainsworth (H.): Annotations on the Pentateuch. Very good.
1849.	Townsend (G.): Scriptural Communion with God. Good.
1643-6.	Jackson (A.): A Help for the Understanding of the Holy Scripture. Good.
1765-6.	Patrick (S.), Bp. of Ely: Commentary on the Historical Books of the O.T.

GOOD COMMENTARIES ON GENESIS

1578.	Calvin (J.): Commentary on Genesis, translated by T. Tymme. Superb.
1633.	Willet (A.): Hexapla in Genesim et Exodum.
1616.	Ainsworth (H.): Annotations upon Genesis. Very good.
1707.	Henry (M.): Exposition of the Five Books of Moses.
1835.	Sibthorpe (R. W.): Book of Genesis.
1841-3.	Blunt (H.): Family Exposition of the Pentateuch.
1868.	Lange (J. P.): Genesis, translated by T. Lewis and A. Gosman.
1877.	Inglis (J.): Notes on the Book of Genesis.
1882.	Dods (M.): Book of Genesis.
1885.	Wordsworth (C.): Genesis and Exodus.
1946.	Griffith Thomas (W. H.): Genesis: Devotional Commentary.

"He said unto them, Therefore every scribe which is instructed unto the Kingdom of Heaven, is like unto a man that is an householder, which bringeth forth out of his treasure things new and old" (Matthew 13. 52).

"Study to show thyself approved unto God — a workman that needeth not to be ashamed, rightly dividing the Word of Truth" (2 Timothy 2. 15).

GENESIS

THE Book of Genesis stands appropriately at the beginning of the
Bible. It starts at the beginning of time and of all things. An
account of creation (1. 1-2. 3) is followed by an account of the origins
of human life (2. 4-25) and this by the story of the fall of man (3).
These three first chapters are introductory to the whole Bible, and
form the foundation on which the story of redemption is built. The
story of Cain (4) is followed by a genealogy linking Adam with Noah
(5) and this by the account of the deluge (6-9). Chapter 10 consists
of a table of Noah's descendants and their distribution in the world.
Next comes the story of the tower of Babel (11. 1-9), and after this
a genealogy connecting Shem with Abraham (11. 10-26).

The whole of the rest of the book is occupied with the lives of
four generations of the patriarchs beginning with the call of Abram
(11. 27-12. 5) and ending with the death of Joseph (50. 26). Theirs
was the family chosen by God to be the source of the nation of Israel,
from whom Christ the Saviour of the world was to spring. The book
covers thousands of years. It reveals God as Creator and Moral Being
concerned with righteousness. It shows us the moral nature of man,
and it begins the story of the outworking of God's purpose of redemption in the history of the human race. It provides us with much
devotional material in the account of the spiritual lives of the individual patriarchs and like every other book of the Old Testament it is
full of pictures of Christ and the Gospel.

The book is anonymous. Its name *Genesis* is Greek and means
Origins. It was given to it when it was translated from Hebrew into
Greek by Jews of Alexandria in Egypt in the third century B.C. The
name was probably the translation of the Hebrew name of the book,
Book of Creation. Jewish and Christian tradition made Moses the
author. Possibly, however, at least as far as the end of Chapter 38,
the book antedated Moses. It is divided into twelve sections, which
are separated from each other by the formula, ' These are the generations of . . . ' (see 2. 4; 5. 1; 6. 9; 10. 1; 11. 10; 11. 27; 25. 12;
25. 19; 36. 1; 36. 9; 37. 2). It is usually thought that the formula
heads the section that follows it, though it is possible that it concludes
that which precedes. Possibly each of these sections was written separately at a time immediately subsequent to the events that it narrates
and added to the preceding ones to form a growing collection.

It is even possible that the earliest sections were written originally
in the Sumerian language. In the earliest chapters of the book a few
words of Sumerian origin occur. Thus the collection would be handed

down in the family of the patriarchs, until it reached the hands of Moses, who perhaps translated it into classical Hebrew and used it as an introduction to his written Law. Alternatively the book may represent an inspired Hebrew abstract made by Moses from earlier documents, which were originally fuller.

God has not answered for us the question of authorship, and it is best to be content with the anonymity in which He has left it. We know that behind Moses or any earlier human authors stands God the Holy Ghost, Who with this book has opened His revelation in the Bible. It is He Who has given unity to the book as a whole and has set it in its place in the unity of the entire Bible.

CHAPTER 1

IN this chapter we have the account of creation. Verse 1 tells us the fact of creation, verse 2 describes the condition of the earth when first created, verses 3-31 are an account of the process of creation, which is set before us as orderly and gradual, occupying six periods called ' days '. The section is continued over chapter 2. 1-3, where it is rounded off with a statement of the completion of creation.

VERSE 1. The opening words of the Bible tell us that time, the world and all life, as we know it, had a *beginning*. Once no universe existed. At the outset God's revelation sweeps away the idea that the universe has existed for ever. *God* is presented to us primarily as creator. The existence of God is not proved. His existence is not even stated, though it is implied in the statement of His activity. We begin with God. ' Of Him . . . are all things ' (Rom. 11. 36). This is the only place where any right view of life can begin and the only foundation on which right moral conduct can be built. We sinners generally begin with ourselves, at the circumference instead of at the centre. This naturally produces confused thinking and irresponsible conduct. As the Scriptures begin with God and the world begins with God, so ought God to be the fountain-head of our individual lives. Is God first in our lives?

The opening statement of the Bible relates not to God's existence, but to His activity. This sets the key for the view of God that we shall find throughout the Bible. It is the record of His acts. God is always acting towards us and for us. His fundamental action is essentially creation. He is always making something new, calling some new thing into existence. Thus, day by day He renews His people's spiritual lives, and continually by the Gospel He is creating spiritual life in dead souls. One day He will create a new creation.

This verse answers the question, when did God create? The answer is, In the beginning of time and of all things. How did God create? This chapter as a whole, by describing the process, answers the questions to a limited extent. But we never get, and should never expect, any real answer to the question *how?* in relation to the activity of God. His activity, like His Being and His power, are incomprehensible to us, except in so far as He has chosen to reveal them. Why did God create? The answer is found in Rev. 4. 11. Creation is for God's pleasure. This at once gives meaning and direction to our own lives. We are created for God's pleasure, and we ought to live for it. It is a wonderful thing also to remember that creation, so far as personal beings are concerned, was an act of Love. In some sense, which we can never fully fathom, the creation of personal beings with the power of moral choice set limits to the sovereignty of God. By creative acts God limited Himself in love. Creation itself set up that tension between the sovereignty of God and the free will of the creature, of which the evangelist is acutely aware.

The objects of God's creation were *the heaven and the earth,* that is to say, the whole universe invisible and visible, the astronomical universe with its distances that makes the brain reel, and the equally immense field of the microscope, known only to man through the magnifying instruments that his skill has constructed. Beyond both these and outside their dimensions is the eternal world of spiritual realities, in which live the angels in countless thousands, beings superior to man. All this the *heaven* includes. The *earth,* whose astronomical insignificance we know, is mentioned alongside the *heaven* because the Bible is written for man in language relative to man and intelligible to him, in the language that he himself speaks. It always takes the point of view of man. The emphasis of the word *earth* is not upon what we know as the planet, but rather upon the land, as opposed to the sky on one hand and the sea on the other.

VERSE 2. After the first sentence the account of creation becomes greatly concentrated. Our attention is narrowed to be fixed upon the *earth.* Modern astronomical knowledge gives us some conception of the immense extent of this concentration, and when we realise that the word *heaven* includes the worlds of angels and other spiritual beings, the extent of the concentration becomes immeasurable. It is the first step in a process of continuous narrowing. The purpose of God becomes concentrated, as we read the Bible, upon a single nation, then upon a single family within it, and finally upon a lonely sublime individual figure hanging in anguish on Calvary's Cross. There the purpose widens again step by step, till it finally embraces a whole creation, a new heaven and a new earth.

A wide range of modern interpreters have explained the first sentence of this verse to mean that the earth was not originally in the condition here described. They point out that the Hebrew verb is not a simple verb *to be,* but rather corresponds to Greek *egeneto,* and may be translated 'became'. They believe that between verses 1 and 2 a judicial catastrophe took place, and that in verse 2 the earth is introduced to us in the condition into which it fell as the result of a tremendous cataclysm. They point to the words of Isa. 45. 18, 'He created it not in vain', where the words 'in vain' represent the same Hebrew word *tohu,* as do the words 'without form' here. In favour of this view is perhaps the point of parallel seen here with the work of the Spirit of God upon a soul in the darkness of sin preparatory to beginning His new creation within it. That soul is a fallen soul. Does not this verse then describe a fallen world? The best known and probably the original advocate of this view was G. H. Pember in the nineteenth century, followed more recently by G. H. Lang, and at the present day by L. Merson Davies.

This view of the relationship of verses 1 and 2 seem however rather forced. We might translate the Hebrew verb as 'came into being'. The statement in Isa. 45. 18 refers to God's ultimate purpose in creation, not to the condition in which it came into being. Again the parallel with the work of the Spirit upon the individual soul goes deeper than is indicated above. The soul is brought from death to life, from a condition in which, relative to eternal life, it does not exist at all. Pember's view causes a violent wrench in the continuity of the chapter, which unjustifiably breaks the thread of the narrative.

The force of the two adjectives that here describe the earth is that the earth was at the time uninhabited and there was no life upon it. Astronomically this may point to a gaseous or fluid condition. The earth was wrapped in darkness, and the mention of the *deep* seems to imply that it was covered with water. The parallel with God's creative act of grace in the regeneration of the sinner, which is found throughout this chapter, begins with this verse. The natural man in his sinful fallen state is *without form*. His life is purposeless, unrelated to the aim of God in making him, and unrecognisable as formed in the image of God. He is also *void*, that is to say empty, without faith, without love, without hope, without God, indeed without real manhood. His life is full of *darkness*. Sin is spiritual darkness. He knows nothing of the light of life. He is blind and groping. In the life of the natural man this darkness is *upon the face of the deep*. ' The wicked are like the troubled sea, whose waters cast up mire and dirt ' (Isa. 57. 20).

In this primeval state intervenes the ' *Spirit of God* '. This is the third Person of the Holy Trinity, present with the first and second Persons in the process of creation. He is seen in the Old Testament inspiring the prophets. In the New He descends upon Jesus at the time of His baptism to equip Him for His ministry, and after the Lord's death and resurrection He comes on the day of Pentecost to indwell and fill the whole of redeemed humanity. It is He that works upon the sinner's heart while still in darkness and death, to convict him of sin and point him to the Saviour. So here He moves *upon the face of the waters*. He does not indwell them. He is not within the world, He is outside it, moving over it. In the same way He is not within the sinner till the moment of conversion. He is working upon him, and the heart which is spiritually dead is no more conscious of His working, however much it may feel strange external currents of power, than were the waters of primeval earth. Yet this movement may be presumed to have had some effect. We may see it as a

cooling, a shaping, a preparation. Throughout the unconverted life of the elect the Spirit is active in such a way as this. His work begins in the womb. (Gal. 1. 15).

VERSE 3. The Jewish eleventh-century commentator Rashi reads verses 1-3 as follows: he places ' when ' before ' God ' in verse 1, and begins verse 2 with ' when ' instead of ' and '. The Hebrew will bear this construction, which makes the creation of light the first act of all creation. Under it, however, the interpretation of verse 2 is awkward, as it is implied that the state of the earth there described was antecedent to creation. This does not seem possible.

With verse 2 begins the first step in the process by which the earth was brought from primeval darkness and chaos to be the dwelling-place of man. It should be carefully noted that this process applies only to the earth. The account of it is written from the point of view of an imaginary person standing on the surface of the earth. It is also worth noting that in no circumstances could this process have become known to any human being first hand. It must be the subject of a revelation from God, or it must be completely worthless because if not revealed it could only arise in the imagination of man.

The whole process consists in a series of acts of God, which are described as words of command. ' By the word of the Lord were the heavens made ' (Ps. 33. 6). The word spoken by God is pictured as possessing creative power. Some of the miracles of the Lord Jesus Christ provide a parallel to this, for example, the healing of the man with the withered hand, where the command to stretch forth the hand supplied the power for obedience (Mt. 12. 13). We may ask what exactly is intended by the words *God said*. Is it legitimate to use such language of God? The answer is that we have no other language to use. The first act of God mentioned in verse 1 is an act that He alone can perform. Man cannot create in the literal sense of the word. Because this is an act which God alone can perform, there is a mystery about its meaning that can never be fully solved. The act itself is supernatural. Saying is not in itself supernatural. It is an act of man, but it is used to describe a corresponding act of God in the supernatural sphere. From this verse on throughout the Bible the acts and attributes of God are described in language which means literally the corresponding acts and attributes of man. The technical name for this is anthropomorphism. Critics have called it crude. It is not so. No act or attribute of God can be described at all except in this language. It is the mark of pure Israelite monotheism in the face of surrounding heathenism, where false gods were often described in terms of the animal creation. It is man that is made in the image of the true and living God.

The first movement of God's creative power towards the earth was the bringing of *light* into being. The light may have come direct from the Divine throne, or it may have been light from distant stars, or it may have been due to what are now called cosmic rays, or it may have been the light of the sun, not yet distinguishable as an object in the heavens through the vapours encircling the cooling earth. In the same way, the first step in spiritual creation of the individual is for God to shine in his heart (2 Cor. 4. 6). The impression given by our verse is that the primeval *light* shone out instantaneously when God's Word was spoken, though it is possible that the words cover a more gradual process. It is certain that in the spiritual creation of the individual there is a moment when the soul passes from darkness to light, from death to life. This light of life is the foundation of spiritual life.

VERSE 4. The word *saw* is proper to man or to any creature with eyes. It is used of God as the word 'said' is used in verse 3. *God saw the light.* Man can see objects with the aid of

light. God can see the light itself, and not only see it but form an estimate of it. To see that it was good means to take pleasure in it. (Rev. 4. 11). What could it be but good, coming, as it did, from the hand of God? Here we see the Creator in the pleasure of His work, a pleasure that on a low and finite scale man, even fallen man, can also know.

The simplest interpretation of the second sentence of this verse is that God caused an alternation of light and darkness. This would be caused by the ordinary rotation of the earth, and the statement lends strength to the view that the light mentioned in verse 3 was the light of the sun.

VERSE 5. When, why, and to whom did *God* call *the light and the darkness* by these names? Did He do so in the secret of His own infinite mind? No, it would be unnecessary. God does not need human names by which to call the things that He has created. Did He do so to angels assumed to be watching the creation of the earth? Perhaps, but probably not. The names *Day* and *Night* are human names, words in a human language. There seems no reason why a conversation with angels should be recorded. The most natural inference is that God used these terms when making His revelation of the facts of creation to the man, to whom He first made it. This could not have been Moses, as the names long antedated him. The natural meaning is that the terms were given by God to the first man. This means that we have here in this chapter the oldest story in the world. How soon it was written down we cannot tell. It may have been handed down orally for generations, but it seems to be the story of the first man. The use here of the Hebrew terms *Day* and *Night* does not mean that the terms first used were Hebrew. The Hebrew is a translation of an older language, perhaps Sumerian, in which the terms may have been translated from an older language still. This sentence seems also to imply that the origin of the human language was at least partially Divine. God gave man at least some of His vocabulary.

The alternation of day and night, essential for the proper functioning of nature in the present world, presents a contrast to the eternal world to come. There there is no night (Rev. 21. 25; 22. 5), but one long day without alternations (Zech. 14. 7). The function of alternation is partly to de-limit time, but the constant return of darkness serves to remind man that he does not live in the final or perfect world. The alternation is a constant reminder, from which no one can escape, of the contrast between good and evil. It is one among the indications which go to show that nature in the present world was so arranged by the Creator as to provide a number of moral lessons.

The last sentence of the verse may be alternatively, and perhaps more accurately, rendered, ' And there was evening and there was morning, one day.' The evening is first mentioned because the Hebrew day began with the evening at sunset and ran till the following sunset. The close connection of this mark of time with the calling by God of the names of light and darkness may indicate that the account of creation by day by day during a literal week of seven days of twenty-four hours each. But this cannot be the only meaning of this primitive time mark, even if it is legitimate interpretation at all. The week as a period, ending with the sabbath, is somehow intimately woven with the period of creation. It is noteworthy that the week is an artificial time period. It is not, like the year and month, created by the movements of the heavenly bodies. While it may well be that the rest of every seventh day is beneficial, or even necessary, for both man and beast, it is improbable that early man would have found this fact so vital a part of his experience, as to have driven him to mark off the week as the most essential part of his calendar. The only adequate explanation of the hold obtained by the week in

the life of man is that it was religious and primitive in origin. The Bible implies that it was given to man as a microscopic picture and permanent reminder of the process of creation. The last sentence of verse 5 may thus be interpreted in three ways: (1) the *day* is a literal day, and the picture is put for the reality that it illustrates; (2) ' evening ' and ' morning ' mean ' beginning ' and ' end ' as we talk of the ' morning of the year ', or ' evening of life '; (3) the meaning may be that evening and morning followed one another continually on and on through an immense period of the process of creation. God's day is to man of immense length. See Ps. 90. 4, where we can scarcely take ' a thousand years ' in an exact sense. They rather mean an immeasurably long period of time, as when a child speaks of ' a hundred miles '. II Pet. 3. 8 provides an additional indication that we are dealing here in creation with long periods of time. Our Lord's words in Jo. 5. 17, spoken to justify a work of mercy on the sabbath, seem to imply that the present time, in which the Father is working in redemptive mercy, is for Him a continual sabbath. If so, it is the sabbath following the ' week ' of creation, the days of which are likely to have been long periods also.

VERSE 6. The second day is marked by division. The word ' firmament ' giving the impression of a solid roof, is derived from Latin *firmamentum*, which is a translation of the Greek *stereoma*. The Hebrew word means *expanse*. The *waters* mentioned are the same as those in verse 2. This verse probably refers to the earth's atmosphere. Division, or separation, forms an early part of the Holy Spirit's work in the regenerate soul after it has been brought from darkness to light. The Spirit teaches separation from sin and from the world, and a deep and definite line of demarcation passes through the inner being of every regenerate person, dividing the spirit, or new nature, from the soul, or old nature. Separation from all that displeases God is one of the greatest factors in holiness.

VERSE 7. The word *made* not only implies a process, but also, in contrast to the term *created,* that the firmament was made out of previously existing materials. This may apply to the atmosphere. *The waters under the firmament* include the oceans. *The waters above the firmament* seem to mean the clouds. The last sentence of this verse occurs in the Septuagint (the Greek version of the Old Testament made in the third century B.C.) at the end of verse 6. Wherever it stands, it tells us of the perfect fulfilment of God's purpose without hindrance or frustration. What God intended came to pass. This is the case with all His purposes and promises, whether of redemption or creation. He, who foreknew His people predestinated them to be conformed to the image of His Son. He who predestinated them called them. He also justified those whom He called and glorified those whom He justified. (Rom. 8. 29, 30). It will not be long before we look back on this purpose and say ' And it was so.'

VERSE 8. On the words *God called* see on verse 5. The word *Heaven* in this verse has not the same meaning as in verse 1. There we must believe it to include the whole astronomical universe and probably also the unseen spiritual world. Here it seems to be confined to the earth's atmosphere. The double sense is natural. The creation is described from the point of view of earth, and to this day we speak of the atmosphere as well as the universe of stars as the sky. In Hebrew, as in Greek, a single word covered the meanings of our two words ' sky ' and ' heaven '. On the last sentence of this verse see on verse 5.

It is noteworthy that in the description of the second day alone of all the days the words ' God saw that it was good ', are omitted (contrast

verses 4, 12, 18, 21, 25). It has been suggested that the reason lies in the fact that the firmament then was, or subsequently became, the abode of the devil and his angels (see Eph. 2. 2). This explanation however seems inconsistent with the statement of verse 31 of this chapter. Perhaps the reason is that all that was made on the second day was an expanse. Nothing actually new is described as having been created or made. The work of the second day was merely an arrangement.

VERSE 9. The restraining hand of God was laid upon the water. Something of this process, by which the dry land was forced by violent convulsive movements upwards through the water, is known to geologists. On the last sentence of this verse see on verse 7.

VERSE 10. *God called.* See on verse 5. *Seas.* In the eternal world there will be no more sea (Rev. 21. 1). The sea therefore, like the alternating darkness, is another sign of the imperfection of the present world. This life is a school, and nature has been constructed to teach moral lessons. The impression given by the sea, in spite of its beauty and attraction, is that of lack of rest. It is a picture of the heart of the wicked (Isa. 57. 20), and its waves and billows are a picture of the wrath of God (Jo. 2. 3; Ps. 42. 7). *God saw that it was good.* See on verse 4.

VERSE 11. This short verse describes and conceals a miracle of nature. The expression *Let the earth bring forth* implies that the Creator had placed within the ground the potentialities of plant life. All vegetation is dependent upon the soil. The soil is the picture of the human heart. (Mt. 13. 3-9; 19-23; Heb. 6. 7). The Word of God is sown in the heart. If received by faith, it brings forth fruit to the glory of God. The fruit consists of the ninefold virtues of the Spirit (Gal. 5. 22). We have here therefore a further parallel between the creation of the natural world and the creation of the spiritual life in the sinner's heart. One of the purposes of regeneration is that the regenerate soul should bring forth fruit in the worship and service of God (Rom. 7. 4).

Three kinds of vegetation are named here. The first is *grass*. Grass is a picture of the fallen human life in the flesh (Isa. 40. 6-8). It is short lived and withers away. Even in England a rainless summer will turn the grass brown, and the withering of the grass is a more frequent phenomenon in the hotter eastern countries. In the presence of grass widespread through the world we find the occasion for a further moral lesson. It should speak to us of death, and remind us that life is short. The second kind of vegetation is *herb*. This is edible (verse 29). It is brought forth by the regenerate heart, when that heart is nourished by showers of Divine blessing (Heb. 6. 7). It is perhaps a picture of the lowlier more practical service that most Christians are called upon to give. It can nourish and build up others. It yields seed. Thus it has the power to increase itself and perhaps to sow itself in the hearts of others. The third kind is the *tree*. This is the picture of the regenerate person (Jer. 17. 8; Ps. 1. 3), and yields the fruit of the Spirit.

The word *tree* is a generic term. Many kinds were created. Each brings forth fruit *after his kind*, or ' in the several kinds thereof '. Each kind is needed to make up the variety and beauty of creation. So in the new creation God needs every one of His regenerate children. *It was so*. See on verse 7.

VERSE 12. This verse describes the exact fulfilment of the purpose of God which was expressed in verse 11. Every detail happened exactly as God decreed. Except for the necessary grammatical changes one verse repeats the other almost exactly. Here is a wonderful correspondence between command and fulfilment. God's inanimate creation can render Him

this perfect obedience. It remains for us moral beings, whose obedience is so much more valuable, to rebel and refuse and complain. In heaven, when the Holy Spirit has finished His work in our hearts, we too shall be able to render this perfect obedience. God give us grace to render it now in this life up to the very last point at which it is possible for saved sinners.

On the last sentence of the verse see on verse 4.

VERSE 13. See on verse 5.

VERSE 14. With this verse we reach the fourth day. If we divide the six days into two parts of three days each, we shall see that there is a correspondence in the two sections. Each one deals first with light, next with water, and finally with dry land. This being so, it has sometimes been suggested that with the fourth day we return to the point at which verse 3 begins and pass over the same ground again from another viewpoint and in greater detail. This however seems unlikely. It would rule out the interpretation of the days as actual periods of creation and oblige us to regard them as no more than literal days of a week in the lifetime of the man to whom the revelation of creation was made. The second series of days, though, it is true, dealing with the same series in the same order as the first, carries us much further in the process of creation. If we think of the description of creation as being made from the point of view of an imaginary watcher standing upon the surface of the earth, the appearance of the heavenly bodies on the fourth day presents no difficulty. It is not till then that they would be seen through the thick clouds which surrounded the cooling earth.

The word *firmament* has a wider meaning in this verse than it had in verses 6 and 7. There it seems to be confined to the earth's atmosphere. Here it refers to the whole expanse of sky visible from the earth's surface. The purpose of the heavenly bodies

was *to divide the day from the night*.
This they had been doing during the
whole history of the earth (verse 4),
and the repetition of the fact here
again strengthens the view that the
light of verses 3 and 4 has reference
to the earth and is the light of the
sun. During the whole description
of the fourth day the heavenly bodies
are pictured as having a function in
relation to the earth. Astronomically
the sun is the centre of a system in
which the earth plays a small part.
Yet it is the earth that sustains life,
including human life, and not the
sun. Furthermore the earth was to
be one day the scene of the incarnation of the Son of God. The earth,
not the sun, is the centre of God's
purpose of redemption, a purpose
that relates not to man only, but to
the whole creation. The Bible is
therefore right in describing the functions of the heavenly bodies as relative to the earth. We watch a train
passing along a railway line. It is
the train that we see, the train that
determines the motion and direction
of the passengers within it. Yet the
train exists for the passenger, and
apart from the passenger there is no
reason for its existence. The relation
of the sun to the earth is similar.

The purpose of the heavenly bodies
is fourfold. First they are to be for
signs. This is intelligible in an agricultural community. The position of
the sun gives the sign for sowing or
ploughing, which depend upon the
seasons. Farmers still speak of spring
sowing or autumn sowing. Thus the
heavenly bodies provide guidance to
the farmer. Secondly they are to be
seasons. The revolution of the earth
round the sun causes the alternation
of the seasons, necessary for the
healthy growth of crops and probably necessary for the health of
animals and men. Thirdly they are
to be for *days*. The rotation of the
earth, causing the apparent rising and
setting of the sun, brings about the
alternation of day and night with its
fundamental influence upon human
and animal life and its deeper moral
message (see verse 5). Lastly the

heavenly bodies are to determine
years. The round of seasons brings
about the solar year, one revolution
of the earth, by which we reckon
years in modern times. The Hebrews
and others among the ancients reckoned the years by the moon, twelve
revolutions of the moon making up
their year with an extra month inserted at intervals to make agreement
with the sun and seasons. The moon
has its influence also on the seasons,
its times of rising at the full being
more even at the equinox, so that it
provides light for gathering in the
harvest.

VERSE 15. This verse tells us the
second, and perhaps more obvious,
function of the heavenly bodies,
which is to give light. In the eternal
world the Lord Jesus Christ is Himself the Sun of righteousness (Mal. 4.
2), giving the light of life to His
people's hearts. Do we submit to His
regular guidance of our lives? Is He
to us for signs of blessing and glory
in the world to come, for seasons of
refreshing from the presence of the
Lord, for days of happy service and
years of growth in grace? If He is
the Sun, His church below is like the
moon, reflecting His light in the dark
world (Phil. 2. 15, 16). We know
now, as the ancients probably did not,
that the moon has no light of her
own, but reflects that of the sun. In
the eternal world there will be no
mediated light. The sun and moon
will have passed away. The glory of
God and the Lamb Himself will be
the source of light there. The heavenly bodies may therefore speak to us
of the need of mediation and so remind us that God's light and life can
only come to us through Jesus Christ.
It was so. See on verse 7.

VERSE 16. The word ' made ' implies
that the heavenly bodies were formed
out of material already existing, and
this agrees with present astronomical
theory. *Two great lights.* This may
be translated ' *The* two great lights '.
It has been pointed out that this
chapter is perhaps the only document

surviving in which reference is made to the sun and moon without calling them by their names. This fact may perhaps indicate that the chapter is of very great antiquity, first written or spoken before the heavenly bodies were given their names. We cannot press this however in view of the occurrence of the word 'stars' at the end of the verse.

To rule. The existence and length of the day are entirely dependent on the sun. The length of the night is not dependent on the moon, but its nature is determined by it. Even modern artificial lighting has not yet quite abolished the dependence of the country people on the moon. *The stars also.* The stars are mentioned here because with the sun and moon they became visible at this point in the process of creation to the imaginary figure watching from the standpoint of the surface of the earth. They had all been actually *made* at far distant periods in the ages of the past.

Verse 17. The stars and sun, if not the moon, may have had other functions and long histories, but they were given a place in the firmament, that is to say, they were set in relation to the earth, for definite purposes that had to do with the earth. In this and the following verse three of the four functions of the heavenly bodies are repeated in a different, and more natural, order. In this verse they are said *to give light,* illustrating Christ as the giver of life to His people.

Verse 18. The heavenly bodies are here shown to illustrate Christ as the guide and controller of His people's lives, and secondly (thirdly in the complete series) as the final judge between light and darkness, that is to say, between the righteous and the wicked.

In the sphere of the new creation the work of the fourth day expresses the work of the Spirit in introducing discipline and regular service into the life of the regenerate. Every child of God is called to service, as is clear from the account of the conversion of

the apostle Paul (Acts 26. 16-18), and is bound to submit himself through the Spirit's activity in his heart to Christ as his King and Master.

God saw that it was good. See on verse 4.

Verse 19. See on verse 5.

Verse 20. The fifth day like the second deals with the *waters. Let the waters bring forth abundantly the moving creature that hath life.* In our version we have a parallel expression to that in verse 11. There it was implied that there may perhaps have been potentialities in the earth, from which plant life could spring. It was thus possible, though not certain, that the primitive material of the universe had the potentiality of developing into electrons, they into atoms, they into molecules, and they possibly, given suitable complex combinations, into vegetable life. Here in this verse we have a different picture. The original Hebrew says literally, ' Let the waters swarm with a swarm of living souls '. There is no question here of a development of animal life out of water. The conception brought before us is of a sudden filling of the oceans with living creatures of a thousand kinds by the word and act of God. This is borne out by the next verse, as we shall see. Biological science seems to have satisfied itself in agreement with this verse that animal life began in the sea.

Moving. Here lies the distinction between animal life and plant life. Plants are fixed to one spot and are rooted in the earth. Animals are free to move about within the limits that God has fixed for them.

Creature that hath life. The Hebrew says, ' living soul '. Here is the first occurrence of the great Hebrew word *nephesh,* meaning ' soul ', but often translated ' life ', ' creature ', or even ' body '. This word with its Greek equivalent *psuche* always lies behind the English word ' soul ' in the Bible. The Biblical meaning of ' soul ' is different from the meaning in common use. Our sense of 'soul' is derived from the Greeks, chiefly from the great fourth-century thinker and teacher, Plato, who regarded the soul as a distinct immaterial and immortal entity imprisoned in the body and released from it at death, and carrying the actual human personality. It was in this sense that Plato and the Greeks used the word *psuche*. In the New Testament however, as in the Septuagint version of the Old Testament, the Greek word, like other prominent terms, is used as the equivalent of the Hebrew word which it translates. The words may be Greek, but the conception is Hebrew. The Old Testament knows nothing of a soul in the Platonic sense. The word 'nephesh' means a living animal entity. It may be applied to a human being, in which case it means 'person', a sense in which it may still sometimes be used in English. It may equally, as in this verse, be applied to an animal, in which case it means 'creature'. There is a great difference between a man and an animal, but this difference does not lie in the possession by the one, but not by the other, of a soul. Both are souls, their soul consisting in the natural or animal life, which both in their separate spheres and in greatly different quality enjoy.

Fowl that may fly. In our version the implication is that the waters brought forth the fowl as well as the other creatures. A better translation is, 'Let fowl fly.' At the word of God the air was filled with birds, as the waters had been filled with sea-creatures. *In the open firmament of heaven.* The Hebrew says, 'In the face of the firmament of heaven'. This may mean either *on its surface,* or *before* it. In either case it implies what is literally true, that the birds fly in that part of the great expanse of heaven that is immediately *above the earth*.

VERSE 21. *Created*. This is the second of three occasions on which this word is used in this chapter (see verses 1, 27). It irresistibly suggests

a new departure, implying that animal life was separately created by God and had no generic connection with the plant life that preceded it. *Whales*. These are not the sea-animals scientifically classified today as whales, but sea - monsters of various kinds. *Creature*: Hebrew *nephesh*, meaning 'soul' (see on verse 20). *Which the waters brought forth abundantly.* The Hebrew says literally, 'wherewith the waters swarmed' (see on verse 20). The sea-creatures and the birds were each created 'after his kind'. This implies that a variety of separate creations was made, and that the 'kinds' could not and cannot interbreed. We cannot tell whether the separately created 'kinds' were families, genera or species, or whether they overlapped modern scientific classification. On the last sentence see on verse 4.

VERSE 22. Happy birds and fish to be the first to be blessed by God. This first reference to blessing in the Bible connects it with increase. God blesses all His creatures from the first humble animal forms swarming in the sea to the people of His love and choice. He has 'blessed us with all spiritual blessings in the heavenly places in Christ Jesus' (Eph. 1. 3). This means that He has made us fruitful in the fruit of the Spirit, in the knowledge of Christ, and in the increase of the church. The animals were unconscious of God's blessing. It was seen at work in their lives. So were we unconscious of the blessing given us before the world began. God's blessing gave these creatures the power of reproduction. He had made His world to be inhabited and He intended that the sea should be filled with fish and the air stocked with birds. God's lavish blessing and royal bounty are seen in the words, 'fruitful', 'multiply', and 'fill'.

The work of the Spirit in the regenerate heart that is parallel to the work of the fifth day is a bestowal of blessing in soul-winning. Every child of God is called upon to serve God in the winning of others, and has God's gifts bestowed upon him to that end, whether it be a gift of direct evangelisation, public or personal, or that of building up and feeding the church to fit it for such service.

Verse 23. See on verse 5.

Verse 24. The language of verse 11 is repeated in this verse. As in that verse, it is possible to think of a process similar to that suggested in the case of plant life. It is possible, though not certain, that the primitive material of the universe was created with the potentialities of development into electrons, they into atoms, they into molecules, and they in suitable circumstances into life. There is no hint in this verse of generic connection between the beasts and cattle on the one hand, and the sea-creatures and the birds of the fifth day on the other. Had such an idea been intended, we might have expected the words, 'Let the fowl bring forth'. The implication of the verse seems to be that the land animals had a different origin from the fish and birds, but not necessarily like them direct from the hand of God. They are not said to have been directly created. They came from God, but perhaps by a process of development.

Living creature: living souls (see on verse 20). Like the fish and birds the land animals appeared after their kind, in a variety of different forms, separated from each other by strict lines of demarcation. The classification of the animals does not follow modern scientific lines, which shows that the modern classification has nothing fundamental or absolute about it. They are classified along phenomenal lines and according to their relationship to man, domestic animals, reptiles and smaller creeping things and wild beasts. *It was so*. See on verse 7.

Verse 25. *Made*. The word 'created' is not used. This confirms the impression given by verse 24, that the land animals sprang, either by descent or otherwise, from material which

was in existence before. On the other hand no more need perhaps be meant than that the land animals were not the earliest forms of animal life. When animal life was new, the word ' create ' is suitable, not so when it merely appeared under different, if higher, forms.

God saw that it was good. See on verse 4.

Verse 26. The first question that arises in this verse is to whom was God speaking when He said, *Let us make man*. There is only one answer that fits both the words, *God said*, and the plural pronoun, *US*. It is true that the ordinary word for God in Hebrew, *Elohim*, which is used throughout this chapter, is plural in form, but it takes a singular verb. The pronoun *US* therefore suggests in itself a plurality of persons. The verse is one of the most outstanding foreshadowings in the Old Testament of the doctrine of the Trinity in Unity. One Person of the Godhead is addressing another.

The first word used in connection with the bringing of man into being is the word *make*. This suggests that material already in existence was used in the making of man, though it is by no means a necessary conclusion that he is related to lower animal forms by descent. The next chapter tells us that the material from which he was made was the dust of the ground, and the next verse, by the use of the word ' create ', implies that man had no physical relationship with any creature that preceded him.

The verse next tells us the essential nature of man. He is made in God's *image*, after His *likeness*. It has sometimes been suggested that the image and the likeness are two separate things, or at any rate two different aspects of the same thing. It seems more probable however that we have here two expressions of the same idea after the usual Hebrew habit of parallelism or repetition. What does it mean to be made in the image of God and after His likeness? If we look back over what this chapter has already taught us about God, we shall see that (1) God creates. In the absolute sense man cannot of course do this. It belongs to God alone. But man can create in a relative sense by making original combinations from the material in the world, which God has put at his disposal, and introducing beauty and design into such combinations. He can also give expressions to original conceptions in music, art or literature. And in all these things he can take a creative pleasure. Such powers are denied to the lower animals. (2) God speaks a word. Man has the corresponding gift of language, not indeed the divine creative language, but a language of communication, capable of expressing command, desire, statement, or question, and clothing his thoughts in such a way as to prove him a rational being. Man is capable of abstract thought. Lower animals have memory. They can associate concrete objects and events and act upon the associations. They do not possess the power of abstract thought. Man is self-conscious. The lower animals are not known to be so. (3) God approves the good. Hitherto in this chapter God's approval has only been given to the inanimate or to the non-moral, but one of the most obvious characteristics of God in the Bible is His approval of what is morally good and His abhorrence of the morally evil. God reveals Himself to us in the Bible as moral by choosing the right and abhorring the evil. Man too is a moral being. He was made a being capable of moral choice, and his ultimate happiness is bound up with the nature of the choice. The moral side of his being is the fundamental side. To be made in the image of God thus means that man is a creative, rational, moral being. He has creative emotions, a rational intellect, and a moral volition. These three correspond to what under the great commandment are called his soul, his mind and his heart respectively. (Mk. 12. 30).

This verse goes on to tell us of the function of man. He was to have *dominion*. He was to be God's vice-regent on earth. David knew this passage (as we should expect), and quoted it (Ps. 8. 6-8). Man lost his dominion by his fall. We do not yet see it restored, nor God's purpose for man's dominion yet fully accomplished, ' but we see Jesus ', the last Adam, crowned already with glory and honour as man's representative, a fact that pledges and guarantees the accomplishment of God's purpose. The dominion over the animals on earth was to be only a training and preparation for dominion in the world to come, and the final fulfilment of God's purpose for man in this respect will come when the promise to the redeemed finds its fulfilment. ' They shall reign for ever and ever ' (Rev. 22. 5).

Over all the earth: the Peshitto Syriac version has ' over all the beasts of the earth ', a reading that seems to be required to balance the phraseology, but has no authority in any extant Hebrew text, or in the Greek version. We cannot tell whether the Syriac translators had a Hebrew text that contained this reading before them, or whether they inserted it in their version because they judged that it ought to have been there. They may perhaps have been influenced by a Targum.

VERSE 27. *So*. The first thing that we see in this verse is that God's act follows from His decision. What He purposes, as what He promises, He is able also to perform, and does and will ever perform to the glory of His Name and the eternal good of His people. He has purposed to call us and *so* we have been called. He has purposed to glorify us, and *so* just as surely shall we be glorified.

Created. This is the third and last time that this word occurs in this chapter (see verses 1, 21). The word occurs at the beginning of animal life and in connection with here the origin of man. It implies a break in whatever continuity may have previously existed. It need not have the meaning of bringing into being out of nothing, and in fact it does not in the case of man (see chapter 2. 7). Its emphasis is on the new departure always caused by creation. See for instance Num. 16. 30, where the words, ' Make a new thing,' represent a literal Hebrew, ' Create a creation '. Man is therefore as different from the lower animals which preceded him, as they are from the plants.

In his own image. For the meaning of this see on verse 26. Man still bears this image, although it is marred by the fall. The degree to which it is marred may differ, at least outwardly, from one individual to another. One man may be the helpless slave of degrading vices, another may be an intelligent and efficient leader of men. Most men are capable on occasion of kind, noble or sacrificial deeds. This is due to having been created in God's image. Yet this occasional performance is man's condemnation, for what he can sometimes perform, and is therefore capable of performing, is due from him always. Yet the fact of creation in God's image gives him a dignity and a sanctity which ought to silence all of the evil-speaking of one member of his race against another (Jas. 3. 9).

The marred *image* is renewed in the redeemed. The new nature which the regenerate sinner puts on is renewed in the image of Christ, the God-man, his Creator and Redeemer. When the work of renewal is complete, as it will be on the day of resurrection, the regenerate will be perfectly like Christ. In the redeemed ' Christ is all and in all ' (Col. 3. 9-11). It will be noticed that the implication of the apostle's words is that the image is spiritual and moral, and this gives us an important clue to the meaning of our verse.

The statement of creation in God's image is repeated. This fact emphasises its importance (see Gen. 41. 32), but the second statement takes a different turn. The pronoun ' him ' at the end of it is in designed contrast to the pronoun ' them ' at the end of the following sentence. The whole human race is of course in the general

sense made in the image of God, but this verse emphasises what the next chapter makes explicit, that it is man, not woman, who was originally created as the image and glory of God. This fact is borne out first by the use of pronouns that denote the male sex in reference to God throughout the Bible. The attributes of the Divine character revealed to us throughout the Bible, while not excluding the tenderness and even delicacy generally, but not always, rightly associated with woman, are more consonant with the personality of man. In experience we find the same thing. While it would be untrue to say that there is any difference between the sexes in the moral implications of the image, the basic and most important ones, the subsidiary implications (the first two that we noticed above on verse 26) are more marked in man than in woman. His creative and rational powers are greater than hers. Further the functions of the human race in having ' dominion ' on earth as God's vice-regent are more properly and easily carried by the man than by the woman. The human nature taken in incarnation by the Divine Word was that of the man, not the woman. The man is the human norm. The woman has a nature modified in inessentials and adapted to a special end. The Christian man therefore ought to pray and worship, in contrast to the woman, with his head uncovered, because he is the image and glory of God (1 Cor. 11. 7).

The work of the sixth day corresponds to the crowning work of the Spirit in the child of God. In the old creation the sixth day saw man created in the image of God. In the new it sees the image of Christ perfectly renewed in the believer. ' When He shall appear, we shall be like Him; for we shall see Him as He is ' (1 Jo. 3. 2). We have been predestinated to be conformed to the image of God's Son (Rom. 8. 29) and after a long work of the Spirit in our hearts, while we are still here on earth, Christ will be formed in us (Gal. 4. 19).

Male and female. The last sentence of this verse tells us the second of two fundamental facts about human nature. The first is that man is made in the image of God, that is to say, essentially a moral being. The second is that he was made in two sexes. God had two purposes in making the human race in this way. Firstly He intended that it should reproduce its kind. This important function is confined, so far as we know, to the inhabitants of this earth. It is not shared by angels (Mt. 22. 30; Mk. 12. 25; Lk. 20. 36). It has far reaching effects. It unites the human race in a single bundle of life, making of it a unity impossible in the case of angels who appear to be separately created individual beings. It is this unity that the Bible refers to when it speaks of our being 'in Adam' (1 Cor. 15. 22). The united humanity in Adam is a symbol and picture of redeemed humanity, similarly united, though by different means and a closer bond, in Christ. This unity enables the one act of redemption performed by Christ to become effective towards the whole human race, just as the whole race has been affected as such by the one act of disobedience on Adam's part that constituted the fall. The power of reproduction also made possible the incarnation of Christ, which was essentially preparatory to the act of redemption. While He was not begotten by the ordinary method of generation, it remains true that the reproductive functions of the human race alone made it possible for Him to assume human nature. This He did as the true child of Mary, through whom He took human nature from Adam. These facts enable us to speculate on the possibility that, seeing that moral evil was already in the universe before man's creation through the devil's fall, God may from the beginning have intended the creation of the human race to be a step in the redemption of the universe as a whole.

The second purpose of God in creating the human race in two sexes was to enable it thereby to reflect the eternal relationship between Christ and His church. The apostle explains this in considerable detail in Eph. 5. 25-33. The rapture, affection and love, the mutual confidence and regard of normal sexual life of man and woman have their spiritual counterparts. They will be absent in the world to come (Mt. 22. 30), but their place will be taken by a deeper and more rapturous reality (Isa. 62. 5). Creation in two sexes necessarily made the family the normal centre of human life, and family life by the mutual affection of its various members provides an illustration of various aspects of the love of God, denied to beings for whom no family is possible. God is a Father, and He pictures Himself as a husband (see e.g. Hos. 2. 7, 19, 20). Christ is His Father's Son. So close a picture is seen in the human family of the sacred relationship of the first and second Persons of the Holy Trinity and of relationships in which God graciously sets Himself with His people, that it is difficult not to think that without family life it would not have been possible for man to have been made wholly in the image of God.

The Lord appeals to this statement in this verse as proof of the sanctity of marriage (Mt. 19. 4; Mk. 10. 6). He goes over the head of Moses back to this primitive standard of Genesis. For Him this verse carried the implication of a purpose of God in the relationship of man and woman, which can only be fulfilled by life-long exclusive mutual faithfulness. Every departure from this standard annuls the original purpose of God.

VERSE 28. As God blessed the fish and birds, so He blesses man. As with them, God's blessing relates to physical increase. The enormous multiplication of the human race and the happiness that family life can bring to man, even in his fallen condition, are evidence of the initial power and continuous operation of the blessing of God. In man's case the blessing went farther than it did with the animals. It extended to the dominion which God had announced was His intention for man (see on verse 26). Man was to *subdue* the earth. His fall has prevented his successful accomplishment of this purpose of his Creator, but he instinctively seeks to carry it out, for the most part, as history shows, in great outbursts of exploratory or inventive activity. Evidence of this are his discovery of the use of fire, his domestication of animals, his practice of agriculture, his mastery of the mechanics of building, his development of the wheel from the fallen log, his successful experiments in navigation, his acquisition of the art of writing and the immense range of his inventions which have revolutionised his manner of life during the last five hundred years. His fall has also prevented his complete subjugation and domestication of the lower animals, which fear him in his savagery and separation from God, but his power over them is sufficiently seen to testify to the efficacy of the initial blessing of God.

God has blessed His elect with all spiritual blessings in the heavenly places in Christ (Eph. 1. 3). The range of these blessings is immensely greater than that of the primitive blessing that we read of in this verse. Yet in conformity with that it must contain the blessing of fruitfulness. And so we see the Holy Spirit bringing forth fruit in the lives of the elect to the glory of God, the spread of the Gospel resulting in the winning of souls, and the people of God set free from the dominion of sin and made to ' reign in life by the one man Jesus Christ ' (Rom. 5. 17).

VERSE 29. This verse shows us God's first gracious provision for man's need. The herbs and trees belong to God by virtue of their having been made by Him. They are *given* by Him to man. This first dealing of God with man is characteristic of all. God always gives and never sells. Fallen man tries constantly to buy spiritual gifts from God by religious observances of great variety or by the

veneer of a decent life through which there often break the violent and passionate forces of a depraved nature within. Yet all the time God gives and seeks our acceptance of His gifts (Ps. 116. 12-13). He gives what man needs physically and much else besides. He gives home and health, the beauties of nature, intellectual pleasures, the delights of craftsmanship and a thousand things more. His spiritual gifts cannot be numbered and when at last nothing else could meet the sinner's need, He gave the unspeakable gift of His only begotten Son, ' that whosoever believeth in Him should not perish, but have everlasting life ' (Jo. 3. 16). And with Him He has graciously given us all things (Rom. 8. 32), not least Himself again in the Person of the Holy Spirit (Acts 2. 33).

Primitive man's diet was intended by God to be vegetarian. He was given first the *herb-bearing seed*. A double provision was made here by God for man's need. First the herb bears seed, that is to say, it reproduces itself and will never fail. Secondly the herb is *upon the face of all the earth*. However far he travelled, man would find provision made for him. Next man was given *every tree*. If the herb were the staple foundation of his diet, the tree provided him with fruit to quench his thirst and to delight his taste. No mention is made here of corn or bread, produced by the labour of man, nor of flesh food. Those are the diet of workers and hunters. In the herb we may perhaps see a picture of the wonders and beauties of nature supporting and establishing the soul of unfallen man, and in the tree with its fruit the riches of fellowship with God, which sustain his spirit. Man's food in the world to come will be fruit of this sort (Rev. 22. 2).

Meat is of course older English for *food*.

VERSE 30. Beasts, birds and reptiles are also given the herb for food. In their case the tree is not mentioned. It is reserved for man. This may mean that even those animals that prey upon others were vegetarian at first, and that changes took place in them after and in consequence of the fall of man. There is so much hidden however behind this brief, if sublime, account, that such a view may be too crude. Even the preying animals derive their nourishment ultimately from the plants, through they do not do so directly. It comes through the animals that they eat, which have taken it in. The teeth and digestive organs of the flesh-eating animals appear to be fitted only for a flesh diet, and if these animals really ate plants and vegetables originally, the changes that must have taken place in them are so revolutionary, that the creature must now be unrecognisable for what it was at creation. It seems more likely that these animals had their present habits from the beginning and form part of those natural phenomena intended to teach moral lessons. We have already seen some of them in the course of this chapter.

It was so. See on verse 7.

VERSE 31. If each part of the creation as it was made was good, the whole was *very good.* See on verse 4. For the last sentence see on verse 5.

CHAPTER 2

IN this chapter we have first the conclusion of the process of creation described in chapter 1 in three verses which belong properly to that chapter and end the section beginning with 1. 1. This is followed by an account from another aspect of the origin of man, consisting of an introduction (4-6), the formation of man (7), the description of the garden of Eden (8-17), the creation of woman (18-23), and the institution of marriage (24, 25).

VERSE 1. The word *heavens* is here in the plural in contrast to 1. 1. There the whole of creation apart from the earth is probably to be thought of, including the spiritual world and the astronomical heaven. In the course of the account of the process of creation the firmament was introduced and a new meaning given

to the word *heaven* (see 1-8). The *heavens* here probably refer to the atmosphere of the earth and to the wider astronomical heavens, hardly to the spiritual world, which antedates the time referred to in 1. 2. *Finished.* There is never a purpose or act of God which is not brought to a successful end. He knows all from the beginning and can never be frustrated or disappointed. His redemption of His people will one day be as successfully accomplished. The Saviour was able to say ' I have finished the work which thou gavest me to do ' (Jo. 17. 4). His redemptive work was perfectly accomplished and finished on the cross (Jo. 19. 30). And if we are conscious that the Holy Spirit has begun a work in our own hearts, we have the assurance of its accomplishment, for ' he which hath begun a good work in you will perform it until the day of Jesus Christ ' (Phil. 1. 6).

All the host of them. This probably means all the stars. Some of their innumerable multitude and of the immense distances associated with them have become known to the modern scientist, although probably the half has not yet been told. This greatly enhances the wonder of the creation and our view of the majesty and power of the Creator. The Bible writers often speak of the host, or hosts of heaven, and one of their titles for God is Jahweh Sebaioth, Lord of hosts. The expression sometimes refers to the stars, in which case it alludes to their immense numbers, and sometimes to angels, when the conception of armies is added to that of multitude. We still use the word *host* in both these senses. As the stars fill the heavens, each in its place, moving into its proper path and order, so the angels fill the spiritual world, each also in its proper place and order. The common use of this word *hosts* seems to be the basis of a connection of thought which we can sometimes detect in the Scriptures between angels and stars. It is quite unnecessary to suppose any mythical connection between them.

VERSE 2. *The seventh day*. If the six days of creation are long periods of time, it is reasonable to suppose the seventh to be the same. The words of the Lord recorded in Jo. 5. 17 seem to imply that the seventh day is still in progress. He asserts His right to do redemptive work on the sabbath in imitation of His Father, Who is doing so on His sabbath. The seventh day, on which creation has ceased, will be followed by the eternal eighth day, the beginning of the new creation. God did not end His work until it was finished. In the same way He will never lay down His purpose of redemption for His church or for any individual member of it, until He has brought every one to glory. There is no proper room for doubt in the trusting saint. *Made*. This word confirms the view that the work here spoken of as finished is that which began in 1. 2. The original creation of 1. 1 must have been made out of nothing, and, even if we accept the subtle view that in some sense it was made out of God, the word *made* is still unsuitable as a substitute for *created*. The material was already present from which God made the earth and firmament.

He rested. This is not the rest of exhaustion (God is never weary) (Isa. 40. 28), but the rest of satisfaction. The emphasis of meaning is rather upon *ceasing* than upon *resting*. The associated word in English is the word ' pause ', the word *rest* being used in something of the same sense, as it is today in the technical language of music. This verse however gives no impression of a *temporary* pause. The work is finished, not interrupted, a fact that proves to us that now that this creation is corrupted by human sin, God will never do anything more to it to reform or restore it. All expectations of any coming of the kingdom of God in this world are vain and unscriptural (1 Cor. 15. 50). God has finished His work upon this creation. That work was perfect, and there is nothing that He can add to it. The promises will be realised in a new and perfect world. *On the*

seventh day, that is the seventh period of time which followed the process of creation and continues in progress. *All his work*. Nothing whatever remained or remains to be done. It is God's purpose that His people should share with Him this perfect rest of satisfaction. The writer of the Epistle to the Hebrews shows from the 95th Psalm that God has a rest in store for His people, which was missed by those who were disobedient and rebellious in the wilderness. The promise remains open under the Gospel, but it is still possible to miss the rest by unbelief. Believers come into the rest. The writer then identifies the rest of the promise, obtainable by faith, with the rest of God spoken of in our verse here. He goes on to argue that the rest could not have come with the conquest of Canaan under Joshua, because the entry into it was still future in the days of David, when Psalm 95 was written. The rest is for us Christians who believe in the Lord Jesus Christ, and it is worth making every conceivable effort and sacrifice to enter it (Heb. 3. 7—4, 11). The writer to the Hebrews tells us that the mark of entry into the rest is to have ceased from one's own works, as this verse tells us God ceased from His (Heb. 4. 10). This rest of faith, the sabbath-keeping that remains for the people of God, comes in the world to come when the toil of service, the heat of battle, and the intricacies of witness in the wicked world are over, when the believer can look back, as the apostle did, over his life, and say, ' I have fought a good fight, I have finished my course, I have kept the faith ' (2 Tim. 4. 7), and when he hears the Lord's words, ' Well done, good and faithful servant; enter thou into the joy of thy Lord ' (Mt. 25. 21). That will be a true rest of satisfaction, never with self-effort, but with the grace of God constantly acting to will and to do after His good pleasure. Yet in a different sense that rest can be anticipated now. The believer enters into it in his heart, when he finally abandons his wicked self, and casts himself in perfect trust on the Saviour, Whose finished work alone can bring him God's pardon, deliverance from guilt and the curse, redemption from the dominion of sin, and sure and certain hope of salvation from death, and a glorious resurrection to eternal life.

VERSE 3. *God blessed the seventh day*. This seventh day is the weekly sabbath established by revelation from God in the beginning of the world. The week with its sabbath was established in human life as a perpetual reminder of two things. Firstly the whole week looks back to the past and is intended to bring constantly before our minds the fact of creation and the debt that we owe to God for the gift of existence. Secondly the sabbath is a recurring picture of the future rest that is in store for the people of God. God did two things for the seventh day. First of all he *blessed* it. The word ' bless ', as it has been hitherto used in the course of chapter 1, has entailed two things: (1) fruitfulness and (2) dominion. God therefore intended the seventh day to be the means of producing spiritual fruit in the lives of His people. Its opportunities for rest and worship were to draw them near to Himself, bring out their love and trust, strengthen their faith by attention to His Word, teach them to worship, and build up their spiritual lives. The day was also to be the dominating factor in the lives of the people of God. So it has always proved, and has in addition exercised far-reaching influence in the life of the world at large. The week revolves round the sabbath, and the week as a mark of time has governed the major part of the activities of the most advanced nations of the world.

Secondly God *sanctified* the seventh day. This means that He set it apart from the rest and consecrated it to activities connected in a special sense with Himself and His worship. The believer's whole life is consecrated to God, but the consecration of the day means that he is intended to engage upon it in the service of direct approach to God and to give direct attention to spiritual needs, not always possible during the six days of activity. The consecration of the day has always involved the assembly of the people of God for acts of common worship, again not possible while each is engaged on his ordinary duties.

The reason for the blessing and sanctification of the day lies in a movement of God Himself. It is true that ' the sabbath was made for man ' (Mk. 2. 27), but it was made for him in order to associate his life with a fundamental activity of God. As always, God did not bless and sanctify because of anything that man had done, but to reflect an activity of His own. The source of the blessing lay with Him, the initiative was His. Man's sabbath is a microscopic picture of God's, just as everything in man's life, if only he had not rebelled, was intended to be the same.

The principle of the sabbath, which thus goes back to creation and long antedates the law, has survived the supersession of the old covenant by the new. The church retained the principle, but instinctively changed the day from the seventh to the first as the expression of her witness that the eternal Messianic age had begun with the resurrection of Jesus and the regenerative activity of the Spirit. The old gave way to the new in Christ, and no more practical or realistic way could have been found to bring home the significance of the change than the alteration of the day round which the common week revolved. The New Testament does not directly command this change, but sanctions it as a fact accomplished (see e.g. Acts 20. 7; Rev. 1. 10).

The closing sentence of this verse and of the whole section, which began with 1. 1, unites the two great words that denote the creative activity of God. He *created*, that is to say, He brought into being things that were totally new. This applies to animal life and to man, as well of course as to the whole process of the creation of all things, heaven and earth, visible and invisible, regarded as a unity, a complete work of the Almighty Creator. In the course of this process He also *made*. By this is meant that He designed and built up out of material which in simpler forms He had previously brought into being. This applies to much of nature on this earth and even in a limited sense to man.

VERSE 4. We here begin a completely new section, written in a more colourful style than the previous, which continues at least up to the end of chapter 3. It is dangerous to draw conclusions about authorship from differences of style, because a writer's style may alter greatly according to the subject about which he is writing. In this case however the atmosphere differs so greatly from that of 1. 1—2. 3, that we may be justified in suspecting that the section on which we are entering came from a different source. Whether this is so, or not, the same Holy Spirit, Who spoke through the prophets, is the ultimate author of this chapter, as of the last, and it is His inspiration and guidance that unify the whole. Whatever be the truth about the human authorship, the view that has so strongly held the field, which sees in this chapter a contradictory account of the origin of man and the world, derived from a discrepant source, and loosely tacked on to chapter 1, is completely unjustified. The introduction of a new Divine Name in this section cannot bear the weight that liberal theory has placed upon it. The criterion of the Divine Name goes back to a French disciple of the infidel Voltaire in the eighteenth century, and has proved merely a convenient means of sheltering materialistic views. The change of Divine Name is consonant with the requirements of the narrative.

The verse begins with the formula that occurs eleven times in Genesis and divides the sections from each other (see 5. 1; 6. 9; 10. 1; 11. 10; 11. 27; 25. 12; 25. 19; 36. 9; 37. 2).

Opinion has differed whether the formula closes the preceding section, or opens the following. The Hebrew word occurs outside the Pentateuch once in the book of Ruth and a few times in Chronicles. In the latter book it seems sometimes to look backwards, while in Ruth (4. 18) it clearly looks forward. Elsewhere in Genesis it clearly looks forward, and since its position must be uniform in all eleven sections, this fact seems to determine its direction throughout. The meaning of the Hebrew word translated *generations* is not easy to determine exactly. Different contexts appear to give it differing senses. The normal sense seems to be, ' story of the family '. It is always used of human beings except in the verse before us, and here its use seems to be determined by a rather bold figure of speech. Its use in this verse has been regarded as a support to the theory of evolutionary development of all life, including, as the context would oblige us, man, from the first material ever created. Apart, however, from the theories of the origin of life which are current today and have as their real raison d'être the exclusion of God from His creation, it does not seem that any reader of this passage would draw such a conclusion. It is more likely that the word is used in this verse as a poetic and intelligible figure of speech, though it may conceal some of the mysteries of the origin of life, and would be consonant with the idea that the original stuff of the universe contained in itself the potentialities of development.

The occurrence of the formula at the head of eleven of the twelve sections of the book proves the unity of Genesis. The sections may have come from separate and very early sources, but they are all bound together into a single narrative by the deliberate repetition of the formula. The insertion and repetition of the formula may be the work of Moses, who may have been the editor of the book and the translator of some of its parts. It may have been the work of one separate patriarchal writer after another in imitation of his pre-decessors. In either case the unity of design is the work of the Holy Ghost.

The heavens and the earth are said by a bold and poetic conception to have generations, that is to say, a family history, which is embodied in the section 2. 4—4. 26. The narra-tive records the creation of man and woman, the fall of the race, the wicked history of Cain, and in the closing two verses the beginning of the line of descent that led eventually to the Saviour. This may well mean that God's purpose in the creation of this earth with its surrounding and attendant heavens was that it may be the scene where in the human race the conflict between good and evil might be brought to a head. The earth was designed from the begin-ning to be the scene of the incarna-tion and passion of the Lord, for these *generations* begin *when* the heavens and earth *were created.* This helps to explain the hints we met with in the first chapter that nature was designed in some respects to teach moral lessons.

The punctuation and reading of verses 4-7 are difficult. The most natural arrangement would be to place a full stop after the word *created* in verse 4. If this is done however, we are obliged to read the particle at the beginning of verse 5 as ' and when ', to continue the long sentence governed by ' when ' to the end of verse 6, and begin verse 7 with the word ' then '. This and other arrangements have been attempted by various commentators. On the whole the punctuation of the Revised Ver-sion is best. This places a full stop at the end of verse 4, and makes better sense of the first two sentences of verse 5. Thus the whole of verse 4 goes closely together.

In the day that. This means ' when '. It is jejune to pretend that the writer thought of the earth and heavens as being made in a single day in contrast to the account in chapter 1. *The Lord God.* The Divine Name appears here for the first time pre-ceding the name *Elohim* (God), which had been used alone through-out chapter 1 and to the end of the first section in 2. 3. When this name appears in English, it takes the form Jehovah. The reason for this is that the real name came to be regarded with such veneration by the Jews that they feared to pronounce it. Their alphabet contained only con-sonants, a system of small signs called points being later invented as a guide to pronunciation. The Divine Name was given the vowel-points of the usual Hebrew word meaning ' Lord ' and the consonants with these points made the form which is *transliterated* in English as Jehovah. The usual *translation* in our versions of the name is LORD in capital letters. The original form of the name is not exactly known. It is usually thought to have been Jahweh. The form is connected with the root of the verb ' to be ', and may have originally meant ' the Eternal '. It will be found that generally speaking throughout the Old Testament the name *Elohim* has a wide meaning and is properly used of God as the Creator, as in the first chapter of this book, while the name Jahweh (Jehovah, or Lord) is the name in special connection with the covenant made with Israel. Thus God is Elohim as Creator, Jehovah as Redeemer. The introduction of the Name therefore at this point em-phasises the fact that the section, on which we are entering, deals with re-demption in contrast to section one. This is most proper, as the section contains the account of the fall and of the first promise of redemption. The change of name is required by the narrative, as always in this and other books. The idea that the dif-ferent names were used by different sections of the populace in the time of the kingdom (e.g. by the northern tribes and by Judah), and thus repre-sent contradictory writers drawn from those sections, whose work was later patched together, has no foundation in fact.

Difficulty has been caused (and much exaggerated by liberal critics)

over the statement in Exod. 6. 3 that
God was not known to the patriarchs
by the name of Jehovah. The passage
implies that the name was first revealed to Moses at the time of the
Exodus. If this is the correct meaning of Exod. 6. 3, the occurrence of
the name Jehovah here in Genesis 2. 4
and often later in the book would be
due to Moses, who might easily have
used it to translate a name or title
used in Sumerian or other ancient
pre-Hebrew language. Again if he
had been himself composing any part
of the book of Genesis, it is natural
to think of him using the Name that
was familiar to him, even if it had
not been revealed at the time of which
he was writing.

Made. The two terms *created* and
made appear in this verse corresponding to their use in chapter 1.

VERSE 5. *And no plant of the field
was yet in the earth, and no herb of
the field was yet sprung up.* This
statement takes us back to the beginning of the third day of creation (1.
9). The point of verses 5 and 6 seems
to be that from the very beginning it
was God's purpose to make man, and
that he was made (verse 7) direct from
virgin soil. The earth from which
man sprang was the primeval earth,
prepared and ready as soon as it appeared from the primeval waters. The
existence and growth of plants and
herbs did not effect the composition
of man. He is not dependent upon
them for existence. He was not affected by the descent of rain from the
clouds. The earth from which he
was made was there in its entirety
before a drop of rain fell. Above all
no man had any hand in the making
of man. 'There was not a man to
till the ground'. 'It is he that hath
made us, and not we ourselves' (Ps.
100. 3).

VERSE 6. This verse is in the same
strain. The necessary watering of the
earth was done by a mist which went
up from it and returned to the same
place. The earth did its own watering. No foreign element entered in.

So that when we come to the formation of man, nothing lies behind but
the Creator Himself and the virgin
earth of which He formed him. These
facts prove two things: (1) that the
creation of man was the real purpose
of God in making the earth at the
very beginning; (2) that man has no
connection by descent or otherwise
with the plant or animal life that preceded him. The implication is that
they were all made for him, to supply
his need, to afford him pleasure, or
to teach moral lessons.

What a picture we may see in
verses 5 and 6 of a soul dead in trespasses and sin. The soul is a recognised picture in the Bible of the
human heart (Mt. 13. 3-8; Heb. 6. 7,
etc.) Here is a dead earth. No plant
or herb could be found on its barren
surface. No fruit of the Spirit was
brought forth to God's glory. There
was no increase or fruitfulness, because there was no spark of life. No
rain descended on this desolate surface. There were no showers of
blessing (Ezek. 34. 26; Jas. 5. 7).
Above all there was no man. The
Man Christ Jesus does not dwell by
faith in dead hearts, and the hard soil
has no attention from the heavenly
farmer. This lifeless ground obtained
its water from a mist which went up
from itself, the mist of self-righteousness, of superstition, or false
philosophy, of worldly pleasures, or
carnal passions, which when exuded
has the effect of concealing the real
condition of the ground and restores
to it no more than it took. This is
the condition of every unconverted
human heart around us today.

VERSE 7. This verse gives us the
Scriptural description of the origin of
man, and the Scriptural view of man's
nature. In two essential respects this
first Adam stands in contrast to the
'last Adam' or 'second man' (1
Cor. 15. 45-47). First, the man was
formed of the *dust of the ground*.

Formed means 'moulded'. Attempts have been made to see behind
this statement the idea of a long
development of the body of man from

the lower animals, and behind them from primitive life forms. It has been said that man's body was moulded by long generations of physical descent. We cannot, however, read this idea into this verse without doing violence to the language. The verse is speaking emphatically of an individual. This is not only seen by the use of the Hebrew article (*man* in each case in the verse is ' the man '), but also by the statement that the breath of life was breathed into the nostrils. If man had living sub-human and non-human ancestors, he was never as man quickened by the breath of life, and the statement becomes meaningless. We need not imagine Divine hands moulding clay, as if they were human hands. The process may have been brought about by the Divine Word. We must not forget that we are dealing here with the sixth day of creation, not with the sabbath of rest. Creation was still in progress. We are still in the realm of the supernatural. The basic mistake of the modern evolutionist is that he refuses to take account of the supernatural and seeks to carry the merely natural back into a realm where it does not belong. In consequence he is finding his problem insoluble and becomes involved in endless and fruitless discussion, because the solution of the question of the origin of life inevitably escapes him. The analogy to the creative act of God in the formation of man lies in the Lord's miracles. These were instantaneous and complete. Lazarus was called in perfect health from his grave. Men blind or lame from birth were suddenly healed, a process involving complicated, but no less instantaneous, adjustments of the mental powers and brain centres, enabling those on whom the miracles were wrought to walk without learning to do so, or to see without a long process of accustoming themselves to the world around them. This was the exercise of creative supernatural power, and it was by the exercise of the same power that the first man awoke to life in perfect accommodation to his sur-

roundings. Man is made *of the dust of the ground*. He is ' of the earth earthy ' (1 Cor. 15. 47). He is but dust and ashes (Gen. 18. 27; Job 4. 19). He is essentially a creature of this earth, and the members of his race are the same (1 Cor. 15. 48, 49). In contrast to this the head of the redeemed humanity is ' from heaven ', and those who belong to the redeemed race have a heavenly origin in Him (1 Cor. 15. 47-49). The two different sections of humanity betray their separate origins by their desires, their appetites, their ambitions and their affections. The principle that governs their lives is in the one case earthly and in the other heavenly.

Can we see any purpose of the Creator in moulding the body of man to the shape in which it was formed? The image of God does not lie in the physical. It is moral and spiritual as we have seen. It is true that the upright position and the dignity of the human body (beauty he shares with the lower creation) fit a being on whom is stamped the image of God. But there may be a more definite factor than this. When the First-begotten came into the world, He said, ' A body hast thou prepared for me ' (Heb. 10. 5). It was not in the womb of the virgin that this body was prepared. It was down the generations from Adam to Mary. And was it not also in the formation of man? In other words man's body was originally formed in such a way that, reproduced from generation after generation, it might eventually be the right, suitable and perfect form to be assumed by the Son of God, when He took our nature upon Him. Adam's body was formed with a view to the incarnation.

When the body had been moulded from the clay, the Lord God *breathed into* man's *nostrils the breath of life*. This was not an act peculiar to man. This spirit (Hebrew *ruach*), or life principle, is shared by everything living. Animals possess it as much as man (Gen. 7. 22). It is the principle of natural life. It is a mistake to see in this statement the idea that a spiritual nature, akin to the Divine and not shared by the lower creation, was imparted to man. The image of God does not consist in the possession of this life principle, but in the quality of it. Not the possession of this spirit, but the quality of it, differentiates man from the animals. It has sometimes been thought that the impartation of the life principle, as it is brought before us in this verse, entailed immortality of the spirit or soul. It has been said that to be made in the image of God involves immortality. The Bible never says so. If it involves immortality, why does it not also involve omniscience or omnipresence, or any other quality or attribute of the Infinite? Why should one alone be singled out? The breath of life was not breathed into man's heart, but into his nostrils. It involved physical life. Throughout the Bible man, apart from Christ, is conceived of as made of dust and ashes, a physical creature, to whom is lent by God a principle of life. The Greek thinkers tended to think of man as an immortal soul imprisoned in a body. This emphasis is the opposite to that of the Bible, but has found a wide place in Christian thought. Modern psychological science tends to vindicate the Biblical view.

The combination of the clay with the life principle made the man *a living soul*. This is the same word as is used in 1. 20, 21 of the marine creatures and in 1. 24 of the animals. It denotes man's natural life. The blood is the seat of the soul. (Lev. 17. 11, 14) and from the soul spring the appetites of the natural life (Mt. 6. 25). (The Hebrew and Greek words meaning *soul* are often translated ' life '). In the New Testament this natural life, or life of the soul, is often contrasted with spiritual life. It is in this respect that the ' last Adam ' is contrasted in the second place with the first man. Adam was made ' a living soul ', but the last Adam is ' a quickening spirit ' (1 Cor. 15. 44-6). Thus man is made unlike the animals a moral and spiritual being, but like the animals a creature of

the earth. His creation was a preparation for the incarnation and may in itself have been a step towards the ultimate redemption of the universe.

VERSE 8. The garden of Eden is a type and picture of the garden, or paradise, of God, which will be on the new earth created by God for the redeemed in the world to come (Rev. 2. 7). The old Eden was planted in a corner of the earth. The new paradise will cover the whole earth. We are still in the sixth day of creation, in the realm of the supernatural, and the garden is in consequence planted directly by the Divine hands. So will the eternal paradise be a creation and gift of God.

The name *Eden* is geographical and local, but it is now impossible to know the site. Tradition places it in Mesopotamia. *Eastward* must mean to the east of Palestine, or even of Mesopotamia itself. There is some substance in the idea that it was in the mountains to the north of Mesopotamia.

There he put the man. Here is proof of God's love and goodness. The man was placed in surroundings that would every moment fill him with delight. The situation is typical of that of redeemed humanity in the world to come. How the man was put into the garden we do not know. He may have been carried there by the hand of God before gaining consciousness, or have been led through the open gate. In the garden he was in the most favourable situation possible for the coming struggle with evil, and we may contrast the situation of the Lord, Who met Satan in a wilderness after being long deprived of food.

VERSE 9. *Out of the ground,* that is to say, in the garden. The situation of the garden may have been adapted to trees already growing there, or a special creation of trees may have been made for it. *Every tree.* In the eternal paradise these trees with their good food are combined with the tree of life (Rev. 22. 2). There is good reason for this. Christ is the eternal tree of life and the trees are the people of God. 'The trees of the Lord are full of sap' (Ps. 104. 16). (For the people of God as trees see Jer. 17. 8; Ps. 1. 3). In the world to come Christ and His people are one for ever. All spring from the root of the tree of life. The trees of Eden appealed to the unfallen senses. They were *pleasant to the sight*. This probably does not mean that they were beautiful in an aesthetic sense. The Bible speaks little of that aspect. It associates the eyes with desire, and the sense here probably is that the sight of the trees roused the appetite for their fruit. Thus desire for God is roused in the heart of the elect when the eye of faith perceives Christ, and sometimes those on whose heart the Holy Spirit is beginning to work, although still unconverted, are enabled to see the transformed lives of the children of God and to desire to be like them. The trees were also *good for food*. The necessary vitamins and other chemical combinations, of whose very existence man was not to know till thousands of years had passed, had been hidden in them by the Creator. *The tree of life*. This is the picture of Christ Himself, Who came that we might have life and have it more abundantly (Jo. 10. 10). In Him was life (Jo. 1. 4) and He is the life (Jo. 14. 6). In dying for us on the cross He gave His flesh to eat, and whoever takes advantage of this death and receives and assimilates the gift of Christ's flesh in his heart by coming to Him in simple faith for pardon there and then enters into eternal life. Thus we may walk now in our hearts by faith in the paradise, where we shall be openly in the world to come, and feed now on the tree of life, which we shall eat unhindered on the new earth (Rev. 2. 7; 22. 2). This means that we shall enjoy and assimilate the presence of Christ for ever. The only condition is that we wash our robes (Rev. 22. 14, R.V.). The tree of life was in *the midst of the garden*. So Christ is in the midst of His believing people's lives and hearts and the centre of the glory of the world to come, the

source of all its joys, and the pivot round which it moves. The nature of the typical tree of life in the primitive Eden it does not seem possible to determine. The idea that it was not a literal tree is difficult in view of the fact that the man, the woman, the garden and the other trees were all material and objective. If it were an actual tree, it must have been unique. The most reasonable speculation perhaps is that, assuming there had been no fall, its fruit was intended to be eaten by men and women to arrest physical decline and possibly as a safeguard against disease. As the human race reproduced itself, its individual members must be removed from the earth to prevent overpopulation, and it is possible that the tree of life would change their nature and prepare them for translation to another world, as in the case of Enoch (Heb. 11. 5), Elijah (2 Ki. 2. 11), or the saints alive at the coming of the Lord (1 Thess. 4. 17).

The *tree of knowledge of good and evil* has no counterpart in the world to come. It is not necessary to think of it as a unique kind of tree like the tree of life. It is more likely to have been one of the fruit trees which was appointed by God to provide a moral test. It was not the nature of the tree that was different. Its importance lay in the fact that it was the subject of a command of God. In the eternal world no moral test is necessary. The victory over evil has been finally won, not by Adam, but by Jesus Christ, his descendant and representative. The primitive Eden lay in front of the moral test. The paradise of God lies beyond it.

VERSE 10. The *river* that *went out of Eden* is the type and picture of the river of the water of life, proceeding from the throne of God and of the Lamb (Ezek. 47. 1-5; Rev. 22. 1), the river whose streams shall make glad the city of God (Ps. 46. 4). This river is God the Holy Ghost (Jo. 7. 38, 39), the Lord and Giver of life, Who is already flowing from the inmost being of the believer. The purpose of the river was to irrigate the garden, but as it flowed out of Eden a secondary use was perhaps to carry away surplus material and prevent the collection of dust or refuse. On leaving the garden the river divided into four streams. This indicates that Eden was situated at a high altitude in the mountains.

Verse 11. The names of the four streams help us to locate Eden geographically. *Pison.* It has been suggested that this may be identical with one of two rivers called by the ancient Greeks Phasis. One river Phasis rose in the Caucasus and flowed into the east of the Black Sea. Another was a tributary of the Araxes, rising in the Armenian mountains. By *Havilah* is meant the Northern Havilah, lying between the Black and Caspian Seas. Gold and precious stones are found there. The fame of the gold is reflected in the Greek legend of the expedition of Jason to find the golden fleece. The expedition went to Colchis, which was the name of the district to the east of the Black Sea, through which the first Phasis flowed. There was also a city called Colchis situated on the shores of Lake Van.

Verse 12. Of course, *the gold of that land* was *good* before the fall of man. Gold is a picture of the glory of God which will appear to the redeemed in all its brightness in the world to come. Precious stones such as the two here mentioned are the picture of the precious sons of Zion, who will be the Lord's in the day that He makes up His jewels (Mal. 3. 17).

Verse 13. If Pison is Phasis, *Gihon* is one of the rivers rising in the Anti-Taurus, or the mountains of Upper Armenia and flowing into the Caspian Sea, perhaps the river called by the ancients Araxes, or that to the north of it which was called Cynus. This river compassed *the whole land of Ethiopia.* No river can entirely encircle a tract of land, but the word ' compass ' well describes the winding

courses of the rivers in this district, whose valleys in some cases describe semi-circles. *Ethiopia* is the rendering of the Hebrew ' Cush '. This Cush was the northern, not the African, Cush, the name given to the peoples who lived south of the Caucasus between the Black and Caspian Seas.

Verse 14. The Hiddekel is the Tigris. *Toward the east of.* This renders Hebrew ' in front of ', which was the normal Hebrew way of expressing ' to the east '. The Tigris however does not flow east of Assyria. The simplest resolution of this difficulty is to take the Hebrew expression literally in this instance and translate, ' in front of ', with the Revised Version, imagining the writer's standpoint to be to the west. The Tigris would in that case flow between him and Assyria.

A glance at a map of this region will show that the Euphrates, the Tigris, the second river Phasis and the Araxes, or Cynus, all rise in the Armenian mountains within measurable distance of each other. If the first Phasis is meant by Pison, the area is not much extended. We may therefore perhaps think of the mountains of Armenia as at one time the site of Eden. Many commentators and readers have been betrayed by the translation ' Ethiopia ' (verse 13) into identifying the second river as the Nile. This makes nonsense of verse 10, because the source of the Nile is thousands of miles from those of the Tigris and Euphrates, and the rivers do not belong to the same area. It is perhaps significant that the earliest men known to history, inhabitants of the Mesopotamiam plain, are thought to have descended on it out of the mountains of the north.

Verse 15. The statement of verse 8 is here repeated, in order to pick up the thread of the narrative. In the same way the Lord God has taken every one of us who believe and has put us by unmerited grace into His paradise, which we enjoy already in our hearts by faith and one day shall enjoy openly and outwardly. The purpose of man's being put into the garden is here expressed. It was *to dress it and keep it*. The man was not to be idle. An activity was provided for him. To dress and keep the garden in such circumstances would be a permanent and satisfying task. Since his fall man has lost the power to dress and keep the garden of his own heart. But as Adam dressed and kept the garden in which he lived, so the Holy Spirit, Who lives in the hearts of the redeemed, does for us what we are helpless to do ourselves. Adam's activity in Eden finds its counterpart in the world to come, where ' His servants shall serve Him ' (Rev. 22. 3).

VERSE 16. In this and the following verse we have the record of God's first commandment. It was a simple commandment, given in primitive conditions to a man who was completely inexperienced and was conscious through his senses only of his immediate surroundings. It is a commandment that suits the childhood of the race.

VERSE 17. Here we have the first moral demand made by God upon man. Since man was created a moral being ' in the image of God ', the making of such a demand could not be long delayed. Had it not been made, the man could never have found his manhood, nor reflected the nature of his Creator. *The tree of the knowledge of good and evil* was therefore, as its name implies, set apart to form the occasion of the moral test. The test was a negative one. Man was commanded *not* to do a certain thing. This implies that evil was already in the universe. The importance of the test did not lie in the action prohibited. There was nothing intrinsically evil in eating the fruit of a tree. The point of the prohibition was that it was God Who made it. We thus learn at once that God Himself is the source of right and wrong and the sole arbiter of creation. A thing is right if God commands it, and wrong if He forbids it, and there is no other ultimate

criterion. God's actions are not governed by laws of right and wrong outside of, or behind, Himself. He is Himself the source of right and wrong. He commands and forbids at will. On the other hand He is in His own nature and Being eternally consistent morally. With Him there is ' no shadow of turning ' (Jas. 1. 17). He is arbitrary in the sense that He is responsible to no one (Isa. 40. 13, 14; Rom. 11. 34, 35), but He is not arbitrary in the sense of waywardness in which that word is sometimes used. In giving this prohibition to Adam then God set up a test of relationship *with Himself*. This is the test that occurs throughout the Bible. God continually demanded of Israel faithfulness to Himself. This is the test with which every responsible human being in the world is faced in various degrees. It is the ultimate test of the Gospel, for the question that faces every sinner to whom the Gospel is presented is really, ' What shall I do with Jesus?'

To assist the man in his childlike state and to strengthen his resistance by calling upon his fears to co-operate with his nascent sense of duty and with the trust that he might naturally be expected to place in his Maker and Friend, God gave him a clear warning of the consequences of disobedience, and here we have the first expression of the great scriptural principle that death is inseparable from sin. It is expressed in Ezek. 18. 4, 20 : ' the soul that sinneth, it shall die,' or again in Rom. 6. 23 : ' the wages of sin is death.' It means that God and sin are incompatible, that where God is, there ultimately sin cannot be. In its widest application it means that God must put out of being a creation that is spoilt or corrupted by sin. What did this warning convey to Adam? If the words *in the day that* are taken literally as they stand in English, the warning can only refer to the spiritual state of guilt, separation from God, and slavery to sin, which the New Testament calls ' being dead in trespasses and sins ' (Eph. 2. 1). It is true that

35

Adam entered this state at the moment of his fall, and it would be foolish to exclude this meaning altogether from this verse. On the contrary it is unlikely that Adam could conceive of any such meaning in the words. He was in a state of innocence, and it is scarcely possible to suppose that he could understand the simplest doctrine of sin. Death however he could well understand, or at least would very soon understand it. He could see it taking place among animals and plants. Perhaps he had already watched the river of Eden carrying away dead insects or dead twigs. He would therefore realise that upon disobedience what he saw taking place naturally among animals would overtake him. The warning therefore most probably in the first place refers to physical death, and as Adam knew of no other life but the physical life that he was living, he would understand that death meant the end. We may then either regard the words *in the day that* as a general mark of time (see on verse 4) equivalent to ' when thou hast eaten,' or if we prefer to regard them as literal, immediate and definite, we shall see in the words *thou shalt surely die* the equivalent of ' become subject to death '. To us has been revealed the truth that physical death is not the end, but that one day ' all that are in the graves ' shall hear the voice of the Son of God and shall come forth (Jo. 5. 28, 29), and that the dead will stand before Christ's throne (Rev. 20. 12) After this there remains for the unrepentant sinner the second final, irremediable eternal death (Rev. 20. 14, 15). The second death is undoubtedly included potentially in the warning given to Adam. It is well to notice that it was not said to Adam, ' In the day that thou eatest thereof, thou shalt suffer eternal conscious torment.' If this is what the Lord God meant, surely here of all places He would say it clearly. On the contrary if we think for a moment of the analogy on which Adam would understand the word ' death ' (as explained above), we shall see more

clearly the nature and meaning of the second death, which is ' everlasting destruction ' (2 Thess. 1. 9).

VERSE 18. *The Lord God said.* When did He say this? Certainly not as an afterthought, but rather in planning His eternal purpose in the immutability of His counsel (Heb. 6. 17). *It is not good.* In every sense it was not good, but contrary to man's nature, that he should be alone. He had physical needs. He had in his heart potential emotions that could only be called forth in family life. Above all he could only give true expression to his nature as made in the image of God by social relationships of various and intricate kinds with other members of his race. God therefore determines to supply the need.

I will make. Man could not supply his own need. He cannot create life. No more can we bring life to souls dead in trespasses and sin. This is the work of God alone. *An help.* Woman was to *help* man. She was to help him serve and worship God, and she was to help him in his daily activity. This is exactly what she actually does, when she is true to her own nature. She was also to co-operate with him in the reproduction of the race. *Meet for him.* This means ' to match him '. Woman is the counterpart of man. Man and woman, when true to themselves, fit into each other and respond to each other.

VERSE 19. This verse begins with a summary of part of the work of the fifth and sixth days. It is perverse to argue that this chapter contradicts chapter 1 by making the formation of the animals subsequent to that of man. Elementary knowledge of Hebrew tells us that the translation ' had formed ' represents the original as faithfully as *formed*. This verse does however for the first time use the word *formed* in connection with the beasts and birds. It may carry a hidden meaning, but it seems more likely that we should think of the process as analogous to the formation of man (see verse 7).

Brought. This chapter gives an over-all picture of continuous fellowship between God and Adam. God took him and put him in the garden. He gave him a command, and now He brought the animals to him. *To see.* This is a favourite scriptural figure of speech, which uses of God language appropriate to man. God knew from the beginning what Adam would say. *Adam.* From henceforth in this section of the narrative the Hebrew word hitherto rendered ' the man ' is translated *Adam. Call.* There is a deep mystery behind this incident of giving names to the animals. Names in the Bible, and among the ancient Semites generally, are not artificial. They express, or are intended to express, the real characteristic of the person or object named. Firstly we may conclude that unfallen man possessed an instinctive perception of the true nature and being of the animal. This is something that seems quite unknown to us in our fallen state. The race may have possessed powers, which were lost at the fall except for occasional remnants, such as telepathy, or the instinctive interpretation of another's thought. Secondly we may ask ourselves to what extent linguistics are involved in this incident of naming the animals. A word in any one of the multifarious languages of the world today is completely artificial. It has no intrinsic connection with the object it represents. It is only by a series of accidents of linguistic history that a dog is called ' dog ', or ' chien ', or ' hund ', or ' cane ', or was once called ' kuon ' or ' canis '. Did unfallen man possess an instinctive, natural language, which in itself and of itself expressed basic realities? We can do no more than pose this question, but if the answer were ever found to be yes, the immense distance between man unfallen and fallen would be illustrated and emphasised. *Creature.* (See on 1. 20).

VERSE 20. *Adam gave names.* This close inspection of the animals and birds probably enabled Adam to observe that they all went in pairs and thus to realise his own need. *There was not found.* Here is Adam's realisation of his need. God knows what ways and means to use today in order to bring the sinner to a realisation of his own much greater need.

VERSE 21. This and the following verse describe the making of the woman. Why was she made from man in this way? There seems no precedent among the animals. The reason was to preserve the picture and type of the relationship of Christ and His church. It is not to be supposed that Adam and Eve understood this. In the case of Adam the particular manner of the woman's creation had the effect of giving him a close sense of proprietorship. Yet if the spiritual meaning were hidden from those who were most concerned in the making of the type, it unfolded itself increasingly to later generations, until under the Gospel it is completely understood. The serious consequences that fell upon Moses for breaking a type by striking the rock a second time (Num. 20. 11, 12) reveal the importance of exactitude in the types, and we may wonder whether, apart from the function of the type as an illustration to men, it may not be a necessity of the Divine nature to demand accuracy in the types as the expression of His purpose. We may compare Ex. 25. 40; Heb. 8. 5.

A deep sleep. The sleep of Adam, through which Eve was created, is the picture of the death of Christ, through which His church was brought into being. Adam was put to sleep presumably for the same reason as an anæsthetic is given today, to avoid suffering and inconvenience. The Lord in contrast deliberately took on Himself the suffering and death due to His people for their sins.

One of his ribs. It does not seem clear that ' rib ' is the correct translation of the Hebrew, which means ' side '. How much of Adam's side, or exactly what part of it, was used in this operation is not clear. Ingenious guesses, made in the light of modern knowledge of genetics, that a chromosome, or gene, was meant seemed ruled out by the last statement of the verse. An operation, the nature of which is not exactly defined, was performed on Adam's body. But the antitype is clear. Christ's church was taken from His wounded side. The blood that flowed from that side made atonement for His people and cleansed them from all iniquity (Jo. 19. 34; 1 Jo. 1. 7; 5. 6).

Closed up the flesh. Adam was healed and restored. So the Lord was raised from the dead to be the eternal Head of His people.

VERSE 22. *The rib . . . taken from man.* In the same way the very life of the true church is the life of Christ, her Lord and heavenly bridegroom. She is 'partaker of the Divine nature'. (2 Pet. 1. 4). The life is begotten in the hearts of her members by the operation of the Divine Spirit using the seed of the Word. *Made.* The Hebrew is ' builded '. Exactly so the church is built up. The process is still going on. The Gospel goes out into the world to quarry the stones, which are fashioned by the Divine Spirit to take their place in the building (1 Pet. 2. 4, 5), and the church is growing into a holy temple for the habitation of God by the Spirit (Eph. 2. 20-22).

Brought her unto the man. In the same way God the Father, having foreknown and predestinated the whole church in eternity past (Rom. 8. 29), brings the individual members as a gift to Christ (Jo. 6. 37; 17. 6), Who undertakes to lose not one of them, but raise each one up at the last day (Jo. 6. 39).

VERSE 23. *Bone of my bones, and flesh of my flesh.* Many old texts and versions quote this verse in Eph. 5. 30 in the form ' of his flesh and of his bones ' to explain and amplify the statement, ' We are members of his body '. The relationship of the believer to Christ is even closer than was Eve's to Adam. The union is

spiritual. The spiritual life of the Christian is the resurrection life of Christ, appropriated by faith and expressed through the lives and conduct of the separate believers. Christ and His people move as an organic whole. This unity is a fact in spite of appearances to the contrary and in spite of the corrupt nature still remaining in the believer. Its seat is the depth of the heart, where a new nature, justified and sinless, has been implanted. It will be evident in the world to come, where its working will be unhindered. Christ thus has greater proprietary rights over and in His people than Adam had in Eve.

She shall be called. Here is an instance of the giving of a name that expressed the origin and nature of the recipient. *Woman* is in Hebrew ' isha ', and *man* in this instance is ' ish '. Thus the name expresses the essential humanity of the woman, her close relationship to man, and the fact that she is his counterpart. This instance helps us to understand verses 19 and 20, and we can perhaps see the primitive human language being built up. God gave the first names (1. 5, 10), among which perhaps the name for man found a place. Man extended the language further by building on these root names. The play on words, which must have existed in the primitive language, is carried on in the Hebrew, into which the passage was finally translated, by the use of the terms ' ish ' and ' isha '.

VERSE 24. This verse contains the basic charter of marriage. The future tenses may be regarded as expressing not merely a simple statement relating to the future, but an expression of the purpose of God. God has so constituted human nature, that this purpose is instinctively carried out from one generation to another. The man sets out to found a family of his own, and the race continually reproduces itself. The process will continue to the end of the world (Lk. 17. 27). *They shall be one flesh.* The Septuagint Greek version, the

Peshitto Syriac version, the Latin Vulgate, and one recension of the Jerusalem Targum, read ' they two '. The Samaritan recension of the Hebrew text has much the same. The passage is quoted in the New Testament from the Septuagint as ' they two ', and this is likely to have been the original Hebrew reading, accidentally modified in the Massoretic Hebrew.

We learn from this verse (1) the inviolability of marriage. The Lord quotes this passage (alongside 1. 27) in His discussion with the Pharisees about divorce. He goes back over the head of Moses, who had allowed divorce as a concession, to this primitive standard set up before the fall of man (Mt. 19. 5; Mk. 10. 6). He interprets these words as a command of God. They appear here in our verse as a statement in the ordinary course of the text. The Lord says that they are God's words, which man has no right to undo. This verse, therefore, as interpreted by our Lord, teaches the non-existence of divorce in the sight of God.

We learn from this verse, as interpreted by the apostle Paul, (2) the manner in which the two become one. It is by the act of sexual intercourse. The apostle makes this explicit by his statement that sexual intercourse even with a prostitute brings the principle laid down in this verse into operation (1 Cor. 6. 16). Thus the purpose of God declared in this verse is brought and worked out through nature. An instinctive natural urge draws the man away from his parents to join his life with that of his wife, and a natural act, for which God has made provision in the constitution of the sexes, is the means of effecting His purpose of making both one. It is the sexual act that constitutes marriage. Legal systems still recognise this by providing for a 'nullity' if after legal marriage the sexual act is not performed. And in God's eyes, once the sexual act has been performed, a man and woman are united for life. Here lies the key to the supposed contradiction between

the two records of the Lord's declaration on divorce (Mt. 19. 9 and Mk. 10. 11, 12). The former is supposed to be modified by an excepting clause. But this clause does not allow divorce for unfaithfulness. It speaks of ' fornication ', not of adultery. It means that if a man finds his wife not to be a virgin, he *must* put her away, because she does not belong to him. There can be no marriage. She is already one with another, and if he lives with her, he can only live in adultery. The verse goes on to say that by putting away his wife and marrying another he is making out his first wife to be an adulteress, that is to say, acting as if she were not a virgin, in which case she could not marry him, but only live in adultery with him. This is the primitive ideal of marriage, from which the evil passions of fallen man's corrupt nature draw him further and further away, to which, however, the Saviour calls His own people to return, promising and providing for them power to obey God's law and maintain this ideal.

We learn from this verse (3) the nature of the relationship between Christ and His church, the spiritual antitype and counterpart of marriage. The apostle quotes the verse in the course of his instructions to Christian husbands (Eph. 5. 31). He is emphasising to them the sanctity of marriage on the ground that it is the picture of Christ's relationship with His church. The apostle says that the principle stated in this verse is a great mystery, but that it is explained by reference to Christ and His church (Eph. 5. 32). We can in fact see a double analogy. As a man leaves his father and his mother, so Christ left His Father's home in heaven to seek and win His church, to which He cleaves for ever. On the glorious day of resurrection, when the marriage of the Lamb is come (Rev. 19. 7), He will be united for ever to His people, who, being partakers of the Divine nature (2 Pet. 1. 4) will live and move with Him as one.

VERSE 25. *Both naked*. Open to the

eyes of all, their hearts were open to God. They were innocent and simple. *Not ashamed.* There is nothing to be ashamed of in nakedness as such. Shame is the outcome of a guilty heart.

CHAPTER 3

IN this chapter we have the story of the fall of man. The temptation and fall (1. 7) are followed by the colloquy between God and Adam (8-13) and the pronouncement of the curse with the promise of redemption (14-19). Then comes the naming of Eve (20), the provision of God of clothing for man (21), and lastly the expulsion from Eden (22-24).

VERSE 1. The serpent is introduced into the story with the same unexpected suddenness with which he perhaps appeared in Eden. This serpent was no snake. He is identified in the last book of the Bible with the devil, and Satan (Rev. 12. 9; 20. 2, where the expression ' old serpent ' means in Greek 'the original serpent'). The snake, whose creation was for the purpose of one of those moral lessons of which we saw evidence in nature in dealing with chapters 1 and 2, is intended to remind us of him. The devil was a creature of God, whose creation fell in the period referred to in Gen. 1. 1. He was a moral being of exalted nature, and the first in whom moral evil manifested itself. We read of his creation and life before his fall, his fall itself and his final annihilation in Ezek. 28. 11-19. His name Satan means that he is the adversary and accuser of the people of God, and his Greek name of ' devil ' emphasises his part in separating God and man. Our Lord calls him ' the prince of this world ' (Jo. 12. 31; 14. 30; 16. 11), and the apostle Paul ' the god of this age ' (2 Cor. 4. 4). The apostle also speaks of him as ' the prince of the power of the air, the spirit that now worketh in the children of disobedience ' (Eph. 2. 2). The Lord also said that the devil was a murderer from the beginning and a liar and the source of falsehood (Jo. 8. 44). The word translated ' murderer ' has a special reference to the killing of men. Here then in Eden we see the devil beginning his work of destroying the human race and luring it to death by falsehood. Sophisticated modern thought shrinks from regarding the devil as a fallen personal being. There are passages in the Bible which in isolation permit of his being thought of as a symbol of sin, or an impersonation of evil. A subtle line of modern thought gives him a kind of ghost personality, the concentration or sum of all evil personalities. But the Bible knows no sophistries like this. It seems impossible to assemble all that the Bible says about him without coming to the conclusion that he is a super-human personal being of a high order, created perfect like all God's creatures, but the author of evil through the conception of an evil thought and the formation of an evil choice in his will. Indeed it is impossible to conceive of the entrance of moral evil into God's creation apart from the existence of such a personality. The only form of evil that could enter the universe is moral evil. Evil could not enter through inanimate things, or through non-moral living creatures, which are all under the direct and continuous control of God. It could enter only through the making of a wrong choice by a being created with the power to do good, and therefore in the nature of the case with the power not to do it. Once within creation moral evil spread to other moral beings and produced other forms of evil, such as sorrow, sickness and death. *More subtil.* In Ezek. 28. 12 we read of the fulness of the devil's wisdom. By his fall this wisdom was perverted into subtlety and craftiness. It is more than enough for the intellect of man, especially of fallen man. By it he deceives the whole world (Rev. 12. 9), having gained an ascendancy over the human race owing to his success in the garden of Eden. *Beast of the field.* Why is the devil compared with animals? (1) Because he is referred to in this passage as *the serpent*, that is to say, as the antitype or counterpart of the snake; (2) Because such a comparison fits the situation of Adam and Eve, who apart from their Creator knew of no other being but animals. This was therefore the only comparison that it was possible for them to make; (3) Perhaps because according to Ezekiel 28. 14 the devil was a cherub, and the cherubim have some essential connection with animals. The cherub was conceived of as a composite being, but the actual or essential part of it was an ox. In the Apocalypse the cherubim are regularly referred to as animals (Greek *zoa*, meaning ' living creatures ', in the A.V. translated ' beasts ', Rev. 4. 6, etc.) *Which the Lord God had made*. These words state the creaturehood of the serpent. The Lord God had made him, as He had made everything else. The Bible never teaches dualism, the doctrine of two forces of evil and good, with separate leaders, engaged in a permanent struggle, whose outcome is doubtful, or at least immensely distant. The devil, though the source of evil and referred to as ' the evil one ', is all the time a creature of God and subject to His Divine sovereignty and restraint. This is comforting for the people of God.

He said unto the woman. This statement raises two questions: (1) How was it that the serpent entered Eden? (2) In what way did he speak to the woman? First then how was the serpent found in the garden? We need not ask *why* he was there. The rest of the chapter plainly describes what his malicious purpose was. But to ask *how* brings up a mystery, which cannot be completely solved. No one who knows God and understands the Bible will suppose that the serpent entered the garden when God's back was turned, or that he insisted on entering in opposition to the will of God. He entered at the very least with the permission and knowledge of God. For all we know there may have been previously in

heaven a conversation similar to that recorded in Job 1. 6-12; 2. 1-6. In this instance God twice took the initiative in drawing Satan's attention to Job. The issues in Eden however were so momentous, and the Bible is so insistent upon the sovereignty of God, that we are probably right in believing that Satan entered Eden as part of the pre-determinate counsel and foreknowledge of God. ' Known unto God are all his works from the beginning of the world ' (Acts 15. 18). Can we learn anything of this purpose of God? We have already seen that there are hints in the Bible that, evil being already in existence in the universe, the very creation of man may have been a step towards the redemption of all. We now know that the defeat of Satan is an essential step towards restoration. Evil in Satan had to be met and overcome. We also know that it is in the human race that the battle against Satan has been fought out and won. If this was God's purpose from the beginning — and it seems impossible to doubt it — Satan must be brought into contact with the human race. Could that battle have been won by Adam? In one sense our answer must be yes. Adam and Eve according to 1 Cor. 10. 13 could have withstood the temptation. Whatever view we take of the eternal purpose of God, we must never lose sight of the fact that Adam and Eve made a wrong moral choice. They sold themselves to do evil, became guilty before God and separate from His fellowship, and justly deserving of eternal death. But having said that, we must further say that, whether or not they could have resisted, in actual fact they did not, and God knew from eternity that they would not. Without, therefore, for one moment abandoning a full belief in the volition and guilt of Adam and Eve, it is possible to see in the fall of Adam a further step in the hidden eternal purpose of the God Who ' works all things together for good to them that love ' Him (Rom. 8. 28). Perhaps it was the fall that made possible a redemption in Christ, which stretches beyond the bounds of the human race, affects the spirit world (Col. 2. 15), and will finally deliver the creation from the bondage of corruption (Rom. 8. 21). We must repeat however that we shall go beyond the teaching of the Bible, if such a view leads us to suppose that the fall of Adam and Eve was inevitable. God, Who has infinite variations of method at His disposal to suit the possibilities of choice that He has given to His creatures, could, it goes without saying, have carried out His eternal purpose with equal facility and success, had the first man and woman resisted the devil.

We must next ask how the serpent spoke to Eve. Commentators and interpreters in the past have sometimes thought that a snake addressed Eve in human speech, and this had led on to the idea that animals possessed the power of speech at the beginning. The identification of the serpent in the Apocalypse with the devil destroys such crude speculation. This particular serpent was not a snake. He was a spiritual being. Did he then speak inwardly to Eve by suggestion to her mind? This is possible, but does not seem likely. It is true that the devil has access to the minds of sinners, but it is not easy to suppose that he had similar access to innocent minds. The simplest explanation is perhaps to take the hint offered us in 2 Cor. 11. 14, where we read that Satan is transformed into an angel of light. In making this statement the apostle seems to refer back to his reference to the deception of Eve in verse 3 of the same chapter. Perhaps, therefore, the serpent appeared to Eve's eyes in the garden as a shining angel and carried on the conversation with her in that form.

Yea, hath God said? This was not a genuine question, but a suggestive sneer, ' So God has said you are not to eat, has He?' This was the first shot in a campaign of lies. The question threw doubt on God's goodness. The devil has taken this line ever since. Many men and women today have in their minds false and uncon-

genial ideas of God, which come ultimately from the devil, in whom the whole world lies (1 Jo. 5. 19). *Every tree.* This seems better translated ' any tree '. The suggestion was quite false, as they could eat of all the trees but one, and it was corrected at once by the woman.

VERSE 2. The woman's answer is better understood if we read ' any ' for ' every ' in the preceding verse. It was a true and sensible answer. *We.* The woman knew that she was associated with her husband in the prohibition, which he had evidently faithfully passed on to her.

VERSE 3. *In the midst of the garden.* Like the tree of life the tree of the knowledge of good and evil was made conspicuous by its position. It is still *in the midst of the garden.* The difference between right and wrong is the hinge of human life, and the moral is the plane on which all true human life is lived. The poor good man is happier than the rich bad man.
Neither shall ye touch. Eve has been accused of adding to the Word of God by the utterance of this phrase, but the charge is not necessarily just. She may have been interpreting the prohibition, and her interpretation seems a sensible one. There was no object in touching the tree, and it would obviously be safer not to do so. The man and woman seem wisely to have decided not to go near the tree. If fallen sinners today were only to give temptation as wide a berth as this, there would be less tragedy in the world.
Lest ye die. This is exactly what the serpent wanted to happen.

VERSE 4. The serpent gives the lie direct to God, and the same is done by many a fallen sinner in the darkness of unbelief (1 Jo. 1. 10). This statement of the serpent's at once opened a conflict in the woman's mind. Was God or the serpent speaking the truth? Eve had enough light to answer this question, and she ought to have known. If the devil had confined himself to this categorical statement, he may not have convinced her, but he gives for it in the next verse a plausible and suggestive reason. This lie of the devil's is widely believed among sinners today, and has been so believed in every generation. Apart from the convicting power of the Holy Ghost acting upon his heart no one can believe that he is perishing. Some give little thought to spiritual things. Others believe that religious observance will set them right with God. Thousands believe in false religions and untrue ways of life. Many believe vaguely that all will come right in the end. But God's Word could not be clearer: 'the soul that sinneth, it shall die' (Ezek. 18. 4).

VERSE 5. *God.* Notice that in the conversation between the serpent and the woman the single name *Elohim,* God, is used, not, 'the Lord God'. This does not fit with the critical theories, but it exactly fits the story. The serpent would not use the Divine name, Jahweh. He is not, and never will be, in the sphere of redemption.

Your eyes shall be opened. This was literally true, but in a different sense from that which the devil implied (see verse 7). The serpent made Eve believe that an immense access of wisdom would follow the act of eating of the tree and its fruit, whereas the importance of the tree really lay in the fact that it was the subject of a command of God. The tree did not matter, as the devil pretended. It was God's command that mattered, and the serpent was careful to draw the attention of the woman away from God and His command and focus it on the tree. In the same way today the attention of the world is drawn away from God and concentrated on the truth or error of any particular way of life, as if any truth could be found anywhere except in God.

Gods. The Hebrew is Elohim, and probably refers to the true God. The serpent was suggesting to the woman the same wicked thought as came into his own heart and brought about his downfall (Isa. 14. 14). *Knowing*

good and evil. This also is literally true (see verse 22), but the knowledge meant something very different from what the serpent implied. God knows evil only to abhor it. Innocent man could only know evil to participate in it and perish by it.

VERSE 6. This verse gives us the first example of the truth of the principle expressed in Jas. 1. 14. Eve was tempted, being drawn away of her own lust and enticed. She had given true and sensible answers to the serpent. Her first sin was to look at the tree at the devil's suggestion that it was a tree of an extraordinary nature, which God was denying her arbitrarily out of envy or spite. She turned her eyes away from God on to the tree. And when she looked at it she *saw,* or thought she saw, three things. She saw these things in conformity with the three principles, which the apostle John tells us compose the wicked fallen world. These principles appear to have come into operation the very moment that Eve turned her head towards the tree and toyed with the devil's suggestions instead of rejecting them outright. *She saw that the tree was good for food.* This was the 'lust of the flesh' (1 Jo. 2. 16). She saw *that it was pleasant to the eyes.* This is 'the lust of the eyes' (*ibid.*) She saw that it was *a tree to be desired to make one wise.* This is 'the pride of life' (*ibid*). So that by one sinful, perhaps hesitant, look Eve brought into being the whole corrupt wicked world and enthroned the devil as the prince of it. These are the three principles that with differing emphasis and in a variety of forms govern the lives of every unconverted person today, and thrust their head into the heart of the believer also, if he is not careful to watch against them. Eve's look at the tree of knowledge, fraught with such catastrophic consequences, is in contrast to the look of faith that the sinner may take at the tree of Calvary, a look that by virtue of the Saviour's propitiatory death and in conformity with God's promise by the Gospel repeals and reverses the harm done by Eve and procures everlasting life.

She took. The evil principle worked out in practice. ' Lust, when it hath conceived, bringeth forth sin ' (Jas. 1. 15).

And did eat. As the fruit was digested and assimilated by Eve's body, so is the poison of sin assimilated by the human spirit. In contrast to Eve's taking and eating the forbidden fruit the sinner may take and eat the bread that came down from heaven and obtain everlasting life (Jo. 6. 51).

Gave also unto her husband. Sin is always social and infectious. No sinner can sin alone. His sin affects directly or indirectly all with whom he comes in contact, however remotely. Every sinner makes other sinners, or, if they are made already, entices them to further sin.

He did eat. The statement made by the apostle that ' Adam was not deceived ' (1 Tim. 2. 14) has sometimes been interpreted to mean that he deliberately took the fruit and ate it, knowing that the serpent had lied, but preferring to perish with his wife than to remain alone faithful to God. This seems unlikely. The statement of 1 Tim. 2. 14, taken in the context, may well mean to say that it was not Adam who was *originally* deceived. In that and the previous verse the apostle is stating that Adam had priority in creation and Eve in transgression.

There is nothing in the whole Bible to lead us to suppose that we have not here the story of two actual trees in an actual garden. In contending for this view we have to resist on the one hand the whole trend of sophisticated modern theology, influenced by rationalistic science and philosophy, which regards the whole chapter as unhistorical and mythical (myth being conceived in a special sense). On the other hand we have to resist that strain in medieval exposition, probably derived from patristic sources, which explained the eating of the fruit as symbolic of the sexual act. This idea arises from heathen ascetism, which had taken hold of the medieval church and caused it to exalt celibacy and virginity and equate them with chastity and to regard sexual desire as such as essentially evil. This is not the scriptural view of sex. (See on 2. 24).

VERSE 7. *Opened*. The serpent had said that their eyes would be opened, and when they were, the man and woman became conscious, not of any exalted sphere of Divine life to which they had expected to be raised, but of guilt and shame. This was their knowledge of evil.

Naked. This sentence means that the pair were overcome by a deep and embarrassing sense of self-consciousness. Clothes seem generally to have been connected in the human mind with sex, and ornamental clothing has much to do with sexual desire. But this aspect need not be fundamental. A sense of shame is conventional. Primitive tribesmen for example, previously unaccustomed to wearing any clothes at all, feel the same embarrassment at appearing clothed in public as does civilised man at stripping. The root of this feeling lies in acute self-consciousness, and this seems to be one of the fundamental aspects of sin. The sinner is self-conscious, where he should be God-conscious. His life revolves round himself as centre instead of round God. In the case of the first pair their sense of nakedness was a symptom of self-consciousness arising from a guilty heart. The outward nakedness was the counterpart of a guilty heart, which was naked before God and exposed to His holy wrath.

Their action in sewing the fig leaves together and making aprons to cover their nakedness is the picture of the general procedure of the sinner, conscious of his spiritual nakedness. He attempts by self-effort to clothe himself before God. He may seek to assuage the unrest of his guilty conscience by religious observance. Every religious system in the world, except the true faith of Jesus Christ based on the Bible, exists to supply a particular prescription for the purpose. The raw heathen rites, the pilgrimage to Mecca, the ablutions in the Ganges, the 'sacrament' of penance, are all variations of the same theme. A common method of sewing the fig leaves is by seeking to do 'kind deeds'. Religion and self-righteousness of many sorts are attempted outlets for the ferment of a guilty conscience within. The Jews of our Lord's time provided the most striking example of determined attempts to incur the favour of God by what the Apostle Paul called 'the works of the law', and it is exactly by these that no flesh shall be justified before God (Rom. 3. 20). So many are the aprons of self-righteousness.

Verse 8. *Voice*. This may be translated 'sound' and may refer to the sound of footsteps. It is clear that if the Lord God walked in the garden, and if His voice or the sound of His footstep could be heard, He was accustomed to showing Himself in visible form to Adam and Eve. This was the 'Angel of the Lord', the pre-incarnate Christ, 'Whose delights were with the sons of men' (Prov. 8. 31), Who appeared often to Moses and at least once to Joshua (Josh. 5. 13), to Gideon (Jud. 6. 12), or to the wife of Manoah (Jud. 13. 3). He is the second Person of the Holy Trinity.

Cool of the day. Differences of temperature did not affect the Lord God. Here is one of the first examples of the grace and goodness of God in meeting man on his own ground. He came at a time when it would be pleasant and comfortable for man.

Hide themselves. This is the way of sinners from that day to this. The inner sense of shame and guilt forces the sinner to avoid God, and, if unchecked, would thereby cut him off from the only source of salvation. The sinner today the world over raises the barricade of worldliness, of intellectual activity, of family life, but if we can pierce these barriers and reach his heart, we shall find it full of guilt. This guilt acting in a vicious circle keeps man from God. It is the cause of hatred of 'religion', and among many religious people of hatred of the true Gospel and of scriptural faith. Everywhere we see the sinner vainly seeking to hide from God. Adam and his wife *hid themselves amongst the trees of the garden*. They used good right legitimate things that had been created for their pleasure as barricades behind which to hide themselves. But 'can any hide himself in secret places that I shall not see him? saith the Lord' (Jer. 23. 24). 'Though they dig into hell, thence shall mine hand take them; though they climb up to heaven, thence will I bring them down: and though they hide themselves in the top of Carmel, I will search and take them out thence' (Am. 9. 2, 3). And the last picture that we find of sinners on the day of judgment is their calling upon the mountains and rocks to fall upon them and hide them (Rev. 6. 16).

Verse 9. *The Lord God called*. Here is the picture in miniature of the hiding sinner and the seeking Saviour. We learn from this verse that God takes the initiative and seeks the sinner. No move came from the guilty pair. They were silent, hidden, and presumably motionless. 'Thus saith the Lord God: Behold, I, even I, will both search my sheep, and seek them out' (Ezek. 34. 11). And at last He came 'to seek and to save that which was lost' (Lk. 19. 10). We next learn that God cares for the sinner. The question asked, 'Where art thou?' does not express desire for information. It is a moving question. It rings through this verse, quivering with the grief of the Divine heart. This is the heart of Jesus, which was so often 'moved with compassion' (Mt. 9. 36). It is to be noted that, apart from the serpent's scornful question, which was no real question at all, this is the first question of the Old Testament. It is the question of God seeking the sinner. Corresponding to it is the first question of the New Testament, ' Where is he?' (Mt. 2. 2), the question of the sinner seeking the Saviour. Thirdly we learn that God makes contact with the sinner. He asks him an intelligible question. This question was not only intended to reveal the care of God, but was also a convicting question. It could only be answered correctly by a confession of guilt. All these things are essential elements in the Gospel approach today.

VERSE 10. This verse reveals the ravaging effects of sin on the sinner's heart, mind and conscience. He is made aware of God's approach, and he seeks to answer Him, but the answer is irrelevant. *I was afraid.* This is the shrinking fear of guilt. It lies at the bottom of the sinner's aversion to the Gospel today. It is not that fear of the Lord which ' is the beginning of wisdom ' (Ps. 111. 10). The reverent and adoring familiarity of the fellowship of the garden, which is restored in the redeemed through the Gospel, had given place to guilty terror. The reason that Adam gave for his fear, though correct so far as it went, was quite inadequate. His nakedness was the outward symptom of a much deeper malaise, to which sin had blinded him. The case of the sinner today is the same. He is blinded by his sin to the real nature of his sin, and, though he is aware that there is something wrong, his sin appears to him much lighter than it really is, and his condition far less grave. Further than this, Adam's answer like that of all sinners avoids the real point at issue. He points to the symptom, the consequence, he avoids mention of the sinful act. In his heart he knew that he had eaten of the tree, and he foolishly hoped that he could keep the knowledge of it from God. There was more excuse for Adam in his inexperience than there is for the sinner today, who, whatever he does not know about God, knows that He is omniscient.

VERSE 11. *Who told thee?* This

brings home to Adam the fact that his sense of shame came from within, arising from his own sense of guilt and the corruption of his nature. Outwardly he was the same as before. In innocence he had been naked without knowing it. Now he knows good and evil, and the whole aspect of his life changes, as sin makes present to his mind a whole series of new facts and relationships.

Hast thou eaten? God goes right to the point with Adam, just as the Holy Spirit in pleading with men today seeks to put His finger on unconfessed sin. There can be no remedy, till this is dealt with. We find the Lord doing exactly the same thing in His conversation with the woman of Samaria (Jo. 4. 16-19).

I commanded thee. By this statement God sets before Adam the real moral issue at stake. The sin lay, not in eating fruit as such, but in breaking God's commandment, whatever that commandment might be. The liberal theologian speaks with contempt of the directions of the apostle about the short hair and uncovered head of men in contrast with the long hair and covered head of women (1 Cor. 11. 2-16). He considers that these instructions can be safely ignored and are not to be compared with the great commandments of the law. It may well be that the matters about which God gives commandments vary, and vary widely, in importance. But the fundamental point, missed by the liberal, in which the great commandments of the law and the instructions of 1 Cor. 11 are on an equal footing, is that all are *commandments of God.* The vital moral issue lies in the fact of the commandment, not in the matter about which the commandment is made. Adam might as well have said that a commandment not to eat fruit from a tree was of little importance. VERSE 12. In this verse we notice three things: (1) Adam spoke the truth in answer to this straight and terrible question. If he thought like all sinners that he could hide himself from God behind a tree, he may well have thought that by lying he could conceal the truth from God. But he did not do so, and in this fact we see the first effect of the convicting power brought to bear upon him by the God Who was so earnestly seeking him in his lost condition. The first step towards salvation is when the sinner decides to speak the truth to God. (2) Adam like every frightened guilty sinner sought to lay what blame he could on another. What he said was true, but perhaps he need not have volunteered it. Like all sinners he had an excuse ready. He had done wrong certainly, but it was not entirely his fault. He had been led into sin by his wife. He had had considerable provocation. So he seems instinctively to have argued. (3) In spite of his seeking to lay the blame on his wife he confessed his sin. *I did eat.* This confession made a bridge for mercy and formed a link from which God was able to build a way of salvation for Adam. ' If we confess our sins, he is faithful and just to forgive us our sins ' (1 Jo. 1. 9). Adam's confession is a model of the confession required by God from every sinner in at least one respect. It was made directly to God and to Him alone. The monstrous practice of confession by one sinner to another, who commits the added sin of falsely assuming authority to receive such confession and pretending to be a priest, is unknown to the Word of God.

VERSE 13. *What is this?* What is it indeed? The true nature of sin is never realised by the sinner until the Holy Ghost brings it home to his heart. Sin is defiance of God and spiritual suicide, something of immeasurable influence in this life and of eternal effect in the world to come. *Done.* Sin shows itself in acts in everyday life. ' He that doeth righteousness is righteous . . . . he that doeth sin is of the devil ' (1 Jo. 3. 7, 8).

The same considerations apply to the woman's answer as to Adam's. (See on verse 12). She spoke the

truth, she passed on the blame to the serpent (with more reason and justice), and she confessed her sin. *The serpent beguiled me.* The same serpent as beguiled Eve is ready to corrupt the minds of Christian believers today from the simplicity and purity that is in Christ. How often he succeeds in doing so. He can preach another Jesus, one who is not the Son of God or Saviour of the world, but no more than a great moral teacher. Above all he can preach a Jesus to be worshipped under strange material forms. He can give another spirit, a spirit that sometimes supplies great religious power and appreciation of music, art and sensuous beauty, and exercises a deep moral influence in the lives of religiously minded individuals. He can provide another Gospel, the gospel of compromise and hail-fellow-well-met, the gospel of justification by faith *and works,* the gospel of the sacraments, the gospel of just doing kind deeds. (See 1 Cor. 11. 3, 4).

VERSE 14. No question is asked of the serpent, and that for two reasons. (1) Confession in his case is impossible and irrelevant, because redemption and restoration are impossible. (2) If any question had been necessary, it had been asked ages previously at the time of his fall. The Lord God therefore proceeds to pronounce the serpent's doom. We may ask why it was that this pronouncement was made at this juncture, if the fall of the devil had taken place long before the creation of man. Again we may see two possible reasons. (1) In tempting the man and woman to their fall the devil had, as so often since, over-reached himself. He had taken a step which brought redemption nearer, if it did not actually help to make it possible, because it opened the way to the crucifixion of Christ, and the redemptive work of Christ reaches beyond the human sphere and undoes the harm done by the devil (1 Jo. 3. 8). The curse was therefore

47

pronounced, not perhaps for the first time, at a time when the devil's own action had made its fulfilment nearer. (2) The curse was pronounced at this juncture for the benefit of man, to whom this verse and the next are indirectly addressed. *Because thou hast done this*. The original fall of the devil must have brought on him the curse of God (see Ezek. 28. 16-19), but the corruption of man brought on him a further curse, and ironically made nearer the fulfilment of the original curse.

Cursed. Curse is the opposite of blessing. It brings withering destruction and ruin. It results from the reaction of God's holy nature against sin. The sinner is accursed (Isa. 65. 20). The disobedient are cursed (Deut. 27. 26; Gal. 3. 10). We as sinners were under the curse of God, till the Saviour became a curse in our stead and brought us the blessing (Gal. 3. 13, 14). The curse of God brings the wrath of God pouring down on the head of the sinner. *Above all cattle and above every beast*. The Hebrew literally means ' out of '. This may mean ' above ', as in our versions, or it might mean ' among '. If the former, the implication is that the cattle and beasts are cursed, but not so greatly as the serpent. If the latter, the meaning seems to be that the others are not cursed at all, but that the curse is a distinguishing mark of the serpent. For reasons why the devil is compared with cattle and beasts see on verse 1.

Upon thy belly shalt thou go. This is a sign of degradation. The devil henceforth would have a mark of degradation upon him in the eyes of all creation. The reptile, though created long before, was made in order to symbolise him, another proof that nature is full of lessons and examples of moral and spiritual realities. Sin always degrades. It detracts from true manhood and womanhood.

Dust shalt thou eat. In nature no snake does this. The words apply only to the devil, and they are the pictorial expression of humiliation and defeat. The devil has never been able to hinder the purpose of God. His corruption of man, as already mentioned, made possible his own defeat. His attack upon Job brought to Job double the blessing that he had had before (Job 42. 10, 12). His resistance to Joshua, the high priest, brought on himself rebuke, but forgiveness to Joshua (Zech. 3. 1-5). His temptation of David secured the site for the temple (1 Chron. 21. 1, 24-26). His temptation of the Saviour brought him utter defeat (Mt. 4. 1-11), and when he came again, he could find ' nothing in Him ' (Jo. 14. 30). His use of Judas Iscariot to bring about the betrayal of the Lord into the hand of His enemies (Jo. 13. 27) only procured his own destruction by the death of the Saviour on the cross. He goes about, ' like a roaring lion, seeking whom he may devour ', but he can be resisted stedfastly by faith (1 Pet. 5. 8, 9). He can hinder the apostle (1 Thess. 2. 18), but in doing so can do no more than bring into operation the great principle that ' all things work together for good to them that love God ' (Rom. 8. 28). And finally he will be bruised under our feet (Rom. 16. 20) and cast for ever into the lake of fire (Rev. 20. 10). From the days of Eden onwards his whole career has been one long series of damaging defeats, the more vexatious inasmuch as he often appears to be outwardly victorious, whether or not to himself, certainly to us in the weakness of our faith.

Verse 15. This verse is the mountain peak and climax of this chapter. It contains the first promise and prophecy of redemption, outlining in two pregnant sentences the two main features of its course, ' the sufferings of Christ, and the glory that should follow ' (1 Pet. 1. 11). About the verse as a whole we notice two things. (1) It was spoken to the devil, although in the audience of man. This means that the great drama of redemption has repercussions and consequences beyond the human race.

The cross of Christ meant the defeat of the devil, and the deliverance of creation from his deadly grip and blighting power (1 Jo. 3. 8; Rom. 8. 20, 21; Col. 2. 15). Yet the promise of the verse is essentially human. We may presume that Adam and Eve heard the words first spoken. Whether the devil had stood by all this time to watch the results of his attack and now was paralysed and speechless in the presence of the Divine Majesty we do not know. But if Adam and Eve did not hear the words spoken, they soon became aware of their significance, and the words at any rate stand in God's Word written for the comfort and edification of the people of God in every generation. (2) We notice that this promise of redemption was made immediately upon the fall of man. Nothing could illustrate the love, goodness and grace of God better than this. This was the first movement in grace towards the sinner. No word of blame was uttered, and even before the announcement of the temporal consequences that God has caused to follow the sin, the promise of final restoration and victory is made. The friend of sinners stood that day in Eden.

I will put enmity between thee and the woman. The woman here represents redeemed humanity. She is spoken of *in persona ecclesie,* merged into that which she represents, as was the case with ' the seventh day ' in 2. 2, 3, and so often in the language of the Old Testament. Thus in Psalm 16 and many other places David speaks *in persona Christi,* and in Ezek. 40. 48 and many other passages the world to come is spoken of in language applicable to Palestine. At the time of her creation Eve symbolised the true church (2. 23). Between the devil and the church of the firstborn God has put an eternal enmity, and there is continual warfare between them. The devil seeks to exterminate the church by persecution, or by allurement into sin. The church overcomes by faith. In Eph. 6. 10-18 we have an account of the weapons with which the church fights the devil, and in Rev. 12. 7-11 we see the warfare in progress. As the devil hates the church, so the church hates the devil and strives to deliver Christ's lost sheep from his grip and power. This enmity is wholly after the mind of God. It was established by Him and is maintained by Him. *Thy seed and her seed.* Here we find the first reference to the two classes into which the Bible divides humanity. Neither racial, nor social, nor any other artificial differences are taken account of by God. On the other hand these two fundamental sections are commonly ignored by man. ' Thy seed ', the seed of the serpent, consists of unredeemed humanity, all unconverted persons who die unrepentant. The first of their number was Cain (1 Jo. 3. 12), and the Jews of our Lord's day were his brothers (Jo. 8. 44). The relationship is of course spiritual and moral. The Bible never suggests the physical paternity of the devil. The two classes are sometimes called wise and foolish, sometimes just and unjust, sometimes believers and unbelievers, among other terms. We find them frequently contrasted in the Psalms, notably in Psalm 37. The *seed* of the woman is first of all Christ Himself, just as later, when the line of descent was concentrated in the family of Abraham, it is Christ Who is pre-eminently Abraham's seed (Gal. 3. 16). But Christ's people are closely associated with Him as the seed (Gal. 3. 29). Redeemed humanity is the seed of the woman, just as unredeemed humanity is the seed of the devil. ' This is the generation of them that seek him, even of them that seek thy face, O God of Jacob ' (Ps. 24. 6, marg.). This is the seed that will serve the Lord and will be accounted to the Lord for a generation (Ps. 22. 30). It is the true and new Israel, the true and redeemed humanity. Enmity is established between these two seeds, not a personal enmity of the righteous for the wicked, but an incompatibility of outlook and principle. The wicked hate the Gospel and the truth. They often hate the believers also. The righteous hate the world and its ways, though never the individual people who compose it (Jas. 4. 4; 1 Jo. 2. 15). The rather strange expression *her seed*, that is, seed of the *woman*, may well conceal the truth of the virgin birth of Christ. At least light is thrown on the expression by the event. *It shall bruise*. *It* refers to the seed of the woman, that is to say, to Christ. The Hebrew word rendered *bruise* (shuph) only occurs on two other occasions in the Old Testament, and its meaning is not easily determined. There is a rather more frequent form, presumably of the same root (shaaph), which means to desire to swallow up, and it is this form which the Septuagint translators appear to have read here. The idea seems to be that of pursuit and bitter enmity. Whatever the exact meaning of the verb, the picture seems to be clear. To bruise the head is a picture of fatal and final destruction. To bruise the heel is a picture of damage, which is neither fatal nor final. Thus Christ destroys the devil. His victory was won in His passion and resurrection, it is applied in the ingathering of His elect and in the hearts of individual believers, and will be consummated in the destruction of Satan after the end of the world. On the cross Satan bruised the heel of Christ by causing Him damage and suffering. But this damage was not final. Christ rose victorious, never to suffer or die again. Both the victory of Christ and the suffering of Christ are shared by His people. God will bruise Satan under our feet, because the victory of Christ is imputed to us and worked out through us and in us (Rom. 16. 20). And while in this world we share the sufferings of Christ (*never* of course in the propitiatory sense), being exposed, as God permits, to the malice of Satan, and possessing the privilege of being instruments in the proclamation of the Gospel (Phi. 3. 8-11).

VERSE 16. *Unto the woman he said*. The temporal judgments now pronounced must have been greatly softened in their effects by the promise of final victory that had just been made. They express in the experience and history of every generation the principle that sorrow and death follow sin, and they bear permanent witness to the fact that our race is fallen. *Thy sorrow and thy conception*. The most natural way to understand this double expression is to take it as meaning ' the sorrow that accompanies thy conception '. We should not understand the word ' *multiply* ' to imply that sorrow existed beforehand and would now be greatly increased. It means ' make for thee very great sorrow '. This will guard us from taking the two expressions separately and supposing that conception was to be multiplied, that is to say, that more children were to be born as a result of the fall than would have otherwise been the case. If there is any difference, the contrary is more likely to be true. No. Sorrow would not exist apart from the fall, but conception would. If, therefore, the expressions are separate, the word *multiply* must mean something different in either case, and this it could not bear. *Sorrow*. There is scarcely ever found, if at all, in the Old Testament, a word carrying the conception of our physical pain. Pain is always described as sorrow. The growing realisation by the most modern science of the close connection between the mental and the physical is thus well in accord with the biblical conception of man. The body is governed by the state of the mind more than has been realised in the past. *Conception*. This means here the whole process of female reproduction through pregnancy to birth. *In sorrow*, that is to say, in pain. *Bring forth*. This is the actual birth. The sentence concentrates and defines the meaning of the previous one. Every childbirth with its difficulty and anguish is a witness to the fall of man, a reminder that all is not well, and a call to repentance and conversion. *Thy desire shall be to thy husband*. The most natural way to understand these words is as the margin — 'subject to thy husband', that is to say the woman would not be free to possess and attain her desires without the permission of her husband.

He shall rule over thee, as in the east generally in ancient and modern times, and in Mohammedanism in particular. Even in the west until the present century all public and large spheres of social life have been dominated by man, and women's interests have not been greatly considered. This rule of life has not always been followed. There is evidence of civilisations in which women were supreme, that have been displaced by the social life which has been dominant in Europe for thousands of years, and have left strange traces of their existence. Such a type of public and social life gave rise to many abuses. The revolt of woman today, is persisted in, must either be the herald of a new order, or help towards the destruction of civilisation. The dominance and tyranny of man are evidence of the fall of the race.

VERSE 17. *The voice of thy wife.* Though we have seen that Adam was probably deceived, as his wife had been before him, it remains true that had he listened to God instead of to her, he might have saved them both. ' If any man cometh after me, and hateth not . . . wife . . . he cannot be my disciple' (Lk. 14. 26), where to ' hate' means ' not to prefer'. God demands that He should be supreme over every other person and interest in our lives.

I commanded thee. Here lies the moral issue, as we have seen. (See on 2. 16; 3. 3, 11).

Cursed is the ground. Difficulties caused by supposing that some physical change must have been brought about in the soil are perhaps lessened by remembering that all life and the forces of nature are maintained moment by moment by the Creator's will and power. His blessing is the cause of fruitfulness (see on 1. 22). He has but to remove His hand or diminish His sustaining power, and

the lowered fertility of nature, which constitutes the curse, is brought into being.

In sorrow. If Eve's sorrow was directly physical, Adam's was due to anxiety, pressure and lack of respite. ' The way of transgressors is hard ' (Prov. 13. 15).

VERSE 18. *Thorns also and thistles.* The production of these may be due to the lowered vitality of nature consequent upon the withdrawal or diminishing of God's sustaining power. However that may be, they are typical of the ugly moral and spiritual growths that spring up in every fallen heart. The curse of God is on these things, and the end of them and the soil from which they grow is to be burned (Heb. 6. 8). Weeds in the garden and weeds in the heart all provide evidence of the fall of man.

VERSE 19. *In the sweat of thy face.* Man can only sustain himself by labour and toil in place of eating the fruits of Eden. The simple trust and dependence upon God in which unfallen man lived are replaced by the self-effort of fallen man. In things physical and economic this self-effort in God's providence is not unfruitful. In spiritual things it is utterly barren. Thus since the fall the road to success in this world has been hard work (2 Thess. 3. 10). In addition to (1) the pains of childbirth and (2) the subjection of woman, here is (3) the necessity for hard toil in order to make a living as evidence of the fall of man. We ought to allow these things to give us their evidence and teach us the right lessons, and try to direct the minds of men and women everywhere to the facts which God has provided these sad things to speak of. *Till thou return unto the ground.* Here is the fourth, the saddest, indeed the supreme witness to the fall of man. No one can avoid hearing its voice. Its incidence is universal. ' The wages of sin is death ' (Rom. 6. 23). The description of death in this verse is in harmony with the whole general outlook of the Bible upon the nature of man and the meaning of death. Here is God's original explanation to man of the fact of death. No word is said about any separation of man's person from his body to go on living discarnate in a state of suffering, or on repentance of blessedness. If this is what death means it is difficult to understand why it was not mentioned and clearly explained here. Man was taken from the ground. He is dust and returns to dust. The book of Ecclesiastes, describing the same event with obvious reference to the present passage, adds, ' And the spirit shall return unto God who gave it ' (Eccl. 12. 7). At death the life principle, breathed into man at the first (Gen. 2. 7), returns to the Giver, and man is left a lifeless corpse to disintegrate and mingle once more with the ground. This verse proclaims the failure and tragedy of natural life on earth. Death proves its failure. Yet the promise of verse 15 with its announcement of final victory includes the abolition of death for the people of God by a glorious resurrection at the last day. This is the great victory over death proclaimed in the Bible, and the only way to circumvent death that is there taught. This verse also encourages, if it does not demand, the practice of Christian burial. The proper place for the dead is in the ground. Of course provision is made for the final resurrection of all the dead on the day of judgment, whether buried or not (Rev. 20. 13). Lack of burial does not affect resurrection. It does however mean disgrace to the dead, and the Bible always conceives of refusal to bury as lack of reverence (1 Ki. 21. 23; 2 Ki. 9. 36, 37; Jer. 22. 19; 36. 3). In contrast to the heathen around them, who have often burned their dead, Jews and Christians have rightly persisted in the custom of burial.

VERSE 20. The brevity of this account of such stupendous events which is the product of literary creative genius and the inspiration of the Holy Ghost, sometimes makes this verse at first appear isolated and disjointed. It is however neither. The great name *Eve* represents Hebrew *chava,* which means ' life ', or ' living '. The life mentioned in this verse is in designed contrast to the death of the previous verse. *Adam called.* This is the expression of Adam's faith in the promise made by God in verse 15. He evidently believed that the seed of the woman would bruise the serpent's head. He further realised that this victory included the reversal of the sentence of death, which his sin had brought upon him and his race. It would not have been necessary to refer specially to Eve as the ancestress of the whole human race. This she obviously is. Adam discerned that she had been set by God in opposition to the serpent, and that her seed would consist of all those who possessed eternal life. In face of the curse and in face of the death sentence he therefore gave her the triumphant name of Eve, a reminder to himself, to her and to her children that death would one day be finally overcome.

She was the mother of all living. In this capacity, as in the manner of her creation and in her enmity to the serpent, she still represents the true church of Christ. She is the type of Jerusalem, which is above, which is the mother of us all (Gal. 4. 26).

VERSE 21. This verse follows from the last. In it God reveals the *way* of the final victory over death, in which Adam and Eve believed. The verse is in designed contrast to verse 7. There we find the guilty pair seeking to assuage their conscience, cover their shame, and set themselves right with God by inadequate and futile self-effort. Here is revealed the right way. *Did the Lord God make.* This is the first essential. All adequate and effective covering for the sinful heart, which will conceal its guilt and make it acceptable to God, must be provided by God Himself. Man is helpless in this fundamental matter. ' God will provide himself a lamb for a burnt offering ' (Gen. 22.

8). ' Behold, the Lamb of God, which taketh away the sin of the world ' (Jo. 1. 29). God gave His Son for a perishing world, sent Him to redeem it, provided in Him of His free grace a refuge for the sinner, and stirs the heart of the lost to appropriate and take advantage of it. *Coats of skins*. Here is the second essential. The provision of skins had necessitated the death of an animal, so that we have a complete illustration in practice of the fundamental biblical principle that ' without shedding of blood is no remission ' (Heb. 9. 22). The death of this animal was the first picture of the death of Christ, in virtue of which alone the believer is justified, clothed, set in his right mind and given access to God. The coats provided by God to clothe the guilty pair are the picture of the robe of Christ's righteousness and the garment of salvation, won for the people of God by Christ on the cross, applied through the Gospel, and appropriated by faith.

Clothed them. Notice that God not only killed the animal, wove the coats and presented them to Adam and Eve. He actually clothed them. He did not offer them to them for acceptance. He did not finish this work of grace and mercy until they were standing completely clothed. This must have involved the removal of the fig-leaf aprons, if they had not already worn threadbare. Just the same God does for His people. He does not offer them shelter and salvation and leave it to chance whether or not they will accept them. Presumably Adam and Eve could have resisted God's action, but, if it was God's purpose and will to clothe them, who cannot easily say who would have prevailed? Thus God never leaves His people. From beginning to end salvation is a work of His grace. He provides the Lamb, slays it at infinite cost, weaves the coats, and clothes His people, not satisfied till they stand complete in Christ, having perfect access and acceptance.

There can be little doubt that the act of God in putting this animal to death was the origin of sacrifice. In this way God ordained it at the beginning of the world, so that men in every generation might have before them the illustration of God's way of salvation. It was known and practised in the next generation (Gen. 4), and although it was much later organised under the Mosaic law, it is found still today among peoples and tribes the world over. Could man have thought out this practice and imposed it upon his descendants as a universal custom, if it had not been revealed in the beginning by God?

VERSE 22. *The Lord God said*. The conversation is again between the Persons of the Holy Trinity, as in 1. 26.

Become as one of us to know good and evil. In the fact of the knowledge man had become like God, but in the manner of the knowledge he was utterly different. God knows good and evil by eternally choosing the good and abhorring the evil. Man knows them by the guilty experience of an evil choice. All human life is coloured by this double knowledge. The scientific knowledge of today, for example, has brought immense good in the relief of suffering and the healing of disease, but hand in hand with these discoveries have gone inventions of unimaginable destruction. The laboratories, in which war is waged on disease, have at the same time produced material for what is known as bacteriological warfare after the devil's own heart. The workshops that have abolished distance and put friend in touch with friend, immeasurably lightening the missionaries' task, have made weapons of destruction already powerful enough to blow the whole human race into eternity and perhaps set the very planet adrift from its orbit. ' The wicked is snared in the work of his own hands ' (Ps. 9. 16).

Put forth his hand. The hand that could not refrain from taking of the tree of knowledge of good and evil must be restrained from taking of the tree of life.

Live for ever. Had man been able to eat of the tree of life, the sentence of death, pronounced in verse 19, would presumably have been nullified. An eternal life in sin would be an offence to God and a misery to any who lived it. Death mercifully closes the corrupt life of fallen man. But though man in flesh and blood is debarred from the tree of life (1 Cor. 15. 50), the believer may eat of it now in his heart by faith (Jo. 6. 54), and one day in a glorified body will enjoy its fruit for ever.

Verse 23. *Sent him forth.* It was sad enough to be shut out of the garden of Eden and to look back on its lost delights while wrestling with the stubborn soil. It is sadder still to be shut out from the presence of God, to have no access, to hear of Him ' by the hearing of the ear ' Job 42. 5), but only to know Him as silent and absent. But this is the sinner's state. *To till the ground.* God mercifully provides for man an exacting occupation, which will prevent him from having the leisure to indulge his sinful propensities to the full. Idleness is the parent of vice (Ezek. 16. 49). *From whence he was taken.* There is a tragic irony in these words.

Verse 24. *Drove out.* The anger of the Lord is scarcely restrained at the sight of sin. *At the east.* This was presumably the direction in which man was driven. He would find himself in northern Persia, or perhaps on the Russian steppe. What loneliness and desolation! One man and one woman with a boundless earth stretching to the horizon around them! *Cherubims.* These are beings of a type that we might call spiritual animals. They symbolise the presence of God, and were thought of (and seen by the prophets) as providing a kind of chariot on which He rode (2 Sam. 22. 11; Ezek. 1). In the vision of Ezekiel the Lord was com-

ing to judgment. Figures of the cherubim were carved of a piece with the lid of the ark of the covenant, and like it overlaid with gold, their faces being directed towards the blood-stained mercy seat. Here they again symbolise the presence of God at the place where He met with men in redemptive mercy (Ex. 25. 18-22). In the Apocalypse the *cherubim* are seen in the midst of and around the throne of God, and they render Him unceasing praise and worship (Rev. 4. 6-8). The cherubim are fourfold beings. They have the face of a lion, an ox, a man, and an eagle. In this respect they appear in the four Gospels, which tell the story of the presence of God on earth in Christ. Jesus Christ is portrayed in the Gospels under the four aspects symbolised by the faces, a king, a servant, a man and the Son of God. So here in this verse the cherubim manifest the presence of God, from which man has been shut out by sin. The *flaming sword which turned every way* is the symbol of the wrath of God. Nothing can escape it. It searches every cranny and reaches to every corner: ' His eyes behold, his eyelids try the children of men ' (Ps. 11. 4). His wrath forbids the sinner access to His presence, and will pursue and devour sin, till no vestige of it is left in His creation. ' If I whet my glittering sword, and mine hand take hold on judgment; I will render vengeance to my enemies, and reward them that hate me ' (Deut. 32. 41). So the wrath and the vengeance and the judgment of God keep the way to the tree of life, and fallen man cannot reach it. But it will be restored one day. It is in the midst of the paradise of God, and its fruit is promised to the overcomer (Rev. 2. 7). It stands on either side of the river of life, which flows through the new Jerusalem. Only the tree of life to come is the eternal reality, the Lord Jesus Christ Himself, while that of Eden was a symbol. Man gains in Christ more than what he lost in Adam.

CHAPTER 4

THIS chapter gives us the story of Cain. The birth of Cain and Abel (verses 1 and 2) is followed by the story of their offerings (verses 3-7), leading up to the murder of Abel (verse 8). Cain's punishment follows (verses 9-15). After this comes a brief account of Cain's family (verses 16-24), and the last two verses (25, 26) describe the birth of Seth. With the end of the chapter the section which began at 2. 4 concludes. The chapter follows closely on the last. It reveals the effects of the fall in the production of a murderer in the first generation, and illustrates the division of the race into the two seeds mentioned in 3. 15.

VERSE 1. *Knew.* This special reference to sexual intercourse implies that it was the first time that it occurred. From this we may make two possible deductions. The first is that the period during which the man and woman lived in Eden before the fall was short. We can in fact understand why the old commentators so often asserted that the fall took place on the same day as the creation. We need however scarcely be reduced to this conclusion, for a second possible deduction from the first statement of this verse is that in the slow tempo of the life of our first parents with their perfect health and immense span of age (5. 5) intercourse took place much less often than under the conditions of life as we know them today. It is possible that it took place only at special times or certain periods of life.

Cain. The name is said to mean ' Gotten ' or ' Acquired ' (see A.V. margin). Probably it is not directly derived from the actual Hebrew root of that meaning, but is sufficiently near to it in sound as to suggest it and to make a play upon it. This kind of assonance is frequent in Hebrew.

I have gotten a man from the Lord. This is the reading of the Targum of Onkelos (3rd cent. A.D.). It requires the addition of a Hebrew letter not found in the Massoretic Hebrew text. The reading of the Revised Version, ' with the help of the Lord ' is probably correct. Eve rightly acknowledged the hand of the Lord in the birth of her child. The Divine Name used here and henceforward in the chapter is Jahweh alone. The use of the names in chapters 1 to 4 shows a significance and design that confounds the foolish theories of differing original documents based on the Divine Names. In chapter 1 the Creator is Elohim. In chapters 2 and 3 the combination Jahweh Elohim (Lord God) identifies Elohim of chapter 1 with Jahweh the Redeemer of chapter 4.

VERSE 2. Abel is the first attested member of redeemed humanity, or the seed of the woman.

Keeper of sheep . . . tiller of the ground. The domestication of animals and the practice of agriculture were thus taking place in the first generation of mankind. The theory of modern anthropologists that long ages of human prehistory elapsed, during which man lived by hunting and fishing before acquiring the knowledge of agriculture, is therefore false. Modern anthropology asserts that agriculture first appeared in Mesopotamia in the fourth or fifth millennium B.C. This might agree well with the Bible narrative, were not inferior cultures held to have been in existence during thousands of years previously. Perhaps the truth is that the inferior cultures have been seriously antedated, and that they are really contemporary with the higher. An alternative theory that human or semi-human beings existed independently of Adam and long before him seems to raise more difficulties than it solves and to be unsatisfactory both to the Christian and to the scientist.

VERSE 3. *In process of time.* The Hebrew has literally ' at the end of days '. As both brothers appear to have brought their offerings together, and the occasion seems to have been special, these words may refer to a typical festival of the kind established under the Mosaic ritual law. It has been suggested that the phrase refers to the sabbath, but this seems unlikely, as the impression given by the text is that the offering was special or unique rather than regular. In any case a primitive revelation is implied, and a localised sanctuary appears to have been established similar to the Mosaic tabernacle. In this way the facts of redemption and the coming of the Redeemer were foreshadowed from the very first by a Divine revelation.

The fruit of the ground. The ground had been cursed by God, and its fruit could not be accepted by Him. *Offering.* This is literally in the original ' gift '. The only present that God requires or desires from men is the surrender of their whole lives and hearts to His service and obedience.

VERSE 4. *The firstlings of his flock and of the fat.* The fat was regarded as the richest and best portion. Abel therefore brought to the Lord the first and the best of what he had. This is the true spirit of obedience and offering. It is true that we have nothing to give and that it is our duty to give all, but it is essential, if only to maintain life, that we use for ourselves much of what God gives us. In this practical sense we ought to give back to Him the best and to give it as a first charge, before we make any use of His gifts for ourselves, the first tenth of our income, the best of our talents and powers, the first assignment of our time.

The Lord had respect. See on verse 5.

VERSE 5. *He had no respect.* Notice here that both the offerers and the offerings were involved in the contrast. First of all the *offerers* were different. ' Cain was of that wicked one ' (1 Jo. 3. 12). He was of the seed of the serpent (Gen. 3. 15), not physically (Gen. 4. 1), but spiritually and morally. He was not reckoned of the seed of the devil because he

was a murderer. He was a murderer because he was a child of the devil. His murder was the fruit of his evil nature. So it is with every sinner. No man is a sinner because he sins. He sins because he is a sinner. Cain, born after the fall, was conceived and born in sin (Ps. 51. 5). Abel, on the other hand, was of ' the seed of the woman '. Our Lord calls him ' righteous Abel ' (Mt. 23. 35). There is only one way in which Abel could have been righteous. Like Cain he too was conceived and born in sin. Every believer knows the way, and the Epistle to the Hebrews states it categorically. It was ' by faith ' (Heb. 11. 4). Abel had believed, no doubt through his parents, the promise of God made at the time of the fall (Gen. 3. 15). He was the first to see the promises afar off, to salute them and to embrace them (Heb. 11. 13). Believing the promise of God, he was justified by faith, and became the first trophy of grace gathered in from a lost and fallen race. Abel was therefore accepted by God because of faith itself the gift of God (Eph. 2. 8), and Cain was rejected because of unbelief.

In the second place there was a difference in the actual *offerings.* No doubt it was natural for Cain to offer the fruits of his own toil for he was a tiller of the ground, and no doubt Abel's offering was equally appropriate. The real reason for the acceptance by God of the one offering and His rejection of the other lay in the spiritual condition of the offerers, on which we have just dwelt (Heb. 11. 4). At the same time it is clear that the offerings themselves are presented to us in the narrative as contrasted types of spiritual realities. Cain's offering, the result of self-effort and hard toil, and bloodless, corresponds to the fig-leaves of 3. 7. Abel's offering on the other hand was a bleeding lamb. His offering must have been killed, or he could not have presented the fat. It corresponds to the coats of skins of 3. 21, and is the first type and picture (apart from the slain animals of 3.

21 whose kind we do not know) of the Lamb of God, that taketh away the sin of the world (Jo. 1. 29). We do not know to what extent, if to any, Abel understood the type, but in bringing his sheep or lamb he was conforming to the method of worship instituted by revelation from God at the beginning (3. 21). Obedience thus went hand in hand with his faith, as it always does (Rom. 16. 26). *Cain was very wroth.* In this we recognise fallen human nature, as we know it today. Cain was jealous, and it is important to notice that the whole controversy that aroused his jealousy was *religious* in character. Cain was unwilling to believe in God, or to obey God. Like all sinners he turned to his own way (Jude 11), and supposed it to be best. At the same time he could not bear to see his brother enjoying the favour of God, which his guilty conscience told him was denied to himself. The satanic hatred of the righteous, of their faith, their Gospel, their worship and their ways which in varying degrees is common to all the unregenerate, flared up in his heart. This is the true source of religious persecution.

VERSE 6. *The Lord said.* We do not know how the Lord manifested Himself to the two brothers, either in the acceptance and rejection of their respective offerings or in the communication now made to Cain. The natural implication of the text is that He spoke in some outward way, as He had done to Adam and Eve in the garden, rather than in the conscience or heart. *Why?* The purpose of these questions was to bring home to Cain the unreasonableness of his jealousy, and how unnecessary it was. All sin is unreasonable and unnecessary. Sometimes a direct question of this sort may reach the sinner's heart and turn him to repentance.

VERSE 7. This verse supplies the proof of the unreasonableness of Cain's jealousy. *If thou doest well.* We must not read into these words

any legal doctrine of acceptance by works. They express in the broadest sense the basic moral relationship between God and man. To do well means to believe on the One Whom God has sent, whether in the full light of the Gospel or in the shadows of the legal, or the primitive, revelation (Jo. 6. 29; 1 Jo. 3. 23; Rom. 2. 7).

Shalt thou not be accepted? Cain might have been accepted on the same terms as those upon which Abel was accepted, by simple justifying faith. It is to be noticed that the same influences towards repentance and faith, which had been brought to bear with success in the case of Abel, were being exercised towards Cain. Here is no doctrine of reprobation. Nothing shut out Cain from blessing but his own unbelief. And here the Lord pleads with Cain to believe, as Abel had believed, declaring that the same acceptance as Abel enjoyed awaited him also on his repentance. All who are ultimately lost are responsible for losing themselves.

Sin lieth at the door. For ' lieth ' the Revised Version has ' coucheth ', conceiving sin to be figured here as a beast of prey lying at the door of Cain's heart in readiness to spring upon him and devour him. Evidently the point of the wild beast's spring is thought of as the irreparable murder of Abel. This is a powerful and valuable conception, but it scarcely does justice to the meaning of the verse. In fact it is open to more than one objection. If the wild beast waiting to spring is the sin of murdering Abel, we have something approaching a suggestion by the Lord to Cain that the murder was inevitable. The murder certainly is not definitely mentioned, but even an approach to a hint of it seems open to objection. Again Cain was already in the grip of sin. He was of the seed of Satan, and conceived and born in sin. Sin in the biblical sense is the root, the sinful nature, not a specific deed, however heinous. Further still, this interpretation breaks the context and obscures the point of the verse, which is that Cain's anger and jealousy are needless, because he is in the same position as Abel as touching acceptance with God. It is much better to take the Hebrew word meaning ' sin ' in the sense of ' sin-offering ', which it often bears. This falls into line with the rest of the verse. It means that God has provided for Cain, as much as for Abel, a propitiation for sin. Abel had taken advantage of it, so also may Cain. The typical sin-offering was the bleeding lamb, which Abel had already brought. The essential and substantial sin-offering is ' the Lamb of God, which taketh away the sin of the world '. The *door* at which the sin-offering lies is then the door of access to the presence of God. Here the holy eternal sin-offering perpetually lies, available for every sinner, and sees His seed, when the sinner makes His soul an offering for sin (Isa. 53. 10). He is Himself the door of His sheepfold, lying across its entrance to protect His sheep (Jo. 10. 7). Thus no one can enter the fold without passing over, or, as it were, through, Him. But every sinner who pleads the Saviour's merits and lays his sin on His head has thereafter for ever perfect freedom of access to the glory of the Father's presence.

Unto thee shall be his desire. If we adopt the interpretation of the Revised Version, we shall explain the pronoun ' his ' as referring to sin, the wild beast crouching at the door, whose desire is set on devouring Cain, and we shall render the following sentence, ' But thou shouldest reign over him ', that is to say, ' But instead of allowing sin to fulfil its desire of devouring you, you should have the mastery over it '. The Hebrew forms will bear this sense. Again however it does not seem to be the natural meaning. The words of the last two sentences of the verse are substantially the same as those spoken to Eve (3. 16), and it is difficult not to think that they have the same meaning. In this case the pro-

nouns ' his ' and ' him ' refer to Abel. If Cain would repent and believe, and take advantage of the propitiation provided, he would not only be made right with God, but his relations with his fellow-man and brother would be set right also. Cain was the elder brother. Perhaps it was his duty to act as family priest. Perhaps he felt affronted at the very fact that Abel made an offering at all, and regarded his doing so as insubordination and contempt of his own religious functions. In any case, if Cain put himself right with God, he would regain his proper ascendancy over his younger brother. It might be that, if he were willing to offer the proper typical propitiatory sacrifice on behalf of the family as a whole, there would be no need for Abel to offer another. We should note that this verse brings out the fact that right relationship between man and man depends upon right relationship between man and God.

VERSE 8. *Talked with.* The Hebrew says, ' said unto ', but in the Massoretic text, from which the Authorised Version was taken, no words follow to express what was said. They dropped out by mistake at an early stage, but are supplied by the Samaritan recension, which dates from the time of King Hezekiah, the Septuagint Greek version, the Peshitto Syriac version, and the Jerusalem Targum all of which drew upon an earlier text, which was doubtless original. In these versions the sentence reads, ' And Cain said unto Abel his brother, Let us go into the field '. The next sentence thus follows on easily in its place. These words bring out the fact that the murder of Abel was planned and premeditated.

Slew him. ' Cain was of that evil one, and slew his brother ' (1 Jo. 3. 12). In the same verse the apostle tells us the motive. The contrast between his own evil deeds and his brother's righteous ones was more than he could bear. This is the first and typical example of the general attitude of the devil's children towards the children of God. It lies behind the murder of the prophets, the crucifixion of the Lord, and the outbreaks of murderous persecution against the church by Rome pagan and so-called Christian.

VERSE 9. *The Lord*. Cain may have supposed that the deed he had done concerned only himself and his brother. If so, he was wrong. God is concerned with every relationship between man and man. Sin against a fellow man is sin against God (compare 2 Sam. 11. 1-12, 14 with Ps. 51. 4). The Lord therefore intervenes to demand of the murderer an account of what had happened to His child.

Where is Abel? He was beyond the reach of Cain sleeping safely and securely in his grave till the day of resurrection and glory, free from the troubles of the wicked, knowing nothing of the long passage of time through which his race were to wait for redemption, ignorant of most of the trials and horrors that the devil was to bring upon mankind.

I know not. Cain knew nothing of this, but his answer was none the less a lie. He did not like Adam confess his sin. He sought to conceal it in the vain hope that he could keep it from his Creator's all-seeing eye. This hope of his is shared by many other foolish sinners. Cain is a living symbol of the work of the poison of sin. His unreasonable anger, bitter jealousy, helplessness before his violent passions, folly in supposing he could hide his crime from God, form an epitome of fallen human nature, as we know it now, and as it always has been in the world.

Am I my brother's keeper? Cain asked this question in defiance. He disclaimed responsibility. But the question is one that each of us ought to ask. The right answer is yes. We have a responsibility for our fellowmen. This responsibility was present under the law (Lev. 19. 17). It is greatly increased under the Gospel

(Rom. 1. 14). The thought of opportunities missed, and the fact that many may, humanly speaking, be finally lost for lack of a word that we might have spoken, would be unbearable, if we did not know that God overrules all.

VERSE 10. *What hast thou done?* God asks of Cain the same question that He asked of Eve (3. 13). It is a convicting question, a shaft aimed at the heart. *The voice of thy brother's blood*. Abel did not consciously cry. The expression is a vivid Hebrew figure, the meaning of which is clear. The murder cried out for vengeance. Like all sin it outraged God's righteous law, and it cries in His ears till the wrong is put right. In this respect Abel is typical of the martyrs of all time. In Rev. 6. 10 we find the souls of the martyrs of Jesus crying to God from the ground beneath the altar on which they were slain. Their cry for vengeance has sometimes puzzled readers of the Apocalypse. But it is not a conscious cry. The soul is identical with the blood (Lev. 17. 11, 14, Hebrew). The clamour in the ears of God must now be becoming unbearable. So this gentle character passes from the earthly scene, faithful, obedient, unresisting, justified by faith, the first to give his life for his God and for righteousness. Not only does his unconscious blood cry out to God for retribution, but his testimony speaks to every age. He blazed a trail and set an example. Few could have had less light on the Gospel, but what he had he followed and obeyed. 'He being dead yet speaketh' (Heb. 11. 4).

VERSE 11. *Cursed*. Sin as always brings its curse (see 3. 17). The very cursed ground now disdains the one who had committed such an outrage.

Earth. We may equally well translate this 'land'. The earth in the Bible never means the planet, but the dry land as opposed to the sea, and the Hebrew word often refers to a particular land or country.

VERSE 12. *The Ground.* A further curse is set upon all ground touched by Cain. In this verse we have a picture of the twofold consequences of sin. Firstly *it shall not henceforth yield unto thee her strength.* The sinner's life and effort are largely wasted, even in the course of his ordinary occupation by which he makes his living. No sinner does his work perfectly. Few do it well. The sinner's natural powers and talents are eaten away by sin. He is constantly battling with the unquiet of his own heart. His energies are dissipated, his life spoiled, and the purpose of His Creator for him left largely unfulfilled. He is very far from getting out of life what the Creator put into it for him. He is never satisfied, and his powers of enjoyment are warped.

The second characteristic of the sinner is that he is *a fugitive and a vagabond in the earth.* He is never settled and never still. He is for ever seeking to escape from God, or from himself. He has no assured hope and no permanent resting-place. He goes from one amusement to another, from one hobby to another, often even from one occupation to another, seeking rest and finding none. The ghosts that inhabit his guilty heart pursue him and drive him here and there. No sinner need wait for the world to come to experience what it means to be a lost soul.

VERSE 13. *My punishment is greater than I can bear.* The marginal rendering is *Mine iniquity is greater than that it may be forgiven.* Which ever be the rendering, Cain was wrong. The reading of the text charges God with inequity, even with cruelty. But the sentiment is on the lips of many sinners. We may notice the significant fact that the death penalty was not awarded for this first of murders. At a later date it was brought in to illustrate the principle of strict retaliation (Gen. 9. 6). But the fact that it did not follow this first of all murders is enough to prove that in the purpose of God the death penalty

is not fundamentally interlocked as a moral necessity with murder. This should deter those who clamour for it today, among whom it is sad to find many Christian people, who owe their salvation to the grace of God. Natural and spiritual death are fundamentally attached to all sin, but not so judicial death to the sin of murder only.

The readings of the margin, if correct, proves that Cain had given way to despair. It is a strange fact that many sinners would rather despair than humble themselves to ask forgiveness of God.

VERSE 14. Cain's attitude is not that of repentance. He may have felt remorse. He is occupied with fear and complaint at his punishment, and is pursued by his persistent sense of grievance. *Earth.* The word is best taken here in the sense of *land.*

From thy face. Cain is probably referring to a local sanctuary, which may have been set up (see on verse 3). He thought that if he was denied access to this, he would be cut off from God. He is certainly expressing a spiritual principle, and there is much pathos in the fact that he was grieved at the raising of a barrier between himself and his God.

Everyone that findeth me shall slay me. It is unlikely that any principle of retaliation had been directly revealed at so early a stage in the history of the world. Such a promulgation is rendered the more unlikely by the fact that the death penalty was not inflicted on Cain. He sensed instinctively the moral propriety of retribution, and knew the principle of retaliation, because he was a moral being, made in the image of God, and had the work of the law written on his heart (Rom. 2. 14, 15). Sinners know in their hearts what is right and what is wrong more clearly than they realise, they are condemned by their own heart, and are subject to an uneasy conscience. In his heart the sinner knows that he has done wrong.

VERSE 15. *Therefore.* Notice the goodness and mercy of God in listening to Cain's complaint and providing against his fears. This murderer was actually preserved from retaliation by a special decree of God. He is slow to anger and abundant in goodness and truth. The purpose of this goodness to Cain was the same as that of His goodness to every sinner. ' The goodness of God leadeth thee to repentance ' (Rom. 2. 4). It was still possible for Cain to turn to the God Who loved him and from Whom he was sad at parting.

Sevenfold. The purpose of going beyond the balanced standard of retribution was to provide a deterrent, and in this fact we see the second of the principles involved in punishment. The first is retribution. The second is the prevention of further crime by awakening the fears of the sinner. (See Deut. 13. 11; 17. 13; 19. 20).

Set a mark. It is difficult to know what this means. Mark means literally ' sign '. Some commentators, including W. Gesenius, think that the meaning is that God gave Cain some sign in confirmation of His promise of protection. The advantage of this interpretation lies in its simplicity, but it seems merely to cut the knot. The Revised Version has ' appointed a sign for Cain '. This seems to mean that if Cain's fears were aroused, he was to utter some recognised cry, or perform some recognised action, which would deter others from attacking him. The rendering of the Authorised Version carries this idea further, and implies that some visible mark was set on Cain's body, which could presumably be recognised at the distance of a bowshot. If this is the true interpretation, the nature of the mark is a matter of speculation. Could it have been a black skin? The mark set on Cain, whatever it may have been historically, is a type and picture of the mark that sin makes on every sinner, manifest in his face, revealed in his manner of life, and expressed in his actions. We may notice incidentally that, if the interpretation of either of our versions is correct, the prevalence of violence and murder is implied. Cain had many imitators.

VERSE 16. *Went out from the presence of the Lord.* He left the land in which a local sanctuary had presumably been set up, and had no further access to it (see on verses 3, 14). In the same way every sinner is debarred from the presence of the Lord, to which access can be had only in Christ (Rom. 5. 1, 2), and will one day be punished with everlasting destruction from it (2 Thess. 1. 9).

The land of Nod. This is an ancient name, evidently unknown to the first Hebrew readers of this passage, because its position has to be explained to them. If it was *on the east of Eden,* it might have been anywhere to the east of the Caspian Sea. It represents the land of spiritual darkness, destitution and death in which every sinner dwells. But it is *on the east.* Perhaps it is not too highly speculative to suppose that this implies the possibility of a morning of regeneration and resurrection to life in Christ (Eph. 5. 14), while the sinner is still in this world.

VERSE 17. *Cain knew his wife.* The childish problem of the identity of Cain's wife was part of the stock-in-trade of Tom Paine and the nineteenth century infidels, and is not unknown to have been given a derisive turn by rationalists of the twentieth century, including theologians. Our passage does not say that Cain found his wife in the land of Nod, but implies on balance that he took her with him. She must have been a daughter of Adam and Eve (see 5. 4). So long as we allow that the human race sprang from a single pair, as the Bible teaches, no moral problem attaches to the inevitable intermarriage of the first generations. On the implications of this sentence see on verse 1.

He builded a city. It was in the

line of Cain, cut off from the presence of the Lord, that the simple pastoral and agricultural life was first left for the organised and complicated activities of a city. Cain turned the family into the state. He introduced the political and social problems that absorb so much of man's life. Public life with its cares, and the artificial set of relationships which it introduced, did not originate from God, but from fallen rebellious man. The first city was built by a condemned murderer. It is good to remind ourselves that this side of life is essentially part of the world. At the same time the conclusion that God calls on His people to forsake it entirely and to set up their own simpler communities, which has sometimes been drawn and acted upon, is extravagant. We are to make to ourselves friends of the mammon of unrighteousness (Lk. 16. 9), and we are to carry the Gospel deep into the cities of the world.

VERSE 18. The murderer's children multiplied, and family after family came into being, deprived of the knowledge of God, doubtless in increasing forgetfulness of the traditions of Eden, certainly in increasing ignorance of the true God and His way of life. In the background of this verse we can see the great heathen systems and godless states of the world coming into being.

VERSE 19. *Two wives.* In the fifth generation from Cain came the first recorded instance of polygamy. Its origin in the family of Cain is appropriate. Though this practice was tolerated by the patriarchs and under the law, it was against the primitive purpose of God. This is made clear by the prophet Malachi who accuses the Jewish priests of unfaithfulness to their wives, and quaintly says that God had enough spirit to make more than one woman in the beginning, had He been so minded (Mal. 2. 14-16). Polygamy destroys true family life and domestic happiness. Apart from the indirect word of Malachi,

just referred to, there is no direct prohibition of polygamy in the Bible, but we are left to infer from the narratives its unsatisfactory nature and the unhappiness that it causes. The bitter quarrels of Sarah and Hagar, the troubles made for Jacob by the wrangling sisters and their maidservants, or the suggestion of deep loneliness that steals through the story of David's life, all tell the same tale and point to the same conclusion.

VERSE 20. This verse tells us the origin of the nomad life and of the domestication of *cattle.* The *cattle* are presumably oxen, as opposed to sheep and goats, which were already known (see verse 2). Thus cultures were initiated, and progress was made, all in the family of Cain. Human life can expand in this way apart from the knowledge of God, and this passage makes it clear that such expansion can take place without His blessing. Material progress, culture, and invention are not necessarily a sign of His approval or a proof of His co-operation. These verses carry an important, but unheeded, lesson for the civilisation of the present day.

VERSE 21. Father means inventor and originator. *Harp.* This was a primitive stringed instrument, probably a small lyre with three strings. *Organ.* This was a pipe or reed. Thus music was originally a worldly invention, and though it has a large place in the spread of the Gospel, the Holy Spirit is more apt to use the human voice, which can sing the Gospel more intelligibly, than an instrument.

VERSE 22. *Instructor of every artificer.* The literal meaning of the Hebrew word translated *instructor* is ' whetter '. This should more naturally be followed by a word meaning an instrument rather than a person, and the Revised Version renders boldly, but perhaps without sufficient basis, ' forger of every instrument '.

Whatever be the exact meaning of the phrase, it is clear that Tubal-Cain was the inventor and originator of metal working. The view of archæologists today is that the use of metals, which must have revolutionised life, succeeded neolithic cultures at a comparatively late date. Two considerations however enter into the interpretation of this passage. The first is the possibility that metals and their use were kept a guarded secret in the possession of a single family or clan for many generations. The second is our ignorance of the date of Tubal-Cain. In the genealogy given in these verses he is sixth in descent from Cain, but there is no guarantee that links are not omitted in ancient genealogies (see Mt. 1. 8). There may therefore be many names omitted between those mentioned in verses 17-22. Besides this, we do not know the date of Cain, nor that of the creation. We have no right to cavil at the statement of this verse, till we know the date to which it refers and the part of the world in which this culture is depicted as starting. The mention of *brass and iron* together creates a difficulty in our present state of knowledge, but like many other difficulties in the Bible it is likely to vanish with fuller archæological light. *Brass*, as mentioned here, is copper. *Naamah*. The mention of women in ancient genealogies is so rare, that Naamah is likely to have been pre-eminent for some reason unknown to us, but possibly known to the first readers of this section. As the Holy Ghost has done no more than mention her name and has hidden from us the reason for the allusion, we must not dwell upon it. The occurrence of the name however provokes three speculations. (1) This woman may have been married into the line of Seth. (2) She may have been notorious as the first to indulge in the practices mentioned in 6. 1-4. (3) She may have been outstanding in the line of Cain as having embraced the faith and worship of the true God. This would be best of all.

Verse 23. This and the following verse are in poetic form in Hebrew, and contain three pairs of parallelisms. The poetic form may be derived from the original pre-Hebrew text, if such, as seems likely, existed, and may represent a very old recitative, possibly Sumerian, which may have preserved the name and deeds of Lamech for generations.

I have slain. The memory of Cain's murder of Abel was preserved in his family, and seems by now to have become a cause for boastful pride. Lamech is proud of his own violence. *To.* An alternative rendering is *because of,* which makes better sense. Someone had attacked Lamech in a way which he regarded as a violation of the pact made with Cain (see verse 15), and he had retaliated by taking the law into his own hands.

Verse 24. Lamech invokes the pact with Cain, but goes wilfully far beyond its terms. The little poem as a whole gives the impression of strong self-will and defiance of God. On this note the history of Cain's race ends. The evil beginning led on to an evil climax. From the natural point of view it was a brilliant race. It organised political life, domesticated cattle, introduced the musical arts and devised the use of metals. It thus possessed a high and progressive civilisation. But it was characterised by sexual excess and self-willed violence. It presents in miniature the picture of this whole corrupt wicked world, which is likely to lead up to a similar climax on a larger scale (2 Pet. 3. 5-7; 2 Tim. 3. 1-13).

Seventy and sevenfold. The Septuagint Greek version and the Vulgate Latin have ' seventy times seven '. If this is the original reading, there may be a reference to it, and a designed contrast, in Mt. 18. 22.

Verse 25. *Adam knew his wife.* See on verse 1. *Seth.* The consonants of this name suggest the Hebrew root and form which mean ' appointed '. *Hath appointed me another seed.* Here is an instance of a principle, which permeates the whole of God's purpose of redemption as it is unfolded in the Bible, and as it has been worked out in history. God did not restore Abel. He appointed a new seed. Thus when Adam and his posterity fail, He does not restore them as such, but appoints the Lord Jesus Christ as the Head of a new redeemed humanity. When the old Israel fails, He appoints a new one, the true church, gathered in from every race (Mt. 21. 43; Gal. 6. 16). When the old covenant fails, He does not restore it, but appoints a new one (Mt. 26. 28). When the law fails, He appoints the Gospel. When Aaron's priesthood fails, He appoints Christ a priest for ever after the order of Melchizedek (Heb. 9. 6-14). When flesh and blood fail, He appoints instead of it resurrection glory. When the old corrupt nature fails, He appoints a regenerate nature for His people, indwelt by the Holy Ghost, and constantly renewed with power from on high.

VERSE 26. *Enos.* This name resembles that of Enoch, the son of Cain, though it is not identical with it. It is the first sign of an inclination to imitate the race of Cain, a trimming of the sails, and a sailing near the wind. It betokens an admiration for that evil race, and a desire to copy it as far as possible without going the whole length. The next chapter will show us more of this attitude and will reveal how the race of Seth was led to within an ace of ruin and extinction, and how God's purpose was almost frustrated by Seth's failure to separate utterly from Cain.

To call upon the name of the Lord. This seems a doubtful rendering of the Hebrew, and it is difficult to see the point of the sentence, as it stands in the text. The true God was known in Eden and if the name Jahweh was not known in the beginning, it was not known, it seems, till Moses' time. The margin has, ' to call themselves by the name of the Lord '. The word *themselves* is not

expressed in the original, there being no object to the verb *call*. If this is the right sense, the sentence denotes defiance of God an an attempt by man to assume the attributes and position of the Most High. This might refer to the rise of a heathen priesthood, which, like its direct successor, descendant and representative, the Romish priesthood of medieval and modern times, blasphemously appropriated to itself functions, such as powers of absolution and regeneration which belong to God alone. The late E. W. Bullinger, D.D., who, though late in life he fell into dispensational extravagance, was an able scholar, substituted for *themselves* the words ' their gods ' in this sentence. He interpreted the sentence as referring to the rise of a blasphemous heathen idolatry, which finally brought the ante-diluvian world to destruction. He had a brilliant insight, and he may well have been correct.

CHAPTER 5

WITH this chapter begins the third section of the book, which is called ' the book of the generations of Adam '. It continues to 6. 8. The chapter consists of an elaborate genealogical table, which links Adam with Noah. It is like a skeleton to the narrative. It is varied only by the story of Enoch.

VERSE 1. *This is the book of the generations of Adam.* This is the title of the third section of Genesis, which lasts till 6. 8. The title differs in form from the titles of other sections by the insertion of the words *the book.* This implies that when the title was given it, it was compiled in writing. In the nature of the case the material is likely to have been handed down orally and added to as the generations passed. It was not written till the time of Noah, when writing may already have been in use in Mesopotamia.

In the day. See on 2. 4. This and the next verse link up with 1. 26-28, thus helping to make a literary unity of the whole book. The earlier account of man's creation is summarised here, in order that we may have before our mind the purpose of God in creating man as we read the table of generations, and perhaps specially as we read the latter part of the section, which is found in 6. 1-8.

VERSE 2. *Called their name Adam*. In this statement we notice two things. First, it was God Who gave man his name. Adam was able to give the animals their names (2. 19, 20). He could take their measure. Only God is able to reveal to man his true nature and the purpose of his creation. Since the fall this has been doubly true. The Greeks said, *Gnothi seauton, know thyself*, but this is what man cannot do. He has a wrong estimate of himself, which governs his conduct and attitude to life. We are dependent as much today as ever upon the revelation of God's Spirit through His Word for a true picture of what we are. We get it in such a passage as Jer. 17. 9, and it is only by the grace of God that we are able to accept it. Secondly, we notice that Adam was the name not of the man only, but of the whole race. The woman was made from Adam, bone of his bone, and flesh of his flesh. Thus in the great New Testament theological references to Adam the whole race is included. The woman was the first to be deceived and had the pre-eminence in the transgression. But this makes no difference to the fact that 'in Adam all die' (1 Cor. 15. 22). The fall was a single racial event, although there were several steps in the process.

VERSE 3. Here begins the genealogical table. Its arrangement is uniform in each generation. First are given the number of years lived by the father until the birth of the son through whom the genealogy is carried on. This is followed by the number of years that make up the rest of the father's life, and the statement of the birth of more sons and daughters. Then the total age of the individual in each generation is stated. The standing difficulty felt by all modern readers of the chapter lies in the immense length of the lives of these ten patriarchs, which mostly lie beyond or just about nine hundred years, and range from seven hundred and seventy-seven in the case of Lamech (verse 31) to nine hundred and sixty-nine in the case of Methuselah (verse 27). There are two obvious ways of getting over the difficulty, and each has been tried. Firstly, it has been suggested by one acquainted with modern Arabian genealogies and family histories, often accurately passed down by word of mouth from generation to generation, that the names in this table with their attendant length of years refer to clans, not individuals only. If this were the case, verses 9-11 (for example) would mean that after ninety years of the existence of the clan founded by Enos and called by his name, a clan was founded separately by one of its members called Cainan, who was in the line of descent from Enos. This clan broke away, no doubt owing to increase in population, and after its departure the Enos clan continued to exist for eight hundred and fifteen years. To regard the names as those of clans does not mean to deny that an individual was in each case the founder of a clan which took his name. We have actually a similar case in Scripture. In Acts 7. 16 the name ' Abraham ' refers to the clan, or family, of Abraham, the patriarch himself, who founded it, being dead when the transaction referred to took place.

This theory is not rationalistic, but reverent. Tempting however as it is, it does not seem that it can be reconciled with the statements made here and elsewhere in Scripture. We know that Seth was an individual, born of Adam and Eve (4. 25). The first statement of verse 3 must therefore refer to the individual Adam's life. Adam must have been a hundred-and-thirty at the birth of Seth.

Furthermore we know that Enoch was an individual and was translated (verses 21-24; Heb. 11. 5). We also know that Noah was an individual, and the statements of great age, made later (7. 11), must refer to him as such.

The second way of resolving the difficulty, which often occurs to readers' minds, is to regard the years as much shorter than the normal solar year of our experience. A recent fascinating American book has sought to show that changes in the motions of the heavenly bodies have occurred from time to time, which would materially alter the length of the year. Such a theory however seems hardly capable of sober proof. And if it were true, it would take us a very little way. Suppose for instance we take these years to be normal lunar months. Very good results appear in the case of the aggregate length of the lives. Adam would be seventy-seven, Methusaleh, the oldest, eighty-two, and Lamech sixty-five. But this will not work out for the years at which the sons were born. It would make Adam the father of Seth at ten (after the murder of Abel) and Mahalaleel and Enoch fathers at five. Neither will it work out for the log of the flood, which gives the months of Noah's six hundredth year.

It seems clear that the Scripture means us to understand that the individuals mentioned in this table did actually live to these immense ages. We have hints and scraps of evidence from secular sources that human life was once longer than it is now, notably in the Vedic hymns, which are estimated to date from the fourteenth century B.C., and were probably produced in the Indus Valley. No length of life as long as this is however ever recorded elsewhere. We must remember that these early men lived in what the Apostle Peter regarded as a different world (2 Pet. 3. 6). The race was in its infancy. There was no history of the ravages of sin or disease, and climatic conditions and forms of life in the past history of the earth, and we must ac-

cept the information that the Holy Spirit gives us. It should lead us to consider the shortness of our own lives and to realise more nearly the urgency of evangelising the unsaved and of using every moment of our time in the service of God.

The number of years given for each generation in our Authorised Version are those of the Hebrew Massoretic text. The figures both in the Samaritan recension and the Septuagint Greek version differ from the Massoretic, and are even greater. While it is generally considered that the Massoretic text is more likely to have preserved the original, we cannot be certain in the cases of difference which reading is correct.

By simply adding up the relevant figures in these ten generations we get a chronology from Adam to Noah. This was the basis of the famous calculations of Archbishop Ussher which appear at the head of the margins of our Bibles. He dated the creation 4004 B.C. The Samaritan and Septuagint figures would carry it back to the sixth millennium. This dating is remarkably short. In fact we cannot rely upon this table as a basis for chronological calculations, because there is no certainty that generations, perhaps many generations, are not missed out. As an example of this we have the Lord's genealogy in Mt. 1. 1-17, where comparison with the Old Testament shows at once that at least two generations were missed out. They are Ahaziah and Joash between Joram and Uzziah in Mt. 1. 8. Similarly in the genealogies in the first book of Chronicles there are occasions where abbreviation takes place. Therefore here as well it may be that only ten prominent figures out of a much larger number of generations are mentioned. We have here family history, not chronology, and there is nothing in the Bible to prevent us from placing the creation of man as far back in time as archæological and anthropological evidence warrants. We do not know how long the antediluvial world lasted. It may have been many thousands of years. *In his own likeness after his image.* These words are probably intended to contrast with verse 1. The original image of God was now marred, and Adam's son was like Adam, not like God. Thus the evil effects of the fall have been passed on through each generation to the present day, creating in every man's heart a bias that makes it easy and inevitable to do evil and impossible to do what is right.

VERSE 5. *And he died.* The cumulative effect of this simple phrase (verses 8, 11, 14, 17, 20, 27, 31) is impressive. Its repetition brings home the universality and inevitability of death. A sense of the vanity and frustration of this present life begins to steal over us thus early in the Bible, as we read this chapter. Generation by generation the full tragedy of the fall unfolds itself more and more. Even the patriarchs through all their long lives were ' all their lifetime subject to bondage ' through fear of death (Heb. 2. 15). The hold of death upon men could not be broken till through death the Redeemer destroyed the devil, who had the power of death (Heb. 2. 14).

VERSE 6. *Enos.* See on 4. 26.

VERSE 12. *Mahalaleel.* This name seems to show a faint half-hearted imitation of that of Mehujael in the family of Cain (4. 18).

VERSE 15. *Jared.* Again there is a half-frightened imitation of the name of Irad, Cain's descendant (4. 18).

VERSE 18. *Enoch.* The Apostle Jude calls Enoch ' the seventh from Adam ' (Jude 14), by which he means the seventh in this list. His statement is quite consistent with the possible omission of links in the genealogy. It distinguishes him from the son of Cain.

VERSE 22. *Walked with God.* Here is the vivid Hebrew way of describing a saintly life. The name Enoch is

identical with that of Cain's son (4. 17), a fact that seems to show that the compromise and imitation, indulged in by Seth's line, had now blossomed into identity with the world. God's answer to this was His call of Enoch, the greatest saint, prophet and witness of the antediluvian world. The Septuagint version renders *walked with God* by ' pleased God ', and this is the form in which the sentence is quoted in the Epistle to the Hebrews (Heb. 11. 5, 6). The fact that Enoch pleased God is proof to the writer to the Hebrews of Enoch's faith. He was a believer, as Abel had been, and his faith looked beyond the wicked world in which he lived to the promise of redemption and the eternal glories. Like Abel he becomes one of the heroes of faith. Enoch was not only (1) a consistent believer of saintly life lived in continual communication with God. He was also (2) a fearless prophet and witness. The Apostle Jude tells us that he denounced the prevalent wickedness and foretold the second coming of Christ to judgment at the end of the world (Jude 14, 15). How did the Apostle know this? The words attributed to Enoch in Jude 14, 15 appear in the apocryphal Book of Enoch, which is generally regarded as having been written about the beginning of the Christian era, and the critics tell us that the Apostle quoted from it. The approved dates of the book of Enoch and of the Epistle of Jude are so close, that there seems no reason why we should not suppose Enoch to be quoting from Jude rather than viceversa. This however does not explain the source of the Apostle's knowledge, which is unlikely to have been a direct revelation of the Holy Ghost. Now the book of Enoch is accepted by the Ethiopian church as canonical, and the book was long known in an Ethiopic version only. What is the reason for this mistaken reverence for the book in Ethiopia? There are strong traditions connecting Ethiopia with King Solomon. The imperial house believes itself descended from

Solomon and the Queen of Sheba. There exists in the country a colony of Jews, the Falashas, who regard themselves as the descendants of Israelite merchants, who settled in the country in Solomon's time. They possess the Pentateuch and carry out its ritual laws with precision. If this tradition with regard to Enoch's preaching, and this summary of his message were original, and if it were handed down in writing or orally through the patriarchs and Moses to Solomon's time, might it not have been taken to Ethiopia by the ancestors of the Falashas? The apocryphal book might have been written round it, and the antiquity of the tradition might have originated the Ethiopic reverence for the book. Whatever the source of the Apostle's knowledge, and whatever the difficulty in understanding the connection of his words with the apocryphal book, we have every right and duty to accept the Apostle's words as inspired by the Holy Ghost and therefore to be humbly received and believed.

Begat sons and daughters. Enoch was no monk or mystic. Like other members of his family he undertook the responsibilities of parenthood. The wickedness of the world in which he lived and his certainty of final judgment did not deter him from bringing children into the world, because he knew that God was Sovereign, was able to call and protect them, and would be finally victorious.

VERSE 24. *Walked with God.* See on verse 22. Where others ' lived ', Enoch *walked with God*. In his own day and with far less light he was like the apostle, who said, ' To me to live is Christ ' (Phil. 1. 21). This is the life that God intends us all to live. *He was not; for God took him.* Enoch was not only (1) a faithful believer, and (2) a bold prophet, preacher and witness. He also (3) was translated to glory without seeing death. This is the interpretation put by the writer to the Hebrews

upon our sentence (Hebrews 11. 5). His translation was the culmination of his life of faith. Enoch like Moses seems to have enjoyed a peculiar intimacy with God. Of all the millions of mankind he and one other, the prophet Elijah (2 Ki. 2. 11), have alone escaped physical death. It is possible that Moses might have done so also, had his disobedience not obliged him to die before entering Palestine (Num. 20. 12; Deut. 4. 22; 34. 5, 6). He was however raised from the dead (Jude 9; Mt. 17. 3, 4). The purpose of God in translating Enoch and Elijah was twofold, so far as we can understand it from the Scripture. (1) Their translation demonstrated that victory over death was included in the promise of redemption given to the human race. (2) Their translation prefigured the rapture and translation of all living saints, which is to take place at the second coming of our Lord Jesus Christ at the end of the world (Jo. 11. 26; 1 Cor. 15. 52; 1 Thess. 4. 17). Enoch lives today beyond space and time, perhaps watching with wonder the outfolding of the purpose of redemption, still walking with the God to Whom his earthly life was devoted, and awaiting the fulfilment of his own prediction of the second coming.

VERSE 25. *Methuselah.* The name of Enoch was completely identical with that of a member of the race of Cain (4. 17). That of Methuselah resembled that of Methusael (4. 18). From this we may gather that in naming his son, and by his bold witness, Enoch had been able to stem the tide of apostasy and compromise, but not entirely to arrest it.

Lamech. Here we find again complete identity of name with one of the most defiant and godless members of the race of Cain (4. 18-24), and behind this identity of name there must have been admiration and respect and a desire to imitate. Even today, when names are artificial and have nothing in common with the characters or aspirations of their owners, children are named after those for whom their parents feel admiration and respect. No one would give his child today such a name as Hitler, and no Christian man would call his son Mohammed. Modern biblical critics have been unable to see anything more in the likeness of the names in the two tables but a confusion and misunderstanding of a single early document. Their obsession with the rationalistic approach has prevented them from seeing what the Holy Spirit has to teach us in a comparison of the two genealogies. The story of the church in the antediluvial world has been repeated in that of Old Testament Israel and in that of the visible Christian church. Each began to leave its abiding-place in Christ, to divest itself of its holiness and separation. Each began to go astray after the world, to seek to imitate the world, to take the names and character of the world. The distinguishing line between the church and the world became less and less distinctive, until in the end, as in the case of Lamech, complete identity was reached. When that stage comes final judgment is near. It came in the time of Lamech's son.

VERSE 27. *Nine hundred sixty and nine years.* If there are no missing links in the genealogy between Methuselah and Lamech, we shall find that Methuselah died in the year of the deluge. God would not bring judgment till he was gone, and he was the longest-lived of any known member of the human race. Already God revealed Himself as ' slow to anger, and abundant in mercy and truth '.

VERSE 29. *Noah.* The consonants of the name make a play upon those of the Hebrew root meaning *to comfort.* In the language of the antediluvian world, whatever it may have been, the name must actually have meant this. The name is preserved in differing forms in several Asiatic languages as the hero of the deluge.

Comfort us concerning our work

and toil. Here is a simple picture of a father taking comfort in his children and home life as a relief from the difficulties of making a living from a reluctant soil. *Because of the ground.* This means that the toil arises because of the state of the ground.

Cursed. Sin was the cause of the curse, and the curse was the cause of the toil. So when the sinner becomes conscious of the curse that lies on the soil of his heart, which can produce only the noxious weeds of the works of the flesh, and can be altered by no toil of self-effort, he may find eternal comfort in the Child Who was born in Bethlehem and afterwards died on Calvary, in order that the Father's power might be aplied to the sinful heart, and that the Holy Ghost might have access to it, in order to turn the curse into a blessing.

VERSE 32. *Was five hundred years,* either when this record was written, or when God made the announcement recorded in 6. 7.

Noah begat. The sense is ' Noah was the father of '. It is unreasonable to interpret the text to mean that the three sons were all born at that particular year of Noah's life, or immediately following it.

CHAPTER 6

THIS chapter opens with the account of the traffic of the sons of God with the daughters of men, leading up to the corruption that determined God to destroy the world (verses 1-8). With verse 9 begins the fourth section of Genesis, the story of Noah and his deluge, which continues to the end of chapter 9. In verses 9-22 we have God's announcement of the coming flood to Noah and His instructions to build the ark.

VERSE 1. This verse with the following seven describes the state of the world before the flood.

Men began to multiply. The blessing of fruitfulness given to man at his creation (1-28) was not withdrawn on account of the fall. It was the purpose of God to create a race and to draw from among its members a redeemed humanity, itself a multitude that no man could number (Rev. 7. 9). Every individual conforms to the life and nature of the race, but each is sufficiently different to be marked off as an individual and known to God and loved by Him as such.

VERSE 2. *The sons of God*. Who are these *sons of God?* A natural interpretation, adopted by many, is that this verse refers to the two races, that of Cain and that of Seth. The imitation of the former by the latter, implied in chapter 5, would lead on to inter-marriage, and identification of religious outlook is achieved in no better way than this. There seems some evidence that in early Mesopotamian history the superior Sumerian race were apt to refer to themselves as ' sons of God ' in contradistinction to the Accadians. In this case the expression ' sons of God ' would refer to the race of Cain. This would be a surprising description, not paralelled in Scripture, in which alone we ought to look for the explanation of its own terms. Again the expression ' sons of God ' is not very suitable for the race of Seth as a whole. It might be expected to apply properly only to believers, such as Abel or Enoch. Elsewhere in the Old Testament the expression ' sons of God ' refers to angelic or spiritual beings (Job 1. 6; 2. 1), and it is in this sense that the apostles Peter and Jude, who are alone of New Testament writers in referring to this passage, appear to interpret it. The Apostle Peter speaks of spirits, who were disobedient at the time that the ark was being constructed (1 Pet. 3. 19, 20). Later he speaks of angels that sinned (2 Pet. 2. 4). The Apostle Jude is more explicit. He describes the same angels as failing to keep their own estate, but leaving their proper habitation, and in referring immediately afterwards to Sodom and Gomorrha, he says that the sins of lust, of which

those cities were guilty, were the same as the sins of the angels (Jude 6, 7). The references in these three epistles seem unmistakably to be to these verses in Genesis 6. Such a conception is not easy in view of the Lord's words that angels have no sex (Mt. 22. 30), but the apostles had heard Him say this, and yet felt no inconsistency between this truth and their interpretation. The Lord was alluding to a normal state of things without prejudice to a violation of it in special circumstances. If however we accept the interpretation of the ' sons of God ' in this verse as angels, the difficulty of understanding how this sexual intercourse can have taken place remains. The apostle Jude's words perhaps supply the clue. He says that these angels did not keep their own estate, but left their proper habitation. What habitation did they occupy instead? Perhaps the answer is that like the devils of Gospel times they possessed men's bodies, and through them came into touch with the women, stirring up in the minds of the possessed those hideous passions and lusts, to which fallen man so often becomes a victim (Rom. 1. 24, 26; 6. 19; 7. 5). The possessing demons are often called in the Gospels unclean spirits, and the word *unclean* is in Greek the same as is often used by the Apostle Paul to describe lust (Rom. 1. 24; Eph. 5. 3; Col. 3. 5). We can only surmise that this is the explanation of the statement in our verse, but if it is the true one, we can imagine constant attacks upon women taking place throughout all the known world by devil-possessed men.

VERSE 3. *My spirit shall not always strive with man*. This rendering requires us to take the word *spirit* to refer to the Holy Spirit. The conception is then much the same as that we find in the prophetical narrative books, where we see the Lord perpetually striving with a rebellious and disobedient Israel. The idea is often applied to the attitude and action of the Spirit of God towards sinners in the present Gospel age, which will end in judgment, when God's patience is, as it were, exhausted, just as the ancient world ended in the judgment of the flood. The idea is scriptural, true and valuable. We cannot however be certain that it properly appears in this verse. The Hebrew verb *doon* translated 'strive' occurs nowhere else in the Bible, and its meaning is not certain. The Septuagint Greek version, the Targum of Onkelos, the Peshitto Syriac and the Vulgate Latin all translate this verb ' dwell in '. In this case the *spirit* is the life principle, breathed into man at his creation (2. 7), and the sentence means that the race to whom God lent life will be destroyed. In either case we have here the first expression in the Bible of the principle that a limit or term is set by God to the opportunity to sin. Sinners continue with apparent impunity up to a point, but when a certain pitch is reached, judgment falls (see Gen. 15, 16; 2 Chron. 36. 15, 16; 2 Pet. 3. 9, 10).

He also is flesh. Man by his fall and its evident and fearful consequences had deprived himself of the eternal future intended for him by God, and reduced himself to the condition of the animals. It seems evident that it is to the animals that the word ' also ' alludes. ' Man being in honour abideth not: he is like the beasts that perish ' (Ps. 49. 12, 20). Created in the image of God, man did not abide in his privileged position, but became like the animals subject to death and a creature of ' flesh ', that is to say, of this world only. The use of the word ' flesh ' in this verse in this connection does not go so far as the Apostle Paul's familiar use of the word in contrast to spirit to denote the corrupt and fallen nature of man, but it forms a basis for it.

Yet. The Hebrew literally is 'and'. We could translate ' therefore ' and preserve the sense. *His days shall be.* This is a Divine imperative — ' his days are to be '. *An hundred and twenty years.* The allusion is prob-

ably to the deluge, and has been generally accepted by commentators as such. In one hundred and twenty years judgment would fall. There is nothing in the passage to suggest that the period was made known to mankind as a whole. The reference to man in the third person suggests the opposite. It may have been made known to Noah, but the spoken word here introduced by ' the Lord said ' is more probably parallel to such passages as 1. 26; 2. 18. Here we learn that the time of God's judgment is known and determined by Him beforehand. Undoubtedly we may believe the same to be true of the final and greater judgment at the end of the world, of which the deluge was a type. It will come neither before or after the time appointed.

Verse 4. *Giants.* The Hebrew is *Nephilim.* They are the same people as in a later age the spies, sent in to search the promised land, saw, or professed to see (Num. 13. 33). They may have been men like Goliath of Gath, who was a freak of nature, gigantic in size, or like the giant who possessed six fingers and toes on each hand and foot respectively (1 Sam. 17. 4; 21. 19, 20). The remains of a man of enormous stature have been discovered at Grimaldi on the Mediterranean coast by the Franco-Italian frontier. These men seem to have been giants in wickedness as well as in physical characteristics.

Also after that. The long history of this ancient active populous and wicked world is told here with such brevity that the exact sense of these words is difficult to determine. They may mean (1) that early in the history of the ancient world an interference of fallen angels with the human race produced the *giants,* and that a second, or continued interference ' after that ' produced the ' mighty men '. Or (2) the ' giants ' may have been sub-human beings, who were on the earth previous to the creation of Adam, the words ' after that ' in that case referring to the events described in verse 2, which would have produced a second set of creatures like the 'giants'. The first alternative seems to be the more likely and less speculative. The second might harmonise with some modern theory and help to explain certain discoveries of the past, but it is difficult to think that if a sub-human race existed, it would not somewhere have been mentioned in the course of the creation accounts in chapters 1 and 2.

Sons of God. See on verse 2.

Became mighty men. This is better translated 'were the mighty men'. *Men.* This again is better rendered 'the men'. The Greek myths of heroes, born of unions between divine beings and women, such as Hercules, may be echoes of these times and events.

VERSE 5. *God.* This is one of the rare cases in which the Hebrew name Jahweh is translated *God* instead of as usual, 'the Lord'. *Saw.* God looks down from heaven upon the children of men, perpetually watching their ways. He created man for His glory, and man has no reason for existence apart from the glory of God. God cares deeply and unceasingly how man behaves. He has sovereign control over His creature.

The wickedness. This is the outward conduct, which is the fruit of a fallen nature within. We shall find a list of the things that it consists of in Galatians 5. 19-21. These wicked works are the evidence of a corrupt nature, and will be brought in as witnesses on the day of judgment (Rev. 20. 12, 13). *Man.* Fallen angels may have been responsible for the wickedness described in verses 2 and 4, but if they were, man had sold himself to them to work evil and placed himself under their power. We can plead no excuse before God for the wicked things that we do. We must answer for them.

Every imagination. As the margin states, this includes both purposes and desires. The mind of man was totally corrupt as a result of the fall, and this corruption rested on a deeper corruption of *heart*. This is

the seat of the will and the place of the deepest springs of the personality. Man is not only a sinner by nature, he is also a sinner by choice. Notice (1) that every imagination without exception was evil. (2) That every imagination was nothing but evil, not partly good, but 'only' evil. (3) That every imagination was nothing but evil always, without intermission, every day of life. This is our own state apart from Christ, and the condition of every unconverted sinner in the world today. Unless we preach this total corruption, and preach to men whom we know to be totally corrupt, we do not preach a full Gospel. This is one of the great statements of the Bible about the corrupt nature of man. Others are to be found in Ps. 51. 5; 58. 3; Gen. 8. 21; Jer. 17. 9.

VERSE 6. *It repented the Lord.* This is a powerful anthropomorphic figure of speech. In an absolute sense God never repents (1 Sam. 15. 29). In a relative sense He allows Himself to be spoken of in terms that apply to His creature. See 1 Sam. 15. 11, 35, where we find declarations that are the more striking, because they come one on either side of that just quoted. The figure gives us a vivid sense of the anger and disappointment of the Creator.

Grieved. Sin always grieves God, whether in the unbeliever or the believer. In Eph. 4. 30 we are told not to grieve the Holy Spirit of God, and there seems to be a connection with the following verse, which mentions bitterness, wrath, anger, clamour, evil speaking and malice. *At his heart.* The eternal God has no heart, but draws Himself near to the creature that He loves by speaking of Himself in language that a man can understand. There are precious eternal incomprehensible realities corresponding to this heart and to this grief, revealed once and for all to men in the human life of Jesus.

VERSE 7. *I will destroy.* 'The wages of sin is death' (Rom. 6. 23).

Created. The Creator, and He alone, has the right to destroy what He created. It seems obvious that the words ' create ' and ' destroy ' stand here in simple contrast to each other. To create means to bring into being, to destroy means to put out of being.

Man . . . beast . . . creeping thing . . . fowls. It seems clear that the meaning of destruction is the same in the case of each of these classes of creatures. The lower creation is involved in the fall of man to the extent that, if the human race is destroyed, the animals are destroyed too. They are on earth for man's pleasure. In them he may watch the wonderful works of his Creator, and by studying their ways he can learn moral lessons.

It repenteth me. See on verse 6.

VERSE 8. *Found grace.* The point of this statement is that Noah was to be excepted from the general destruction. The grace of God is always the only foundation of salvation. On what grounds did Noah find grace? Certainly not on those of his own deserts. If he had approached the Lord on these grounds, he could never have found grace, because implicit in the very term is the idea of favour or kindness to the undeserving. He could only have found wrath. The only ground on which he found grace is the sovereign eternal purpose of God Himself to bless him which was manifested to him in grace. (See Titus 3. 4, 5). The manifestation of the grace was made morally possible by the death of the Lord Jesus Christ, which atoned for the sins of Noah and those of all his people. In Noah's day this death was future in time, but an accomplished fact in the purpose and knowledge of God. The grace shown to Noah, which saved him from the destruction of the deluge (and indeed saved him also from the eternal destruction of the second death) is typical of the grace shown to all the people of God, saving them all from the wrath due to sin.

VERSE 9. *The generations of Noah.* This is the title of the next section of the book, which extends to the end of chapter 9. It tells the story of the deluge and of the covenant afterwards made with Noah. Its sections are as follows: (1) background, 6. 9-13; (2) preparations for the flood, 6. 14-7. 10; (3) the flood, 7. 11-8. 14; (4) Noah's sacrifice, 8. 15-22; (5) the covenant with Noah, 9. 1-17; (6) Noah's drunkenness, 9. 18-29.

Noah. In this verse we are told three things about Noah. (1) He was *just.* This means that like Abel he was righteous. This righteousness was not Noah's own, and did not rest upon any desert of his, for he had none. It was the only righteousness known to the Bible by which a man can be accepted by God, the righteousness, which is by faith of Jesus Christ unto all and upon all them that believe (Rom. 3. 22). Noah could not believe in Jesus Christ, because He had not yet come, but he could and did believe the Word of God about the judgment of the world, and acted upon it. He saw the promises afar off, and embraced them, and confessed that he was a stranger and a pilgrim in the earth, and he looked for the heavenly country (Heb. 11. 7, 13-16). If Noah was *just,* the claims of God's law were satisfied against him as a sinner, and this could only be through the death of the Saviour on Calvary, Who paid Noah's debt and set him free. (2) Noah was *perfect in his generations.* While this may mean, or include, the fact that Noah came of a line that had not been corrupted by any of the practices mentioned in verses 2 and 4, it is more probable that it means that he was upright among his contemporaries. ' Whosoever is born of God sinneth not ' (1 Jo. 5. 18). Noah was exceptional as an upright man in a wicked world, as all the people of God are exceptional in the same way. (3) Noah was not only justified, not only lived a life of moral uprightness among men. *He walked with God,* that is to say, like Enoch he had an inner life of communion and devotion with his God. In these three principles he showed the marks that always distinguish a true child of God.

VERSE 10. Like Enoch Noah was a man whose piety did not prevent him undertaking family responsibilities.

VERSE 11. *The earth.* This is put for the people who lived on it. *Corrupt.* At the fall a spiritual rot set in at the heart of human nature, which brought moral corruption. Sin stinks in God's nostrils. Moral corruption resulted in physical corruption, the body growing old, losing its powers, and succumbing to death. *Filled with violence.* Cain's example was widely followed. Satan was a murderer from the beginning, and having sold themselves into his power, men became murderers like him. It is perhaps to this period that we may look to fit into history the savage races, such as Neanderthal man, which modern discovery has brought to life.

VERSE 12. *God looked,* as He is always doing (see Ps. 14. 2; 53. 2, 3). He searches the earth and the depths of the individual sinner's heart. Nothing is hid from Him, and His assessment is perfect. *Corrupt.* See on verse 11.

Flesh. See on verse 3. *His way.* This may be (1) God's way. God has a purpose for mankind and for every individual among them, a way in which He intends that each one should walk. This is the way of holiness. The sinner corrupts this way. Sin eats into the purpose of God for him, and prevents him from enjoying its blessings or reaching its end. To corrupt God's way is an affront to God. Or (2) the way is the way of all flesh. The result is the same, whichever of the two we understand. The true way of all flesh is God's way for each and all. Or (3) to corrupt his way may mean ' to walk in a corrupt way '. In this case the way is the perverse way of each individual

sinner, to which we have all turned, going astray like sheep (Isa. 53. 6).

VERSE 13. *God said.* We do not know how God communicated with Noah. It seems most reasonable to suppose that He did so in a vision or dream, as later to the prophets.

The end. Thank God that all sin, evil, sorrow, trouble, and suffering will one day come to a final end. God pleads with the sinner for a limited period, and then the day of grace ends. The end of apostate Israel came (Ezek. 7. 2, 3, 6), and ' the end of all things is at hand ' (1 Pet. 4. 7).

Come before me. The time had come near, and the end, if we may say so with reverence, was now in God's mind. It was impossible to allow the evil to go any further.

Violence. Violence and corruption are characteristics of the earth today. The wars and weapons of destruction today are more horrible and violent than they have ever been in the history of mankind.

I will destroy. The deluge is one of the two great Old Testament events to which our Lord points as pictures of the day of judgment (Mt. 24. 37-39; Lk. 17. 26, 27). The end of the old world is therefore a type of the end of the present one, and the destruction of sinners that took place in the flood is a picture of the eternal destruction of the disobedient and guiltily ignorant from the presence of the Lord (2 Thess. 1. 9). *With the earth.* The marginal rendering seems more likely to be right, ' from the earth '.

VERSE 14. *Make thee an ark.* The ark is the picture of Christ, not the church. We owe the idea that the ark represents the church to mediæval superstition, and even the Book of Common Prayer, substantially so scriptural, is wrong over this. The Lord Jesus Christ, and He alone, is the eternal refuge of His people, and outside Him there is no salvation. In Him they are safe from all the waves and billows of the wrath of God. Although the ark represents Christ, it was to be made by Noah. In this respect we see the human nature of Christ. Jesus Christ was as much man as if He had never been God, just as He was as much God as if He had never been man. In a limited sense man made Him. He was a child of Adam, for whom a body had been prepared through all the generations from the beginning (Heb. 10. 5). In another sense men made Him a Saviour by crucifying Him, and some among those who had done so afterwards put their trust in Him. *Gopher*. It has been suggested that this is not the name for a kind of wood, but a noun meaning 'boat', which should go more closely with the word 'ark'. An *ark gopher* would then mean a boat with a deck. *Wood*. Wood always points to the cross. Christ 'bare our sins in His own body on the tree' (1 Pet. 2. 24), where the Greek for tree is *to xulon*, meaning 'wood'. The ark was made of wood. The Saviour in Whom we take refuge is a crucified Saviour. It is because He was crucified, and only because of it, that He is our Saviour.

We now learn from this and the following verses six things about the ark. (1) *Rooms shalt thou make*. The literal Hebrew is 'nests'. In Christ is a nest for each one of His children, a place of his own in the Saviour's heart. In this nest the child of God may rest and nestle down and take refuge. When a babe in Christ, he is sheltered in the nest and given his food there. When adult, he may use the nest for breeding. In it he brings up spiritual progeny, leading sinners to Christ and nurturing them up in the true doctrines of the Word. (2) *Shalt pitch it within and without with pitch*. The word translated 'pitch' seems literally to mean 'to cover'. The root is the same as that used in Hebrew for covering sins by atonement. As the ark is pitched with pitch, so the Saviour makes atonement. The ark was to be pitched within and without. Within the atoning sufferings of Christ shelter His people. They are continually be-

fore their eyes. They do not see the wood, but only the pitch. It is to Christ's atoning sufferings that they continually look, and trust to them to cover all their sins. The ark was also to be pitched without. So it is the atoning sufferings of the Saviour that turn their face to all the fierce waters of the wrath of God to which they are exposed, and form a barrier between them and His people. The cross with the atonement made upon it eternally protects the children of God from the Divine judgment.

VERSE 15. This verse tells us (3) the dimensions of the ark. These were sufficient and suitable for a double purpose, firstly, to ride on the waters and take the strain of the weather from without, and secondly to accommodate as suitably and comfortably as possible those who were within. Thus the Son of God took a human body, perfectly suited to undergo death and pay the penalty of sin, and passed through such suffering, that He became a perfect and sympathetic high priest (1 Pet. 2. 24; Heb. 2. 17; 4. 14, 15). The dimensions, 300 x 50 x 30, are on a closely proportionate scale. Their highest common factor is ten, a number which has been associated with the idea of glory, when it is used in the Bible. If we divide each of the dimensions by five, a number which is often associated with grace, we shall find that the results are respectively 6 x 10, 10, and 6. As six is a number associated with man in the Bible, we find that the ark was constructed to be a symbol of the Redeemer, Who was to bring man by grace to glory. In the three dimensions we may perhaps see God's grace, mercy and peace (1 Tim. 1. 2). His grace is as long as eternity, His mercy is as wide as the sinner's need, and His peace is as high as His own throne in heaven. The dimensions of the literal ark were enormous. A cubit was in length nearly, or about, two feet, so that it was six hundred feet long, a hundred feet broad, and sixty feet high. Presumably it had no keel, but was flat-bottomed.

VERSE 16. (4) *A window shalt thou make.* This was literally a ' light ', not an aperture such as is mentioned later (8. 6). Albert Schultens in the eighteenth century was the first to suggest, from the analogy of an Arabic root, that the whole roof may have been constructed of transparent material to form a huge skylight. The next sentence however, which runs in Hebrew, ' unto a cubit shalt thou finish it from above ', seems to mean that the window was to run round the whole length and breadth of the ark a cubit (two feet) below the roof, or that it was to be a cubit in height. However that may be, those who are secure in Christ have a window towards heaven, through which comes light from the throne of God. With the eyes of faith they look up in prayer, as their Ark rides the storm.

(5) *The door of the ark.* There was only one door, and it was in the side, just as the only way of access to God in Christ is through the pierced side of the Saviour. The door set in the side of the ark reminds us of the side of Adam, from which Eve was taken (2. 21, 22). Out of the Saviour's pierced side came the cleansing blood and the regenerating water. These alone make salvation possible.

(6) *With lower, second, and third stories shalt thou make it.* Finally there is progress for those who are in Christ. They enter by the only door on the first storey. They may pass on to the security and assurance of the second storey, and thence to the place of prayer by the window on the third storey.

VERSE 17. *I, even I.* Our God is the God of nature. He could and did bring the flood at the moment that His purpose required it. Similarly it is He and He alone Who will bring about the end of the world. To Him alone man is responsible, and He is the Creator, Sovereign, and Judge of all. *A flood of waters.* The old world was destroyed by water. The present world will be destroyed by fire (2 Pet. 3. 6, 7). *The earth.*

This may be as well translated ' the land '. The narrative of the flood leaves us uncertain whether the deluge was confined to Mesopotamia, or affected the whole planet. If the former, was the whole human race destroyed? How far was it spread over the earth at the period? Was the flood a very severe example of the inundations that periodically affected Mesopotamia? We have achæological evidence that such a flood took place. If so, the narrative is written relative to Mesopotamia. On the other hand, was the flood a phenomenon of the nature of a geological upheaval, spreading over the whole planet, or the whole Europe-Asia-Africa land block? The existence of marsupial animals in Australia goes a long way to prove that Australia was never affected by a flood, as it seems likely that the animals were created there. The details of the deluge given in 7. 11, 12 seems to make the latter alternative the more probable, and the passage in 2 Pet. 3. 6, 7, already referred to, is scarcely capable of any other interpretation. *To destroy all flesh.* So at the second coming of the Lord Jesus Christ the wicked will be punished with everlasting destruction (2 Thess. 1. 9).

The breath of life. See on 2. 7.

Shall die. The death of all flesh at the time of the deluge is typical of the second death, eternal and irremediable, which will engulf all those whose names are not found written in the book of life (Rev. 20. 14, 15).

VERSE 18. *Establish my covenant.* God's covenants are not so much agreements between equals, as settlements by God as benefactor upon man as beneficiary. This was a covenant of salvation from a natural disaster, but it is in line with, and typical of, the great spiritual covenants of scripture. So God has established His new covenant in the blood of Jesus with all His people, promising of His free grace and mercy to change His people's hearts, to be their God, to open Himself to them to such an extent that all will know Him experimentally, and to forgive and forget all their sins (Jer. 31. 33, 34; Heb. 8. 8-12). It is solemn to notice that out of the many thousands then living God's covenant was made with eight persons only (1 Pet. 3. 20). Similarly of all the thousands of Israelites in the wilderness at the time of the exodus, who were over twenty on leaving Egypt, only two passed through to the promised land (Num. 13, 14; 1 Cor. 10. 1-12). This is typical of the fact that in a corrupt and evil world believers are few. Are we certain that we have our standing and place among the little flock to whom the Father is giving the Kingdom (Lk. 12. 32)?

Thou shalt come into the ark. This in type is a Gospel promise. God invites man in Christ. The Lord Jesus said, 'Come unto me' (Mt. 11. 28). 'The Spirit and the bride say, Come. And whosoever heareth let him come. And let him that is athirst come' (Rev. 22. 17). Notice that this is an invitation to come *into* the ark, that is to say, to be identified with Christ. So far as the flood outside was concerned, those who were in the ark were one with the ark, in a sense, part of it. So the true believer, in accepting the Divine invitation, becomes a member of a body of which Christ is the Head, and a branch of the spiritual vine, which IS Christ. Thus to be identified with Christ implies identification of oneself with His cause here on earth as a rejected Saviour. On the other side God looks at Christ, and sees the believer completely identified with Him. Christ's death was the believer's death, Christ's resurrection was the believer's resurrection, and Christ's session at God's right hand is the believer's session. *Thou . . . sons . . . wife . . . sons' wives.* All in the ark were members of a single family. This is a type of the spiritual family, of which all in Christ are members. All believers are children of God (Jo. 1. 12), and all are brethren of Christ (Heb. 2. 11, 12). Redeemed humanity is a family, and heaven is a home.

Those who have been cut off from members of their earthly families for Christ's sake will not find that they have lost this happy relationship even in this world (Mk. 10. 30).

VERSE 19. Noah and his family were not alone in the ark. They were to *bring* others. There are four spiritual realities, of which in whole or in part the animals may be typical. (1) We may regard them simply as souls won for Christ, 'brought' into the ark by the original believers. (2) In the vision given to Peter on the housetop at Joppa the Gentiles, to whom the Gospel was going, were pictured as animals of various kinds (Acts 10. 9-16). We may see therefore in the animals in the ark the picture of Gentiles sharing salvation with the covenant people of God (Rom. 11. 17, 24; Eph. 2. 19-22). (3) The animals did not like Noah enter the ark by faith. They were creatures incapable of faith. They were in the ark by the mercy of God, because He had a purpose for their future. They may therefore typify such irresponsible members of the human race who are saved by Christ's death, which cancels Adam's sin, many millions of infants and perhaps idiots and the like. (4) The animals may typify creation as a whole, which will one day be delivered from the bondage of corruption into the glorious liberty of the sons of God (Rom. 8. 21). This does not mean that every human being will ultimately be saved, nor any individual animal raised from the dead. The statement looks forward to the new heavens and earth, when creation will as a whole be finally delivered from evil.

To keep them alive. The purpose of the ark was to preserve life. So all those who take refuge in Christ will be preserved safe through the day of judgment and brought to everlasting life, while all out of Christ will be destroyed. Our Lord Jesus Christ died for us, that we should live together with Him (1 Thess. 5. 10).

Verse 20. *Shall come unto thee.* In verse 19 we are told that Noah was to bring them. Here we are told that they will come. This is exactly the situation with those who believe in Christ. They are brought by the faithful ministrations of the Word, and the prayers of Christians. But they also come. ' All that the Father giveth me shall come to me ' (Jo. 6. 37).

Verse 21. The storing of the food was an insurance for the future. It was an act of wisdom and foresight. In the same way, although this is far from being its only aspect, faith in Christ is a wise insurance against condemnation on the day of judgement and eternal destruction. The insurance is ' for them ' as well as ' for thee '. A father's faith may often affect his child's eternal destiny, not automatically, but because the child has the opportunity, denied to those brought up in ungodly homes, of hearing and believing the Gospel, and watching the example of Christian living.

Verse 22. *Thus did Noah.* This was the obedience of faith. Noah not only heard the Word, but he did it (Mt. 7. 24, 26). In this way he proved himself righteous (1 Jo. 3. 7). The Bible knows no faith that is not obedient, and no righteousness that is not practical.

All that God commanded. Noah's obedience was complete, which is more than ours often is. He did not pick and choose among the commandments of God. He believed unquestionably that they were wise and right, and in that faith he carried them out. His life, and the lives of his family, to say nothing of the beasts, depended upon that obedience, just as our happiness and spiritual usefulness depend upon ours and the eternal life of the sinner depends upon his faith and obedience to the Gospel.

CHAPTER 7

THE story of Noah is continued in this chapter. Verses 1-6 deal with the command to Noah to enter the ark. In verses 7-10 he goes in, and verses 11-24 describe the deluge and its extent, repeating the account of the entry of Noah and his family into the ark. The chapter gives us a picture of the final judgment and destruction of the ungodly, and at the same time one of the security to be found in Christ.

Verse 1. *Come thou.* This is a Divine invitation and command. The Lord Jesus said, ' Come unto me ' (Mt. 11. 28). The deep, voiceless, irresistible attraction of the Father gives the same invitation in the sinner's heart (Jo. 6. 37, 44). The Spirit echoes the invitation through the church (Rev. 22. 17) and one day the Saviour's voice will be heard saying to those on His right hand, ' Come, ye blessed of My Father ' (Mt. 25. 34). Noah was not carried into the ark, nor compelled in any outward sense to enter it. He went in of his own free will in obedient faith, being convinced of the goodness of God's purpose for him. All eight persons must have entered of their own free will. Yet God's purpose through them for the world was perfectly carried out. The situation is exactly the same with believers in the Gospel. All come of their own free will in obedience to the Father's command and the Spirit's invitation. Yet the numbers of those who come will in the end be found to fulfil exactly the eternal purpose of God. *All thy house.* Noah's family was granted to his faith. No man can guarantee the salvation of all his children, and it is a matter of experience that whole families are not always saved, but the promises in the Bible on this matter are enough to urge a man to persevering prayer for all his family and to prove that God desires families to be united in spiritual blessing and to be all together in

the world to come. *Into the ark.*
Only faith could obey the command
to leave a world, which was going on
as usual, and face confinement in the
ark. Noah and his family were not
being invited to a scene of luxury or
comfort. They had to leave behind
their homes and property, and face
a situation in which nothing but their
barest necessities would be provided.
The exigencies of the situation demanded this. So, if a man is to be
saved, he must leave the world and
identify his interests with those of
a rejected Christ. The ark and its
occupants would require all Noah's
attention, so long as he was in it.

For. We must not read legalistic
doctrine into this sentence, or take it
to mean that God delivered Noah
because he possessed self-righteousness. Noah possessed the only
righteousness that is acceptable to
God, the gift of righteousness appropriated by faith (see on 6. 9). Still
less does the passage mean that a
man is invited to accept Christ on
the ground of a righteousness that he
already possesses. It is only acceptance of the gospel that makes a man
righteous, and the invitation is addressed to sinners (Mt. 9. 13; 1 Pet.
2. 24). What the passage means, in
its spiritual and anti-typical setting,
is that only the righteous will be delivered from wrath and destruction on
the day of judgment. *Righteous
before me.* The only true righteousness is that which is accounted to be
so by God. The opinion of man
does not matter. It is often wrong,
hailing as righteous those who before
God are dead in trespasses and sins.
The Christian lives to please God, not
men. The only righteousness accepted
by God is the righteousness of Christ,
worked out in a spotless life on earth,
made available to sinners on Calvary,
and applied to them by the Holy
Ghost through the Gospel in response
to faith. *In this generation.* The
righteousness of the true believer,
which is unreal unless worked out in
practice, stands out against the background of the wicked world in which
he lives (Phil. 2. 15, 16).

VERSE 2. *Clean beast.* The distinction between clean and unclean, later
to be elaborately worked out in the
law of Moses (Lev. 11. 1-47; Deut.
14. 1-20), was known to Noah, and
had probably been the subject of a
primitive revelation to Adam and
Eve. The distinction is typical and
artificial, and is entirely removed
under the Gospel (1 Tim. 4. 4, 5).
Clean animals were those which
might be eaten and sacrificed, in the
case of unclean animals neither was
permitted. The distinction was made
under the law in order to teach a
practical lesson on the difference
between holiness and unholiness.
Sevens. The Hebrew says, ' Seven,
seven ', emphasising that there were
to be seven pairs. Other animals
were to be represented by a single
pair.

VERSE 3. *By sevens.* The Samaritan
recension, the Septuagint Greek version, and the Peshitto Syriac, all add
before this the phrase, ' which are
clean '. As the sentence stands in our
version, it is implied that there were
seven pairs of every kind of bird.
The versions have probably preserved the original reading. *To keep
seed alive.* The purpose of God in
Christ is to preserve the lives of His
people in a wicked world and through
the day of judgment, till He brings
them safe at last to the new heavens
and new earth, which He has prepared for those that love Him (2 Pet.
3. 13; 1 Cor. 2. 9).

VERSE 4. *Yet seven days.* There is
an interval between the time of the
entry of the believing soul into Christ
by faith and the day when judgment
falls on the world. In the case of
the last soul saved there will still be
an interval, however short it is. The
day of wrath will fall with instantaneous suddenness, and there will
not be one moment for repentance.
To rain. A continuous rain of
forty days is exceptional in any
climate. It would have swollen the
great rivers, and caused them to in-
undate the Mesopotamian plain, but

it would not have carried the ark to the mountains of Ararat, or have had effects sufficiently sudden to cut off all escape. It was accompanied by violent convulsions (see verse 11). It was no normal rain, but part of an extraordinary astronomical, meteorological, or geological, phenomenon. It was quite outside the normal order of things. So will the day of judgment be. A type seldom fits its antitype perfectly, and here the long continuance of the rain is in contrast to the suddenness with which the Bible leads us to expect that day of the Lord will come (1 Thess. 5. 2).

Destroy. The keynote of the day of judgment is again emphasised (2 Thess. 1. 9). The word ' destroy ' is in designed contrast with ' make '.

VERSE 5. The statement of Noah's practical obedience is repeated. He not only heard, but did (Mt. 7. 24; 1 Jo. 3. 7).

VERSE 6. *Six hundred years old.* On the longevity of the patriarchs see on 5. 3.

VERSE 7. *Noah went in.* He fled for refuge to lay hold of the hope that lay before him (Heb. 6. 18). *Into the ark.* He entered safe into Christ, and identified himself with the Saviour. There every true believer has eternal security. *Because of the waters of the flood.* Not because they had already appeared, but because they were coming. So the believer flees to Christ for refuge, because he believes the Word of God, which warns him of judgment to come.

VERSE 8. *Clean . . . not clean.* Condition and character make no difference to entering the ark. Christ's invitation goes to the apparently clean, the religious and the respectable, as well as to the gross sinner. Outside of Christ no one is clean in God's sight. Every kind of person is invited. Racial, social, or religious, or linguistic differences make not the slightest difference.

VERSE 9. *As God had commanded Noah.* Notice that in verses 1 and 5 the Divine Name Jahweh is used, because the passage is dealing with Noah, who is in the sphere of redemption, and with clean beasts and birds, intended for sacrifice, which prefigures redemption. Here in verse 9 we are dealing with the ordinary beasts, which are outside the sphere of redemption. We therefore rightly have the Creative Name. This does not fit with the foolish theories popularised by Wellhausen, but is in harmony with the narrative and its requirements. The words *two and two* at the beginning of the verse refer to the seven pairs of clean animals and the one pair of others.

VERSE 10. *After seven days.* Although Noah knew the time when the flood would come (verse 4), the delay must have seemed wearisome and long. The final judgment is also greatly delayed, but ' the Lord is not slack concerning his promise, as some men count slackness ' (2 Pet. 3. 9). The purpose of the delay, as the apostle tells us in the same verse, is to provide opportunity for sinners to repent and be saved. This may have been the reason for the seven days of delay in Noah's case. It was no longer possible to enter the ark, but at this last moment sinners might turn in their hearts to God. *The waters of the flood were upon the earth.* ' But the day of the Lord will come as a thief in the night ' (2 Pet. 3. 10). There may be long delay, but God's Word can never fail.

VERSE 11. *The seventeenth day of the month.* The exact day of God's purpose arrived, as it will finally arrive at the end of the world. The only warning of this day, that had been given to the world, was the faithful preaching of Noah (2 Pet. 2. 5), just as today the universal preaching of the Gospel is the only warning given of judgment to come (Mt. 24. 14). Noah recorded the exact day, and kept a careful log of the voyage in the ark (see 8. 4, 5, 13, 14).

The fountains of the great deep. This is ancient poetical, not modern scientific, language. The deep means the ocean (see 1. 2), and the word is often used in the Old Testament to denote the sea. The breaking up of the fountains of the great deep is a vivid expression for the breaking of its bounds by the ocean. Tidal waves swept round the earth high enough to cover the tops of the mountains. A great upheaval of the earth's crust took place. This was accompanied by atmospherical disturbances causing continuous torrential rain. It is noteworthy that, if the year is reckoned in this verse as beginning at the autumn equinox, the flood took place in November, which is the normal month for rain in Mesopotamia. If it is reckoned as beginning with the month Nisan at the spring equinox, the flood took place in May, the period of the yearly inundation of the country. In either case the occurrences were quite abnormal. The great deep represents the waves and billows of the wrath of God, which broke in their entirety over the Saviour, as He hung on the cross (Ps. 42. 7; 88. 7). They are restrained during the day of grace, but in the judgment the wells will be broken up, and they will burst out upon every sinner, over whom they will not have already passed in the Person of the Saviour, and will overwhelm him eternally. The sinner is also exposed to the rain. This is the rain of the Gospel invitation, intended for the sinner's blessing (Isa. 55. 10, 11; Ezek. 34. 26), but, if rejected by him, clinching his condemnation at the judgment, and turned into a ' witness against him ' (Mt. 24. 14; Jo. 12. 46).

VERSE 12. The rain did not cease, till it had fully accomplished what God sent it to do. So, on the last day God's judgment will be fully comprehensive and completely destructive.

VERSE 13. *In the selfsame day.* This does not mean that Noah and his family and the animals entered the ark on the same day as the flood started. They did so seven days before that day (verses 4, 10). The statement means that they all went in together on the same day. Thus the whole family of God enters into Christ on the same day of grace, and were chosen together to do so in the eternal counsel of God before the foundation of the world (Eph. 1. 4; Rev. 13. 8; 17. 8). The simultaneous entry emphasises the oneness of the family of God. There is one body, and one God and Father of all (Eph. 4. 4, 6). Notice how the individuals are named: Noah, Shem, Ham, Japheth, Noah's wife, the sons' wives, beast, cattle, creeping thing, fowl. The church is a unity, a single society, precious to God as such. At the same time each individual member is known to Him, named by Him, cared for by Him, and loved by Him. Each one was foreknown and predestinated. Each one was called. Each one was tenderly comforted, trained, and dealt with according to his particular need, given his particular place in the service of God, and will finally be brought through in triumph to glory. ' Of all that thou hast given me have I lost not one ' (Jo. 6. 39).

VERSE 14. Here we have the description of what sinners are like, when they come to Christ, accept His invitation, and enter into Him. Some are raging beasts, fierce, selfish and destructive. Some are cattle, perhaps patient, gentle and industrious, but utterly stupid and without spiritual understanding. Some are lustful and earth-bound, creeping about in darkness and shame, and some like the fowls of the air in the Lord's parable (Mt. 13. 4, 19), bitter enemies of the Gospel, placing themselves at the devil's disposal in futile but malicious attempts to destroy and uproot it. The animals came out of Noah's ark unchanged, but sinners of all these various sorts, who enter into Christ, will come out in glory, utterly changed and conformed to

81

the image of God's Son (Rom. 8. 29).

VERSE 15. *Unto Noah.* Here we learn the essential part played by Noah in bringing the animals into the ark. It would have been difficult to force them in, and it seems clear that there was no necessity to do so. *They went in unto Noah.* He had so won their confidence, that they were not afraid, but followed him into the ark. This means that the animals, which are generally shy and sometimes fierce, were well acquainted with Noah. He must have taken much trouble with them. In the same way the believer must win the confidence of the unconverted, so that they will come to Christ at his bidding. This he can only do by the grace, and in the power, of the Holy Ghost. *Two and Two.* The mates went in together. So, there is no happier example of the Holy Spirit's working, than when husband and wife, or several members of a family, find Christ together. *Of all flesh.* Not one relevant species was left out. In the same way the church of Christ is gathered in from every nation, tribe, people and tongue (Rev. 7. 9). *The breath of life.* This is mentioned to emphasise the fact that the purpose of God was to preserve life. The race that He created will not perish, but will be brought through Christ to eternal life, though, as in the case of Noah's animals, only an elect number will find salvation.

VERSE 16. *As God had commanded him.* Notice Noah's responsibility in carrying out the purpose of God in saving life. Noah had on his shoulders the organisation of this strange assembly, the selection and collection of the animals, the preparation of food, the driving or coaxing of them in. In the same way the Lord has laid a command upon His church to go into all the world and preach the Gospel to every creature (Mt. 28. 19). We are responsible under God for bringing to Christ such as should be saved (Ezek.

33. 1-9; Prov. 24. 11, 12). It is of the utmost importance to ask ourselves whether we are exercising this responsibility.

The Lord shut him in. Noah could not have got out of the ark, even if he had wished to, or tried to. So the believer is secure in Christ. Once he has entered, God has shut him in. The believer's assurance is based upon God's sovereign purpose to save him. The child of God is safe in the arms of Jesus. He is shut in to salvation in Christ, as he passes through the dangers and temptations of the present world, and he is shut up to salvation at the end of the world and on the day of judgment. No Christian should play with the idea that he is not eternally safe in Christ. Once born again, he cannot contrive to be unborn, nor can he change his Father any more than he could in the natural sphere. Shut in by the Father to security and assurance, he cannot pass out again through a door barred by God Himself, and indeed no more than Noah did, does he wish to leave his refuge for the raging seas of sin, disquiet, and destruction outside.

VERSE 17. *Forty days.* This great judgment did not cease, until it had accomplished the whole purpose of God in sending it. It will be the same at the end of the world. Though the Lord's second coming will be sudden and instantaneous, like a thief in the night (Mt. 24. 42-44; 2 Pet. 3. 10; 1 Thess. 5. 2; Rev. 3. 3; 16. 15), yet there are hints that the day of judgment itself may be a process, occupying at least a thousand years (Rev. 19. 17-20; 15).

The waters increased. In the same way the shadow of the cross deepened throughout the Saviour's earthly life From His youth up He was afflicted and ready to die, as the terrors of the Lord increased about Him (Ps. 88. 15). At last the Lord's fierce wrath went over Him, and His terrors cut Him off.

Bare up the ark. In all these terrors the Saviour's spirit was born up constantly in prayer to His Father in heaven, and they culminated in Gethsemane. *Lift up above the earth.* At length the waves and billows of the wrath and curse of God against sin, as it was borne in its entirety by man's Saviour and representative, lifted Him up on the cross, to the place where He could draw all men unto Him (Jo. 12. 32). Reckoned with Him, and safe as it were within Him, as He passed through death and resurrection, were all those who had been chosen in Him before the foundation of the world, riding with Him to safety on the very waves, which destroy all those who are out of Him. The wrath, which fell upon Christ, is the guarantee of His people's salvation.

Verse 18. *The waters prevailed,* as they will prevail on the day of judgment, until they bring to destruction all who are opposed to Christ. Yet all the time *the ark* with its freight *went upon the face of the waters.* The Saviour was all the time fulfilling His Father's purpose for the world. He like the ark was fully exposed to the rains and storms. The waters were above and below Him, but no drop reached those who in the Father's purpose were safe within Him.

Verse 19. The waters not only increased (verse 17), and prevailed (verse 18), but they *prevailed exceedingly.*
All the high hills. The waters of God's wrath, flowing over the Lord Jesus Christ on the cross covered and destroyed the high hills that exalt themselves against the sovereignty and righteousness of God. Satan and sin and death were there defeated once for all. They will prevail again exceedingly on the day of wrath and destroy for ever all the enemies of God and man. Nothing can finally escape them.
Under the whole heaven, that is to say, all that is in the sphere of natural life, all the pomps and vanities of this present world, and all the

pride and boastings of men. God in His holiness and in His sovereign purpose will ultimately prevail.

Verse 21. *All flesh died.* Under the floods of the judgment of God Christ Himself was put to death in the flesh (1 Pet. 3. 18). With Him and in Him all His people died to sin, that they might live to righteousness (1 Pet. 2. 24; Rom. 6. 3-7; Gal. 5. 24). On the day of judgment *all flesh* will finally perish, those who do not possess spiritual life in Christ finding no place among the glories of the world to come. God's holiness can but condemn to death all who infringe His laws, and destroy 'flesh', which is the evil, fallen nature of man. On that day all *fowl* will be destroyed, those who busy themselves in snatching away the Gospel from men's minds, and hindering its success in every possible way. To the 'fowls' belong the false prophets, the teachers of a false Gospel, the leaders of the false religions, the communists, the rationalists and the atheists. All will meet their end, and never be found again. The *cattle* will be destroyed on that day, harmless and stupid, interested only in their fodder, living circumscribed lives without troubling over their responsibility to God. The 'beasts' will be destroyed, fierce, malicious, savage and cruel, exploiting their fellow-men, trampling on the interests of others, roving the earth and devouring their prey. The *creeping thing* will be destroyed on that day, earthbound, and following 'the hidden works of darkness', of which 'it is a shame even to speak' (Eph. 5. 11, 12). The margin of the Revised Version calls it a 'swarming thing', and so it is, here, there and everywhere, corrupting and polluting the life of the world. *And every man,* those who have ears to hear, but will not hear, who know the Gospel and refuse it, who face the issue, so far as possible, and choose self and sin in preference to the service of God.

Verse 22. *The dry land.* The fish

were not affected. The judgment of the flood was partial and temporary, a picture of the true. On the day of judgment there will be no exceptions.

VERSE 23. *The face of the ground.* On that day all that possess nothing but the life of earth will be swept from existence. The list of creatures is again repeated for emphasis, and in a different order, to enhance the warning of coming judgment, which we all so badly need.

From the earth. This present actual world will be burnt up (2 Pet. 3. 7), but in the world to come there will be an earth for the habitation of man, which will be the seat of righteousness and peace (Ps. 37. 11; 2 Pet. 3. 13). But nothing that defiles will find a place on this new earth.

Noah only . . . in the ark. Only those, who are in Christ, the eternal ark of safety, will remain alive through the day of judgment. ' There is no other name under heaven, given among men, whereby we must be saved ' and there is no salvation in any other (Acts 4. 12). Notice the exceedingly small proportion of those who were saved, only eight persons in a whole world. It is not for us to ask if finally there will be only a few saved, but it is for us to strive to enter in by the strait gate, that leads to life, to cast all behind us if we can but find Christ, to suffer, if necessary, the loss of all things, that we might gain Him, and be found in Him (Lk. 13. 23, 24; Phil. 3. 8, 9).

VERSE 24. *An hundred and fifty days. The waters prevailed* until the work of judgment and destruction was complete. So at Calvary *the waters prevailed,* until the conquest of Satan, sin and death was complete, and so on the day of judgment they will prevail, until Satan, sin and death are destroyed, all obdurate sinners swept away, and redeemed humanity brought safely through by God's infinite grace to the glories of the world to come.

CHAPTER 8

IN this chapter we continue the story of Noah. The floods abated (verses 1-5), Noah sends out birds in order to ascertain the condition of the earth (verses 6-12), and at last was able to uncover the ark and see that the earth was dry (verses 13, 14). He comes out of the ark at God's command (verses 15-19), builds an altar, and receives a promise from God (verses 20-22).

VERSE 1. *God remembered Noah.* His thoughts are always for His own. The mother may sometimes forget her own child, yet God will never forget us. We are graven on the palms of His hands (Isa. 49. 15, 16). He thought of us in eternity past and predestinated us to be conformed to the image of His Son. He remembered us, when we were lost in Adam, and sent His own Son to seek and to save us (Lk. 19. 10). He thinks of us every day, as we pass through the dangers of the world, and never for a moment remits His care of us. Nor will He forget us on the day of judgment, but will send His angels to gather us together, and will set us down safely in the eternal paradise (Mt. 24. 31; Lk. 23. 42, 43). *Every living thing.* God remembers all who possess the life that is life indeed (1 Tim. 6. 19), the life that is to be found only in Christ and is possessed only by those who have the Son of God (1 Jo. 5. 12). *The cattle.* God remembers every kind of creature, but the Holy Spirit here singles out for mention *the cattle,* which represent the weak and ignorant incapable of spiritual reception. In doing so it seems that He means to turn our thoughts specially towards the masses of ignorant heathen cut off from the Gospel and the truth. *With him in the ark.* In the same way the Lord gave to the Apostle Paul all those who were with him in the ship (Acts 27. 24). God remembered and saved the living things and cattle that were in the ark for Noah's sake. Even so, God remembers and saves us for Christ's sake, not for any merit or claim of our own, but simply because we are identified with Christ.

A wind. This is a picture of the Holy Ghost as the Lord and Giver of life. The waters of wrath and judgment, manifested upon Calvary, were assuaged, when the life of God swept like a wind from heaven through the lifeless body of the Lord Jesus Christ, as He lay in the tomb. Similarly they will be assuaged at the last day, when death, the last enemy, is destroyed, and His people appear in His eternal kingdom in resurrection glory (1 Cor. 15. 26). When the same Divine wind sweeps over the heart of the sinner, which is like a troubled sea (Isa. 57. 20), the waters of sin and disquiet are assuaged, and the peace of God takes their place.

VERSE 2. *Stopped.* The fountains and windows had accomplished their purpose. The day of judgment will also accomplish its purpose.

VERSE 3. *Continually.* The Hebrew is ' in going and returning '. This confirms the impression that during the flood tidal waves swept round the earth. At this stage they became less and less high. *Hundred and fifty days.* This is the measure of the five months from the seventeenth day of the second month to the seventeenth day of the seventh (7. 11; 8. 4). This means that an artificial month of thirty days was in use, making a year that fell midway between the solar and the lunar. At regular periods this year must have been adjusted to the solar year. The ordinary Hebrew year was lunar with the insertion of an extra month when necessary for adjustment to the solar, but there seems to be evidence of the use of the artificial year in some of the calendars of ancient Egypt. The number of 360 days accords well with the Babylonian custom of reckoning by twelve and sixes.

VERSE 4. *The ark rested.* So, when the fight with sin and death was over,

and the battle won, the Saviour rests at God's right hand, having brought through those for whom He died safe from death to life. He rests in a more exalted place than *the mountains of Ararat.* He is on the throne of the universe, highly exalted by His Father, so that in the Name of Jesus every knee shall bow, whether of things in heaven, or on the earth, or under the earth (Phil. 2. 9-11).

VERSE 5. *Decreased continually.* The Hebrew is ' in going and decreasing '. This is a continuation of the process mentioned in verse 3, the recurrent waves becoming smaller and smaller.

The tenth month, on the first day of the month, that is to say, two months and a half from the resting of the ark. *The tops of the mountains seen.* There were seven separate steps, or pieces of evidence, by which Noah could be assured that the danger was over, and that he would soon be brought through to a restored earth. The first was the resting of the ark (verse 4), which we have seen corresponds to the resting of the Saviour in heaven at God's right hand. The resurrection of Jesus and His passage into heaven as our Forerunner are certain signs that we shall follow Him there (Heb. 6. 19, 20). In this verse we find the second pledge of the good things to come (Heb. 9. 11). The tops of the mountains are seen. Here was visible evidence. In the same way we can see certain pledges of the coming glory in the work of the Holy Spirit in transforming and sanctifying His people's lives, while they are still in this world. The day of release has not yet come, but where before there was nothing but a raging sea of sin and judgment and curse, we may see a work of God unmistakably begun in our own lives, and those of all His children, which is the earnest of a perfect work in the world to come. If He has begun to make us like Jesus, He will never cease, till we bear His perfect image. ' He that hath begun a good work in you shall continue it until the day of Christ Jesus ' (Phil. 1. 6).

VERSE 6. *Opened the window.* This is not the same as the roof window or skylight mentioned in 6. 16. The Hebrew word is different. It was an aperture, formed perhaps by the removal of a small panel of wood, which could be taken away altogether, or could open on a hinge. In the same way the child of God may open the window of his heart and look up to God in prayer, or may survey the whole spiritual scene of judgment and mercy, promise and warning by the light shed by God's Spirit on His Word.

VERSE 7. *A raven.* This is an unclean bird (Lev. 11. 15). It is a picture of sin and the sinner, and in its behaviour we find the third pledge that Noah had of the fulfilment of God's promises to him. The raven *went to and fro.* The literal Hebrew is, ' went in going and returning '. In other words the raven came constantly back to the ark, making it its base and its home. Now the fact that the black sinner dwells during this Gospel age in Christ and goes continually to and fro on the Master's service is the proof of the finished work of Christ. Unless Christ's perfection covered him, he could have no fellowship with God at all. And the perfect justification is proof of the glorification to come (Rom. 8. 30). So the raven goes to and fro, till the earth is dried, the judgment past, and the sinner transformed and brought finally safe to heaven.

VERSE 8. The fourth, fifth and sixth pledges to Noah of the drying up of the waters of judgment are found in verses 8 to 12. They are given through the behaviour of the dove. If the raven represents the sinner, the *dove* represents the spiritual life of the believer. This is *sent forth,* as it were, from the window of the heart, and lifted in prayer to God.

VERSE 9. *The dove found no rest.* The spirit of the believer finds no rest among the troubled waves of this present evil world. It knows that it is on pilgrimage, and that it has a home in God in the world to come. *She returned.* The spirit of the child of God can rest only in Christ, as it journeys through the darkness and waste of the world.

The waters. The whole world lies in the evil one (1 Jo. 5. 19), and as such lies under the curse of condemnation of God. It is uncongenial to the child of God, because he belongs to the Father (1 Jo. 2. 15, 16).

Put forth his hand . . . took . . . pulled. In the same way the Saviour draws His child to Himself, pulling him in to peace and assurance.

VERSE 10. *Seven days.* The Holy Spirit spends time in working upon the heart of the child of God, and transforming it from within.

Again he sent forth. Her faith perhaps is stronger, and she is able to penetrate farther.

VERSE 11. *An olive leaf.* Here is a promise laid hold of by the dove, or the evidence of a soul won, or the whisper of the Spirit in the heart. She has the witness in herself that she is a child of God (Rom. 8. 16), and she knows that before long the earth will be dry (Rom. 8. 22-25).

VERSE 12. *Returned not again.* The spirit reaches a stage in the spiritual life, in which it abides with Christ in the heavenly places, and finds that, while still on pilgrimage, it lives in heaven.

VERSE 13. *In the first month, the first day of the month.* This is the picture of a new beginning. ' If any man be in Christ, he is a new creature ' (2 Cor. 5. 17). He walks in newness of life (Rom. 6. 4), he puts on the new man (Col. 3. 10), a new song in his mouth (Ps. 40. 3), and he looks for a new heaven and a new earth (2 Pet. 3. 13). The Lord has made a new covenant with him (Heb. 8. 8, 13). It seems never to be God's purpose to patch up or reform what is old, but to create something new in its place. *The waters were dried up*. Every manifestation of God's wrath is temporary. ' He keepeth not his anger for ever ' (Ps. 103. 9). Even the great day of judgment will accomplish its purpose and come to an end, and every manifestation of God's wrath will be over.

Removed the covering of the ark, and looked. At last the day will come, when faith is exchanged for sight. ' We shall see him as he is ' (1 Jo. 3. 2). ' And when ye see this, your heart shall rejoice, and your bones shall flourish like an herb; and the hand of the Lord shall be known towards his servants, and his indignation toward his enemies ' (Isa. 66. 14).

The face of the ground. As yet only the surface was dry, and Noah must wait a little yet for full and final possession. So, after the day of resurrection the judgment must run its course, until the quelling of the final rebellion and the destruction of the last enemy, death (1 Cor. 15. 26; Rev. 20. 1-15).

VERSE 14. *The seven and twentieth day*. The last interval was one of fifty-six days, at the end of which the new earth was ready for Noah. In the same way the elect will be brought through to a perfect sanctification in the new heavens and new earth (1 Jo. 3. 2).

VERSE 15. *God spake*. Notice that during the whole story the initiative was God's. All took place, as He commanded. It is the same with our salvation. He foreordained us (Eph. 1. 4, 5), He created us, He saved us, and called us with a holy calling according to His own mercy and His own purpose and grace (2 Tim. 1. 9; Tit. 3. 5). He has justified us, and promised to glorify us (Rom. 8. 30). He tells us that He will never cast us out, but will raise up every one on the last day (Jo. 6. 37-39). As Noah's salvation from the deluge was the work of God from beginning to end, so is our salvation from His wrath and curse and judgment (1 Thess. 5. 9, 10).

VERSE 16. *Go forth*. The interior of the ark is exchanged for the freedom and range of the new world. So on the redemption of the believer's body (Rom. 8. 23) the cross will be exchanged for the crown, rejection by the world will give place to acceptance in the heavenlies. It will no longer be necessary to take up the cross daily. But we must never forget that the ark is the only way to glory. Are we safe in Christ?

VERSE 17. *Bring forth*. In the same way the earnest expectation of creation awaits the revelation of the sons of God. When Noah came out of the ark, the animals came out with him. They could not come out before. So, when the redemption of the sons of God is complete on the day of resurrection, God's creation will cease to be subject to the bondage of corruption (Rom. 8. 21, 22).

That they may breed. The purpose of the animals' deliverance was that they might fulfil the intention of God at their creation, and the purpose was one of blessing. In the same way the purpose of God in redeeming humanity is that they might fulfil the function, for which they were created, namely, to glorify God and enjoy Him for ever. The original image (1. 27), defaced by the fall, is restored in Christ (Col. 3. 10), and God's blessing, changed by sin into a curse, is given back to the redeemed in abundant measure, more extensive than would have been possible in a natural life of innocence.

VERSE 18. *Noah went forth*. So on the day of resurrection the believer will go forth from the burden of the flesh, leaving behind him for ever his corrupt nature, and enter into the freedom of the glory of the children of God (Rom. 8. 21).

VERSE 19. *Kinds*. The Hebrew word is ' families '. There are plenty of hints in the Bible that God wants to see families re-united in glory. We rightly sing of the day of redemption, ' Orphan no longer fatherless, nor widow desolate'. 'God setteth the solitary in families' (Ps. 68. 6).

VERSE 20. The deluge is now over, and with this verse we begin the account of God's dealings with Noah, as a new start is made in the history of the human race. *Noah builded an altar*. Noah had learnt the meaning and necessity of sacrifice from his ancestors. The practice had been handed down from the days of Abel (4. 4), and was the subject of a revelation in the garden of Eden at the time of the fall (3. 21). Notice that the altar and the offering upon it were the foundation and beginning of the new life which Noah was beginning, of his relationship with God in the new world, and of the covenant and promises which God made. It is the same with our own spiritual life. Our entire relationship with God, our forgiveness, our salvation, our victory in the spiritual sphere, our future resurrection and glory, all depend upon the offering of Himself made once and for all on Calvary by Christ. Altars were needed throughout the Old Testament period before the coming of Christ to prefigure His one eternal offering. Now that it has been made, altars have no more place in Christian worship or service, and any claim that they have is based on false and erroneous premises. *The Lord*. Hitherto in the chapter the Divine title has been God (Heb. Elohim), because the subject matter has related to the creative sphere, the deluge and the animals. As soon as the altar is mentioned, we enter the redemptive sphere, and the proper title, Jahweh, is used. The basing of the documentary theory upon the difference in the Divine Names is crude and irrelevant, and is the result of prejudice and pre-conception, which could have been corrected by proper study of the text.

Clean. Only that which is clean may be offered to the Lord. The division of the animals and birds into clean and unclean, though a subject of revelation in the days before the Gospel, was artificial. It had no final

reality (1 Tim. 4. 4). It was a God-given picture of the real difference between holiness and unholiness in the spiritual sphere. No man has ever been clean in God's sight in himself except the Lord Jesus Christ alone. He only was fit to be an offering. He was the sinless Saviour. He suffered, the Just for the unjust (1 Pet. 3. 18). He was the Lamb of God without blemish and without spot (1 Pet. 1. 19).

Offered burnt offerings on the altar. Here we learn (1) the nature of the act of offering; (2) the meaning of the offering. (1) There were two major parts to the act of offering, (a) the killing of the victim, (b) the burning of the victim on the altar. Both these essentials were present in the one offering of Christ on Calvary. (a) Christ was put to death. He died the death due to sin (Rom. 6. 23) as the sinner's representative and substitute. His death, which was the just punishment of sin, vindicated the holy law of God, which is outraged by sin, and destroyed the barrier of enmity between God and the sinner, enabling God to make peace righteously with the sinner, receive him, and forgive his sins (Isa. 53. 5). The Saviour died the death which is due to us sinners. (b) The fire at Calvary was not literal, but spiritual. The significance is that the Saviour as sin-bearer with our sins laid on Him was consumed. The sins were burnt up, destroyed and obliterated for ever (Jer. 31. 34). Calvary was a supreme manifestation and demonstration of the wrath of God, which was acutely felt by the Saviour (Ps. 18. 7-15), Who was cut off by it from His Father's presence and fellowship (Mt. 27. 46). The eternal Spirit, Who is a burning fire (Mt. 3. 11), was present at Calvary (Heb. 9. 14). It was at Calvary, 'when the flame went up toward heaven from off the altar, that the Angel of the Lord ascended in the flame of the altar' (Jud. 13. 20). (2) The significance of the burnt offering (as opposed to the sin offering and other offerings of the Levitical law) appears to have been the devotion to God of a whole life without reserve to do His will. Such an offering Christ made. He came to do God's will (Heb. 10. 7, 9). The believer may also make a burnt offering, in fact he is called upon to do so (Rom. 12. 1). In Christ's case alone the will of God was that He should make atonement on the cross for the sins of the world. In the believer's case God's will for him is a life and death of service and witness. But the principle of the burnt offering is the same. The believer dies daily (Lk. 9. 23; 1 Cor. 15. 31), and the Holy Spirit perpetually burns on the altar of his heart.

VERSE 21. *A sweet savour*. Liberal theologians have often expressed, and generally hold, the view that the Lord is conceived of here as sniffing the smoke that literally arose from Noah's altar, as the idolator conceives of his crude, heathen gods. Such an interpretation is both irreverent and irrelevant. It is due to the inability of the natural man to perceive the things of the Spirit of God (1 Cor. 2. 14). The sweet savour here smelled by the true and living God was Christ (Eph. 5. 2), of Whose love and offering Noah's sacrifice was a pattern and picture. As the burnt offering is not confined (like the sin offering) to Christ, but is shared by the believers, so the sacrificial gifts of believers are perceived by God as a sweet savour (Phil. 4. 18). Thus the Lord here smelled or perceived (1) the one eternal offering of Christ, which was to take place on Calvary, (2) the devotion of Noah's heart, expressed in the offerings which he made. The Hebrew expression is ' a savour of rest '. The Saviour's offering was the means by which the Lord obtains eternal rest from the presence of evil in His creation, by which also man obtains eternal rest in heaven.

Said in his heart. This anthropomorphism, which is the only means of expression open to us, means that a resolution was taken by God, a purpose formed and undertaken. Such a purpose was undertaken in consequence of the offering. Thus the offering of Christ lies at the root of the eternal purpose of God to call, justify and glorify His elect, who are written in the book of life of the Lamb slain from the foundation of the world (Rev. 13. 8; 17. 8).

I will not again curse. No. The curse was exhausted, when Christ Jesus was made a curse for us in order that the blessing might be ours (Gal. 3. 13). *The ground*. This seems to imply that some of the difficulties that beset the agriculturist before the flood were removed after it.

For. If this is the right rendering, the sense is that there would be no purpose in further cursing the earth, because man's nature is in any case incurably wicked. The marginal rendering is ' though '. In this case the emphasis is upon the mercy of God. In spite of man's sinfulness the efficacy of Christ's sacrifice is such, that God will take no further penal action against man. *The imagination* of man's heart is evil from his youth. Compare the statement in 6. 5. This is the second of the great Bible statements of the sinful condition of man. Ps. 51. 5 deals with him at conception, Ps. 58. 3 with him at birth, this passage with his youth, and Gen. 6. 5 and Jer. 17. 9 with the adult, finished product. *The imagination* is the purpose. A young man makes wrong plans for his future, has wrong ambitions, wrong desires day by day. He leaves God out of his plans, takes no care to see whether or not they conflict with the interests of others, and centres them all in himself. These evil imaginations, or purposes, come from the *heart*, that is to say, the deepest-seated part of human nature, corresponding largely to what we now call the will. They are the fruit of a fallen nature, corrupt at the core, and of deliberate evil intent. *Neither will I again smite*. No wrath, no judgment, no destruction remain for those who have taken advantage by

faith of the sacrifice of Christ made
on their behalf. Christ has suffered
all in their stead and on their behalf.
' God hath not appointed us to
wrath, but to obtain salvation by our
Lord Jesus Christ, Who died for us '
(1 Thess. 5. 9, 10). *Everything
living.* To smite everything living
means to put it to a violent death.
This is what will happen on the day
of judgment to *every thing* out of
Christ.

VERSE 22. In this verse we have the
great charter of man's existence on
earth. The promise has been, and
still today is being, fulfilled to the
letter. The seasons caused by the
earth's revolution, and the alternation of day and night caused by its
rotation, have never ceased. Round
both these man's life is centred.
There is no great event, or series of
events, in history, that is not affected
in its incidence by the weather, or by
the hour at which it took place.
Notice that the expression *seed time
and harvest* implies the co-operation
of man. God gives the opportunity,
and man must take advantage of it.
If he does not sow, he will not reap,
and if he does not reap, he will not
eat. It is the same with the spiritual
sowing and the spiritual harvest. The
seed is the Word of God. He gives
the seed and the season, but we must
sow. If we do so, we shall reap a
harvest of souls. The promise of
this verse relates strictly to the present world. It belongs to unbelievers
as well as believers. In the world to
come there will be no seasons (Rev.
7. 16; 22. 5) and no alternation of
day and night (Zech. 14. 7; Rev. 21.
23, 25).

CHAPTER NINE

THE story of Noah is further continued until the end of this chapter. God gives His blessing to Noah
(ver. 1, 2), provides for his diet (ver.
3), and explains the sanctity of blood
(verses 4-7). God makes His covenant with Noah, promising that there
would never be destruction by a flood

again, and gives the rainbow as the
token of the covenant (verses 8-17).
The mention of the names of Noah's
three sons leads up to the incident of
his drunkenness and the disgraceful
conduct of Ham, followed by the
curse pronounced on Canaan and the
blessing on Shem and Japheth
(verses 18-27). The story ends with
Noah's age and death (verses 28, 29).

VERSE 1. *God.* The writer now
naturally and fittingly returns to the
Divine Name, Elohim, as this part
of the story is dealing with things
temporal. The blessing, the diet, the
covenant, the blood, the destiny of
the three sons are all matters concerning human life on earth. They
fall within the creative sphere. On
the other hand the altar and the
offerings were in the redemptive
sphere (8. 20-22). The narrative itself
provides the true reason for the distinction of the Divine Names. Only
hearts seeking to clutch at any straw
to rid them of the authority and demands of the Scripture would
swallow the crude, foolish documentary theory.

This verse and the six that follow,
to the end of verse 7, look back to
creation, and renew or expand what
was said and given to Adam. (1) We
have the blessing of fruitfulness.
This blessing was given to the first
pair, when they were created (1. 28).
It is renewed in Noah, the head of
the renewed world. In the same way
the redeemed obtain from God the
blessing of spiritual fruitfulness, corresponding to the natural blessing,
which God gave to Adam and his
race. The fruit that God intends us
to bring forth is twofold, firstly, the
fruit of the Spirit consisting of the
nine virtues (Gal. 5. 22), and secondly
the fruit of souls won for Christ (Jo.
15, 16).

VERSE 2. *The fear of you.* In this
verse we find (2) the renewal of the
blessing of dominion, which was
given to Adam (1. 28). Man was
intended to be God's vice-regent (Ps.
8. 6-8). This privilege has been tem-

porarily frustrated by the fall, but it will be fulfilled in the world to come, and is receiving its fulfilment at this moment in Jesus (Heb. 2. 5-9), Who is on the throne of God (Rev. 3. 21) and reigning over all things in heaven and earth (Mt. 28. 18). In the spiritual sphere, the child of God, armed with the Gospel, is given dominion over every beast, the savage governments and fierce intolerant individuals in the world, over *every fowl*, all the opponents of the Gospel, over *all that moveth upon the earth*, earth-born men of worldly interests, *and upon all the fishes*, creatures not affected by the flood, those standing outside the stream of revelation in ignorance of the covenants, the teeming millions of heathen, spread over the world. This dominion is exercised by the preaching of the Word and the proclamation of the Gospel, and all are delivered, as God pleases, into the hand of the redeemed.

VERSE 3. We have (3) the provision of food, made for Adam, renewed for Noah (1. 29), but added to. The new humanity still has the food of the natural man to sustain the body during the earthly pilgrimage. But ' man doth not live by bread only, but by every word that proceedeth out of the mouth of the Lord doth man live ' (Deut. 8. 3). This is the bread of God that came down from heaven to give His life for the world (Jo. 6. 33). On this living bread redeemed humanity lives, feeding upon Christ in His Word (Jo. 6. 33).

VERSE 4. The purpose of the prohibition of this verse, which is repeated and expanded in the Mosaic legislation, is to teach the sanctity of blood. The blood is the life-essence of the natural creature, human, and animal. The blood is not given for food, but for purposes of atonment (Lev. 17. 11). *Life* is in Hebrew ' soul ', which is the natural life, as opposed to the spiritual (1 Cor. 2. 14; Heb. 4. 12). The prohibition then, when applied in the spiritual life, shows us that we do

not feed upon Christ in any literal sense, as He was during His incarnation. We feed upon Him spiritually by faith. This is the principle that the Lord was at pains to explain (John 6. 63). It is only after His ascension that He becomes spiritual food. But it is the very principle misunderstood and defied by the unreformed Christian churches, which profess to change bread and wine into the very flesh and blood of Jesus Christ. The heavenly bread is eaten only by faith in the heart, and in no sense outwardly. In the true scriptural Lord's Supper symbols of this spiritual truth are used.

VERSE 5. This and the following verse contain (4) provision made to deal with any situation that might arise in Noah's family, or among his descendants like the case of Cain and Abel. *Your blood of your lives*. The Hebrew is ' of your souls ', and the emphasis is upon human blood as opposed to that of animals, which had been mentioned in the previous verse. *Will I require*. This is the requirement of a judge, and we have here one of the earliest of the many emphatic passages in the Bible, which represent God as the supreme Judge and Lawgiver. Man as a moral being is responsible to God as judge, and it is an erroneous idea of the Gospel to suppose that this responsibility and relationship are ever superseded. The Gospel does not tell us that God had ceased to be judge. It tells us that His just requirements as judge have been met on our behalf by the Lord Jesus Christ. The requirements are basic and eternal. So here everyone who sheds human blood is responsible to God for what he has done. There is nothing here to limit the responsibility to acts, which in some narrow sense may be called ' personal '. Individual murders may broaden into feuds, and these again into wars. The guilt and responsibility of murder is not said here to be removed, if it is done indiscriminately in company with troops of others. Nor are we told that it is removed, if the murder is committed on the orders of any authority. In any circumstances the shedding of human blood creates a guilt and a responsibility before God. We have no right to confine the implications of this passage to what is legally called murder. Accidental homicide, as the Mosaic legislation makes clear, carries a form of guilt but no responsibility (Deut. 19. 4-6), but only an artificial exegesis can exclude from this passage the sin of war.

At the hand of every beast will I require it. This does not mean that a beast is a responsible, moral being. The sentence emphasises the sanctity of human life. Its propriety can be seen at once in the case of some pet or domestic animal that should cause the death of a child of the family. Decency would require its being done away with.

At the hand of man. One day the criminal must give account. But will the soldier escape, or the bomber, or the maker of the lethal weapon, or the scientist who invents it? Not only violence and murder, but all sin and wrongdoing will be required by God. And the day will come when every mouth will be stopped, and the whole world brought in guilty before God (Rom. 3. 19).

At the hand of every man's brother will I require the life of man. Life again is literally ' soul '. This sentence has been interpreted as meaning that God requires a man's *brother,* that is to say, his ' kinsman ', to avenge his death. Now it is true that the avenger of blood is allowed for, and taken for granted under the Mosaic law (Num. 35. 12; Deut. 19. 6). Among the ancient Semites family blood feuds may have existed, as they have existed from time immemorial until the present century among the mountain tribes of Albania. It is also true that God pronounced through the prophets vengeance upon flagrant murderers, and raised up agents to carry it out (2 Ki. 9. 24-26). But the act of slaying the murderer was not final. In God's eyes it required itself to be

avenged (Hos. 1. 4). It is more likely that the sentence means that God will hold every slayer responsibile for the blood that he sheds, not that He will require someone to avenge the blood. The word *brother* in the first place looks back to Cain and Abel. The introduction of the whole passage seems intended to prevent a similar occurrence. But in the second place the word *brother* appears to have the normal Hebrew sense of ' another ', ' anyone else '. We use it in this sense, when we speak of ' brother man '. The sentence would then mean, that every human being in the world is held responsible by God for any human life taken by him in any circumstances other than accidental.

VERSE 6. *Shall his blood be shed.* This is best thought of as what we may call a Divine imperative, on the borderline between a command and a statement. It is a command that will certainly be obeyed, a statement that will certainly come to pass, the declaration of a moral principle. It is akin to similar expressions occurring in certain of the Psalms, which are regarded in the New Testament as prophetic statements of the future and find their fulfilment in Gospel events. See for instance Pss. 69. 25; 109. 8, and the fulfilment in Acts 1. 20. The fulfilment of the present principle comes in three ways: (1) It is fulfilled in history by the action of man. Murder in the ancient east inevitably produced the revenger of blood, and the blood-feud with its unending savage repercussions has been the curse of certain primitive tribes till modern times. In the more settled communities the state has taken upon itself the avenging of blood, and has often interpreted the present verse as binding it to the infliction of the death penalty. But it seems clear from Hos. 1. 4, referred to above, that no action by man finally carries out this great principle. Instead it creates further problems. (2) The principle will be vindicated on the great day of judgment at the end of the world. Then every slayer will receive his deserts, and receive them at the hands of *man*. The Judge on that day will be a man. The Father has given the judgment into the hands of the Son, because He is the Son of man (Jo. 5. 27). The reason for entrusting the judgment to the Son may be in order that this very principle of our verse may thus be fulfilled. (3) Many murderers and slayers have, thank God, repented and come to salvation by faith in Christ. Many Christian men have honestly and conscientiously made themselves responsible for the blood of their fellow-men by taking part in war. What happens in such cases? The principle still finds its fulfilment. The death of Christ, the believer's representative and substitute, at the hands of men and for men fully vindicates the outraged law of God, and all blood shed before conversion or in ignorance by any child of God is avenged to the full in the death of his Surety. This is one of the reasons, though not the only one, for the emphasis of the Bible upon the blood of Christ, as opposed to the mere reference to His death. *In the image of God.* This sentence gives us the reason for the sanctity of human life. Man is not sacred for what he is, or might be, in himself. His value does not lie there. His life is sacred, because he is made in the image of His Creator, Who lends to man's worthless life something of His own holiness. The image, though disfigured, is still retained by fallen man, whose natural life, sinful and corrupt though it is, still remains sacred.

VERSE 7. The blessing of verse 1 is repeated for emphasis. The statements about the dominion (verse 2), the diet (verses 3, 4), and the sanctity of human life (verses 5, 6) are subsidiary to the blessing. Their fulfilment is necessary to its proper carrying out. The blessing has been wonderfully safeguarded and fulfilled. The eight persons of Genesis 9 have increased today to about two thousand million, notwithstanding the fact that, until the recent spread of medi-

cal science, about eighty per cent of the members of the human race is likely to have died in infancy. Each one of these persons, however short his life, however remote, however savage, however ignorant, is fully known in every detail by God, his Creator. Each one will appear among the righteous, or among the wicked, on the day of judgment.

VERSE 8. In verses 8-17 we have the account of the first great covenant mentioned in the Bible. *God spake.* Notice that the initiative, as always, comes from God. Noah did not propose a covenant, nor ask for one. It is the same with all God's covenants, including the everlasting one that He has made with us in the blood of Jesus. God's love and grace took the initiative in them all. None was an afterthought. God purposed our salvation before the world began, and took all steps to bring it about. *To his sons.* A covenant is not made with an individual only, but with a family, group, fellowship, or company of men. If we have subscribed to the everlasting covenant made with us in the blood of Jesus, we have been drawn into the family of God, and will remain for eternity in that holy fellowship.

VERSE 9. *I.* This is emphasised by being doubled. Not only is the initiative God's, but the power is His. He can and does fulfil His covenants.

I establish. The covenant is therefore grounded and sure. We need never doubt it, but can trust to it fully. Noah's covenant was established in the power and mercy of God. It dealt only with temporal things. Our covenant is established in the shed blood of Jesus, which can never fail. It perfectly satisfies God's moral demands, it perfectly cleanses the sinner and it will ' never lose its power, till all the ransomed church of God be saved to sin no more ', as William Cowper truly sang.

Covenant. The great covenants of the Bible are not agreements between equals. They are rather settlements by a benefactor upon beneficiaries. God is the great Benefactor. Jesus Christ is the great Testator, Whose will, or testament, leaving to His faithful people eternal salvation, everlasting life, perfect ultimate sanctification, and all other benefits of His passion, was brought into effect by His death (Heb. 9. 15, 16). We are the unworthy beneficiaries. *With you and with your seed*. Thus God's covenant is made with Christ and with all those vitally joined to Him in spirit. ' Behold, I and the children, which God hath given me ' (Heb. 2. 13).

VERSE 10. *Every living creature that is with you*. The word translated ' creature ' is in Hebrew ' soul '. The covenant is not made with Noah and his family only, but with every creature that is with them. So the everlasting covenant is made ' with you and with many ' (Mt. 26. 28). Every one that is with us in the true fold shares the blessings of the covenant, the bitter opponents of the Gospel, the indifferent, the selfish and savage, as soon as they come to repentance and faith. *The ark*. It is with those who were in the ark that the covenant is established. The everlasting covenant is established only with those in Christ. It is they alone who were foreknown and predestinated in eternity past, they who are effectually called, they alone who are justified and glorified. With them the everlasting covenant is made for the remission of sins, and the sins of all those who believe are fully and freely forgiven and forgotten (Jer. 31. 34). The sins of those outside the covenant cannot be forgiven. They will stand before the judge on the great day guilty and unjustified. But the covenant is made *from all that go out of the ark, to every beast of the earth*, from the Jews who first trusted in Christ (Eph. 1. 12) to every subsequent generation of believing Gentiles, from the believers of today to all those whom they will lead to Christ. *Every beast of the earth* with

which the covenant is made is the descendant of the original pair of its kind that came out of the ark. So everyone led to Christ is brought into the same family as every believer that has gone before him. Each one, as he comes to Christ, is related organically in Christ to the whole company of faithful people. With this spiritual family, this seed that serves God (Ps. 22. 30), this true church, this redeemed humanity the covenant is made.

VERSE 11. *I will establish*. God takes the initiative and announces His purpose of mercy and grace. The covenant is established, ' ordered in all things and sure '. It is firmly rooted in the blood of Jesus. It has moral foundations, conformable to the holiness of God. It is founded on the Father's eternal purpose, and applied to the individual soul by the Spirit.

The covenant has two clauses, which in conformity with the usual Hebrew parallelism have substantially the same meaning. Yet we can see in the second an advance upon the first. The first clause says that no flesh *shall be cut off any more by the waters of a flood*. This, taken by itself, might be held to mean that, even assuming the coming of another flood in the future, the race would not be destroyed by it. In this sense it is true of all those in Christ. Another flood will come. The great day of judgment is future. No believer will be cut off by it. Having heard God's Word, and believed on Him Who sent Christ, he has passed from death unto life, and will not come into condemnation (Jo. 5. 24).

The second clause of the covenant makes a stronger and more definite affirmation. It says that there shall not ' any more be a flood to destroy the earth '. For the people of God, there will be no more flood. The flood is passed. It overwhelmed the believers' Surety. It condemned and destroyed sin in the body of Christ on the tree. ' There is now therefore no condemnation to them which are in Christ Jesus ' (Rom. 8. 1). The law is already vindicated, and the holiness of God satisfied. There can be no more condemnation and no more judgment for the sinner who rests all on the finished work of Christ. The manifestation of wrath on the day of judgment cannot touch him.

VERSE 12. *The token.* God not only established the covenant, but gives a sign to man that He has done so. He not only justifies the sinner who believes in Christ, but gives him the evidence and assurance that He has done so. There are several means of assurance, but the token here mentioned emphasises one. *Between me.* The covenant rests on God's pledged Word, and may be received by the believer in trustful assurance. *And you.* That is to say, the believer already safe in Christ. *And every living creature* (Heb. *soul*) *that is with you,* that is to say, every sinner who in the future will repent and believe. *For perpetual generations.* The covenant is everlasting, and will never be revoked or fail. Christ is responsible for the ' eternal salvation ' of all who obey Him (Heb. 5. 9).

VERSE 13. The rainbow is the token of the covenant then made with Noah. This does not mean that the rainbow did not exist, or had not been seen, before the deluge, but that now for the first time it was vested with significance. As we see it in its beauty, we may and should remind ourselves that God has made this covenant in His mercy with the whole human race living now in natural bodies on this earth, and with the animals as well. Whatever natural disasters take place, we have the assurance that we shall never be destroyed again by a flood of the magnitude of Noah's deluge. In the spiritual sphere the beautiful token appears also in the cloud. The Sun of righteousness (Mal. 4. 2), Who is the Saviour Himself, shining upon the shower of blessing (Ezek. 34. 26), creates in the regenerate soul the life

and beauty, which are a token of the covenant.

VERSE 14. *When I bring a cloud.* When is this? Cloud and darkness were brought over the earth, when the Saviour hung dying on Calvary, but the bow was seen in the cloud. There the love of God was demonstrated to the extreme limit. When the Saviour ascended, a cloud was brought over the earth to receive Him from sight, but the bow was seen in the cloud. The Saviour's departure from the world meant the accomplishment of His mission of redemption, and made possible the coming of the Holy Ghost. At the time of a temporal judgment, the clash and subjugation of nations, the Lord rides to judgment on a cloud (Isa. 19. 1). Thus in the terrible wars and convulsions of this twentieth century we may say that a cloud is brought over the earth, but the bow is seen in the cloud. Crisis after crisis turns out to the ultimate furtherance of the Gospel. In God's working in all these things, as well as in the revival showers, we see the token of the everlasting covenant made with redeemed humanity in the blood of Jesus Christ. The bow will never shine more brightly than in the last day, when the clouds of eternal judgment are brought over the earth, and the Son of man appears upon them in glory. That will be the day when in judgment mercy is remembered, and the redeemed are received in virtue of the covenant into eternal glory. Thus the token of the covenant runs like a streak of beauty through all the great events of redemption, and through all God's dealings with men.

VERSE 15. *I will remember.* The rainbow was to be not only an assurance to men, but a reminder to God. This does not mean that God needs to be reminded, but that the rainbow was in some sense the symbol of the moral basis of the covenant. In this sense it is a picture of the love of God, which was demonstrated at Calvary, and there alone (1 Jo. 4. 9,

10). The blood of Jesus is the basis of the everlasting covenant, and the presence of Jesus at the Father's right hand is the perpetual reminder to the Father of the covenant. Nothing done by anyone claiming to be a priest on earth can remind God of anything. He looks on the face of the Anointed, and the mediating Presence in heaven is the pledge that the covenant has been established and will be eternally in force.

The water shall no more become a flood to destroy. God's holiness is an essential part of His character and being, but once it has broken out in holy wrath upon the head of our Surety, it can never become a flood to destroy us again. Having thus broken out, it becomes our eternal protection, working hand in hand in harmony with the love of God.

VERSE 16. This verse repeats and emphasises (1) the fact of the presence of the bow. Every redemptive event is shot through with the mercy of God, based on the shed blood of Jesus; (2) the fact that God, not man only, looks at the bow. Here the bow is the symbol of the Lamb of God, on Whom the Father looks perpetually too see all His believing children. (3) The purpose of God's looking on Christ. It is that He may continually have before His mind (to speak in human language) the basis of His covenant, and continually be reminded by the presence of Christ in heaven, where He has gone by His own blood, of that which makes the covenant possible.

VERSE 17. This verse repeats and emphasises the statements of verse 12. The bow is a token to man as well as a reminder to God. The love of God, seen and proved on Calvary, where we were reconciled, when enemies to God, is the sure sign of final salvation in the risen life of Christ (Rom. 5. 10).

VERSE 18. In this and the following verse we have a note of Noah's posterity. Canaan is mentioned because he inhabited Palestine, and thus came into close relationship with Israel. By the mention of Canaan we are reminded that human nature emerged from the ark unchanged. The awful heritage of Adam was not altered nor minimised. To remove sin and its curse it took that of which the ark was only a picture.

VERSE 19. The sons of Noah here again represent redeemed humanity, with whom the whole of the new earth is overspread.

VERSE 20. This and the following seven verses give us the shameful story of Noah's drunkenness and the contumacious behaviour of his son Ham. The incident teaches us (1) that there is no man, not even among the children of God, the Lord Jesus Christ alone excepted, whose nature is not corrupt, and into whose life sin does not intrude (1 Ki. 8. 46); (2) that one sinful act may have incalulable consequences, and may affect the lives of very many beside the sinner. The two things told us in this verse of Noah are quite right and proper, but they show us that opportunities for sinful and even vicious behaviour lurk in our everyday occupations.

VERSE 21. *He drank of the wine.* It is conceivable that Noah did not know the properties of wine, either because previous to the deluge he had never cultivated the vine, or possibly because climatic conditions were so different after the flood from what they were before it, that fermentation was increased. Whether Noah's sin was committed in ignorance, or thoughtlessly, or deliberately, we notice that the consequences were the same. The evil that follows sin is the result of sin as such.

Was drunken. Drunkenness is sin (Prov. 23. 29-35; Eph. 5. 18).

Uncovered. As in the case of Adam and Eve (3.7), this is a picture of guilt, or spiritual nakedness in the sight of God. The sinner is intoxicated with the pleasures of the world, or with its greed and cares, with intellectual pride, or with the lusts of the flesh. Thus he lies uncovered in the sight of God within the tent of his body, and if he appears still in that condition on the day of judgment, his mouth will be stopped and he will be declared guilty before God (Rom. 3. 19).

VERSE 22. *Ham . . . saw.* Like all fools he made a mock of sin (Prov. 14. 9). The situation was probably that described in Hab. 2. 15, 16. His mockery was the more sinful in that the one at whom he mocked was his own father, to whom he should have shown filial reverence. He was breaking the spirit of the fifth commandment, which had not yet been given in so many words. Ham is like every sinner when confronted with gross sin in his fellow-men. He can mock at it, jeer at it, take a secret pleasure in seeing it (Rom. 1. 32), but he can do nothing to help or relieve the sinner.

Told his two brethren. This implies that he intended to share the joke with them, and supposed that they would be glad to share it with him. Here also Ham was behaving typically.

VERSE 23. *Took a garment.* The Hebrew may imply that it was the upper garment of Noah. There is only one garment that can cover the sinner's nakedness, and that is the robe of Christ's righteousness, and with this the Lord has covered His people (Isa. 61. 10). Clothed in this perfect robe, the sinner stands justified for eternity before his God.

Laid it upon both their shoulders, just as two or more believers may take upon them the burden of prayer and of sacrifice necessary to bring an unconverted fellow-sinner to the Saviour. Noah possessed the robe, which was his and could have covered his nakedness. So every sinner has the robe of Christ's righteousness made and fitted for him. But Noah was too helpless to put it on. He could only be covered by it, as his

two sons took on themselves the burden of bringing it to him. This is our work as servants of Christ and ministers of the Gospel.

Went backward. The evangelist does not pry into the sinner's sin. He does not see him as he is, in all his hideous guilt. His eyes are fixed on Christ as he seeks to bring salvation to the sinner, and he sees him by the eye of faith as God means him to be. Covered the nakedness. ' Charity shall cover the multitude of sins ' (1 Pet. 4. 8) and ' he which converteth the sinner from the error of his way, shall save a soul from death, and shall hide a multitude of sins ' (Jas. 5. 20). Sins actually committed against the believer are covered, as he forgives in love those who trespass against him. Sins committed against God are covered by the robe of Christ's righteousness, as the evangelist brings the Gospel of God's love and salvation to the penitent. Sins that might have been committed are destroyed at the root, as the life of the newly-converted man is transformed and sanctified under the influence of the Holy Spirit. So we have in the action of these two brothers an inspired picture of the work of love in the ministry of the Gospel.

Their faces were backward. The believer's face is turned away from sin and the world, and fixed upon the throne of God and Jesus, exalted to His right hand. *They saw not.* They treated their father with the respect and reverence due to him. In the same way the servant of Christ treats the sinner, to whom he takes the Gospel, with the reverence due to him as a man made in the image of God, and a potential child of the heavenly Father.

VERSE 24. *Noah awoke.* So does the sinner, when he comes to Christ, awake from the sleep of sin to the life of righteousness (Eph. 5. 14).

Knew. The sinner knows only too well those who cannot help him, and those whose conduct tends to aggravate his sin. He will certainly know it, when he awakes on the day of judgment, and will point an accusing finger at all those who will have helped him on the way to hell.

VERSE 25. *Cursed.* So on the day of judgment the curse of God will fall on those who fail to recognise the service due to Christ in the need of the unconverted, or who help their fellow-men to hell by regarding sin lightly (Mt. 25. 41-46). Till then, under the Gospel, the love and goodness of God seek to win men.

Canaan. Notice that the curse is pronounced not on the guilty father himself, but on his child. Every sinner exercises a frightful influence over all those with whom he comes in touch, especially those nearest to him. Sin is infectious, but righteousness is not transmissible (Ezek. 18. 19, 20). Many a parent is humanly speaking responsible for sending his child to hell, because the home is carried on without reference to God. The curse of the worldly father comes to fruition in his child. Here is the origin of the manners of the Canaanites (Lev. 18. 27; 20. 23), and their enmity towards Israel, and their judgment by the sword of Joshua.

A servant of servants. Sin always reduces a sinner to slavery. ' He that committeth sin is the servant of sin ' (Jo. 8. 34; Rom. 6. 16, 20). The sinner is the slave of himself, of his own lusts and passions, and of the suggestions and temptations of the wicked around him. The primary reference of this passage is to the then future history of the nations of the world. It may be seen fulfilled literally in the servitude to which the surviving Canaanites were reduced by Israel (Josh. 9. 23; 1 Ki. 9. 20, 21). On a wider scale it has been true throughout the history of the world, that the races and peoples descended from Ham or Canaan have been those who have often been exploited and regarded as inferior by others.

VERSE 26. *The Lord God of Shem.* Notice that in a chapter in which the Divine Name throughout has been Elohim, the redemptive Name *Jahweh* occurs in an appropriate setting in this verse. The careful use of the Names by reference to the context seems so obvious to the unbiassed reader, that it is difficult to see how intelligent men could ever have proposed or accepted the differentiation in their use as the basis of the documentary theory. Only strong prejudice could have brought them to do so. The double title *Jahweh* Elohim is used here, as in chapter 3, in an obviously redemptive context. The Lord was to be in a special sense the God of Shem, because from Shem's descendants was to come first, Abraham, the father of the faithful, and the special family, holy to the Lord, of which Abraham was the ancestor; but above all because in the fulness of time the Son of God was to become incarnate in that family and effect by His death and resurrection the salvation of the world. This great train of events was not incidentally assigned to take place in the family of Shem as a reward for his upright behaviour on this occasion. The story makes no difference between him and his brother Japheth, unless the putting of his name first in verse 23 implies that he was the instigator of the good deed. It was planned and purposed by God from all eternity, and He no doubt laid His hand upon the personal Shem and gave him such grace and such a character, that a righteous influence might be brought to bear on his descendants, and a pure tradition flow down to them.

Canaan shall be his servant. This verb and the three in the following verse are Hebrew imperatives, and may be translated *let* or *must.* The meaning is very little different, as Hebrew imperatives have the force of statement prophetic of the future (see on verse 6). Not only were the Canaanites literally the servants of the Semites, but in the spiritual sense all that the Canaanites stand for, Satan and his world of sin, are brought unwittingly into the service of God's redemptive plan. Satan's attack on Job succeeded only in bringing the patriarch after his trial into greater blessing than he had enjoyed before. The wicked hands that murdered the Lord achieved the salvation of the world. The tests and trials and heresies that the believer meets with in this world, provided he clings to his Saviour, only bring about the strengthening of his faith and character. ' All things work together for good to them that love God ' (Rom. 8. 28).

VERSE 27. *Enlarge.* The table in the following chapter shows that the descendants of Japheth are generally speaking the nations of Europe. The enlargements of these nations has been one of the most conspicuous features in the history of the world. It may be seen in the domination of most of Europe by the peoples who spread from a region between the Black Sea and Denmark in the third and second millennia B.C. imposing their language almost wherever they went. It may be seen in the Greek colonisation, in the construction of the Roman empire, and in the virtual domination of the world in modern times by the peoples of Europe and their descendants in America.

He shall dwell in the tents of Shem. If the pronoun refers to God (Who has the creative title, when Japheth is being dealt with, as opposed to the redemptive in the case of Shem), the sentence is a prophecy first of God's dwelling in the Mosaic tabernacle and the temple of Solomon among Israel, and second and supremely of the incarnation of our Lord Jesus as a Jew among the Jews. However, if we consider the context and connection of the three sentences which compose this verse, it is more natural to take the pronoun as referring to Japheth, and most commentators appear to understand the sentence in

this way. The statement would then mean that Japheth would be associated with Shem, particularly perhaps in the worship of the true God. In this case we have a prediction of the evangelisation of the nations and their grafting into Israel (Rom. 11. 17-24; Eph. 2. 13, 19; 3. 6). The Gentiles who were first evangelised and are spoken of in the New Testament were predominantly Japhetic nations, and are in fact sometimes called by the apostle Greeks, a name that is put for all Gentiles, and is specifically Jahphetic (Rom. 1. 14, 16). We may also perhaps see some significance in view of this prediction in the fact that it is the nations of Europe and their offshoots who have been regarded for centuries as ' Christian nations '. Spiritually this amounts to very little, indeed it may be a spiritual liability, but it at least means that the descendants of Japheth have for long made an outward profession of worshipping Shem's God.

Canaan shall be his servant. The nations of Europe have been quick to exploit the Hamitic races, and in the past have reduced numbers of them to slavery. Spiritually the same applies here, as was said on the previous verse.

VERSE 28. Noah had a long day of grace in which to witness to his children and descendants and to recount the wonderful works of God.

VERSE 29. Here we fall back into the language of chapter 5, and this verse virtually completes the genealogical table there. The chapter ends with the tragic refrain, the reiteration of which in chapter 5 produces a cumulative effect. Death is the wages of sin (Rom. 6. 23), and is the ' way of all flesh ' (Josh. 23. 14; 1 Ki. 2. 21).

CHAPTER 10

WITH the beginning of this chapter begins the fourth section of Genesis, the generations, or story, of the sons of Noah. The section divides into two parts (1) the ethnic table (10. 1-32), and (2) the story of the tower of Babel (11. 1-9). Our chapter consists of the ethnic table which is divided into three sub-sections: the sons of Japheth (2-5), of Ham (6-20), and of Shem (21-31). Shem is placed last, because the narrative that follows is concerned with his descendants. Of the others Japheth, who was blessed (9. 27), naturally precedes Ham, who was cursed (9. 25). Apart from the names of the sons of Noah themselves the names in the tables are those of peoples who are usually called in accordance with Hebrew custom by the name of an individual, who may or may not have actually existed as an ancestor. This was the case with Israel itself. The date of the table was before the destruction of the cities of the plain (ver. 19). It could not therefore have been composed later than the time of Abraham, whose date lay between 2000 and 1500 B.C., perhaps rather earlier in that period than later. At the same time the table could not have been compiled relatively very much earlier than the time of Abraham. The Greeks were inhabiting the islands and coasts of the Aegæan sea (verse 4). This they probably did not do before the beginning of the second millennium B.C. The Medes were known as a separate people (verse 2), but the other Japhetic peoples appear to be placed in the regions north of the Black Sea (verses 2, 3). Indo-European migrations eastward through Asia Minor, which might account for the mention of the Medes, perhaps took place about 2000 B.C. Indications of various sorts thus appear to point to the date of the compilation of the table being about, or slightly later than, 2000 B.C. The compiler was a Semite.

VERSE 1. *The sons of Noah*, of whom the whole earth was overspread (verse 19). *Shem, Ham and Japheth*. This is the order, in which the sons have been mentioned since 5. 32.

Sons born. The blessing of fruitfulness (9. 1) was fulfilled. What God has promised He is able also to perform (Rom. 4. 21). If God has promised to us spiritual fruitfulness in His service, He is able to carry out His promise, and in faith we may expect Him to do so.

VERSE 2. *Japheth*. The three sons appear in the table in reverse order, in order that Shem may be given prominence at the end.

Gomer. These are the people known as Cimmerians, who lived to the north, perhaps to the north west of the Black Sea. It is possible that their name survives in the ethnic name of the Welsh people, Cymru.

Magog. These were a people of south Russia, who have been identified with the Scythians.

Madai. These are the Medes, who lived to the east of Mesopotamia and later in collaboration with the Persians built a world empire. They spoke an Indo-European language, which had been brought in migration from eastern Europe. *Javan*. These are the Greeks. The name is that of Ionians, the Greeks who lived on the west coast of Asia Minor, with whom the eastern peoples first came into contact. *Tubal and Meshech*. These people are mentioned together in Ezek. 38. 2, and appear to have lived in Russia. The name Moscow or Muscovy, probably derives from Meshech. Possibly the name of the city Tobolsk comes from the name Tubal. *Tiras*. This people does not seem to be identifiable.

VERSE 3. *Ashkenaz*. Modern Jews identify these with the Germans. *Togarmah*. This was a northern people. (Ezek. 38. 6).

VERSE 4. *Elishah*. This may be a Semitic form of the name Hellas, by which the Greeks called their own country. If so, it proves the table to have been compiled after the occupation by the Greeks of the north western parts of their mainland, where the name probably arose, and after the differentiation of their language from the common Indo-European stock. This fact again seems to set the beginning of the second millennium as a *terminus a quo*. *Tarshish*. This is usually identified as Tartessus in Spain, but, wide as was Greek colonisation, no people of Greek language is known to scholars in that part of the world. *Kittim*. This is the island of Cyprus. *Dodanim*. The correct reading according to the Septuagint Greek version, the Samaritan recension of the Pentateuch, and the Hebrew text in the parallel passage in 1 Chron. 1. 7, is *Rodanim*. The characters in Hebrew representing D and R are alike, and confusion has arisen in copying in this case. The people referred to are the inhabitants of the island of Rhodes.

VERSE 5. *By these*. It is possible to render 'from' instead of *by*. *These* may refer to the sons of Javan only, or to all the sons of Japheth. The expression 'the isles', which refers to coastal districts as well as islands, seems to fit the Greeks alone better than all the peoples mentioned in the preceding verses. The apostle Paul sometimes uses the term 'Greeks' as a synonym for all Gentiles (Rom. 1. 16). If the phrase 'the isles of the Gentiles' in this verse refers to the Aegæan Sea, his phraseology may be an echo of this passage. *Divided*. 'Were . . . divided' may be rendered 'separated themselves'. *In their lands*. In the corresponding passages in verses 20 and 31 these words go with the conclusion to the whole sub-section. It is possible that similarly here they may belong after the words 'every one'. *After his tongue*. The peoples are regarded from four different aspects, geographical (*in their lands*), linguistic, racial and political. There is nothing to

show that the compiler of the table thought of these as exactly overlapping. In actual historical experience they seldom, if ever, have. Divergent races are bound together by unity of language, as in the case of the English language today, and different languages may be spoken by peoples who are racially akin. An example may be found in modern India. This is equally true, and more obvious, in the case of political association and racial kinship. By mentioning these four distinct methods of dividing the peoples of the world the writer guarded himself against giving the impression that he thought of the peoples whom he mentioned together as necessarily racially akin. Naturally some of them were, but it would be contrary to the tendency of Hebrew thought to take the words 'sons' in verses 2, 3 and 4 necessarily in a genealogical sense. 'Sons' may mean 'successors'. The languages of the sons of Japheth, though probably mainly of the Indo-European family, cannot all now be identified. It is interesting that the writer does not associate Crete (see on verse 14) with Greece. This great table of associated nations emphasises the fact, as we stand on the brink of the account of the call of Abraham, that God is the God of all the nations of the world. It is He that set the bounds of their habitations (Deut. 32. 8; Acts 17. 26), His purpose being that they should seek God and one day find Him (Acts 17. 27). Indeed the call of Abraham was the first step in the long process of preparation for redemption, as a result of which the Gentiles might one day be brought within the scope of evangelical blessing.

VERSE 6. *Cush*. These are the Negro peoples, particularly the Ethiopians, but there was another Cush in the region of the Caucasus (see on 2. 13). *Mizraim*. This is the regular Hebrew name for Egypt. *Phut*. These are generally considered to be the peoples of North Africa west of Egypt. *Canaan* inhabited Palestine, and gave the country one of its permanent names.

VERSE 7. The names in this verse are not easily identifiable. There was a *Havilah* near the Caucasus (2. 11), and another between southern Palestine and Egypt (25. 18. 1 Sam. 15. 7).

Sheba and Dedan are usually associated with the country today called Ethiopia or Abyssinia. The name Ethiopia in the Bible usually refers to the Kingdom of Meroë in upper Egypt.

VERSE 8. *Began to be a mighty one.* Nimrod was the first to found and rule a world-empire. He sought domination over his fellow-men for his own profit and pride. It is possible that he may be the same as the great figure known in ancient history as Sargon I, who ruled from Assyria to the western coast of Asia Minor. His evil example has been followed ever since by the Egyptians, Assyrians, Babylonians, Medo - Persians, Macedonians, Greeks, Romans and various nations of the modern world.

VERSE 9. *A mighty hunter,* of men not of animals, in the sense which we find in Micah 7. 2. In robbing men and peoples of their independence and freedom he is pronounced by the Holy Ghost to be a hunter, snaring, entangling, murdering and devouring. Such is the Bible view of world empire. Note that he was a hunter *before the Lord.* This reminds us of 6. 11, and the phrase here seems used in exactly the same sense. It is noteworthy that we have in this verse the redemptive Name Jahweh, *the Lord.* This fact establishes a connection between world empire and the redemptive purpose and covenants. The succession of world empires, later brought before us in the Bible, although always regarded as evil, all played an important part in the purpose of redemption. Egypt was closely associated with Israel in the bondage and the exodus, Assyria

and Babylonia were used as instruments of God's judgment to purge the Jews of idolatry. Persian kings permitted the return of the Jews from exile, and ordered the rebuilding of the temple. The Greeks under Alexander and his successors brought a common language to the eastern Mediterranean, and so laid the linguistic foundations of the New Testament. Rome unified the world, and by means of her mighty roads and the peace that she imposed made the spread of the Gospel possible. Modern nations and empires have been used by God in similar ways as unconscious, or even unwilling, instruments for the furtherance of the Gospel. We do not know in what way the empire of Nimrod furthered, or sought to frustrate, God's plans for the redemption of man in Christ, but with many other examples in history before us, we may be assured that even in those early days it was somehow used by the Lord.

Wherefore it is said. The empire and evil name of Nimrod became proverbial among the Semites and Israelites. The influence of this mighty evil man was not forgotten. His name became a byword. His evil reputation follows him among men, and his wickedness will accuse him on the day of judgment and in the presence of his many victims drag him down to hell. ' Seekest thou great things for thyself? Seek them not ' (Jer. 45. 5).

VERSE 10. *Babel.* This may suggest that Nimrod was connected with the incident of the tower of Babel described in the following chapter. Or again he may have founded his empire immediately after the dispersion of the people, which began there. The reference to Babel as the beginning of his kingdom may lend some colour to the idea that he was the founder of an idolatrous system of religion, but there is no real evidence in Scripture that this was so. Again there is no evidence, beyond a partial similarity of name, to connect him with the

Ninus mentioned by Herodotus, or with Queen Semiramis. The hunting of which he was guilty might however include the snaring of men's spiritual lives through idolatry. *Shinar*. This is the ancient name for Mesopotamia.

VERSE 11. *Went forth Asshur*. It is better to read with the Revised Version, ' he went forth into Assyria ', that is, Nimrod went forth.

Builded Nineveh. As in the case of Cain (4. 17), the building of cities is connected with the wicked. Perhaps the narrative implies that God's intention for man was a simple agricultural life. *The city Rehoboth*. This may be rendered as the text or as the A.V. margin, ' the streets of the city ', in which case it refers to Nineveh, or as a double name, ' Rehoboth-Ir '.

VERSE 12. *A great city*. Greatness in the eyes of the world does not necessarily correspond to greatness in the eyes of God. In God's eyes the values of the world are reversed (see Luke 1. 51-53).

VERSE 13. *Mizraim*, that is Egypt. *Begat*. This implies that the seven peoples, mentioned in this and the following verse, sprang originally as colonists from Egypt. *Ludim*. These are the Lydians. The district of southern Asia Minor was called Lydia in classical times. The remaining three people mentioned in this verse do not seem to be identifiable.

VERSE 14. *Pathrusim*. These are the inhabitants of Pathros in Upper Egypt. It is evident that the name of the country long antedates its Greek form. *Casluhim*. The identity of these people is not known. In this passage and in 1 Chron. 1. 12, which is probably copied from it, they are said to be the ancestors of the Philistines. However in Deut. 2. 23 the Caphtorim, who are the people mentioned next in this verse, are obviously identified with the Philistines, and in Amos 9. 7 the Philistines are

said to have come from Caphtor. There is no evidence of displacement in the text of the verse, and the explanation perhaps is that Casluhim and Caphtorim were branches of the same people.

Philistim. These are the Philistines, who gave their name to Palestine. In the days of Samson, Saul and David they were a strong people, occupying the maritime plain in the south-west of Palestine, and were strong and bitter enemies of Israel. Archæologists have dated their arrival in Palestine about the twelfth century B.C. This does not agree with the mention of them here in this table, nor with their presence in Gerar in the time of Abraham and Isaac (20. 34; 26. 8, 14-18). The explanation perhaps is that previous to the twelfth century they colonised isolated settlements, but did not till then occupy the whole land.

Caphtorim. These are usually considered to be the Cretans, whose ancient and magnificent culture was first laid bare by the British scholar, Sir Arthur Evans. They are the people known to archæologists as Minoans, whose capital was at Cnossos. Their island, after centuries of brilliance, was finally taken by Greeks from the mainland, and their influence was widespread in Greece. It is in agreement with the known facts, that the compiler of this table does not connect them with the Greeks. We can tell from this passage that they were a Hamitic people with connections with Egypt.

VERSE 15. *Sidon*. This is the city on the Mediterranean coast of Syria north of Palestine, often closely connected with Tyre. Its inhabitants were Phenicians, and all evidence goes to show that they were Canaanites, exactly as we are told here. *Heth*. These are the Hittites. In the Bible they are usually known as one of the seven nations inhabiting Canaan, who were to be driven out before the Israelites. While these Hittite settlements existed in Palestine, the Hittites ruled an empire in Asia Minor and northern Syria during the third and second millennia B.C., about which much has been learnt during the last fifty years.

VERSE 16. The three peoples named in this verse were among the pre-Israelite inhabitants of Palestine. The Jebusites were the occupiers of Jerusalem.

VERSE 17. *Hivite.* These were among the seven pre-Israelite inhabitants of Canaan (see Ex. 3. 8; Josh. 12. 8). Their name has been identified by some scholars with that of the Achæans, Homer's *Achaioi.* *Arkite.* This name does not seem to be identified. *Sinite.* This appears to be the same name as that of the Chinese. Perhaps it was once a common name for all of Mongolian stock, or for all speakers of the Tai languages.

VERSE 18. The three names mentioned in this verse are perhaps those of Syrian peoples.

Spread abroad. We know that the Hittites spread to Asia Minor, where they ruled an empire extending from Assyria to the Mediterranean. If the people called Sinite (verse 17) were really the ancestors of the Chinese, Canaanite migrations were exceedingly far-flung. Notice that of all the peoples mentioned in this chapter the Canaanites are the only ones of whom it is said that they were spread abroad. Satan saw to it that the people who were cursed permeated the world. He had these wicked people (see Lev. 18 and 20) ready placed to counteract the truth, wherever it might appear, so that he might use them to frustrate God's purpose of redemption, which he feared. Like the Canaanites, sin and the influence of Satan spread among men. Sin is infectious and ubiquitous. Wherever the Gospel is taken, it finds Satan entrenched and ready to oppose it with all his might and main. In spite of this we may thank God that greater is He that is in us, than he that is in

the world (1 Jo. 4. 4).

VERSE 19. The borders here mentioned are practically those of the Holy Land, afterwards promised to Abraham and his children. The Canaanite was not only spread through the world, he was also concentrated in the inheritance of the redeemed. In the same way the devil and his armies occupy the heavenly places, which the Israel of God is one day to occupy (Eph. 6. 12), and they are now being driven out of them by the victorious warfare of the Gospel (Eph. 6. 10-20; Rev. 12. 10, 11).

Sodom and Gomorrah. The cities of the plain, which were afterwards destroyed (chapter 19), were still in existence when this table was compiled. *Lasha* is nowhere else mentioned in the Bible. It was perhaps a very ancient place, which later disappeared.

VERSE 20. See on verse 5.

VERSE 21. *Eber.* This is the ancestor of the Hebrews. The verse tells us that all Hebrews are Semites. The Hebrews included many peoples living to the east of Palestine. *The brother of Japheth the elder.* The R.V. renders the text ' the elder brother of Japheth '. Either is apparently a good rendering of the Hebrew. The Massoretic text accents the words, so as to give the A.V. rendering. The age of Shem, as it is given in 11. 10, compared with that of his father as stated in 5. 32, appears to be that of the youngest of the three brothers. The A.V. rendering of this verse is therefore probably correct.

VERSE 22. *Elam.* The Elamites often appear in the Old Testament. They lived in the mountains bordering on Mesopotamia. *Asshur.* These are the Assyrians, who later built a great empire and carried away captive the northern kingdom of Israel (2 Ki. 17). They are noted for their cruelty. *Arphaxad* was in the direct line of the Hebrews and Abraham (see 11. 11-13). *Lud.* These are perhaps the Lydians of Asia Minor. *Aram.* This is the regular Hebrew name for Syria. The language spoken in Syria in early times, which later spread far afield and was spoken in Palestine, when the Lord was on earth, ·is called Aramaic.

Verse 23. The people mentioned in this verse are probably different Syrian tribes.

Verse 24. We know nothing of *Salah* except what we are told in 11. 12-15.

Eber. From this name that of the Hebrews is derived.

Verse 25. *Peleg.* This name in Hebrew means ' division '. *Divided.* The division referred to seems to be that which occurred after the incident of the tower of Babel (11. 1-9). In this we have another example of the power and influence of sin. Sin is the greatest of all divisive forces. It separates man from God (Isa. 59. 2), and in consequence it separates man from his fellow-man. This process is reversed in redemption. Christ became our peace on the cross, and broke down the barrier between God and sinners (Eph. 2. 14). As a result nothing can ever separate the child of God from his Father and Saviour (Rom. 8. 37, 38). In Christ the redeemed are brought into an eternal fellowship with each other, which is rooted in their fellowship with God (1 Jo. 1. 3).

Verse 26. The thirteen children of Joktan, mentioned in this and the following three verses, were probably inhabitants of Arabia. Their descendants remain there today. Here in Scripture they are nothing but a list of names, but God their Creator knew, and knows, all about them. loves them all, and from the beginning was preparing their redemption, although they knew nothing of it, and became early cut off from the

knowledge of the true God and His purposes. For centuries now in these latter days the blight of Islam has descended upon them. Christian unfaithfulness in the past has made the task of bringing salvation to them far harder than it might have been.

Verse 28. *Sheba.* The occurrence of this name, as well as that of Havilah in the following verse, among both Hamites (verse 7) and Semites shows to what extent these peoples and races became mingled. We have the same story as that of the families of Seth and Cain (see on 5. 9-27). Where God would keep His people holy and separate, their tendency is towards compromise, co-operation and confusion.

Verse 29. *Ophir* was noted for its gold. (1 Ki. 10. 11).

Verse 30. The district referred to here seems to have been south-east of Palestine. The statement seems to imply that the table was compiled in Palestine, and it seems reasonable that the compiler may have been Abraham himself. A list of peoples and nations, such as this, could suitably accompany the great promises made to Abraham of the future blessing of the Gentiles through him and his seed.

Verse 31. See on verse 5.

Verse 32. Notice (1) that families are the foundation of human society. As the generations pass on, families may become nations, but the family still remains the basis of all healthy human life. One of the blights of modern life is that the family is being reverenced and regarded less and less, and its place is being taken by the nation or state. This is so not only in avowedly totalitarian countries. The increase of divorce, the trend of the educational system, and in spite of its advantages certain aspects of the so-called welfare state, all tend in the democratic countries to weaken family life and so to loosen the foundations of healthy society. (2) The society that grew among the descendants of Noah, although showing many contrasts to the final society of the redeemed, may yet be said to be typical of it. That society will consist of a single universal family. All its members will be children of God by faith in Christ Jesus (Jo. 1. 12; Gal. 3. 26). Yet in the unity of the world to come there will be variety. There will be ' the nations of them that are saved ' (Rev. 21. 24). All will walk in the same light, and all will be united in the glory and wonder of the presence and love of their Creator and Redeemer. (3) The nations who were descended from Noah were *divided*. Deep divisions still separate them today, jealousies, suspicions and fears. The division existing between the nations of the world is based upon their universal separation from God, and this can be remedied only by the Gospel. There will be no remedy in this present evil world. The division is healed now in the Christian society, and will be perfectly healed in the world to come.

CHAPTER 11

In this chapter we complete the fourth section of Genesis, which is the story of the sons of Noah and began at 10. 1. This is followed by the fifth section, ' the generations of Shem ' (verses 10-26). The last six verses of the chapter form the introduction to the long central sixth section of the book, ' the generations of Terah ', which continues to 25. 11 and consists of the life story of Abraham. The story of the tower of Babel (1-9) recounts the presumption of man and the intervention of God to save man from himself and prevent the frustration of the purpose of redemption.

VERSE 1. Language was not mentioned in 10. 32, because it is dealt with in these verses. *Of one langu-*

age and of one speech. The Hebrew word translated ' language ' means literally ' lip ', and that translated ' speech ' means literally ' words '. Perhaps the former refers to phonetics, the actual sounds and their pronunciation, and the latter to vocabulary. The importance of language in the life and history of man can scarcely be exaggerated. The power of speech differentiates man from the animals. It is the sign and expression of rational thought and of a reasoning mind. The cries of animals are instinctive expressions of emotion, capable of arousing a response of an emotional kind in another animal, but not capable of conveying thought, conclusion, or intention. At the same time differentiation of language has proved one of the most divisive forces in human history. People fear or despise those who speak a different language and cannot speak their own. Language has played a part of fundamental importance in the work of redemption, for the Gospel is conveyed by the spoken word, and it has pleased God by the foolishness of preaching to save such as believe (1 Cor. 1. 21). ' Faith cometh of hearing, and hearing by the Word of God ' (Rom. 10. 17).

VERSE 2. *As they journeyed*. The context seems to leave it an open question whether the reference here is to the whole race, or to a section of it. If to the former, the events recorded here must have taken place at a relatively short period after the deluge. *From the east*. The R.V. translates ' eastward '. Here again the A.V. seems more likely to be right.

Shinar. This is the ancient name for Mesopotamia. *They dwelt there*. It is better to dwell in Christ than in Shinar.

VERSE 3. *They said one to another*. Here we have co-operation. So sinners have always conspired and co-operated in doing what is evil and seeking to deprive God of His glory and bestow it on man. *They had brick for stone, and slime had they for mortar.* In so doing they were an unwitting picture of the sinner of all generations. The sinner substitutes what is artificial for what is natural. Instead of trying to build with God's living stones (1 Pet. 2. 4, 5), he builds a world with the material of his own wicked works, with what is man-made instead of what is God-created. Man's religion, his civilisation, his legal systems, his social customs, his government, and all the variegated activities of his life, have been built ever since upon his own ideas and opinions apart from God's revelation. As a result he has made a busy, but miserable world.

Again, not only does he substitute his own brick for God's stone. Instead of the mortar of faith in God and love to one's neighbour, which binds together the redeemed society in the true church, he has the cohesive slime of sin. His society is united in the bonds of a false religion, or by a common aggressive purpose, or by the filthy mirth-producing communications of unclean minds. To what sort of society do we belong? Are we bound to our neighbours by a common faith and a mutual love? Or are we united by unworthy aims with some section of the world? Are we using slime or mortar? Brick and slime were the common building materials of Mesopotamia as opposed to stone and mortar, which were in use in Palestine.

VERSE 4. *A city.* Again the building of a city is associated with the wicked, as it was in the case of Cain (4. 17) and Nimrod (10. 11). *A tower.* This was probably the kind of temple tower, common to the cities of Mesopotamia and known as a zigurrat.

Unto heaven. This (1) may be a figure of speech for exceptional height, as in Deut. 1. 28. Or (2) the whole phrase may mean that the

signs of the zodiac were printed on the inside of the roof at the top of the tower, which was made to resemble the dome of heaven, for purposes of idolatrous worship. It seems likely that the intention was to establish a centre of heathen religion.

A name, lest we be scattered. The purpose of building the city and tower seems to have been to create a memorial, which could perhaps be visited from all quarters of the earth, and would constitute a permanent monument to those who might be separated from each other in the course of the increase of population, and might be forgotten by each other. They may also have supposed that the tower would provide them with a name or standing with God. If so, they were woefully ignorant. There is only one Name, in virtue of which man can approach God, and that is the Name that is above every name. In the Name of Jesus every knee shall bow (Phil. 2. 10). Christ is now seated at God's right hand in the heavenly places, far above every name that is named, not only in this world, but also in that which is to come. (Eph. 1. 21).

VERSE 5. *The Lord.* This is Jahweh, God's Name in connection with redemption. The city and tower were perhaps the centre of a scheme by which the devil intended to produce an attractive alternative to the city and place where one day God would place His Name (1 Ki. 8. 16-20). Babel was to be for the name of man what Jerusalem was to become for the Name of God. The spirit of Babel has pursued the Israel of God ever since. Under the Gospel we have the spiritual Babylon at Rome (Rev. 17 and 18), a city and church built for the glory of man, where the Bishop of Rome sits in in the place of God. The church of Rome glorifies the pope, the church of Christ glorifies her Saviour. *Came down to see,* just as later He came down to see and to know about Sodom (18. 21). This is a figure of speech, but a very gracious one. It means that God will not judge or destroy evil without condescending to investigate it. He knows all from the beginning. He has no need to see and learn, but by allowing such a figure to be used about Himself He emphasises the fairness of His judgments. True and righteous are Thy judgments (Rev. 16. 7).

The children of men builded. All that man builds is false. Only God can build the true city. It was the city which hath foundations, whose builder and maker is God, for which Abraham looked (Heb. 11. 10). It is the new Jerusalem, the city and church of all the redeemed (Heb. 12. 23; Rev. 21. 2, 10; Gal. 4. 26), the only permanent and happy society, foreknown by the Father, purchased by the Son, and called by the Spirit.

VERSE 6. *The people is one.* There is a great danger in the unity of sinners. If all the enemies of the Gospel were joined in one, we should humanly speaking be destroyed off the earth, and the light of the Gospel would be put out. But God keeps them apart.

One language. Their common language facilitated their co-operation. Their minds ran in the same groove. One day God ' will turn to the people a pure language ' (Zeph. 3. 9).

They begin. Sin begins but it does not stop. It goes on to a consummation. When it is finished, it brings forth death (Jas. 1. 15). Therefore we learn from this passage the importance of stopping the career of sin at an early stage. The power of sin grows stronger, and the edifice that it erects grows more and more solid. In the case of a community only some signal judgment, falling in time, can prevent its disastrous consequences. The judgment of Babel is an example. Economic and military disasters, disposed by the sovereignty of God and falling in time, may prevent worse things. The recent defeat of Germany is perhaps an

example. In the case of an individual, conversion to Christ in youth is the only sure shield against moral decadence in this life and eternal destruction in the world to come.

Nothing will be restrained, that is, nothing will be unattainable. These possibilities were present owing to the unity of purpose given to the community by its common language. A combination of sinners is a great danger. Mercifully God has divided men and given them many opposing loyalties, religious, national and social, so that they cannot combine to exterminate the Gospel.

Imagined. Sin begins in the imagination. Its seat is in the corrupt heart, the fruit of which is seen in actions. Lust, when it hath conceived, bringeth forth sin (Jas. 1. 15). The Lord taught us that murder and adultery were committed in the heart before ever any act took place (Matt. 5. 22, 28), and it is out of the abundance of the heart that the mouth speaketh (Matt. 12. 34). Therefore we need to obey the Holy Ghost, when He tells us, ' Keep thy heart with all diligence ' (Prov. 4. 23). The word *imagined* in this verse means, as so often, ' purposed '. These people conceived a plan of future action in their hearts, which was contrary to God's will, and which they intended to carry out.

VERSE 7. *Let us go down.* We have here the same form of language as in 1. 26. This is a record of a conversation between the Persons of the Holy Trinity, all of Whom are concerned together in perfect and eternal harmony with the work of salvation and redemption. The frustration of evil plans at Babel was necessary for the completion of the purpose of redemption. Had man been unrestrained, he would have succeeded in preventing the fruition of God's plan in some way, which naturally we do not know.

Confound their language. Thus the greatest divisive force in human life was brought into being. How was this brought about? First we should notice the connection in this passage between the confounding of the language and the scattering abroad (verses 8, 9). The statement at the beginning of verse 8 may imply that the scattering was the method used by the Lord to bring about the confusion of language. Now one of the basic maxims of modern linguistic science is that it is isolation that causes differentiation of language. The language of a single community is preserved as a unity because of the necessity for all the members of the community to be intelligible to one another. Even so it is broken up into dialects, used among sections of the community. If the community breaks up by migration, by violence, or by political or social change, these dialects develop into languages among the isolated sections of the former community. Linguists are able to trace this development in the Indo-European languages of Europe and Asia, which had their origin in a single language-continuum, probably spoken in the third millennium B.C. In historical times the Latin language has broken up in the same way and developed into the Romance languages of modern Europe and South America. Linguists have not been able to trace a common origin for the various great linguistic families of the world, but links between certain of them have been found, which make it conceivable that a few of them may be derived from the same source in a remote past. It is very far from being proved that this is the case with all, and it probably never can or will be proved. But a common origin at a remote epoch is conceivable. This may then be the process concealed behind the story of Babel. It is a natural process, but this is no reason why the God of nature should not have made use of it. Such an interpretation has however the disadvantage of leaving unexplained the means by which the dispersion was effected. We may be able to think of means, but there is

nothing in the story to tell us which of them, if any, were used.

Secondly however we should notice that the emphasis in our verse is not upon speaking, but upon understanding. This reminds us of the gift of tongues bestowed by the Holy Spirit on the church on the day of Pentecost. A careful reading of Acts 2. 4-13 will show that, while there were no more than twelve men at most who spoke, what they said was understood in at least fifteen languages. This means that the miracle was performed between the lips of the speakers, who would all thus speak their native Galilean, and the ears of the hearers. The gift of tongues was operative in the early church. Its purpose was mysterious to unbelievers, and it created confusion in the mind of the unlearned (1 Cor. 14. 23). This implies that one who was 'learned' in foreign languages might understand the tongue, from which it follows that the unknown tongue was a human language, somewhere spoken in the world. The gift of tongues still occasionally operates. A minister of the Church of England, well known fifty or sixty years ago as a gifted preacher, preached one Sunday evening in his London church in English a sermon, which was the means of the conversion of a Norwegian sailor, who was present and knew no English. The whole sermon was heard by him in Norwegian. Now this Pentecostal gift, which was designed to facilitate the spread of the Gospel, seems to be a definite reversal of what took place at Babel. We must not exclude the possibility therefore that the intervention of the Lord at Babel was entirely in the sphere of the supernatural. Possibly some instantaneous operation was performed upon the minds, brains, speech organs, or ears of the community, similar to that at Pentecost, but in the reverse direction, which brought suddenly into being certain of the great families of human speech. The resulting confusion would be the means of the break-up of the community into a series of smaller ones, whose members were mutually intelligible. These would naturally separate from each other. Isolation would bring into operation the natural laws of linguistic development, which have been at work from that day to this. Notice how this judgment made the salvation of the sinner more difficult by preventing him from understanding the language of revelation without a translation, but at the same time made it possible for salvation to be brought to men.

VERSE 8. *Scattered them abroad*. See on verse 7. *They left off*. The work of the sinner will never be brought to completion, but will fall into ruins, or be left as the monument of futile and godless effort.

VERSE 9. *Babel*. In Aramaic this name appears to mean *the gate of God*, and Assyrian inscriptions show this meaning. In Hebrew the consonants were the same as those of a root meaning 'confusion', and a play of words therefore arose on this meaning. Here is a great parable. What to the heathen is the gate of God is confusion to the Christian. This is specially true of the modern Babylon (the name Babylon being of course only the Greek form of Babel). To the Romanist the church of Rome is the gate of God. To the Christian it is confusion.

If in verse 8 the implication might be that the scattering was the cause of the confusion of language, here in verse 9 the confusion precedes the scattering. The only inference that we can draw is that there was a close connection between the two. Thus the proud combined effort at rebellion ended in confusion. This is the end of all sin and of every sinner. But 'he that believeth shall not be ashamed' (Rom. 10. 11). Instead of being gathered into the garner of God sinners will be scattered in outer darkness. '. Scatter thou the people that delight in war' (Ps. 68. 30).

VERSE 10. Verses 10-26 form the fifth section of the book of Genesis, the 'generations' of Shem. It consists only of a genealogy. This slender thread is the link that binds the narrative together, and the story of redemption hangs in these verses upon it. With regard to this genealogy we notice (1) that, as in the case of 5. 3-32, there may be gaps in it (see Matt. 1. 8). It ought not therefore to be used as a chronology, as has sometimes been the case in the past. For all we know thousands of years may have elapsed between Noah and Abraham. (2) The family represented in this genealogy was God's instrument for fulfilling His promise of redemption to the race. The men mentioned in these verses are all ancestors of Christ (Lk. 3. 34-36). All genealogies of the Bible point to Christ. In this family the purpose of God was being quietly carried out in spite of the threatening events of Babel and of any other opposition of Satan. The same is true today. God is working quietly and deeply in the world in the hearts of men. The fury of the adversary cannot prevent the advance of the Gospel. (3) The members of this family, who were carrying out the redemptive purpose of God, are likely, in some cases at least, to have been unconscious of it. Some perhaps were believers, who followed the will of God step by step. Certainly some were heathen. From these things we gather that we cannot know the extent of our influence, nor how much, or in what way, God will make use of us. If we remain faithful in service and obedience, the power and will of God are the only limits to the result. In the same way God in His sovereign disposition of power can use and overrule wicked men for the accomplishment of His purposes of salvation. Notice that in the first generation after Shem the length of human life was more than halved. Three generations later (verse 19) it was halved again. Man's days on the earth are but a shadow, and there is none abiding

(1 Chron. 29. 15).

VERSE 12. *Begat Salah.* The Septuagint Greek version inserts another generation and the name of Cainan between Arphaxad and Salah, and is followed in so doing by the evangelist in the Lord's genealogy (Lk. 3. 36). As the translators of the Septuagint are unlikely to have invented the name, they must have found it in the Hebrew text from which they made their version. It is therefore probable that it had been inadvertently dropped out from the texts that lay behind the Massoretic.

VERSE 14. *Eber* was the ancestor of the Hebrews.

VERSE 16. *Peleg* was alive at the time of the confusion of languages (see 10. 25).

VERSE 26. *Begat.* As in the case of Noah (5. 32), this means ' was the father of '. It does not necessarily mean that all three sons were born in the same year of Terah's life, a possibility in the polygamous conditions of the day. As in the case of the genealogy in chapter 5, the figures in this genealogy are different in the Samaritan recension of the Pentateuch and the Septuagint Greek version, especially in the latter, from what they are in the Massoretic Hebrew text, from which our translation was made. The numbers are greater in the Samaritan and Septuagint. Accuracy in the transmission of figures in the ancient languages was difficult to attain, and though it has generally been considered that the Massoretic text has been more likely to preserve the original, we cannot now be certain what the right reading should be.

VERSE 27. Here we begin the great central sixth section of Genesis, which deals with the life of Abraham. It continues till 25. 11. The closing six verses of the present chapter form an introduction to this section and deal with Terah's family. This verse repeats the statement of verse 26. The repetition is an indication that a new start is made at verse 27. We may have a separate writer, or a document by the same writer begun at a later time. It is also conceivable that the repetition served to show that the place of this section came immediately after the last, which ended at verse 26. This would be necessary, if the documents were originally written on a series of clay tablets. It seems to have been the custom not to number the tablets, but to mark their sequence by a repetition at the beginning of one of words used at the end of the preceding.

Haran begat Lot. Lot is to play a large part in the story that follows.

VERSE 28. *Haran died.* This fact bears upon the story of Abraham in two ways. First it forms a background to the story of Lot, explaining, at least in part, how it was that he accompanied Abraham to Palestine. Secondly it emphasises the fact that later, when Abraham was seeking a wife for his son from among the members of his own family, only the descendants of his brother Nahor were left. *Ur of the Chaldees.* Ur was one of the great cities of the Mesopotamian plain, and was a centre of the worship of the moon god. It was a prosperous city of high culture and a luxurious mode of life for the rich. Terah and his family were settled here. Knowledge recently gained by archæological discovery about Ur emphasises the settled comfort which Abraham forsook at the call of God.

VERSE 29. *Wives.* Each wife was a close relation of her husband. This Semite family, living in an environment which was probably mainly Sumerian (perhaps, that is to say, Canaanite), seems to have taken pains to preserve its racial purity. Perhaps there was a tradition coming down from the time of Shem, which enjoined such a step. The attitude seems in any case to have been fully in line with the purpose of God, Who in any age, under primitive conditions, under law, or under Gospel, has called on His people to be separate from the world. *Sarai* was the daughter of Terah by a different mother from Abraham (20. 12), and *Milcah* was her husband's niece, the daughter of his brother Haran.

VERSE 30. *·Sarai was barren.* Sarai was to illustrate in herself the wonderful work of the Spirit of God in giving life to a dead soul and raising it from the death of sin to the life of righteousness. In God's purpose she was barren. Her condition typifies the spiritual barrenness of the unconverted soul, which can produce no fruit of the Spirit, but is in the sight of God like a dry wilderness. No one is ever won to Christ by one who is unconverted himself, unless he is the unwilling, unconscious or mechanical vehicle of the Word of Life. ' They that are in the flesh cannot please God ' (Rom. 8. 8).

She had no child. Sarai would be all the time instinctively conscious of her need, and this would probably account for her jealousy of Hagar (16. 5, 6) and her sensitiveness over Ishmael (21. 9). The sinner, who is conscious of dissatisfaction and emptiness, often manifests his feelings in bitterness towards those who are converted, while all the time in the depth of his heart he is longing to have what he sees they possess.

VERSE 31. It is with this verse that Stephen in his speech begins the story of the covenant nation. Notice that it was to Abraham that God originally appeared (Acts 7. 2). It was Abraham who received the call. Yet in this verse we read *Terah took Abram his son.* Terah was either seeking to share in a blessing to which he had not been called, or alternatively was attempting by taking matters into his own hands to frustrate God's purpose for his son. The call of Abraham made action necessary. Terah therefore took action, in order that Abraham might not.

They went forth with them. The Peshitto Syriac version reads, ' he went forth with them '. The Septuagint Greek version, the Samaritan recension of the Pentateuch and the Vulgate Latin read, ' he brought them forth '. Both these readings make better sense than that of our version. *To go into the land of Canaan.* This was their professed purpose.

They came unto Haran, and dwelt there. They were in fact like large numbers of religious people, who declare their purpose of journeying to heaven, but they get no further than half way. They leave Ur and go out. They make a profession of religion. They take an actual journey, but they stop short of the right place. We do not know why Terah stopped in Haran. Perhaps he did not want to go too far away from what had been his home. Perhaps he found Haran a convenient place. He could live there under settled conditions, and had no need to live in tents. Yet he could say that he had received a·call of God and had acted on it. Perhaps he had considered himself virtuous in leaving Ur. He could keep an eye on his son and prevent his giving way to an exaggerated enthusiasm. He effected a compromise which he hoped would satisfy his son and be sufficient obedience to God's call. In fact for many years he held Abram back from blessing. How many professing Christians reach Haran and get no farther. They go halfway and settle where they are comfortable. They cripple the spiritual lives of any over whom they have influence. They had better not have left Ur. Like Terah they are those who received no call, but have gratuitously associated themselves with God's redemptive purposes. In which of the three places are we in our spiritual lives? Are we unashamedly still in Ur? Are we settled comfortably in Haran, enjoying the prestige of having answered the Gospel call? Or have we burnt our boats and launched out into Canaan, there to bear costly and unmistakable witness to the Saviour and His Gospel?

VERSE 32. *The days of Terah.* As long as Terah was alive progress seemed impossible.

Terah died. The death of Terah meant the cutting of ties. It was not till after his father's death that Abraham was able to move into Palestine (Acts 7. 4). So with us. If we would obtain God's blessing, and realise the promises that He makes, and answer His call, we must make a clean cut with the world, the flesh and the devil. We must take up the cross and follow Christ (Mt. 10. 37-39). We must go out unto Him without the camp, bearing His reproach (Heb. 13. 13). We must renounce all our possessions (Lk. 14. 33). We must allow no one to come between us and the Saviour's call (Lk. 14. 26). God broke Abraham's tie, and in the same way He will break ours. Just as the death of Terah supervened in the case of Abraham, so we must die with Christ (2 Cor. 5. 14) and be crucified to the world (Gal. 6. 14).

GENESIS 12

IN this chapter we have the first phase of the story of Abraham, the father of the faithful. His life history is a parable of the spiritual life. We read here of his call (verse 1), the promises made to him (verses 2, 3), his obedience and departure (verses 4, 5), his journey and a further promise (verses 6-9). Verses 10 to 20 describe his escape from famine into Egypt and the serious compromise, of which he was guilty there.

VERSE 1. *The Lord had said.* Notice that, as ever, the initiative came from God, Who moved at this point in sovereign power in pursuance of His purpose of redemption. The Holy Spirit, speaking through Stephen (Acts 7. 3), declares that this call took place when Abraham was still in Ur. It therefore explains the action of Terah in leaving Ur (11. 31), although he failed to reach the place that God had appointed for his son. The call thus came without Abraham having taken a single step towards altering the life that he had lived in heathenism from the beginning. God broke into his life. So it is with every child of God. No one can move, however short a way, towards God, until He has first called him. The call of God breaks into a man's sinful life. ' Whom He predestinated, them He also called ' (Rom. 8. 30).

Get thee out. This is the pattern of the call that comes to every child of God at the beginning of his Christian life. God is taking *out* of the Gentiles a people to His Name (Acts 15. 14). He has chosen us *out* of this present wicked world (Gal. 1. 4), and He tells us to come out of the midst of them and be separate (2 Cor. 6. 17). The call of God is always away from the world, away from sin, away from the old life. Our verse tells us of three things that Abraham was to leave. They are (1) his *country.* For him this meant the literal, physical, geographical severance of ties. He was to take a journey and to become henceforward a pilgrim. In the case of the Christian a literal departure of this sort is sometimes involved in God's call. This is so in the case of the missionary called to the foreign field. In the spiritual sense this is always true. The call of God involves a break with the old life, social or political, the old life of thought, ambition and outlook. (2) Abram was to leave *his kindred.* This also is true of the Christian. No family interest is to come between him and the will of God. (3) He was to leave his *father's house.* ' Whoso loveth father or mother more than Me ', said the Saviour, ' is not worthy of Me ' (Matt. 10. 37). We notice that this third severance was too great for Abram's spiritual strength, so that he never moved out into the fulness of the blessing which God had for him, until after his father's death. We notice that all the three things which Abram was to leave were good, not sinful.

Thus discipleship involves the renouncing of the right and legitimate things of the world, just as the Saviour renounced His Father's eternal home, in order to come to redeem us. *Unto a land.* The call had a positive, as well as a negative, side, and this was by far the more important. So it is with the Christian. He is not called to forsake the world simply for the sake of renouncing. The separation is a means to an end, a necessary means. If Abraham had never left Ur, he could never have reached Palestine. In the same way God calls His people to a country, a heavenly country, of which Palestine is the shadow and symbol, and gives them great and precious promises, as He did to Abraham.

I will shew thee. The heavenly country is the subject of a revelation by God. It is on this passage that the writer to the Hebrews bases his statement that Abraham went out, not knowing whither he went. This does not mean that he did not know that he was going to the land of Canaan, but that he had never seen it and was dependent upon a revelation of God for his knowledge of it. So it is with us. We know that we are going to the heavenly country, but we do not know where it is nor what it is like. We are entirely dependent upon the promises and revelation of God. Palestine is the consistent type throughout the Old Testament of the heavenly land, which is promised to the redeemed. The heavenly country is in fact called the 'new earth', or new *land*, in contrast with Palestine which is the old land and no more than a type (Isa. 65. 17; 2 Pet. 3. 13; Rev. 21. 1).

VERSE 2. In this and the following verse we have the first seven of the fourteen great promises to Abraham, recorded between chapters 12 and 22 of Genesis. These promises are of fundamental importance for understanding God's plan of redemption, and are the basis of the Gospel (Heb. 6. 13-20). They are in the line of the first promise made to Adam and

Eve at the time of the fall (3. 15), and they lie behind the national consciousness of Old Testament Israel, its looking forward to better things, and behind the message of the prophets of blessing to come. We notice that in his call and obedience Abraham was both blessed himself and made a blessing to others. This is true of every Christian. No one can be blessed without being made a channel of blessing to others, and no one can be a blessing to others without being blessed himself.

The key to the meaning of the promises is to be found in the interpretation set upon the seventh of them (verse 3) by the Holy Ghost in the New Testament (Acts 3. 25; Gal. 3. 8). They are fulfilled in the Christian church and the Gospel. *A great nation.* Old Testament Israel experienced a flash of greatness and glory under David and Solomon, lasting in all about fifty or sixty years, from which they entered into a decline, until they lost their independence, which they have never permanently recovered. This transient brilliance cannot be said to fulfil this promise. They were replaced by another nation, as the Lord had predicted (Mt. 21. 43). The Lord's words are explained by the apostle Peter, who heard them, in the same context of ideas, the living stone, rejected by the builders, but made by God the head of the corner (Mt. 21. 42; 1 Pet. 2. 4-8). He says that Christians are the holy nation (1 Pet. 2. 9), and in so saying he applies to the church the words spoken to Old Testament Israel under the old covenant (Ex. 19. 6). Now those who belong to Christ are Abraham's seed (Gal. 3. 29), and we therefore have no difficulty in identifying the *great nation* as the 'holy nation', that is to say, the Christian Church, or whole company of the redeemed. This nation is immensely great in numbers (Rev. 7. 9), and it is great in estimation, being 'saved by the Lord' (Dt. 33. 29). The Lord here reveals to Abraham His purpose to gather out a redeemed nation, of which Abraham was the ancestor, because he was the ancestor of Christ.

I will bless thee. The second promise is one of personal blessing to Abraham himself. It was fulfilled in his justification by faith, recorded in Gen. 15. 6. Abraham received no temporal blessing, apart from the maintenance of his life and the provision of his needs. He was a stranger and pilgrim all his life. He did not even receive a square foot of land, on which to tread (Acts 7. 5). His blessing was the far deeper and greater one of a perfect standing with God. This fact reveals the nature and meaning of the word ' blessing ', as it occurs in these promises, and indeed, unless qualified by the context, throughout the Bible. God's blessing means His forgiveness and salvation in Christ.

Make thy name great. In accordance with this promise Abram has become one of the outstanding figures of the world. He is honoured by Christians, Jews and Mohammedans.

Thou shalt be a blessing. This fourth promise is fulfilled in the fact that Abram was one of the most prominent human channels, through whom Christ came into the world. In the Person of Christ Abram has become a blessing. He has been a means of salvation to countless thousands. It is this blessing that is brought to us Gentiles in Jesus Christ, Who was made a curse for us, in order that we might receive it (Gal. 3. 13, 14), and the apostle identifies it with the receiving of the Spirit through faith. We should consider well the apostle's words in Gal. 3. 13. The blessing is ours, only because Christ was made a curse. It follows that, when God made the promises to Abram, He was committing Himself to Calvary.

VERSE 3. *I will bless them that bless thee.* This is a promise that those who bless and honour Christ and His people will be themselves blessed. Whoever confesses Christ before men will be acknowledged by Christ in the presence of His Father (Mt. 10.

33). Whoever honours Christ will be honoured by the Father (Jo. 12. 26). Those who show kindness to Christ in the persons of His brethren when in need are the blessed of His Father, who inherit the Kingdom (Mt. 25. 34-40).

Curse him that curseth thee. This sixth promise goes naturally with the fifth. It alone demonstrates that the promises relate to eternal and spiritual things. God's curse is never given arbitrarily. It is directed against unrepentant sinners, and finds its fulfilment in the fearful sentence to be pronounced on the day of judgment (Mt. 25. 41). On that day the curse of God will reach to the innermost depths of the being of every enemy of Christ and His people, the callous, the persecutors, those who despise and oppose the Gospel, and all who have been indifferent to the Saviour's love and death.

In thee shall all families of the earth be blessed. This last of the seven promises is quoted, explained and amplified in two passages in the New Testament. It is sad to note in passing that several nineteenth-century theological commentators attempted to deprive this promise of its spiritual meaning and Gospel content by reducing the sense to that of the Gentiles blessing themselves by the use of Abraham's name. This sorry missing of the point will be found in the commentaries among others of C. A. Briggs, Franz Delitzsch († 1890), August Dillman, Heinrich Ewald († 1875), W. Gesenius († 1842), and Eduard Riehm († 1888). The answer to these suggestions is found in the explanation given to the passage by the apostles. The apostle Peter applies the passage at the close of the sermon which he preached in Jerusalem after the healing of the lame man (Acts 3. 25). He tells us that the Jews are the first of the families of the earth to be offered the blessing. This implies that they are not offered it exclusively. He then says that the blessing consists in being turned away from one's iniquities, in other words, in conversion and repentance. The apostle Paul also tells us that the promise relates to the justification of the Gentiles by faith, and that it is believers who are blessed with faithful Abraham (Gal. 3. 8, 9). The promise is not quoted in any other place in the New Testament, and no other meaning is put upon it in Scripture. It is thus quite clear that this promise relates to the Gospel, and the remainder naturally accompany it.

VERSE 4. This and the following verse give us the record of Abraham's obedience to the Lord's call. Like the apostle, he was ' not disobedient to the heavenly vision ' (Acts 26. 19). The writer to the Hebrews comments on this verse, that Abraham obeyed to go out. He works this fact into the scheme of his teaching about faith, and says that it was by faith that Abraham obeyed (Heb. 11. 8). Here then is the first great act of faith in Abraham's life. He ' departed.' It is the first act of faith of every child of God. Conversion means a departure, a break with the former life, the beginning of a journey along the narrow way from earth to heaven.

As the Lord had spoken unto him. Every call, every conversion, is a word from God. The beginning of every spiritual life is this speaking of God. The word of God has power to create the world (1. 3) and power to heal the sick (Mt. 12. 13). No true spiritual pilgrimage can begin, unless it has a command of God behind it.

Lot. ' Righteous Lot ' (2 Pet. 2. 7) went voluntarily and went with conviction. He had heard the same call as Abram, and he probably went with high hopes. But he was to turn out a hindrance and a disappointment. We find in his life the following downward steps: (1) a wrong choice (13. 11); (2) he pitched his tent toward Sodom (13. 12); (3) he dwelt in Sodom (14. 12); (4) he sat in the gate of Sodom, that is to say, exercised leadership in it (19. 1); (5)

though he escaped destruction, he is last seen in degradation and misery (19. 30-36). Lot is the illustration and example of the worldly Christian, who possesses salvation, but escapes by the skin of his teeth and loses all in the process.

Seventy and five. We do not know how long Terah and Abram lived in Haran, but Abram had lived three-sevenths of his life, before he was able to step out in obedience to God's call. While we can clearly see that harm might have been done by Terah's compromise (see on 11. 31), yet the impression given us by the narrative is that God's purpose was not retarded. Then, as now, God works all things together for good to them that love God, and are called according to His purpose (Rom. 8. 28).

Out of Haran. He was able to leave the halfway house of compromise and set out on the pilgrimage to which he had been called, as soon as every tie had been cut by his father's death.

VERSE 5. Abram took Sarai his wife. This faithful woman accompanied her husband on his pilgrimage. Any married man, who is called by God and converted, may reasonably hope that what God has done for him He will also do for his wife. God made the family, and does not want to see it divided. In contrast to this, a Christian man who contrary to God's command (1 Cor. 7. 39) marries an unsaved woman, should never expect that his witness will lead her to Christ. Such action is tempting and defying God, trying to force His hand. What power can any attempt at witness have, when his whole relationship with her is based on disobedience?

Lot. ' Lot went ' (verse 4), but Abram took him. The two statements, taken together, imply that it was through Abram's faith and witness that Lot heard the call of God and voluntarily obeyed it.

All their substance that they had gathered, and the souls that they had *gotten in Haran.* Neither substance nor souls were left in the place of compromise. If they had been, they would have drawn Abram back. In starting on his pilgrimage he dedicated to God all that he possessed, his family, his household, and his property. He took all with him to use in the service of his God.

To go into the land of Canaan. Their purpose was the same as when they left Ur (11. 31). God's plan for our lives does not alter. It was fixed when we were chosen in eternity past (Eph. 1. 11), and its working begins in our lives at birth (Gal. 1. 15). God is always calling to us to carry it out, His aim is always the same. If we shrink from His calling, or fail to go forward, He will not alter His plan. He calls us again to the same place. *Into the land of Canaan they came.* Contrast 11. 31. Notice the patience and persistence of God, and the final success of His call and vindication of His purpose. The difficulties that detained Abram at Haran were known to Him and allowed for. He did not abandon Abram. He kept the call continually before him, until the circumstances were ripe for its fruition. He will deal with us in the same way.

VERSE 6. *Passed through the land.* After this Abram only once left the land, but he was continually journeying from place to place in it. This is a precise picture of the Christian believer in the present life. In heart and spirit by faith he is in the land, yet he does not yet actually or outwardly possess it, and he is perpetually travelling. *Sichem.* This was near the centre of the land. *Plain.* The R.V. interprets this as oak (text), or terebinth (margin).

The Canaanite. The foe was already in possession. In the same way the world rulers of this darkness, spiritual forces of wickedness, are in the heavenly places before us (Eph. 6. 12). By the advance of the Gospel the devil is displaced and cast out (Lk. 10. 17, 18; Rev. 12. 9-11).

VERSE 7. *The Lord appeared.* This was an appearance of the Word of God, the pre-incarnate Christ, often called in the Old Testament the Angel of the Lord. ' No man hath seen God at any time. The only-begotten Son, Who is in the bosom of the Father, He hath revealed Him ' (Jo. 1. 18).

Unto thy seed will I give this land. This is the eighth promise made to Abraham. It is renewed and extended in 13. 15. Notice that it is not attached to the seven promises of verses 2 and 3, which relate to eternal and spiritual things, but stands apart from them, being temporal in scope and in fulfilment. Stephen in his speech emphasises in connection with this promise the fact that, when it was made, Abraham did not possess a square foot of the land. This is again a parable of the Gospel. We too possess nothing of the new heaven and the new earth. Round us Satan, his spiritual hosts, and his worldlings possess the earth. But the promise of better things, actually to be possessed in the future, is made to us in a deeper and greater sense than that in which it was made to Abraham. Who were the seed to whom the promise was made? Ishmael was Abraham's seed (21. 13), but the promise did not apply to him. Esau was Abraham's seed, but no more did it apply to him. It was fulfilled in Isaac alone (21. 12), and of Isaac's two sons in Israel alone. It was the children of Israel who possessed the land. All this is again a parable. The final seed of Abraham, who will inherit the promises and possess the new land, of which Palestine is the type, are Christ (Gal. 3, 16) and His people (Gal. 3. 29).

Altar. Abram's altar was in line with that of Noah (9. 20) and of the primitive revelation in Eden (3. 21). He was reminded by it of the need of death in order to obtain access to God, of the fire of the Holy Ghost consuming and accepting the victim on the altar, and of the ascent as a column of smoke of the free-will offering of a dedicated life. The

altar is always a picture of the one
offering of Christ on Calvary for our
sins. No doubt as he made his offering, Abram dedicated his life afresh
to the call and service of God. No
doubt also he looked upon his offering as a thank-offering.

Unto the Lord. In a sea of hideous
polytheism the child of God acknowledges the one true and living God.
This is what Israel was intended to
do during their life in Palestine,
though they succeeded very imperfectly.

VERSE 8. *He removed.* So, each day
sees the child of God moving nearer
and nearer to the heavenly home.
There is no settled life for the Christian in the world. *A mountain.* The
wonder and inspiration of the offering
on Calvary, if we contemplate it, will
bring us to a mountain-top experience, where we live in the presence
of God. *Bethel.* This means House
of God. We too shall find ourselves
near to the house of God.

Pitched his tent. Again we have a
parable of the believer in this world.
He is living in the body, a tent, which
will one day be put off (2 Pet. 1. 13,
14). One day he will have a building
from God, a house not made with
hands, eternal in the heavens (2 Cor.
5. 1). The hymn is true, which says
of him that he nightly pitches his
moving tent a day's march nearer
home. *Bethel on the west, and Hai
on the east.* Bethel means House of
God, and Hai means Ruin. Every
man stands between these two. He
may set out on the narrow way, that
leads to the city and house of God,
there to dwell for evermore, or he
may move out along the broad way
that leads to ruin and destruction
(Mt. 7. 13, 14). At this spot Abram
did the right thing. *He builded an
altar,* that is to say, he resorted to
Calvary. He offered a sacrifice that
was a picture of the one eternal
sacrifice offered by the Saviour once
for all. Having built the altar, from
between its horns, as it were, he
called upon the name of the Lord.
He therefore had no fear of not go-

ing the right way. Every child of
God must do the same. At the beginning of his spiritual life, when he
steps from the death of sin to the
life of righteousness, he can do so
only at Calvary. That is the only
place from which to call upon the
name of the Lord. That is the place
of access, the place where every believer is sure of acceptance. Moreover during his spiritual life at any
place of doubt or on any necessity
for decision he must call from the
same place upon the name of the
Lord. To call upon the name of the
Lord means (1) to invoke the Lord
for what He is, this being shown in
its fulness at Calvary and nowhere
else. (2) It means to claim an interest in the Lord, to acknowledge that
one belongs to Him, and to make
one's request on the strength of so
belonging. Thus Abram takes each
step with sacrifice and prayer.

VERSE 9. *Abram journeyed.* He did
not stop short, till he had passed
through the whole length of the land.
He answered God's call to the full.
He went literally the full length. We
too must go the whole way with God,
and not stop short of the place
where He wants to lead us, and of
the blessing which He has in store
for us. *The south,* that is to say,
the Negeb, the undulating country to
the south of what was subsequently
'the territory of Judah.

VERSE 10. Verses 10-20 tell us the
story of Abraham's sad mistake. *A
famine.* This was not the cause of
Abram's sin. It was sent from God,
and we may conjecture that the reason for His sending it was either (1)
to drive Abram into Egypt, so that
he might give a witness there, or (2)
to test his faith, so that he might
cast himself on the Lord alone for
protection and provision. The first
alternative will only hold good, if we
feel that Abram did right in going
down into Egypt. We too shall meet
with famines in the course of our
spiritual lives. They may be due to
lack of Christian fellowship, to poor
spiritual food week by week, or day

by day, or to one or other of the troubles and sorrows of this world. Yet we may be certain that, if the famine is not of our own choosing, or the result of our own act, our heavenly Father sends it to test our faith, or to bring us out into a place of greater happiness and blessing.

Went down into Egypt. This was not necessarily the cause of Abram's sin, though it might have been. Our text does not tell us whether he was right or wrong to go. Egypt is usually in the Bible the type of the world, but the believer may use the world, so long as he does not become entangled in it (1 Cor. 7. 31). He may do business in it, make his living in it, use its monetary systems, and by its resources may under God protect himself from physical harm or loss. He may for instance make use of a savings bank, or an insurance system, and may take advantage of social services. All these may on occasion be God's appointment for him. Abram may therefore have been quite right in going down into Egypt. It may have been the Lord's provision for him. The famine may even have been sent in order to drive him there to give a good witness. On the other hand, though we cannot deduce it, we may suspect that he should not have gone. The Lord had called him to Canaan. Ought he to have gone outside it? Did he take the line of least resistance, do the natural thing? It is fatally easy for us to do so. Ought he not to have cast himself upon the Lord, and trusted Him to support him and his household? Did the very fact of going down into Egypt carry with it the seeds of the weakness, which he showed? We cannot tell, but we can take the warning and learn the lesson.

Grievous. However grievous, the Lord, Who sent it, could deal with it. The intensity of any trouble or difficulty is no reason for abandoning trust in God, as if He could only cope with small things, or for taking a wrong course with regard to it. A grievous famine ought to call forth stronger faith and deeper trust.

VERSE 11. *Come near to enter into Egypt.* The influence of Egypt overwhelmed Abram on its threshold. The spirit of the world will overtake us, if we go too near to it. Some Christians live on the threshold of the world, and take part in as many of its activities as they dare. In time its spirit overcomes them. The only safe course is to live in Canaan, as far as possible from the frontiers of the world. If there is a four thousand-and-foot precipice on one side of the road along which one, is driving, it is better not to drive with the wheels on the edge.

He said unto Sarai his wife. Abram's fear drove him to compelling his wife to become his partner in deceit. We do not know what her thoughts were. Her affection for her husband may have led her to welcome the ruse and to take part in it gladly. On the other hand she may have felt the disgrace acutely, and been very apprehensive of the result. As nothing is said about her feelings, it is likely that they were never consulted, a fact that added selfishness to the meanness of Abram's conduct. *A fair woman.* Sarai's beauty and attractions were the source of Abram's fear.

VERSE 12. In this verse we find the source of Abram's act. It was fear of man. The lack of faith, which perhaps began to be called forth by the famine, now seemed to deepen, till it was quite unrestrained. He had every right to expect that the God Who had called him and given him the promises would protect him and his wife from the sort of evil that he dreaded. ' The fear of man bringeth a snare: but whoso putteth his trust in the Lord shall be safe ' (Prov. 29. 35). This verse might have been written to meet Abram's situation. The world today is full of fear of man by man, and the snare that it has brought is all too plain for all to see. Fear of man besets us in various forms in the course of our spiritual lives. It may prevent our witness in times of persecution, but any day it may creep in and shut our mouths, when we ought to be speaking for Christ.

VERSE 13. The fear of man in Abram's heart gave birth to an act of incredible meanness. He resolved to save his own life at the expense of his wife's honour. No doubt standards differed from today, but quite insufficiently to excuse such an act. The account of this action illustrates for us the fact that ' there is no man that sinneth not ' (1 Ki. '8. 46). No single child of God is presented to us in the Bible with unblemished character. Only the Saviour Himself is sinless. Before Abram's day we have read of Abel and Noah. The fact that Abel offered a lamb shows that he was conscious of sin, and in the case of Noah we have the account of his drunkenness (9. 20-27). We shall find sin and imperfection in the life story of every child of God, whether in the Old Testament or the New. Perfect sanctification has not been granted us in this world. It will be ours on the day of judgment. *Say, I pray thee, thou art my sister.* This was the truth (20. 12), but not the whole truth, and therefore as false as if it had been a lie.

That it may be well with me for thy sake; and my soul shall live because of thee. Notice *me* and *my*. Abram was concerned with his own safety. It is difficult to judge whether or not Sarai could have refused to co-operate with her husband. It is possible that she could not have properly refused.

VERSE 14. *The Egyptians.* Abram knew enough of the world to judge of it. What he anticipated came to pass. He was not wrong in his judgment, nor wrong in taking precautions. It was his method that was sinful.

VERSE 15. *Commended.* The commendation of the world, especially of those who are great in it, may prove the spiritual ruin of the

believer. ' Woe unto you, when all men speak well of you ' (Lk 6. 26). Thus the commendation of the Egyptian princes would have ruined Sarai, if the Lord had not intervened: *Pharaoh's house.* Notice that what was probably the highest honour that the world could bestow was a disgrace to Sarai. In spiritual things all values are reversed. Worldly honour holds no prospects for the child of God.

VERSE 16. *He entreated Abram well.* Abram obtained this good treatment at the expense of his own and his wife's honour. The praise and flattery and material kindness of the world are at times greater temptations to the believer than its hatred and persecution. *Sheep . . . and camels.* These possessions were illgotten. They were like treasures heaped up on earth. Abram's enjoyment of the gifts must have been blighted by an evil conscience.

VERSE 17. *The Lord.* This verse tells us the comforting fact that in spite of Abram's mistake the Lord intervened to save him from the consequences of the wrong step that he had taken. We learn that the Lord does not abandon His children, when their corrupt nature asserts itself. He is for ever watching over them to deliver them from the evils that they are prone to bring upon themselves. Abram had entangled his own feet in a net, but the Lord cut the meshes, not because Abram deserved such intervention, but in pursuance of His own purpose of sovereign grace, which Abram's folly could not frustrate or turn aside, any more than can ours. *Plagued Pharaoh.* Pharaoh's plagues were kinder than Abram's good treatment. The latter was the result of dishonesty, meanness and deceit. The former were the means of keeping the king from sin. How often may plagues, as they fall in judgment around us, or descend on our heads and break into our own lives, be intended to keep us from sin. How often, for all we know, may they succeed. Here is a partial explanation of the calamities of the world. Some of them are intended to awaken the conscience and inform the mind, so that men may be kept from sinning against God, perhaps irrevocably, before it is too late.

VERSE 18. *Pharaoh called Abram.* We do not know what led him to connect the plagues with his abduction of Sarai. The Lord, Who sent them, was able to explain their purpose, and did so, in a way that He has not revealed.

What is this that thou hast done? There is no sadder situation in the world than when a worldling rebukes a Christian for conduct which he would not have undertaken himself and appears to him to be wrong. Any Christian man in such a position needs to hang his head in shame. The world is quick to expect and demand consistent behaviour in a professing Christian.

Why didst thou not tell me? To add to Abram's humiliation, he could now see that he need never have had any fear. Apart from the care and protection of the Lord, to which he ought to have trusted under the worst circumstances, he had no real ground for fear. If he had been honest with Pharaoh, Pharaoh would have been honest with him. In the same way the fears of the child of God are often groundless.

VERSE 19. *So I might have taken.* Pharaoh implies that he would not have planned to take Sarai, had he known the real facts of the case, and expresses relief that he had been saved from the wrong step. Here is an honest heathen man embarrassing the child of God by showing a better character than he. The whole incident was needless.

Go thy way. Pharaoh is afraid of Abram's company. We have the sad situation in which a man of the world wants to be rid of the company of a godly man, because he despises him, and because his presence has

brought him no good. Abram had brought plagues on Pharaoh, shame and humiliation on himself, and distress on Sarai. Now he is sent away from a place where he might have given a good witness, where also it is likely that his testimony might have been well received.

VERSE 20. *His men.* We do not know the numbers of these men, but they are not likely to have been ignorant of the circumstances of Abram's departure. He therefore has to leave in humiliated silence, despised, and possibly ridiculed, by those to whom he might have told the goodness of God and the circumstances of his call and pilgrimage. *They sent him away.* So he leaves Egypt, materially enriched, but spiritually poor, humiliated, yet thankful to the Lord for an intervention which had saved him from disaster. In spite of all it is scarcely possible that he cannot have been strengthened in his faith by the realisation that the Lord had not deserted him, but was ready to intervene to extricate him from difficulties which were of his own sinful making.

CHAPTER 13

IN this chapter the story of Abram is continued. Verses 1-4 record his return from Egypt to Bethel. This is followed by the separation of Abram and Lot and the fatal choice of Lot, which was the first step on the wrong road which he travelled (5-13). In verses 14-17 we have the promise of Palestine made to Abram and his seed, and the last verse (18) records Abram's removal to Hebron.

VERSE 1. *Went up out of Egypt.* Abram never left Canaan again till the day of his death. One excursion into Egypt was enough for him. May it be the same with us. *His wife,* Sarai, was safely brought out of danger and dishonour that were not of her own making. *All that he had.* Again Abram left nothing in the world. He dedicated to the service of God all his possessions and used them for the purposes of his pilgrim life. In the same way God requires all that we have, and does us the honour of demanding what He pleases in the service of the Gospel. *Lot with him.* This means that Lot had gone down into Egypt, and it may well be that the experience first turned his mind in a worldly direction. Perhaps he never forgot the attractions of Egypt, but nurtured a secret longing for them in his soul. Though his heart was the Lord's (2 Pet. 2. 7), his desires were fixed on ' the great city, which is called spiritually Sodom and Egypt, where also ' one day his Lord was to be crucified (Rev. 11. 8). *The south,* that is, the Negeb between Egypt and what was one day to be the territory of Judah.

VERSE 2. *Very rich.* Materially he was the richer for his sojourn in Egypt, but spiritually the poorer. The child of God, who allows his interests to wander into the world, often finds this to be so. At the same time his riches were such as could be used in the service of God. In cattle he had abundant opportunity for sacrifice, in silver he had ' plentiful redemption ' (Ps. 130. 7), and in gold he had the likeness of the glory of God. Each child of God is rich in these things, because they are the gift of God to him apart from all desert on his part.

VERSE 3. *On his journeys.* Abram resumes the pilgrim life, to which he had been called by God. Our spiritual life also consists of a journey through the world. *The south,* that is, the Negeb (see on verse 1). *Bethel,* that is, the house of God. He was right to go to this place. It meant that his heart was fixed on abiding in the Lord. He knew that he had been called to dwell in the house of the Lord for ever (Ps. 23. 6). The ultimate purpose of the salvation of the elect is that each may abide with God in His home for all eternity.

At the beginning. Here is an additional good reason for Abram's journey to Bethel. After the unhappy episode in Egypt he retraced his steps to the place where he had first gone wrong. We must do the same in similar circumstances. We must renounce our wandering and all that has come of it and return to the will of God, going back to the point at which we were conscious of having departed from it. *Between Bethel and Hai.* We must go back to the place of our first decision, and make again, as it were, the initial choice between the house of God on the one hand and ruin on the other. Not that a real choice, once made, can ever be repeated. A decision for Christ is made once and for all. But it can be re-affirmed, and allowed to exercise a deeper power in the life than hitherto.

VERSE 4. *Unto the place of the altar, which he made there at the first.* Abram not only went to Bethel, the house of God, and not only to the place of his initial decision between the house of God on the one hand and ruin (Hai) on the other. The same place was the place of the altar. He went back to Calvary, where he started his spiritual life. He reviewed everything afresh in its light. He renewed his vows, as it were. *Called on the name of the Lord.* This means that he once again invoked God for what He is, known to Abram at the altar, and to us much more fully at Calvary. Abram once more realised that he belonged to God. He sought and found protection, and identified his own interests with those of the Lord. In similar circumstances we must do exactly the same.

VERSE 5. Verses 5-13 tell us of the separation of Abram and Lot. Each had great possessions. From this fact a jealous quarrel arose among their servants. As this was a bad witness to the people of the land, Abram suggested their separation, and asked Lot to choose where he would like to go. Lot chose the Jordan valley, and Abram remained in Canaan.

Lot also. Lot had heard the call of God to accompany Abram, and who knows whether he might not have been incorporated in some way in Israel? He had gone down with the patriarch on the unfortunate visit to Egypt, and now he had become worldly-minded. *Flocks and herds and tents.* He possessed, that is to say, abundant material for sacrifice and ample opportunity for living the pilgrim life. We too possess these things from God. His flocks and herds were not of much use to him in Sodom, and there was certainly no scope for his tents there. Perhaps he turned them all into money, in order to purchase or build the grand house in which he is later found living, large enough to bring up a family of at least four, and probably six, and rich enough for the entertainment of angels.

VERSE 6. The facts recorded in this verse may well be due to the increase of riches that Abram received in Egypt as gifts from Pharaoh. If this is so, one of the first consequences of Abram's shameful conduct in Egypt was an enforced separation between him and Lot. This turned out to be Lot's spiritual ruin. We may get right back to true fellowship with God, as Abram did at Bethel, after an intrusion of sin into our lives, but we cannot always escape the natural consequences of sinful actions. In this case, as so often, such actions affected seriously the spiritual life of a fellow-believer.

Could not dwell together. There is no more tragic situation than when two fellow-servants of Christ find it impossible to live and work together. This happened in the case of Barnabas and Saul (Acts 15. 37-40).

VERSE 7. *A strife.* Disunity in the household of faith is a great evil. If it happened in the case of the apostles Barnabas and Paul, we may well expect it to happen among humbler

believers, and experience shows that unfortunately it often does. *The Canaanite and the Perizzite.* This statement appears here perhaps for two reasons. (1) It implies a reason why the herds of Abram and Lot were restricted. Only limited space was available to them owing to the presence of the settled inhabitants. So today too often the peoples and governments of the world will find means of restricting the evangelistic or pastoral activities of the pilgrim believers. (2) The statement implies that the quarrel made an unfortunate impression on the inhabitants. This is very true to experience. Any lack of unity among Christians, or in fact any inconsistency whatever on their part, spoils any testimony that they seek to give to the world. The people of the world are extraordinarily quick to mark any inconsistency in the lives of Christians. By it they are given an excuse (though not a reason) for refusing the Gospel, and are often hardened in their opposition and their sin.

VERSE 8. Abram realised the tragedy and danger of the situation, and refused to be a party to the quarrel.

Brethren. Abram and Lot were natural kinsmen, a fact that made any quarrel between them the more unfortunate. As such, they were types of the members of the Christian family, who are ' all sons of God by faith in Christ Jesus ' (Gal. 3. 26). The family of God ought to be the most harmonious in the world, as it will be in the glory of the new heavens and new earth.

VERSE 9. *Is not the whole land before thee?* This question brings out Abram's generosity and nobility of character. He gave Lot the first choice, though he had every right, as the older man and head of the clan, to take it himself. In this condecension Abram was like the Lord Jesus Christ, Who came down from heaven, not to do His own will (Jo. 6. 38). Abram left the result of the choice to God, and evidently determined to see God's guidance in it. We too can afford to do the same.

VERSE 10. This and the following verse record the first of the wrong steps taken by ' righteous Lot ' towards spiritual ruin. He did not insist on his uncle choosing, but took advantage of the older man's generosity. The attractions of Egypt were by now in his blood, and he decided to leave the dull pilgrim life of Canaan for the gaudy worldliness of Sodom. *Plain.* This means literally ' circle '. It seems to have been the designation of a district in the Jordan valley, which comprised the five wicked cities and included Jericho (Deut. 34. 3). *Jordan.* The Jordan throughout the Bible is consistently a type of death. Its passage was necessary in order to enter Palestine from the east (Josh. 1. 11), but to dwell in its valley is spiritually unhealthy. Lot therefore chose death instead of life, not that we are to suppose that a man whom the apostle refers to as ' righteous ' (2 Pet. 2. 7) finally lost his salvation, but he lived from the spiritual point of view a living death, and ultimately lost everything but his life.

Well watered. The plain was watered from Jordan, the river of death. So is the world. This good irrigation makes it an attractive place. It is full of entertainment and interest.

Before the Lord destroyed Sodom and Gomorrah. The attractions of the world last until the day of judgment, and no further. Lot left out of his reckoning the great judgment that was relatively soon to come. So does the worldling, never giving it a thought. His plans for personal advancement as well as his loftier ideals for the improvement of the world, all leave the great day of judgment out of account. ' The world passeth away, and the lust thereof ' (1 Jo. 2. 17).

As the garden of the Lord. The man of the world looks back to the natural delights of an earthly paradise without taking account of its deeper joys, which lay in the habitual presence of God and in constant fellowship with Him. He looks backward to what is lost for ever instead of forward to the better thing that will be possessed for ever. *Like the land of Egypt.* Here is more than a hint of the origin of Lot's spiritual decline. He had seen Egypt, and it appealed to him. It had turned him away from the pilgrim life. Now he wishes to reproduce its pleasures in his own surroundings. Under the circumstances he could not return to Egypt, but he sees a country like it, and determines to make it his abode.

Zoar. This was the name of the fifth city of the plain (19. 22). Its occurrence is therefore natural in this context. It may be original. The sentence would then mean that Lot could see, or the writer had in mind, the district which reached as far as the city of Zoar. The Peshitto Syriac version however reads *Zoan.* which is the name of a district of Egypt. This appears to make better sense, continuing and rendering more detailed the comparison with Egypt.

VERSE 11. *Lot chose him.* Here was a selfish choice, made through the lust of the eyes (verse 10; 1 Jo. 2. 16), without reference to the will of God and without consulting the interests of the older man, to whom he owed so much Following, perhaps unconsciously, the instincts of his old corrupt nature, he went astray like a sheep, and turned to his own way (Isa. 53. 6). *Plain.* See on verse 10. *Jordan.* Lot chose a land that was watered by the river of death. He chose to live on the wrong side of the river. The inhabitant of Canaan has the river behind him, as does every believer today, having died with Christ from the elements of the world (Col. 2. 20). Lot's position was like that of the worldly-minded widow (1 Tim. 5. 6).

Lot journeyed. He left the land of promise, and was never to see it again. The attractions of Egypt had destroyed his interest in it.

They separated themselves. This

was by mutual consent. Their interests were incompatible. Abram was looking for the heavenly country and the city which hath foundations, whose maker and builder is God (Heb. 11. 10, 16). Lot, though a member of the heavenly city, wished to reach it without engaging on the pilgrim life. The love of the world was in Him, and he hoped for the pleasures of Egypt and Sodom, as long as it was possible for him to enjoy them. The faithful Christian and the worldly-minded Christian always reach a point, where they separate from each other. Each is a drag on the other's activities. 'Can two walk together except they be agreed?' (Amos 3. 3). Thus we find two kinds of churches, those engaged in amusing the goats, and those engaged in feeding the sheep; and in the ranks of a Christian Union the exercise among a minority of a constant pressure towards a broader and more inclusive curriculum.

Verse 12. *Abram dwelled in the land of Canaan.* This was a happy place to dwell, even though he was only a stranger and a sojourner. He had the presence and the promises of the Lord. Like Abram we believers also dwell in the land of promise in our hearts by faith, although like him we are strangers and pilgrims on earth. 'Here we have no abiding city, but we seek one to come' (Heb. 13. 14). *Lot dwelled in the cities of the plain,* that is to say, in the orbit of the cities of the plain, for he was still in a tent. Here he lived in danger and distress (2 Pet. 2. 7), seeking the best of both worlds, but enjoying neither, afraid to pay the cost of the pilgrim life, but miserable in the worldly surroundings. This is the situation of every true child of God who allows himself to be worldly-minded. *Pitched his tent toward Sodom.* He kept up the pretence of being a stranger and pilgrim by retaining his tent life, but he pitched the tent in a position where he could take advantage of the luxuries and amusements of the city.

Doubtless he did not intend at this stage to abandon his tent and make the city his home. He meant to go as near to the world as possible without actually becoming a part of it, but the natural trend of his life moved on, and the current proved too strong for him, as it does for all who are in a similar position. We next find him dwelling in Sodom (14. 12).

Verse 13. This was a notorious fact, which must have been perfectly well known to Lot, yet it did not deter him from associating with them. He did not intend to be like them, and as a matter of fact he never became so (2 Pet. 2. 7). His eye was on the 'fulness of bread and abundance of idleness', or, as the R.V. renders it, 'prosperous ease' (Ezek. 16. 49). Yet his first consideration in choosing somewhere to live should have been the moral condition of the place to which he was going. Material interests governed his choice. God's interests might come in, where they could, if they could. How many Christian people have chosen to live where it was easy or pleasant to live, without giving a thought to the question whether there is or is not an evangelical church in the neighbourhood, or a need for their service and witness.

Verse 14. *The Lord said.* The Lord took the opportunity of reassuring Abram that the separation had been right, and that His blessing was still with him. *After that Lot was separated.* Another tie with the world had been cut. The narrative of the following chapters shows that Abram had an affectionate interest in Lot and an intense loyalty to his family relationship. Undoubtedly therefore he was grieved at the separation, but he allowed nothing to stand on the way of the will of God or of the completion of the purpose of the call, which he had received. The separation was necessary for Abram's spiritual health, and when it had been made, the Lord was able to confirm and extend the promises. *Lift up now thine eye.* When Lot did this (verse 10) ,he lifted them up in the lust of the eyes. Abram now lifted up the eye of faith.

Northward, and southward, and eastward, and westward. The believer may do the same. He may look northward to Mount Zion, the joy of the whole earth, the city of the great king (Ps. 48. 2). He may look to the south, whence the wind blows, that the spices may flow out from the garden of his heart to please the Lord, to Whom it belongs (Cant. 4. 16). He may look eastward to Eden (2. 8) and to the Sun of righteousness rising upon it with healing in His wings (Mal. 4. 2), or he may look westward to the evening time, when it will be light as noonday, because there is no night there (Zech. 14. 7; Rev. 21. 25), and he may realise that all these things will be his, because God has promised them in Christ.

VERSE 15. In this verse we have the eighth of the fourteen promises made to Abram. It is much expanded from the form in which it appears in 12. 7. *All the land which thou seest, to thee will I give it, and to thy seed for ever.* We shall notice two additions to this promise in the form in which it appears here, as compared with the first announcement of it in 12. 7. They are (1) that the land is promised to Abram personally, as well as to his seed; (2) that the promise is made ' for ever '. This promise cannot be understood literally. Palestine, as part of the present earth, will be burnt up on the day of judgment, when the heavens and earth, that are now, are destroyed by fire (2 Pet. 3. 7, 10-12). We must therefore either take the land literally and the expression ' for ever ' metaphorically, or the expression literally and the land metaphorically. (1) If we take the land literally, we may think of the expression as parallel with the ' everlasting priesthood ' of Aaron and his sons (Ex. 40. 15; Num. 25. 13). In

the former of these two passages the expression ' everlasting priesthood ' is, or may be, qualified by the words ' in their generations '. In any case however Aaron's priesthood was completely superseded by that of Christ (Heb. 7. 11-28). It was typical and temporal. The expression ' everlasting priesthood ' therefore, as applied to Aaron's office, must mean ' so long as the typical priesthood shall last ', or ' until the Messianic age '. It does not even mean ' until the end of the world '. Now we may regard the gift of the land to Abram and his seed for ever in this light. He and they, in this case, were to have it, so long as it should exist, or until the Messianic age. Palestine still exists, and presumably will do so, until the end of the world, but Abram and his seed have not possessed it. If we take the expression as meaning ' until the Messianic age ', we obtain an equally unsatisfactory result. Aaron's priesthood was in being and exercised from the time of Moses until the time of Christ with the exception of a short interval of seventy years at most during the Babylonian exile, and even in captivity its function may not have entirely ceased. It was not the same with Israel's possession of the land. They had it from Joshua's day till that of Nebuchadnezzar. After that, though a remnant of them returned to live in it, they did not own it. They were the subjects and servants of Gentile empires, to whom they paid tribute, except again for the short Maccabean period in the second and first centuries B.C. Occupation of the land as the subjects of Gentile rulers can hardly satisfy the promise of a gift of the land. Again, even if we feel that Abram's seed possessed Palestine during this Old Testament and inter-Testament period, Abram himself died without possessing a square foot of it (Acts 7. 5). Such an interpretation thus fails to meet the requirements of the fulfilment of the promise. (2) The alternative is to take the eternity as literal and the land as metaphorical.

This raises the promise to the level of those that deal with spiritual and eternal things. But in what sense is it fulfilled? Abram looked for a heavenly country (Heb. 11. 16). This heavenly country is the new earth or new land (Heb. eretz, Greek gé), of which Palestine, the land of promise, was the consistent Old Testament type. The prophets often foretell the blessings of the world to come in language which expresses the geography of Palestine (see for instance Ezek. 47 and 48). Palestine, as the typical land of promise, is thought of as one with the antitypical land, just as typical Old Testament Israel is sometimes thought of as one with the anti-typical spiritual Israel. Abram is thus promised the gift of the world to come, of which the land of promise, to which he had been called was the type. The seed, to which it is promised together with Abram himself personally, is Christ (Gal. 3. 16) and His people (Gal. 3. 29). It was in this sense that the apostle Paul understood and interpreted the passage, when he said that Abraham was ' heir of the world ' (Rom. 4. 13). The promise is not however exhausted even here. There is a sense in which the literal Palestine is given to Abram and his spiritual seed for ever. To them it is the Holy Land. It was the scene of the incarnation, earthly life, death, resurrection and ascension of the Son of God. These things are eternal things, and inasmuch as they occurred in the literal Palestine, they raise it, as it were, to an eternal status. Palestine lives in the eternal things of which it was the scene, and in the eternal effects of those things. The church triumphant will be eternally singing of Calvary, and in this sense eternally singing of Palestine. So we may regard this as a fulfilment of the promise also.

VERSE 16. I will make thy seed as the dust of the earth. This is the ninth of the fourteen promises. It has a partial fulfilment in the large numbers of Abram's natural descend-ants. There are the Ishmaelites, the children of Keturah, and the Edomites in addition to the Israelites, who are spoken of as a people of immense numbers (Deut. 1. 10; 28. 62), but the ultimate fulfilment lies in the great multitude of redeemed humanity, that no man can number (Rev. 7. 9), who are all the seed of Abraham, because they are Christ's (Gal. 3. 29). Though in each generation on earth the saved are in a small minority, in that day they will comprise an innumerable multitude. They may in fact greatly outnumber the lost, if the countless number of members of the human race (perhaps, taken all in all, about eighty per cent of it), who have died in infancy, are included, as seems probable, among them.

VERSE 17. Arise, walk through the land. Thus faith takes possession. Abram's walk was a triumphant claiming of what he had been promised. The only basis for his claim was the promise of God. In the same way our faith may triumph because of what God has promised us. Our faith rests on His Word. We may count our blessings and claim our possessions, rejoice in assured anticipation and take possession in our hearts. Like Abram's, our walk should be a walk of faith. True witness, and true spiritual life, consist of this triumphant faith.

I will give it unto thee. In these words we find (1) the sovereignty of God. God owns what He will give. The Canaanites imagined that the land was theirs. In fact it was the Lord's. The peoples and governments of the world imagine that it is theirs, but the whole of it belongs to God, and He gives it to whomsoever He will. (2) We find the principle of grace. If ever God enters into a transaction, the conveyance, or the covenant, is a gift on His part. God never sells. He gives freely His own Son, His own Spirit, the water of life, the Gospel. The door is closed to the many who seek to buy from God by the offer of their own supposed merits. (3) We find that God dispenses His grace to whomsoever He will. There is no reason why He should not have given the land to Lot, or Pharaoh, or Nahor — or humanly speaking there is no reason, no reason that we can see — instead of to Abram, except His own sovereign electing grace, inscrutable wisdom and divine counsel. There was nothing in Abram, any more than there is anything in us. God made Abram what he was, and makes us what we are. Yet such is the perfection of God's grace, counsel and wisdom, that though we cannot tell why He should choose Abraham, we know that His choice was the right one, the best, the perfect choice.

VERSE 18. *Removed his tent*. He started on another stage of the walk of faith.

In the plain. Another rendering is ' by the oaks '.

Built there an altar. He still clung to Calvary. At Sichem, at Bethel, and at Hebron, he builds altars. He feels the constant need of cleansing from sin, and he desires at every stage of his pilgrimage to dedicate his life again to God. He knew something of the real meaning of what the altar typified. He rejoiced to see Christ's day, and ' he saw it, and was glad ' (Jo. 8. 36).

CHAPTER 14

IN this chapter we have the story of the slaughter of the kings and the episode of Melchizedek. A confederacy of Mesopotamian kings made a raid into the Jordan valley and the districts south-east of Palestine. At the Dead Sea they were met by the kings of the five cities of the plain, who had been their tributaries, but now rebelled. The Canaanite kings were defeated, and the invaders carried away spoil and captives, among whom was Lot. On the news being brought to Abram, he armed his household, pursued the kings, and recaptured the spoil. He re-

fused to keep what he had won, and was met by Melchizedek, king of Salem, who blessed him, and was given tithes of the spoil. The atmosphere of the chapter is different from the rest of the story of Abram. It contains a new name of God, El Elyon, the most high God (verses 18-20, 22), Whom Abram identifies with Jehovah (verse 22). Abram is called ' the Hebrew ' (verse 13), and the chapter appears to have been written from the point of view of Melchizedek.

VERSE 1. Here is an impressive list of kings with high-sounding names, such as the world loves. Its records are full of lists like this. In their own eyes and in those of their subjects these kings were very great, but in the eyes of God they were nothing. It is exactly the same in the world today. We often read in the newspapers of ' the great powers '. These powers seem to us mighty. The Americans or the Russians seem able to do what they like in the world. But God is the supreme sovereign of them all, disposing their hearts and minds to carry out His will and directing the actions of all their governments. The activities of the four kings mentioned in our verse had a purpose, of which they knew nothing. God intended the campaign to be a warning and a chastening to Lot, and used it to bring Abram in touch with Melchizedek. *Amraphel*. The identity of this king with Hammurabi, the great law-giver, seems to be considered untenable on chronological grounds. *Shinar*. This is the ancient name of Mesopotamia. *Arioch*. This seems to be a Semitic name. *Ellasar*. This was a city north of Ur in the Mesopotamian plain. *Elam* was the mountainous district east of Chaldea. *Tidal*. This is thought to have been a Hittite name. *Nations*. This may be a title, assumed as emperor over different peoples. The R.V. keeps the Hebrew as a proper name, Goiim, but this does not help to locate the kingdom.

VERSE 2. Expeditions like this are known from secular records to have taken place at this period. The Mesopotamian kings occasionally ranged as far as the Mediterranean coast. Their object on this occasion seems to have been the subjugation of the five cities of the plain. Before the destruction of those cities there was a well-used highway running down from Damascus through Gilead and Bashan to the east of Jordan as far as Sodom and Gomorrah, where it crossed a route running east from the Mediterranean. It appears to have been the situation of Sodom at this junction of trade routes that brought her her wealth (Ezek. 16. 49).

VERSE 3. *All these*. The context seems to make it plain that these are the five kings of Sodom and Gomorrah, Admah, Zeboiim and Bela. *Joined together*. This was a natural, but unholy alliance. Their united forces could not hinder the purpose of God. *The vale of Siddim, which is the salt sea*. The salt sea is the Dead Sea. The level of its water has been rising for generations, so that in the time of Abram the sea was much smaller than it is now. The valley where this battle was fought and the whole area where the cities of the plain stood is now under water. The sea is a perpetual memorial of the destruction of the cities and of their wickedness.

VERSE 4. *They served*. Sinners are always in bondage. The servitude of Sodom to Chedorlaomer was by no means as great as its servitude to its sin. ' He that committeth sin is the servant of sin ' (Jo. 8. 34). *They rebelled*. The sinner's rebellion against the dominion of sin is fruitless and hopeless (Rom. 7. 14-24).

VERSE 5. *Rephaims*. These were people of gigantic size, of whom there seem to have been several colonies in various parts of Palestine. *Ashteroth-Karnaim* was in Bashan, a long distance east of the Sea of Galilee. *Zuzims*. These also are thought to have been a gigantic people. The proper name does not occur elsewhere in the Bible, a proof of the early date of this chapter. *Ham*. This was near the Ammonite Rabbah, north-east of the Dead Sea. *Emims*. This people lived in what was afterwards the land of Moab (Dt. 2 .10). *Shaveh Kiriathaim*. or the plain of Kiriathaim, was to the east of the Dead Sea.

VERSE 6. *Horites*. These were the inhabitants of Seir before the Edomites, who dispossessed them (Dt. 2. 12, 22). *Mount Seir*. The kings continued southwards, till they reached Mount Seir, which lay between the Dead Sea and the Red Sea. *El-paran. which is by the wilderness*. This was the southernmost point reached by the kings. It lay on the edge of the wilderness of Paran, which occupied the north-eastern portion of the peninsula of Sinai.

VERSE 7. *They returned*. If the cities of the plain thought that they had escaped, they were mistaken. The kings came northward again on the western side of the valley.
En-misphat. The name means ' spring of judgment '. The kings were unconsciously carrying out the judgment of God, Who, we may believe, intended by these events to give a warning to Lot and perhaps also to Sodom and Gomorrah. The name En-mishpat was apparently an early one, and is here glossed by the familiar name Kadesh. The glossator was presumably Moses. The effect is the same as if we said, ' They came to Eboracum, which is York.'
Smote all the country of the Amalekites. As the avenging sword came nearer and nearer, Lot had the opportunity to repent of his choice and to return to Abram, or at least to Canaan, but he did not learn his lesson. The people of Sodom might also have had a chance to repent. The judgments and catastrophies that happen daily in the world. acci-

dents, sickness, scarcity, death, are sent by God to lead men to repentance. The accumulation of misery that there is in the world under the best circumstances ought to speak to men of the real nature of sin. The Amalekites, who were the descendants of Esau (36. 12), were not in existence at the time of these events. They later inhabited the Negeb. The hand that has glossed the names has introduced them, in order that his readers might understand what country is meant. There was presumably an ancient name, which is not here glossed, but is omitted. Possibly it was unknown to Moses, who therefore did not pass it on, but rendered it in Hebrew, by the name of the Amalekites. Esau and his descendants are in the Bible types of the flesh. We therefore see in this incident a picture of God's judgment by temporal disaster upon man's corrupt nature. *Amorites.* These were Canaanites, or akin to them, original inhabitants of the land. *Hazezon-Tamar.* This lay on what is now the west coast of the Dead Sea at a point which is now at about the centre of the coast. In Abram's day it may have been at the southern end.

VERSE 8. *Joined battle.* Fallen human nature seeks to join battle with the judgments of God and miseries of the world and to defeat them, but always to no avail.

VERSE 9. For the names of the kings and their countries see on verse 1. *Four kings with five.* The scales seemed weighted in favour of the Canaanites. They ought to have been able to defeat an enemy, whose inferior numbers are implied. But ' the race is not to the swift, nor the battle to the strong' (Eccl. 9. 11). God disposes of all battles by controlling the many factors which are out of the reach of man. Thus man's ingenuity has not been able to rid him of disease, accidents, or disaster.

VERSE 10. *The vale of Siddim was*

full of slimepits. The slimepits represent the filth of the flesh, in which the people of Sodom lived (1 Pet. 3. 21). Their country was full of them.

Fell there. The slimepits were a snare to them, and became the occasion of their fall.

Fled to the mountain. Here they would live a primitive, uncomfortable life. So the sinner is incapable of living the life that God intended for man.

VERSE 11. *All the goods of Sodom and Gomorrah.* The dominion of sin and the consequent judgments of God take from man all the gifts of God. *All their victuals.* Sin and the consequent judgments of God take from man even what is necessary for the maintenance of life, and in consequence he comes to the grave.

VERSE 12. *They took Lot.* Here was the warning and chastening of God, sent to bring Lot to repentance. His choice brought this trouble upon him. He threw in his lot with the wicked, and he shared the judgment that came upon them. God in His love brings chastening into the lives of backsliders (Heb. 12. 5-13). *Abram's brother's son.* The capture of Lot was a matter of interest to Abram. They were members of the same family, and 'if one member suffer, all the members suffer with it' (1 Cor. 12. 26). In the same way we should make the troubles of our fellow-Christians our own. We are all members of the family of God. *Who dwelt in Sodom.* These words show us the next downward step of Lot's career. It inevitably followed on the last, though Lot was too blind to realise that it would be so. In 13. 12 we find Lot pitching his tent toward Sodom. He did not intend to live in it. He kept up the appearance of being a pilgrim. But such a compromise could not last long. Now, as we might expect, we find him dwelling in Sodom. The tent has gone. There is no more pretence of being a stranger or sojourner (though the men of Sodom always regarded him as such (19. 9). He has identified himself with the wicked city, and made himself a citizen of it. The same steps are invariably seen in the life of the worldly Christian. He goes near the world. He means still to live in his tent, but, if he once compromises, he can never resist the allurements of sin, and his life becomes less and less distinguishable from that of the man of the world.

And his goods. In God's mercy he lost everything. All that had been bought with the money gained from the sale of the cattle and the tents was gone. God often brings His backsliding children to worldly loss. Lot laid up for himself treasure upon earth, and the thieves broke through and stole (Mt. 6. 19). If he had stayed in Canaan, nothing would have been touched.

Departed, taking Lot with them to a cruel death or a lifelong captivity, a prospect to which his worldliness had brought him. Many a backsliding Christian has been brought to the brink of ruin like this.

Verse 13. *One that had escaped.* This is the picture of a saved soul. Each one of us has fled for refuge to lay hold on the hope set before us (Heb. 6. 18). The one who had escaped had an intense interest in those who had been taken captive.

Told Abram, the Hebrew. The one who has escaped comes to seek help from the man, whose interests he believes to be affected. So we ought to have a poignant interest in our fellow-men, who are still captives to the power of sin, from which by God's mercy and grace we ourselves have escaped. We ought also to seek help for them both from the Lord Himself and from those of our fellow-Christians, who are able to bring them help.

Confederate. God had given the pilgrim friends among the people of the land. In the same way He sometimes gives His children friends among the people of the world, whom He disposes to do them some special kindness, or supply some need. Those who are kind to the people of God may certainly expect some blessing.

Verse 14. *When Abram heard that his brother was taken captive.* The news provoked immediate response. Does the realisation that there are millions without Christ, captives to Satan, sin and death, provoke a similar response in us?

He armed his trained servants. He collected a band of men round him in order to lead them to the rescue of the captives. Notice that these servants were ' trained '. They were therefore ready for the emergency, whenever it arose. Are we trained for the work of God, ready whereever we are needed? The necessary training consists of knowledge of the Scriptures (2 Tim. 3. 15-17). *In his own house,* that is to say, either in Ur or in Haran. These were all men, who had come out to share the pilgrim life with Abram. *Three hundred and eighteen.* This is a small number for an army to defeat four powerful kings, but God is able to save by many or by few (Jud. 7. 7; 1 Sam. 14. 6). At the same time it has been suggested that the three hundred and eighteen were themselves heads of bands of retainers. It scarcely seems likely that Abram's following would have consisted of large enough numbers to make room for this.

Dan. The only city known to the Old Testament by this name is that first called Laish, seized and occupied by members of the tribe of Dan in the days of the judges (Jud. 18, specially verse 29). This city lies near the source of the Jordan and south of Lebanon. It is in the right direction for Abram's pursuit. It was however apparently not called Dan till its occupation by the Danites long after the time of Abram. This is one of the indications eagerly seized on by liberal critics and theologians in order to discredit the Pentateuch and its Mosaic authorship. They argue that this chapter must have been written after the time of the Judges. Their conclusions are too sweeping, though easily arrived at because of their prejudice. There are three possibilities with regard to the occurrence of this name in this verse. (1) The city may be quite another and older one of the same name. (2) The name Dan may gloss an older name. If the Pentateuch were a living book, read during the whole of Israel's history, it would be natural to keep it up to date by glossing ancient and obsolete names by their then modern equivalent. In the same way the Amalekites are mentioned in verse 7 of this chapter. (3) This chapter, which seems so different from those around it, may be a record made by Melchizedek and found in Jebus on its capture by David, who would have it placed in sequence in Genesis. This suggestion is not without difficulties, but it seems possible to conceive of its being in harmony with a proper view of inspiration, if Melchizedek himself were the human author. The suggestion has been made by Mr. F. F. Bruce. It would then be easy to think of David glossing and correcting the passage under the inspiration of the Holy Ghost.

Verse 15. *Divided himself against them.* This is the principle on which to carry on the Gospel war against the devil. All cannot do the same work, nor would it be right for all to be concentrated at the same place. Some preach, others pray, others give personal witness. Some organise and plan, others fit into detailed tasks. There are differences of gifts and ministries and activities (1 Cor. 12. 4-6). All have their part in the great campaign.

By night. Notice the secret preparations and deployments, that took place before the actual battle. They were essential for success. It is the same in the Gospel warfare. Before battle is joined, the work of prayer must be undertaken in secret, unknown to the enemy, sometimes actually at night. Praying and watch-

ing go together (Mt. 26. 40, 41). *Smote them.* We also must smite with the sword of the Spirit, which is the Word of God (Eph. 6. 17). *Pursued them.* We must never be slack in following up the enemy. Souls are sometimes retained in the devil's grasp, because, humanly speaking, we do not follow them up far enough. We rouse their interest and then let them go. Often much persistence is needed in order to win a soul.

Hobah, which is on the left hand of Damascus. Left means north, so that the distance covered by Abram was very great. He had a long way to go and an arduous task to perform. It will be the same with us. Some of us may have literally a long way to go, if called to the foreign mission field.

Verse 16. *He brought back all the goods.* The goods represent precious human beings, captured by the enemy, and in need of rescue (Isa. 66. 20; Rom. 15. 16). *His brother Lot.* This was the chief object of Abram's expedition. Here was a righteous man, who had fallen into the hands of the enemy. Although it was chiefly owing to his own fault, Abram, who knew this, took no account of of the fact. *And his goods.* Lot's possessions were also rescued, in order that he might use them thenceforward for God, but he did not do so. He profited nothing by this bitter experience, but returned instead to his former worldly life. We may suspect that his wife and family had much to do with his unwillingness to take up the pilgrim life. His wife was devoted to the wicked city (19. 26), of which it is possible that she may have been a native. We shall also learn later, that his sons were so engrossed in the life of the city, that he apparently did not even consider urging them to share his escape. His married daughters and their husbands refused to believe his testimony of the coming judgment, and his two unmarried daughters turned out to be shamelessly immoral.

The women also. Abram did not forget them, as Christ has not forgotten them. Their position in society has been immeasurably altered by the Gospel.

The people. A successful Gospel campaign relieves the social conditions even of those, who are not converted, by raising the standard of morals and improving the principles upon which society is conducted.

VERSE 17. *The King of Sodom went out to meet him.* Notice how the forces of evil exploited Abram's victory, and made it out to be their own. Notice also how the victory actually benefited the King of Sodom, and restored him his kingdom and property. Mission campaigns, as well as great revivals, generally benefit the life and conditions of the unconverted, and are often taken advantage of by them. The action of the king of Sodom did not however detract from the victory, which was brought about by God and accomplished His purpose in the restoration of Lot (Isa. 41. 2, 3). So long as the world lasts, Satan will exploit the victories of the Gospel. The improvement in social conditions, which is a by-product of evangelisation, will temporarily make the particular place or district more comfortable for the unconverted to go on sinning in. Such a result can probably never be avoided and ought in no way to deter us.

The King's dale. This is where Absalom set up his monument (2 Sam. 18. 18). The name is no proof that the passage dates from the time of King David only. It may have been a very old name connected with a Canaanite king.

VERSE 18. *Melchizedek* . In Melchizedek we have the next personal type of the Lord Jesus Christ after Adam. Though Adam was a type of Christ in certain respects (Rom. 5. 14), he exhibited many contrasts to Christ. Melchizedek on the contrary is a complete type. Apart from the present three verses Melchizedek is mentioned in Scripture only in Ps. 110. 4 and in Heb. 5. 10; 6. 20; 7. 1-17. In the Psalm the Holy Spirit speaks through David to Christ, and declares that God has sworn that He shall be a priest for ever after the order of Melchizedek. The passages in the Epistle to the Hebrews take up this prediction in the Psalm, and use it as a proof that in Christ God has set up a new order of *priesthood, which supersedes that of Aaron. The writer quotes extensively from this passage of Genesis to bring out the comparison between Melchizedek and Christ and to prove that his priesthood was greater than Aaron's. A sense of mystery surrounds the figure of Melchizedek in this passage, and attempts have been made to identify him with (1) the Lord Himself, in which case we should have here a theophany, or (2) with Shem, who might still be living, if the genealogy of Gen. 11. 10-26 be taken in a strictly chronological sense. These identifications are partly due to the fact that the Holy Spirit in the Epistle to the Hebrews describes Melchizedek as ' without father, without mother ' (Heb. 7. 3). It does not however seem possible that these words can be intended to have a historical meaning. They refer to the fact that Melchizedek appears *in Scripture* without antecedents and disappears equally suddenly, no statement being made of his birth or age, nor of the time of his death (Heb. 7. 3). Historically he may perhaps have been an Amorite chieftain, ruler of Jebus, or Salem, a worshipper of the supreme God of the Semites, El Elyon, Whom Abram is careful to identify with Jahweh. If this was the case, his coming to meet Abram is explained by his relief at the averting of danger from his city, and the deference paid to him by Abram is explained by the fact that the latter was a landless stranger and pligrim in the country to which Melchizedek belonged.

In verses 18 to 20 six points of comparison between type and antitype appear. (1) The name Melchizedek means in Hebrew, king of righteousness. He reigns in righteousness (Isa. 32. 1). He judges the poor with righteousness (Isa. 11. 4), and righteousness is the girdle of his loins (Isa. 11. 5). By identifying Himself with us sinners and dying for us on the cross He fulfilled all righteousness (Mt. 3. 15). His death made possible the gift of God's righteousness to all His believing people (Rom. 3. 21-26). He now reigns in righteousness over all who acknowledge Him (Mt. 28. 18; 1 Cor. 15. 25).

(2) Melchizedek was *King of Salem*. Salem means peace, and in this sense he is a type of the Saviour (Heb. 7. 1, 2). The Lord Jesus Christ is the Prince of Peace (Isa. 9. 6). At His birth the angels proclaimed peace and goodwill to men (Lk. 2. 14). This peace is based on righteousness. Apart from righteousness its existence is not possible. At the cross ' righteousness and peace kissed each other ' (Ps. 85. 10). The Saviour's death made possible peace between God and man (Eph. 2. 14-18). It made possible the sovereignty of God's peace in the believer's heart (Phil. 4. 7; Col. 3. 15), and it made possible peace with all men (Heb. 12. 14). In the world to come ' the meek shall inherit the earth, and delight themselves in the abundance of peace ' (Ps. 37. 11). Where Jesus reigns there is righteousness and peace.

(3) Melchizedek *brought forth bread and wine*. This was for the sustenance of the weary but victorious warriors. It is a picture of the flesh and blood of Christ, on which the believer feeds (Jo. 6. 53-58). Melchizedek's bread and wine are the more appropriate figures of the spiritual food, inasmuch as the same symbols were chosen by the Lord to represent it under the new covenant (Mr. 26. 26-28; 1 Cor. 11. 23-26). The horrible superstition with which the unreformed churches have corrupted the Lord's Supper makes it necessary to emphasise that the Lord

denied outright that the eating of His flesh and the drinking of His blood was literal (Jo. 6. 63). These actions are done by believing and receiving the words spoken by Jesus (Jo. 6. 63), and they are illustrated by two Old Testament passages, in which they are introduced with the meaning of *deriving advantage from a person's death* (Ps. 27. 2; 1 Chron. 11-19). This determines the meaning of the phrases, when they occur in the New Testament. The bread and wine of the Lord's Supper are pictures and symbols of the body and blood of Christ, which remind us of what He has done for us, and confirm our faith in Him. They are no more, and never have been any more. In any ceremony in which these elements are regarded as anything more there is no true Supper of the Lord. As the Paschal Lamb was eaten after it was killed, so the Saviour after His death becomes the spiritual sustenance of every true believer, giving him everlasting life with the first mouthful, and ever after keeping his spiritual life strong and healthy. The child of God feeds by reading, studying, believing and appropriating the Scriptures. It is the function of Christ as king of righteousness and king of peace to feed His people with this spiritual food.

(4) Melchizedek *was the priest of the most high God*. It is in this capacity that he is singled out both in Ps. 110. 4 and in the Epistle to the Hebrews to be the type and representative of Christ. Jesus Christ is High Priest of an order superior to that of Aaron. He is a priest for ever. As priest He offered Himself without spot to God (Heb. 9. 14). As priest He is able to save to the uttermost them that come unto God by Him, seeing He ever liveth to intercede for them (Heb. 7. 25). As priest He reigns now as King upon His throne (Zech. 6. 13). Apart from the priesthood of all believers (1 Pet. 2. 9; Rev. 1. 6; 5. 10), there is no other priest in the Christian Church but Christ. The pretensions to priesthood made by Romanists, Anglo-Roman-

ists and other unreformed bodies, are heathen in origin, unreal in practice, derogatory to the Lord Jesus Christ, and blasphemous against God.

VERSE 19. (5) Melchizedek *blessed* Abram. The Holy Spirit uses this fact in the Epistle to the Hebrews to prove that Melchizedek was greater than Abraham (Heb. 7. 7). In this respect also he is a type of Christ. It is from the Lord Jesus Christ that all blessing flows. In Him alone and because of Him and through His death and resurrection His people prosper. They can only please God as Christ dwells by faith in their hearts (Eph. 3. 17). Christ is the source of that blessing, by which the church multiplies and grows. Christ is greater than every creature, being seated at the right hand of God and given all authority and power.

Blessed be Abram of the most high God. Notice that in blessing Abram Melchizedek, who was not Christ, but a humble and probably unconscious type of Him, is careful not to assume in himself the power to bless, as do Romanist and Anglo - Romanist priests. He calls upon God, the source of all blessing, to bless him. In the same way the formularies of the Church of England oblige the minister only to declare and pronounce God's forgiveness, and state that *God* pardoneth and absolveth all them that truly repent and unfeignedly believe His holy Gospel. But in this sense also Melchizedek was a type of Christ, Who is the Mediator between God and man (1 Tim. 2. 5), and the channel through which God's blessing comes to man. God can make contact with man only in Christ. *Possessor of heaven and earth.* Melchizedek recognises that God is the Maker, Owner and Sovereign of the world. From the resources of the world He could bless Abram materially, and from the infinite resources of His own eternal Being He could pour spiritual blessing upon Him. So He does with us, through the channel of Calvary. If God is the Possessor of heaven and

earth, it follows that all that we possess is held from Him. This means that it is entrusted to us for use in His service to the blessing of our fellow-men.

VERSE 20. *Blessed be the most high God.* When the word ' bless ' is used of man, it means to cause to prosper. When it is used of God, it means to praise. Perhaps the idea that links these senses is that of giving joy. Man is made happy by God's blessing, and God is made happy by the praise, reverence and friendship of human hearts (Prov. 8. 31).

Which hath delivered thine enemies into thine hand. God is consistently recognised throughout the Bible to be the disposer of battles and warfare, just as of any other human activity or event. This is true in secular history (2 Ki. 19. 25). It was true of the wars engaged in by Old Testament Israel (1 Ki. 8. 44, 45). It is abundantly true of the warfare of the Gospel against the devil for the souls of men. At Calvary God won in Christ the decisive victory, and on the grounds of that victory has promised the final victory of all His elect people (Rom. 8. 37; 16. 20; Rev. 12. 11). God in Christ has won for His people victory over the dominion of sin (Rom. 6. 14), and has already defeated death on their behalf in a victory which will be applied universally to the elect on the day of resurrection (1 Cor. 15. 54, 55). Every child of God may experience like Abram the deliverance of his enemies into his hand.

(6) The last point, in which Melchizedek is here presented as a type of Christ, is that Abram *gave him tithes of all.* In the Epistle to the Hebrews the Holy Spirit connects this fact closely with Melchizedek's blessing to demonstrate the greatness of Melchizedek. The Old Testament giving of tithes is a picture of the dedication of himself by the believer to Christ. In the financial sphere, which belongs to earth, it is a happy thing to follow this principle literally. If every believer gave regularly a

tenth of his income, or such other proportion of it as he was clearly shown of God, Christian work would be hindered far less from lack of means than is often the case. The Christian who gives regularly in this way often (perhaps usually) finds himself blessed financially and prospered materially. At the same time the spiritual principle under the Gospel, of which tithing is the type, is the dedication of oneself, one's life, time, talents, money and resources to the service of God. There is a parallel dualism in the meaning of the sabbath. The rest and holiness of the seventh day under the old covenants is the symbol of the spiritual rest of the believer here on earth and his eternal holiness and rest in the world to come. At the same time the principle of the weekly sabbath needs application literally, so long as the believer is here on earth. This is satisfied by the proper observance of the Lord's day.

Verse 21. The wicked king felt under an obligation. Immensely relieved at the recovery of what he had lost, he offered Abram his expenses, as it were. His offer seems generous, because he had a bargaining spirit, and may have had at the back of his mind the least that he himself would have taken under similar circumstances. It would not be surprising, if he thought that the *goods* had probaby been damaged in transit. His demand for the *persons* (Hebrew, ' souls '), among whom there were women (verse 16), may be suspected of having some connection with the lust and wickedness, for which his city was notorious.

Verse 22. *I have lift up mine hand.* This means ' I have taken an oath '. The hand was lifted up in swearing among the ancient peoples (compare Rev. 10. 6). *The Lord.* Abram deliberately identified the true God, Whom he knew, with El Elyon, the most high God, possessor of heaven and earth. Whether he actually used the title Jahweh does not seem certain in view of the revelation of that name made to Moses (Ex. 6. 3). That revelation may mean that Abraham knew the name, but had no experience of its redemptive meaning in the sense in which it was realised at the Exodus. It may however mean that Abraham did not know or use the name, but used the title El Shaddai (God Almighty). In that case the occurrence of the name Jahweh in the text of Genesis would be due to Moses, who would have rendered the older title into Hebrew by this name. Whatever name Abraham actually used, and whatever language he actually spoke (it was probably Aramaic), he undoubtedly identifies Melchizedek's El Elyon with the true and living God. In so doing he gives a valuable piece of testimony. It is much as if a Christian were to say, ' Jesus is the true God '. The testimony may have been valuable to Melechizedek, who now disappears from history, and in so doing becomes in a *seventh* manner a type of the Lord Jesus Christ, ' without father, without mother, without genealogy, having neither beginning of days, nor end of life, but likened unto the Son of God.'

Verse 23. *I will not take.* Perhaps Abram remembered the gifts of Pharaoh (12. 6) and their unfortunate result. He had learnt that no good comes from accepting gifts and rewards from worldly people. He gave his service freely to God in a cause which he believed to be His. If he was to be rich, he would take riches only from God. He would give no opportunity to the world to whisper that there were selfish motives in what he did. His spirit was the same as that of the apostle, who refused to take advantage of the reward, to which he was justly entitled, rather than create the impression that his service was not completely disinterested (1 Cor. 9. 11-15; 2 Cor. 11. 7-9). Our spirit should be the same. It is better to suffer loss, than to make the world think that we serve God for financial, or material, reward. God will supply our needs and see that we do not lose by such an attitude.

VERSE 24. *Save only that which the young men have eaten.* These were out-of-pocket expenses, which Abram felt justified in taking. *The men which went with me.* We were told (verse 13) that Aner, Eshcol, and Mamre were confederate with Abram, but this verse gives us the first intimation that they accompanied him on the expedition. They helped in the campaign, and were in the same position as governors, who give permission for the preaching of the Gospel, or any who assist in practical arrangements, such as printing, cleaning, advertising, or transport during a Gospel campaign. Being Amorites, they would not understand the principle of taking no reward. Abram sees that they receive what they expect and what is rightly due to them. We should be careful to see to the same. Underlying the verse is a certain generosity and nobility of character apparent on Abram's part. He had a high aristocratic code of honour and conduct. This would be appreciated by the three confederates and would help to incline them to receive whatever testimony of the true God Abram had to give them.

CHAPTER 15

THIS chapter tells of further promises and predictions made to Abram. The Lord makes a personal promise to Abram (verse 1), who complains that he has no child (verses 2, 3). The Lord promises him a son of his own, and declares the multiplication of his descendants (verses 4 and 5). Abram believes this, and is justified by faith (verse 6). The Lord promises him Canaan for an inheritance (verse 7), and over a covenant sacrifice foretells the bondage in Egypt, the exodus, and the conquest of the land (verses 8-21).

VERSE 1. *After these things.* If it be really true that chapter 14 was

written by Melchizedek and preserved in Jebus till the time of David, these words would follow 13. 18. The Lord's words to Abram about the shield and reward would then have reference to Lot's choice and Abram's sacrificial generosity. They are not out of place in such a connection, but they appear to fit better the end of chapter 14. Abram had been in danger in battle. The Lord therefore reminds him that He is his shield. In particular Abram had refused reward for what he had done (14. 22, 23), and the Lord therefore appropriately tells him that He Himself is his reward. *The word of the Lord.* The spoken word, just as later it came to the prophets, conveyed perhaps by the Living Word, but certainly by the Holy Ghost, Who spake by the prophets. Abram was a prophet (20. 7). *In a vision.* Here is a second means, by which the Lord communicated with Abram. We have already met with instances of theophany. Notice that the title for God continues through this chapter to be Jahweh, the redemptive name. This is to be expected by all who realise that the difference in name fits the context, and are not carried away by the prejudice that supports the foolish documentary theory. The chapter deals with redemptive issues.

Fear not. Believers have nothing to fear except to offend God. ' Underneath are the everlasting arms ' (Dt. 33. 27). The worst that man can do to them is to kill the body, but he cannot touch the real person (Mt. 10. 28). Jesus Christ has all power on earth (Mt. 28. 18). Therefore popery, communism, and atom bombs may all do their worst, and yet not a hair of the believer's head will perish (Mt. 10. 30). If they need not fear man, so are they delivered from all fear of the wrath and judgment of God. Their Saviour is responsible for their eternal salvation (Heb. 5. 9). Nor need they fear the attempts of Satan to draw them away from faith in their Saviour. They need have no fear that their own corrupt nature will get the final victory over them. ' The blood of Jesus Christ cleanseth from all sin ' (1 Jo. 1. 7).

*Jesus, Thy blood and righteousness
My beauty are, my glorious dress.
Midst flaming worlds in these
    arrayed,
With joy shall I lift up my head.'*
The grounds for Abram's confidence are immediately stated to him by the Lord. *I am thy shield, and thy exceeding great reward.* Jahweh here promises to be two things to Abram, (1) for the present his shield, and (2) for the future his reward. We have nothing to fear in this world, if we have God Himself interposed between us and our enemies. The greatest interposition was made at Calvary. Here Christ Jesus placed Himself between us and Satan, between us and sin, between us and the curse of God, between us and death. There the whole force of God's righteous wrath and the whole fury of our enemies fell upon our Shield and Saviour. On the basis of this divine interposition the Lord remains our shield continually, as we pass along the whole of our journey through the world. (2) God Himself is our final reward. He created us to enjoy Him for ever. No wonder that such a reward is called ' exceeding great '. In God is perfect, infinite and increasing satisfaction for every one of His creatures. ' His servants shall serve Him, and they shall see His face ' (Rev. 22. 4). The essence of eternal life is to know Him (Jo. 17. 3).

VERSE 2. *Lord God.* This is not the same name in the original, as that used in chapters 2 and 3. There the expression ' Lord God ' represented the combination Jahweh Elohim. It was a connecting bridge between the name of the Creator, Elohim, and that of the Redeemer, Jahweh. Here the expression, as so often in the prophets, is Adonai Jahweh, Lord Jahweh. The first constituent in it is a title of reverence. The name is essentially redemptive. *What wilt*

thou give me? For the moment the great promises seemed to have little effect upon Abram. His attention was concentrated on his supreme personal problem. Is this not often the case with us? God makes to us from His Word precious promises, intended to embrace and cover and provide for all our problems and needs and much more besides. But we overlook them, because we suppose we have a supreme need, and we want it specifically dealt with. Abram appears almost to have questioned the possibility of reward, so long as his need of a child was not satisfied. *Go.* This means to go out of the world, to die. Abram was now of an age, when he had little reasonable expectation of becoming a father. In spite of God's promise of fruitfulness Abram was afraid of remaining barren to the end. Is not this sometimes the case with us? Our spiritual lives are barren of virtues and barren of souls won, when provision has been made for their fruitfulness. *Steward,* that is, possessor. The Hebrew says idiomatically, ' son of possession '. Abram meant that, as he had no child, Eliezer would possess all he had, after he had gone. The Hebrew for possession in this verse is *meshek.* Notice Abram's use of the word ' house '. Though it was meant as a collective term for his dependents and belongings; it yet seems an echo of the old life in Ur and Haran. Abram's question perhaps shows that at the moment his faith was not at its highest, and in such circumstances the old life started to reassert itself. We shall have similar experiences. *Is this Eliezer of Damascus.* The targum of Onkelos, the Peshitto Syriac version and the margin of the Revised Version read, ' is Eliezer the Damascene '. The text is open to slight doubt, the Hebrew for Damascus being Dammesek, where we have a repetition of the word meaning ' possession ' (Heb. meshek). An intended play on the words would however be very much in the Hebrew genius. We hear no more of Eliezer.

He is often identified with the servant who went to fetch Rebekah (chap. 24), but the identification is nowhere stated.

VERSE 3. The atmosphere of this verse seems to be different from that of the last. Abram's words read more like a delicately-phrased prayer than a complaint. It is possible that the words of verse 2 were spoken in the ' vision ' in immediate answer to the Lord's promise of verse 1. Those of verse 3, introduced by a further ' And Abram said ', may have been spoken when Abram had woken up, or resumed normal sensibility. His mind was full of his vision. God's promise brought to a head what was uppermost in his mind. Already he had been promised seed. Yet he had waited and longed for so long a time. In verse 3 he simply states to the Lord what was filling his thoughts. This is a form of prayer in which God delights, and we should find greater spiritual blessing, if we made these simple statements to God more often. The great prayer of the Lord Jesus Christ recorded in Jo. 17 has as many affirmations as petitions. But if this is the spirit in which Abram said these words, he must have uttered them in faith. He had no doubt that the Lord was able to give him a child. If we have a fear, a longing, a problem, something that overmasters our lives, as Abram had, why do we not lay it in simple faith before God? Our utterance of the need implies a petition for its satisfaction.

VERSE 4. Jahweh's answer to Abram's faith was immediate and ample. He gave him the promise that his need would be satisfied and his petition answered. *The word of the Lord came unto him.* It came to him, as it came to all prophets with the authority and inspiration of the Holy Ghost. Nothing is said in this verse, as in verse 1, of a vision. We do not know how the word came in this instance. The word of the Lord is not only, or even chiefly, concerned

with Abram's personal blessing. It has to do with God's eternal purpose in redemption, and it seems that Abram understood this. Notice that God's answer to Abram's prayer was direct, definite and detailed. The Holy Spirit had given Abram the faith and knowledge to ask for something that was in line with God's will and purpose. We too may expect such direct, definite and detailed answers, especially if we ask the Holy Spirit to help our infirmities by showing us what to pray for, as we ought (1 Jo. 5. 14, 15; Rom. 8. 25, 26).

VERSE 5. In this verse we have in another form a repetition of the ninth of the fourteen promises made to Abram. This promise of multiplication was first made in 13. 16. *He brought him forth abroad.* Abram was brought out to be alone with God on this momentous occasion. Faith, prayer, promises made through the Word are for the individual soul, holding communion with God alone. ' The faith that thou hast, have it to thyself before God ' (Rom. 15. 22). Similarly each man separately will give an account of himself to God (Rom. 15. 12). *Look now toward heaven, and tell the stars.* Abram could not number even the small proportion of stars that he could see with the naked eye. What would he have said, if he had been possessed of a modern telescope? There was much more concealed in God's promise than Abram could even conceive. He could have no idea of its extent. It is the same with us, when God gives us promises.

So shall thy seed be. Abraham's seed consists of all who belong to Christ (Gal. 3. 29), and these will one day be a great multitude that no man can number (Rev. 7. 9). This promise of God was embraced by Abram by faith, laid hold of, received and believed. It was an anchor to his faith when the days came in which it seemed that its fulfilment was impossible (Rom. 4. 18). The fulfilment was made possible (in the human sphere) by the co-operating faith of Sarah (Heb. 11. 11, 12). We Christians know, what the scientist does not, that the criterion of the possible is not experience nor natural law, but the power and promises of God. ' What He hath promised He is able also to perform ' (Rom. 4. 21).

VERSE 6. This is one of the great verses of the Bible. The fundamental principle of justification by faith is stated in it definitely and explicitly for the first time. The text is appealed to by the apostle Paul, as he expounds the Gospel truth of salvation by faith in Christ (Rom. 4. 3, 9, 22, 23; Gal. 3. 6). *He believed in the Lord*. Notice that it does not say, ' He believed the Lord ', but ' He believed *in* the Lord '. The former is of course included in the latter. Abram's faith consisted of two parts. (1) He believed the fact. He was thereafter convinced that he would have a son. (2) He acted on that belief by committing himself to God. Undoubtedly the faith of Abram rested on all that is recorded in the course of this chapter as having been said to him. He committed himself to God as his shield and reward. Justifying faith can only be concerned with eternal issues. Belief of a promise that a certain earthly country would one day be the believer's possession could scarcely justify. We may notice that twice in the preceding verses of this chapter the expression ' the word of the Lord ' occurs (verses 1, 4). It was on this ' word of the Lord ' that Abram's faith rested, and to which it responded. ' Faith cometh of hearing, and hearing by the word of God ' (Rom. 10. 17). Now this word of the Lord had told Abram four things, and on these things he rested his faith. (1) That the Lord was his shield. While this is always true in the case of all dangers, the supreme fulfilment lies in the interposition of Christ between believers and their enemies at Calvary. We may well believe that in some sense up to his lights Abram understood this fact. Here he saw the day of Christ and

was glad (Jo. 8. 56). (2) Abram believed that the Lord was his reward. He looked to the heavenly country (Heb. 11. 16), to being received to glory (Ps. 73. 24), and to dwelling in the house of the Lord for ever (Ps. 23. 6), and this belief became the pivot of his life. (3) He believed that a child of his own would be his heir. This was to him no mere personal matter. He connected this seed to come with the seed of the woman, foretold at the time of the fall of man, and believed that it had a part to play in the redemptive purpose of God. Already perhaps he looked beyond Isaac to Christ. (4) He believed the promise of the multiplication of his seed, that is to say, he believed, up to his lights and so far as he was able to comprehend, in a redeemed humanity to come resting on the victory of Christ. The promise of a multiplied seed, which could not have meant large numbers condemned ultimately to die, reversed the condemnation of the fall and fulfilled the mystical promise that Eve would be the mother of all living (3. 20). Abram therefore believed in the ultimate fulfilment of the redemptive purposes of God, and that he himself would share in the blessings of that fulfilment. His faith therefore related to spiritual and eternal things, and as such was a justifying faith.

He counted it to him for righteousness. He refers to the Lord. *Counted.* This means to set down in the balance on the credit side for purposes of judgment. Abram, being like all men a moral personality, stands before God for approval or condemnation. Being a sinner, he can of his own self meet only with condemnation. But God places in the scales of judgment something that weighs them down on the credit side. *It.* To what does this important word refer? Not to Abram's faith as such in the sense that its exercise was meritorious. We shall notice that the word ' faith ' does not occur in the previous sentence. *It* refers to *the fact that he believed in the Lord.* This belief in the Lord implies the acknowledgment by Abram that he possessed no righteousness of his own, in other words, that he was a justly condemned sinner. It also implies that he looked to the Lord to supply what he needed and did not possess. He *relied* for righteousness upon the Lord. *For righteousness.* Notice again that it does not say ' as righteousness.' The faith was not a meritorious equivalent of righteousness, nor was it something that God accepted in the place of meritorious works. It was *for righteousness,* not for it in the sense of being instead of it, but for it in the sense of being the means by which the righteousness was appropriated, or obtained. It was an effective instrument, or channel, or coupling, which linked Abram with the righteousness that he needed. *Righteousness,* as used in this verse, means a right standing with God and before the bar of His justice. It means the position of one in whose case the claims of God's law are satisfied. In the eyes of human law a man possesses this righteousness, (1) if he is acquitted by a judge and jury, or (2) when he has completed a sentence imposed upon him to vindicate or satisfy justice. In the case of a capital sentence he is not justified till he is dead. This last is the case of the sinner (Rom. 6. 7). The righteousness which God imputed to Abram was based on the satisfaction of all the claims of God's law against him made by Jesus Christ on the cross of Calvary, which God foresaw and anticipated and acted upon. There is no other way, by which the claims of God's law can be satisfied in the case of any sinner in the whole course of the world. These facts are interpreted and explained by the Holy Ghost through the apostle Paul. In Rom. 4. 3 the apostle quotes this verse. In Rom. 4. 5 he says that not faith as such is reckoned in the place of righteousness, but that the faith of the one, who believes in, trusts to, relies on the God Who justifies the ungodly, is reckoned as the means to righteousness. Here again we have acknowledgment of personal ungodliness and need, and reliance upon God to supply righteousness. The apostle says that such faith believes that what God promises He is able to perform (Rom. 4. 22), and that under the Gospel justifying faith is concentrated on the atoning death and resurrection of Jesus our Lord (Rom. 4. 23). The apostle also says that Abram was justified in believing what he heard (Gal. 3. 5, 6). We have already noticed the four facts, mentioned in verses 1, 4 and 5 of this chapter, which Abram believed. The apostle James also mentions Abram's faith ,and explains that it was a living faith issuing in devoted obedience (Jas. 2. 23).

VERSE 7. The point of this verse seems to be that in proclaiming Himself as Jahweh God proclaims Himself as the author and agent of redemption, and thus connects the call of Abram and the possession of Palestine with the purpose of redemption. They fall into their place as steps in that purpose. The possession of Palestine is no more an end in itself than is the call of Abram. Both were means towards the coming of Christ.

I am the Lord. Compare Ex. 20. 2. This fact is the basis of the law, of redemption, of grace, of faith, of righteousness, of sanctification, of glory to come, and of every other gift and blessing. All these things are so because God is what He is (Ex. 3. 14), especially because He is Jahweh, the Redeemer.

Brought thee out. This is what the Lord has done for every one of His children. He has brought us out, not from Ur, but from this present evil world (Gal. 1. 4), from the power of Satan (1 Jo. 3. 8) and from bondage to sin (Tit. 2. 14). *To give thee this land.* To us He has given, not Palestine, but that of which it is a type, a new heaven, and a new earth, wherein dwelleth righteousness (2 Pet. 3. 13). We have it today in prospect, just as Abram had Palestine in prospect.

VERSE 8. *Lord God*. See on verse 2. *Whereby shall I know*. We ought not to attribute Abram's question to any lack of faith, or weakness of it. If that had been the case, it is unlikely that it would have received the full answer that was given to it. He may have wished to know in greater detail how the promise would be fulfilled. This the answer certainly explained. Alternatively, or in addition, he may have wanted assurance, although his faith was already strong. It is very proper for believers to desire assurance, and they are expressly given it by God (1 Jo. 5. 13). If Abram was seeking assurance, he found it in the gracious act of God of making a covenant with him (verse 18).

Inherit. This is the function of an heir, and if Abram was an heir, he was a child of God (Rom. 8. 17). His inheritance embraced the world (Rom. 4. 13).

VERSE 9. The account of the making of the covenant, which occupies verses 9-21 of this chapter, is not free from mystery, and some of its details are obscure. At the same time the following facts emerge clearly: (1) A solemn covenant was entered into, involving promise and guarantee on Jahweh's part (verses 17, 18). (2) The covenant involved blood-shedding (verse 10). It therefore becomes once again a type and picture of the new covenant made in the blood of Jesus (Mt. 26. 28), and the animals, whose blood was shed, become naturally a type of Him. (3) A detailed prediction of the bondage in Egypt, the exodus and the acquisition of Palestine was made at the institution of the covenant. (4) The context of the passage (particularly verse 6) and the apostle's statement about Abram's inheritance (Rom. 4. 13) connect these events with eternal redemption, and they are seen to be (a) steps towards the accomplishment of that redemption, and (b) types of its major

features.

Take me. These animals were not strictly to be sacrificed in the sense of the levitical law. If they had been, we should not have expected the words ' take me '. God alone can provide a lamb for an offering (Jo. 1. 29), as Abraham himself was later to be shown in a particularly poignant manner (Gen. 22. 8, 13). Here we learn that the institution of the covenant was to cost Abram something. His flocks and herds were held at the disposal of God. In the same way no one can enter into the benefits of the new covenant, until he is prepared to hand himself over to the service of God.

In the animals and birds, whose blood was to be shed, we see a fourfold picture of Christ, fourfold, not fivefold, as the birds form a pair and a single item (verse 10). The three animals were each to be three years old in contrast to those of the levitical law, which were to be one year, where age was specified (Ex. 12. 5). There is no need to see hidden mystery in the number three. No more need be meant than that the animals were to be in their prime strength. *An heifer*. This is a picture of Christ as the servant of God, bearing the yoke of sorrow and weariness and labour, represented in the face of an ox in the cherubim. *A she goat*. This represents Christ as the source of His people's spiritual nourishment and their tender guardian. *A ram*. This represents Christ as the conqueror in His strength and power (Rev. 5. 5; 6. 2; 19. 11-16). *A turtle-dove, and a young pigeon*. These represent the tenderness and gentleness of Christ (Mt. 12. 19, 20), filled, as He was, by the Holy Ghost, Who descended upon Him in the form of a dove (Mt. 3. 16).

VERSE 10. *He took unto him*. In the previous verse he is told to take them for Jahweh. In practice he takes them unto himself. This is always the case. Whatever we devote to God redounds in blessing upon ourselves. The advantage is always ours.

Divided. The usual method of making a covenant was to cut an animal into two parts. The parties to the covenant, or at any rate one of them, then solemnly walked between the two parts (see Jer. 34. 18). So was the Saviour divided, as it were, and broken on the cross.

The birds divided he not. Instead of one animal divided into two parts, which were then placed facing each other, the two birds were placed in the same relative position. This made four separate pairs. If we are to see any significance in the number four, it may be that it brought home to Abram the fact of the four generations, mentioned in verse 16.

VERSE 11. *Fowls,* that is, birds of prey. During the whole day Abram kept watch over the carcases. The long wait is perhaps a picture of the long interval between Abram's day and the accomplishment of God's redemptive purpose in Christ. During this time Satan, sin and death made constant attempts to prevent the fulfilment of God's purpose and invalidate His covenant.

Abram drove them away. The attempts of the devil to frustrate the purposes of God in Christ were successfully resisted, under the providence of God, by the faith and watchfulness of successive generations of a faithful remnant of Abram's seed.

VERSE 12. *The sun was going down.* The delay was protracted as far as possible. The day of the world was ending, and its sun was going down. All hope for it was gone, when once in the end of the ages Christ appeared to put away sin by the offering of Himself (Heb. 9. 26).

A deep sleep. By this experience something of the implications of the covenant was brought home to Abram. It is an obvious picture of death. In order to bring us safely through to resurrection ground the Saviour had to pass through the deep sleep of death.

An horror of great darkness. This may or may not have been an anticipation in Abram's experience of the servitude in Egypt. It certainly brought home to him, like the deep sleep which induced it, something of the meaning of Calvary. It was exactly such a horror that enveloped the Saviour, as He became our sin-bearer on the cross. His prayer was unanswered (Ps. 22. 2), and He was forsaken by His Father (Mt. 27. 46), Who is of purer eyes than to behold iniquity (Hab. 1. 13). The horror of great darkness was caused in the experience of Christ by His identification with us and our sin. He was made to be sin for us (2 Cor. 5. 21), and became a curse for us (Gal. 3. 13). By these means Abram learnt something of the meaning of redemption, and perhaps came to understand the basis of the righteousness, which he had laid hold of by faith (verse 6). Adam had a similar experience of deep sleep at the time of the creation of Eve (2. 21), a fact from which we learn that Christ's church was created in and through His death.

VERSE 13. *Know of a surety.* Here is the answer to Abram's question of verse 6. God graciously gave him confirmation and assurance.

Thy seed. Abram's true seed is Christ and His people (Gal. 3. 16, 29). Of this seed the natural seed, Old Testament Israel, was in many respects typical. Here we have the prediction of typical happenings to the typical seed, which illustrate and foreshadow the events of eternal redemption. Notice the four stages in the history of the typical seed, here predicted: (1) bondage and affliction in a strange land. (2) Judgment on the enemies of the seed. (3) The deliverance of the seed. (4) The return of the seed to their inheritance (verse 16). The sojourn of the seed in a foreign land and their service and affliction there is a prediction of the sojourn and bondage of Israel in Egypt, described in Ex. 1-12, which is typical of the service given by the people of God to sin in their natural state before their redemption. 'We were all by nature children of wrath, even as others' (Eph. 2. 3). We were strangers in a double sense. At that time we were aliens from the commonwealth of Israel, and strangers to the covenants of promise (Eph. 2. 12). Also if we think of the redeemed as known to God, and loved by Him, in eternity past (Rom. 8. 29, 30; Eph. 1. 4, 5), they are in their natural state, when lost in Adam, strangers in a strange land. Every sinner is in bondage to sin (Jo. 8. 34; Rom. 6. 16), and the service of sin produces bitterness and affliction. 'The way of transgressors is hard' (Prov. 13. 15).

Four hundred years. Our ignorance of the chronology makes the interpretation of this period difficult. The verse reads naturally as if the bondage and affliction in Egypt lasted four hundred years, or at least that the four hundred years lay between the entry into Egypt (Gen. 46. 1-7) and the exodus, and many have interpreted it in this way. With this agrees in round numbers the statement of Ex. 12. 40, as it stands in the Massoretic Hebrew text, and as we have it in the Authorised Version. The apostle Paul however in Gal. 3. 17 says that the law, which immediately followed the exodus, came four hundred and thirty years after the covenant with Abraham. He evidently thought of the period in Egypt as lasting about half that period. In this calculation he follows the Septuagint Greek version, which with the Samaritan recension substitutes for the words 'in Egypt' in Ex. 12. 40 the words 'in the land of Egypt and the land of Canaan.' The recension and the version thus interpret the four hundred and thirty years of Ex. 12. 40 as beginning with the entry of Abraham into Canaan (Gen. 12) and ending at the exodus. It seems in English to be a strain on language to call this 'the sojourning of the children of Israel,' though it is perhaps more natural in Hebrew or Greek, and it does not seem right to say that in so short a summary such

language is impossible. Taking together the references in both Testaments and in the versions, we conclude that the period of four hundred and thirty years begins with the birth of Isaac. How then are we to read the four hundred years of this verse? It seems difficult to take the words 'a land' as referring to anything wider than Egypt. If the sojourn of the patriarchs in Canaan were included, should we not expect the reading 'lands'? The meaning of the words 'four hundred years' seems to be, 'and they shall afflict them until a time, which is four hundred years from now.'

VERSE 14. *That nation* is Egypt. Egypt is often seen in the Bible as the type of the world. God's people before redemption are the slaves of sin and the world.

Will I judge. This was fulfilled in the ten plagues of Egypt (Ex. 7-12). These plagues have their counterpart in the temporal judgments which constantly appear in the world in the course of history and are aimed at assisting the Gospel (see Rev. 8. 7-12, the judgment of the Roman empire, and Rev. 16. 2-21, the judgment of the papacy and Roman church. For the relationship of the plagues to the witness of the Gospel see Rev. 11. 4-6). The world will be destroyed on the great day of judgment (2 Pet. 3. 10-12; 2 Thess. 1. 7-9; Rev. 20. 11).

Afterward shall they come out. This was fulfilled at the exodus (Ex. 12. 41). The true people of God are also redeemed from the world by means of the Gospel under the blood of Christ, the true Paschal Lamb, Who redeems us from all iniquity (Tit. 2. 14). *With great substance.* This was fulfilled in the spoiling of the Egyptians (Ex. 3. 22; 11. 2; 12. 35, 36). In the same way the kings of the earth bring their glory and honour into the new Jerusalem (Rev. 21. 24).

VERSE 15. The outline of the great typical events of the then future is interrupted by a gracious personal promise to Abram. The time for his own inheritance would not come until the distant future. He without us was not to be made perfect (Heb. 11. 40). He must await his resurrection at the end of the world.

Thou shalt go to thy fathers. Abram's fathers were idolaters (Josh. 24. 2). There is therefore no question of Abram's spirit surviving death and joining those of his fathers in another world, and this statement introduces no such conception. Abram was to join his fathers in the grave. *In peace.* In these words lies the promise. Abram would die at peace with God through the blood of the cross, which he had dimly foreseen, but in which he had placed all his faith. He would die also with the peace of God reigning in his heart and mind and with the assurance of a blessed resurrection from the dead to inherit the heavenly city, for which he looked (Heb. 11. 16). The promise also means that he would spend his old age in peace and would leave the world before the servitude and affliction, which God was foretelling, should begin.

Thou shalt be buried. In the Bible burial is regarded as the only honourable means of disposing of a dead body. To lie unburied was a dishonour and degradation (Jer. 22. 19; 36. 30). The Moabites were to be severely punished, because they burnt the bones of the king of Edom into lime (Am. 2. 1). The modern obsession with cremation is unscriptural and non-Christian, materialistic in origin and irreverent to the dead. The very use of the word ' cremation ' shows this. It is a euphemism for ' burning ', and the conscience and decency of man revolt from the use of the straightforward word. To cremate means to burn the dead. *In a good old age.* Here is the second of the two promises. Long life in this world, when accompanied by God's blessing and lived in His fear, is a type of everlasting life, ' even length of days for ever and ever ' (Ps. 21. 4). Thus even in the fact of his being preserved in peace to a good old age

the life of faithful Abraham was typical of the blessings to be received by his seed.

VERSE 16. The prediction of the great typical events is resumed in this verse, the personal promise to Abram being inserted immediately after the reference to the servitude and affliction in order to relieve him of any fear that he would suffer this personally. *In the fourth generation.* The exact meaning of this phrase is not easily discoverable. It may be (1) quite literal. In the genealogies in Exodus exactly four generations appear between Levi, who with his son Kohath went down into Egypt with Jacob (Gen. 46. 8, 11), and Moses, who led the people out (Ex. 6. 16-20). The four generations might thus be reckoned as Levi, Kohath, Amram, Moses. But if we begin with Levi, why not with Jacob himself? This can be done by taking literally the expressions ' a daughter of Levi ' (Ex. 2. 1) and ' his father's sister ' (Ex. 6. 20). We could then reckon Jacob, Levi, Jochebed, Moses. Neither of these reckonings is however satisfactory. Not only is the second counted through a woman, but neither allows sufficient time for the two hundred and fifteen years, which, allowing for the Septuagint interpretation, is the shortest time covered by the sojourn in Egypt. It is more likely that omissions have been made in the genealogy in Ex. 6. 16-25 (see on Gen. 11. 10 and on chapter 5). It is more likely, for example, that Jochebed was a member merely of the same tribe as Amram's father, than that she was actually his aunt. It would therefore be possible to begin the four generations with Kohath, who came into Egypt from Canaan (Gen. 46. 8, 11). Amram might then be the third link and Moses the fourth and last, especially as he was born eighty years before the exodus (Ex. 7. 7). But (2) the Hebrew word *dor*, translated ' generation ', is not of such exact meaning as the English. The reference may therefore be parallel with the four hundred years of verse 13. *They shall come hither again.* After the bitter experiences of Egypt the seed would undoubtedly enter into the promised inheritance. They themselves had never personally been in Canaan, when they entered it under Joshua. But they are regarded as being all one with Abraham and as having been in Canaan in him (Heb. 7. 9, 10). In the same way the true seed are one with Christ (Gal. 3. 28, 29). When therefore we are redeemed we return with Christ and in Christ to the place where Christ was from all eternity, and where we too were in the purpose of God in Him (Eph. 1. 4).

The iniquity of the Amorites is not yet full. Here we have another expression of the important principle, which we first met with in 6. 3. Sin accumulates, till there comes a time when God's anger and judgment break out upon it (2 Chron. 36. 16). The sinner treasures up for himself wrath in the day of wrath (Rom. 2. 5), heaping it up, as he goes on sinning without repentance day by day. God waits in mercy, seeking to lead men to repentance (2 Pet. 3. 9; Rom. 2. 4). But a point will come, when His judgment will break out. The patience of God is well illustrated in this passage by the fact that He waited four hundred years before destroying the Amorites. This was finally done (or should have been finally done) by the sword of Israel under Joshua. Notice that the people of God suffered long in Egypt, while He was waiting with a yearning heart over the Amorites. This is always the principle on which God acts. He leaves the ninety and nine saved sheep in the wilderness, while He goes after the one that is lost (Lk. 15. 4). So today for generations God has left His own people exposed to the temptations and dangers of the present evil world, while He seeks for lost sinners through the Gospel. Such is His love for fallen men, and such should be our love too.

A sad reference is made to this principle as expressed in this verse

by the apostle Paul in 1 Thess. 2. 16. There, ironically enough, he uses the same words of the Jews themselves. The same final judgment, which their own ancestors had been raised up to inflict on the Amorites, the Jews had now brought upon themselves by their murder of the Lord Jesus and the prophets, and their antagonism to the Gospel.

VERSE 17. This verse describes the establishment of the covenant, which was formally accomplished by at least one of the parties passing between the corresponding pieces of the slain animals, which were placed opposite to each other (Jer. 34. 18). *When the sun went down.* God makes His covenant, when man's sun is set and the day of his natural life is eclipsed by the fall. Adam and his race are lost, and there is no more hope for them morally or spiritually as such. The sun of God's blessing and favour has ceased to shine on the race.

It was dark. Man lives in the darkness of sin, which issues in 'the unfruitful works of darkness' (Eph. 5. 11). It was this same darkness of sin, wrath, judgment and death, that enveloped the Saviour on the cross, when the covenant was established (Mt. 27. 45, 46). This is the spiritual night, counterpart of the physical, into which Judas Iscariot went out (Jo. 13. 30). It is at this point that God comes to man in this state, and makes with him the new covenant in Jesus' blood.

A smoking furnace. This represents the righteous wrath of God, which fell upon the Lord Jesus Christ on the cross. Unless this had happened, no covenant could have been made. Abram was taught by this experience the basis of the covenant, which is grounded in the righteousness of God. This same smoking furnace of the wrath of God will one day burn up the wicked in the lake of fire, though the death of Jesus 'for every man' (Heb. 2. 9) has made it unnecessary for any man to suffer eternal punishment. Any man may repent and believe.

A burning lamp. This represents the light of life (Jo. 8. 12). The descent of God's wrath upon Jesus on Calvary brings this light of life to everyone of His followers. The two go together. The believer's life is rooted in the death of Jesus. At the cross mercy and truth met together, and righteousness and peace kissed each other (Ps. 85. 10). They worked together in harmony to effect the believer's salvation. Abram was thus taught that God made a covenant with his seed, in which by the exercise of His wrath and judgment He brought them light and life.

Passed between those pieces. The symbols of the furnace and the lamp indicated that Jahweh Himself was passing between the pieces, as the One Who initiated, established and assured the covenant. So it is with us. Our salvation and our assurance rest on His' act and His word.

VERSE 18. *In the same day.* On the very day that the Saviour died the new covenant was established with us and became effective. *The Lord made a covenant.* The Lord's covenants are not agreements between equals, but settlements by a benefactor upon beneficiaries.

Unto thy seed have I given this land. Palestine was given to the old Israel as a type of the new land to be given to the new Israel (see on 13. 15). *The river of Egypt.* This is not the Nile, but the stream that formed the frontier of Egypt. *Unto the great river, the river Euphrates.* Israel possessed the land within these exact boundaries in Solomon's time (1 Ki. 4. 21), and might have kept it for ever, had not persistent rebellion and disobedience so soon set in.

VERSE 19. This and the two following verses mention ten nations, into whose inheritance Israel entered. This is the longest list that is anywhere given. They represent the foes of the church, at present in the heavenly places (Eph. 6. 12), who are being dispossessed by the advance of the Gospel and the faith of the saints, the initial, deadly, irretrievable blow having been dealt them on Calvary.

VERSE 20. *Rephaims.* These are formidable foes being of gigantic stature, but not too strong for the Lord.

VERSE 21. *Jebusites.* These were the inhabitants of Jerusalem. They were not dispossessed till David's time (2 Sam. 5. 6-10). It is only the heavenly David Who can lead us successfully against our foes.

CHAPTER 16

WE now come to the story of Abram's second great mistake. Hagar, the Egyptian slave-woman, is introduced into the narrative, and under persuasion from Sarai Abram takes the step of making Hagar his concubine and becoming by her the father of a son. This practice was recognized by the law and custom of the time, and Abram's act should not be regarded in the same light as similar action would be today. It is difficult to assess his motive. He may have despaired of an heir by Sarai and persuaded himself that this was the way in which God intended His promises to be fulfilled. Hagar's pregnancy caused her to adopt a superior air towards her mistress. Sarai grew angry and ill-treated her, and Hagar ran away. As she was wandering in the wilderness, she was met by the Angel of the Lord, Who made promises for her and her child, and sent her back to Sarai. Hagar and her child are the picture of the old covenant, made at Sinai, the members of which are in bondage, and of Jerusalem in Palestine, in contrast to the new covenant of the Gospel and the heavenly Jerusalem (Gal. 4. 21-31).

VERSE 1. *Bare him no children.* This barrenness is the state of the natural, fallen, sinful human heart. It can produce no fruit to the glory of God. ' They that are in the flesh cannot please God ' (Rom. 8. 8).

An handmaid, that is a bondslave, or slave-woman. Bond-service is the condition of every sinner. ' He that committeth sin is the servant of sin ' (Jo. 8. 34). Thus the chapter opens sadly with two women, one barren, the other a bondslave. The first represents the child of God before conversion, lost in Adam, dead in trespasses and sins, and under wrath as others (Eph. 2. 1-3). The second represents the dead legalist, who seeks to win merit by the works of the law, but is all the time the slave of sin.

An Egyptian, that is, belonging to the world, of which Egypt is throughout the Bible a type. The fact that Hagar was an Egyptian connects this second mistake of Abram's with the unfortunate visit to Egypt, where Abram made his first mistake (12. 10-20). We have no direct statement, but it seems likely that Sarai acquired her slave in Egypt, and that Hagar may have been among the ' maidservants ' (12. 16), whom Pharaoh gave to Abram.

Verse 2. *The Lord hath restrained me from bearing.* Notice that Sarai rightly attributed her condition to Jahweh, Whom she recognized as being the sovereign and supreme disposer of men and of nature. Her condition itself is that of the true church before the coming of the Gospel.

Go in unto my maid. Abram's relationship with Hagar did not alter her condition of bondage. In the same way the fact that the law was given by God Himself from Mount Sinai through the mediation of angels (Gal. 3. 19; Heb. 2. 2) did not mean that it could deliver from slavery to sin (Rom. 8. 3; Gal. 3. 21, 22).

Obtain children by her. The Hebrew says, ' be builded by her ' (see margin). At best this was a second-hand and artificial method, but Sarai would have had to be content with it, if God had not afterwards wrought a miracle in her life. So those under the law hoped that a redeemed humanity might be built through

obedience to the law.

Abram hearkened to the voice of Sarai. He was wrong to do so, just as Adam had been (3. 17). His faith weakened, his understanding grew clouded, and he was overborne. In the same way human persuasion may be a snare to us, especially when it comes from those with whom we are linked by natural affection, whom we are accustomed to trust, or whom we find it difficult to deny.

Verse 3. *Hagar her maid, the Egyptian.* The union was anomalous from the beginning. Hagar was an Egyptian, a woman of the world. In the story of this marriage with its disastrous consequences and tragic aftermath, we see a reinforcement of the apostle's warning, ' Be not unequally yoked together with unbelievers ' (2 Cor. 6. 14).

Ten years. This sentence teaches us two things: (1) That Abram's patience began to be exhausted. If we become impatient with God, we shall not find answers to our prayers, and we may even be led to interfere in God's purpose and dealings with us to our own sorrow and disadvantage. We are called to ' wait for God's Son from heaven,' and when He comes, all prayers will be answered (if not before), and all purposes completed (1 Thess. 1. 10). ' I waited patiently for the Lord, and He inclined unto me and heard my calling ' (Ps. 40. 1). ' Wait on the Lord; be of good courage, and He shall strengthen thy heart; wait, I say, on the Lord ' (Ps. 27. 14). (2) The sentence teaches us that a long experience of walking with God and experiencing His guidance and His promises does not render us immune from a lapse of faith, a weak decision, or a spiritual blunder. Continual dependence on God is our only safeguard.

To her husband Abram. Abram and Sarai were husband and wife. Sarai's action therefore only introduced confusion and disharmony. This is always the case, when the law is brought in alongside of the

149

Gospel. Works cannot be added to faith, where justification is in question. Similar confusion is often introduced today by a Jewish interpretation of Old Testament promises and prophecies in place of the Christian interpretation, supplied by the New Testament.

VERSE 4. *She conceived*. She was like the first covenant, which gendered to bondage (Gen. 4. 24). Her child was a slave like herself. The first covenant was a true covenant of God, but it could not set free.

Her mistress was despised. Instead of being builded (verse 2) Sarai found that she was cold-shouldered. Similarly the Jew despised the Gentile. Instead of helping and serving he looked down with contempt from the height of Sinai.

VERSE 5. These events are full of natural human interplay. Sarai blamed Abram, when the suggestion, which she herself had made, turned out to have the opposite effect from what she had intended.

VERSE 6. Abram implies that the remedy is in Sarai's own hands. In the whole of this story we find the purpose of God being worked out through ordinary human reactions. Personality stands for much in the work of God.

As it pleaseth thee. The Hebrew says ' good in thine eyes ' (see margin). Notice Sarai's *hand*, standing for authority, her *eyes*, standing for desire, and her *face*, standing for resentment and anger.

She fled. So in the days of the Old Testament the Jews sought to evade their obligation under the old covenant.

VERSE 7. *The angel of the Lord*. This is the first time that this expression occurs in the Bible. The meaning of the word ' angel ' in both testaments is sometimes representative, or exact replica (see for instance Acts 12. 15), and this seems to be its sense when used in this title. The angel of the Lord was recognised in the Old Testament to be Jahweh Himself (see for instance, Judg. 13. 3, 9, 13, 15, 16, 17, 18, 20, 21 and especially 22), and yet the very expression shows that He was thought of as a counterpart or replica of Jahweh. He was the pre-incarnate Christ, and the expression ' Angel of the Lord ' puts in short compass the exact conception, which we find in Heb. 1. 3. Christ is the brightness of the Father's glory and the express image of His Person. He is from all eternity the Word, or Revealer, of God.

Found her. True to His eternal character and ways, exactly as we find Him in the Gospels when incarnate, He came to seek the lost and found her, as He has found so many since. It is characteristic that He came to seek a slave-girl, a Gentile, who had put herself in the wrong by running away. ' The Son of man is come to seek and to save that which is lost ' (Lk. 19. 10).

By a fountain of water. This situation reveals a sense of need, and the lost sinner with such a sense is the one who is found by the Lord. *In the wilderness*. This is where every sinner wanders, lost, aimless and lonely. Here into the wilderness of sin and sadness comes the Saviour to find him. Notice that Hagar, like every sinner, had fled from the household to which she belonged, and wandered out into this wilderness of her own accord. She alone was responsible for her being there.

By the fountain in the way to Shur. If her place by the fountain revealed her sense of need, she was by the wrong fountain. It was in the way to Shur, which ' is over against Egypt ' (1 Sam. 15. 7). Her face was turned towards the world and the flesh pots of Egypt, where she wrongly hoped to find respite from the burden that oppressed her. She knew nothing of the fountain of living waters, but sought for the broken cisterns instead (Jer. 2. 13). If she had known of the true fountain, she had no more desire for it, being driven away by Sarai's treatment. But where his servant failed in witness, the Lord Himself came to seek the one who had been driven away.

VERSE 8. *Hagar, Sarai's maid.* By addressing her by name the Lord revealed that He knew her personally and all the facts of her life. So He did in the case of the Samaritan woman by the well (Jo. 4. 29). So He does with us. So He does with every lost sinner. *Whence camest thou?* The Lord asks the sinner whence he came, and by doing so arouses in him the longing for the fellowship with God, which his race has forfeited by sin, and the unfallen state, left irretrievably behind. *Whither wilt thou go?* Notice that the question is not, 'Where are you going?' God knows the answer to that question better than the sinner, who is going, usually without realising it, to hell and eternal death. That is not the question. It is, 'Where do you want to go?' This question in some form or another is asked by the Lord of every sinner, when He meets him and faces him with decision. It corresponds to the question that He asked of the impotent man, 'Wilt thou be made whole?' (Jo. 5. 6). Does the sinner want to go on to a life of sin in the world with eternal death at its end, or does he want to go to eternal life and to the throne and presence of God? The question is revealing, because it reminds the sinner that a goal and a destiny await him at the end of the way of life. *And she said.* Notice that Hagar answered openly and frankly the first of the two questions that were asked her. She did not prevaricate. She knew what lay behind her, and what she wanted to escape. This is an important stage for a sinner to reach at his first encounter with Christ through the Gospel. But she made no answer to the second. Perhaps she felt a strong attraction towards Egypt, but was afraid to acknowledge it. Perhaps she actually did not know in which of the two directions open to her she really

wanted to go. Here she was like many a sinner, who is challenged by the Gospel, and has reached a watershed in his life.

VERSE 9. *Return to thy mistress.* A command from the Lord breaks her indecision, and comes to her with authoritative power.

Submit thyself under her hands. Hagar represents the old covenant made at Sinai, and the old Jerusalem below (Gal. 4. 24, 25). The only rightful place of the old covenant is in service to the new. The law is not an end in itself. It serves the Gospel. The old covenant was not an end in itself, but prepared the way for the new. The old Jerusalem with her religions and national privileges was not an end in herself, though there are many today inclined to think and teach so. She was a type of the new. She had no reason for existing but to prepare the way for the new.

VERSE 10. *I will multiply thy seed.* The old covenant was a revelation from God. It stood within the orbit of redemption. It could engender, though only to bondage. Hagar's seed was the seed of Abraham after the flesh, and as such shared the blessing of prosperity and multiplication.

VERSE 11. *Thou art with child.* The heart of every sinner at the moment when he is challenged by the Gospel and faced with decision is pregnant with destiny.

Ishmael. The meaning of this name is 'God shall hear' (see margin). The fundamental fact of the converted man's life is that God has heard his affliction, and brought him from death to life, from condemnation to righteousness, from uncleanness to holiness, and from darkness to light. This fact is a pledge that God will hear him in any affliction, necessarily lighter, which may come upon him in the future.

VERSE 12. *A wild man,* literally, a wild ass among men. The wild ass is a symbol of savagery and carnality. There was no promise that Hagar's child would be a blessing in the world. She and her son were to play their part in the purpose of God by prefiguring the old covenant and Israel after the flesh (Gal. 4. 22-25).

His hand will be against every man. This is true of the unconverted Jews, of whom Ishmael was a type (1 Thess. 2. 15). The old Israel, which might have been a blessing, has become a curse to the world.

And every man's hand against him. History has proved this statement to apply to the unconverted Jews, of whom Ishmael was a type, throughout almost all the Christian era. Ishmael was born as an intruder into Abram's family, and it seems as if men everywhere regarded him in the same light. Judaism is likewise an intruder into the family of God, as it were. It is a revealed religion in origin, but it has perverted the revelation and misunderstood its purpose. It is obstinately opposed to the Gospel, and has never repented of its murder of the Lord. Like Ishmael, Jews and Judaism have generally been regarded as intruders by the rest of the world. But this is part of the purpose of God, directed towards leading the Jew to the Gospel, in which, as in the case of all others, lies his only hope.

In the presence of. The Hebrew has literally, ' before the face of '. The phrase is difficult, and it does not seem possible to be certain of its meaning. The most likely interpretation is that it means ' to the east of '. This was literally true of Ishmael and his descendants. Perhaps however there is also a sense, in which it applies to the antitype. Jews have been scattered throughout the world since the time of the exile in the sixth century B.C., and to a greater extent since the first century A.D. There are few civilised nations, among whose inhabitants they are not represented. They ' dwell in the presence of all ' their brethren, exposed to their contempt and unable to escape their enmity.

VERSE 13. *She called the name of the Lord.* This means that she had an insight, either a new one, or for the first time, into the character and being of God. She understood what God was like, as she had never done before. Every sinner, whom God finds, and to whom He speaks, does the same. Only the man who has been found by God and has heard the voice of God has any real understanding of God.

Thou God seest me. The revelation that came to Hagar, as it does to every sinner, is that God is interested in him. God sees him, knows him, loves him, and plans for him. Until his conversion his eyes are not open to see this, and he does not understand it. The fact that God could see her came as a revelation to Hagar, which was evidently full of comfort to her, and enabled her to return to the life that she feared. If God had seen her and provided for her in the wilderness, He could see her and protect her in Sarai's tent.

Hagar uses the name El, adding to it the form Roi, which means ' seeing ', to make a new and illuminating divine title. She could say El-Roi ,just as Melchizedek could say ' El-Elyon ' (14. 18). Notice that she does not use the name Jahweh, which either she had never heard, or was not natural to her. The holy inspiring Spirit uses the name Jahweh throughout the description of the incident, because Jahweh was working to carry out His redemptive purposes, not only in Hagar individually, but indirectly also in the birth of Ishmael as a type of the old covenant of Sinai, which was still to come. But Hagar, at any rate until this moment, knew Him only as Creator in the same sense in which the unconverted know of Him.

Have I also here looked after him that seeth me? The meaning of Hagar's question is not easy to determine except in the very general sense that her heart was full of wonder and praise. Some of the learned commentators, who have no objection to tampering with the text, have tried to turn the active words ' that seeth me' into a passive 'that is seen of me'. We have no need to follow them. Probably the question — or statement, as it really is — may have one of the two alternative meanings that follow: (1) the words 'to look after' may mean 'to see' in the sense of 'to see the light', and thus 'to live'. In this case Hagar is expressing surprise that she is still alive after having been in the presence of God. The same conception occurs in Judg. 6. 22; 13. 22, although in the later cases the persons in question speak of their seeing God and not His seeing them. This conception is a true one. It is the reaction of the convicted sinner on realising the holiness of God, and we find it expressed in other words by Simon Peter in Luke 5. 8. (2) Alternatively Hagar's words may mean — on the whole more probably—that she looked *after* the God Who had been seeing her all the time, in other words, that she had never realised that He had been seeing and caring, until *after* all this long time she had looked and seen. This also is a very true sentiment. The sinner, when he is brought to God in regeneration and conversion, wonders how it is that he has never seen Him before.

VERSE 14. The well, that is to say, the place, where Hagar had been vainly seeking for satisfaction, transformed by her meeting with God into the greatest experience of her life, was given a new name. Thenceforward it meant something different to Hagar, just as the place and time of his conversion do to every sinner. *Beer-lahai-roi*, that is, the well of Him that liveth and seeth me (marg.) The expression 'well of' may refer to possession. To Hagar it was God's well, because there He had met with her. This implies that she realised that God made the well, set it in the place where it was, and brought her to it. All that was true of Hagar, as in the spiritual sense it is true of the converted sinner. Alternatively the expression may mean 'the well, which has the name of'. In

this case, though it amounts to the same thing, Hagar is recognising by the name which she gave to the well, that in all her experience God was the mover and actor. Him that liveth. This is the great realisation of the converted sinner. At his conversion God becomes real to him. Christ becomes his living Saviour and Friend. So with Hagar. She had heard the name of God mentioned again and again in the tents of Abram and Sarai. Perhaps she realised that He was real to Abram at least. But He had never been real to her herself. It needed a personal experience before the God Whom she knew by hearsay became to her the *living* God. *And seeth me*. This is the second realisation that comes to the sinner at conversion. His eyes are opened to see that God cares for him, knows all his life, and has been watching him. Before his conversion he was tempted to think that God took no interest in him. Now he knows that He sees and judges and loves. 'Thou art about my path and about my bed, and spiest out all may ways' (Ps. 139. 3). Every true conversion commemorates the well Beer-lahai-roi. Is the reader certain that he has been to the well?

It is between Kadesh and Bered. The well was an actual well, really existing, in a place where it could still be traced and found. The story of Hagar is no legend. It was sober historical fact. The scene was known. There is therefore no question that the God Who found and cared for Hagar is the True and Living God, Who could do the same for the readers of the story, and can do the same for us. He is a God, Who acts in this present life among living men and women. Here lies the significance of the true historicity of the narrative of the Bible. These things are not things that the writers represented God out of their own imaginations as doing, nor are they moral stories without basis in fact told to illustrate the character and actions of God. They are real, and their truth ought to be to us a source of assurance and encouragement. If God did these things for these actual living persons on our plane of life, He will do them for us as well. In the same way to meet with God in conversion, to be found by Him, is the actual experience of many. It happens every day. We have only to walk the road from Kadesh to Bered in order to have proof. We need only ask real living men and women.

VERSE 15. *Hagar bare Abram a son.* So the old covenant produced an Israel, God's firstborn (Ex. 4. 22). There was a ' church in the wilderness ' (Acts 7. 38). There was a ' people of the Lord ' (2 Sam. 1. 12). They dwelt alone, and were not reckoned among the nations (Num. 23. 9). Yet they were gendered to bondage (Gal. 4. 24). They broke the Lord's covenant, because they had no moral power to keep it (Jer. 31. 32).

Ishmael. This means ' God hears '. Abram recognised an answer to prayer in Ishmael's birth. It was an answer, which like others gave Abram what he asked for, but not the very best, which he might have had, if he had not wanted and asked for something less than the best. We are very much like him.

VERSE 16. *Fourscore and six years old.* This was a long time to wait, but not as long as God intended. Abram's faith had again failed him, for he felt that the time was past when God could act, and that he must take matters into his own hands. As a matter of fact the time had not yet come.

CHAPTER 17

IN this important chapter we have the account of the covenant of circumcision. The Lord appears to Abram, renews the covenant and promises, and changes his name to Abraham. As a sign and token of the covenant Abraham and all his house are to be circumcised. Sarai's name is also changed to Sarah, and

a son is promised to her. Gracious promises were also made with regard to Ishmael. Then in obedience to God's command Abraham with Ishmael and all his household submitted to circumcision.

VERSE 1. *Ninety years old and nine.* There had been a further thirteen years of waiting, during which life in the tents had gone on without incidents of importance. This follows the pattern on which God worked during Old Testament history. There were intervals between such times of crisis as the exodus, the establishment of the kingdom, or the miracles of Elijah. It is also the pattern to which God usually works in the individual lives of believers.

The Lord. Notice this occurrence of the name Jahweh at the beginning of a chapter, in which the name ' God ' is generally used. This is another piece of evidence that makes critical theories based on the divine names appear improbable. Jahweh appeared to Abram in pursuit of His redemptive purpose.

Appeared. As in 12 .7. Sometimes communication was made by undefined means (13. 14), sometimes by vision (15. 1). So God has more than one way of communicating with us. The normal channel is through Scripture, but He may speak through the providential disposal of our circumstances, or occasionally directly in our hearts.

I am the Almighty God. This fact appears as the basis of the covenant and promises that follow. Everything depends in the first instance upon what God is. Blessing and goodness flow essentially from His nature. The fact of our relationship with Him is the foundation on which all our blessings rest. The Hebrew name is El Shaddai, the name by which God told Moses He was known to the patriarchs (Ex. 6. 3). Thus Jahweh, the Redeemer, appeals to the fact that He is El, the Creator, to Whom the duty of His responsible creatures is owed, Who also is capable of carrying out the promises that He makes by His almighty wisdom and power.

Walk before me, and be thou perfect. These two commands are not left to Abram to obey in his own strength. Like all commands of God they carry with them and in themselves the power and ability for obedience. They are like the Word of God, by which the world was created (Gen. 1. 3), or the word of Christ to the paralysed man, which he was able' instantly to obey (Mt. 12. 13). The two commands cover respectively the life of the believer in this world, and secondly in the world to come. Spiritual life in this world consists of walking before God. The idea of walking arises from the conception of life as a journey, brought about by the passage of time. In Hebrew it expresses conduct or behaviour. To walk before God therefore is to carry out every action, speak every word, and think every thought with the realisation that one is in the presence of God. In the world to come the believer will be perfect. He already has a perfect standing with God, based on the finished work of the Lord Jesus Christ (Col. 1. 12; Heb. 10. 14). On the day of resurrection and thenceforward he will have perfect sanctification (1 Jo. 3. 2; 1 Thess. 5. 23, 24). To be like Christ means to be perfect, and this was the purpose of God for the believer in eternity past (Rom. 8. 29). This same perfection is God's promise and command for believers of this Gospel age, as the Saviour tells us (Mt. 5. 48). In the original Greek the verb is in the future indicative, and may be read either as a command, or as a statement for the future. The application is completely true in both these senses. In the Gospel this perfection is connected with the expression of love (Mt. 5. 43-48). If we choose to take the marginal reading in our verse, *upright,* or *sincere,* we reach the same conclusion, for both these words imply an absence of deviation from performing or willing the will of God. Such a translation would emphasise the uprightness and sincerity of heart that proceed from justification, and we should then see in these two commands the twofold blessing, which God bestows upon every believer in regeneration though in reverse order, sanctification and justification.

VERSE 2. *I will make my covenant.* This means that God would bring Abram into a special relationship with Himself. The scriptural covenants are not agreements between equals, but settlements by a benefactor upon beneficiaries. Our own relationship with God depends upon the new covenant foretold in the Old Testament (Jer. 31. 31), and established by Jesus on the night of His betrayal (Mt. 26. 28), being ratified in His blood.

Multiply. This is always the result of entering into covenant relationship with God. Fruitfulness follows. Flowing from our own relationship with God in Christ comes the blessing of others won for Him. As time goes on, and those whom we have led to Christ bring others, the numbers of those to whom we shall have been a channel of blessing grows larger and larger (Jo. 7. 38).

VERSE 3. *Fell on his face.* This is the attitude of adoration and worship. It implies also the sense of unworthiness to look upon God. It is the right attitude for us all in the presence of God and in the awareness of His grace.

God talked with him, as He loves to talk with all His children. To us He speaks through His Word, or occasionally by the Holy Spirit in our hearts.

VERSE 4. This verse repeats verse 2 in different language. On the covenant see verse 2.

A father of many nations. This is the tenth of the fourteen promises made to Abram. The many nations are believing Gentiles, brought to God through the Gospel by faith in Christ (Rom. 4. 17). Abram is the father of all believers in the sense (1) that he is the exemplar of their faith; (2) that he is the natural ancestor of the Lord Jesus Christ, to Whom all believers are united. Natural descent from Abram carries no promise of blessing (Mt. 3. 9). Thus in this promise the Gospel is foreshadowed and the existence of the predominantly Gentile church predicted.

VERSE 5. *Thy name.* The change of name implied a change of nature and the entrance into a new relationship with God. Abram had possessed the new nature for many years (15. 6), probably since his call in Ur of the Chaldees. The covenant of circumcision was the sign and seal of it. By this covenant Abram and his family entered formally into a new relationship with God. They became Jews, as it were. Every child of God receives this new nature, when he is converted (Eph. 4. 22-24; Col. 3. 9, 10).

Abram. The meaning is ' Exalted Father '.

Abraham. The meaning is ' Father of a great multitude '. The change of name thus has two effects (1) Abram ceased to be exalted. This happens, whenever a sinner is converted to God. Self is abased, and Christ takes its place on the throne of the believer's life. (2) Abraham became the source of blessing to a great multitude. This also happens to a sinner at his conversion. Before it he is barren spiritually. Afterwards he becomes a means of blessing to many.

Have I made thee. The sense is that God had appointed Abraham to be the father of many nations. This was a step in God's purpose of redeeming the world. All through these events we see this purpose moving forward in sovereign power. God's appointment of Abraham as the father of ' the nations of them that are saved ' (Rev. 21. 24) assured the then future salvation of those nations, and in making this promise to Abraham God was carrying out the eternal purpose, that He had formed before the foundation of the world.

VERSE 6. *Exceeding fruitful.* This is a repetition in different words of the promise made to Abraham in 13. 15, 16. Fruitfulness is the central part of God's blessing. He looks for it in the Christian (Jo. 15. 2). It consists (1) of the ninefold fruit of the Spirit (Gal. 5. 22) and (2) of souls won for Christ (Col. 1. 5, 6).

I will make nations of thee. This is the eleventh promise to Abraham. Under the old covenant it was fulfilled in Israel, Edom, the Ishmaelites, Midianites and others. Under the new it is fulfilled in believing Gentiles and Jews, who form ' the nations of them that are saved ' (Rev. 21. 24).

Kings shall come out of thee. This is the twelfth promise. Under the old covenant it was fulfilled in the kings of David's line, the various dynasties that ruled the northern kingdom of Israel, the kings of Edom (Gen. 36. 31-39), and others. Under the new it is fulfilled supremely in Christ (Lk. 1. 32, 33), and also in all the faithful, who are a kingdom of priests (1 Pet. 2. 9; Rev. 5. 10), and will reign for ever and ever (Rev. 22. 5).

VERSE 7. *I will establish my covenant.* God not only made a covenant, He established it, that is to say, He made it firm and sure. It was established by the death of Christ on Calvary, which made its fulfilment possible. In the same way the covenant of salvation made with us is assured and unshakeable.

Me. If God is a party to the covenant, as He is, it can never be broken. *Thee.* Abraham was personally included in the covenant. His personal salvation was assured by it.

Thy seed after thee. This includes the natural seed, to which the ' generations ' refer, but also the spiritual seed, which is Christ (Gal. 3. 16) and His people (Gal. 3. 29).

In their generations. The allusion is to the generations of the Jews, who underwent circumcision till the coming of the Gospel. *An everlasting covenant.* This proves that the covenant ultimately deals with eternal and spiritual things. Mary the mother of Jesus saw its fulfilment brought about by the first coming of Christ (Lk. 1. 55, in the context of the preceding verses), and Zacharias, the father of John the Baptist, saw the same thing in the whole train of events that made up the incarnation and redemption (Lk. 1. 68-73).

To be a God unto thee. Abraham had already entered into a new relationship with God by faith, as do all the justified (15. 6). This covenant of circumcision was the sign and seal of it. God is the God of all men in the sense of being their Creator; but stands in a special relationship to the believer as his Father and Saviour. *And to thy seed after thee.* This promise is fulfilled in both the typical and real seed. In the Old Testament under the old covenant God was in a special sense the God of Israel. Other nations had their idols. Many in Israel followed idols, but Jahweh was the nation's God. References proving this could be multiplied throughout the Old Testament. But the relationship with Old Testament Israel, being a relationship with a nation in the flesh, was but a type and shadow of the new and true. The promise is fulfilled in the relationship into which God enters in Christ with all who come to Him by Christ (Jo. 1. 12).

Verse 8. In this verse the eighth promise to Abraham, which we first find in 13. 15, is repeated.

Unto thee. Abraham never personally possessed Palestine, but he is ' heir of the world ' (Rom. 4. 13), and will possess the world to come. See on 13. 15. *Thy seed after thee.* This was fulfilled (1) in the conquest of Canaan by Joshua, (2) in the entry of the redeemed into the new heaven and new earth. See on 13. 15.

The land wherein thou art a stranger. The Hebrew says literally, ' the land of thy sojournings '. This is a parable of the life of the believer in this world. He is a stranger in it. Here he has no abiding city (Heb.

13. 14), but the world will one day be his.

> ' I am a stranger here,
>   Heaven is my home,
> Only a sojourner,
>   Heaven is my home.
> And I shall one day stand
> Upon my Lord's right hand,
> Heaven is my fatherland,
>   Heaven is my home.'

All the land of Canaan. Though promised to Abraham, the land then belonged to Canaan. In the same way the enemies of the Gospel and of mankind now occupy what will one day be our inheritance in the heavenly places (Eph. 6. 12). *An everlasting possession.* See on 13. 15.

I will be their God. This has a fulfilment under either covenant. See on verse 7.

Verse 9. *God.* The chapter began with the name Jahweh (verse 1). After the use of El in the name El-Shaddai (verse 1) and of Elohim (God) in verses 7 and 8 the narrative passes naturally into the use of Elohim. This does not at all fit the critical theories.

Thou shalt keep my covenant. God asks for co-operation as He does still. Abraham was to set his seal to the covenant and sign his name, as it were, beneath that of the Almighty Benefactor. *Thy seed after thee in their generations.* The whole family came within the covenant, and each member of it was to set his seal to it. This was to be done ' in their generations '. There are no generations in the world to come (Mt. 22. 30), and the expression therefore proves that the covenant was temporary and had reference to this world only.

Verse 10. *This is my covenant.* This means that this is the part that Abraham and his seed are to play in the keeping of the covenant.

Between me. God's part in the covenant was to be a God to the family and nation and to give them the land of Canaan. *You.* The word is plural. It refers to the then existing members of Abraham's house. Ishmael was brought within the covenant of circumcision (verse 23) and the whole household was included (verse 23). *Thy seed,* that is to say, the direct descendants of Abraham. From the beginning the covenant was wider in scope than the actual seed. Thus in every generation many underwent circumcision, who were outside the true seed of Abraham (Rom. 2. 28, 29). *Every man child.* Not only was the covenant of circumcision temporary and not eternal, it also was concerned with only one sex. This does not mean that the women among the seed of Abraham were outside the covenant and unable to look at Jahweh as their God. It means that the one sex was appointed as representative of the whole. The man underwent circumcision. The woman was within the covenant, because she was represented by those in whom the covenant was sealed. This is a faint picture of our own standing before God. The Lord Jesus has undergone death for us, and we are within the covenant, because represented by Him. *Shall be circumcised.* Circumcision has no place under the Gospel (1 Cor. 7. 19; Gal. 5. 6; 6. 15; Col. 3. 11). It is replaced by baptism. Circumcision was for everyone born into the old covenant, which he entered by natural birth. Baptism is for everyone born into the new covenant, which is entered by spiritual birth.

Verse 11. *The flesh.* Circumcision was in the flesh, and the sign of a covenant in the flesh, which is a shadow and type of the new covenant.

A token. This is more than a proof or pledge. It is both a pledge and a sign, or picture. Thus the apostle Paul says that circumcision was a sign, and also a seal of Abraham's righteousness. In what sense was circumcision a token, or sign? (1) It was normally seen and known only by the circumcised individual himself. It was not a mark intended to be seen by others. This fact emphasised to the individual (a) God's care for him personally and reception of him

personally as a partaker in the covenant blessings; (b) his individual responsibilities as a member of the covenant. (2) Being situated in the organ of generation the mark of circumcision brought home to the circumcised man that he was a member of a whole family, which was in special relationship with God, and that he would pass on to his children this covenant relationship and have the responsibility of bringing them up in it. (3) It would be a permanent reminder to the one who had undergone it that he was conscrated to God, and its situation in his body would be a peculiar and emphatic reminder to him that God required the ' putting off the body of the sins of the · flesh ' (Col. 2. 11), which under the Gospel is the permanent spiritual reality, of which circumcision under the old covenant was the type. Circumcision was thus a sign, token or picture of the meaning of the covenant and of the inner spiritual realities, to which it pointed. In these things circumcision shows a contrast to baptism, which took its place under the Gospel (Col. 2. 11, 12). Unlike circumcision baptism was not secret. It is an open acknowledgment and confession. The open light of the Gospel has been shed on the darkness of sin. Unlike circumcision baptism leaves no permanent mark on the baptised. It is concerned with the spirit. It expresses the fact, especially when considered in contrast with circumcision, that the blessings of the Gospel are received in the heart and not in the flesh. In common with circumcision however baptism speaks emphatically, though in quite different words, as it were, of the ' putting off the body of the sins of the flesh.' The apostle Paul tells us that circumcision was not only a sign of the covenant, but also a *seal* of the righteousness, which previously belonged to Abraham by faith (Rom. 4. 11). We are probably justified in regarding the seal in two distinct senses. (1) The covenant with its attendant circumcision was a *confirmation by God* of His gift of righteousness to Abraham in the nature of a permanent reminder to him and encouragement to his faith. In the case of all the circumcised descendants it was not a proof of individual justification. It remained a proof of the justification of their ancestor Abraham, but in the case of all those who came to be properly instructed as to its meaning it would be a call to follow the example of Abraham's faith and appropriate God's gift of righteousness. Its presence in the body might serve to stimulate enquiry about its meaning. (2) The act of circumcision was a seal set *by Abraham* to his faith in God and of his appropriation of it by faith. Both these aspects of the seal appear in baptism. It is something tangible, appointed by God, as a seal and proof to the believer of the spiritual change that has been wrought in his heart. The confession made by the believer at his baptism is also his own seal to his acceptance by faith of God's gift of righteousness.

VERSE 12. In this verse we have a fourfold description of the proper subjects for circumcision. The whole is typical of spiritual realities. The first subject of circumcision is *he that is eight days old*. It is easy to become fanciful about the significance of numbers in the Bible and speculative notions of their meaning ought to be avoided. At the same time it is clear that seven is the round number of the Bible. Counting goes by sevens in the same sense as ours goes by tens. This being so, it is easy to see that at eight a new start is made, and there are enough examples of this in Scripture to enable us to take the number eight as sometimes significant of regeneration and newness of life. It is difficult not to think that this is the point of the fixing of the eighth day as the time for circumcision. The fact tells us that those who are in covenant relationship with God are regenerate and living in newness of life.

The second subject for circum-

cision is *every man child in your generations*. (This covers of course the same class as the first). The emphasis here is upon the individual converted and brought into the family of Christ as the generations of the church proceed. This man enters into covenant relationship with God.

He that is born in the house. This covers the same ground as the last, but the emphasis is slightly different. The words ' your generations' perhaps stressed the part played by the Christian in bringing others in. These words emphasise the fact of regeneration. Everyone, who is in special covenant relationship with God, is born in His house, begotten by Him to everlasting life through the operation of the Holy Ghost in his heart by the seed of the Word (Jo. 3. 3, 7; Jas. 1. 18; 1 Pet. 1. 23; Eph. 5. 26; Tit. 3. 5).

Bought with money. Here is another typical description of the elect. They are redeemed, not indeed with corruptible things such as silver and gold, but with the precious blood of Christ (1 Pet. 1. 19). They are bought *of any stranger*. Before their redemption they were slaves to Satan and sin, and of their vain conversation delivered unto them by their fathers (1 Pet. 1. 18). Being redeemed, they are brought into covenant relationship with God in Christ.

Which is not of thy seed. The redeemed are not born into the world of the seed of Abraham, or children of God. They are ' children of wrath, even as others' (Eph. 2. 3), but they are given the right to become children of God (Jo. 1. 12). There is a special application to Gentiles, who were aliens to the commonwealth of Israel and strangers to the covenants of promise (Eph. 2. 12). All are brought safely in and given the right to the circumcision of Christ (Col. 2. 11).

VERSE 13. *He that is born in thy house, and he that is bought with thy money.* See on verse 12.

Must needs be circumcised. The covenant requires co-operation on the part of the redeemed. All of the seed of Abraham who failed to be circumcised invalidated the covenant in their own case (verse 14). God requires of the Christian the putting off the body of the sins of the flesh, and burial and resurrection with Christ (Col. 2. 11, 12), that is to say, the renunciation of self (Mt. 16. 24) and the dedication of the life to the One Who died for him and rose again (2 Cor. 5. 15). No one who does not realise that his conversion involves this, or who is unwilling to undertake it, is truly converted (Lk. 14. 26, 27, 33).

In your flesh for an everlasting covenant. Notice that it does not say ' *as* an everlasting covenant ', but *for* one. No covenant in flesh could be an everlasting covenant. ' All flesh is grass . . . The grass withereth, the flower fadeth ' (Isa. 40. 6, 7). The covenant of circumcision was *for* an everlasting covenant, that is to say, (1) It typically represented the everlasting covenant established by Christ, circumcision being a type and picture of the Christian circumcision mentioned in Col. 2. 11; and 2. It led on, and pointed, to the everlasting covenant. It was preparatory to it. It was intended to represent to Old Testament Israel the principles on which the new covenant would be made. It was not in itself an everlasting covenant (1 Cor. 7. 19; Gal. 5. 2, 3, 6; 6. 15).

VERSE 14. *The uncircumcised man child,* that is to say, the one who fails to avail himself of the covenant mercy and blessings. God did not cut off in judgment the eight-day child. That was the normal time for circumcision. But there were exceptions. The people born in the wilderness were not circumcised as infants, but underwent the rite on the borders of Canaan, before they could inherit the land (Josh. 5. 2-9).

That soul shall be cut off from his people. All who neglect God's great salvation will be blotted out of the book of life and eternally lost (Heb. 2. 3; Psa. 69. 28). The Bible

teaches that Christ died for all men, not only for the elect (1 Jo. 2. 2), for the former potentially, and for the latter actually. The names of all ever born are thus *potentially* written in the book of life. Neglect to take advantage of Christ's offer of salvation and of the benefits of His passion causes the name to be blotted out from the book.

Broken my covenant, that is to say, invalidated it, so far as he himself is concerned.

VERSE 15. *Sarai.* The meaning of this name does not seem to be clear. ' Combatant ', or ' Heroine ', has been suggested.

Sarah shall her name be. The change of name given to Sarai at the same time as to Abram shows that she too was brought into covenant relationship with God. The covenant blessings were not restricted to Abraham and his male descendants, but Sarah was included. The change of name represents a change of status, and is typical of the change of nature, received in regeneration. ' Sarah ' means Princess or Queen. In contrast with Hagar she represents the free Jerusalem above (Gal. 4. 26), the bride of Christ (Rev. 21. 2, 9). She is therefore rightly called the queen. ' Upon thy right hand did stand the queen in gold of Ophir ' (Ps. 45. 9).

VERSE 16. *I will bless her.* God's blessing turns barrenness into fertility. The consequence of His blessing us must be spiritual fertility. the winning of others to the Saviour.

Give thee a son. Notice that children are gifts of God, and that the sex of the child is determined by God. This means direct divine control of the inner secret forces in the body of the father. Nothing happens by chance. God is sovereign of all His creation, and maintains it from moment to moment by the Word of His power.

She shall be a mother of nations. The Hebrew is, ' She shall become nations '. From Sarah descended Edom, Israel and Judah. As mother of the seed of Abraham she is the mother of all believing Gentiles, and finally of ' the nations of them that are saved ' (Rev. 21. 24).

Kings of people shall be of her. ' People ' is plural in Hebrew. The kings are those of Edom (Gen. 36. 31-39), Saul and the various northern dynasties, the house of David, and above all the Lord Jesus Christ and His people, who are kings (Rev. 1. 6: 22. 5).

VERSE 17. *Fell upon his face.* This attitude of worship is the proper one for a creature before his Creator, a sinner before his Judge, or a redeemed being before his Redeemer. Perfect love casts out fear (1 Jo. 4. 18), but the duty of worship can never be superseded in this world, or in that which is to come (see Rev. 4. 8-11).

Laughed. Was this the laugh of contemptuous unbelief, as was the case with Sarah in 18. 12, or that of exultant joy, as was the case with her in 21. 6? Taken in isolation, or with the immediate context alone, the passage seems to read more naturally like the former. If this is so, however. it is difficult to see how the promise could have been repeated and expanded immediately afterwards. Moreover Sarah asked a similar question at the time of her laugh of exaltation (21. 7). If this was a laugh of unbelief, God dealt with it very mercifully. It was this very promise that the apostle Paul tells us was received by Abraham with triumphant faith. He says that he was fully confident that God was able to overcome the physical difficulties (Rom. 4. 19-21). It is therefore reasonable to conclude that this laugh of Abraham's arose from triumphant faith and exultant joy. We too may laugh for the same reason, and shall certainly do so in the world to come (Isa. 65. 13. 14; 66. 14).

Said in his heart. Perhaps he did not intend to express his pent-up feelings to God, Who heard however the thoughts of his heart, as if they had been spoken aloud.

Shall a child be born unto him that is an hundred years old? And shall Sarah that is ninety years old, bear? In asking these questions. Abraham disregarded the physical impossibilities, showed himself strong in faith, and gave glory to God (Rom. 4. 19, 20).

VERSE 18. *O that Ishmael might live before thee.* Those who think that the laugh of verse 17 was an expression of unbelief interpret these words as a prayer that Ishmael might inherit the promises in view of Abraham's mistaken notion that he could never have a son by Sarah. More reasonably they are a prayer that in view of the coming birth of a son to Sarah Ishmael might not be altogether excluded. The words *live before thee* may mean (1) spend his life in the conscious presence of God, and be a worshipper of, and believer in, Jahweh. This is a prayer worthy of Abraham. (2) The words may mean ' receive eternal life '. This also is a prayer worthy of Abraham, but it perhaps savours too much of the later Gospel age. (3) The words may mean ' be alive in the eyes of God ' rather than dead and unnoticed, be real to God, and thus be the object of God's care. If the words can mean this, it would seem well in agreement with Hebrew idiom. It is a prayer that any godly father might well pray for his child. It is a prayer which accords with deeper principles, of which Abraham may have known only very little. The elect are those who ' live before ' God.

VERSE 19. God turns to reassure Abraham about the birth of Isaac before answering his request for Ishmael. *Sarah thy wife.* Notice that this promise is (1) definite, (2) detailed, (3) emphatic. ' Sing. O barren, thou that didst not bear ' (Isa. 54. 1). Sarah is Jerusalem above (Gal. 4. 26), which before the time of the Gospel was quite barren. *Isaac.* This means ' laughter '. The commemoration of the laughter of verse 17 seems conclusive proof that it sprang from exultant faith.

I will establish my covenant with him. Isaac was to be in a special relationship with God, which Ishmael did not experience. *For an everlasting covenant.* This relationship was to lead on to the new and everlasting covenant, established in the blood of Jesus. *His seed after him.* Israel after the flesh was in a special relationship with God under the old covenant. The Lord Jesus Christ was in a unique relationship, and the church is in a special relationship under the new covenant.

VERSE 20. *As for Ishmael.* Ishmael and his blessing were, so to speak, by-products of the covenant. In the same way blessing in the earthly and material sphere have accompanied the Gospel in the world. A man converted from a life of vice is blessed in his home life. The home of the converted drunkard is immeasurably changed. Happiness and order take the place of discomfort and misery. The man who dedicates his substance to God is often greatly blessed materially. The nation that recognises the Gospel officially accepts or establishes it, or encourages its spread, knows a dignity and freedom, that are absent where the Gospel is suppressed or unknown. These things are by-products. They are not the real purpose or aim of the Gospel, but they are valuable evidence of its truth. Thus Ishmael's blessing, though outside the covenant, might well have provided proof that the God of Abraham was the true and living God. *I have heard thee.* God shows that He attends to, and answers, the prayers of His faithful people.

Five statements are made about Ishmael. (1) *I have blessed him.* It would not be proper to draw too definite a conclusion from the tense of this statement, Hebrew construction being so different from our own. At the same time there is no need to overlook the fact that it is in the past. God had already blessed Ishmael. We may consider this to have been (a) in the formation of His sovereign purposes in eternity past,

purposes which embrace not only the elect, but all things; (b) as the immediate response to Abraham's prayer, made at the moment of its utterance (Dan. 9. 23; 10. 12), or even before it was uttered (Isa. 65. 24).

(2) *Will make him fruitful.* Blessing and fruitfulness are inextricably intertwined in Scripture and in the purpose of God. Ishmael's fruitfulness was in the natural, not the spiritual sphere, but it was part of the fulfilment of the promise made to Abraham (verse 6).

(3) *Will multiply him exceedingly.* Again this was in the natural sphere. We catch a glimpse of its fulfilment in Jud. 6. 5 compared with Jud. 8. 24. Multiplication is the normal result of blessing (see on 1. 22), and if we have been blessed with all spiritual blessings in the heavenlies in Christ (Eph. 1. 3), we shall multiply spiritually by the winning of souls for Him.

(4) *Twelve princes.* God sets the bounds of the nations and determines the numbers of the peoples and the increase of families. Ishmael's children were themselves to be leaders. The blessing was to be worthy of the One Who bestowed it, and of the promises made to Abraham.

(5) *A great nation.* So he became. His descendants interfered from time to time in the history of Israel, generally in a hostile sense (Gen. 37. 25, 28; Jud. 6-8).

In considering this blessing we must not forget that Ishmael was a type of the old covenant, of Jerusalem that is now, and of Israel after the flesh (Gal. 4. 25). The blessings of Abraham overflowed to Israel after the flesh, although as a nation they have never been under the new and everlasting covenant. They too were blessed in the purpose of God. They too were fruitful and multiplied (Ex. 1. 7). They too produced princes and leaders, and they too became a great nation (1 Ki. 4. 20, 21), and but for disobedience might have remained so.

VERSE 21. *My covenant.* Isaac was to be the ancestor of Christ. His descendants, and not Ishmael's, were to be in special relationship with God. He was to be the heir of the blessings and promises, which go eventually back to the primitive pronouncement recorded in 3. 15. Notice what this verse teaches us of the sovereign election of God. He chooses Isaac and excludes Ishmael.

At this set time. This is not a reference to the period of gestation. Isaac was not conceived immediately, the events described in chapters 18-20 taking place first (see 21. 1, 2). The expression fixes a definite date (see 21. 2) in the following year, which may have been mentioned to Abraham in terms of the Mesopotamian calendar, to which he was accustomed. When the passage came to be edited, presumably by Moses, and perhaps translated into Hebrew, we can understand the omission of the date, if it was expressed in terms which the Israelites would not understand. Again God's sovereign purpose is seen at work, fixing the proper moment for Isaac's birth. 'My times are in Thy hand.'

VERSE 22. *Left off talking.* God says no single word that is unnecessary. His Word is perfect, and cannot be added to without being corrupted.

Went up. Spatial movement in a strict sense is irrelevant in the case of the Divine Being, Who fills heaven and earth (Jer. 23. 24), but the movement that here took place, or that appeared to take place, was significant in two ways. (1) As a *departure* it exemplified and reinforced the fact of God's separation from man because of sin. God visits man in mercy and grace in order to explain and forward His purposes of love, but He cannot dwell with him. That will take place in the world to come, when all barriers between God and the redeemed will have been broken down (Rev. 21. 3). To the extent to which they are already broken down He dwells now in the heart of the believer by faith (Jo. 14. 23; Eph. 3. 17). (2) As an ascension God's movement from Abraham signified

that He dwells *above* man, as is consistently taught throughout the Bible. God is in heaven, from the viewpoint of this world beyond the sky, man is on earth. This means that God is higher and greater than man. God reigns above. God is a king. Man owes Him worship and reverence. In the unseen world at the centre of all being is the almighty and eternal throne of God. The actual effect upon our minds of this conception may be measured to some extent by considering the opposite, if we may do so for one moment for this specific purpose without irreverence or blasphemy before dismissing the picture for ever. Think then of a theophany concluding by a descent into the ground.

VERSE 23. *Ishmael his son.* Ishmael was not included within the scope of the covenant (verse 21), yet he was circumcised because of his natural descent from Abraham. The situation is the same in the case of Old Testament Israel, which Ishmael represents (Gal. 4. 25).

Born in his house. See verse 12.

Bought with his money. See on verse 12.

Every male. The one sex was representative of the whole.

Circumcised. See on verse 11.

The selfsame day. This was a great act of faith. It meant that for some days all the males were incapacitated and the little community helpless in a foreign land among potential enemies and actual strangers. Compare Gen. 34. 24-26. This is the exact situation of the church of Christ. By her spiritual circumcision, in which she puts off the body of the sins of the flesh (Col. 2. 11), she is debarred from the use of violence, guile, or any other worldly method in self-defence. Her members are sent out into the world as lambs in the midst of wolves (Mt. 10. 16). She is humanly speaking as helpless among her enemies in the world, as was Abraham and his household immediately after their circumcision. The blood of her martyrs has freely flowed in almost every generation. It has been said that on a conservative estimate the church of Rome alone is responsible for fifty million of them. But this helplessness is only apparent. She is protected and sustained by mighty unseen forces (2 Ki. 6. 17; 1 Jo. 4. 4), so that it falls out that the blood of the martyrs and the sufferings of the church become signs of strength rather than weakness and greatly assist the cause of the Gospel rather than hindering it.

As God had said unto him. Here is the foundation, upon which Abraham's faith rested. His trust in God's Word led him and enabled him to perform an act, which natural common sense might have suggested to be the height of folly. His faith in God demanded obedience to God's command, and gave him the assurance that he would gain rather than lose by obeying it. Exactly the same principles sustain the church of Christ in the Gospel age. In actual fact no danger, or harm, came to Abraham, or his household.

VERSE 24. *Ninety years old and nine.* No age is too great to receive blessing from God, or to enter into new ways of obedience, especially in the case of those accustomed to years of simple trust.

VERSE 25. *Thirteen years old.* Ishmael was at the threshold of his manhood, when this formal entry into covenant relationship would be likely to make the greatest impression upon him. All his life thenceforward he would carry in his body a reminder of his father's God, so that he would have no excuse for unbelief, disobedience or rebellion. In a better state still is the boy in whose heart the seed of the Word and the knowledge of God have been sown. There is material in the heart on which the Holy Spirit can work at any later period in life.

VERSE 26. *In the selfsame day.* See on verse 23. Notice also that Abraham's obedience was immediate. He

did not dally, or procrastinate. He obeyed directly and at once. This is the pattern to which our obedience as Christians should conform.

VERSE 27. *Born in the house.* See on verse 12.

Bought with money of the stranger. See on verse 12.

CHAPTER 18

THIS important chapter divides into two sections: (1) the promise to Sarah of a son (1-15), and (2) the intercession of Abraham for Sodom (16-33). Jahweh Himself with two angels appears to Abraham, who offers them hospitality without at first realising their identity. The promise of Isaac's birth is overheard by Sarah, who laughs at it, and is rebuked for doing so. The Lord announces to Abraham the coming destruction of Sodom, and the angels pass on towards the city, while Abraham remains with Jahweh, interceding for any righteous that there might be in the city. The two great lessons to be found in the chapter are (1) the almighty sovereign power of the Lord and His ability to perform what He promises in the face of apparently insurmountable difficulties (verse 14), and (2) the efficacy of persistent intercessory prayer.

VERSE 1. *The Lord appeared.* He was, and is, always present, but as a rule unseen. Now He makes Himself visible. This was undoubtedly an appearance of the second Person of the Holy Trinity, the pre-incarnate Christ, often called the Angel of the Lord (see on 16. 7). No man has seen, or can see, the Father (1 Tim. 6. 16), but the only-begotten Son, Who is in His bosom, has revealed Him (Jo. 1. 18). The theophany was, as always, for the purpose of promise. and blessing. If God in any sense shows Himself to us, we may be certain that such is His purpose.

In the plains. The true meaning is perhaps ' by the oaks '.

He sat in the tent door. Note the

occasion on which the Lord appeared. It was not when Abraham was busily engaged, but when he was at rest. In the quiet of noonday with its opportunities for meditation Abraham was in a position to receive the Lord. Notice also that the interruption of his daily labours was caused by the natural circumstance of the heat of the day. In the same way our own activity may be interrupted by a cause which appears natural and ordinary, or by illness or ill-health, or even for purposes of recreation. The heat of the sun is often in the Bible a picture of pressure, tribulation, or trouble (Isa. 49. 10; Rev. 7. 16). So if we find that pressure of any sort is interrupting our activity and forcing us to rest, we may be certain that the hand of the Lord is at work, and we may suspect that we are being prepared to receive some particular revelation, or blessing.

VERSE 2. *He lift up his eyes.* Abraham seems to have looked up, before he was aware of the presence of his visitors. If so, the implication is that he was in a state of expectancy. If we are expecting blessing, and if we lift up our eyes and look to God for it, we are likely to receive it.

Three men. The patristic interpretation of the three men as the three Persons of the Holy Trinity was adopted by many of the Reformers, and Archbishop Cranmer placed this passage in the lectionary of the Church of England as an alternative for the evening of Trinity Sunday. The interpretation, though it is faithful to scriptural truth, may be said to be not without nobility of conception, and should be regarded with respect on the ground that it appealed to the great reformers, seems yet to be open to at least three objections: (1) There is a suspicion of crudity about it. (2) It tends towards tritheism. (3) Most important of all, it is difficult to see that it does not contradict 1 John 1. 18 and 1 Tim. 6. 16. It is more satisfactory to take the central figure of the three to be the second Person of the Trinity (see

on verse 1), and the other two as attendant angels, identical with those who afterwards ' went toward Sodom ' (verse 22), and eventually arrived there (19. 1) and rescued Lot (19. 15).

He ran. In spite of the heat, which he forgot in his desire to entertain his guests. If our heart is right with God, we too shall run in His service without regard to difficulty or trouble. As Abraham ran to meet and serve his God, so the Father runs to meet the returning sinner (Lk. 15. 20).

Bowed himself. Our first duty to God is submission and worship.

VERSE 3. *My Lord.* The Hebrew is Adonai, a title of respect which is often used of God in conjunction, or not, with Jahweh, to which divine name it gives its vowel points to form the hybrid, but familiar, word Jehovah. Like its Greek counterpart Kurios the title is often applied to men, so that its use here does not imply that Abraham was aware of his Visitor's identity. Indeed if Hebrews 13. 2 be a reference to this incident, we know that he was not. *If now I have found favour in thy sight.* On Abraham's lips these words seem to have part of the polite phraseology of hospitality, but they have a deep theological significance. We can receive no blessing from God, till we have found favour in His sight, and this we can only do by the exercise of His sovereign grace made available to us by ' the redemption, that is in Christ Jesus ' (Rom. 3. 24).

Pass not away. This is a prayer of fundamental gravity and importance. If the Lord passes away from us without blessing us, we are lost, and lost for ever. In many lives, perhaps at some time or other in every life, He draws near and passes by, as Jesus did at Jericho (Lk. 18. 37). It is strange and sad that so few are on the watch for this rare opportunity, and that so many neglect it when it occurs, allowing Jesus to pass away from them and missing the opportunity of seeking His blessing.

VERSE 4. In this and the following

verse we note that Abraham offered his visitors three things: (1) water, (2) rest, (3) food. These are the things that the Saviour wants of us, when He seeks the hospitality of our hearts. (1) The *water* was for washing the feet after the dust and stains of a hot journey. The Saviour has travelled far to reach us, ' out of the ivory palaces into a world of woe ', past and through the anguish of Calvary. He seeks from us first the recognition of this fact and the performance of the service that arises because of it. He Himself is willing to perform this menial service for His own servants (Jo. 13. 1-17). How much more is it our duty to perform it for Him in the person of those who belong to Him. (2) The Saviour desires the *rest* that is provided in the home of our hearts. ' The Spirit of glory and of God resteth upon you ' (1 Pet. 4. 14), the implication being that the Spirit turns from the hardness of the unregenerate heart and from contending with the wickedness of the world to take delight and refreshment in the hearts of those who love Him. *Under the tree.* In the marvellous condescension of God the hearts of His people supply Him with the shelter and shade of loving fellowship.

Verse 5. (3) *A morsel of bread.* When the Saviour comes into a heart, He comes to sup (Rev. 3. 20). He is fed by the sacrifice of His people (notice that in Lev. 21. 21 the levitical sacrifices are called ' the bread of his God '), offered as their reasonable service (Rom. 12. 1).

Comfort ye your hearts. According to the Bible the spiritual and the physical in man are inextricably bound together in the unity of the personality. Food comforts the heart. It is a common experience that a good meal may set a hungry man in good spirits.

After that ye shall pass on. When we are sure of having received Christ into our hearts, we may let Him go in the sense of passing on to bless others. In another and very real

sense He remains for ever.

Therefore are ye come. God's purpose in visiting the human heart is to enjoy fellowship with it. ' Come to my heart, Lord Jesus, there is room in my heart for Thee.'

So do as thou hast said. Are we so much in touch with the divine mind, that our suggestions and proposals are commended by the Lord, and we are commanded to carry them out?

Verse 6. *Abraham hastened.* ' The king's business requireth haste.' It is always good not to lose a minute in carrying out the Master's service. *Unto Sarah.* Sarah was to co-operate in doing service to the guests. Notice in this verse and the next the team work, or community of service.

Quickly. Sarah was to share the urgency. Have we this sense of urgency in the service of the Lord? *Three measures.* This probably means one measure for each of the guests. *Fine meal.* This represents righteousness in the sense of standing with God, as seems so often to be the case in the levitical types, and is the first thing that the heavenly Visitor looks for in our hearts.

Knead it. ' Work out your own salvation '. With the believer's co-operation justification is worked out in practical righteousness.

Make cakes upon the hearth. Notice that to do what was required the fire of the hearth was necessary. Fire represents the Holy Spirit (Mt. 3. 11; Acts 2. 3), and reliance upon Him is essential, if we are to complete any service to satisfy the Master.

Verse 7. *Abraham ran.* Compare this with ' hastened ' and ' quickly ' in the previous verse.

A calf tender and good. After the fine meal this is the next thing that the heavenly Visitor looks for. It represents a burnt offering, and for this we must offer our bodies, a living sacrifice (Rom. 12. 1). The calf was tender, young, pliable, trustful, softhearted, just as we must be in simple faith and reliance on the Lord. It was also good. In ourselves we are not good. We have no goodness of our own, but only that which we derive from the Saviour. This is a perfect goodness however, and satisfying to Him, as He sees it at work in our hearts.

Gave it unto a young man. By ourselves alone we have no opportunity to offer our lives as a living sacrifice to God. We must ' give ' them to others in love and service, and thus they become ' dressed ' and ready for the Master's use and enjoyment.

Butter. This is the third thing for which the Lord looks, when He visits the human heart. It represents richness and fatness, and this means the best. All that we have is His, but He looks for the exercise in His service of the best of the gifts that He has given us and for the best that our personality can be. *Milk.* This generally represents the Word (1 Pet. 2. 2), and the Lord takes pleasure in the reflection of His own Word in the hearts of His people.

Set it before them. This is exactly what we too are to do. We are to take our sacrificed lives and set them before the Lord.

He stood by them, waiting to attend on their needs. This is the right attitude of the servant of the Lord (Psa. 123. 2). Do we stand continually by Him?

Under the tree. This is the only place where it is possible to stand, under the shadow of the cross. Our service must be performed in the light of the cross. It must be the service of those who trust in a crucified Saviour and have made the cross their own (Mt. 10. 38; Jo. 12. 26).

They did eat. We cannot properly deduce from the statement, any more than from Luke 24. 41-43, that it is necessary for angels to eat, or that we ourselves shall need food, when in resurrection glory. We may, or may not. The act in this case was one of condescension and fellowship, symbolising the satisfaction taken by the Lord in fellowship with His people.

VERSE 9. *Where is Sarah thy wife?* If Abraham had not realised the identity of his Guest, he was now no longer left in doubt. The Guest knew all about him and his wife. Perhaps, when standing by under the tree, he had suspected Who He was.

In the tent. Sarah was a pilgrim. She had no permanent home. She represents Jerusalem, which is above (Gal. 4. 22-26), and this promise is made to her, while she is still in this present life, a stranger, dwelling in tents.

VERSE 10. *I will certainly return unto thee.* The fulfilment of the promise and the realisation of the blessing depend on the presence of the Lord. It is when He comes to us, that barrenness is turned into fruitfulness. His coming would perhaps be unseen, but no less real. Similarly it is because His Spirit has come to our hearts, that spiritual fertility is possible for us. *According to the time of life.* The Hebrew says, ' when the season lives '. The A.V. interprets this as here, the R.V. saying, ' When the season cometh round '. The expression is not parallel to the words ' at this set time ', for both these phrases occur together in verse 14. The A.V. rendering suggests that the words may refer to Sarah's physical condition. She had passed her change of life (verse 11), but her ' season ' of childbearing was to live, or revive. The R.V. rendering suggests the time of year. It was the heat of summer (verse 1). The words perhaps mean that Sarah would conceive, when the weather revived after the heat. On the whole the A.V. rendering seems to fit the context best, and we may thus perhaps see in the words a reference to Sarah. Here is a great principle. Life must precede fruitfulness. We cannot bring forth fruit to the glory of God's name, until we have appropriated by faith the life of Christ.

Sarah thy wife shall have a son. The Holy Spirit through the apostle Paul points to these words as the crucial promise which distinguishes

Isaac, the child of promise, from Ishmael, the child of the flesh (Rom. 9. 9). Thus we have God's promise leading on to the appropriation of life, and life leading on to fruitfulness. This is the regular spiritual order. *Sarah heard*. The women's quarters were only separated by a flap, and Sarah was able to overhear the whole conversation, although she herself was unseen. This it seems she was intended to do. If we listen for the Lord's voice, we may sometimes hear it in some word, or circumstances, that does not seem to be aimed directly at us. Yet the Lord has us in mind all the time.

Verse 11. *Old and well stricken in age*. The Lord had brought them to this condition, where fruitfulness was no longer naturally possible, in order that His work upon them physically might symbolise the work of the Holy Ghost spiritually in the sinner's heart.

It ceased to be with Sarah after the manner of women. Sarah had passed her change of life, and was therefore in a condition relative to motherhood identical with that in which fallen human nature stands relative to pleasing God (Rom. 8. 8). The opportunity of doing so has irrevocably passed.

Verse 12. *Sarah laughed*. This was a laugh of unbelief and incredulity in direct contrast to Abraham's laugh of faith (see 17. 17). Sarah had overheard the conversation, but was hidden inside the tent. She had not seen the Visitor, as her husband had. She was therefore probably still ignorant of His identity.

Shall I have pleasure. This probably means (1) sexual pleasure, (2) the joys of motherhood. *My lord*. She means her husband, and the apostle Peter draws attention to her words (1 Pet. 3. 6) as being the expression of ' a meek and quiet spirit ' (1 Pet. 3. 4). He uses them as an encouragement to Christian women to submit themselves to their husbands, and calls Sarah by implication one of the holy women who hope in God

(1 Pet. 3. 5).

Verse 13. *Wherefore did Sarah laugh*. The laugh had been only ' within herself ' (verse 12), but it was heard by, and known to, the One before Whom all things are naked and open (Heb. 4. 13). ' The Lord looketh on the heart ' (1 Sam. 16. 7). He knows the thoughts of all our hearts, as He knew those of Sarah's. From Him ' no secrets can be hid '. This knowledge opened Sarah's eyes, and her realisation of it was the first step in turning her from incredulity to the faith by which ' she received strength to conceive seed ' (Heb. 11. 11). The more we realise how much open our hearts and lives are to the gaze of God, the more our faith is likely to be strengthened, and the more power we are likely to receive. The knowledge is convicting, humbling, and conducive to holiness and obedience.

Verse 14. *Is anything too hard for the Lord?* This is one of the great sentences of the Bible. As so often in Hebrew, the negative is expressed in interrogative form. It is a comforting, life-giving question. Nothing is too hard for the Lord. The creation and preservation of the world are not too hard for Him, nor the judgment of the sinner, above all the redemption and salvation of His believing people and their deliverance from the power of Satan, sin and death, although that redemption cost the life of His Son and, as may be said, shook the very Godhead to its foundations. No single miraculous act, as in Sarah's case, is too hard for Him, nor is the obstinacy of any individual. Each can be, and is, broken, and brought to saving faith by grace, or to eternal condemnation, according as the sovereign righteous purpose of God has decreed. The Hebrew word translated ' hard ' means literally ' wonderful ', and is appropriately the same as is used for the Messianic title ' Wonderful ' in Isa. 9. 6. This great passage is quoted in the case of Elisabeth (Lk. 1. 37), which was similar to that of Sarah (though, as we do not know Elisabeth's age, we cannot say whether the same miracle was necessary in her case). It is also quoted by the Lord in a context of great significance (Mt. 19. 26; Mk. 10. 27). He tells the disciples that salvation is impossible with men. No man can do anything to bring about his own salvation, or that of others, by any means, whether religious exercise, moral effort, or fervent prayer. But with God all things are possible. By the allusion in these words to Gen. 18. 14 the Lord makes clear as daylight two facts: (1) the condition of fallen man, which in relation to salvation is the same as was Sarah's in relation to motherhood after her change of life. All hope and opportunity were past. Without the miraculous intervention of God the hopes of salvation, so foolishly and so frequently indulged in even by professing Christians, are absolutely unavailing. Since his fall man has been 'dead in trespasses and sins' (Eph. 2. 1). (2) By the same allusion the Lord makes clear that every conversion is a miracle and lies in the sphere of the supernatural. It is brought about by the work of the Holy Spirit, sovereign and unaided, in the sinner's heart, a work that from man's point of view is 'too hard' and too wonderful.

At the time appointed. R.V. has 'at the set time'. See on 17. 21.

I will return. See on verse 10.

According to the time of life. See on verse 10.

VERSE 15. *Sarah denied.* There could be no doubt now in Sarah's mind of the identity of the Visitor. She knew that it was the Lord. The realisation that God Himself has visited the soul and is seeking to deal with it is one of the first steps towards faith. *She was afraid.* 'The fear of the Lord is the beginning of wisdom' (Prov. 9. 10), but Sarah's fear was a guilty one, and caused her to attempt to conceal her sin.

Nay: but thou didst laugh. If Sarah tried to hide her sin, the Lord did not gloss over it. He challenged her with it, as He does in the case of every sinner. He forces him to a realisation of it, and seeks to bring him to confess it. It is evident that Sarah accepted the verdict and confessed in her heart, for she was brought triumphantly from unbelief to faith, whereby she received the power to conceive seed (Heb. 11. 11). No doubt her incredulity was due to ignorance of the identity of the One Who made the pronouncement. We may compare Jo. 4. 10. How many in the world today are incredulous of the promise of redemption and contemptuous of the Gospel, because they are ignorant of the facts, lacking a light and a knowledge, which we might have supplied. Abraham had only to whisper through the folds of the tent, 'It is the Lord', for Sarah to be spared her incredulity and the humiliation of its exposure.

VERSE 16. With this verse we begin the second section of the chapter, which deals with a different subject. Sarah is left in the tent to ponder over the wonderful promise, and our attention is drawn to the wicked cities of the plain. *The men,* that is either the Lord and the two angels, or the two angels alone, as in verse 22.

Looked towards Sodom. A guilty people may well tremble, when the Lord's attention is directed in this way towards their sin. He waits a long time. He waited for the Amorites four hundred years (15. 13-16). He waited for Judah, till there was no remedy (2 Chron. 36. 16). He is waiting still for a wicked Christendom and an apostate church (Rev. 16. 19), and He is mercifully patient over the world at large, although 'the day of the Lord will come' (2 Pet. 3. 9, 10). Perhaps He is looking toward western Europe and at the same time towards the world at large.

Abraham went with them. This was an act of courtesy, which led to a superb opportunity for intercession.

VERSE 17. *Shall I hide.* 'The secret

of the Lord is with them, that fear Him' (Psa. 25. 14). Here is a marvellous instance of the condescending desire of the Lord to share His secret purposes in fellowship with men. 'He shewed His ways unto Moses', but only His works unto the rebellious children of Israel (Psa. 103. 7). Do we know something of His ways, or do we only know His works? Do we share His secret purposes of spreading the Gospel in the world?

Verse 18. This verse gives us the reason for the Lord's condescension in revealing to Abraham what He was going to do. It is that Abraham had been caught up in the purpose of redemption. It is the same with us. As believers, 'called according to His purpose' (Rom. 8. 28), we each have our place in God's plan for blessing the world. If we are faithfully fulfilling the plan, as God gives us light and ability, we may expect that He will seek to show us something of His mind, not only the general principles of it, as they are revealed in His Word, but some of the particulars and details, which He wants us as individuals to carry out. We may seek these from Him in prayer.

A great and mighty nation. This is the Christian church, the true Israel (Mt. 21. 43), the holy nation (1 Pet. 2. 9), which in the world to come will be 'a great multitude that no man can number' (Rev. 7. 9).

All the nations of the earth shall be blessed in Him. This is fulfilled in the justification of the Gentiles by faith (Gal. 3. 8), as the Gospel goes out through the world. Notice that this blessing extends to 'all the nations'. This does not mean every individual among them. It is the same fact as that referred to by our Lord, when He said that the Gospel would be preached to all nations (Mt. 24. 14), and by the apostle, when he said that the great multitude comes from every nation and tribe and people and tongue (Rev. 7. 9).

Verse 19. As this verse stands in the A.V., it makes the fulfilment of the promises made to Abraham dependent upon his own and his family's obedience. The R.V. however gives it a different turn, translating as follows: 'For I have known him, to the end that he may command . . .' and later: 'that they may keep the way of the Lord . . . to the end that the Lord may bring . . .' The condition in the A.V. is regarded as certain of fulfilment in the knowledge of God. In the R.V. it is not so certain that such a condition is intended. The Lord declares that His purpose in making Himself known to Abraham was that he and his family might walk in God's ways. The R.V. says nothing about the fulfilment, or the lapse, of this purpose. The last sentence of the verse, beginning in the R.V. with the words 'to the end that', may be taken in one of two alternative ways. (1) The sentence may be parallel to the former one, 'to the end that he may command', both following and depending on the words 'I have known', and together expressing two reasons why the Lord had made Himself known to Abraham. The second sentence however does not seem to make very good sense, when taken as parallel with the first. The Lord scarcely made Himself known to Abraham, in order to bring upon him what He had spoken. He rather made Himself known by speaking. The second sentence is therefore better taken (2) in the same sense as the A.V., that is to say, as a purpose dependent upon Abraham's obedience. If we take the second sentence in this way, we may prefer the R.V.'s translation of the verse. God's purpose in making Himself known to Abraham was that He might bring into being a family, that would give witness to Him by consistency of moral conduct, enabling Him to fulfil the promises that He had made.

Command his children. Notice the responsibility of parents and the necessity of training children and evangelising each generation. Notice that God's purpose was to bring into being a family or nation, which would witness as a group to His righteousness. The old Israel failed Him in this respect. The true church, which has the indwelling Holy Spirit, carries out His purpose. *Keep the way of the Lord.* This means to live a consistent sanctified life. To keep in this connection means (1) to exercise diligence; (2) to believe the Lord's Word; (3) to obey His commands; (4) to keep to the way without turning off it to the left or the right; (5) to continue doing so all one's life. *The way* means the way of life, or line of conduct, laid down by the Lord for man to follow, as he passes through this world. *To do justice and judgment.* As always, the Bible here strikes a practical note. Keeping the way consists in *doing.* The way lies through the practical daily tasks, which are made by God into opportunities and tests, and thus lifted out of the trivial. Justice and judgment are the fundamental moral requirements. They are equivalent to practical righteousness. *Justice* means (1) that which God has declared to be right; (2) that which is right and fair and open in relationship with men. *Judgment* means that which the will decides to be right in reliance upon the revealed will of God. It involves deliberate association with what is right and deliberate dissociation from persons and courses which are wrong.

That the Lord may bring. It is very important to notice that the fulfilment of the promises to Abraham is dependent upon obedience and consistency on the part of his descendants. If this were not the case, the situation would have been one of flagrant antinomianism. The old Israel forfeited the promises because of disobedience and inconsistency (Jer. 31. 32; Mt. 21. 43), and they have been embodied in the new covenant, which ensures obedience and consistency to all who receive it (Heb. 8. 10-12).

VERSE 20. *The Lord said.* The general purpose of this revelation seems to have been the condescending desire to share it in fellowship. The immediate purpose may well have been to call forth the powerful intercession that followed it.

The cry of Sodom and Gomorrah. The picture is that of an increasingly loud noise rising to heaven and forcing itself upon the attention of God. The same thing is happening in the case of modern Christendom, the Babylon of the New Testament (Rev. 18. 5). The idea is the same as that expressed by the mounting up of sin till it reaches breaking point (see on verse 16). This takes place in the case of individuals as well as nations (Rom. 2. 5). If only the sinner could for a moment hear this noise, as it sounds in heaven!

Their sin is very grievous. All sin is grievous and abominable to God by the reaction of His holiness.

VERSE 21. *I will go down now, and see.* Here we have the same figure as in 11. 7. The underlying idea is that God takes no action in judgment except upon the strictest assessment of the facts. *I will know.* God knows all without the necessity of finding out. This whole verse is an expression of the purpose of God in human terms. This shows (1) the condescension of God; (2) the terminology is intended to make us understand the principles on which God moves in His dealings with men. Compare Mt. 6. 8, 32.

VERSE 22. *The men.* The two angels are described as men, because they appeared in the form of men. Angels sometimes appear as horses and chariots of fire (2 Ki. 2. 11; 6. 17; Ps. 68. 17).

Went toward Sodom. This fact and that of the subsequent arrival of the angels (19. 1) throw some light on the statements of verse 21. The angels had been charged with the execution of God's judgment upon the guilty cities. It was they who went down and saw (verse 21) as God's representatives.

Abraham stood yet before the Lord. Notice that Abraham waited till he was alone with God before making his intercession. True prayer requires undisturbed access to God without distraction, or the presence of others. Prayer lies between God and the individual. Of course there is a place for corporate prayer. According to Jewish tradition the text read originally, ' The Lord stood yet before Abraham '. This rests on no manuscript record, but reflects deep insight. It would follow the previous sentence more easily. It would give a moving impression of condescension, and it expresses a conception, which is not without truth. It is sufficient to realise that God and man are brought together in this moving scene in intimate fellowship, the one opening his heart on behalf of a friend, and the Other anxious to answer and bless.

VERSE 23. *Abraham drew near.* Nearness to God is essential for successful prayer. See Jas. 4. 8. This essential nearness to God, without which prayer is impossible, is brought about by the blood of Christ (Eph. 2. 13). There is no other agency that can bring those who are at a distance from God by reason of sin into a relationship of nearness to Him. No priest, no mass, no religious rite or ordinance, no effort, no self-denial, no alms-giving can break the barrier, which separates the sinner from God. Nothing can do so but the blood of Jesus, personally received and appropriated by an act of faith. Through our Lord Jesus Christ we have access by faith (Rom. 5. 1, 2; Eph. 2. 18), and in the assurance of this access we are to come with boldness to the throne of grace, as Abraham did (Heb. 4. 16).

With the remainder of this verse we have the beginning of Abraham's intercessory prayer, which continues until verse 32. Notice that it was (1) reverent. Abraham had an objective in his mind, but he did not mention it all at once. He reached it in six separate steps. These may have represented an increase in his faith, though this does not seem to be the impression given. They certainly expressed a rising confidence. Abraham felt his way. We may contrast this very careful approach with our own encouragement in Christ to come with boldness to the throne of grace (Heb. 4. 16) and to make our requests known unto God (Phil. 4. 6), but we ought to follow the example of Abraham's reverence and sense of unworthiness. (2) The prayer was definite. Much of our own prayer is vague. Definite prayer — to which we are encouraged by many examples in the Bible — obtains definite answers. (3) The prayer was persevering. Abraham continued till he reached his objective. Ours ought to be so also (Lk. 18. 1; Eph. 6. 18; Col. 4. 2; 1 Thess. 5. 17). We shall also see later that Abraham was (4) mistaken over the facts on which he based his prayer, but that this did not prevent an abundant answer being given. *Wilt thou also destroy.* Abraham based his petition on his knowledge of the character of God, that is to say, on His righteousness, and we ought to do the same. Our prayers, to be successful, must be in conformity with the revealed will of God and with the principles on which He acts towards men (1 Jo. 5. 14, 15). Abraham's prayer was concerned with the salvation of the righteous from destruction. This same thing should be the main theme of our own prayers. He based his petition on the righteousness of God. We also must do the same in clearer Gospel light. We must base our intercessions on the fact of Christ's atoning death, which both revealed and satisfied the righteousness of God.

The righteous. Abraham was thinking of Lot (19. 29). It is therefore clear that he understood what constituted righteousness in the sight of God. He knew Lot's personal character well enough by experience. It was not a character that showed much personal or practical righteousness. He knew that like himself Lot had been justified by faith, and therefore had a perfect standing with God and a claim upon Him as the possessor of it (2 Pet. 2. 7).

VERSE 24. *Spare the place.* Abraham asks for the whole city to be spared for the sake of the righteous in it. During the Gospel age the whole world has been spared from judgment for the sake of the elect, who are still in it.

VERSE 25. *That be far from thee.* These words bring out the extreme boldness of this prayer. Abraham is so closely in touch with the mind of God, that he knows how He will act and pleads with Him on the ground of the impossibility of His acting contrary to His nature and principles.

The righteous with the wicked. Abraham is aware that there are two classes of mankind, distinguished since the first pronouncement about the seed of the woman and the seed of the serpent (3. 15) and since the story of Cain and Abel (Chap. 4). These classes are distinguished right through the Bible (see for instance Ps. 37). The distinction, which is the only substantial one made in the Bible between sections of the human race, shows that the fundamental issue in human life is moral. In ourselves we all belong to ' the wicked '. By faith in Christ we may pass into the other class and may appropriate to ourselves the perfect righteousness of Christ. None but those who possess this righteousness can ever be numbered among the righteous. Abraham also knew that the destiny of the two classes was different. The wicked will one day be slain eternally (Rev. 20. 15). The righteous will enter into life (Rom. 2. 7-10).

That the righteous should be as the wicked. The law distinguished clearly between them (Ex. 23. 7; Prov. 17. 15), and they will be clearly distinguished on the day of judgment (Mt. 25. 46).

Shall not the Judge of all the earth do right? These words are sometimes quoted in a fatalistic sense, as if whatever happens will work out well in the end, and so inaction on our part will be justified, but it should be noticed that the words are uttered to justify an earnest prayer for the salvation of those in danger. They are used as a basis for action, not for inaction. Abraham knew God to be the *Judge*, not only, or necessarily, at the end of the world, but now in all the affairs of men. The very first relationship, in which God stands to men, whom He made moral beings, is that of Judge. All are responsible to Him (see Ps. 14. 2). Abraham also knew that God was the Judge of *all the earth*, not of one family, one race, or one people only, but of all men. In saying this he acknowledged that there is only one true and living God. He also knew that God's dealings with men were perfectly right and just. This meant that he could trust himself to God and rejoice in all His acts.

VERSE 26. Notice that the Lord gave to Abraham the exact answer to his prayer. For all we know, he might have stopped praying at that point and received nothing more. A definite answer to prayer is thus not necessarily intended to be final, but to inspire to further prayer. *All the place.* The righteous are the salt of the earth (Mt. 5. 13), preserving it, while they remain in it, from destruction.

VERSE 27. *I have taken upon me.* Abraham's sense that he was daring in approaching the Lord illustrates the difference between the law and the Gospel. While the barrier was standing, while the veil was in existence and temporary sacrificial expedients had to be resorted to in order to keep contact with the Lord, the sinner might well feel, in spite of an assurance that he was a recipient of grace, a diffidence in approaching to a holy God. Now that the barrier is broken (Eph. 2. 14), the veil torn in two (Mt. 27. 51), and we have a great High Priest in heaven itself (Heb. 4. 14), we may come — are invited to come, and ought to come — with boldness to the throne of grace (Heb. 4. 16). At the same time it is our duty to imitate Abraham's ' reverence and godly fear ' (Heb. 12. 28).

Which am but dust and ashes.
Notice Abraham's proper sense of unworthiness. He seems to have felt his distance from God as creature from Creator rather than as sinner from the Holy One. This we too should always feel, and we may perhaps continue to do so in the world to come. In this description of himself Abraham emphasises that he is (1) earthly (1 Cor. 15. 45-49), and (2) mortal (Rom. 5. 12). God on the other hand is heavenly (Mt. 5. 48) and immortal.

VERSE 28. *For lack of five.* This is a bold, persuasive, challenging and even subtle note in these words. They present the question in a strong light and with a definite emphasis. Prayer is like the pleadings of the child with the parent.

If I find there forty and five. Here is a second definite answer to a definite petition, which again is not final.

VERSE 29. *I will not do it for forty's sake.* This is a third definite answer in the terms of the petition, again not final.

VERSE 30. *Oh let not the Lord be angry.* Abraham need not have feared. The Lord loves to hear and answer prayer.

I will not do it, if I find thirty there. Here is a fourth definite answer to a definite prayer, which again does not indicate finality. These affirmative answers illustrate increasingly the loving-kindness and mercy of the Lord. He is more concerned to spare the few righteous than to destroy the many wicked.

VERSE 31. *I have taken upon me.* See on verse 27.

I will not destroy it for twenty's sake. This is a fifth definite answer in so many words, which yet is not final.

VERSE 32. *Oh let not the Lord be angry.* See on verse 30.

This once. Abraham had nearly reached the objective at which he had been aiming all the time.

Ten. Abraham had in mind Lot and his wife, his sons, presumably two in number (19. 12), his four daughters, two married (19. 14), two unmarried (19. 12, 15, 31) and his two sons-in-law (19. 14). This makes a total of ten. He was right in regarding Lot as ' righteous ' (2 Pet. 2. 7), that is to say, one who was justified by faith in spite of unworthy conduct. He naturally concluded that the members of a righteous man's family might be numbered among the righteous as well. But he was wrong. Lot's wife was finally lost (19. 26). Lot's sons were so indifferent, that he did not even think it worth while to give them a warning. His sons-in-law refused to listen to him (19. 14). His married daughters perished with their husbands. His two unmarried daughters, though brought safely out of Sodom with their father, proved by their shameless conduct that they were unrepentant women of the world (19. 30-38). Thus Abraham's facts were wrong. He was praying on false premises. But he was praying sincerely and up to his lights, and it is both important and encouraging to notice that his prayer was answered, though not in the way that he expected, for which he had asked (19. 29). What Abraham wanted was Lot's salvation with all that belonged to him who were righteous. This was the meaning, the kernel, of his prayer, and he obtained it, although he was ignorant of the fact that there were none but Lot alone who were righteous.

VERSE 33. *The Lord went his way.* This is an anthropomorphic figure of speech, which assists the expression of communion between friends which this wonderful incident gives us.

Abraham returned into his place, but in so doing did not leave the Presence, which was no longer visible to him.

CHAPTER 19

IN this chapter we have the dramatic account of the destruction of Sodom and Gomorrah, which is the second of the two Old Testament incidents referred to by our Lord as illustrations of the day of judgment at the end of the world (Lk. 17. 28-30). The first is Noah's flood. The account also supplies the anticlimax and end of the story of the life of Lot. The persons in the story are the two angels, Lot, the men of Sodom, Lot's wife and Lot's two daughters. Abraham is watching, as it were, in the background, and has a close connection with the event (verse 29). The angels arrive in Sodom, are entertained in Lot's house, and are the object of a vile and brutal attack, which endangered Lot himself. He was rescued by the angels, and urged to leave the city. He failed to persuade any of his family to accompany him except his wife and two daughters. During the escape his wife was overwhelmed and lost. Urged to escape to the mountains, he begged to be allowed to go to Zoar, and was permitted to do so. Immediately on his entry the guilty cities were destroyed by a conflagration. Feeling insecure Lot withdrew with his daughters to a cave and we last see him in degrading circumstances, helpless in the hands of the wicked daughters.

There are two principal lessons to be drawn from the chapter: (1) the example and certainty of the final destruction of the wicked; (2) the miserable end and failure of the life of the worldly Christian, illustrated by Lot.

VERSE 1. *There came two angels.* The R.V. gives a better connection with the previous chapter by rendering, 'The two angels came'. They are the two who had visited Abraham with their Divine Master (18. 2, 16, 22).

To Sodom. It is extraordinary to find angels in Sodom, but not so extraordinary as to find the Lord of glory, the Holy One, our Saviour as a man in this world.

At even. Night was falling upon Sodom, just as eternal night is falling upon this world (Jo. 9. 4). *Lot sat in the gate.* This means that he was a magistrate in the place of authority. This is the position that he had reached. From pitching his tent near Sodom (13. 12) he had come to dwell there (14. 12) and now finally to assume authority there. This is a perfect parable of the life of the worldly Christian.

Rose up to meet them: and he bowed himself. The very proper courtesy of these actions cannot conceal the fact that Lot was doing the honours of Sodom.

VERSE 2. *Turn in.* Though Lot was worldly enough to live in Sodom, he was righteous enough to loathe its ways (2 Pet. 2. 7). While there was no doubt true hospitality in this invitation there was also apprehension for the strangers, which is shortly seen to be not ill-founded. Lot seeks to conceal from the strangers the true condition of the city, of which he is ashamed, and in so doing to deceive himself about it also, so as to justify to his conscience his being there.

We will abide in the street. This may have been (1) a polite refusal of Lot's invitation in oriental bargaining style, leading on to an ultimate acceptance; (2) a genuine refusal because of the undoubtedly uncongenial atmosphere of Lot's household. Angels could scarcely be happy staying in a house, of which Lot's wife was mistress, or where the two daughters were at home. If the times had been modern, we can well imagine the red-lipped daughters with dirty cigarette ends hanging from their mouths and the sons-in-law dropping in last thing at night for a glass of whisky on their way home from the pictures; (3) an intention to fulfil the purpose for which they had been sent to Sodom, namely to ' go down ' and ' see ' (18. 21). Either (1) or (2) and (3) might be combined.

VERSE 3. *He pressed upon them greatly.* Lot was genuinely horrified at this proposal, a fact that proves that he knew well the condition of the city in which he lived, and must have experienced a continual conflict of heart and conscience, as the apostle Peter's statement suggests was the case (2 Pet. 2. 5).

They turned in unto him. Perhaps they realised that in, or from, Lot's house they would ' see ' all they need.

He made them a feast. By this time we may suspect that he had begun to guess who they were. In any case the lavish and generous hospitality might, he felt, set him right in the eyes of his guests and demonstrate that he was on the right side. Lot must have felt as uncomfortable in the presence of the angels, as the worldly Christian feels today at a prayer meeting.

Did bake unleavened bread. This may mean, ' Had it baked '. On the other hand the implication may be that he baked it himself, and if so, we may see that he had no co-operation from his wife. This is in contrast with Abraham in similar circumstances (18. 6). Lot's wife, whose final loss (verse 26) proves her to have been unconverted, may have refused to bake it, or may have expressed open disdain for the godly guests. Or Lot may have shrunk from asking her. If the latter be the case, we may suspect a reason. Notice that the bread was *unleavened,* that is to say, it was holy and pure from pollution. Lot guessed, or realised, that this kind of bread would be congenial to his visitors. If he was true to type, he may have sought to give them the impression that he was accustomed to eating unleavened bread. His wife would scarcely be the person to bake it, even if she knew how. *They did eat.* The acceptance of Lot's hospitality was a gracious action, which expressed good will and must have tended to break the ice. In similar circumstances we may do well to follow the angel's example. Notice that the angels did not patronise Lot,

but put themselves under an obligation to him.

VERSE 4. This verse describes a dangerous, brutal and indecent assault, made by men who were doubtless angered by Lot's protection of the strangers and probably took the opportunity to vent their anger and hatred against Lot. Those in Lot's position cut themselves off from the righteous, as Lot had done from Abraham, but generally incur the resentment of the unconverted. They fall between two stools.

VERSE 5. *Know them.* This means carnal knowledge. This demand was shamelessly made as if it was a right.

VERSE 6. *The door.* It is a fact of significance that Canaanite houses of the bronze age period, in which this story is set, had heavy doors, of which hinges have occasionally been discovered in situ. Later in the iron age during the Israelite occupation of Palestine no such door existed, nothing but a curtain being usually hung at the entrance to a house. This confirms by incidental evidence the truth of this narrative and demonstrates its derivation from a contemporary source.

Shut the door. He not only wished to protect his guests, but to put a barrier between himself and them, while he parleyed with his worldly acquaintances.

VERSE 7. *I pray you, brethren.* Lot is not ashamed to address these wicked men as brethren, and allows a weak, polite and futile protest to take the place of earnest rebuke.

VERSE 8. *I have two daughters.* Lot is reduced by the compromising attitude which he had adopted throughout his life, and the entanglements in which he had fastened himself, to this desperate expedient. It is a suggestion that no truly self-respecting man, certainly no godly man, could make. He found himself in the same sort of predicament to which worldly compromise sooner or later leads every Christian who indulges in it.

For therefore came they under the shadow of my roof. Lot states openly why he had pressed the strangers to accept his hospitality, a reason that had been implied in the narrative and suspected by the citizens. Its open declaration enraged them.

Verse 9. *Stand back.* Lot could not have expected that his mild protest would succeed. He cannot have been surprised at this outburst of rage.

Came in to sojourn. The men of the city knew that Lot did not belong to them. Worldlings always regard the worldly Christian as a stranger, however much he may try to woo them.

He will needs be a judge. Lot tried, as the worldly Christian so often tries, to clean up the world in which he wanted to live. Such an attitude exasperates the man of the world.

Came near to break the door. Satan and the men of the world, as soon as they become roused, seek to break down the last barrier between themselves and the compromising Christian.

Verse 10. *The men put forth their hand.* The two angels now took the situation in hand, and in similar circumstances is it not our duty to do so? Are we ready and willing to put forth a helping hand to the Christian who is losing himself in worldly compromise, and in danger from the enemy, and to pull him safe into the house of faith with us?

Shut to the door. We too, if we can, must set up a barrier between our compromising brethren and the world. Notice that God protects the believer from danger, while he is still in the wicked world.

Verse 11. *Blindness.* God turns the plans of the wicked against the elect to confusion. He prevents them from realising their aim and keeps them from seeing it clearly, occupying them with a variety of trivial or irrelevant matters. They do not know which way to turn.

Both small and great. The ordinary people of the world as well as the leaders are affected with judicial blindness.

They wearied themselves. This is a true picture of the people of the world (see Jer. 9. 5; Jo. 6. 27).

Verse 12. *Hast thou here any besides?* The angels were seeking to make up the numbers of Abraham's ten righteous (18. 32). An important principle is involved here. God promises to save the family of the righteous with him (compare Acts 2. 39; 16. 32, 33), but their actual salvation depends upon their individual willingness to believe and escape (verses 14. 26). Thus we see that promises made to the family or children of a believer involve no violation of the ordinary principle of individual faith, which is the only way of salvation.

Son-in-law. Lot had at least two sons-in-law (verse 14). *Thy sons.* The plural shows that he had at least two sons. It is noteworthy that they are never mentioned again. Lot did not appear to think it worth while even to warn them, as he did the sons-in-law (verse 14), and the most reasonable conclusion is that he knew them to be so abandoned, as to be beyond warning. What else could any father expect, who marries an unconverted woman, possibly a native of Sodom, and brings up his children in the polluted and evil atmosphere of such a city, when he ought to have made any sacrifice to keep them away from it? The children of the worldly Christian often turn out like this. *Thy daughters.* Lot had at least four daughters, two unmarried, who lived at home with him, and at least two married (see verse 14). He had allowed his daughters to marry inhabitants of Sodom.

Whatsoever thou hast in the city. The R.V. says 'Whomsoever', which we may take to be the more accurate reading. Persons are being referred to, not property. No property can be taken out of the world by the believer (1 Tim. 6. 7), but by God's mercy and grace he can take his children and family safely out with him, provided they consent to come. The same principle was at work in the case of Rahab (Josh. 2. 13; 6. 23).

Bring them out of this place. Sodom is the picture of the whole world, and the message of the Gospel continually goes out, like the word of the two angels, to deliver men from ' this present evil world ' (Gal. 1. 4), to call them to be reconciled to God (2 Cor. 5. 20), and to urge them to flee for refuge to the Saviour (Heb. 6. 18) and escape, before destruction and judgment burst upon the world. Contrast with the *place* of destruction the *place* by the Lord in a clift of the rock (Ex. 33. 21, 22), and the *place* of which the Lord said, I will give it you (Num. 10. 29).

Verse 13. *We will destroy this place.* So will the world be one day destroyed (2 Pet. 3. 10, 12). The destruction of Sodom and Gomorrah is a standing warning and example of this coming destruction of the world (Jude 7).

The cry of them is waxen great before the face of the Lord. This is the mounting clamour of sin, which claims inevitable attention at the last.

The Lord hath sent us to destroy it. The angels of destruction may even now be in the world, awaiting the gathering out of the elect. The destruction of Sodom, when it took place, seems to have been effected by natural means. Perhaps some vast astronomical disaster is being prepared, or perhaps even man in his wickedness is being left to destroy himself by his wanton invention of destructive weapons.

Verse 14. *Lot went out.* In order to reach his sons-in-law in their need Lot had to leave home at night, when it was time to go to bed (verse 4), in circumstances of great difficulty and possible danger. We shall find our own situation to be much the same, but we are not always willing to go.

Spake unto his sons-in-law. We must not only go to sinners, we must also speak to them. It is by the foolishness of preaching that salvation comes to those who believe (1 Cor. 1. 21). ' Faith cometh by hearing, and hearing by the word of God ' (Rom. 10. 17), ' but how shall they hear without a preacher?' (Rom. 10. 14).

Up, get you out of this place. Here is the fundamental message of the Gospel, sometimes missed in the preaching of today. We sometimes make our Gospel exclusively a message of moral power. That is undoubtedly included in it, but is not fundamental. God calls on men in Christ to a separation from sinners (Heb. 7. 26), to newness of life and consecration to His service, and to safety in Christ from the wrath to come (1 Thess. 1. 10).

The Lord will destroy this city. Our message to sinners will be incomplete, unless we include in it the theme of coming judgment and the inevitable condemnation of sin apart from Christ. *He seemed as one that mocked unto his sons-in-law.* This is the normal experience of the worldly and compromising Christian. There is no power, nor effectiveness, in his message. His manner of life betrays him, and the unconverted, who are well able to judge it, draw the conclusion that there is no reality in his Gospel. Successful evangelism depends upon separation from the world and consecration to God.

Verse 15. *When the morning arose.* Lot may have spent the whole night arguing with his sons-in-law, perhaps in trying to prepare his wife to leave, perhaps in busy futile distractions. We do not know. He does not seem to have spent it in peaceful sleep, certainly not in prayer. In any case it was wasted and gone. More sin had been committed in the city to outrage the majesty of a holy God, merciful destruction during sleep had been denied to many. The day with its activities had begun. Some of the guilty citizens, if the day advanced far, might leave the city and put themselves out of reach of judgment. Strangers and traders might enter the area and become involved.

Hastened Lot. This is in accord with the urgency of the Gospel. It is our business to hasten the sinner, if we can. If he delays, he may be overtaken by death, by judicial blindness, or even by the judgment itself.

Which are here. The Hebrew says, ' Are found '. So we are to do our diligence to be found of Him in peace without spot and blameless (2 Pet. 3. 14). May we be found, not lost.

Lest thou be consumed. The Gospel offers the alternatives of urgent escape and destruction.

VERSE 16. *While he lingered.* It seems incredible that he should linger, but in doing so he showed himself one with many a sinner, who has no sense of urgency in relation to God, either about judgment, or repentance. We too are often guilty of the lack of a sense of urgency with regard to the salvation of others. The sinner leaves the world and its attractions tardily, loth to believe in its coming destruction.

Laid hold upon his hand. It is the same with the sinner. Of our own accord we should never have left sin and the world, even at the urgent call of the Gospel. An invisible Hand takes hold of ours and draws us to the Saviour (Jo. 6. 44).

The Lord being merciful unto him. ' It is not of him that willeth, nor of him that runneth, but of God that showeth mercy ' (Rom. 9. 16). The mercy of God lies behind our salvation, and is the prime mover in bringing it about. God's mercy initiated the plan of redemption, that satisfied His justice. Mercy implies (1) lack of desert on the sinner's part and (2) his helplessness. Is this mercy shown in an arbitrary manner? No, because (1) Christ died potentially for all (1 Jo. 2. 2). (2) Why then are all not saved? We have not, and we ought not to expect, an explanation of

the inscrutable decrees of God, but here in the story of Lot we find the veil partially lifted. (2) Lot was saved in answer to the prayer of Abraham. It is intercession that makes the vital difference in the response made to the Gospel. This is true to experience. Those who are prayed for are often saved. In the story of Lot's deliverance from Sodom we have an example of emphatic lack of merit and of powerful intercession. *They brought him forth.* We too have been brought out, that we might be brought in. We have been brought from under the bondage of sin and delivered from guilt and curse.

Set him without the city. We too have been set in Christ safe outside the city of destruction, though we do not always realise the separation from the world that is implied in our acceptance of the Gospel.

VERSE 17. *When they had brought them forth abroad.* This corresponds to the deliverance of the sinner by faith through the Gospel. The tie with the evil world is now broken. The verse tells us four things that the rescued sinner is to do: (1) *Escape for thy life.* Here we find implied (a) the urgency of the Gospel, and the way of salvation. ' Strive to enter in by the strait gate ' (Lk. 13. 24); (b) the reality and severity of the judgment; (c) the fact that the issue is one of life and death. (2) *Look not behind thee.* A longing or a covetous look back to the world may endanger the whole of a man's spiritual life. (3) *Neither stay thou in all the plain.* There must be no pause in the Christian race. The rescued sinner must not seek to settle in the endangered area of the wicked world. He must ' press on unto the prize of the high calling of God in Christ Jesus ' (Phil. 3. 14). (4) *Escape to the mountain.* The rescued sinner must not pause till he is secure in ' the mountain of the Lord's house ', out of all harm's way and safe beyond the fires of judgment.

VERSE 18. *Oh, not so, my Lord.* True to his character, Lot seeks the way of compromise. How many a Christian has followed him. He is unwilling to go as far as possible from sin and the world. Instead he wants to stay as near as possible. Perhaps his wife and daughters complained. Lot makes an appeal to God's grace and past mercy for indulgence. He draws a wrong conclusion, and mistakes both the nature and purpose of grace and mercy. But he is followed by many a Christian.

VERSE 19. *Found grace in thy sight.* See on 6. 8.

Thou hast magnified thy mercy, that is, shown great mercy. God's mercy to every vile sinner is great.

Saving my life. The city was not yet destroyed, but Lot knew by faith that his life had been saved from a judgment which had not yet fallen. The believer knows the same. ' God hath not appointed us unto wrath, but to obtain salvation through our Lord Jesus Christ, Who died for us ' (1 Thess. 5. 9, 10).

Lest some evil take me, and I die. Lot's argument was false and flimsy. If the Lord had magnified His mercy to him in saving his life, it is not likely that He would give him a direction that he could not obey without reversing the purpose of God toward him, already made clear. Yet many Christians are of Lot's mind. Probably he did not think he would actually be in danger on the mountain, but hankered still after the comfort of a city, and sought to retain as much of the world as possible.

VERSE 20. *This city is near.* These words contain the two reasons why Lot wanted to go to Zoar. (1) It was a city. He would, he thought, be able to live in it the life that he had been accustomed to live in the world. Many Christians expect their Christian life to be as like as possible to their old one. (2) Zoar was near. The journey would be less arduous. He could settle down in safety near, or in, the world

It is a little one. Lot foolishly thought that this fact was sufficient to turn away God's wrath. He tried to persuade God for his own sake to overlook something, because it was small.

Let me escape. Lot realised the necessity for escape. He was quite prepared not to stay in Sodom, but he wanted to choose for himself where he should go instead of accepting the Lord's choice. Many of us are like him.

My soul shall live. Notice the Hebrew usage of the word nephesh, meaning *soul*. The expression ' my soul ' is equivalent to ' I '. Lot understood that the issue was one of life and death. He was willing to escape from judgment, but not to go too far away from the world. He would not make a clean break with it.

VERSE 21. *I have accepted thee.* God granted Lot's request, but ' sent leanness into his soul ' (Ps. 106. 15). He soon left Zoar of his own accord for the place to which God had told him to go at the first (verse 30). The situation turned out to be the opposite of what he had thought. His fears were aroused in Zoar, where he had deceived himself into thinking that he would be secure. *I will not overthrow.* We may see two sides to this fact. (1) Lot's procrastination prevented, or at least delayed, the proper execution of God's judgment. (2) The whole city was spared because of Lot's presence in it. This is what it means to be ' the salt of the earth ' (Mt. 5. 13).

For the which thou hast spoken. Here is another example of the power and efficacy of prayer. Zoar was spared entirely, humanly speaking, because Lot had spoken for it.

VERSE 22. *Haste thee.* Again the urgency of the Gospel is emphasised. Our sloth and procrastination delay the ripe judgment of the world and allow sin and sorrow to mount up ever higher, when we ought to be ' looking unto and hastening the coming of the day of God, wherein the heavens being on fire shall be dissolved, and the elements shall melt with fervent heat ' (2 Pet. 3. 12).

I cannot do anything till thou be come thither. God had limited Himself by the prayer of Abraham. In the same way He cannot destroy the world, till every one of His elect, foreknown from all eternity, is safely gathered out (Mt. 24. 14).

Zoar means ' Litt e'. Zoar, where many Christians dwell, is only a little way out of the world. Only a little service for God can be done in Zoar. It is a place of little faith, little consecration and little joy.

Verse 23. *The sun was risen upon the earth.* The purpose of this statement is to emphasise the length of the delay and the lateness of the hour. ' The night is far spent, the day is at hand ' (Rom. 13. 12).

Verse 24. Our conception of the manner in which this destruction took place will be governed by our interpretation of the words ' out of heaven '. If they refer (1) to the eternal heaven, where the throne of God is, then the whole phenomenon was miraculous and supernatural, a breaking in of eternity upon time and a very special and fitting illustration of the final judgment at the end of the world. There is nothing in the verse to prevent us holding such a view. It is perhaps however more probable that the words mean (2) ' out of the sky '. In this case the overthrow was a natural phenomenon, brought about by the God of nature at the exact moment necessary for His purposes. It seems that a gas, or vapour, escapes, or used to do so, from the ground in this district, which is combustible, and would cause an explosion of tremendous force, if ignited. It is suggested that ignition, which would be unlikely, occurred (by the agency of the two angels?). The brimstone and fire, which destroyed Sodom and Gomorrah, stand as a permanent prototype of the fire which will destroy the

world on the day of judgment. The apostle Jude calls the fire of Sodom ' eternal fire ' (Jude 7). He says that the cities are set forth as an ensample, suffering the vengeance of eternal fire. He cannot be referring to the inhabitants of the cities in another world, because they are not set forth as an ensample. His words must mean that there exists in the world an illustration and warning of the meaning of eternal fire. The condition of the cities of the plain throughout history until the present day is the example to which he refers. The fire that caused it is ' eternal.' It is important to notice that it is not burning today. It burnt for only a few hours, but it did so with eternal results. What it consumed has been consumed for ever. This is the scriptural picture of eternal fire, and ought to make quite plain to us that eternal fire consumes once for all with an irrevocable result, and does not continue burning for ever. Not only does our Lord select the destruction of these cities as an illustration of the final judgment (Lk. 17. 28-30), but the language of this passage is taken up in the Apocalypse to describe the same thing (Rev. 14. 10; 19. 20; 20. 10; 21. 8).

Verse 25. *Those cities* now lie underneath the Dead Sea. *All the plain* is now a desolate region. *All the inhabitants* were swept in their monstrous wickedness to death and judgment.

Verse 26. *His wife looked back.* She did one of the two things that Lot had been warned not to do (verse 17), and the ' look ' probably involved a ' stay ' (verse 17). This must have taken place on the way to Zoar before the destruction of the cities. She may have stood on some eminence, looking back at the city with its roof tops ablaze in the beauty of the rising sun, the city, of which she was perhaps a native, which she loved in her heart. She may have felt incredulous about the destruction, or she may have wished to take one last look at the city before it was destroyed. Whatever her motive, her action was fatal. She was lost in the catastrophe that overwhelmed the area. The Lord gives us a solemn warning to remember her (Lk. 17. 31). Humanly speaking, it is possible for us to take such a look on the spiritual plane, to forget the urgency and necessity for our journey and the company with which we are travelling, and become involved, as she was, in final destruction. This will happen to all those who profess to undertake the Christian journey with unchanged heart and without newness of life. The unconverted can never reach the end of the journey or the final security.

She became a pillar of salt. This statement confirms the view that the destruction of the cities was a natural phenomenon. The soil was filled with salt, a fact still illustrated by the condition of the Dead Sea, and much of this would be blown up in the explosion and fall in the form of ash. It was with this ash that Lot's wife was overwhelmed.

VERSE 27. This is an example that every Christian ought to follow, if his spiritual life is to be strong. Early in the morning we all ought to stand before the Lord. We need no particular place for the purpose, only undisturbed privacy.

VERSE 28. *The smoke of the country went up as the smoke of a furnace.* This was the proof that the 'eternal fire' (Jude 7) had done its work, and the cities were completely destroyed. In the same way the smoke of Idumea will go up for ever (Isa. 34. 10), and the smoke of those that worship the beast (Rev. 14. 11), and the smoke of Babylon (Rev. 19. 3). In each case this is evidence of destruction.

VERSE 29. *God remembered Abraham.* It was for Abraham's sake that Lot was rescued, just as now it is for Christ's sake that believers are sent out of the midst of the overthrow, when God destroys and overthrows

the world. No believer deserves to be saved from destruction any more than Lot deserved to be rescued from Sodom.

VERSE 30. *Lot went up out of Zoar, and dwelt in the mountain.* He now does of his own accord what the angels had advised him to do at the beginning. He was allowed to do what he wanted, but it did not satisfy him.

He feared to dwell in Zoar. In doing so he showed lack of faith, as God had told him He would not overthrow Zoar (verse 21). Weakness of faith goes inevitably with compromise and worldliness, and Lot was a prey to fears and anxieties. If he could not trust God, he had nothing but the premises of the natural man to build on.

He dwelt in a cave. He had despised the pilgrim's tent and preferred the luxury of Sodom. Now he is reduced to a cave on the mountain side. Many a worldly Christian finds himself at last in the same predicament.

VERSE 31. *The firstborn said unto the younger.* The unchaste suggestion, made in this and the following verse, is worthy of a woman brought up in the atmosphere of Sodom. Lot had not thought of what he was exposing his children to, when he decided to make the wicked city his home. The worldly Christian of today often forgets the same thing. The disrespect here shown to their father by these two women can scarcely be wondered at in view of the callous suggestion which he himself had made with regard to them (verse 8). No father, who could contemplate such a course in reference to his daughters, could expect affection or respect from them. *Our father is old.* The point of this remark may be (1) that on his death they would be left alone and unprovided for, if they could not raise a family; or (2) that what they contemplated must be done without delay.

There is not a man in the earth. Their outlook was limited to the cities of the plain, whose inhabitants had been destroyed. Had they gone up to Abraham and consented to join his household and live the pilgrim life, they might have been cared for and provided with godly husbands. This course however could scarcely have been to their liking.

Verse 32. *Wine.* Whatever else they could, or could not, procure in the cave, they had taken care to bring a good cellar up from Zoar. *That we may preserve seed.* We need not doubt that this was genuinely their purpose, but this does not make the means which they took to attain it less immodest.

Verse 33. *They made their father drink wine.* Weak, fear-ridden, helpless, worn out by shock, lonely, disappointed, burdened in conscience, the old man was in the power of these unscrupulous women. Many a worldly Christian finds himself at the end in a similar situation.

He perceived not. He was drugged, deceived and taken advantage of. He had forgotten what he had once known in youth, how to depend on God's care. He had long ceased to cultivate a spirit of trust, or to appropriate the strength that is mediated through faith.

Verse 34. *The firstborn.* The elder daughter seems to have been the moving spirit throughout.

Verse 35. See on verse 33.

Verse 36. Lot ended his days not only in poverty and discomfort, but also in disgrace.

Verse 37. *The Moabites unto this day.* This is a note that may well have been inserted by Moses, when editing the narratives. The Moabites lived to the south-east of Israel, and were constantly a thorn in their side. Thus the consequences of Lot's decision to forsake the pilgrim life and to compromise with the world lived on, and permanently hampered the people of God. This fact also is,

alas! true to type. The witness of the church is weakened today by the aftermath of many a compromise in the past.

Verse 38. *The children of Ammon.* The Ammonites lived to the east of Jordan and north of Moab. They too were a thorn in Israel's side.

CHAPTER 20

THIS chapter provides a serious warning to the experienced Christian. In it we find Abraham repeating the mistake that he made in Egypt at the beginning of his sojourn in Palestine (12. 10-20). In each case he gave way to fear of man, which brings a snare (Prov. 29. 25). If this was understandable at the beginning of his career, it seems surprising that after having received so many promises, learnt to walk with God, believed against hope that God would perform what was humanly impossible, and become a powerful and prevailing intercessor, he should repeat this sin of lack of faith in circumstances far more dangerous than at the beginning. The lesson of the chapter is that the corrupt nature in the believer remains corrupt. However great his spiritual experience, he remains liable to fall into the same temptations as ensnared him at the beginning of his Christian life. He possesses no immunity. His safety does not depend upon his experience, or his progress in the Christian life—though spiritual growth creates and increases a habit of trust in God — but, as always, upon the continual keeping power of God, on which alone he can safely rely.

Verse 1. *Abraham journeyed.* We do not know what motive he had in making this journey. There is nothing to say that it was undertaken in the will of God, or as the result of prayer. He may have felt safer at a distance from the area that had been destroyed. While we cannot say that Abraham did wrong in making the journey, it may be that his departure was the first step out of God's will.

South country. The Hebrew is the Negeb, the rolling country to the south of Judah.

Kadesh and Shur. This was the road on which Hagar had travelled (16. 7, 14). It led to Egypt, and was therefore in a dangerous area. *Gerar.* This was in the south-west of Palestine in what was later Philistine territory.

VERSE 2. *Sarah his wife.* It is possible that Sarah's youth had been miraculously renewed (see 18. 13, 14). *She is my sister.* This was a quibble, intellectually accurate, but deceptive.

Took Sarah. Abraham's deceit brought about this immediate result. He must have foreseen the possibility of it, and again he was ready to save his skin at the cost of his wife's honour, and seems to have taken no account of the bitter distress caused to her. What followed showed that, even from the selfish point of view, Abraham's fears were needless.

VERSE 3. *God.* Notice the use of the divine name Elohim. In chapter 19 we had the Lord, Jahweh, being merciful to Lot. As long as the narrative was told from Lot's point of view, this name was used. It gave place to Elohim in verse 29, where a general statement of the destruction of the cities was made. In this chapter we have Elohim throughout except in the last verse, where Jahweh occurs once. This fits the narrative exactly. Abimelech is outside the sphere of redemption. God deals with him as his Creator, but in the last verse He is seen to have been acting on Abraham's and Sarah's behalf as the covenant Redeemer. This is the proper explanation of the use of the names. It is consistent with common sense and with the integrity of the writer, or editor. The critical theories are based on prejudice, and are quite arbitrary. *Came to Abimelech in a dream.* Here we have a direct intervention of God in order to protect His servant from his own

folly and to ensure the accomplishment of His declared purpose. It is comforting and encouraging to notice that Abraham was not abandoned to the consequences of his foolish act. Folly and sin did not rob him of God's protection, nor deflect God's blessing from him. We often find ourselves in a similar position, but we need not fear that we shall forfeit God's favour, nor lose the blessings which He has given us in Christ. We never had any merit to lose. Dreams are to this day a means of revelation to eastern people.

Thou art but a dead man. This is a vivid expression of the great scriptural principle that ' the soul that sinneth, it shall die ' (Ezek. 18. 4, 20), or ' the wages of sin is death ' (Rom. 6. 23).

She is a man's wife. The seventh commandment had not yet been formulated, and was not to be for another four hundred years, yet Abimelech was one of those who have the work of the law written on their hearts (Rom. 2. 15). He was, like all men, a moral being, and his conscience was his law. As the result of a primitive revelation, long tradition and common sense, he knew that adultery was wrong. It is evident that he consented instinctively to what God said to him.

VERSE 4. *Lord.* This is Hebrew Adonai, not Jahweh.

A righteous nation. In the strict redemptive sense of ' righteous ' Abimelech was wrong. ' There is none righteous, no, not one ' (Rom. 3. 10). He meant that he was innocent of this particular offence. Like all those who do not know the Gospel Abimelech thought of his life as made up of a series of separate acts, some good and some bad. Only the revelation of the Holy Spirit can bring home to a man the fact that separate acts are the fruit of a root within, an evil heart. It is what a man is that matters in God's sight. What he does is the evidence of what he is. It is interesting that, as their ruler, Abimelech identified his people with himself. He felt that a personal act of his own committed his people. This illustrates the strong conception of group unity felt by the ancient orientals. The idea of the covenant people of God, both in the Old and New Testaments, builds upon this sense. It is brought to its highest point in the great New Testament teaching of the oneness of Christ with His church and His headship over it. This enlightened ruler felt himself to be the king and father of his people, and little knew that he was supplying a faint picture of God's coming anointed King.

VERSE 5. Abimelech's question was only too true. If disaster had overtaken Abimelech, Abraham would have been responsible. We do not realise the far-reaching effects of our weaknesses and sins.

She, even she herself. We cannot tell what grief and bitterness of spirit lay behind this statement of Sarah's. It was probably impossible for her to do otherwise. Her motives may have been mingled fear and affection for her husband. We cannot tell to what extent, if any, she prayed, trusted, or rested on God's promises.

Integrity. The margin suggests 'simplicity', or 'sincerity'. He means that he was ignorant that he was doing anything wrong.

Innocency. Abimelech was honestly deceived.

VERSE 6. *Yea, I know.* God knows all hearts and their motives. Nothing is hidden from Him. He reads thoughts and hearts infinitely better than we read a book.

In the integrity of thy heart. It may be that by repeating this phrase of Abimelech's, but omitting the one that dealt with innocency of hands, God intended to bring home to Abimelech that it is integrity of heart that matters fundamentally.

I also withheld thee from sinning against me. We do not know the actual circumstances in which this intervention of God took place, nor what reason Abimelech gave to him-self for leaving Sarah alone. We find in this incident however another of the biblical proofs of the absolute sovereignty of God over human actions and states of mind. Before He spoke in the dream to Abimelech, God had been acting. He allowed Abimelech to take Sarah. This would bring home to Abraham something of the folly of his action, but he prevented Abimelech from doing any harm. God was already committed by His promises to Sarah, so that the whole purpose of redemption was at stake. If God can withhold a heathen ruler from sinning against Him, how much more is He able to keep us from falling and present us faultless before the presence of His glory with exceeding joy (Jude 24).

Suffered I thee not to touch her. God's sovereign power and providence extended to the practical protection of Sarah by means unknown to us, which appear to have been of the sort which we should call today guidance by circumstances.

VERSE 7. *Now therefore restore.* Notice that this is the third of three steps taken by God in relationship to Abimelech. (1) He permitted sin in ignorance to take place. This has a close connection with the sin and fear of Abraham. God allowed a dangerous situation to follow Abraham's weakness. (2) He intervened, but not apparently in a supernatural way, to prevent irretrievable consequences. (3) He called upon the sinner to restore. True conversion is a restoration of right relations between God and His creature. It is the removal of sin with its curse and the barrier that it causes between God and the sinner, and the setting of the sinner where he was before the fall, though it is more than that. True conversion must also be followed by the restoration of any wrong done to another.

He is a prophet. This is the first occasion in the Bible on which this word is used. A prophet was the mouthpiece of God (see Ex. 4. 15, 16; 7. 1, 2). The prophets of Israel were clothed with the Holy Spirit and spoke the words of God to the people. They were the channel through which the canonical Scriptures were given to Israel and to the church. It is sometimes said that the church gave us the Scriptures, or that God gave us the Scriptures through the church. Nothing is farther from the truth. For one thing we ourselves are part of the church. God gave the Scriptures to the church through His prophets, whom He filled with His Spirit for the purpose. The word ' prophet ' would not be likely to be a new one in the ears of Abimelech. Prophecy was a very ancient phenomenon, and there seem to have been prophets attached to the courts of many ancient Semitic and other oriental rulers. There was an inspiration which came from the devil (Acts 16. 16), which may have been a perversion of a provision made by God in a primitive revelation. We know in any case that Enoch was a ' prophet (Jude 14). The anonymous author of Ps. 105 seems to have had this verse, Gen. 20. 7, in mind, when, describing God's protection of Abraham, he wrote, ' Touch not mine anointed, and do my prophets no harm ' (Ps. 105. 15). There does not seem to be a reference in the narrative to any inspired utterance by Abraham, but the fact that he is described here as a prophet may encourage us to believe that he may have been the original author of this part of the Genesis narrative.

He shall pray for thee. This being the first instance of the occurrence of the word ' prophet ' in the Bible, prayer is the first function of the prophet of which we are told. This suggests that the Holy Spirit regards prayer as more fundamental and important than utterance, and possibly as indispensable to inspired utterance. We may think of Elijah, the greatest of prophets, as a man of prevailing power in prayer (1 Ki. 18. 42-45; Jas. 5. 17, 18), and if prayer is the basic function of a prophet, light is thrown upon the intentions of God for His humblest servants and handmaids by His pouring out

of His Spirit upon them (Acts 2. 17, 18). God has given us His Holy Spirit, in order that before anything else He might make us men and women of prayer.

Thou shalt live. The prophet's prayer gives life to the one condemned to die. This is an exact type and parallel to the situation seen in 1 Jo. 5. 16, where God promises to give life to the brother who sins a sin not unto death, in answer to a believer's prayer. The sin of Abimelech, which was committed in ignorance and innocence, is the sort of sin that is meant by sin not unto death. Sin unto death is sin committed deliberately against the light. Under the law no sin offering availed for it (Num. 15. 27-31). It amounted to blasphemy against the Lord (Num. 15. 30, R.V.; Mt. 12. 31, 32). Under the Gospel this sin is that of refusal of the Gospel (Heb. 10. 26-31). This promise should encourage, indeed oblige, us to pray for the unconverted, so long as they have not to our knowledge finally refused the Gospel.

If thou restore her not. Notice that the prophet's prayer for life for the sinner only avails if the sinner does his proper part in restoration. Life cannot be given in answer to prayer apart from repentance and conversion. The sinner's destiny, humanly speaking, is in his own hands, and rests upon the choice that he makes.

Thou shalt surely die. Death is the ultimate consequence of all disobedience to God's commands (Gen. 2. 17; Ezek. 18. 4, 20; Rom. 6. 23).

All that are thine. Sin is social, and every sinner brings down many another with him, just as Adam brought all his posterity with him to the grave (Rom. 5. 12; 1 Cor. 15. 22).

VERSE 8. *Abimelech rose early.* He wisely lost no time in taking steps to comply with God's demands and avert his doom. It is the duty of every sinner to do the same. *Called all his servants, and told all these things.* He did wisely and right to inform those affected of their danger and consult with them. It is rare to find sinners moving together in genuine repentance towards God.

Sore afraid. They had before them the recent example of the destruction of the cities of the plain. This fear of God's judgment is a good thing, and a sign of dawning faith.

Verse 9. *What hast thou done unto us?* Such reproach from one outside the covenant must have been very bitter to Abraham.

Thou hast brought on me and on my kingdom a great sin. The consequence of Abraham's weak and thoughtless conduct was far greater than he had anticipated. To bring sin upon another is very dangerous and very hateful in the eyes of God (Mt. 18. 6; Lk. 17. 1, 2). Yet it is to be feared that we all thoughtlessly do it more often than we are aware.

Deeds . . . that ought not to be done. It is a sad thing for a believer to fall in his conduct below the standard recognised by unbelievers.

Verse 10. *What sawest thou.* The irony of this reproach makes it very bitter.

Verse 11. As was to be expected, Abraham has no real answer for Abimelech. He had three things to say. The first of them is in this verse. It was a sorry sentiment, and ·must have sounded to Abimelech hypocritical and patronising. He thought that Abimelech did not fear God, and said so openly. He was mistaken. Ignorance existed, but the fear of God clearly manifested itself. Fear that these heathen were abandoned in wickedness led Abraham to a course of conduct which might very well have stifled the fear of God that they actually possessed. Abraham was right in thinking that he stood in a different relationship to God from Abimelech, but he seems to have fallen into the temptation of thinking of himself as superior for this reason. Events proved him wrong.

Verse 12. This verse gives us the second of Abraham's three answers to Abimelech. It was a verbal quibble. His description of Sarah had been verbally accurate, but actually deceitful.

Verse 13. This is the third of Abraham's three answers. It did not follow that, because he had made a pact with Sarah, he should have deceived Abimelech. He should never have made the pact.

Verse 14. The reason for Abimelech's friendship with Abraham was not the influence of Abraham, or respect for him, but the intervention and revelation of God, Who could as easily have intervened to protect him and Sarah. Abimelech's gift, made in addition to the restoration, to which he was bound, was a proof of genuine repentance.

Verse 15. Abimelech felt that Abraham's presence might bring him blessing. This feeling was again based on what God had told him. God is able to give us favour in the sight of the ungodly, to protect us, and to carry out His purpose through us.

Verse 16. *Thy brother.* This was an ironical reproof.

. A thousand pieces of silver. This seems to have been given in recognition of the wrong done to him.

He is to thee a covering of the eyes unto all that are with thee. This is a difficult statement. It may mean (1) that the existence of Abraham as her husband is a covering to Sarah's eyes, so that she cannot look wrongly at any other man. This is a true and proper sentiment, but not one that it seems likely that Abimelech would have expressed at this moment. There is no evidence in the narrative that Sarah had sought any company besides her husband's, or that she was anything but unwilling to have been taken into Abimelech's house. If there had been no connivance on the part of Sarah — and it is incredible to suppose that there was — the sentiment is very jejune. (2) Alternatively, and more likely, the statement may mean that Abraham, being Sarah's husband, was a protection to her as a metaphorical covering over the eyes of all men who saw her, preventing them from looking lustfully at her. That is more satisfactory than the first. It would imply that Sarah had been foolish in referring to Abraham as her brother, and would have found protection, if she had honestly said that he was her husband. (3) As a second alternative we may adopt the R.V. reading, which is as follows: *It is for thee a covering of the eyes to all that are with thee*. This means that the gift of the thousand pieces of silver was intended to cover the eyes of Sarah's husband and his household in the sense that they would forget the wrong done to her and not think of it again. This interpretation seems to bring out best the sense of the words ' with thee '. Apart from this there is little to choose between Nos. (2) and (3).

And with all other: *thus she was reproved*. The first words in the A.V. are awkward, and the R.V. seems to make better sense. It reads as follows: ' and in respect of all thou art righted ', with a marginal reading ' before all men ' for ' in respect of all '. This means that Sarah's position and honour have been fully restored, the gifts given by Abimelech to Abraham being evidence to all that she is restored without any harm having been done to her. Thus ' all things work together for good to them that love God ' (Rom. 8. 28). Abraham was the better for the incident. The reproof, we may hope, purged his fear of man. In any case he had experienced the power and ability of God to protect him. Sarah was the better for the incident. She was brought triumphantly through a trying experience. Abimelech was the better for the incident. He received a revelation from the true God and got the benefit of Abraham's prayers. We and all the church of Christ are the better for the incident, the account

of which has been written for our learning and has provided us with yet another example of the wonderful working of our gracious Sovereign Lord.

Verse 17. *So Abraham prayed*. What else could he do? He rightly went to the throne of grace, where he could lay bare his heart and ensure blessing for the future.

God healed. He always longs to heal in answer to prayer, and the prayers He loves best are those made on behalf of the sin-sick.

They bare children. Abimelech had had a practical proof of God's displeasure in this sign of barrenness. Every sinner is spiritually barren. ' They that are in the flesh cannot please God ' (Rom. 8. 8). Repentance and restoration change barrenness into fertility.

Verse 18. *The Lord*. The Redeemer had been active in defence of His covenant people and His purpose of redemption. Sarah must, it seems, have been at least a month in Abimelech's house.

Sarah, Abraham's wife. She is a picture of the true church (Gal. 4. 26), the wife of the Lamb (Rev. 21. 9). Though she passes through times of apparent danger, the Lord will protect her by frustrating all the activities of those who seek to ensnare her. His purpose for her and through her will never fail.

CHAPTER 21

This chapter falls into three sections. First we have the account of the birth of Isaac (1-7). In close connection with this comes the expulsion of Hagar and Ishmael (8-21), and this is followed by the covenant made at Beersheba between Abraham and Abimelech (22-33). The lessons of the chapter are (1) the ability of God to perform what He had promised, although it was impossible in the natural sphere. (2) The purpose of God, illustrated by a natural typical occurrence, to annul the old covenant and replace it by the new. (3) In the concluding section we have an illustration of a covenant and its meaning.

VERSE 1. *The Lord.* Notice that in verses 1-7 it is Jahweh Who performs the quickening regenerating act in accordance with the terms of His promise and His purpose of redemption. In verses 2, 4 and 6 however the Divine title is Elohim, a fact that emphasises the Creator's providence and power. To say that verse 1 derives from a different source from verses 2-7 is to show the straits to which criticism can be reduced by prejudice. The six verses would not make sense apart from verse 1. Notice the two things that are said of Jahweh. First He *visited,* then He *did.* The Lord's action is preceded by His presence. He Himself comes first to visit. He gives Himself, and after He has come, He puts forth His power. He will do nothing in our own hearts, till He has first come into them Himself. Then we shall feel the force of His regenerating and vivifying power, of which His action towards Sarah in the physical sphere is an illustration.

As he had said . . . as he had spoken. God's great acts of blessing do not come because in the first place we ask for them. We may indeed pray for His blessing, when we know what His will is. But His acts of blessing come, because He has promised them. He fulfils His Word, and ' what He has promised He is able also to perform ' (Rom. 4. 21).

VERSE 2. *Sarah conceived and bare.* Barrenness was turned into fruitfulness, as it always is by the life-giving touch of the Lord. Sarah represents the free Jerusalem above, which is the mother of us all (Gal. 4. 22, 26). She was barren, as it were, all through the days of the old covenant, till the Holy Spirit descended upon her in power on the day of Pentecost. Since then she has borne millions of children of promise. *In his old age.* It has not been until the time of the old age of the world that the children

of the free Jerusalem have been born. It was not till the fulness of time came that God sent forth His Son. *At the set time.* God is the Lord and Sovereign of time. The fact that this event happened ' at the set time ' is proof that it was ordered by God and was the fulfilment of His promise.

VERSE 3. *Isaac.* This means ' laughter '. The name commemorates Abraham's outburst of triumphant joy, when the promise was made to him (17. 17). The fulfilment of God's promise is, and always will be, the cause of the same happy laughter to believers

VERSE 4. *Abraham circumcised his son Isaac.* The child was born within the covenant, and its seal was set on him as a natural descendant of Abraham. His birth entitled him to all the blessings of the old covenant, the eventual possession of Palestine and the material prosperity connected with it. Neither his birth nor his circumcision entitled him to spiritual blessing (Mt. 3. 9; Rom. 2. 28, 29). Its counterpart under the new covenant is baptism, which belongs to everyone born by regeneration into the family of God. True circumcision is that of the heart (Rom. 2. 29).

Being eight days old. The number eight, which points to regeneration, connects circumcision with the new covenant and the power of the Spirit. It was a picture of the putting off of sins of the flesh (Col. 2. 11).

As God had commanded him. There is no true religious rite which is not the subject of God's command and revelation. Nothing in worship invented by man has any validity before God or power to please Him. Yet the visible church has always indulged in such inventions, and many of them are practised today.

VERSE 5. *Abraham was an hundred years old.* This was to teach the necessity of waiting for God's blessing. It was not till the fulness of time was come that God sent forth His Son (Gal. 4. 4). We too, who have turned to God, must spend our lives waiting for His Son from heaven (1 Thess 1. 10). Abraham had to wait, until it was clear beyond contradiction that the blessing was due to God's intervention alone. In the same way God's grace intervenes in the hearts and lives of sinners, when it is clear that their condition without it is hopeless.

VERSE 6. *God hath made me to laugh.* Sarah was now able to share her husband's triumphant joy. He rejoiced at the promise (17. 17), and she at the performance. So when God's promises are all finally fulfilled for His servants they will rejoice and sing for joy of heart (Isa. 65. 13, 14).

All that hear will laugh with me. The believer's joy is infectious. If we can show our joy and explain its source, the Holy Spirit enables us to communicate it to others, so that they too may be enabled to 'joy in God' (Rom. 5. 11), and 'rejoice in the hope of the glory of God' (Rom. 5. 2).

VERSE 7. *Who would have said unto Abraham.* The last two words are important. Anyone who did not know the circumstances might well have said that it was quite natural and very likely that Sarah should have given children suck. The people of the world often think if they do not say, that it is quite natural for the sinner to enable himself to please God, and very likely that he will attain to happiness in the world to come. But no one who knows the true circumstances says such a thing as this. No one says it 'unto Abraham'. The sinner who knows his own nature and anyone who believes what God's Word says about the nature of sin and the condition of mankind will consider it an astounding thing that a sinful heart can ever be made to bring forth fruit unto holiness (Rom. 6. 22) to the glory of God, and will realise that it is only possible by divine action working in grace. *Sarah should have given children suck.* If this implies that Sarah herself fed her child, emphasis

is laid upon the extent of the miracle wrought in her and the completeness of the renewal of her youth. 'They that wait upon the Lord shall renew their strength' (Isa. 40. 31). So in Christ powers lost in Adam are renewed and restored.

In his old age. What had happened was a sense of wonder to all who knew the truth about Abraham's and Sarah's age. The sinner, brought to Christ when dead in trespasses and sins, is enabled to bring forth fruit to the glory of God (Eph. 2. 1; Rom. 7. 4).

VERSE 8. With this verse begins the second section of this chapter, which continues to the end of verse 21. It is the story of the expulsion of Hagar and Ishmael, used by the apostle Paul as an allegory of the replacement of the old covenant by the new and of Jerusalem below by Jerusalem above (Gal. 4. 21-31). It is needless to say that in speaking of these things as allegories (Gal. 4. 24) the apostle does not imply that the story is legendary. He means that both the event itself and its embodiment in the Scriptures were so ordered, as was so often the case in the narrative of the Bible, as to be an illustration of spiritual truth. The persons in the story are Abraham, Isaac, Sarah, Ishmael and Hagar. Abraham here stands for his great descendant, the Lord Jesus Christ, Isaac for all those truly born again through the Gospel, Sarah for the true church and new covenant, Ishmael for the Jews, and Hagar for the old covenant and for Jerusalem in Palestine.

The child grew. So after the day of Pentecost the infant church grew (Acts 2. 41; 5. 14). *And was weaned.* The time came in the history of the early church, when it broke the bounds of Judaism.

Abraham made a great feast. We cannot tell what joy there is in the presence of the angels of God over one sinner repenting (Lk. 15. 7, 10).

VERSE 9. *Sarah saw the son of Hagar.* Ishmael represents the natural descendants of Abraham, born after the flesh (Gal. 4. 23), children of the earthly Jerusalem (Gal. 4. 25). *The Egyptian*. Though she had been so long in Abraham's house, Hagar remains an Egyptian. She was essentially of the world, of which Egypt is a consistent Scriptural type. In the same way the old covenant was essentially in the flesh. It was made with a people in the flesh, and it was maintained by carnal ordinances (Heb. 9. 10).

Which she had born unto Abraham. As Ishmael was a child of Abraham, so the old covenant was ordained of God, and had its place in the purpose of redemption. Its ordinances are illumined by the light of the Gospel and give out a radiance to all who read them in that light.

Mocking. The R.V. has ' playing ', suggesting an indifferent and innocent child and implying an unreasoning jealousy on Sarah's part. But the A.V. rendering is borne out by the apostle Paul in Gal. 4. 29. This is the only word from which in the whole passage he could infer the fact of persecution, and we see the Holy Ghost interpreting His own narrative through the apostle.

VERSE 10. *She said unto Abraham*. The Holy Ghost through the apostle Paul ignores the fact that the words which follow were originally spoken by Sarah. The apostle calls them the words of Scripture (Gal. 4. 30), as they undoubtedly are, and implies that their embodiment in the Scripture gives them vital force and turns them into a prophecy of the action of God in repudiating the old covenant.

Cast out this bondwoman and her son. As soon as the Gospel came and the Christian church was established, the old covenant, on which were based all the privileges of Judaism, was abrogated, and the new took its place. The Lord had said that the kingdom of God would be taken from the Jews and given to a nation (Mt. 21. 43), which the apostle Peter identifies with the Christian church (1 Pet. 2. 9). The Lord Himself by the

oblation of Himself once offered caused the sacrifice and oblation to cease (Dan. 9. 27), and the privileges of Judaism with its law, its ritual and its priesthood are gone for ever (Heb. 9). The old covenant made slaves of those with whom it was made by setting before them impossible moral demands (Rom. 7. 7-14). The Jews clung to their privileges, refused to recognise the change, and persecuted the church, until God sent the Romans in A.D. 70 to burn the temple and destroy the Jerusalem ' that now is ' (Gal. 4. 25; Lk. 19. 41-44).

The son of this bondwoman shall not be heir with my son. There cannot be two heirs, nor more than one people of God. The apostle in Gal. 4. 30 reinforces from this verse his direction to the Galatians not to subject themselves to Jewish law, ordinances, or ritual. We are not to be in bondage to these things, but free from them in Christ. Notice that the blessing which we receive from God is an inheritance, coming to us because we are His children and members of His family.

VERSE 11. If the casting out of Ishmael to make room for Isaac was *very grievous* to Abraham, how much more grievous was the casting out of the old Israel, in order to make room for the Christian church, in the sight of God. We remember how the Lord grieved and wept over Jerusalem (Mt. 23. 37-39; Lk. 19. 41-44).

VERSE 12. *Let it not be grievous*. The knowledge that any course is in the will of God takes away all grief and burden connected with it. So finally there was nothing but good to come out of the supersession of the old covenant and the Mosaic law.

Hearken unto her voice. God had been behind Sarah's request. Through her His will was being made known to Abraham. God often uses human agencies in making known His will. *In Isaac shall thy seed be called*. This means that it would be the descendants of Abraham through Isaac who would receive the promises and the blessings and be called to be the channels of God's grace to the world. The apostle Paul points out that the purpose of God for the seed of Abraham was selective from the first generation (Rom. 9. 7). No one can claim a right to the promise on the mere ground of natural descent from Abraham. If such were the case, Ishmael and Esau and their descendants could claim them. God has finally narrowed down the seed to Christ, but with and in Christ all those who believe. The writer to the Hebrews emphasises the preciousness of Isaac to Abraham in view of this selective pronouncement of God (Heb. 11. 18).

VERSE 13. *Also of the son of the bondwoman will I make a nation*. If Ishmael represents the children of the old covenant and of the law, he is typical in respect of these words also. The old Israel was a nation. It consisted of Israelites, to whom belonged the adoption and glory and the covenants and the giving of the law and the service and the promises, whose are the fathers (Rom. 9. 4, 5). The old Israel was called at the beginning of her history into a special relationship with God, she received and preserved the ancient scriptures, she stood out as an island of monotheism in the midst of a raging sea of corrupt heathen polytheism, and she produced a line of heroic prophets. Though her unbending obstinacy and blindness caused the destruction of her capital and of its inhabitants and the dispersal of her remnant through the world, she has remained a force in civilisation. She has never been absorbed. Members of her race have worked their way to positions of influence in many of the nations, and at the present day a nucleus of enthusiasts has returned to Palestine and inaugurated a state there, which has been recognised as sovereign independent by the nations of the world. *Because he is thy seed*. The blessing of Ishmael was a by-product of the call of Abraham, just as the Gospel has by-products. The material environment and educational opportunities of those who believe are improved. The home and family life of the converted drunkard are transformed, and the nations which permit or recognise the Gospel and encourage the reading of the Bible enjoy a much higher standard of living than those who refuse to do so, or are ignorant of it.

VERSE 14. *Rose early in the morning*. Notice Abraham's habit of immediate obedience.
Bread and a bottle of water. These are the two necessities for sustaining life. In the same way the spiritual life must be sustained by the bread of life, which came down from heaven (Jo. 6. 32-35), the Lord Jesus Christ Himself, on Whom we must feed in His Word (Jo. 6. 63), and the water of life, which is the Holy Spirit of God (Jo. 7. 37-39).
Gave it unto Hagar. The living Bread and the Water of Life are free gifts of God to every poor wanderer and sinner (Jo. 6. 32; Rev. 21. 6; 22. 17). *Putting it on her shoulder*. The water of life is put into the bottle of the Scriptures and made available for the wayfaring man to carry with him. *The child*. Not only was the old covenant annulled, but the Jewish nation, which it had engendered to bondage (Gal. 4. 24), was sent away as such from its privileged position in the household of God (Mt. 21. 43).
Wandered in the wilderness. In the same way ever since the dispersion the Jew has been wandering in the wilderness of the world. *Beersheba*. This was the place where the covenant had just been made, or was about to be made, with the Gentiles (verse 32). To the Jew, who clings to the old covenant, this territory is only a wilderness. Yet it is in this 'wilderness of the peoples' that God will meet with His people (Ezek. 20. 35; Hos. 2. 14).

VERSE 15. *The water was spent in the bottle*. The old covenant could give life no more, and the Old Testament Scriptures come to an end as a channel of blessing, if they are used in isolation after the fulfilment of the promises to which they witness.

She cast the child under one of the shrubs. The old covenant can do no more for its children than leave them to die.

VERSE 16. *Let me not see the death of the child.* The old covenant was intended to lead on to the life to be found in the new. ' The end of the law is Christ ' (Rom. 10. 4).

VERSE 17. *God heard.* There is never a cry from the heart that He does not hear. The sinner's cry of despair particularly claims His attention.

The angel of God called to Hagar out of heaven. Hagar knew this voice, and had heard it before (see 16. 7-11). Notice that while Hagar was still in Abraham's house and therefore within the ambit of the covenant, the Angel is the Angel of Jahweh. Now that she has been cast out, the Angel is the Angel of God. God calls today out of heaven through the Gospel to the wanderer in his despair. *What aileth thee, Hagar? fear not; for God hath heard.* When the sinner cries, and God hears, there is nothing to be afraid of.

VERSE 18. *I will make him a great nation.* There is no hint in the Bible that this promise to Ishmael carried with it spiritual blessing or any assurance of life in the world to come, but when God makes a promise to the sinner through the Gospel, He gives Him faith, righteousness, life, power and immortality.

VERSE 19. *God opened her eyes.* This is one of the first acts of the Holy Spirit in dealing with the soul which He turns from darkness to light (Acts 26. 18). The blindness of sin gives place to the vision of God. *She saw a well of water.* Both Jew and Gentile, when their eyes are opened by the Holy Ghost, see a well of water of life, of whose presence they were unaware before.

Filled the bottle with water. When the Holy Spirit enlightens the heart, the water of life flows through the Scriptures to the regenerate soul.

VERSE 20. Notice the four statements of this verse about the dying sinner who has been revived by the water of life. (1) *God was with* him. In the same way He is with every man and woman, lad or lass, who drinks of the water of life and is born again. Every conceivable blessing is contained in that simple word. If God is with us, we have protection, power and life, and the supply of all our needs.

(2) *He grew.* So every normal Christian grows up from spiritual infancy to manhood (2 Pet. 3. 18), until he will finally reach the measure of the fulness of the stature of Christ (Eph. 4. 13).

(3) He *dwelt in the wilderness.* Every Christian during the state of his growth dwells in the wilderness of this world. Here his needs are supplied by his Father in heaven and his character is strengthened and sanctified by the Holy Ghost.

(4) He *became an archer.* He learns to shoot the arrows of God at the hearts of the unsaved and win them as prey for the Saviour.

VERSE 21. In this verse Ishmael and Hagar revert to their original type. The last four verses had shown us the goodness and mercy of God to the wandering and dying sinner, a habitual characteristic of the nature of God, which the Bible takes every opportunity of emphasising. This verse begins with the repetition of the statement that Ishmael dwelt in the wilderness, suggesting a hint of double spiritual meaning. This verse reminds us that Ishmael was outside the covenant. He dwelt in the wilderness of Paran, which was to the south-east of Palestine, not in the promised land. All the unconverted dwell in the wilderness. ' The way of transgressors is hard ' (Prov. 13. 15).

The land of Egypt. Thus Ishmael was definitely linked with the world. This is true of the unconverted Jew, since the old covenant has been superseded . His mother was a Hittite (Ezek. 16. 3), and she has, as it were, taken him a wife from among her own kin. The Jew is a child of Abraham in the same sense as Ishmael, but he is outside the new covenant (though it is open to him to enter it through the Gospel). He does not dwell in the promised land, but in the world, and his associations are with the world.

VERSE 22. Beginning with this verse and extending to the end of the chapter we have an account of the covenant entered into at Beersheba between Abraham and the Gentiles. In this action of Abimelech and Phichol we see a shadow of the new covenant, by which we Gentiles have been brought into the household of God. The incident fittingly follows that of the expulsion of Hagar and Ishmael, which the Apostle Paul explains as a picture of the annulment of the old covenant.

Abimelech and Phichol the chief captain of his host spake unto Abraham. Notice that the initiative was taken by the Gentile rulers. In the same way God uses His people's witness to stir the hearts of the unconverted to seek Him.

God is with thee in all that thou doest. This was the fact that brought Abimelech to ask for the covenant. Again and again those who do not know God are given a desire to do so by watching the blessing that God gives to His people. They can see that Christians possess spiritual power and joy, of which they know nothing themselves.

VERSE 12. Abimelech appears to have felt that the future lay with Abraham. Perhaps he knew of the promises. Perhaps he drew his conclusion simply from what he saw of the blessing of God in Abraham's life. Similarly, the unconverted man who seeks God realises that the future lies with Christ and His people.

VERSE 24. Abraham willingly enters

into the covenant, just as Christ and His people are only too willing and glad to receive Gentile sinners into covenant relationship. ' The Spirit and the bride say, Come ' (Rev. 22. 17).

VERSE 25. *Abraham reproved Abimelech.* The covenant could not be made until differences were settled. Similarly the sinner cannot enter into relationship with Christ, till the differences between them have been settled and the sin question dealt with. *A well of water.* This is like the sinner's own life, of which he has robbed God. He must be prepared to restore it, before he can enter into covenant relationship with Christ.

VERSE 26. Abimelech was ignorant of the robbery. So is the sinner, until he is convicted by the Holy Ghost of living a selfish life and using for himself time and talents that belong to God.

VERSE 27. Notice that the gifts came from Abraham's side. The sinner has nothing to give to God. God gives all to him. The animals that were given were probably intended for sacrifice in the making of the covenant. So God gives to the sinner His own Son to be a sacrifice for sin and to make the covenant possible by the shedding of His own blood.

Both of them made a covenant. It requires two to make a covenant. Before the new covenant in the blood of Jesus can become effective for the individual sinner, he must ratify it for himself by appropriating its benefits by faith.

VERSE 28. *Seven ewe lambs.* In these ewe lambs we may see a picture of the Holy Spirit, with Whom the number seven is sometimes closely associated (see e.g. Zech. 3. 9; Rev. 4. 5). Being female, they were not intended for sacrifice, but for fertility. In the same way the Holy Spirit, as the Comforter, is that Person of the Holy Trinity, Who is compared to a mother. ' As one whom his mother comforteth, so will I comfort you ' (Isa. 66. 13). The work of the Holy Spirit in the world is to increase the church through the Gospel. The lambs are set by themselves. In the same way the Spirit of God is holy.

Verse 29. In Abimelech's question we may see a reflection of the seeking sinner's enquiry about the work of the Holy Spirit, as he sees it going on in the lives and service of believers. Notice that he emphasises the segregation of the lambs. In the same way the sinner often notices that the believer's life and activity differ from those of the world.

Verse 30. The lambs were to be (1) a gift. So the Holy Spirit is God's gift of Himself to mankind. They were also to be (2) a witness to the fact that the well had been digged by Abraham and belonged to him. In the same way the Holy Spirit is God's advocate in our heart and the witness that we are children of God (Rom. 8. 16).

Verse 31. *Beer-sheba*. This name means (1) Well of the oath. To Hagar, who was outside the covenant, there was a wilderness there, but to Abimelech, with whom this covenant was made, the place, which was not his own but Abraham's (verse 30), became not only the perpetual monument of the covenant made with him in spite of his deserts, but also (2) Well of the seven, that is to say, the place, where in virtue of Jesus' death and glorification he received (though to him all was in dim shadow and figure) the Holy Ghost (Jo. 7. 39).

They sware both of them. God has taken an oath for the believer's blessing and security (Heb. 6. 13-18), and the believer in response dedicates and devotes himself to God's service.

Verse 32. *They made a covenant.* God has made with the believer a new and everlasting covenant in the blood of Jesus (Jer. 31. 31; Zech. 9. 11; Lk. 22. 20), and the believer

makes it effective in his own case by individual appropriation of its benefits. *Abimelech rose up.* So the believer, as soon as he ratifies the covenant, awakes and rises from the dead (Eph. 5. 14).

They returned into the land of the Philistines, to live their life on a different plane and to witness to their own people of the great things that God had done for them (Mk. 5. 19, 20).

An archaeological difficulty is caused by the mention here and in verse 34 of the Philistines. In the present state of knowledge it is held that the Philistines, who were invaders from Crete or the Aegean, did not enter Palestine until the twelfth century, six or seven hundred years perhaps later than the time of Abraham. So far as the present chapter is concerned, we may note that Abimelech and Phichol are not described as Philistines. The expression ' the land of the Philistines ' might well be used by one, such as Moses, living in a time when the actual inhabitants were Philistines, exactly as we speak today of Picts formerly living in Scotland, or Bulgarians invading the Balkans. In view of the fact however that in chapter 26 the same Abimelech, or his son or grandson, and his people are themselves called Philistines, the solution may be that the Philistines planted small colonies in Palestine a long time before they invaded and occupied the land in force.

Verse 33. *Grove.* The margin says ' tree ', and the R.V. ' tamarisk tree '. ' Tree ' is likely to be the right meaning. The tree points to the cross (1 Pet. 2. 24). *In Beersheba.* The cross is the place where the covenant is made.

Called there on the name of the Lord. It is at the cross where every sinner must call, and whoever calls there on the name of the Lord is sure of an answer. *The everlasting God.* ' From everlasting to everlasting Thou art God ' (Ps. 90. 2). At the cross the sinner, a lost creature of time, faced with death and extinction, enters into eternal relations with the everlasting God. At the cross he is saved with an everlasting salvation (Isa. 45. 17; Heb. 5. 9), and there he obtains everlasting life. The fact that Abraham called on the everlasting God shows that he sought and hoped for everlasting things, as the New Testament tells us (Jo. 8. 56; Heb. 11. 10).

VERSE 34. *Abraham sojourned in the Philistines' land many days.* So is the believer a stranger and a sojourner in the earth (Ps. 39. 12; 1 Pet. 2. 11). We are in the Philistines' land, that is to say, among those who are Gentiles and naturally, or potentially, hostile; and we are here for ' many days ', not so much perhaps in our own individual lives, but in regard to the whole history on earth of the people of God and church of Christ.

CHAPTER 22

THIS is one of the great chapters of the Bible, and may be thought of as the climax or mountain top of the Book of Genesis. It is certainly the climax of the story of Abraham's life. It brings him to the final test of his faith, and when this is over, the story of Abraham draws immediately to its close. The great lessons of the chapter are (1) that the final test of faith is its readiness to abandon and devote all to God. (2) We have a vivid parable and picture of the devotion by God the Father of His only Son for the redemption of the world. (3) We see a type of sub-stitutionary atonement.

The main section of the chapter ends at verse 19. Verses 20-24 really form the prologue to the final section of the story of Abraham's life, which is more concerned with Isaac.

VERSE 1. *After these things.* These words are not insignificant. The testing came after the fulfilment of the promise in the birth of Isaac and his establishment as the heir and after the expulsion of Ishmael, of whom Abraham had been fond. The test thus came, not to a weak, but to a triumphant faith.

Tempt. The word means 'test' or 'prove'. We usually reserve the word 'tempt' for a malicious seduction into sin or error. A tempter desires his subjects to fail, but the one who tests desires him to succeed.

Said unto him, Abraham. God calls by name the individual with whom He has business. He is just as much able to make His will known to any one of us.

Behold, here I am. Notice Abraham's immediate and ready response. Are we as ready to respond to the call and command of God?

VERSE 2. *Thy son.* The analogy between Abraham and God Himself in this incident begins at once. God Himself has a Son. Human fatherhood and sonship are shadows of this central divine relationship, which belongs to the Being of the Godhead. *Thine only son Isaac.* So Christ is God's only Son, Who was in His bosom, Whom He did not spare, but delivered Him up for us all (Jo. 1. 18; Rom. 8. 32).

Whom thou lovest. In the same way God the Father loves His Son (Jo. 10. 17; Col. 1. 13). Notice the emphasis in the phraseology of this verse upon the extent of the sacrifice that was asked for.

The land of Moriah. This is generally considered to be the district round Jerusalem, where the temple was much later built (see 2 Chron. 3. 1). If this is correct, a further analogy appears with the sacrifice of Christ, which took place at Jerusalem.

Offer him there for a burnt offering. In the same way Christ offered Himself without spot to God (Eph. 5. 2; Heb. 9. 14). There are two things essential for the offering of a burnt offering. The first is that it be offered freely and voluntarily (Lev. 1. 3). Thus Christ came to do the Father's will, which demanded the sacrifice of His life (Heb. 10. 7; Mt. 26. 39). The second is that it be offered whole, or entire (Lev. 1. 9). Nothing must be kept back. Christ kept nothing back, and we too are called upon to offer all that we have and are (Rom. 12. 1). The example of Abraham in this chapter shows that such an offering is the final corollary of faith.

Upon one of the mountains. The offering was to be made on a high and exposed place, not in a corner. In the same way Christ was set forth as a propitiation (Rom. 3. 25), openly crucified on a hill-top against the sky-line. The transaction also was the most open of all events in the course of human history, being the dividing point for the reckoning of the eras of time. *Which I will tell thee of.* In the same way the circumstances of the crucifixion were all governed by God (Acts 2. 23), its place (Lk. 13. 33), and its time (Jo. 7. 30; 8. 20; 13. 1).

VERSE 3. *Abraham rose up early in the morning.* Notice Abraham's quick and unhesitating obedience.

Saddled his ass. He took practical steps to carry out God's will.

Two of his young men. The point of their introduction into the story will appear in verse 5.

Isaac his son, whom he would fain have left behind. So, if righteousness could have come by the law, it would have come (Gal. 3. 21). God did not send His Son to die for nothing, but because no other way of salvation for men was possible. *Clave the wood.* So God made the trees (Gen. 1. 11), from which one day the wood was to come to make the cross, on which His Son was crucified.

Rose up, and went unto the place. The Father pre-determined the crucifixion of His Son (Acts 2. 23), and moved, as it were, down the ages, till He came to the place after a journey which did not begin merely at the time of the fall, nor even at the time of creation, but in eternity past. Jesus Himself set His face as a flint to go up to Jerusalem (Mk. 10. 32; Lk. 9. 51).

VERSE 4. *On the third day.* Perhaps we may compare this to the third year of the journey, which the Saviour took from the Jordan to Calvary. *Saw the place afar off.* God the Father had seen it from eternity past, and the thought of it overshadowed the Saviour from His youth up (Ps. 88. 15).

VERSE 5. *I and the lad will go yonder and worship, and come again to you.* This statement was an expression of a superb faith, and the two young men to whom it was spoken, though they had no idea of its meaning at the time, appear in the story, in order that this testimony may be recorded. It is the basis of the declaration of the writer to the Hebrews that Abraham reckoned that God was able to raise Isaac from the dead (Heb. 11. 19). Thus this incident was not only the climax of Abraham's life of faith, when God's demand was made for all

that he had, but it was also the summit of his faith in the God of the impossible. He had believed in God's promise of Isaac's supernatural birth (Rom. 4. 18-21). Now he believed in God's power to raise him from the dead, for which he had no promise, though he was ready to believe it was implicit in what God had told him to do.

VERSE 6. *The wood.* This stands for the cross (see 1 Pet. 2. 24).

Laid it upon Isaac his son. In the same way Jesus went out, bearing His cross (Jo. 19. 17). In spirit He had borne it all His earthly life.

He took the fire in his hand, and a knife. If the Son carried the cross, the Father, as it were, took the fire and the knife. The fire stands for the Holy Ghost, through Whom the Saviour offered Himself without spot to God (Heb. 9. 14), and the knife perhaps for the Roman power. The actual historical events and practical details were in the Father's hand.

They went both of them together. So did the divine Father and Son pass together in perfect accord to the sacrifice of the cross (2 Cor. 5. 19).

VERSE 7. *Where is the lamb?* Abraham had not yet judged it right to tell Isaac what God had commanded. The lad therefore had no horrible anticipation, especially as he had heard his father's remark to the two young men (see verse 5). This was in contrast to the Saviour, to Whom the cross was an agonising anticipation during the whole course of His earthly life (Ps. 88. 15). Yet in another respect the situation was similar. The Saviour was aware of the fire, as soon as the Spirit came upon Him on the banks of Jordan and led Him straight through the ministry to the cross (Mt. 3. 16—4. 1). He was aware of the wood, as His language to His disciples more than once implied (Mt. 10. 38; 16. 24), but He could nowhere see a lamb, and knew that there was none but Himself.

VERSE 8. *God will provide Himself a*

lamb. This is one of the most profound evangelical statements of the Bible. No one could provide a lamb for the salvation of mankind but God Himself. No creature could be that lamb. Certainly a race of sinners could not provide one. But God provided His only Son, the lamb of God, that taketh away the sin of the world (Jo. 1. 29). We may compare God's provision of the skins for Adam and Eve (Gen. 3. 21).

They went both of them together. See on verse 6.

VERSE 9. *They came to the place*. So the divine Father and Son reached it together (Jo. 16. 32).

Built an altar. In the antitype this means to bring about the whole circumstances of the sacrifice. In another sense Christ Himself is the living altar in the living temple.

Laid the wood in order. This was actually done by the hands of the Roman soldiers.

Bound Isaac his son. It was the love of God for men that bound Christ to the cross (Jo. 3. 16).

Laid him on the altar upon the wood. Though in practice it was by wicked hands that Christ was crucified and slain, it was God Who brought it about (Acts 2. 23).

VERSE 10. *Took the knife to slay his son*. Notice the meek and unresisting part played by Isaac in this transaction. In this he showed himself a true pattern of his great Descendant. Perhaps in the feelings of Isaac at this moment we may trace a faint shadow of the terrible dereliction of the Saviour, when He was cut off from the presence of the Father, endured His curse, and suffered perdition in our stead (Mt. 27. 46; Gal. 3. 13).

VERSE 11. *The angel of the Lord*. Notice the change of the Divine Name in the middle of the narrative, a fact that cannot be reconciled with the theories of the liberal critics, who suppose the differentiation of names to indicate a difference of origin for the narratives. The name Elohim has been used in the chapter hitherto. This indicates perhaps the cosmic character of the event, of which this story is a picture and type. Now the Redeemer is dealing with Abraham, and is going to renew the redemptive promises to him. We therefore find, as we should expect, the name Jahweh. *Called unto him out of heaven*. Divine intervention took place when it could be delayed no longer. The Lord allowed the test to go its full length.

Abraham, Abraham. There are notes both of triumph and of urgency in this double call.

VERSE 12. *Lay not thine hand upon the lad, neither do thou anything unto him*. There was no last-moment intervention in the case of the Saviour. There was no escape and no possibility of a substitute. Had He willed it, there might have been intervention (Mt. 26. 53).

Now I know. God knew from the beginning, but by using this figure He expresses the fact that the testing of Abraham's faith was exhaustive and conclusive. From the human standpoint Abraham might have failed in this test. It was a real test to him. To God it was a demonstration. The Apostle James says that Abraham was justified by works at this point (Jas. 2. 21). He does not mean by this that Abraham's sacrifice, or anything else that he did, was meritorious in the sight of God, but that it was evidence of the existence of the faith by which he was justified. This is clear from the apostle's context. He says (1) that works are the evidence of faith (Jas. 2. 18). He says (2) that the patriarch's faith co-operated with his works, by which he means that they cannot be thought of as separated, but are to be seen as two sides of the same process, amounting in fact to the same thing (verse 22). He then says (3) that the works perfected or completed the faith, brought it to maturity (verse 22), and from this he draws the conclusion (4) that the sacrifice of Isaac by Abraham was a proof of his justification by faith (verse 23). Notice that the apostle is careful to quote the Scripture, which asserts Abraham's justification *by faith*. This view of faith exactly agrees with that of the writer to the Hebrews, who carefully explains throughout the 11th chapter of his epistle that true faith, both in Abraham's case and in many others, issues in, and expresses itself by, the kind of practical action which the apostle James calls ' works '. The apostle Paul says the same (Gal. 5. 6).

That thou fearest God. This is a general expression meaning a worshipper of the true God and a believer in Him. It holds good today, and aptly describes a Christian.

Seeing thou hast not withheld. The mark of the true believer is that he withholds nothing from God, neither his life, nor anything that he has. In the same way God Himself showed His love for us by sparing not His own Son, but delivering Him up for us all, and with Him freely giving us all things (Rom. 8. 32).

VERSE 13. *Abraham lifted up his eyes, and looked, and behold behind him.* The ram was there behind him all the time, but Abraham had not noticed it. So it is with the sinner. The Saviour has effected atonement for him, but the sinner does not see or know this, till the Holy Spirit has opened his eyes. If the ram was behind Abraham, he must have turned round in order to see it. In the same way the sinner must turn towards God and be converted, before he can see the Saviour with the eyes of faith. Indeed conversion is a sight of the Saviour. *A ram.* The ram in the place of Isaac now becomes the type of Christ. *Caught in a thicket.* In the same way the Saviour was entangled in the sin of man and sent by it, as it were, to the inevitable death of the cross. He was caught up in the great redemptive purpose. He was straitened till His work was accomplished (Lk. 12. 50). In Gethsemane He finally found that the cross could not be avoided (Mt. 26.

39, 42). *By his horns.* The Saviour was bound to the cross by the *strength* of His love.

Offered him up for a burnt offering in the stead of his son. Here appears a vivid picture of the fundamental Gospel truth of substitutionary atonement. Christ has been offered in the sinner's stead, bearing the guilt and punishment due to the sinner (Isa. 53. 5). He was made a curse for us (Gal. 3. 13). Isaac escaped death, and the ram suffered it in his place. So the believer escapes God's condemnation, which falls instead upon the head of the innocent Saviour. Christ indeed died on our behalf, but to say that He died on our behalf, but not in our stead, is to leave His death unexplained and to deprive the Gospel of its power to take away guilt. Christ's death as our substitute was the only way by which the demands of God's law upon us could be satisfied. Notice that the ram was offered as a burnt offering, that is to say, it was offered whole and entire, as a sweet savour, pleasing to God. Christ offered Himself as a burnt offering as well as a sin offering. This means that He offered Himself without reserve right up to the point of death and blood, and also that His offering was pleasing to God. God's love in Christ went out to a lost world. He willingly gave His Son for perishing mankind. The offering and death of Christ were a delight to God's love.

VERSE 14. *Jehovah-jireh.* This means, Jahweh will see, or provide. Calvary is the place where the Lord provided for the sinner's needs, after seeing them. He saw the needs from all eternity and provided for them by sending His own Son in the likeness of sinful flesh, and for sin (Rom. 8. 3), in order that He might die in the sinner's place (Mt. 20. 28), and that the chastisement of our peace might be upon Him (Isa. 53. 5). As He provided the ram for sacrifice in Isaac's place, so He provided the Lamb of God, which taketh away the sin of the world (Jo. 1. 29).

As it is said to this day. The provision once made is permanent and eternal. ' Christ was once offered to bear the sin of many ' (Heb. 9. 28). He ' made one sacrifice for sins for ever ' (Heb. 10. 12). And so to this day ' He is able to save to the uttermost them that come unto God by Him ' (Heb. 7. 25). *In the mount of the Lord it shall be seen.* The mount of the Lord is heaven (Isa. 14. 13, 14). In that mount in eternity past the Lord saw the need of fallen man. During every generation of human history ' the eyes of the Lord run to and fro throughout the whole earth, to shew Himself strong in the behalf of them, whose heart is perfect toward Him ' (2 Chron. 16. 9). From heaven during this Gospel age Christ looks down to see the need of His people as well as the need of a perishing world. For ' it ' the R.V. margin reads ' he '. So it is when the spirit mounts by faith to the mount of God that Christ is seen as Saviour, intercessor, mediator and priest. It was there that in eternity past God the Father saw Him as the lamb slain and the Redeemer of the world. For ' seen ' the R.V. reads ' provided '. In the same way the Saviour was provided in heaven in eternity past (1 Pet. 1. 20).

VERSE 15. In this and the following three verses we have the confirmation and renewal of the promises to Abraham.

The angel of the Lord. This was the pre-incarnate Christ. *Called.* We are not told that Abraham saw the angel. It appears that he merely heard a voice. Here is yet another manner of theophany.

VERSE 16. *By myself have I sworn.* By the remarkable condescension of this oath the Lord gave to Abraham and his heirs the assurance of the fulfilment of the promises. By two immutable things, in neither of which God could lie, namely His promise and His oath, we believers, who are the heirs to Abraham's promises, have strong confirmation, full confidence and assurance that what God

has promised us He will in the end give us (Heb. 6. 13-18). The oath was the greatest and most binding that could be taken, because it was taken by God Himself, the writer to the Hebrews reminding us that there was no other by whom He could swear (Heb. 6. 13).

For because thou hast done this thing. This does not mean that there was merit in what Abraham did, which obliged God to bless him. He had done what was commanded him, and thus was an unprofitable servant (Lk. 17. 10). What he had done was however the evidence of his justifying faith, and in this sense the apostle James tells us that he was justified by works, basing his statement upon this passage, and possibly upon this present verse and sentence (Jas. 2. 21-23).

Hast not withheld thy son. The refusal to withhold from God even the best of all possessions, and that in its entirety, is the final response of true faith to God. We may feel certain, that one of the features of Abraham's act which delighted God was its reflection of Himself. He too ' spared not His only Son, but delivered Him up for us all ' (Rom. 8. 32).

VERSE 17. In this and the following verse we have the last announcement of promises to Abraham. It contains four clauses, three of which are repetitions of former promises in slightly different form, and one is new, making fourteen promises in all.

In blessing I will bless thee. This is an emphatic repetition of the second of the fourteen promises, first made in Genesis 12. 2. It was fulfilled in Abraham's personal justification (15. 6), which, as the apostle James tells us, was demonstrated by this very incident (Jas. 2. 21). It was also fulfilled in Abraham's personal relationship with God (Isa. 41. 8; 2 Chron. 20. 7; Jas. 2. 23). Notice that the devotion of all to God brings renewed and additional personal blessing.

In multiplying I will multiply. This is a repetition of the ninth of the fourteen promises, first made in 13.

16. There the multiplied seed was to be as the dust of the earth. Here are two further powerful figures. The seed is to be multiplied as the stars of heaven. Ancient astronomers vainly thought that they could count the stars. The modern telescope has revealed that, as far as human ability to reckon them goes, they are without number. The sand upon the sea shore consists of countless millions of grains, much as does the dust of the earth. The preliminary fulfilment of this promise is found in the increase of ancient Israel (e.g. Ex. 1. 7), and the final fulfilment in the multitude of the redeemed (Rev. 7. 9).

Thy seed shall possess the gate of his enemies. This is a new promise which completes the fourteen. It is a promise of victory. The final fulfilment comes when the enemies of Christ are put beneath His feet (Ps. 110. 1; 1 Cor. 15. 25), the last to be destroyed being death (1 Cor. 15. 26), but it is fulfilled daily in the life of the Christian, who, being delivered out of the hand of his enemies, serves God without fear in holiness and righteousness before Him all the days of his life (Lk. 1. 73-75).

VERSE 18. *In thy seed shall all the nations of the earth be blessed.* This is a repetition of the seventh promise, first appearing in 12. 3. It is interpreted in two passages of the New Testament. In Acts 3. 25 the apostle Peter tells the Jews that they are the first of all the families to be blessed under the promise. The implication is that blessing on the Gentiles will follow. He also explains that the promised blessing consists of conversion to God from sin (Acts 3. 26). The apostle Paul exactly agrees. He says that the promise predicts the justification of the Gentiles by faith through the Gospel (Gal. 3. 8), and that the seed, to whom and through whom the blessing comes, is Christ (Gal. 3. 16).

Because thou hast obeyed my voice. Abraham's obedience was the expression of his faith. True faith always works itself out in obedience

(Rom. 16. 26). This is true of the ordinary affairs of life. A child obeys a parent whom it trusts. A man obeys a surgeon, lawyer, banker, or superior officer according as he believes in him.

> 'Trust and obey, for there's no other way
> To be happy in Jesus, but to trust and obey.'

VERSE 19. *Abraham returned to his young men* with Isaac, exactly as he had said to them (verse 5).

They rose up and went together to Beer-sheba, to tell Sarah of the wonderful provision of God and to live in the light of the promises, having received a new revelation of the meaning of redemption. *Abraham dwelt at Beer-sheba.* He dwelt in a good place. Beer-sheba means *the Well of the Oath,* or *the Well of the Seven.* First then he dwelt by a well, as the Christian does by the well and source of the living water, which is the Holy Ghost Himself and springs up in his heart to eternal life (Jo. 7. 38, 39; 4. 14). Then he dwelt by the place of the oath of covenant. Similarly the Christian dwells securely in the shadow of the new covenant made with him in Jesus' blood for the remission of sins (Mt. 26. 28). Abraham could also think of Beersheba as the well of the seven, and this points us to the sevenfold gifts and characteristics of the Holy Ghost. The Christian dwells where the Holy Spirit dwells, abiding in Christ and He in him (Jo. 15. 3; 1 Cor. 6. 19; Eph. 3. 17), led by the Spirit (Rom. 8. 14) and taught of Him (Jo. 6. 45).

VERSE 20. At this point the main portion of the narrative of Abraham's life ends. The climax has been reached, and his faith brought to a triumphant conclusion. With this verse the story begins to wind up. The list of Nahor's children is preliminary to the mission of the servant in chapter 24. The list is followed by the account of the death of Sarah (chap. 23), the marriage of Isaac (chapter 24) and the death of

Abraham (25. 1-11).

It was told Abraham. Possibly he sent to enquire, though the more likely inference is that the information came to him unsolicited. It came in any case, just when he needed it, and in this circumstance we may see God's guidance and sovereign care. We may be sure in our own cases that, when we need information for carrying out God's work and God's plans, it will be brought to us. The information was required by Abraham in connection with the selection of a bride for Isaac.

Milcah. She was the daughter of Haran, and thus sister of Lot (11. 29).

Nahor was a son of Terah and thus brother of Abraham (11. 27). He does not appear to have accompanied Terah and Abraham on the migration from Ur to Haran (11. 31) and may have been settled in Syria already.

Verse 21. Nothing is known to us about the bearers of this list of names, except a little about Bethuel, the last of them, who reappears in the story. To us they are nothing but names, but God knows them intimately each one. The appearance of the names in the Scripture reminds us of names written in the book of life (Phil. 4. 3). Nothing, so far as we know, is in that book but names, written there for no merit of their own, but because of the inestimable merit of Christ, and written there from the foundation of the world (Rev. 13. 8; 17. 8).

Uz. Job lived in the country of this man's descendants (Job 1. 1).

Buz. Elihu, the counsellor of Job, was a descendant of this man (Job 32. 2). He is mentioned with Dedan and Tema in Jer. 25. 23, and therefore probably lived in the south.

Aram. This man was the ancestor of the Syrians, who were called in Hebrew Aramaeans. His name is familiar today to all who refer to the Aramaic language. There may never have been an individual however of this name. The allusion may be to the race or nation.

Verse 22. *Bethuel.* He is the last mentioned and is likely to have been the youngest, but he was the one through whom the purpose of God was carried out. This is an instance of a phenomenon that occurs often in the Bible story. We may compare the cases of Jacob, Isaac, Joseph and David. The principle is in accordance with 1 Cor. 1. 27-29.

Verse 23. *Bethuel begat Rebekah.* This is the link that connects this little family tree with the narrative that follows in chapter 24 and subsequently. The purpose of these verses is (1) to introduce Rebekah's family and background, and (2) to show that Isaac's bride was not a foreigner, but a member of Terah's family.

These eight. Of the eight God selected one, and that the youngest. Possibly he was not only the youngest, but weak-minded, or imbecile, as Professor Blunt gave reason to believe in his *Coincidences of Scripture,* written over a hundred years ago.

Verse 24. *His concubine.* Nahor's concubine. Like Abraham, he had secondary wives. We hear no more of this woman or her children. The mention of them here completes the information given to Abraham, but implies that God knew them and loved them. The Holy Spirit mentions them, because He cares for them. The whole world is included in His evangelical purposes, even the despised and outcasts.

CHAPTER 23

THIS chapter tells us of the death of Sarah and of the purchase of a field for a burying-place for her. It looks forward and leads on into the story of Isaac, being preparatory to the account of his marriage, which immediately follows it.

Verse 1. *One hundred and seven and twenty years old.* Sarah is the only woman in the Bible, whose age is given. Since she was about 90 when

Isaac was born, this statement shows that Isaac was about thirty-seven at the time of her death. Sarah is the most outstanding woman in the Bible. A unique miracle was performed for her. She is included by the apostle Peter among the holy women, which hoped in God (1 Pet. 3. 5, 6). Such women did good and had no fear of man (ibid.) The number of her years is a prime number, emphasising the unique happenings in her life. It stands between 126 on the one hand, a number, which is the multiple of 9 and 7 and 2 and implies, if we do not feel it fanciful to see symbolism in Scriptural numbers, that she was heavenly-minded (9), a partaker of the Spirit (7), and holy (2); and 128 on the other, which is the multiple of 8 and 8 and 2, emphasising regeneration and resurrection and holiness a second time. Her death lay — and this is true, whether we choose to find it implied in the number, or not — between a holy, heavenly, Spirit-guided life on the one hand and an abundant and holy resurrection (albeit still future) on the other.

VERSE 2. *The same is Hebron.* Notice how the name is glossed, showing that it had fallen out of use, when the book was edited by Moses. This is one of the proofs of the early date of these portions of Genesis, which were probably written immediately after the events, which they describe.

In the land of Canaan. Sarah died in a foreign land, not having received the promises, but having seen them afar off and saluted them. The child of God still dies in the land of his pilgrimage and sojournings, sometimes done to death by its inhabitants, as was his Master, sometimes worn out by old age and long service, as in Sarah's case.

Abraham came, perhaps to the tent of Isaac, which may have lain at a little distance. The most likely source for the story of these events is Isaac. *To mourn for Sarah, and to weep for her.* Tears and sorrow are the natural accompaniments of death,

the more so in the days before the Gospel, when the hope of resurrection seemed remote. But the Lord God will swallow up death in victory and will wipe away all tears from off all faces (Isa. 25. 8; Rev. 21. 4), and we Christians are told by the Holy Ghost through the apostle not to sorrow as others, who have no hope (1 Thess. 4. 13).

VERSE 3. *Abraham stood up from his dead.* He had been lying on his face in sorrow (compare the action of David (2 Sam. 12. 16; 13. 31)), or kneeling in prayer by Sarah's bedside. *Spake unto the sons of Heth.* This was done immediately owing to the necessity and custom of speedy burial. The fact that he was a sojourner compelled Abraham to parley with the Hittites at a time, when of all others he might have wished to be alone with his son. The sons of Heth are the Hittites, who were among the inhabitants of Palestine.

VERSE 4. *I am a stranger and a sojourner with you.* So is every child of God a stranger and sojourner in the world. The position of Abraham in Palestine is a parable of that of all his spiritual descendants on the larger scale (Ps. 39. 12; 1 Chron. 29. 15; Heb. 11. 13).

Give me a possession of a burying-place. The whole land was Abraham's by promise, just as all things are ours (1 Cor. 3. 21). Yet he had to ask for and purchase the barest necessity of a burying-place. This gives us a moving illustration of the sacrifices which Abraham had made at the call of God, and provides a warning and incentive for ourselves.

Out of my sight. What is dead is not fit to be seen, yet for age after age God endures the sight of souls dead in trespasses and sins. One day all will be safely buried out of His sight.

VERSE 5. *The children of Heth answered.* Abraham was entirely at their mercy, and they might have had no inclination to respond, but God knew the needs of His servant and saw that they were provided.

VERSE 6. *Hear us, my lord.* The Hittites were polite and courteous to Abraham, God having given him favour in their eyes.

Thou art a mighty prince among us. The Hebrew words translated ' a mighty prince ' mean literally ' a prince of God '. The Hittites recognised the power and influence possessed by Abraham, although he was only a sojourner, exactly as Abimelech had before them (see chapter 20). This was as it should be, and it ought to be true of us. Can this be said of us?

In the choice of our sepulchre. They offered the best. Do we follow their example and offer the best to God?

None of us shall withhold. This was very generous, but perhaps their words were not so unworldly as they seem. This way of speaking appears to have been the ordinary way in the ancient east of beginning a bargain, and perhaps they never intended this offer to be literally accepted. This way of speaking is typical of worldly people, who often say what they do not mean and pretend to be generous, when they really are not. A distinguishing feature of the redeemed is that in their mouth is found no guile (Rev. 14. 5).

VERSE 7. *Abraham stood up, and bowed himself.* His purpose in standing up, that is to say, in making himself conspicuous, was to bow, that is to say, to humble himself. In the same way Christ came not to be ministered unto, but to minister (Mt. 20. 28). Notice Abraham's courtesy and humility. He made no rough demands, nor did he attempt to stand on any rights. All this should be an example to us. *The people of the land.* They were still in possession, although all had been promised to Abraham.

VERSE 8. *Intreat for me.* Abraham sought the help of the people of the land, nor should we feel above seeking the help of the people of the world in matters that are right and necessary. Opportunities for witness are provided, in this way.

Ephron the son of Zohar. Abraham had a definite aim and knew clearly what was in his mind. He did not beat about the bush. This is a good example to follow in prayer to God as well as in making requests to men.

VERSE 9. *The cave of Machpelah.* Abraham did not need the whole field but the cave which was in it. So Christ did not need the whole field of the world, but only the treasure which was hidden in it, consisting of the elect (Mt. 13. 44).

Which he hath. The owner of the field possessed the cave before the field was purchased. *Which is in the end of his field.* It was in a corner, and perhaps not thought much of, but it was the one thing needed and valued by Abraham. The elect are not thought much of in the world and are apt to get pushed into its corners, but it is they who are needed and valued by Christ.

For as much money as it is worth. The margin says, ' For full money ', and the R.V. says, ' For the full price '. So Christ paid the full price for the world, which was His own suffering and life blood. Nothing less could redeem, and the awful price that was paid proves the value in God's sight of a single human soul.

For a possession of a burying-place amongst you. Christ bought the world that in it, while it lasts, He might bury His elect. We remember that Sarah represents Jerusalem, which is above, that is to say, the true church (Gal. 4. 26). So the elect are buried with Christ by baptism (Col. 2. 12) amongst the people of the world to await the glorious day of resurrection. Here also beneath the soil of this world most of them lie actually buried.

VERSE 10. *Dwelt among.* The R.V. says, ' was sitting in the midst of ', which makes better sense.

In the audience of the children of

Heth. He wanted witnesses for what he was going to say.

All that went in at the gate of his city. He wanted those who understood his ways to get an impression of his generosity.

VERSE 11. *Give I thee . . . I give it thee . . . Give I it thee.* He never intended to do this. It was a roundabout way of bargaining. This appears to have been the usual way of doing business such as this, and demonstrates the guile of the fallen human heart.

In the presence of the sons of my people. Outwardly he called upon his own people to witness the gift, pretending in his heart that it was for Abraham's sake that he did so. In reality he was parading his generosity in public, even if he scarcely realised that he was doing so.

VERSE 12. *Abraham bowed down himself before the people of the land.* So did the Saviour, Who came not to be ministered unto, but to minister. We are to do the same, and we are to submit ourselves to all in authority in the world (1 Pet. 2. 13, 14; Rom. 13. 1-6; Tit. 3. 1). Humility was part of Abraham's witness, and it is essential to ours.

VERSE 13. *In the audience of the people of the land.* The circumstances were such, that, if Abraham had not spoken publicly, he could not have spoken at all. In so doing he gave public witness to his honesty and openness of purpose.

I will give thee money for the field. The R.V. reads, ' I will give the price of the field.' Notice that in contrast to Ephron and the other Hittites Abraham never altered his purpose or the expression of it. In his mouth ' was found no guile ' (Isa. 53. 9; Zeph. 3. 13; Ps. 32. 2; Rev. 14. 5).

Take it of me, and I will bury my dead. Abraham refused to perform the very necessary office of burial until the money had been properly paid for the field.

VERSE 14. *Ephron answered Abraham* . Although he spoke in a roundabout way, because it was his custom and he knew no better, he seems to have been friendly to Abraham and to have wished to enter into a transaction, which would be of benefit to both sides.

VERSE 15. *The land is worth four hundred shekels of silver.* He names a price, which may well have been too large. He had no doubt had this price in his mind all the time that he was pretending to be willing to give the land.

What is that betwixt me and thee? He now pretends that he is indifferent to the price. This may have been the normal way of bargaining among his people, but, if it was, it betrays a crooked and avaricious heart.

VERSE 16. *Abraham hearkened unto Ephron.* He may have been taken in, but it is better to be so than to take others in. Possibly Ephron expected him to beat him down. In bargains of this kind it is often customary to begin by naming a price which is higher than the seller expects to obtain. If Abraham had ever been inclined to bargain, the circumstances in which he was placed on that sad day might well have been enough to prevent him. By accepting the first price named he showed his honesty, openness and guilelessness, and gave a testimony to his God and His righteous requirements which was well worth any financial loss which he might have sustained.

Abraham weighed to Ephron the silver. Silver often stands in the Bible for redemption, and here our thoughts are turned to the eternal transaction effected by Christ on the cross, which purchased our freedom from Satan, sin and death.

In the audience of the sons of Heth. There were plenty of witnesses that the amount was the same as had been demanded.

Current money with the merchant. The silver was a medium recognised by both sides. In something of the same way the Saviour was a Mediator, bridging God and man, acceptable to God and able to represent man.

This was not the transaction referred to by the martyr Stephen in his speech (Acts 7. 16). It was the purchase of a field in Shechem by Jacob from the children of Hamor to which Stephen was referring. The fact that he says that the purchase was made by Abraham instead of by Jacob has been seized on eagerly by liberal critics and destructive theologians always on the look out to find, if they can, some discrepancy in the Bible. It is quite unnecessary to suppose that Stephen confused two transactions, although, if he did so, we have a very accurate account of his speech, including his mistake, in the inspired narrative. It is however impossible for him to have made a slip, seeing he was full of the Holy Ghost (Acts 7. 55), Who may be expected to have given him the words of his speech in accordance with the Lord's promise for exactly those circumstances (Mt. 10. 19, 20). Stephen was using the name Abraham in the tribal or legal sense, much as the name Israel was used for the nation. He meant that the purchase was made by the family or clan which was associated by the inhabitants of Canaan with the name of Abraham.

Verse 17. *The field of Ephron, which was in Machpelah, which was before Mamre.* Note the precise legal language. The transaction and contract were official and legal. In the same way the transaction by which Christ on the cross acquired the world was in accordance with the law of God and accepted by Him as eternally valid.

The field. ' The field is the world '. (Mt. 13. 38). *The cave which was therein.* This was the burying-place for the sake of which the field was bought. Christ purchased the world for the sake of the elect, who are buried in it.

All the trees that were in the field. The trees represent the people of God (see Jer. 17. 7, 8; Num. 24. 6; Job 29. 19; Ps. 1. 3). ' The trees of the Lord are full of sap; the cedars of Lebanon, which he hath planted ' (Ps. 104. 16). ' The righteous shall flourish like the palm tree ' (Ps. 92. 12).

That were in all the borders round about. The redeemed of the Lord are found in all the borders and corners of the world. They come from every nation and tribe and people and tongue (Rev. 7. 9).

Were made sure. The assurance and security of the redeemed in Christ is absolute. His purchase of them will never be disallowed (Jo. 10. 27-29; Rom. 8. 37, 38; Heb. 6. 13-20). This great and unchangeable fact must not prevent us from doing our diligence to make our calling and election sure (2 Pet. 1. 10). In fact it is through our own co-operation that God works to make it sure. It is He that works within us both to will and to do after His good pleasure (Phil. 2. 13).

Verse 18. *Unto Abraham.* Just as the elect are made sure unto Christ. *For a possession.* So the heathen are Christ's inheritance, and the uttermost parts of the earth are His possession (Ps. 2. 8). ' The Lord's portion is His people, and Jacob is the lot of his inheritance ' (Deut. 32. 9). *In the presence of the children of Heth.* The death and resurrection of Christ did not take place ' in a corner ' (Acts 26. 26). His crucifixion took place openly in the presence of devils and men (Ps. 22. 12, 13). He was ' set forth as a propitiation ' (Rom. 3. 25).

Before all that went in at the gate of his city. As the world goes 'about its business today, the Gospel of Christ's redemption is openly proclaimed before it.

Verse 19. *After this, Abraham buried Sarah his wife.* Immediately after the purchase of the world by the blood of Christ He Himself was buried in it, and all His people with him (Col. 2. 12).

In the cave. So the true church of Christ is safe buried in the cleft of the Rock of Ages.

The same is Hebron in the land of

Canaan. This is an interesting and significant gloss. When the book was edited the name Mamre had been lost, and the place was known as Hebron. This fact is duly noted for the enlightenment of readers, for whom the name Mamre would have no meaning. But in addition the glossator explains that Hebron was in the land of Canaan. This means that he did not live there, and points strongly to Moses, who was never in Canaan, as the editor of the book, as we should expect. Notice that the country is not called ' the land of Israel '. It was still ' the land of Canaan '. This means that the gloss was made before the Israelite conquest under Joshua, and confirms the likelihood of Moses' editorship. The R.V. gives a different emphasis to the sentence. It places the words ' the same is Hebron ' within brackets. They are still a gloss on the name, but the words ' in the land of Canaan ' belong to the original sentence. They remain proof that the passage dates from before the Israelite conquest, but, if the original passage dates from the time of the patriarchs, they cannot be proof of residence outside the land. They would then have the sense of an expression of praise and wonder that Sarah had left Ur of the Chaldees and Haran and reached the land which God had spoken of to die there. Here was a firstfruit of the fulfilment of His promise.

Verse 20. *The field*. This represents the world.

The cave that is therein. This represents the safe hiding-place in Christ for sinners in the world. *Were made sure*. See verse 17. *Unto Abraham for a possession*. See verse 18. *By the sons of Heth*. Devils and men will one day recognise the right of Christ to the sovereignty of the world (Phil. 2. 10, 11).

CHAPTER 24

In this chapter we have a detailed account of the mission of Abraham's servant to find a bride for Isaac. The story is a parable of the mission of God's evangelising servants to gather out from the world a people to His Name to be the bride of Christ. The servant is sometimes regarded as a type of the Holy Spirit, but it seems more likely that he is a type of the evangelist. The context of the narrative has significance. It immediately follows the account of the death of Sarah. Thus the death of Christ must precede the marriage of the Lamb, and death in Christ for the people of God must precede the part they have in the wedding feast of a glorious resurrection. In the actual narrative this chapter has a close connection with its context. The section 22. 20-25. 11 forms the conclusion of the life of Abraham and connects his story with that of Isaac, which follows it. The steps in the connection are: (1) the enumeration of Nahor's family (22. 20-24); (2) the death of Sarah (23); (3) the marriage of Isaac (24); (4) the death of Abraham (25. 1-11).

Verse 1. *Abraham was old and well stricken in age*. This is the background of the chapter. He knew that his life was past, and that the future lay with his son. His own work and witness were finished. In the same way, when the Saviour's work on earth was finished, and He was about to return to His Father, He commissioned His disciples to carry on His evangelising work on earth.

The Lord had blessed Abraham in all things. Even during his sojourning and pilgrimage he had been abundantly blessed. All this was a foretaste of eternal blessing to come. In the same way we have the Lord's promise that everyone who has forsaken loved ones or property for His sake and the Gospel's will receive a hundredfold in this present time (Mk. 10. 29, 30).

Verse 2. *His eldest servant of his house*. He chose for this important mission the most responsible representative that he could find. The Master looks for similar trust and responsibility in us. We can only obtain this by dependence on Him and by abiding so closely in Him that we instinctively know His will. We must have His interests closely at heart, as this servant had his master's.

That ruled over all that he had. All that our Master has is put at our disposal to use in His service. His resources are infinite.

Put, I pray thee, thy hand under my thigh. This means to take hold of the genital organs, which was the solemn and binding method of taking an oath in the ancient eastern world.

VERSE 3. *I will make thee swear.* The servant of God, before being sent out on his evangelistic mission in the world, enters into covenant-relationship with his Master and is called upon to devote himself utterly to His interests. We ourselves too often forget this and seek to enter into half-hearted service, which cannot be acceptable to God.

The Lord, the God of heaven, and the God of the earth. Here Jahweh, the Redeemer, is identified with the Creator, Who rules heaven and earth. Abraham knew with Whom he had to deal. All the forces of heaven and earth, angels, men and nature, are at the disposal of God as instruments for carrying out His purpose. If the servant broke his oath, he would find himself faced with all the resources of God Almighty, which would be brought to bear in retribution against him.

Thou shalt not take a wife unto my son of the daughters of the Canaanites. There are two courses which are forbidden by Abraham. This is the first. There is to be complete separation between those in covenant relationship with God and the heathen around them. This is a parable, and the principle holds good today. We are not to be unequally yoked with unbelievers, but are to come out from among them and be separate (2 Cor. 6. 14, 17). The bride of Christ is a chaste virgin (2 Cor. 11. 2), ' without spot or blemish or any such thing ' (Eph. 5. 27). The Lord Jesus Christ has called us out of this present evil world (Gal. 1. 4). No unrepentant sinner will ever be found among the company, which makes up the bride of Christ. See also verse 6 *Among whom I dwell.* Abraham dwelt among the Canaanites, just as we dwell among the sinners of the world, awaiting our inheritance, which Satan and his children now possess.

VERSE 4. *Thou shalt go unto my country.* Christ's country is the heavenly Sion. All those who form His bride are natives of this country, born again of God (Jo. 1. 12; 3. 3, 7), citizens of Sion (Ps. 87. 5, 6). *And to my kindred.* All those who form the bride of Christ are His kindred, children of God like Himself (Jo. 1. 12; Rom. 8. 14, 16; Gal. 3. 26).

Take a wife unto my son Isaac. This is the purpose of the Gospel mission in the world. A wife is being taken for God's Son (2 Cor. 11. 2; Rev. 19. 11; 21. 9).

VERSE 5. *Peradventure the woman will not be willing.* The Gospel proclamation is always faced with this risk. The majority of those in the world are not willing to accept the claims of Christ. The refusal of the Gospel was foreknown to God and the subject of a prediction by Isaiah, who asks, ' Who hath believed our report?' (Isa. 53. 1). The claims of God were refused by ancient Israel. ' All the day long I have stretched forth my hands to a disobedient and gainsaying people ' (Isa. 65. 2; Rom. 10. 21). *To follow me unto this land.* Many more are willing to appropriate the relief and comfort which are brought by the Gospel than are ready to follow the Lamb whithersoever He goeth (Rev. 14. 4). When it becomes evident that home, friends and country must be forsaken, and that the servant of God must be ready to go out and lead a pilgrim life, many, who have superficially accepted the claims of the Gospel, begin to draw back and refuse to follow the evangelist any further, as he seeks to lead them to Christ (Mt. 13. 20, 21).

Must I needs bring thy son again

unto the land from whence thou camest? This question, which occurred to Abraham's servant, is the same in principle as occurs sometimes to the evangelist. Must the standard of the Gospel be lowered, and the claims of Christ be reduced, to accommodate the weakness and half-heartedness of those who will not accept them in their entirety? The Scriptural answer is an emphatic no, but the opposite answer seems to have been given by the church generally today, and there are evangelicals who have not been afraid to join with others in giving it. The compromise with the world and the accommodation to its standards, so often seen today, would horrify the apostles, and the result is already disastrous.

VERSE 6. *Beware thou that thou bring not my son thither again.* This is the second of the two courses which Abraham forbade his servant to take. The first appeared in verse 3. While there was to be no association with the heathen, there was (2) to be no going back to the old life. The pilgrim life must never be abandoned for a return to the world. If the bride would not come out of the world to the bridegroom, he must never go back to her into the world.

VERSE 7. *The Lord God of heaven.* Abraham rightly looks to God Himself, the source of all power and grace, to bring the mission to a successful accomplishment. We must do the same. In all our evangelistic efforts we must depend upon God to do for us what we cannot do. This is exactly what the Saviour has promised (Mt. 28. 18-20).

In depending upon God Abraham relied upon (1) His action in the past, and (2) His promises for the future. (1) He relies on the fact that God took him from his father's house and from the land of his kindred. God's purpose was quite clear from what Abraham had already experienced. There must be no attempt to reverse it. What He had done for Abraham He could do for another. So, if we

should become discouraged in our Gospel quest, we may look back to our own conversion, and take confidence from what God has done in our case. (2) He relies upon God's promise for the future. He remembers the oath taken by God at the time of the sacrifice of Isaac. He remembers that God has declared His purpose of gathering a redeemed humanity into the inheritance, which He has prepared for it, and he realises that, in order to accomplish this purpose, God will most certainly gather out His own from a sinful world. We may therefore go forward in confidence on our evangelistic mission.

Unto thy seed will I give this land. This is an exact repetition of the promise given in 12. 7. It was fulfilled when the natural seed conquered and inherited the land under Joshua, and it is fulfilled in the seed of promise, Christ and His people, by the great redemptive events which took place in the land, as well as in the final eternal inheritance on the new earth (Rev. 21. 7). *He shall send his angel before thee.* We have someone better than an angel to precede us in our mission, God the Holy Spirit Himself. It is He that convicts the world (Jo. 16. 8). He opens blind eyes and inclines stubborn hearts to accept the Gospel call. The Holy Spirit guarantees the success of the worldwide Gospel campaign.

Thou shalt take a wife unto my son. The church, which is gathered out of the world by the Gospel, is the bride of Christ (2 Cor. 11. 2; Eph. 5. 25-32; Rev. 19. 17).

VERSE 8. *If the woman will not be willing to follow thee.* These words were spoken to meet the objection of the servant, expressed in verse 5. Abraham implies that he is confident by faith that she would be willing. The same believing confidence is necessary for success in evangelism. It means complete dependence upon God.

Then thou shalt be clear from this my oath. The evangelist is not responsible for the decision of the one to whom the call is given. He is responsible for the clear presentation of the call. If he presents the call and it is not accepted, he has done his duty.

Only bring not my son thither again. In these words of warning we may see a double significance. (1) They mean that the standard of the Gospel must never be lowered to accommodate the scruples of those to whom it is presented. (2) They may well mean that God is resolved to go forward with His great plan of redemption, however much His offer of salvation is refused in the world.

VERSE 9. Abraham's servant thus bound himself to carry out his master's wishes. We, too, are bound to our Master's interests by the very terms of our discipleship. He calls us to serve Him and follow Him (Mt. 19. 21; Jo. 12. 26). He promises that if we do so He will make us evangelists (Mt. 4. 19). The apostle Paul at the time of his conversion was called directly into the service of the Lord (Acts 26. 16-18). To place the interests of family, of self, or of property above those of the Master is incompatible with discipleship (Lk. 14. 26, 27, 33).

VERSE 10. *Ten camels.* The camels had no intelligent part in the mission. They performed their part without the slightest realisation of the real meaning of the journey. They were incapable of understanding. Camels in the Bible sometimes stand for the rich. Here they undoubtedly represent the people of the world, who are all under God's control, and contribute in countless ways to the mission of the Gospel. Their trains and ships and aeroplanes carry the missionaries and evangelists. Their presses print Gospel literature. Their commerce provides God's servants with food. Their money buys what is necessary, and it often happens that the more prosperous they are, the more easily the Gospel campaign is carried out. All these resources are placed by God at His servants' disposal, and they may use whatever of them they will.

Departed. The standing order for Christ's servants is, ' Go '. ' Go ye therefore and teach all nations ' (Mt. 28. 19). The apostle Paul was sent to the Gentiles (Acts 26. 17). We too are to go. The journey may be long or short, but what is lost will not be saved, unless it is first sought. The Son of Man Himself came to seek and to save that which was lost (Lk. 19. 10).

All the goods of his master were in his hand. All power is given to Christ in heaven and on earth (Mt. 28. 18). He has at His disposal all the resources of either, and all these things are ours (1 Cor. 3. 21). The key to their actual possession and use is prayer. If we are poor and surrounded by difficulties and obstacles, the probable reason is that we do not pray. If we do, the resources of the world are disposed for our help and use in the mission of the Gospel.

He arose. Too often we sit still and expect the lost to come to us, though they seldom do so. *Went to Mesopotamia, unto the city of Nahor.* Notice that the servant did not wander aimlessly out, speaking for his master to all and sundry whom he might encounter on the road. He had a definite mission to a definite place. Successful evangelism proceeds on the same lines. Each servant of Christ has a definite call to a definite work in a definite place (or a series of such calls), if he is willing and ready to find out by prayer what the call is, and to obey it.

VERSE 11. *He made his camels to kneel down.* This is a valuable by-product of the mission of the Gospel. The camels performed this act unintelligently and in their ordinary routine. They knelt for unloading. But they knelt, and in something of the same way many of the people of the world have been made to kneel owing to the influence of the Gospel brought to bear upon them. This has been especially true in the past in the case of the so-called Christian nations. *Without the city.* Any help that the people of the world may be able to give in a Gospel campaign ends at the threshold. Only the servant of Christ can enter the city, as it were, and do the actual work. *By a well of water*. This is the place at which to wait, and on which to base every Gospel campaign. The servant of God does well to wait at the brink of the well of ever-flowing water of life, where he can constantly procure supplies from the Holy Spirit Himself to refresh and strengthen him in the work that lies before him. *At the time of the evening*, when men are alive to the fact that the world is passing away, and the fashion thereof (1 Jo. 2. 17; 1 Cor. 7. 31), when their business and activities are behind them and they feel that the night of condemnation is descending upon them. In actual fact the evening is usually the best time of day for evangelism. Men are more thoughtful in the evening. The cares of the day are behind them, and they are better able to concentrate their minds.

Even the time that women go out to draw water. Notice (1) that the servant went to the place where he would naturally expect to find those whom he was seeking, at the time when he would expect to find them. He thus showed a common sense which has not always appeared in evangelistic effort. We ought to do the same. Notice (2) that he went at the right time to a place where he would expect to encounter *seekers*. The women would come out to draw water. We too must put ourselves in the path of those who are seeking satisfaction from the broken cisterns of the world, and explain to them that they can only find it in Christ. The well is one of the most fruitful places for personal work (compare the Lord and the Samaritan woman, Jo. 4).

Verse 12. Having put himself in the right position for making contact with those whom he was seeking, the servant took the next essential step. He applied to God in prayer. These are the two steps which are essential for successful evangelism, and between them in the wider sense they embrace all that is necessary. The sight of the servant in an attitude of prayer, surrounded by his kneeling camels, must have been striking, and is likely in itself to have aroused the interest of any who came out of the well.

O Lord. Hebrew Jahweh. As a member of the household of Abraham, and, as such, circumcised (17. 23), the servant was within the covenant and had a right to call upon the covenant God. *God of my master Abraham*. The servant called on the God of the master on whose business he was engaged. We are to do exactly the same. It is as Christ's God and Father that we are to call upon God (Eph. 1. 16; 3. 14).

I pray thee. The heart is lifted in definite prayer, which can be expressed in words.

The rest of the verse is occupied with two general requests, which are really two aspects of the same. The servant again completely identifies himself with his master's interests. His own success is a kindness shown to his master. It is an inspiring fact that success in evangelism, which can only be obtained by God's grace and providence and through the power of the Holy Spriit, is an expression of God's love to Christ. It furthers Christ's interests and advances His glory.

Verse 13. Notice the striking definiteness of the prayer recorded in this and the following verse. In this respect it is like Abraham's prayer for the righteous in Sodom (18. 23-33). Our prayers are sometimes vague through lack of faith and power. Definite prayer tests our faith. Definite prayer obtains a definite answer. In this verse the servant makes two statements (compare our Lord's prayer recorded in Jo. 17). Prayer is not intended to be nothing but asking. In the two statements of this verse the servant places his situation before God. He could scarcely have done so in this way if he had not been aware that he was in the right situation to receive the answer to his prayer. This shows us that one of the conditions of receiving an answer to our prayers is that we should be in the place of God's will and choice, when we make them. The two statements of this verse concern (1) the servant himself. He tells God that he has done his own part and is in the place where he can go no further and do no more. He is standing by the well from which he can draw the living water that he needs and is needed by others. (2) The second statement concerns those whom he is seeking. He mentions them to God, thus revealing where his interest lies. A man will pray for what he wants, not for what he doesn't. This statement also implies that he himself cannot deal with these seekers. God Himself must perform His own will.

VERSE 14. *Let it come to pass.* Whether the servant realised it all, or not, this prayer implied a simple, unwavering faith in the complete sovereign control of God over the hearts and minds of men. This sovereign control is a fact in spite of all that may be said or thought about human free will. It is said of the late well known Christian leader and Keswick speaker, Dr. F. B. Meyer, that on one occasion, when travelling to America, he held a service on board, to which he invited an atheist, with whom he had had conversations. It was necessary to go through the dining saloon to another part of the ship, and in doing so the atheist picked up two oranges and placed them in the hands of a woman, who was asleep on the steerage deck. On his return he found the woman awake, and she told him that she was a Christian and had been praying for an orange. This evidence of God's sovereign control over his own actions led to the atheist's conversion. Such faith in the sovereignty of God must be the basis of all successful prayer.

The damsel to whom I shall say. The request for water was customary. It is a good thing for the evangelist to put himself under an obligation to someone whom he is seeking to win.

Such an action often disposes a man or woman to listen. The Lord did the same thing at the well at Sychar (Jo. 4. 7).

I will give thy camels drink also. It was not the custom to offer water from the well to the camels. Such an unusual offer would be for the servant a special sign from God. About this we may notice two things: (1) Having done all that is humanly possible and reached the place where we can do no more ourselves, we are entitled to ask God for particular guidance in following out the details of His will. There is nothing wrong in asking for a sign, if we are certain that we have exhausted the main principles of guidance and are assured that we are entirely engaged on the Lord's business and not on any of our own. (2) Secondly we may notice that what distinguishes the bride of Christ from others is her solicitude for the camels, that is to say, for the unconverted. To them she offers water from the fountain of life. This is what will distinguish her on the day of judgment (Mt. 25. 34-40).

Thou hast appointed. Here is another indication of the servant's faith in the sovereignty of God. Of all the young women of this city God had appointed one, and the servant desired to be led to her. Success in evangelism often depends on asking God to lay individuals upon one's heart and concentrating one's efforts upon them. As many as are ordained to eternal life believe (Acts 13. 48).

For thy servant Isaac. All who are ordained to eternal life are a gift from the Father to Christ (Jo. 6. 37, 39) and make up His bride.

Thereby shall I know. The servant believed that God was showing this kindness and had based his prayer on that faith, but he had not yet had any demonstration of it. His request for knowledge was not occasioned by lack of faith, but was made in order that he might be certain of God's will and be able to carry it out. *Unto my master.* The servant was completely identified with the interests of his master.

VERSE 15. *Before he had done speaking.* The answer to his prayer, which had been made in accordance with the will of God, was immediate, just as God later promised through the prophet Isaiah (Isa. 65. 24). We are entitled to believe that the answers to our own prayers are immediate, although often in the nature of the case the answer may not be apparent. *Milcah, the wife of Nahor.* The expression is intended to emphasise that like Isaac Bethuel was the child of his father's principal wife, and not of a concubine. *Abraham's brother.* The bride is the bridegroom's kinswoman. So is the heavenly Bridegroom the Kinsman of His bride. He took our nature upon Him and was made man. We also like Him are children of God, He of one substance with the Father by eternal generation (Col. 1. 15), we by the new birth (1 Jo. 3. 1, 2). *With her pitcher upon her shoulder.* This is another of the marks of the bride of Christ. She makes it apparent that she is seeking the water of life in contrast to the world, where no one seeks after God (Rom. 3. 11).

VERSE 16. Here is a twofold descripcription of the bride. We have (1) her beauty, and (2) her purity. *Very fair to look upon.* ' So shall the king greatly desire thy beauty ' (Ps. 45. 11). The church is presented to Christ a glorious church, not having spot or wrinkle or any such thing. Her beauty is the beauty of holiness and is a reflection of the Saviour's beauty (Eph. 5. 27).

A virgin. The church is pure and belongs to Christ alone. She is presented to Him as a pure virgin (2 Cor. 11. 2). She is made up of a company of sinners, who are in themselves utterly impure, but are given by God the righteousness of Christ and a new nature, which is holy (Rom. 3. 21, 22; 6. 4).

Neither had any man known her. This means the same thing, but expands and expounds the former statement. In the same way the redeemed ' are not defiled with women ' (Rev. 14. 4), which means that they have not compromised with any of the heathen religions of the world, nor with any professedly Christian unscriptural system. This description implies single-minded devotion to Christ (Mt. 6. 22). The redeemed are kept by the power of God through faith unto salvation (1 Pet. 1. 5).

She went down to the well. This is the daily regular practice of the bride. The well is the Holy Spirit Himself (Jo. 7. 38, 39). Every day we must go to the Word of God, and to do so we must go down. We must humble ourselves before God and submit to His Word.

Filled her pitcher. By reading and studying the Scripture we can take in the supplies of spiritual sustenance that we need. It is necessary to do this regularly each day.

Came up. From the place of prayer we come back again into daily life, replenished, refreshed and strengthened.

VERSE 17. *The servant ran to meet her.* Here we may see (1) the eagerness aroused in those who have a sense of need as soon as they see that we have a supply of the water of life. (2) More agreeably to the context we may see the eagerness of the evangelist, which we ought to copy. The servant ran, so as not to allow a single moment to slip by, or a single opportunity to escape him. Philip the evangelist later did the same (Acts 8. 30).

Let me, I pray thee, drink a little water of thy pitcher. The servant was now putting Rebekah to the test, although she had no idea of it. Her response to his request would determine whether he claimed her for his master or not. In a different sense this is fundamentally true in the case of the evangelist and the one whom he is seeking.

VERSE 18. *Drink, my Lord.* Any of the young women who came out of the city to draw water would have said as much. This was customary courtesy. *She hasted.* The haste was perhaps characteristic of a generous and sympathetic mind. Perhaps it was an unconscious response to the haste and eagerness of the servant.

Let down . her pitcher upon her hand, that is to say, she brought it down from her shoulder, or possibly from her head, and held it to his lips.

VERSE 19. *I will draw water for thy camels also.* Here was the very sign for which the servant had asked. Such a thing was quite unusual and showed Rebekah to be one who was ready to do more than was required of her, that is to say, to act in grace. It necessitated much labour and trouble. The resolution to draw for the camels may have been a sudden instinct in Rebekah's mind, placed there by God in answer to the servant's prayer. More probably it came naturally to her, God having determined her heredity and upbringing in the light of the purpose which He had for her. It is more likely that it was not the impulse that was peculiar, but the woman herself. God prepares all His people for the purpose that He has for each throughout their lives before even He calls them and before they are aware that He has a purpose for them. The apostle Paul knew that this was so in his own case (Gal. 1. 15). So did the prophet Jeremiah (Jer. 1. 5).

Until they have done drinking. This showed that Rebekah was one who did not look back, if she had once put her hand to the plough. If the servant was a man well acquainted with human nature, as was probably the case, he might have taken in her character at a glance, on hearing these words.

VERSE 20. *She hasted.* She was glad and eager to do this kindness.

Emptied her pitcher into the trough. This is another characteristic of the bride. She emptied the pitcher of the water that she had drawn for herself in order to give it to camels. Thus the redeemed give up to the people of the world what they might have used for themselves.

Ran again unto the well. She was quick and eager to do this kindness.

Drew for all his camels. She did not stop halfway, but supplied the need of all.

VERSE 21. *Wondering at her.* It is always wonderful to see the Holy Ghost at work upon and in a soul. *Held his peace.* The evangelist and Christian worker must learn to exercise restraint. It is possible by pushing oneself forward to interfere with the work of the Holy Ghost.

Prosperous or not. It seemed already evident that the journey was successful, but much still depended humanly speaking upon the young woman's decision. How much happier it is to win a soul than merely to give the witness and fail, although the evangelist may rightly leave results with the Lord. The servant realised here that the prosperity of the journey was in the hands of Jahweh.

VERSE 22. By his action described in this verse the servant claimed Rebekah for his master. The evangelist, on seeing definite answer to prayer and the manifest working of the Holy Ghost, may do the same.

As the camels had done drinking. Rebekah had been ready to do a humble, unusual, menial task. *The man took.* The servant offered Rebekah gifts which his master had sent for her, and she accepted them. In the same way the evangelist offers the soul that he is seeking the gifts of God, which have been entrusted to his keeping.

Earring. The R.V. says ' ring ', and the A.V. margin says, ' a jewel for the forehead '. The ring was worn on the nose. By placing this ring upon Rebekah's nose the servant claimed her face, that is to say, her whole person and her abiding presence for his master. *Of half a shekel weight.* The Hebrew says ' one beka '. The mention of the weight emphasises the value of the gift. *Two bracelets for her hands.* By placing the bracelets on Rebekah's hands the servant claimed her service for his master. Thus the evangelist leads the converted soul both to the love and fellowship and possession of Christ, and also to His service. *Ten shekels.* Ten is the number of glory. The *one* beka emphasises the fact that she now belongs to Christ alone, and the *ten* shekels that she is entering a glorious service. *Of gold.* Gold in the Bible represents the glory of God. As she accepted the gifts which Christ's servant and representative offered her, the glory of God entered into her life and enfolded her. ' Whom He justified, them also He glorified.' (Rom. 8. 30).

VERSE 23. *Whose daughter art thou?* It was still necessary to ask this question in order to make sure that all things had indeed worked together for good (Rom. 8. 28). The servant must have felt that he knew the answer. He was bound by his master's orders to a daughter of Nahor. He might have enquired first of all for Bethuel's house, but he chose the way of prayer. *Is there room.* This is the question that Christ asks of the sinner's heart, and that the evangelist asks of the one whom he is seeking. Is there room in the heart for Christ? Is there room among the cares and business of life for attention to the Gospel?

VERSE 24. The disclosure of her parentage made by Rebekah in this verse proved her to be the very one whom the servant had been sent to seek. How satisfying it is to the evangelist when the same knowledge comes to him. The prayerful soulwinner is directed by God to the very man of His choice.

VERSE 25. *We have both straw and provender enough.* Rebekah was still thinking of the camels. She may have had an exceptional love for animals. Care for the helpless distinguishes the bride of Christ. *Room to lodge in.* Rebekah was willing to take the stranger in. So the repenting sinner answers Christ's call by opening his life and heart to him (Rev. 3. 20).

VERSE 26. The servant's reaction was right. Before anything else he gave the glory to God. Nothing calls forth such adoration, worship and wonder in the heart of a servant of God as the sight of the miraculous work of the Holy Spirit in the life of one to whom he has been sent to offer the Gospel.

VERSE 27. The servant rightly expressed his praise in words. In this verse we find the following points: (1) The servant calls on his master's God. (2) He sees the success of his mission in the light of a kindness shown by God to his master. (3) He blends co-operation with guidance and thus states a principle which the Holy Spirit acts upon and uses to this day.

Blessed be the Lord God of my master Abraham. The corresponding New Testament phrase is, ' Blessed be the God and Father of our Lord Jesus Christ ' (1 Pet. 1. 3; Eph. 1. 3). Jahweh was the servant's God, because He was Abraham's. So God is our God and Father, because He is the God and Father of our Lord Jesus Christ (Jo. 20. 17).

Who hath not left destitute my master of His mercy and truth. Man depends for his life upon God's mercy and truth. Mercy is the expression of God's grace to the undeserving fallen sinner in his helplessness and pitiable state. Truth is God's faithfulness to His pledged word. What He promises He is also able to perform (Rom. 4. 21). God in showing mercy is true to Himself, since He vindicates His righteousness and holiness by the Saviour's death on the cross. It was at the cross that mercy and truth met together (Ps. 85. 10).

I being in the way, the Lord led me. If this version is correct (the R.V. is weaker), we have a striking principle of guidance. The servant is first in the way. He sets out in the right direction as far as he knows it. He goes as far as he can, and while he is in the way, he receives the guidance that he needs. Many a man says that he has never been guided to the mission field. The reason may be that he had never put himself in the way. He had never recognised the general call involved in the Lord's commission to His church (Mt. 28. 19). He had thus never put himself in the way of obeying it and had never received the direct guidance and particular call, which comes when he ' is in the way '.

To the house of my master's brethren. The servant did not know the brethren, nor the house, but God knew, and His angel gave guidance. In the same way the evangelist does not know who are the elect, but if he abides in prayer, as the servant did, and seeks and expects God's guidance, the Holy Spirit will lead him to them.

VERSE 28. *The damsel ran.* She was an eager witness as she had been an eager helper. *And told.* She at once did the right thing and took the right step. The confession of Christ in the world, whether in the God-given opportunity provided for confession in baptism, or by a continual witness by word of mouth, is essential to salvation (Mt. 10. 32; Rom. 10. 9, 10). *Them of her mother's house.* She went to the natural place and told the news in her own home, much as Simon Peter heard the news of Christ from his own brother Andrew (Jo. 1. 41). Notice the expression ' mother's house ', where we might expect ' father's house '. Professor Blunt, in his valuable book, *Coincidences of Scripture.* makes much of this, and seeks to show that the expression is an undesigned coincidence with others in this narrative, which all go to show that Rebekah's father was a nonentity, perhaps a weak-minded man.

VERSE 29. *Rebekah had a brother.* Those who accept Christ are always in this position, for even if they have no immediate relatives, they have thousands of brother men, to whom their conversion is a striking witness. *Laban.* He is afterwards to figure prominently in the story of Rebekah's son. *Laban ran out unto the man, unto the well.* The news that his sister brought him had exactly the right effect upon him. He ran to the evangelist to see for himself, and as the evangelist stood by the well, an ap-

proach to the evangelist was an approach to the living water, the Holy Spirit Himself, as it always is, or should be.

VERSE 30. *When he saw . . . and when he heard.* To make a lasting impression upon a needy sinner both these things are necessary. Notice that there, as often, the seeing came first. Laban could see that his sister had been beautified and her appearance changed. He saw the ring and the bracelets and knew thereby that she had accepted gifts. He may have realised that these gifts signified the devotion of her life. But he not only saw but heard from his sister's lips the explanation of what had happened. It is very important that the meaning of, and reason for, any transformation that a sinner sees, should be explained to him. Otherwise he may give the credit to the one who has been changed instead of to Christ, Who changes him.

Thus spake the man unto me. Rebekah passed on to her brother what had been said to her. In the same way it is the duty and privilege of one who has been transformed and renewed by the Gospel to pass on the Gospel message. *He came unto the man.* So yet another sinner comes to the evangelist as a result of what he sees and hears. The train of events remains the same, even if we think of Laban as stirred by any desire for material advantage, or interested in the jewellery for its own sake. Many a seeking sinner has at first some low idea of the Gospel.

He stood by the camels at the well. There could · be no more precise picture of the ideal position of the evangelist. He formed the link, as it were, between the camels and the well. He stood by his camels. He remained among the people of the world who needed him, with whose welfare he was entrusted, they being helpless. He also stood at the well, at the source of the supply of living water.

VERSE 31. *Come in, thou blessed of*

the Lord. These are welcome words for an evangelist to hear. Notice that the servant was invited to enter the house in the name of his master's God. In giving this invitation to the servant, Laban was giving it to his master, and indeed to Jahweh Himself. The Lord Jesus Christ recognises such an invitation given to one of His servants as given to Himself and to His Father (Mt. 10. 40). The words of Laban may also be considered as a picture of the invitation given by a sinner to the Lord Jesus Christ to enter his heart and life.

Wherefore standest thou without? Until He is invited into a life, Christ stands outside and knocks (Rev. 3. 20).

I have prepared the house. Here is a contrast with the situation of the Gospel. The sinner cannot prepare his heart. He must come to the Saviour just as he is, and the Saviour will come into his life in all its disorder and sordidness and begin at once to put it right. In the literal and material sense a seeker who invites an evangelist into his home is capable of preparing it and often does so carefully. *Room for the camels.* When the Gospel is received and accepted by a household, the people of the world, who may be connected with the household, get benefit.

VERSE 32. Notice in this and the following verse five consequences of the successful presentation of the Gospel. (1) *The man came into the house,* that is to say, shelter for the worker himself. The man who throws himself into work for the master finds his mind often relieved of worldly or personal cares by the incidence of the work itself. (2) *He ungirded his camels,* that is, relief in the material sphere for the unconverted, among whom the Gospel is being preached. A well-known example is the abolition of slavery brought about by the exertions of evangelical Christians more than by any other factor. (3) *And gave straw and provender for the camels,* that is, supply of the needs of the people of the world, where the

Gospel is preached. Honest trade with customers on whom they may confidently rely is brought them, and the standard of life of those in countries where the Gospel is accepted is raised. (4) *And water to wash his feet, and the men's feet that were with him.* Occupation with the work of God keeps His servants free from sin, and helps to keep their walk through the world clean.

VERSE 33. (5) *And there was set meat before him to eat.* Doing the will of God and engaging on His work provide spiritual sustenance to the child of God. Such occupations nourish and strengthen his spiritual life. This was so in the case of the Master Himself (Jo. 4. 32-35).

I will not eat, until I have told mine errand. Notice how the servant set his master's interests before his personal comfort and needs. This is an example to us. We follow it in theory, but not always in practice.

Speak on. Laban was ready to hear. To the sight of his sister's changed appearance and to her personal testimony was now added the impression of the high value and immense importance that the servant obviously set upon his message. The servant's self-denial bore fruit.

VERSE 34. Notice that the servant has no identity to tell. His identity is wrapped up in that of his master. The first thing he mentions in his message is his master's name. The fact that he was his master's servant was the whole basic reason for his journey and his message. We may compare the words of the apostle Paul (Acts 27. 23). We ought to begin our message with the mention of our Master's Name.

VERSE 35. The servant still says nothing about himself. He speaks of the blessing, greatness and possessions of his master.

The Lord hath blessed my master greatly. He had given him personal justification, victory in the trial of faith, a son and heir after years of waiting, many great and precious promises for himself and his family for the future, and great material riches. In the same way God has blessed our Master also. He has given Him a Name that is above every name, that in the Name of Jesus every knee should bow, and every tongue confess that He is Lord (Phil. 2. 9-11). The first thing that we ought to tell the sinner and the seeker is the fact of this blessing, and we ought to aim at raising a desire in him to share it.

He is become great. This is abundantly true of Jesus Christ. ' The head that once was crowned with thorns, is crowned with glory now.' Jesus is crowned with many crowns (Rev. 19. 12), and all power is given unto Him in heaven and on earth (Mt. 28. 18). We ought to tell the sinner of this greatness in order to give him the impression of the power of the Saviour to keep him, save him and protect him, bring him to glory and cause him to share this greatness, if only he will associate himself with Him.

He hath given him. Eight things which God had given Abraham are named, arranged in four pairs. All are pictures of the possessions of the risen and ascended Christ. *Flocks.* The Lord Jesus is the good shepherd. He has sheep of many folds, which He will make into one flock (Jo. 10. 16). The flock of His pasture are men, and He is their Lord God (Ezek. 34. 31). *Herds.* These consist of oxen, who labour for Him and do His service. It is the greatest privilege and freedom to take His yoke upon us (Mt. 11. 28). Both sheep and oxen are animals suitable for sacrifice, and the Saviour's sheep and oxen offer themselves to Him as living sacrifices (Rom. 12. 1). *Silver and gold.* These have been given to the Saviour as personal possessions. Silver is linked in the Bible with money, and carries the thought of redemption. In the silver and gold we have the picture of the suffering and the glory (1 Pet. 1. 11). Christ took a body in order to redeem, and this was prepared for Him by the Father from the creation

of Adam down the generations and given Him in the womb of the virgin (Heb. 10. 5). After His resurrection the Father gave Christ glory (1 Pet. 1. 21) and this is what is pictured by the gold.

Menservants and maidservants. These are much the same as the herds. When pictured as the herd, Christ's servants are thought of as a group controlled by Him, capable of labour and sacrifice. Here their humanity and power to co-operate are emphasised. He desires to be served freely by trustworthy servants, able to take the initiative and act intelligently in His service. *Camels and asses.* These are unclean animals. They represent the people of the world, the camels especially the rich, the asses the ordinary people. All are placed in Christ's control (Mt. 28. 18), and are used freely by Him in the furtherance of the Gospel and the advance of His kingdom, although they are quite ignorant of the fact.

VERSE 36. *Sarah my master's wife.* Sarah is mentioned (1) as one whose name should be known to the family of Nahor (see 11. 29). Sarah was a sister of Abraham and Nahor as well as being Abraham's wife (20. 12). (2) She is mentioned in order to demonstrate the honourable position of Isaac in the family of Abraham. He was not the son of a concubine (see 25. 5, 6). Both these facts would assist in recommending Isaac to Laban and Rebekah. Although God the Father is bringing many sons to glory (Heb. 2. 10), yet the Lord Jesus Christ is His honourable, true and only Son (Jo. 1. 18; Rom. 8. 32).

When she was old. This fact would (1) explain why Isaac was of the age and generation of Rebekah rather than of that of her father, and (2) emphasise the preciousness of Isaac and the affection with which his father regarded him.

All that he hath. God the Father has given all to His Son (Jo. 16. 15; 17. 10).

VERSE 37. *Made me swear.* No one

is sent out on service for Christ who has not devoted himself to His cause.

A wife to my son. The church is the Lamb's wife (Rev. 19. 7; 21. 9). *The Canaanites.* ' There shall in no wise enter into it anything that defileth ' (Rev. 21. 27).

In whose land I dwell. Christ was a sojourner on earth, and so are His people (1 Pet. 2. 11). They live among the wickedness and uncleanness of the world.

VERSE 38. *Unto my father's house.* The elect, who form the bride of Christ, belonged originally to the Father. They were foreknown by Him and chosen in Christ before the foundation of the world (Rom. 8. 29; Eph. 1. 4), and they were given by the Father to Christ (Jo. 17. 6).

To my kindred. The elect are Christ's kindred (1) in Adam. He took our nature upon Him (Heb. 2. 16). (2) They are Christ's kindred as sons of God by faith in Him (Gal. 3. 26; Heb. 2. 11-13).

Take a wife unto my son. ' The kingdom of heaven is like unto a certain King, which made a marriage for his son ' (Mt. 22. 2).

VERSE 39. *Peradventure the woman will not follow me.* The servant, like the evangelist today, could only see the human side, and realised that the success of his mission depended upon the decision made by Rebekah. This was true so far as it went.

VERSE 40. *The Lord.* The woman's decision was not the final factor. The Lord was the sovereign disposer of her heart. The same is true today, and we may be confident, if we go out to win souls on the Lord's business. The two factors are found in the presentation of the Gospel. ' Peradventure the woman will not . . . ' ' The Lord will . . . '

Before whom I walk. If Abraham actually said these words to his servant, they are omitted in verse 7. They may be the servant's paraphrase and interpretation of his master's words. If we put side by side the account of Abraham's words in verse 7 and the servant's report of them in verse 40, we shall see that Abraham speaks of what the Lord had done for him and promised him, and the servant speaks of Abraham's sanctified life. Walk in the Scripture means conduct and behaviour. Abraham lived and acted in the presence of his God. He may also have used the word ' walk ' more readily than the word ' stand ' as Elijah did (1 Ki. 17. 1), because he habitually thought of himself as a sojourner and pilgrim. Abraham regarded life as a journey, and that is what it is.

Will send his angel with thee. The servant had only an angel, a representative. We have God the Holy Spirit Himself. Abraham had told his servant that Jahweh's angel would go *before* him. This was true, and so he did. The servant found that the ground had been prepared for him. When however he comes to relate his master's words, he realises that the angel had been *with* him all the time. The angel had not only prepared the ground, but was guiding the servant himself. Both these aspects are true today. The Holy Spirit goes before us to prepare the ground, and travels with us as our guide.

Prosper thy way. Success in any service for God, or in any evangelistic campaign, is achieved in the unseen sphere, and is due to God alone. *Thou shalt take a wife for my son.* It is good to remind ourselves of the grand purpose of the Gospel. It is to gather out a people for the glory of the Lord Jesus Christ. If we remember this, we shall not be tempted to think that the Gospel has failed, because so many refuse it. Its purpose is not to save the world but to gather out a bride for God's Son.

Of my kindred and of my father's house. See on verse 38.

VERSE 41. *Then thou shalt be clear from this my oath.* The evangelist's responsibility ends when he has given the witness and faithfully presented the Gospel. As long as he has done this, he is not responsible for the decision made by those to whom it is presented.

If they give not thee one, thou shalt be clear. The evangelist's mission and responsibility end when the Gospel is rejected.

VERSE 42. Notice how in this and the following verses the servant simply and artlessly describes the approach that he had made. He concealed nothing, but was perfectly open in stating his purpose and how he had tried to achieve it. The same tactics in evangelism today are often successful. The sinner, or seeker, realises that nothing is going on behind his back and that he is being approached in simplicity and love.

I came this day unto the well. He tells in all simplicity how he came to the place where he expected to meet the one whom he was seeking. *And said.* He unreservedly repeats his prayer in order to demonstrate the reality of the answer to the glory of God.

O Lord God of my master Abraham. He calls upon his master's God just as we call upon the God and Father of our Lord Jesus Christ.

If now thou do prosper. He asks for a sign that he is on the right way, walking in the line of God's will, and that God will give him success in his mission.

VERSE 43. *Behold, I stand by the well of water.* See on verse 13.

It shall come to pass. The R.V. makes better sense. It reads: ' Let it come to pass, that the maiden which cometh forth to draw, to whom I shall say, Give me . . .' The servant faithfully tells of the obligation under which he put himself to Rebekah.

VERSE 44. The servant tells quite simply the sign for which he asked God.

The Lord hath appointed out. These words would have a great effect upon Laban and Rebekah. The realisation of God's appointing hand would make an impression upon them.

VERSE 45. *Speaking in mine heart.* This man knew how to pray. Verse 15 says merely ' speaking '. The servant himself adds the words, ' in mine heart '. God was real to him. He did not need to go to any place or shrine. He was no heathen. He did not need to watch for any notice announcing, ' This church is open for prayer '. He lived in God and God in him. He sanctified the Lord God in his heart (1 Pet. 3. 15). This is true religion and true prayer. *Rebekah came forth.* Rebekah already knew this fact, but did not know the circumstances in which it happened. She could scarcely fail to be convinced that God's hand was upon her.

VERSE 46. The servant openly explains the fulfilment of the sign and the answer to his prayer. By simply telling the facts in this way he gives convincing evidence of the presence of the hand of God. Here is a good hint for the evangelist.

VERSE 47. *The daughter of Bethuel.* She was of kin to the bridegroom, and her identity was made known by her act of grace.

I put the earring upon her face, and the bracelets upon her hands. The R.V. says, ' the ring upon her nose '. By her acceptance of these gifts, Rebekah's life was consecrated to God and her hands dedicated to His service. Notice that the gifts were placed upon her person. She was not first asked whether she would accept them or not. It would have been possible for her to refuse by drawing back and not allowing the servant to approach. In this we see a true picture of the work of the Holy Ghost in the Gospel.

VERSE 48. *I bowed down my head.* The servant knew that he was in God's presence where he stood. So are we. Wherever we are, by night or day, we are in God's presence and may lift up our hearts to Him in prayer, silent or expressed.

Worshipped the Lord. The dominant note of this worship was evidently wonder and praise. His whole heart went out to his God in devotion.

Blessed the Lord God of my master Abraham. The worship consisted of praise and devotion of a more general type. The blessing was more definite. It was thanksgiving for a special act of goodness and grace. Notice that the servant's God was his master's God, just as ours is the God and Father of our Lord Jesus Christ. We can understand something of the reality and example of Abraham's religion from the sincerity of his servant's worship. Is our faith so real that those dependent upon us catch its spirit and are themselves brought into living touch with God through Christ?

Which had led me. The servant's journey is not only a picture of any particular evangelistic mission, but a parable of life. ' As many as are led by the Spirit of God, these are the sons of God ' (Rom. 8. 14). We cannot walk through life in the way that pleases God of our own accord. We must have the Spirit's leading. God has graciously granted it to us, and it is for us to follow it. The same is true in the case of any particular piece of service. We must find by prayer the Spirit's aim and His plan for reaching it, and then follow His lead. *In the right way.* There are many wrong ways in life, and there are wrong ways of doing God's work. Without the Spirit's lead we cannot recognise which is the right way. ' Teach me thy way, O Lord, and lead me in a plain path ' (Ps. 27. 11; 86. 11). ' Lead me in the way everlasting ' (Ps. 139. 24). *To take my master's brother's daughter unto his son.* The final object of service for God in this world is to gather out the bride of Christ. For the significance of the word ' brother ' see on verse 4.

VERSE 49. At the end of his simple narration and explanation the servant makes an appeal. This is a good example for the evangelist to follow. *If ye will deal kindly and truly with my master.* This is the issue in all evangelism. ' What think ye of Christ?' (Mt. 22. 42). To accept the Gospel is to deal kindly with Christ, to return love and faithfulness and loyalty and service for His love. It is to recognise His love in paying the price of redemption and to seek by God's grace to make some return for it. It is also to deal truly with Him, that is, in the only way of our bounden duty towards Him. By refusing the Gospel we play Christ false. The only proper and right response to His love is to appropriate His salvation and enter His service.

Tell me. The evangelist must demand the expression of a decision.

If not. The presentation of the Gospel demands a choice and decision from those who hear it. Acceptance and refusal lie with them.

Tell me. The evangelist is entitled to know if an adverse decision has been made.

That I may turn. A sinner's refusal to accept the Gospel does not bring the task of evangelism to an end. God's servants must go on and offer it to others. When the Jews refused the Word of God, the apostles turned to the Gentiles (Acts 13. 46). If the disciples were persecuted in one city, they were to flee to another (Mt. 10. 23), not to abandon the campaign and return home.

VERSE 50. *Laban and Bethuel.* Professor Blunt in his book on the coincidences of Scripture points out that this is the only passage in the whole narrative from which we may gather that Bethuel was still alive. Even here he is mentioned second to his son. He was evidently a nonentity, and perhaps weak-minded.

The thing proceedeth from the Lord. It is important to notice that what convinced them was the definite answer to prayer. By answering the servant's prayer God has proved to them that the whole matter was being controlled by Him. In the same way we must convince the sinner and seeker that the Holy Spirit is present and at work in his personal case. This happens more readily at times of revival than at any other time.

He gave also to her brother and to her mother precious things. Those connected with the bride always receive some benefit from the preaching and acceptance of the Gospel. Material benefits arise from it. This can be seen by comparing the conditions of life in those countries which have allowed free play to the Gospel, or in which it has been officially established, with those in which it is suppressed or persecuted.

We cannot speak unto thee bad or good. They meant that they felt that the direction had been taken out of their hands, and that God's intervention was so plain that they dared not oppose it, while they had no need to assent to his question as the conclusion was foregone. They felt under a deep sense of the presence and call of God. This is the position in which we should desire to see the sinner.

VERSE 51. They were so deeply convinced of the will of God, that they were ready to give up one who was dear and precious to them. In the same way the sinner must be ready to give up his life and service to Christ.

As the Lord hath spoken. They recognised the voice of God in the answer to prayer and the attendant circumstances. We may therefore learn an important method by which God speaks to us. There has been no direct spoken communication from God. Thus we may look for God's guidance and the making known of His will through answering our prayers.

VERSE 52. Here is the second occasion on which the servant worshipped the Lord. The first was when his prayer was answered (verses 26, 48). The second is when the decision is made in his master's favour. These are the two occasions for praise in the ministry of the Gospel today.

VERSE 53. Now that the decision has been openly made, further gifts are given to Rebekah. The first, though their effect was beauty and adornment, were given as marks and signs of her dedication to her new master and of his possession of her. These are given out of grace and kindness for purposes of adornment. They consist of three things: (1) *Jewels of silver.* These showed the beauty of her redemption. When once his decision is made the sinner becomes one who is not his own, but bought with a price (1 Cor. 6. 20). This fact of his redemption vitally affects his conduct and the whole trend of his life (2 Cor. 5. 15). He becomes adorned with the beauty of the redeemed, which is a gift from his master to him. (2) *Jewels of gold.* These signify the nature and glory of God. The redeemed are partakers of the Divine nature (2 Pet. 1. 4). The glory of God appears in the redeemed by the grace and operation of the Holy Spirit like flashing jewels of gold, beautifying and adorning their characters. (3) *Raiment.* All the redeemed are given gifts of raiment by the heavenly Bridegroom. The first gift is the robe of Christ's righteousness (Isa. 61. 10), and after that the beautiful garments of sanctification (Isa. 52. 1) and the holy garments of consecrated priesthood ' for glory and for beauty ' (Ex. 28. 2).

VERSE 54. *They did eat and drink.* When the mission had been discharged, the servant could turn to the satisfaction of his personal needs. ' The labourer is worthy of his hire ' (Lk. 10. 7), and it was the servant's privilege and duty to accept what was placed before him.

Tarried all night. Rest is another necessity, that hospitality may be provided for the servant of God.

Send me away unto my master. The servant's love and loyalty continued to place his master's interests before everything else. He saw no purpose in staying. He had nothing to do but his master's business. He would ask for no rest and respite from the long journey, but wanted to set off again at once, so that his master's business should be the least possible delayed. This is a good example of zeal. Notice that his desire was to be sent to his master. He was not completely happy when absent from him. In the same way it should be the supreme desire of every servant of Christ to see his Master's face.

VERSE 55. *Let the damsel abide with us a few days, at the least ten.* This is a characteristic request. It was made by those who had had the chief interest in the bride hitherto. It was a subtle request. It seemed a small one. She was about to leave them for life. What were ten days compared with a lifetime? Why should she be in a hurry? Their request probably arose from the simple desire not to part with Rebekah so suddenly and quickly. Yet whether they realised it or not, much depended upon those ten days. They were sufficient to have made Rebekah's resolution fail. It is important that those who make a decision for Christ should step out and act upon it without a moment's delay. To wait and dally are dangerous, and often the influence of those who are nearest and dearest in the natural sphere is set in the direction of delay. A quick and resolute decision is regarded as rashness.

After that she shall go. Rebekah's family did not claim to prevent her going altogether. They probably did not desire to. But they did not want her to go at once, and it may well be that ' after that ' she would not have gone at all. If Satan cannot prevent us making a decision, he will seek to delay our acting upon it, and his most ready instruments are often the members of our own families.

VERSE 56. *Hinder me not.* Delay on Rebekah's part meant delay to the servant. The consummation of the church's mission does not take place

till the bride is gathered out complete. It is not till the Gospel has been preached in the whole world for a witness that the end will come (Mt. 24. 14).

Seeing the Lord hath prospered my way. The evident fact that the Lord had been at work was a strong argument against delay in answering His call.

Send me away that I may go to my master. The servant repeats the request made in verse 54. He wanted to see his master and give an account of his mission. This is exactly what we shall do.

VERSE 57. *We will call the damsel.* This is a wise decision, clearly overruled by God. No one can make a decision for another in spiritual matters. Each individual must make his own decision. Each is capable of doing so, and is called upon to do so.

VERSE 58. *Wilt thou go with this man?* The direct question, which can never in the end be avoided, is put. The repenting sinner must decide whether he will allow the evangelist to lead him to Christ.

I will go. She makes her own decision of her own free will. This definite clear-cut word delights the Lord. He seeks the freely-given fellowship of His creatures. Rebekah's decision was to go at once. By tacitly accepting the servant's gifts she had shown that she consented to go. Now by this simple decision she shows that her interest in the bridegroom is paramount. She is ready to put his call first and to answer it immediately, leaving her mother's house with scarcely an opportunity to say goodbye. She was ready to leave the protection of her home and set off with a stranger on a long journey to be the bride of a man whom she had never seen. Her decision was influenced by (1) the clear evidence of the call of God, seen in a remarkable answer to prayer, and (2) the gifts which the bridegroom had sent her. ' Hearken, O daughter, and consider, and incline thine ear; forget also thine own people, and thy father's house; so shall the king greatly desire thy beauty ' (Ps. 45. 10, 11).

VERSE 59. *They sent away Rebekah.* They accepted the circumstances and respected her choice, though the world does not always do this in the case of the repenting sinner. There is another sense in which the world, even a convert's own family, sometimes sends him away by driving him out and casting him off. *Her nurse.* In Rebekah's nurse we may see the old law, which is our schoolmaster to bring us to Christ (Gal. 3. 24). The nurse fed us in our infancy, before faith came. When the Gospel is revealed, the faithful nurse is not repudiated (Mt. 5. 17-19; Rom. 3. 31; 8. 4), but is absorbed into the bridal train and enters into a more dignified status. *Abraham's servant,* that is, the evangelist. *His men.* These were the helpers and assistants in the mission, without whose presence and aid it could not have taken place. Perhaps they were occupied chiefly in driving the camels.

VERSE 60. *They blessed Rebekah.* They expected her new life to be fruitful, as the people of the world usually do.

Thou art our sister. They sought a share in the blessing that they looked for, and hoped that some of it would reflect on themselves.

Be thou the mother of thousands of millions. They expected exceptional fruitfulness in Rebekah's descendants. They may have heard some rumours of the promises made to Abraham and have believed in their hearts that he took the right course when he went out into the pilgrim life at the call of God. Or they may have heard an account of these promises and of the fulfilment of some of them from the servant in the course of his conversation with them on the previous evening. Or they may have been so much impressed by the answer to prayer and the manifest working of God which they had wit-

nessed as to be convinced that God had a purpose of exceptional blessing for Rebekah. Or two or all of these factors may have worked together in their minds.

Let thy seed possess the gate of those which hate them. This is an echo of the promise made to Abraham in 22. 17. The wishes of Rebekah's family for her blessing were in line with the will of God. They are caught up in the Messianic anticipations which began in the Garden of Eden. Both have been abundantly fulfilled. Rebekah became an ancestress of Christ and a channel of the blessings of Abraham to us. She has become the mother of a great multitude, that no man can number (Rev. 7. 9), the church of the firstborn, whose names are written in heaven (Heb. 12. 23). The second of the two blessings is fulfilled in the victory of Christ, which is shared by His people, over Satan (Col. 2. 15), sin (Rev. 5. 5), the world (Jo. 16. 33) and death (1 Cor. 15. 25-6). Far more lay within the words of Rebekah's mother and brother than they could have realised. The victory of Christ was accomplished by His sacrificial love in offering Himself to God on the cross as man's sin-bearer and redeemer, there to suffer the pains of perdition in man's place. Throughout the Gospel age He is constantly winning the victory by love in the hearts of repenting sinners, and the day will come when the last enemy will be destroyed (1 Cor. 15. 26) and creation handed over to the Father (1 Cor. 15. 28) free from all evil and misery for ever (Rom. 8. 21).

VERSE 61. *Rebekah arose.* She took action, as every sinner who would escape to God, must do. To do nothing is to neglect God's salvation (Heb. 2. 3) and to be lost.

And her damsels. The royal bride of Ps. 45 had ' virgins her companions that follow her ' (Ps. 45. 14). We are probably intended to see in the bride and her maidens together the whole company of the redeemed, and we may like to see in the central figure the original Israelite remnant and the Gentiles who have adhered to the Gospel in the attendants. Or we may think of the damsels in attendance as the innumerable company of angels who form part of the inheritance of the redeemed (Heb. 12. 22).

Followed the man. The repenting sinner is led by God's servant to Christ. The apostle Paul invited his converts to be followers, or imitators, of him, as he was of Christ (1 Cor. 11. 1; Phil. 3. 17). May we all have the grace to set a similar example and to know how to lead the wandering sinner home.

The servant took Rebekah. He brought a rich prize for his master (Rom. 15. 16).

Went his way. He started off on the long journey home at the close of a successful mission, bearing his sheaves with him. He had traded well with the talents that his master had entrusted to him, and he was ready to hear his master's words, ' Well done, good and faithful servant ' (Mt. 25. 20, 21).

VERSE 62. We pass in thought to the other end of the journey. *Isaac came.* As the bride comes to meet the bridegroom, so does he come to meet her, whether into the secret of the individual believer's heart at his conversion, or openly to receive the whole company at the end of the world.

From the way of the well Lahairoi. For this well and its name see 16. 14. It is the well of the Living One Who sees. In this passage it may well signify the presence of the Living God, where the heavenly Bridegroom dwells. From there He came to redeem His bride, and from there He will come to meet her on the last day, when her journey is over. The Septuagint Greek version says, ' Isaac came through the wilderness '. This is true of the heavenly Bridegroom, who came through the wilderness of suffering to find and greet His bride.

The south country. Isaac lived in the farthest part of the land of promise that could be reached by anyone coming in, as Abraham had done, from the north. So our Forerunner has already gone right in to the presence of God for us, and dwells there. We are still on the way, but no further point could ever be reached.

VERSE 63. *To meditate.* The margin says ' to pray '. In the same way, while the bride is making her journey, the Bridegroom is interceding for her in heaven. *In the field.* If the field is the world, this expression speaks to us of the Bridegroom's interest in the world. The context however implies that Isaac went out in order to be alone with God. There is a sense in which our Isaac is alone with God in majesty and glory praying for us His people. *At the eventide.* It will be at the eventide of the world, indeed as eternal night descends upon it, that the Bridegroom will meet the bride.

Behold, the camels were coming. In verse 61 we were told that Rebekah and her damsels were riding upon camels. In the same way the resources of the world are rightly made use of to set forward the Gospel, and it is down the trail of time and upon the events of history that the bride has made her journey. Now the bridegroom, as he surveys the horizon, sees the camels coming. In the same way the world is making progress in time and in resourcefulness as the evening draws on. And the advance of the world is bringing nearer the union of the Bridegroom and the bride.

VERSE 64. *When she saw Isaac, she lighted off the camel.* The first sight of the heavenly Bridegroom causes the bride to detach herself from the world. This is true spiritually of the individual soul. It will be true of the bride, the whole company of the redeemed, at the end of the world. At the sight of Isaac she will be loosed from the world and be rapt away to meet Him in the air (1 Thess. 4. 16, 17).

VERSE 65. As the Bridegroom walks day by day to meet the bride in the field of the world, where she finds Him in the pages of Scripture, His identity is interpreted to her by the evangelist and pastor.

She took a vail, and covered herself. The first contact with the Master means the elimination of self. Rebekah could no longer be seen. She denies herself (Mt. 16. 24) and loses her identity in that of her Lord.

VERSE 66. We shall do the same when the journey is done. How happy it will be to go over with the Lord the whole course of life and service, entering no doubt into the secrets that are now behind the veil, and discovering the many answers to prayer, the protection afforded by the angels, the dangers avoided and the constancy of the sovereign control exercised by the Lord. We shall not only find that all is known, but the way that lies behind will need interpretation to us. The account will be perfectly happy, because the sins and iniquities that marred the way will be remembered no more (Heb. 8. 12).

VERSE 67. *Isaac brought her into his mother Sarah's tent.* The bride took the place of the mother. In the same way the redeemed and regenerate humanity in Christ takes the place of the old humanity, which is dead in Adam, but yet gave birth to Christ, so far as His human nature is concerned.

Took Rebekah. So Christ takes His people to Himself for ever (Jo. 14. 3), that where He is, we may be also.

She became his wife. On the great day the marriage of the Lamb will come (Rev. 19. 7). *He loved her.* Christ has loved His people with an everlasting love (Jer. 31. 3). He loved His own, who were in the world, and loved them unto the end (Jo. 13. 1). He loved the church, and gave Himself for her (Eph. 5. 25), and in the same way He loves every individual member of it (Gal. 2. 20).

Isaac was comforted after his mother's death. So we may believe that the Lord Himself will be comforted for ever after the fall and the loss of Adam, in whom He delighted (Prov. 8. 31), by the presence and company of His redeemed, in whom His soul delights, and we may even now in our imperfect state in this world give Him rest and comfort by opening our hearts to be His abode. Notice how in the last four verses of this chapter Rebekah ceases to be the central and paramount figure. Isaac comes to the fore. Isaac brings her, takes her, loves her. The climax is seen in the comforting of Isaac, for whom Rebekah is brought. The journey was not undertaken with the salvation of Rebekah as its supreme purpose, but to the glory and comfort of Isaac. Rebekah entered into happiness in his happiness, but his needs and his glory are supreme. If we view the Gospel from this angle, we shall understand better some of the mysteries of God's plan of salvation and His great acts of redemption.

CHAPTER 25

THIS chapter divides into three sections. In verses 1-11 we have the conclusion of the story of Abraham. These verses form the last subsection of the final section of Abraham's life, which began at 22.20, and at their close the long sixth division of the book of Genesis, which tells the story of Terah and his family, comes to an end (11.27-25.11). Verses 12-18 give us the very short account of Ishmael and his family, and at verse 19 begins the story of Isaac, which continues to 35.29. These last sixteen verses of the chapter describe the birth of Esau and Jacob and the sale by Esau of his birthright. The two chief lessons of the chapter are concerned with the elective purpose of God, interpreted by the apostle Paul in Rom. 9. 12, and the reversed sense of values that Esau had. This is brought out in the Epistle to the Hebrews 12. 16.

VERSE 1. *Then again Abraham took*

a wife. This rendering implies that Abraham married after the death of Sarah. This however seems very unlikely. When Isaac was born, parenthood was scarcely more possible for Abraham than it was for Sarah (Rom. 4. 19). The R.V. probably gives a more accurate rendering: 'And Abraham took another wife'. For 'took' we should read 'had taken'. Keturah was a concubine, or secondary wife, taken in accordance with the custom of the time.

VERSE 2. *Midian.* This people occurs frequently in the narrative of the Old Testament, sometimes as enemies of Israel. They lived to the south-east of Palestine.

Shuah. Bildad, one of Job's friends, was a descendant of Shuah (Job 2. 11). He was associated with an Edomite, and therefore presumably lived in the same south-easterly direction.

VERSE 3. *Sheba and Dedan.* These names are usually associated with the country today called Ethiopia or Abyssinia. In 10.7 they are said to be descendants of Ham. The repetition of the names here means that the districts were inhabited by a mixed people, perhaps consisting of original Hamites overlaid by a Semite stock. Dedan is mentioned in Jer. 25. 23 with other Semite peoples. The identity of the peoples mentioned as descending from Dedan is unknown.

VERSE 4. *Ephah.* This people is mentioned with Midian and Sheba in Isa. 60. 6. The rest do not seem to be identifiable.

All these. From these two simple words we learn two things: (1) the large numbers of Keturah's sons and descendants were not appointed by God to be heirs of the promise. This privilege was reserved for Isaac, the only son of Sarah. This is in accordance with a principle that we often see at work in the Bible. God saves by Gideon's three hundred (Jud. 7. 7). He chooses the foolish, the weak, the despised, the things that are not,

to bring to nought the things that are (1 Cor. 1. 27, 28). Isaac was almost certainly the youngest of all Abraham's children. (2) Since all these names are inserted in the Bible, we may be certain that God knew and cared all about these men and the tribes, or peoples, into which their descendants grew. We know nothing about most of them. He knows all, and He loves them all. They are a cross-section of the whole human race, every member of which is known and loved by God. Probably they all have descendants alive today, known by different names and speaking different languages, who await the Gospel message. Here in Genesis we find them cut off from the covenant, cast out and sent away. By the Gospel they and all mankind may be called back to God.

The fact that Abraham had other descendants besides Isaac, who drop out of the story, reminds us that God has other creatures besides ourselves, countless angels whose interests He has at heart, and we know not whom besides. He does not forget any of His creatures. The covenant, by which an election is brought into intimate touch with Him, is intended to broaden out into blessing for all who do not refuse God's grace.

VERSE 5. Isaac was Abraham's heir. In the same way God the Father has appointed His only Son the heir of all things (Heb. 1. 2), and has created all things through Him and for Him (Col. 1. 16). All that is the Father's belongs to the Son (Jo. 17. 10).

VERSE 6. *The concubines,* that is, Hagar and Keturah. There may also have been others in accordance with the custom of the day. There was a low standard of social life in these matters owing to the corruption of human nature. ' In the beginning it was not so ' (Mt. 19. 8), and the true standard of monogamy and of happy family life has been restored by Christ in the Gospel (1 Cor. 7. 2; 1 Tim. 3. 2, 12). Until the Spirit of God came with power to deal with human nature and impart newness of life, even believers like Abraham were unable to rise to the original standard.

Abraham gave gifts, and sent them away. These are just the two things that God does to those of His creatures who are outside the covenant. He showers gifts upon them. He is kind both to the just and to the unjust. He gives to sinners sunshine and rain (Mt. 5. 45), life and breath and all things (Acts 17. 25). But He does not allow them to interfere with His great purpose of redemption, and on the last day they will be finally told to depart (Mt. 7. 23).

While he yet lived. Abraham himself made all the right and proper arrangements that he could, while he had the opportunity. He fell in by faith with the purpose of God. He may have been as fond of all his sons as he had been of Ishmael (21. 11), but he did not allow his natural affection, or any desire that he might have had to keep his children with him to interfere with the known purpose of God. He knew that Isaac was the child of promise (Gal. 4. 23), and that in him his seed was called (21. 12).

Eastward, unto the east country. They presumably lived in northern Arabia.

VERSE 7. Abraham lived forty-eight years longer than Sarah had done (23. 1), and as she was about ten years younger than he (17. 7), he was a widower for about forty years.

VERSE 8. *Abraham gave up the ghost, and died.* Death is the wages of sin (Rom. 6. 23), and is the due of every member of our fallen race. Believers cannot escape it, except at the end of the world (1 Thess. 4. 17). But for the believer death is not the end. God is the God of Abraham, and He is not the God of the dead, but of the living (Mt. 22. 32). Abraham lives to God (Lk. 20. 38), and will one day be called from his grave to a glorious resurrection (Mt. 8. 11: 22. 31, 32).

In a good old age. This was a mark of honour and happiness.

Was gathered to his people. This is a Hebrew idiom for death. It perhaps originated in the ancient custom of burying the members of a family together in the courtyard of their house, or in a family grave. Thus one by one the family was gathered into the graveyard. Although the family ceased to be gathered into the same burying ground, the conception and the phrase remained, although the different members of the family may have died and been buried at great distances from each other. They were then thought of as being gathered into a wide vague land of the dead, or state of death. The phrase cannot mean that we are meant to think of the dead being gathered into some abode in another world in a disembodied state. This would mean that Abraham and his ancestors, who were idolators (Josh. 24. 2), were together beyond the grave, and this would be contrary to the teaching of Scripture on the destiny of man.

VERSE 9. *Isaac and Ishmael.* These two men, whose lives and destinies were so separate, were brought together by their common relationship to Abraham and their common interest in his death. In the same way many of different origin and outlook are brought together by a common relationship to Christ and interest in His death.

Buried him. What is dead needs to be buried, and a funeral is the public proof and open demonstration of death. So those who are dead with Christ need to be buried with Him in baptism (Rom. 6. 3, 4).

In the cave of Machpelah. Abraham's body still lies safely sheltered in the cave, over which now stands a mosque. Access to the cave is forbidden, but strangers have occasionally been able to descend to it. Among them is said to have been King Edward VII when Prince of Wales. At least one member of the British Army in Palestine in 1917 was able to enter the cave and in the dim light found stone sarcophagi.

VERSE 10. *Which Abraham pur-*

chased. The burying-place was the only ground that Abraham possessed in the land of promise.

Sarah his wife. For the account of the purchase of the field and the burial of Sarah see chapter 23.

VERSE 11. *After the death of Abraham*. The death of his father made Isaac the head of the family and put the inheritance into his hands. In the same way it is after the death of Christ that inheritance and blessing become ours.

God blessed his son Isaac. God's blessing brings increase, prosperity and success. The blessing given to Isaac was the blessing of Abraham, which belongs to every Christian believer (Gal. 3. 14). It was given to Isaac in contrast to Ishmael and the other sons of Abraham because Isaac was the child of promise (Gal. 4. 23), in whom Abraham's seed was called (Gen. 21. 12; Rom. 9. 7; Heb. 11. 18).

Dwelt by the well Lahai-roi. The name of the well is He that liveth and seeth me (16. 14). Isaac therefore dwelt in the presence and under the eye of the living God. We too are to abide in Christ (Jo. 15. 3). We are to live our lives as those who are always in God's presence.

VERSE 12. This and the following six verses contain the whole of the seventh set of " generations ", the eighth section of the book of Genesis. The section is conspicuous for its smallness, and is little more than a skeleton. It is designedly small in contrast to the coming sections dealing with Isaac and Jacob. The probable reason for the inclusion of " generations of Ishmael " in the book is to show the fulfilment of the promises made to his mother before his birth (16. 11, 12) and to his father (17. 20).

Ishmael, was the child of the flesh, not the child of promise. He and his mother are types of Old Testament Israel after the flesh, living under the Sinai covenant, and cast out before the new Israel (Gal. 4. 22-31).

Hagar, the Egyptian. Ishmael's mother was of the world. She was Egyptian in her sympathies. *Bare unto Abraham*. For the circumstances of Ishmael's birth see chapter 16.

VERSE 13. *The names of the sons of Ishmael*. We know little, if anything, of them but their names. God however knew them through and through, cared for each one, and appointed their destiny. *Nebajoth*. His descendants were a sheep - breeding people, and are mentioned by the prophet Isaiah as being acceptable to the Lord under the Gospel (Isa. 60. 7). If Ishmael was cast out, his descendants are called to repentance in Christ. *Kedar*. These were the best known people among the descendants of Ishmael. They also were sheep-breeders (Ezek. 27. 21), and they also are called to blessing under the Gospel (Isa. 60. 7). They are mentioned several times in the Old Testament (see for instance Ps. 120. 5).

VERSE 14. *Dumah*. Isaiah has a mysterious reference to this people. (Isa. 21. 11, 12), who seem to have been closely connected with Edom and Idumea.

VERSE 15. *Tema*. This was an Arabian people connected by Jeremiah with Dedan (Jer. 25. 23) and in the book of Job with Sheba (Job 6. 19).

The remaining sons of Ishmael are nothing but names.

VERSE 16. *By their towns, and by their castles*. They appear to have had fortified settlements. *Twelve princes*. God fulfilled His word to Abraham (see 17. 20). However great the princes were, it is better to be a humble child of God, one of the weak things of the world and the things that are not (1 Cor. 1. 27-29).

VERSE 17. *An hundred and thirty and seven years*. He lived ten years longer than Sarah and thirty-eight years less than Abraham.

Gave up the ghost. His spirit returned to God Who gave it, and his life was over (Eccl. 12. 7).

Gathered unto his people. See on verse 8.

VERSE 18. *From Havilah unto Shur,* that is to say, south of Palestine.

That is before Egypt. Egypt is in the Bible the picture of the world. This is where we should expect Ishmael and his children to dwell. Like the unbelieving Jew under the old covenant, of whom he is a picture (Gal. 4. 23-25), he did not exactly live in the world, but his inclinations were towards it, and he lived on its borders. *As thou goest toward Assyria.* This probably means that the Ishmaelites lived on and around the caravan route that connected Egypt with Assyria. Later we shall find them making use of one of these routes (37. 25). Assyria is one of the Bible pictures of the domain of the devil, and we thus find those who had been born after the flesh in relationship with the devil as well as with the world.

He died in the presence of all his brethren. This repeats, or partially repeats, the statement of 16. 12. The Hebrew word translated ' died ' means literally ' fell '. The R.V. suggests that the right meaning may be ' abode '. ' In the presence of ' may be translated ' over against ', and the true meaning may be geographical, meaning ' to the east of '. Ishmael did not live or die in the land of promise. He lived ' over against it ', on its borders, in touch with Egypt and Assyria. He left it as a boy, and the only occasion on which we know that he returned to it was the funeral of his father. In all these things he resembles many who are brought up in a Christian home, but leave it for the confines of the world. Yet they often dwell ' over against it ', perhaps with a sad and jealous heart, wishing secretly to be in it, but proudly refusing to abandon the supposed advantages of the world. As in the case of Ishmael, it is often a funeral that brings them back (verse 9). Thus ends the brief sad story of Ishmael,

the child who missed the promises because he mocked at the purpose of God and perhaps sought for himself what was intended for another (21. 9).

VERSE 19. With this verse the story of Isaac and his family begins, and continues to the end of chapter 35. Its length and detail are in definite and intentional contrast to the brief sketch of the history of Ishmael. This section contains the account of the birth of Esau and Jacob (25. 19-26), Esau's selling of his birthright (25. 27-34), Isaac's relations with Abimelech (26. 1-33), Esau's marriages and the blessing of Jacob obtained by deception (26. 34-27. 46), the departure of Jacob to Haran (28), his service and marriage there (29, 30), Jacob's return to Palestine (31), his meeting with the angels, wrestling with God and meeting with Esau (32. 1-33. 16), his purchase of land (33. 17-20), the adventures of Dinah and Shechem (34), Jacob's return to Isaac and Isaac's death (35).

The generations of. See on 2. 4.

Abraham begat Isaac. This is the only case, in which at the beginning of a section of ' generations ' we are carried one step backwards. The reason seems twofold. (1) Abraham was the one first called by God, who entered into the covenant, which governed the lives of his descendants. The phrase ' Abraham's son ' thus implies a certain relationship with God. (2) Isaac seems to have been of a quiet retiring disposition. He may have felt that there was nothing in his own life or personality worth recording. He preferred to be known as Abraham's son. Acts 7. 16 seems to make clear that Abraham gave his name to the whole family or clan.

VERSE 20. *Forty.* This probably means *about* 40, unless we are to suppose that at least three years elapsed between Sarah's death in chapter 23 and Isaac's marriage in chapter 24.

Rebekah. See chapter 24. *The Syrian.* Hebrew says *Aramean.* They spoke Aramaic, as Abraham had done before entering Canaan, where he began to speak Hebrew, which is a Canaanite dialect. 'A Syrian ready to perish was my father' (Deut. 26. 5). *Padan-Aram*. This is the first time this name is mentioned. In Genesis 24 it is called a city of Mesopotamia. It was probably situated near Haran.

VERSE 21. *Entreated the Lord*. This was the right thing to do. Isaac showed himself to be a man of prayer. He could make this request with confidence, because he could rely on the promises of God, and he also knew his own mother's experiences.

She was barren. Yet she was the woman appointed by God to be the bride of Isaac (24. 14, 44). This was a further test for Isaac's faith and a further illustration of the principle that God uses the things that are not to confound the things that are (1 Cor. 1. 27, 28). In the same way God has appointed for His Son a bride who in herself is utterly barren, but derives from the heavenly Bridegroom all her life and power (Jo. 15. 5).

The Lord was entreated of him. Notice the change of the Divine Name from Elohim, the Creator, in verse 11, to Jahweh, the Redeemer, here. In verse 11 the supreme disposer is thought of, the God both of Ishmael and Isaac. Here we are dealing with matters that lie entirely within the covenant. We have here an encouragement to prayer and an example of an answer to it. There was no stupendous miracle resting on a spontaneous promise, as there had been in Sarah's case. There is no suggestion here of supernatural intervention. God is the God of nature and so moved the forces of nature in answer to prayer, that barrenness was overcome. We too may claim and expect answers to prayer in similar circumstances. God often moves where science fails.

Rebekah his wife conceived. This was a gracious and quite definite answer. The barrenness was a blessing, because both mother and children

would realise all their lives that their birth was an answer to prayer and therefore an act of grace and mercy. It ought to have given them a sense of the purpose of God in their lives.

VERSE 22. *Struggled together*. Even before their birth their mutual antipathy became apparent. They were to be different in character and different in destiny. They typify the spirit and the flesh, which are perpetually antagonistic. (Gal. 5. 17).

Why am I thus? Rebekah was early puzzled by this inner struggle. So are those unbelievers in whom an inner heart-struggle occurs. Many unbelievers desire to do right, but realise that they have no power to do it. They find themselves drawn by sin and temptation into acts and words which they hate and, if they could, would banish from their lives. Their experience is the same as that so vividly described by the apostle in the sixth and seventh chapters of Romans. They ask in despair, ' Why am I thus?' The same struggle goes on in the believer, for it seems clear from Gal. 5. 17 that the apostle is speaking in the Epistle to the Romans from the standpoint of a converted man. In the believer the struggle is fiercer and more definite, because in him are two antagonistic natures. In the unbeliever the struggle, when it occurs at all, is set up by his conscience, the mere wraith of what his first forefather once was many thousands of years ago. Every believer possesses two separate natures, the old corrupt one taken at birth from Adam and the new regenerate one received from Christ at his conversion. He has the double advantage over the unbeliever in that he knows the secret of victory over his corrupt nature and finds it wrought in him by the Holy Ghost. He also has a satisfying answer to the question, ' Why am I thus?' He knows from God's Word the origin of the corruption of his nature, he knows too the purposes of God in his redemption, and experiences the regenerating power of the Holy Ghost. If he is conscious of the struggle within, he thanks God that it demonstrates the antipathy of his regenerate nature to sin, and he finds its fierceness continually diminishing as Christ becomes more and more formed within him by the Spirit's gracious and powerful action.

She went to inquire of the Lord. It is difficult to know where she went. The rationalistic critic cuts the knot by saying that the story does not represent facts, but was composed in a later age when it was customary to go to the temple or tabernacle. This is not the way to deal with the statements of Scripture. It is irreverent and crude. Our ignorance of the answer to the question is far from proving the inaccuracy of the text. She may have gone (1) to a heathen shrine, but if she had, it does not seem likely that Jahweh would have met with her there. It is true that His grace and mercy are so great, that He may have had pity on her heathen origin and overlooked her ignorance. (2) There may have been some central point, some special tent, in the little community of Isaac's household, which was set apart for worship, to which she went. (3) She may have gone to some particular person, such as a prophet, but if so, we are quite ignorant who he could be. Perhaps he was some Balaam or some Job. The most likely person of all is perhaps her husband, but if she consulted him, the expression ' went ' is strange. (4) Very likely she went into the secret recesses of her own tent and kneeled before Jahweh, Whom she had learnt during twenty years of married life to dissociate from local shrines and to address in the sanctuary of her own heart (1 Pet. 3. 15). Wherever she went, she seems to have thought of her action in much the same way as her heathen ancestors had done, when they went to enquire at some shrine or oracle.

VERSE 23. However she asked, Jahweh graciously gave her the answer that she required.

Two nations. These are Israel and Edom, typifying the spirit and flesh.

Two manner of people. The one

would be carnal and worldly in outlook. The other would be the unique covenant people. The destinies of both would be quite different.

Stronger. Israel was to be the stronger. The true Israelite is strong in the Lord and in the power of His might. The natural Israelite has retained such strength, that he remains distinct in the world today. Edom has long since perished, and if any of Esau's descendants are left, they cannot be identified today.

The elder shall serve the younger. Edom would serve Israel. Edom was conquered and made tributary in David's time (2 Sam. 8. 14), and remained subservient to Judah through much of the history of the kingdom (see 1 Ki. 22. 47; 2 Ki. 8. 20). These things are typical of spiritual realities. The flesh is older than the spirit. Man is born into the world with it. He acquires a spiritual nature by faith at conversion. The natural precedes the spiritual (1 Cor. 15. 46). It is only in the regenerate man that the two natures co-exist, but where they do, the flesh by God's grace is subservient to the spirit, and sin has no dominion over the true believer. (Rom. 6. 14). The apostle Paul selects this declaration made to Rebekah as an example of the operation of the elective purpose of God. He says that being made before the children's birth, it could not depend upon their merit. It was made, ' that the purpose of God according to election might stand ' (Rom. 9. 11, 12). It is on this principle that God deals in grace with all who come to Him in faith. His grace is independent of merit. The apostle implies that the choice of Jacob and the predestination of the two children were essential for the accomplishment of God's purpose of redemption and blessing. We need thus make no mistake over the purpose of election. Further light is thrown for us upon the purpose of God, when we see that it was the younger of the two who was elected. This is in accordance with the same principle as we see it at work, for example, in the selection of Gideon's three hundred (Jud. 7. 4-7). The principle is embodied in the Gospel and expressed emphatically by the apostle in 1 Cor. 1. 26-29. It prevents any glory being given to the flesh. So far as we can see, God could have as easily moulded Esau to the purpose as Jacob. Esau was a wicked man (Heb. 12. 16), but Jacob was naturally a despicable character. God might also, so far as we can understand, have included both children in the promises and covenant, as He did in the next generation with all twelve sons of Jacob. If we ask why He dealt in this way, we are not likely to receive further light than we do from the considerations which have been mentioned. We may be content to know that in all His elective purposes God acts as He does, (1) to bring glory to Himself, (2) to bring the utmost ultimate blessing on the elect and all mankind, (3) to prevent any glory accruing to the flesh. If we seek to pry further, we are reproached by the Holy Ghost through the apostle for doing so (Rom. 9. 19-21).

VERSE 24. *Twins*. Though both were boys, they were far from being identical twins. Yet both started from the same position and with identical opportunities from the human point of view.

VERSE 25. *Red*. This colour suggests blood, which is the life of the flesh (Lev. 17. 14). Esau's appearance was thus true to his nature and destiny. *All over like an hairy garment*. A hairy or woollen garment is the opposite of fine linen, which represents the robe of Christ's righteousness. (Rev. 19. 8).

Esau. This name appears to resemble a root that has the meaning of ' hairy '.

VERSE 26. *His hand took hold on Esau's heel*. This act was regarded by the prophet Hosea as symbolic of prevailing power. The antagonism of the brothers was apparent at birth. Jacob would one day prevail (Hos. 12. 3).

Jacob. The name means supplanter. The infant's action in taking hold of his brother's heel was symbolic of his final supplanting of him in all privileges and blessing. In the same way, though the flesh precedes the spirit, the new nature gains all that is lost by the old.

Threescore years old. The course of Isaac's life seems to have been slow, quiet and peaceful.

VERSE 27. *The boys grew*. The implication is that they grew up. The same is true of the things that they typify. The believer grows in grace and in the knowledge of our Lord and Saviour Jesus Christ (2 Pet. 3. 18), until he comes to a perfect man, to the measure of the full age of the fulness of Christ (Eph. 4. 13). Sin also, when it is finished, brings forth death (Jas. 1. 15).

A cunning hunter. Esau was like Nimrod (see 10. 9). The flesh knows how to hunt souls to their destruction (1 Pet. 2. 11), and is very cunning at this craft. *A man of the field*. ' The field is the world ' (Mt. 13. 38). All the interests of the flesh are in the world. Its pleasures, ambitions and activities lie there. ' The lust of the flesh ' is one of the constituents of the world (1 Jo. 2. 16).

A plain man. The Hebrew for ' plain ' is tam. It occurs several times in Job, also occasionally in the Psalms, Proverbs and Song of Solomon, and is elsewhere translated ' perfect ', ' upright ' or ' undefiled '. The description can scarcely be meant to imply that Jacob was of blameless character. The subsequent narrative proves that much of his behaviour was inconsistent with such a meaning. The key is probably to be found in the words that follow, *Dwelling in tents*. While Esau's interests were in the world, Jacob was perfectly content to live the pilgrim life. He may have appreciated the promises made to Abraham and the meaning of his call. He must have known the terms of the oracle given to his mother before his birth, and he may have realised that they made him the heir of the promises and of the call. He perhaps understood that he stood in the same relationship to Esau as his father had done to Ishmael. In Heb. 11. 9 it is pointed out that he dwelt in tents with his father and grandfather. Here then we see emphasised one of the chief characteristics of the spiritual life. In contrast to the activity of the flesh the spirit is quiet. In contrast to the materialistic ambitions of the flesh the spirit is content. In contrast to the pursuit of happiness in the present the spirit waits for what is to come. The believer dwells in tents, passing through the world as a stranger and pilgrim (Ps. 39. 12; 1 Chron. 29. 15; Heb. 11. 13).

VERSE 28. *Isaac loved Esau.* This favouritism was wrong and must have made for disharmony in the family. Esau's character was unlike that of his father, and perhaps the father's affection was called out by a sort of attraction of opposites. *Because he did eat of his venison.* This was an unworthy motive. His son's worldliness began to draw Isaac's eye away from the spiritual and invisible, and to occupy him with the cravings of the flesh. In every age, today as much as then, an indulgent parent, though he may be himself a child of God, can easily become blind to worldliness or unbelief in his child.

Rebekah loved Jacob. No reason is given for her partiality. It may have been reaction to Isaac's affection for Esau. In any case it can scarcely have been right and must have made for disharmony and jealousy.

VERSE 29. *Jacob sod pottage.* Jacob was attending to material needs, but his heart was not set upon them, as was Esau's. It is possible to eat and drink to the glory of God (1 Cor. 10. 31).

Esau came from the field, where he had been indulging, as it were, in his worldly pursuits. *He was faint.* The worldling often exhausts himself with the speed and anxiety of his worldly activity. He has no rest in God.

VERSE 30. *Feed me, I pray thee.* Esau grasped at the immediate satisfaction of his bodily need. The Lord Jesus in a similar situation did the opposite and was content to depend upon God (Mt. 4. 3, 4). *That same red pottage.* The Hebrew says ' with that red red '. On the implications of red see on verse 25. Esau was fascinated by the natural life and what it had to offer. He did not care for spiritual things. *For I am faint.* Esau's bodily necessity was his compelling reason. He did not consult the will of God.

Edom. This means ' red '. Esau goes down to history as the one who lives for the things of the soul instead of for those of the spirit (see 1 Cor. 15. 44-46; Heb. 4. 12).

VERSE 31. *Sell me this day thy birthright.* This request reveals (1) Jacob's subtlety. He could outwit his brother, just as his natural descendants have so often been able to outwit their Gentile brethren. Bitter enmity is aroused in either case as a result. (2) The request reveals Jacob's desire to have spiritual blessing and to inherit the promises. His heart was set on the right thing, though he was mistaken (a) in the means he took to obtain it, and (b) in supposing that the blessing went with priority in birth. God had said that it would not. He went about to establish his own righteousness (Rom. 10. 3), but through a long and troubled life he came to learn that all depended on the grace of God.

VERSE 32. *At the point to die; and what profit shall this birthright do to me?* If he had really been at the point of death, the birthright might have been the only thing to profit him. He saw, or thought he saw, all his pleasures fading away from him.

VERSE 33. *Swear to me.* Jacob took advantage of his brother's hunger and desperation. His action was mean, but, unknown to him, the hand of God was behind the transaction. *He sold his birthright unto Jacob.*

The writer to the Hebrews takes Esau and this incident as the type and illustration of the worldling, whose sense of values is reversed (Heb. 12. 16). He calls him a ' profane person '. This means ' worldly-minded '. The morsel of meat stands for the pleasures of the flesh. The satisfaction it gave was immediate, short-lived and temporary. The birthright stands for regeneration and eternal life. Many a man follows Esau in his choice, seeing no value in the spiritual life and the things of God, and will one day like Esau seek them with a desperate desire and find that it is too late to have them (Heb. 12. 17).

VERSE 34. *Jacob gave Esau bread and pottage of lentils.* Esau got his side of the bargain, as is often the case with the worldly man.

He did eat and drink. He obtained his enjoyment and satisfaction. Perhaps the bread gives a hint of the natural religion that is often found in the life of the worldly and carnal man.

Rose up. His satisfaction and pleasure were over. *Went his way.* Even so, when his momentary satisfaction is over, the worldly man goes his way to the grave with all that he lived for behind him.

Despised his birthright. He regarded it as of no value. The temporary satisfaction of his appetite was more important to him. In the same way the man of the world regards as of no importance the fact that he was made in the image of God in order to love, serve and obey his Creator. All this he leaves out of his reckoning. He lives for the pleasures of the moment, and in so doing like Esau he loses all.

CHAPTER 26

THIS chapter gives us the story of Isaac's relations with Abimelech and his life in Gerar. He went there because of a famine (ver. 1). The blessing of Abraham is repeated for him (2-5). Isaac then practises the

same deceit over his wife as his father had done in similar circumstances in the case of Sarah (chapter 20) (6-11). There follows the account of Isaac's well-digging (12-22). The promises and blessing are again repeated (23-25), and then follows the covenant with Abimelech (26-33). The last two verses of the chapter, which tell of Esau's marriages, belong really to the following chapter (34, 35).

VERSE 1. *A famine in the land.* Believers are not immune from the ordinary judgments and natural disasters. They may however expect to be protected from their consequences and to find that they are overruled in the purpose of God to bring blessing. In this case the famine provided a test for Isaac's faith and obedience. This famine did not take place spontaneously, independently of the control of God. His sovereign will and power brought it about.

Beside the first famine that was in the days of Abraham. This is related in 12. 10 and following. This statement deliberately disconnects the two incidents, as if the Holy Ghost foresaw the foolish attempts of liberal critics to make out that the two accounts concern the same original incident. *Abimelech.* The name is probably a title similar to the title Pharaoh, but he may have been the son of the man with whom Abraham made a covenant (21. 22-34). *King of the Philistines.* A difficulty arises over the mention of the Philistines here, as unprejudiced archæological opinion considers their settlement in Palestine not to have taken place till after the conquest under Joshua. If the archæologists are right (and there is always the possibility of further knowledge compelling the revision of an opinion), two explanations are possible. (1) The Philistines may have had isolated colonies or settlements in Palestine among the native population before they conquered and inhabited part of the land. Gerar would be one such colony. (2) Possibly this Abimelech and his people were not actually Philistines, but the name was substi-

236

tuted for that of an earlier people. This might occur if the early name had fallen completely out of use and therefore meant nothing to the readers. In the same way a modern archæological work might refer to a neolithic people living in the Iberian peninsula as Spaniards. If, however, this explanation holds good, the gloss, or alteration of name, must have taken place later than the time of Moses, perhaps in that of David. While it is not impossible that such an alteration might have taken place under the inspiration of the Holy Ghost, especially when we remember that some conservative opinion holds that the Pentateuch attained its final shape in the days of David, we enter on dangerous ground when we think of such alterations to the text being made so late. Our best course is to await further archæological knowledge. On previous occasions this has often elucidated and vindicated the text. *Gerar*. This was in the extreme southwest of Palestine on the brook Besor to the north of the desert of Shur.

VERSE 2. *The Lord*. Here we have Jahweh, the Name of the Redeemer, because God reveals Himself in this chapter as carrying out the promises to Abraham and blessing Isaac within the covenant. *Appeared*. This gracious appearance implied habitual absence. We have no need of such appearances, as we have the constant presence of the Holy Spirit in our hearts and constant access to the throne of grace.

Go not down into Egypt. This was a gracious direct warning not to make the mistake that Abraham had made (see 12. 10-20). It is a warning to us as well. In times of difficulty we ought not to go down into the world and adopt worldly methods of protection or alleviation. Our duty is to rely in all circumstances on our heavenly Father's care and trust in Him to deliver us from trouble and supply all our need. Such an attitude is always inevitably richly rewarded. ' He that believeth on him shall not be ashamed ' (Rom. 9. 33).

Dwell in the land which I shall tell thee of. We ought to dwell (1) in Christ (Jo. 15. 3), (2) in heaven by faith in our hearts (Eph. 2. 6), (3) in that particular place on earth where God's work for us lies and to which the Holy Spirit directs us. God will tell us of it, guiding us there by circumstances or sounding a call through the need of the place.

VERSE 3. In this verse we have a command with a twofold blessing attached, and a twofold reason for the blessing. The command is *Sojourn*. The child of God must always be a stranger and a sojourner on the earth (Ps. 39. 12; 1 Chron. 29. 15). *In this land*. It is the land of promise. One day the meek will inherit the earth (Ps. 37. 11). Accompanying this command are two blessings. (1) *I will be with thee*. There can be no higher good than the presence of God. In Him are all things, and His presence carries every good thing with it. Having Him we have all, and we need nothing but Him. In one sense He is omnipresent (Jer. 23. 24), yet there is a far deeper and more special presence which is denied to the sinner and vouchsafed to the saint (Mt. 28. 20; Jo. 15. 3; Eph. 3. 17). God's presence gives protection from harm and keeps alive a free, reverent, happy relationship of love and fear. (2) *Will bless thee*. God's blessing brings happiness, success, prosperity and especially increase. If a Christian is blessed, it is chiefly seen in his winning of souls.

There are two reasons for God's blessing of Isaac: (1) His purpose, and (2) His promise. (1) *For unto thee, and unto thy seed, I will give all these countries*. God had a great purpose for Isaac, and this was the first reason for His blessing him. In the same way, if we find that God is with us and is blessing us, we may be sure that He has a purpose for us, something to give us. It is an inheritance incorruptible, undefiled, and that fadeth not away, reserved in heaven for us, who are being kept by the power of God through faith unto salvation (1 Pet. 4. 5). Notice that the promise was (a) a personal one to Isaac. It was ' to thee '. During his lifetime Isaac possessed no square foot of the land except the field where his mother and father had been buried, purchased by Abraham from the Hittites. He died a stranger and a sojourner. He did not receive the promises (Heb. 11. 13). The gift of all the countries to Isaac must therefore come to him in resurrection glory. It will be fulfilled in the same way as it will be fulfilled to Abraham, who is made by the promises ' heir of the world ' (Rom. 4. 13). This means that the countries of Palestine and its surroundings are types and symbols of the new heaven and the new earth. The promise was also (b) to Isaac's seed. The true seed is the redeemed humanity which will inherit all things (Rev. 21. 7). The natural seed inherited Palestine under Joshua, and its dominion extended in Solomon's day to the utmost boundaries that had ever been promised to Abraham (Gen. 15. 18; 1 Ki. 4. 21). (2) God was with Isaac and blessed him in order to fulfil a promise that He had made to another in the past. If we are conscious of God's presence and blessing, we may be sure that we enjoy them in fulfilment of God's covenant and promise to the Lord Jesus Christ, to Whom He gave the uttermost parts of the earth for His possession (Ps. 2. 8). God has made Him the head of the heathen, and told Him that a people will serve Him (Ps. 18. 43). God's pledged word to Christ is fulfilled in the blessing which by His grace He gives to us.

I will perform the oath which I sware unto Abraham thy father. The oath had been taken on an occasion which Isaac remembered well. He had heard its terms spoken from heaven immediately after the ram had been offered as a substitute for himself (22. 16-18). The terms were blessing, increase, victory and the privilege of the seed of Abraham being a channel of blessing to the world. It began to be fulfilled in the birth of Christ (Lk. 1. 68-73), and it works out in the deliverance of God's people from their enemies and their sanctified service during all their lives (Lk. 1. 74, 75).

VERSE 4. *I will make thy seed to multiply.* This was fulfilled (1) in the large numbers of Old Testament Israel (Ex. 1. 7) and will be fulfilled (2) in the great countless multitude of redeemed humanity (Rev. 7. 9).

Will give unto thy seed all these countries. See on verse 3.

In thy seed shall all the nations of the earth be blessed. The seed is Christ, and it is in Him that all nations receive the blessing of the Gospel (see Acts 3. 25, 26).

VERSE 5. *Because that Abraham.* Notice that it does not say, ' Because that thou '. Isaac was blessed because of the obedience of another. So are we blessed because of the obedience of Christ, for Whose merits we are justified and obtain salvation.

Obeyed my voice. This is a repetition of 22. 18, where the reference to Abraham's obedience seems especially to belong to his offering of Isaac. This was an act of peculiar obedience, but it was the culmination of a life of obedience, which began in Ur when Abraham first heard the command to leave his country and family and to sojourn in Canaan. Apart from this obedience it would have been impossible for Abraham to have obtained the promises, for he would never have left Ur. *And kept my charge, my commandments, my statutes, and my laws.* It is noteworthy that this is never mentioned to Abraham during his lifetime. If it had been, the conception of merit might have crept in. Nowhere is it said that blessing came to Abraham because he kept God's commandments. The result of his keeping them was that blessing came to Isaac, if only on the practical ground that the obedience in the home nourished Isaac's spiritual life. The spiritual reality is clear. It is because Christ kept God's commandments that we obtain grace and blessing. In the *charge* we may see Abraham's life of faith as a whole, through which he gave continual witness to the existence, character, requirements and purposes of the true and living God. The *commandments* are the particular directions given to Abraham from time to time to guide him in the carrying out of God's purpose. Examples are the initial commandment to leave Ur and Haran and to enter Palestine, or the commandment to expel Hagar, or to offer up Isaac. The The *statutes* probably have a more religious reference and may be illustrated by the sin offering of chapter 15. 9-17, or by circumcision. The *laws* are the great moral principles by which God requires a man to order his life. Abraham observed them by showing faith and obedience and hope, by understanding and appropriating justification and by fixing his hope on the glories of the world to come.

VERSE 6. *Dwelt in Gerar.* This is what Jahweh had told him to do (verses 2, 3), and Isaac simply obeyed.

VERSE 7. In verses 7-11 we find another extraordinary instance of weakness of faith and fear of man. The incident supplies a warning of the persistence of sin in the nature of the justified and the proneness of our hearts to give way to temptation in spite of full knowledge of the danger that had attended identical conduct in the past. It was perhaps in order to avoid this very temptation that Jahweh had forbidden Isaac to go down into Egypt (verse 2), where it had first been a snare to his father (12. 10-20). Here in Gerar Isaac's father had endangered his own birth by the same thing (20). In neither case had there been any need for the deception, God having been clearly present for protection. Both these occasions were well known to Isaac, through whom the record of them must have come down to Israel and eventually to us. Yet he fell into the same snare. *The men of the place asked him of his wife.* Abraham had twice made the suggestion himself to Sarah that she should call herself his sister. Isaac was not guilty of initiating the suggestion. The situation in this case arose as the result of lust.

She is my sister. In spite of his knowledge of the reproach that Abraham's attempts at deception had brought him Isaac evidently took his cue from his father. When Abraham said the same thing about Sarah, he was telling a half-truth (20. 12). Isaac had no such excuse. He might scarcely have thought of the idea of his own accord.

He feared. ' The fear of man bringeth a snare ' (Prov. 29. 25). Isaac forgot, when he was afraid, to trust in the Lord.

Lest, said he. the men of the place kill me for Rebekah. Like Abraham in similar circumstances Isaac was mean enough to be ready to sacrifice his wife's honour to save his own life. He forgot in his fear that God was able to protect him and would never repudiate the promises that He had made to him, and he was foolish enough to suppose that God would have told him to sojourn in Gerar without being aware of the danger to which he thought himself exposed. Thus are we shown from this incident the power of sin to deprive us of common sense and reason. This in its turn led Isaac to dishonour God by acting as if He was incapable of protecting him.

She was fair to look upon. Sin in others turned this gift of God into a danger and· a snare.

VERSE 8. *A long time.* The deception and risk were long drawn out. Isaac's attitude was kept up persistently. During this long time he must have lost much in spiritual power. *Looked out at a window.* A site that is considered to have been the ancient Gerah was excavated some twenty-five years ago, a building that may well have been the chief's residence being found to have stood on the top of the mound. From this spot it is easy to look down on to the tents of the Bedouin, which to this day are pitched round the foot of the mound, and to see into the women's quarters at the rear of the tents. This is probably what Abimelech did. There is nothing in the text to imply that he was spying. The incident was providential.

Sporting. He was making love to her.

VERSE 9. Isaac told the truth.

VERSE 10. *What is this that thou hast done unto us?* Abimelech charges Isaac with wronging his people. His question showed the needlessness of Isaac's fears and the folly of his deception. *One of the people might lightly have lien with thy wife.* This statement reveals a condition of society in which the position of women was degraded. Sin had greatly weakened the sense of moral issues. The Gospel has restored the position of women in society and made men alive to the issue involved.

Thou shouldest have brought guiltiness upon us. Two aspects of Abimelech's outlook are made plain here. (1) He had a conscience, a standard and a sense of guilt. He was clear that adultery was wrong. Thus a heathen man proved himself to be a moral being and more careful to observe a fundamental principle than Isaac himself. (2) He regarded his whole community as a moral unity. The responsibility of the individual before God, which is fundamental to the Gospel, was less realised in the ancient east. The conception of sin bringing guilt and disaster upon a whole community appears clearly in the story of Achan (Josh. 7). The unity of a community in guilt and responsibility before God is seen throughout the Old Testament in the covenant relationship between Israel and God. It is brought to perfection (though no longer in the matter of guilt) in the church which is the body of Christ, the fulness of Him that filleth all in all (Eph. 1. 22, 23).

VERSE 11. Isaac found protection in the very man that he feared, not only for his wife's honour but for his own life. Once again God showed that the fears of his elect are groundless, and

that His care for them is independent of failure in their relationship towards Him. Notice that the authority of an earthly government and the sanctions of an earthly law were used by God for the protection of His people. This fact illustrates the truth of Rom. 13. 1-4.

VERSE 12. In verses 12 to 25 we have a picture of Isaac's manner of life and an account of the way in which God blessed him.

Isaac sowed in that land. The occupation of Abraham and his household seems only to have been pastoral. Isaac now adds agriculture to the keeping of cattle. He sowed in the land of his sojourn. This is an exact picture of the purpose of God for His people under the Gospel. Here in the world in which we sojourn we are to sow the seed of the Word in the hearts of men. The evangelist sows the Word (Mk. 4. 14). *Received in the same year an hundredfold.* The results were immediate and perfect. Success like this does not appear to attend the propagation of the Gospel. The parable of the sower itself tells us of four kinds of soil, of which only one is fruitful. Three quarters of the seed is lost. When the Gospel is preached, only a minority believes and accepts it. Yet we find that some of the seed sown on good ground in fact brought forth an hundredfold. Both in the case of Isaac and the case of the Gospel we must look below the surface. Isaac's hundredfold is not likely to have been attained without the scattering of much unfruitful seed, and though outward failure generally attends much preaching of the Gospel, it remains true that the Word of God does not return to Him void, but accomplishes that whereto He sends it (Isa. 55. 11). God's purpose is never frustrated, and as many as are ordained unto eternal life believe (Acts 13. 48). When we stand among the redeemed in glory and look back upon the sowing of the Gospel message, we shall find that the harvest is a hundredfold.

The Lord blessed him. Only the blessing of God can bring prosperity, and all reaping that we may do in the Gospel is due to it.

VERSE 13. *The man waxed great.* We too are meant to do the same. God intends us to come to a perfect man, to the measure of the stature of the fulness of Christ (Eph. 4. 13). The way to become spiritually great is to receive God's blessing in sowing the seed of the Gospel and reaping souls for Him.

Went forward. We are to do the same. We are to grow in grace and in the knowledge of our Lord and Saviour Jesus Christ (2 Pet. 3. 18). If we do not know more of Christ and His love, or more of the holiness of God, this year than we did last year, there is something wrong with our spiritual lives.

Grew until he became very great. Our ultimate destiny is to be filled with all the fulness of God (Eph. 3. 19). Staggering as this thought is, it is yet not all. It seems that it may be only the beginning of a grace and a greatness that become literally incomprehensible. For immediately after praying this prayer for us, and therefore thinking the thought, the apostle goes on to say that God will do for us more abundantly than we can either ask or think (Eph. 3. 20). The measure of our greatness is the greatness of our Saviour and representative, Who is exalted to the right hand of God (Ps. 110. 1; Phil. 2. 9) and sits enthroned in the highest place that heaven affords.

VERSE 14. *Flocks.* The Saviour is the good shepherd and possesses many sheep (Jo. 10. 14). *Herds.* The cattle represents the Christian worker (1 Cor. 9. 8-11; 1 Tim. 5. 17, 18). *Great store of servants.* All the converted are servants of Christ (Jo. 13. 13), to say nothing of ten thousand times ten thousand and thousands of thousands of angels (Dan. 7. 10; Rev. 5. 11).

The Philistines envied him. The antagonism felt by the people of the world towards the people of God is often due at bottom to envy. They realise that the Christian possesses power and peace, and they envy him both. They envy the success that sometimes accompanies the Christian's industry and honesty.

VERSE 15. This verse gives a picture of the repeated efforts of the devil and the world to block the channels of the water of life, which the Christian digs. This action has been conspicuous during the last half century (before 1952). Organisation after organisation, founded by evangelicals as a channel for the Gospel to reach the world, has been stealthily seized by liberals, modernists, worldlings, or those with unreformed or ecclesiastical leanings, and effectually blocked as a means of evangelism. Often new associations with bases that are proof against all but dishonesty have been formed in their place. The wells have been blocked by the dust and earth of destructive criticism and a gospel of social advancement that denies the necessity of atonement.

VERSE 16. *Go from us.* The world would fain be rid of the people of God. It recognises that the principles of the two are opposed, and it dislikes interference with its own views and aims. *Thou art much mightier than we.* The world fears the people of God. It realises that they can exhibit a power in prayer and a depth of understanding of life which reveals the life of the world to be ungodly and superficial.

VERSE 17. *Isaac departed thence.* He did not stay where he was not wanted. The Lord did not do so either (Mt. 8. 34-9. 1; Mk. 5. 17, 18). Neither will the Holy Spirit stay where His presence is not wanted. God never forces Himself into anyone's life, and a man is free to reject the Gospel.

Pitched his tent. Like his father he lived the life of a sojourner, thus presenting a parable of the life in the world of the people of God.

VERSE 18. The direct statements of

this verse, which say that the same wells were digged a second time and called by the same names, ought to have prevented the destructive critics from putting out the crude story that chapters 20 and 26 are two traditions going back to the same original. The subconscious motive for such theories is to discredit the truth of the Bible.

Digged again. Notice Isaac's faith and persistence. He insisted on opening up again the channels of water of life which the enemy had closed. We too often have the duty and necessity of doing this. *In the days of Abraham his father.* See 21. 25.

After the death of Abraham. When a powerful influence was withdrawn, the enemy took the opportunity of stopping up the channels of blessing. They are always on the watch to do so, and the situation is true to life today.

He called their names after the names by which his father had called them. He did not pretend that they were different, or give them names that he thought might attract a younger generation. He went back, as it were, to the old paths, and walked in the old ways. He was not ashamed of the old names, but was proud to be reviving his father's work. He thereby preserved continuity with his father's work, claimed it as his own, and showed himself to be the rightful heir.

Verse 19. *Isaac's servants digged in the valley.* No channel of water of life can be found and made operative for men without preliminary hard work. The water is there, but it must be made available. This can only be done by long preparation in prayer and much organisation. The work is done in the valley, down among the common walks of life, not on the mountain top of spiritual exaltation. It is here in the valley that the water springs.

A well of springing water. The word translated 'springing' means in Hebrew 'living'. The living water is the Holy Spirit Himself, God's gift of Himself to His people, a well of water springing up in their hearts to eternal life (Jo. 4. 14).

Verse 20. *Didst strive with Isaac's herdmen.* The enemy's strife was not directed against the servants who digged the well, but against the herdmen who used it. The herdmen correspond to the pastors and shepherds. The owners of herds that do not belong to the Lord, and do not work for Him, seek to take the water of life from those to whom it belongs and use it for their own ends. This has often happened during the history of the Gospel.

Esek. This means 'contention'. The adversaries of the Gospel, or those who wish to claim its power and privileges without paying the price, seldom leave the people of God in peace to proclaim the Word.

Verse 21. *They digged another well.* The same process was repeated. The toil was necessary once again, and, it was rewarded with the same bitter results. The process is easily recognisable in the history of the Gospel. We may see it on the largest scale in the capture of the primitive church by the enemies of the Gospel at the time of Constantine the Great, and the total corruption of its organisation. At the Reformation a fresh pure well was dug. After the lapse of time the same enemies have set out to capture and corrupt the reformed churches.

Sitnah. This means 'hatred'. The strife increased and the bitterness redoubled.

Verse 22. *He removed from thence.* This seems to have been the secret of Isaac's success. He did not fight for the wells which had been captured by the enemy or claim them for his own. He did not repeat his mistake of digging a well in the same place as that of which he had been deprived, or tapping the same vein, so to speak. Instead he separated himself from his adversaries. This is what we are constantly called upon to do. 'Come out from among them and be ye separate, saith the Lord . . . and I will receive you' (2 Cor. 6. 17).

Rehoboth. The meaning of this is ' room '.

Two happy results followed Isaac's separation of himself from the Philistines. (1) *The Lord hath made room for us*. Isaac was now free to live his life and to serve and worship the Lord without interference from his adversaries. (2) *We shall be fruitful in the land*. He was now in a position to increase, in the language of the Gospel to win souls. These two results always follow the action of those who are ready to come out and be separate from false religion and to abandon hopeless attempts at co-operation. The greatest demonstration of the truth of this principle that has ever been made in the history of the Gospel is the glorious Reformation.

VERSE 23. *He went up from thence to Beer-sheba*. He returned to the place where the covenant was made. Beersheba means ' the well of the oath ', and we may think of him, after his separation of himself had brought God's blessing upon him, seeking to re-dedicate his life to God.

VERSE 24. *The Lord appeared unto him the same night*. Perhaps this was in a dream, perhaps in a vision. As he sought to renew his covenant obligations, the Lord met with him immediately.

And said. The Lord's words consisted of (1) a statement of the basis on which His promises rested. (2) An encouragement. (3) Three reasons for the encouragement with the reason for His promises. *I am the God of Abraham thy father*. Here we have (1) the basis of God's blessing of Isaac. He was blessed because of a promise made to another. It is the same with every believer in the Gospel dispensation. He is blessed because of the Father's promises to His Son Jesus Christ. The believer's God is the God and Father of our Lord Jesus Christ.

Fear not. (2) This is a command that comes often in the Bible and applies to every believer under the law or under the Gospel. The child of

God has his Father's perfect protection from present evils and dangers and the assurance of His grace to bring him through in perseverance to the blessings of the world to come. ' Perfect love casteth out fear ' (1 Jo. 4. 18). Fear diminishes in proportion to the increase of our love to God. *I am with thee*. This is (3) the first of three reasons why there is no need to fear. The words of the promise are simple, but its range is infinite. If God is with us, we possess all that we need and more. All power and all wisdom are at our disposal. We have an impregnable defence against all enemies and the assurance of everlasting life because the God Who is with us is eternal.

Will bless thee. God's blessing always accompanies His presence. This is a promise that gives a purpose in life for the future.

Multiply thy seed. Blessing and multiplication go so closely together as to be almost identical. If God blesses us, we shall find that we win souls for Christ and are used for the increase of His kingdom. *For my servant Abraham's sake*. Blessing came to Isaac for the sake of another to whom the promises had been made, not for any merit of his own. It is the same with us. We are blessed with all spiritual blessings in heavenly places in Christ Jesus (Eph. 1. 3). We are blessed for Christ's sake.

VERSE 25. This verse tells us of four actions on Isaac's part which typify and illustrate the spiritual life. (1) *He builded an altar there*. We must do the same. We must take one more look at Christ on Calvary and once more make His soul an offering for our sin (Isa. 53. 10). As the need arises, we must plunge again into the fountain that is open for sin and uncleanness (Zech. 13. 1). We must sanctify the Lord Christ in our heart (1 Pet. 3. 15), and there we must offer our bodies as a living sacrifice (Rom. 12. 1) and our continual sacrifice of praise (Heb. 13. 15). There are other sacrifices that we may offer on the

same altar, financial ones for example
(Phil. 4. 18). ' With such sacrifices
God is well pleased ' (Heb. 13. 16).

(2) *He called upon the name of the
Lord*. He identified himself with Jahweh as His servant. He claimed the
protection of His Name, and asserted
a special relationship with Him. By
calling on the Name he took obligations on himself. He bound himself
implicitly to obey and serve the One
to Whom he belonged. We must do
the same. As we go to Calvary and
accept all its benefits, we too must
call upon the Name and not be afraid
to confess His Name. ' Whosoever
shall call upon the Name of the Lord
shall be saved ' (Acts 2. 21).

(3) *And pitched his tent there*. During all our earthly sojourn we must
pitch our tent beside the cross and
dwell at Calvary. ' Beneath the cross
of Jesus I fain would take my stand '.
We can never afford to move away
from it. It is only at the cross that
we obtain resurrection power and
newness of life.

(4) *There Isaac's servants digged a
well*. It is at the cross that the fountain of water of life becomes available
to us. From the wounded side of
Jesus came forth blood to justify and
water to regenerate and sanctify (Jo.
19. 34). We are cleansed by the
washing of water by the word (Eph.
5. 26), but the stream flows from the
cross and springs up in the believing
heart to life eternal (Jo. 4. 14). Notice
that the servants dig the well. In the
same way the servants of Christ go
out with the Gospel to dig as it were
in · the hearts of men, clearing the
ground of the dust and mire of sin,
in order that the living water may be
available and may spring up.

VERSE 26. In the eight verses which
begin here we find an account of the
pact of friendship made between
Abimelech and Isaac.

Abimelech went to him. This was a
great testimony to the grace of God
and the power and blessing evident in
Isaac's life. It is seldom that the
people of the world come to us in this
way. If we lived nearer to the Lord,
perhaps they would come more often.
From Gerar. He took a considerable
journey, which showed that he was in
earnest.

And Ahuzzath one of his friends.
This was a further proof of the impression made by Isaac's godly life.
It was also a demonstration of the
reality of Abimelech's desire. He was
able to persuade at least one of his
friends to go with him to seek blessing from the true God and to enter
into covenant relationship with His
servant. This is a very desirable
situation, which God sometimes
allows us to see in times of revival,
but it does not do for us to depend
upon its arising. We are to *seek* and
to save that which is lost, as the
Master did. The lost are seldom
likely to seek us.

*Phichol the chief captain of his
army*. Abimelech wanted to enter
into this agreement in grand style and
to leave no doubt of its real meaning
to him. He brought one of his officials
with him to show that he was serious.
He had made up his mind what he
wanted to do.

VERSE 27. *Wherefore come ye to me,
seeing ye hate me*. This was a remon-
strance rather than a question, and a
double one at that. Isaac implies the
unreasonableness of the hatred, and
in asking the reason for their coming
he implies a rebuke for their attitude.
Hatred of the people of God by the
world is natural. ' Marvel not if the
world hate you ' (1 Jo. 3. 13). The
world hated the Saviour first (Jo. 15.
18). Such hatred is foolish as well as
wicked, because the Lord and His
people are the greatest friends the
world will ever have. *And have sent
me away from thee*. The world tries
to send God's people to Coventry. It
is galled by their presence and wants
to get as far from them as possible
and to forget their existence. Their
presence rouses its conscience. It
sought to send the Lord away by
crucifying Him, and of one of His
leading servants it called out, ' Away
with such a fellow from the earth,
for it is not fit that he should live '

(Acts 22. 22).

VERSE 28. *We saw certainly that the Lord was with thee.* Abimelech and his company did not deny that they had once hated Isaac and sent him away, but they had become wiser. The evident blessing of God will sometimes in His mercy produce such an effect as this. Revival blessing will bring it about. Power and peace manifested in a Christian's life will impress the world. In this case the Philistines became aware of Jahweh's interest in Isaac and His presence, help and support in his daily life. *Let there be now an oath.* The Philistines were afraid of opposing one who they could see was blessed and prospered by God.

Betwixt us and thee. Whatever others might or might not do, they wanted to insure that they were on the right side. They made a decision and showed a determination which, when shown by a sinner towards the Gospel, carries him through to conversion and salvation.

Let us make a covenant. In the same way many Gentiles have been ready to subscribe to God's new covenant made with them in the blood of Jesus for the remission of sins (Mt. 26. 28).

VERSE 29. *That thou wilt do us no harm.* This Abimelech was not as generous as his father had been when he dealt with Abraham (see 21. 22-32). The request that he makes here seems to have had fear as its motive rather than any desire for spiritual blessing. The last thing that the people of God will do is to injure those in need around them. Abimelech's mind was evidently in darkness.

As we have not touched thee. The example was unfortunate, as Abimelech's servants had twice deprived Isaac of the water which he had found.

As we have done unto thee nothing but good. This statement was even more extraordinary. They had stopped up the wells dug by Abraham and sought to steal those which Isaac had dug in their place. They had also shown envy and hatred. The statements made by Abimelech in this verse exemplify the deceitfulness of sin. Abimelech and his people had behaved badly to Isaac. Sin however had deceived him into the belief that he had treated him well. Sinners usually believe themselves to be in the right and cannot be brought to see that they have wronged others. Abimelech's spirit was that one good turn deserved another.

And have sent thee away in peace. This was the last thing that he had done. He had sent him away in envy (verses 16, 27). Abimelech must have believed that he had actually done these things, for he could hardly have thought that he could have persuaded Isaac to believe the opposite to what had actually happened.

Thou art now blessed of the Lord. He could see this, but it seems to have roused his envy. Like so many people in the world he wanted to share the blessing without the essential conditions of repentance and faith.

VERSE 30. *He made them a feast.* This was very generous of Isaac, but he showed himself like the God Whom he worshipped. God loads His people with benefits and is kind even to the unthankful (Lk. 6. 35). To those who truly enter into covenant relationship with God and open the door of their hearts to Jesus Christ life becomes subsequently a feast (Rev. 3. 20).

They did eat and drink. Though they outwardly partook of the food, there is nothing in the narrative to suggest that their hearts were changed.

VERSE 31. *They rose up betimes.* They were anxious to get their business done and over. Their different motives were compelling.

Sware one to another. They entered into a solemn agreement. Abimelech's motives seem to have been those of fear and policy. He thought that the blessing of Isaac would lead to danger to himself. He did not know Isaac's

God nor His all-embracing purposes of blessing. Our blessing does not mean the cursing of the sinner, but his profit and good. Isaac's motives may well have been a genuine desire that the Philistines should share his blessing and come to know the true God.

Isaac sent them away. They had not the slightest desire to follow the pilgrim life.

They departed from him in peace. They had been impressed, as we should say, but not converted. This is something to the good. They had been challenged by incontrovertible facts. Yet if they continued to refuse their implications, they might end in a place of worse danger than if they had never seen God's hand at work. It is better to have one man converted than a dozen, or even a hundred, impressed. Henceforward they knew the reality of God's work in Isaac, and they were afraid to oppose it. They were ready to be at peace. They may have been deceived into thinking that their attitude would entitle them to a share in spiritual blessing.

VERSE 32. *The same day.* The coincidence gave significance to the discovery of the well.

We have found water. The generous treatment of the sinner and worldling opens the heart to blessing from the Spirit of God. ' He that watereth shall be watered also himself ' (Prov. 11. 25). ' There is a river, the streams whereof shall make glad the city of God ' (Ps. 46. 4). The river is the Holy Spirit Himself flowing from the throne of God and of the Lamb. The same water of life is collected and made available in the Scriptures (Eph. 5. 26).

VERSE 33. *Shebah.* This means ' the oath '. The well and the oath are always connected in the Christian life. The well stands for the water of life, the Holy Ghost Himself springing up in our hearts to everlasting life (Jo. 4. 14), and the oath stands for the dedication of our lives to God, when we enter into covenant relationship with Him. This dedication can only be effected by the Holy Spirit Himself working in our hearts by His grace and power (Phil. 2. 13), and the water of life is only seen in its fulness in the lives of those who have entered into a solemn compact with God.

Beer-sheba. The destructive critics like to maintain that this narrative is a ' duplicate ' of that in chapter 21 (see 21. 31), and that both stories are hazy memories of a single incident in the nature of folk-lore. This would do away with inspiration, which is the critics' aim. The inspiring Spirit has forestalled them with direct statements that there were two famines (verse 1) and that the wells were dug twice and renamed by the same names (verse 18). If the other wells were renamed, why should not Beersheba have been? And what was to prevent a similar incident under similar circumstances from taking place on the same spot?

VERSE 34. The story of Isaac in Gerar is now ended, and this verse with the following opens a section which continues through the next chapter and onwards. This mention of Esau and his wives and of the bitterness caused to his parents by his marriages is preliminary to the story of the appropriation of the blessing. Esau's hostility, and Jacob's departure from home.

Forty years old. This was the same age as Isaac had been when he married Rebekah (25. 20). The ages of the patriarchs were far less than those which appear to have obtained before the flood (see chapter 10), but were double what is the normal life of a man in modern times. Thus Abraham was 175, Isaac was 180 (25. 7; 35. 28) and Jacob 147 (47. 28). So that Esau at the age of forty was a young man who might now be about twenty-five.

Judith the daughter of Beeri the Hittite. The Hittites were inhabitants of Canaan among the very people with whom Abraham had been so anxious that his sons should not intermarry (24. 3). Esau cared nothing for his birthright, and by thus marrying a Hittite woman showed that he wished to abandon the pilgrim life to which his family had been called and to enter the life of the world. His marriage is likely to have been preceded by a close and lengthy association with the Hittites, at least, with the family to which the lady belonged. Beeri would not have given his daughter to a stranger, and a foreigner at that. He would not have given her to one whose ideals and outlook on life were the opposite of his own. This marriage is thus another proof that Esau was a profane man, that is to say, secular-minded (Heb. 12. 16).

And Bashemath. Esau was a polygamist, as Lamech had been before the flood (4. 19). He was a man who could not resist women, and the Epistle to the Hebrews, drawing a severe conclusion from the references to these and subsequent marriages (28. 9), calls him a ' fornicator ' (Heb. 12. 16). His mind was set on the world and the flesh. Spiritual realities had no attraction for him. The grace of God was not at work in his heart, and though he was the child of godly parents and born into an elect race, he showed all the traits and tendencies of the fallen and corrupt nature in which he was conceived and born (Ps. 51. 5; 58. 3). Godly parents cannot pass on godliness by natural birth. They can only bring into the world a child of Adam and prayerfully seek the grace of God for its regeneration, as they had been regenerated themselves. However we care to think of a child, whether in Old or New Testament days, as within the covenant, the Scripture consistently presents the fact that it is born in sin, fallen and guilty, and that it needs the regenerating grace of God to give it spiritual life. This grace the child must one day take to itself by faith at the appropriate time. We may see a partial exception in the case of John the Baptist, about whom there exists the possibility that he was born again before he was born (see Lk. 1. 15, 44). But John was the greatest of all the sons of Adam (Mt.

11. 11), and this fact of an anticipatory filling with the Holy Ghost before the advent of faith may be one of the reasons of his greatness. John's case was special. Esau's case was normal.

VERSE 35. *A grief of mind.* The Hebrew says ' bitterness of spirit ' (see A.V. margin). Both parents shared this grief. Rebekah had entered into the spirit of the pilgrim life and showed an understanding of God's promises and purpose. Isaac's hopes were still wrongly centred on Esau, as the subsequent narrative proves. They now saw him falling away to the world, a man of the flesh, contaminating the family life and putting himself outside the scope of the promises. There seems little doubt that their own favouritism and weakness had contributed to the situation. We may well imagine that Esau's wives despised them and drew him further and further away from them. Their heathen practices no doubt entered his home, and it cannot have been long before he gave up living in tents and began to occupy a house in a Hittite city. In the next chapter, it is true, we find him still apparently with his parents, but, wanderer as he was, it is not long before he went off permanently to Seir. Restless carnal Esau, as Lot had done before him, provides another inspired warning from the Holy Spirit's picture-book of life.

CHAPTER 27

IN this chapter we are shown the sovereign providence of God working His purpose out through a tangled skein of human weakness and deception. The characters in the story are the four members of the patriarchal family. Two of them, Isaac and Esau, seek to frustrate the revealed purpose of God. The remaining two, Rebekah and Jacob, seek to carry out that purpose but from low motives and by wrong methods. Each of the four is rebuked and disappointed. Isaac is deceived and frightened. Esau loses all and cannot regain it by bitter tears. Jacob is driven from his home and mother for a period of twenty years. Nothing more is said about Rebekah, and it may be presumed that she was dead by the time of Jacob's return and never saw her favourite son again. Isaac resolves to give Esau his dying blessing, which, though oral, had testamentary effect. While Esau is out hunting, Jacob is persuaded by his mother to steal the blessing. This arouses Esau's bitter hostility, and Jacob leaves home to escape his brother's anger and sets out for the home of Rebekah's people.

VERSE 1. *Isaac was old*. He felt that the feebleness and despondency of old age were coming upon him. This condition was an illustration of his spiritual weakness, which prevented him from overcoming his natural affection for his elder son and from resolving to walk in the line of God's purpose and will. There is no need for us to be spiritually weak. Full provision is made for our strength, and we may draw upon infinite resources of power in Christ (Eph. 6. 10).

His eyes were dim. Weakness of sight was also typical of Isaac's spiritual condition. He ought to have seen more clearly what God's purpose was and the unfitness of Esau to receive the blessing. His eyes were dim because they had not been continually anointed with the eye-salve of the Holy Ghost (Rev. 3. 18).

He could not see. He could not see the purpose of God, having wilfully blinded himself to it. Self-will causes spiritual blindness, and we all need to have the eyes of our understanding enlightened (Eph. 1. 18).

Esau his eldest son. Esau had sold his birthright very cheaply (25. 31-34), but no doubt both he and his father considered him to be the eldest son. He now pretended that he had never meant to get rid of his birthright in spite of his oath. Esau seems to have brought his Hittite wives to live in tents in the same settlement as his parents, and his domestic life cannot have been happy. The two wives are not likely to have got on well together, and we know that both were disliked by Isaac and Rebekah (26. 35). Esau perhaps clung to his father's affection.

VERSE 2. *I am old*. He intended to make a will, and this was done orally by means of the blessing later delivered (verses 27-29). The terms of such a testamentary blessing were sacred in the family.

I know not the day of my death. This means that he thought his death was near and might overtake him before he was able to give the blessing. As a matter of fact he had about another fifty years to live. He had a long lingering old age of blindness and perhaps of weakness also.

VERSE 3. *Quiver*. The Hebrew word is *t'lee*, and does not occur elsewhere in the Bible. Perhaps it was a sort of javelin.

Go out to the field. 'The field is the world' (Mt. 13. 38). Isaac sent Esau to a place that he knew and loved well. The atmosphere at this point of the story is worldly and carnal.

Take. The Hebrew says 'hunt'. Hunting in the Bible is a worldly occupation typically, and often characterises the enemies of God. (See for instance 10. 9).

VERSE 4. *Savoury meat such as I love*. Isaac seems to have had an inordinate carnal appetite. He was ready to entangle the purpose and promises of God with its satisfaction.

That I may eat. If his appetite was satisfied, he was ready to bless his son. He thought of the food as a sort of stimulation.

My soul. This is an emphatic way of saying 'I', in Hebrew. At the same time the word 'nephesh' (*soul*) suggests the natural plane as opposed to the spiritual. Soul and spirit are different and are sometimes opposed in the Bible (1 Cor. 15. 45; Heb. 4. 12). The word translated 'natural' in 1

Cor. 2. 14, where it is again opposed to ' spiritual ', is derived from the Greek word *psuche*, meaning ' soul ' and corresponding in the New Testament to the Hebrew ' nephesh ' in the Old. The atmosphere of this blessing was thus worldly, natural and carnal.

VERSE 5. *Rebekah heard*. We may imagine her to be quick-witted and on the watch, hovering round to see that nothing was done against the interests of Jacob her favourite son. Her overhearing what she was doubtless not intended to know, or was not supposed to concern her, betrays the existence of suspicion in the family, which was evidently living on a very low spiritual plane. It is the glory of God that with such material, both then and now with us, He brings His purposes to completion and is never frustrated in them.

Esau went to the field. He went out into the world to hunt for what satisfies the carnal appetite, and while he was there, the purpose of God went forward behind his back, and he found that when he was in the world he had lost all. The same is true of every worldling.

Behold, I heard. She uses the knowledge that she ought not to have possessed to further her designs for her son. Yet through this tangle and by means of all these doubtful motives the purpose of God was triumphantly carried out.

VERSE 7. *Venison*. The deer by the law of Moses might be eaten (Deut. 14. 5), but it was not one of those animals which might be offered in sacrifice. This fact gives us a hint of the level on which the life of Isaac and his family was lived. Their mode of life was legitimate but not sacrificial. In other words we may suppose them to be living the respectable life of comfort and integrity that is lived by so many professing, and indeed by some real, Christians. If this was the basis of their life, almost everything that is told us about the individual members of the family is accounted for. The parents' favouritism is consistent with such a life, so is Esau's defection to the world and fall into carnal sin, the fact that Jacob and his mother did not shrink from practising deception, and the chastening of God which so obviously appears in this chapter and the rest of the story of Jacob. There was nothing unclean in the family's standard of life — indeed Esau's sin was a grief to both his parents (26. 35; 27. 46) — at the same time there was nothing sacrificial, no self-dedication to the will of God. Of all this the venison speaks.

Savoury meat. The strange interlocking of the savoury meat with the blessing illustrates the confusion in Isaac's outlook of spiritual and carnal things.

VERSE 8. *Obey my voice*. Rebekah was accustomed to command her son, although he appears to have been between seventy and eighty years of age, corresponding to a man of about forty on the scale of human life at the present day. Jacob's character perhaps suffered from this submission and needed the long training that we see working out in the subsequent narrative.

VERSE 9. *The flock*. Rebekah's motive and method may both have been wrong, but in contrast to Isaac's command to Esau she sent to the right place. Esau went to the field, that is the world (Mt. 13. 38), to fetch something unacceptable for sacrifice. Jacob went to the flock to fetch an animal acceptable to God.

Two good kids of the goats. A kid was used in sacrifice equally with a lamb (Ex. 12. 5). It is therefore a picture of the lamb of God that taketh away the sin of the world (Jo. 1. 29).

Thy father, such as he loveth. Isaac was unable to distinguish the source of the savoury meat. Venison and goats' flesh were the same to him. This suggests failure to discern spiritual things (1 Cor. 2. 14).

VERSE 10. *Thou shalt bring it to thy father*. Jacob was to bring something better than Esau intended.

That he may bless thee. If we children of God desire our Father to bless us, we must bring Him the slain Lamb. Indeed this we cannot do. We must hide in the Lamb, cling to the Lamb and plead the sacrifice of the Lamb.

Before his death. The testamentary blessing was meant.

VERSE 11. *Esau my brother is a hairy man.* Esau had a natural hairy covering, a veneer of self-righteousness, a protection which was no protection, for it grew out of his naked skin and guilty sinfulness, being all the time only part of himself and the product of natural religion.

I am a smooth man. Amid all the schemes and subtlety Jacob yet had the sense that he could not come into his father's presence to seek a blessing because of his smoothness, that is to say, his nakedness. Nakedness is the picture and associate of guilt.

VERSE 12. *Will feel me.* Isaac could not see (verse 1).

A deceiver. This is in fact what his mother intended him to be. The self-description shows that his eyes were open to what he was doing, and is the measure of his lack of faith and that of his mother. If God intended him to have the blessing, as He did, He could have given it to him openly.

A curse upon me, and not a blessing. In Jacob's case this would be if his father discovered his attempts at deceit.

VERSE 13. *Upon me be thy curse, my son.* Her maternal affection was strong enough to risk the curse and to call it down on her own head. The apostle was ready to do the same for the salvation of his Jewish brethren, had it been of any avail (Rom. 9. 3). The Lord Jesus actually took and bore the curse, that the blessing might be ours (Gal. 3. 13, 14).

Only obey my voice. These words reveal something of the power that Rebekah exercised over Jacob. They could well be taken apart from their context as a message of the Spirit to the sinner's heart, the pleading of Christ with sinner or believer.

Go fetch me them. She needed the kids for the purpose in hand. The sinner has a far more desperate need of the Lamb of God, and if we listen in love and sympathy, we may hear his voice appealing to us, ' Go fetch me Him.'

VERSE 14. *He went, and fetched, and brought them to his mother.* He does not seem to have yet been fully aware of her intentions.

VERSE 15. *Goodly raiment of her eldest son Esau.* This may have consisted of the priestly garments of the firstborn. It seems to have belonged to him as the ' eldest '.

Which were with her in the house. Esau's mother had taken care to keep this raiment by her and to look after it. It had not been entrusted to the care of his heathen wives. The words ' in the house ' suggest the possibility that Isaac and Rebekah had forsaken the pilgrim life of the tent and were living in a permanent residence. On the other hand the Hebrew *bayith* has a wide usage and means very much more than a building. Here it may mean no more than ' in her home ', or ' in her care '. *Put them upon Jacob her younger son.* Notice the threefold manner in this and the two following verses in which Jacob was equipped to enter the presence of his father. He was himself elected by God before birth to receive the blessing (Rom. 9. 11). He is here presented to us as a picture of the elect of God coming to the throne of grace (Rom. 5. 2; Heb. 4. 16). (1) He wears the goodly raiment of priesthood (1 Pet. 2. 9; Rev. 1. 6; 5. 10). This fact emphasises (a) that he has access, (b) that in receiving the blessing he represents others who are to receive it with him, to whom he is a channel of blessing. In Jacob's case these were his natural descendants.

VERSE 16. This verse describes the second of the three ways in which the elect are equipped to enter the presence of their Father. (2) The skins of the kids were put upon his hands and the smooth of his neck. The naked sinful idle hands were covered by that which was procured by the death of the kids. This is the covering of sin which comes as the benefit of Christ's passion, exactly the same as was provided by God for Adam and Eve (3. 21). The same covering was put upon the sinner's stiff, obstinate rebellious neck.

VERSE 17. Here is the third thing with which the sinner may have access to the Father, (3) the savoury meat and the bread. Christ is the sweet savour (Eph. 5. 2) with which the people of God are accepted by the Father (Ezek. 20. 41). His perfect obedience and His offering of Himself to death delighted the Father (Mt. 3. 17; 17. 5). This sweet savour extends to, and is imputed to, all who belong to Christ, and ensures their welcome at the throne of grace. Christ is also the bread of God coming down from heaven and giving His life for the world (Jo. 6. 33). As such He is the sum in His own Person of all the levitical typical sacrifices (Lev. 21. 6, 8), the antitype and fulfilment of them all, and a complete satisfaction (the meaning of ' bread ' in this connection) in His death of all the requirements of God's holy law. These were given into the hands of Jacob. So the sinner comes into the presence of God grasping Christ by the hand of faith.

VERSE 18. *He came unto his father.* as does every sinner, both when he repents for the first time and every day thereafter. ' I will arise and go unto my father ' (Lk. 15. 18).

And said, My father. This verse reminds us that, however ignoble was Jacob's method, he was yet entering his father's presence with the genuine and earnest desire to seek a blessing from him.

Who art thou, my son? This is a question that the heavenly Father never asks. It marks a change from the picture of access to God seen in the approach of Jacob to his father

and takes us back to the actual narrative and the crooked interplay of motive practised by the characters in the story. Isaac was blind and could not see which of his sons was talking to him.

VERSE 19. The two answers given by Jacob to his father, recorded in this and the following verse, were lies, but yet beneath the surface contained some substance of truth. *I am Esau thy firstborn.* This was a lie. Jacob was not Esau. Yet by election (Rom. 9. 11, 12) and by a definite transaction, made with his brother's consent (25. 31-34), he was the first-born and was entitled to the blessing. If he had spoken boldly in faith to his father and pointed out these facts, he might well have obtained the blessing. He had not sufficient trust in God to overcome his well-founded fear of his father's intentions, but descended on to his father's own ground.

I have done according as thou badest me. This was a lie and an impersonation of Esau. Jacob had received no bidding.

Venison. He had not brought any venison at all, but he knew that if he called it goats' flesh, his father would not accept it. So he called it venison and put inverted commas, as it were, round the word in his mind. This is a bad example. When we are dealing with the unconverted for instance, it is best to be scrupulously honest and not dress up our message. Even specious titles sometimes tend to give a wrong impression.

That thy soul may bless me. It is clear from these words that Jacob was at a low enough spiritual level to suppose that God's blessing depended upon the satisfaction of his father's appetite. Yet he rightly sought and craved for the blessing.

VERSE 20. *How is it that thou hast found it so quickly?* The question was a suspicious one. Isaac was not certain that he was speaking to Esau.

Because the Lord thy God brought it to me. The answer was brazen and in effect blasphemous. Jacob sought to bolster up his deception by calling in Jahweh's Name. At the same time it was true that the hand of God was in fact at work. He was using and over-ruling these tortuous methods to frustrate Isaac's design and bring His own purpose to fruition.

VERSE 22. *Jacob went near.* Safely covered with the skin of the kids he could approach his father.

The voice is Jacob's voice. The voices of the two brothers seem to have been so much alike, that it was only just possible for their father to tell the difference, so alike that he could believe himself mistaken. It is sad when the voice and message of a Christian are indistinguishable from those of the world. It is even sadder when the voice is Jacob's, but the hands those of Esau, when life and action are inconsistent with an orthodox message. The result is deception and confusion.

VERSE 23. *He discerned him not.* Two lines of thought that seem to be present in these verses are exemplified in this word. We may see in it (1) a warning against conformity with the world. As Christians we must be discernible from the world. (2) We may be reminded by this expression that the eye of our holy God does not see the sin and guilt that is safely covered by the death of Christ.

As his brother Esau's hands. To the man who is spiritually blind Gospel religion and natural religion appear alike.

So he blessed him. Isaac acted wrongly and irresponsibly in doing so, because he thought he was blessing Esau, although God had made known His will that the blessing was not to go to Esau, but to Jacob. Yet God overruled the whole set of circumstances to carry out His purpose according to election.

VERSE 24. *Art thou my very son Esau?* This question gives us a deep impression of the suspicion, fear and perplexity of the poor old man. He could not make out the situation, and the meanness of taking advantage of his blindness is set in high relief.

I am. This was a direct deliberate lie. It marks the depths to which Jacob descended. His faith, if at this stage of his life he had any at all, was so weak and inoperative, that he was anxious to impersonate a worldly and carnal man because he thought that such a man had the advantage.

VERSE 25. *Venison.* Isaac still dwells on the plane on which no sacrifice can enter. See on verse 19.

That my soul may bless thee. This is an expression which again implies the natural plane. Soul is Hebrew *nephesh.* The expression 'my soul' is little more than an emphatic 'I', an expressed ego, but 'nephesh' always implies and sometimes expresses the opposite to the spirit (see Heb. 4. 12). Isaac lived at this time on a natural plane, he expected to give Esau a blessing that would work out on the natural plane, and he seemed to fail to grasp the true meaning of the blessing of Abraham. God however was using and overruling all these mistaken ideas and wrong conduct in order to pass on the blessing where He intended it to go.

He did eat: and he brought him wine and he drank. So far as Isaac was concerned, his willingness to give the blessing rested on the comfort of the satisfaction of his natural appetite. The food and wine put him into a good and expansive frame of mind. The blessing however which God gave Jacob through the lips of Isaac, rested upon His eternal purpose of election made before the world began (Rom. 9. 11; Eph. 1. 4).

VERSE 26. The approach and the kiss signified the acceptance by Isaac of the supposed Esau. Jacob could now be assured that the blessing was his.

VERSE 27. *He came near and kissed him.* Here we have a further picture of the repenting sinner's approach to the Father. Coming near means access, which we have by the blood of

Jesus (Rom. 5. 2; Eph. 3. 12). The kiss we find in Lk. 15. 20. It is a tender expression of welcome and love.

He smelled the smell of his raiment. It was the raiment that smelled sweet. Christ, Who clothes and covers the sinner, is the sweet savour of acceptance before God (Eph. 5. 2). If we put on the Lord Jesus Christ (Rom. 13. 14; Gal. 3. 27), we can be certain of access and acceptance with the Father. *Blessed him.* So Jacob obtained the blessing. If there is one thing that the story makes clear, it is that he did not obtain it on the ground of merit. His conduct was mean and deceitful, his faith very weak. All that can be said of him is that he desired the blessing and had at least some sense of its value. He knew from his mother what the oracle of God had said before his birth, and no doubt he based his case on that Word. And so he obtained the blessing, because he was elect according to the foreknowledge and determinate purpose of God, Who gave him the faith to believe in the value of the promise and the desire to persevere till he obtained the blessing. The blessing had nothing to do with what he had done, either good or bad (Rom. 9. 11). Here is an encouragement to us undeserving sinners seeking God's blessing in Christ, but conscious of the corruption of our nature within.

The smell of my son. In the opening words of Isaac, which occupy the end of this verse, we see the *basis* of the blessing. This is shown by the word 'Therefore' with which the next verse begins. The basis is the smell, that is to say, the sweet savour, which is Christ (Eph. 5. 2). Notice that though the expression used is 'the smell of my son' it was the raiment in which the sweet smell was found. The sinner in himself has no sweet savour. The Christ Whom he puts on (Rom. 13. 14), Whose righteousness covers him (Isa. 61. 10), presents the sweet savour to God, and this is the basis of the sinner's blessing.

The smell of a field which the Lord hath blessed. It is the smell of the harvest field blessed by the Gospel, loved by God (Jo. 3. 16) and redeemed by Christ. Christ Himself as the Head and representative of all the redeemed is Himself in one sense the field. Because He has been blessed the redeemed are blessed. Notice the use of the Divine Name Jahweh, because the blessing is part of the great redemptive purpose.

VERSE 28. In this and the following verse we find the *content* of the blessing. They may be said to be (1) provision, (2) power, (3) victory. This verse gives us the provision. It is threefold. (a) *God give thee of the dew of heaven.* Notice the change of the Divine title from Jahweh to Elohim. On the documentary theory this is fantastic. On the common sense view it is perfectly satisfactory and to be expected. The Name Jahweh is used where spiritual blessing is in view. This is the context of the whole blessing. In this verse in an immediate context of dew, fatness, corn and wine the Name of God as Creator is naturally used. Dew is a symbol of strength, freshness and youth (Ps. 110. 3). The dew of heaven is a gift of God to all His elect. 'They that wait upon the Lord shall renew their strength. They shall mount up with wings as eagles. They shall run and not be weary. They shall walk and not faint' (Isa. 40. 31). 'Who satisfieth thy mouth with good things, so that thy youth is renewed like the eagle's' (Ps. 103. 5). We may confidently expect this blessing. *The fatness of the earth.* In its literal sense this is an Old Testament blessing. Christians have not been promised earthly prosperity. They are rejected, and may be hated, as was their Lord (Jo. 15. 18). This gift will be seen in all its fulness on the new earth (Ps. 37. 11). Yet it has its counterpart for the Christian in the present life. Fatness means the best, and it is the Christian who in the right and deep sense makes the best of both worlds. He has been promised by His Lord a hundredfold now in this present time and in the world to come life everlasting (Mk. 10. 30, 31). *Plenty of corn and wine.* These are types of spiritual blessings which every believer possesses. The corn represents the Saviour Himself, the bread come down from heaven to give life to the world (Jo. 6. 33). The believer may feed on Him day by day as he reads his Bible. Christ as the source of His people's spiritual sustenance never fails. The wine represents the Holy Ghost, with Whom the believer is to be filled, knowing something of the exhilaration caused by wine (Eph. 5. 18).

VERSE 29. In this verse as the blessing continues, we find promises of power and victory. *Let people serve thee and nations bow down to thee.* This prediction was fulfilled in the case of Old Testament Israel through the conquests of David and the rule of Solomon. In the case of the new Israel, the church, it will be fulfilled in the world to come (Rev. 3. 9). In that day kings will bring their glory and honour into the new Jerusalem (Rev. 21. 24, 26).

Let thy mother's sons bow down to thee. We see something of the immediate force of this expression, when we remember that Isaac supposed that he was blessing Esau. Jacob was the favourite of his mother. Isaac was therefore pointedly making Jacob and his descendants the servants of Esau. The purpose of God however was to make Esau the servant of Jacob (25. 23), and this was the actual effect of Isaac's words. The fulfilment came in the subjection of Edom to Israel during the period of the kings, but it goes very much wider and deeper. Just as the blessing of Abraham had so much reference to Christ, so we find the same reference and hidden emphasis here where the blessing passes on to Jacob. It is Christ Whom peoples will serve, to Whom nations will bow down (Ps. 18. 43; 89. 72; Rev. 1. 5; 19. 16). Christ is Lord over His brethren (Jo. 13. 13; Eph. 1. 22; Phil. 2. 9-11).

To Christ His mother's sons will bow down. This is not only the case with His immediate brethren, sons of Joseph and Mary (Jo. 7. 5; Gal. 1. 19). In a wider sense the Lord's mother is the Israel of God (Rev. 12. 1, 2, 5). Again Eve, the mother of all living, may be said to be the mother of Christ, Who is in a special sense her seed (3. 15). Christ is the rightful Lord of all mankind, and on the day of judgment every knee will bow to Him.

Cursed be every one that curseth thee. This and the following sentence are direct echoes of the original blessing of Abraham, which Esau could never have appreciated, had it been passed on to him (12. 3). Jacob is here identified with Christ, his great descendant, just as Abraham had been identified with Him so often when the promises were made to him. Thus we have here a pronouncement of the defeat of the enemies of Christ. No one who does not acknowledge the Lord Jesus Christ as his Saviour and Master can ever receive blessing from God (Acts 4. 12). No one speaking in the Spirit of God can call Jesus accursed (1 Cor. 12. 3). Whoever rejects Jesus and refuses His salvation remains under the wrath, condemnation and curse of God (Jo. 3. 18, 36), and on the last day all such will hear the words, ' Depart from me, ye cursed, into everlasting fire ' (Mt. 25. 41).

Blessed be he that blesseth thee. Blessed in every way is the man who blesses Jacob in the Person of his great descendant, the Lord Jesus Christ, who receives Christ into his heart as his Friend and Saviour, who makes His cause his own, who loves and serves Him with faithful allegiance and seeks to bring Him blessing and glory by winning others to His service. He is blessed with all spiritual blessings in the heavenly places (Eph. 1. 3), with a hundredfold in this present world, and in the world to come with life everlasting (Mk. 10. 30). He is blessed in conscience, in heart, in mind and in body, and on the last day he will hear the happy words, ' Come, ye blessed of My Father, inherit the kingdom prepared for you from the foundation of the world ' (Mt. 25. 34). And all this blessing he rightly ascribes to its Giver and Author (Rev. 7. 12).

VERSE 30. *It came to pass.* Notice the exalted literary quality of this narrative, brought out with great force in this verse. The author is a literary genius, and his story is creative. It is told superbly and unfolds with dramatic power. The inspiring Spirit throughout the Bible makes use of the best human art. We too should follow His example to the small extent that we are able and strive to present the Gospel to sinners with the best devices that we can properly command.

Esau his brother came in from his hunting. Many a sinner comes in from his hunting to a dark death-bed, or will come in on the day of judgment to stand before the God to Whom he has refused to be reconciled. He comes in from a life of hunting and destroying souls with the weapons of his evil influence, his scornful tongue, or his bloodstained hands. Sin is contagious, and the sinner has only to sin to spread the foul moral disease. He has only to sin by omission. He has only to leave God out of his life in a cultured and religious way, only to leave out of his life all thought or real understanding of holiness, to find when he comes in at the end of his career that by his very indifference, by the subtle seeping of his pride through the minds of those he touches, he has kept many a soul outside the Kingdom of God. He may hunt souls by scorn and antagonism to the Gospel. Many a soul is turned aside and driven to everlasting death by the scornful assertions of the destructive Biblical critic, or by the intellectual snares of the atheist and evolutionist. The same result is brought about by the ignorant sneers of a parent or friend. Or the hunter of souls may destroy them by the violent taking of

physical life, especially in the great wars of the present century. He comes in with the confident expectation of receiving a blessing. ' Many shall say unto me in that day, Lord, Lord ' (Mt. 7. 22). So Esau came in from his hunting. The story now changes from comedy to tragedy. Our gaze is concentrated on the trembling, nonplussed old man and his despondent, despairing and finally bitterly hating son. The Holy Ghost takes this story in the Epistle to the Hebrews and holds up Esau as the example of the man who reverses his sense of values, who lives for this world and its pleasures and finds at the end that he has lost everything (Heb. 12. 16, 17).

VERSE 31. *He also had made savoury meat.* But it was made of venison, that which was respectable, cultured, good in the eyes of the world, not unclean, but unacceptable for sacrifice. No blessing comes of such a dish.

Brought it. He brought it without guile, sincerely believing that he was doing what he had been commanded, and without the slightest suspicion that it would not be acceptable to his father. In the same way many a sinner will bring the offering of a religious life and good deeds to God, never doubting the possibility of their acceptance. *That thy soul may bless me.* Esau's venison could not satisfy his father, because he had already eaten of the savoury meat made of the kids. In the same way God can never be satisfied with the sinner's religion and ' good life '. He is but nauseated by them, if 'only for the reason that He is satisfied once for all and for ever by the one eternal sacrifice of His own Son, the Lamb of God that taketh away the sin of the world (Jo. 1. 29). Yet Esau expected the blessing of right. He was the elder son, and the blessing went with the birthright. No real blessing ever belongs to any man of right. All comes of God's unmerited grace and mercy.

VERSE 32. *Thy firstborn Esau.* Esau

forgot that he had sold his birthright (25. 31-34). Like many a sinner he wanted to eat his cake and have it. The birthright meant nothing to him when it had to be paid for by the abandonment of carnal appetite and its satisfaction, but when he needed the blessing he claimed it as belonging to him. Many a sinner who has lived for self and this world will find on the day of judgment that he desperately needs the blessing of God, which he can never have because he has thrown it away during his lifetime on earth.

VERSE 33. *Trembled very exceedingly.* This is a piteous sight. He trembled with fear of his son's anger, through ignorance of the unknown future results of the blessing that he had given, through vexation with himself, and perhaps because he realised that he had been outside the will of God.

Before thou camest. The sinner may think that a decision on his destiny will be taken on the day of judgment. In fact all will have been done and decided before he comes. God is satisfied by the death of Christ, not by the sinner's supposed good deeds, and the death of Christ must be embraced and taken advantage of and made his own by the sinner in this present life, before ever death or the end of the world comes to remove for ever the opportunity to do so.

Have blessed him. God's blessing comes to His elect in this world before the day of judgment. That day reveals it. If a sinner comes to the day of judgment without having received blessing in this life, it will be impossible for him to receive it then.

Yea, and he shall be blessed. Isaac could not recall his dying blessing, which had testamentary effect. In the same way God never recalls His blessing. Whom He blesses is blessed. ' The gifts and calling of God are without repentance ' (Rom. 11. 29). God's blessing, once given, is a comfortable assurance for the future and a pledge of eternal life.

VERSE 34. *He cried with a great and exceeding bitter cry.* In so doing he was an illustration of the lost on the day of judgment, whose astonishment and anguish will be immeasurable, and cast a shadow over the views of glory that brighten the last pages of the Bible. ' There shall be weeping and gnashing of teeth ' (Mt. 8. 12).

Bless me, even me also, O my father! We may compare Mt. 7. 22.

VERSE 35. *Thy brother came with subtlety.* We must not think of God as responsible for the subtlety. Jacob was wrong and held guilty for his deception of his father. But the subtlety was used and over-ruled by God to carry out His purpose. The central illustration of this interlacing of Divine purpose with human sin is the crucifixion of the Lord. It took place by the determinate counsel and foreknowledge of God, yet the hands that accomplished it were no less wicked, responsible or guilty (Acts 2. 23). In this way the Bible shows us again and again that evil and wickedness can never frustrate the purpose of God, but can only serve it and set it forward. Such is the constant bitterness of Satan's defeat. ' For we can do nothing against the truth, but for the truth ' (2 Cor. 13. 8).

Taken away thy blessing. Jacob stole it by dishonourable methods, but God never meant Esau to have it. Isaac's obstinacy in seeking to go against the known will of God was outwitted.

VERSE 36. *Jacob.* The meaning of the name is ' supplanter '. Jacob was given this name because he took his brother by the heel in the womb (25. 26; Hos. 12. 3). His character proved consistent with it.

My birthright . . . . my blessing. The unrepentant sinner loses both. Adam was the son of God (Lk. 3. 38), but he begat a son after his own likeness (Gen. 5. 3). Our fallen race has lost its family relationship to its Creator, and this must be reconstituted in the case of every individual who believes (Jo. 1. 12). With the birthright goes the blessing. Our fallen race is under God's condemnation (Jo. 3. 18) and curse (Gal. 3. 10). Blessing can only be restored to it in Christ (Gal. 3. 14).

Hast thou not reserved a blessing for me? Isaac was able to trump up a blessing for Esau of an inferior and secondary kind, but there will be no blessing whatever for the unsaved sinner on the last day.

VERSE 37. The lordship and dominion could not be mitigated in the nature of things. If Jacob rule, Esau must serve. In the same way we who claim Christ as Lord cannot escape His service. The provision of corn and wine need not necessarily be exclusive. Esau, though serving, must be supplied.

What shall I do? Isaac was able, as it were, to scrape together a subsidiary blessing, but not even this will be possible on the day of judgment for those who will have failed to appropriate the blessing freely offered them in this life.

VERSE 38. In this verse we find the picture which is so graphically taken up by the Holy Ghost in Heb. 12. 17. The verse shows us (1) Esau's passionate longing for the blessing, which he had previously cast away with his birthright, and (2) his bitter cry of despair. In Esau here, as the writer to the Hebrews makes so plain, we have a type of the lost on the day of judgment. On that day the sinner will earnestly desire the blessing that he now despises and throws away, and will realise its irretrievable loss. ' There shall be weeping and gnashing of teeth ' (Mt. 8. 12).

VERSE 39. Isaac contrives a hasty blessing for his disappointed son. *The fatness of the earth, and of the dew of heaven.* Notice that in contrast to Jacob's blessing the earth here comes first and heaven second. Jacob had first the dew of heaven and earthly blessing second in dependence on it (verse 28). This is so in the case of all the elect. They seek first the king-dom of God and His righteousness, and all their earthly needs are added unto them (Mt. 6. 33). They are blessed with all spiritual blessing in the heavenly places in Christ (Eph. 1. 3), and their life is hid with Christ in God (Col. 3. 3). Any prosperity that they may enjoy on earth derives from their relationship with God. With Esau the reverse is the case. The fatness of the earth comes first, just as it is always uppermost in his mind. The dew of heaven from above is his, whether appreciated or not. In God every sinner lives and moves and has his being (Acts 17. 28). God causes His sun to shine on the evil as well as on the good, and sends His rain on the unjust as well as on the just (Mt. 5. 45). But the foundation of the life of the worldly-minded and carnal man is always earthly.

VERSE 40. *By thy sword.* Esau was to live by self-effort, not by faith in God. Neither Esau nor anyone like him can ever say, ' The life that I now live in the flesh I live by faith of the Son of God ' (Gal. 2. 20). He was to live a strenuous and violent life. The sword betokens hate and fear. Yet all this active self-effort was to result in nothing but service to his brother and in such the carrying out of God's purpose. Esau can only carry out God's sovereign counsel and will. What a picture of thousands of sinners in the world today. Man sees only his immediate carnal and material ends. He scarcely understands any deeper meaning of life. He labours for the bread that perishes (Jo. 6. 27). He will not realise until he looks back on life on the great day that all his effort has been directed by an unseen Hand to advance the cause of the Gospel and the good of the elect.

When thou shalt have the dominion. Edom only had the dominion when wickedness manifested itself in Judah. As long as the believer is faithful and obedient, sin, the world and the devil can never have dominion over him.

Thou shalt break his yoke from off thy neck. Here was an outburst of obstinacy and self-will on Isaac's part. He knew God's purpose with regard to the two brothers. The elder was to serve the younger (25. 23). He must already have realised that he had himself been made an unwilling instrument in the carrying out of the purpose. Yet his heart was not with the purpose of God, but with his elder son. He does not consent to the purpose. He would rather it were not carried out. He will do what he can to frustrate it. He wants Esau to have the dominion, and he tries to encourage him to snatch it. He would rather Jacob was unfaithful to his God, if that was the way for his favourite son to get the dominion. No wonder we find that his family was almost immediately broken up and that the remaining fifty years of his life were spent in obscurity.

VERSE 41. *Esau hated Jacob*. This is the hatred with which the world and the flesh always regard the elect. In this way Cain hated Abel (4. 5, 8), Jezebel hated Elijah (1 Ki. 19. 2), and this is the hatred that we are to expect from the world (1 Jo. 3. 13). *The blessing wherewith his father blessed him*. Esau was bitterly envious for that which he had once despised and thrown away. If he had possessed the blessing, he would not have valued the deepest and most real part of it.

Said in his heart. ' From within out of the heart of man proceed murders ' (Mk. 7. 21). Being a child of Adam, Esau, like Cain, had the heart of a murderer, and apart from our redemption in Christ, so far as our flesh is concerned, so have we.

The days of mourning for my father are at hand. His evil nature and murderous spirit turned him into an unnatural son, so that he looked forward to the death of the father who adored him and had sacrificed his own uprightness of character in an attempt to bestow favour upon him. His estimate was however wrong. If his father was ill, he recovered. In any case he lived about another fifty years. Esau's evil desire was there-

fore disappointed, as is so often the case with the sinner. *Then will I slay my brother*. He intended to express the hatred of his heart by an act of murder.

VERSE 42. Notice in this verse the providence and provision of God. His sovereign providence brought Esau's intention to the ears of the watchful mother, and He used her affection and her wisdom as the instruments of His purpose for the preservation of Jacob.

VERSE 43. Rebekah's plan for her son's safety is outlined in this verse, but it is clear from the ensuing narrative that it was God's plan. Rebekah's motives may all have lain on the natural plane. At any rate they were ill-informed, so far as spiritual things were concerned. Yet God used them. We see here an example of God's sovereign disposing power over-ruling and using human hearts and minds. The same power is operative today. It is always perfectly successful and is never frustrated. God had many lessons and a long hard time of training awaiting Jacob in Laban's house at Haran.

VERSE 44. *A few days*. This part of Rebekah's plan was not carried out. God's purpose was different. The few days lengthened to at least twenty years. At the end of this long time Jacob returned to his father (35, 37), but there is no mention of the mother of whom he had been so fond. The inference is that she was dead.

VERSE 45. *Until thy brother's anger turn away from thee, and he forget*. Rebekah seems to have known Esau to be of a fickle disposition, as he well may have been. Alternatively she said what she wished and what she thought would be comfortable to Jacob.

That which thou hast done to him. The inference from these words is that Rebekah admitted that Esau might be justly angry, and that a wrong had been done to him. Her fallen nature reveals itself in her attribution of this act to Jacob alone, while in fact the inspiration and suggestion were entirely her own.

Then I will send, and fetch thee. We do not know what were the circumstances that prevented her sending. Perhaps contrary to her wish and expectation, Esau's anger did not turn away, but was nurtured in a dangerous bitterness. Perhaps Isaac forbade Jacob's return. Perhaps Rebekah's own death took place soon after Jacob's departure. It is enough to know that it was not God's purpose that Jacob should return until many years had elapsed.

Deprived also of you both. The murder of Jacob by Esau would have this effect. Esau might himself have been put to death as a murderer. In any case his continued residence with his parents would have been impossible after the commission of such a deed. She planned to be deprived of one only of them for a short time.

VERSE 46. Rebekah now cleverly urges on Isaac a reason for sending Jacob away. It was a good reason. It is to the credit both of Isaac and Rebekah that they seem to have understood God's purpose, so clearly revealed to Abraham, of keeping the family distinct and forbidding inter-marriage with the heathen. It was this principle that had brought about their own marriage, and this explains the attention that they paid to the principle and the value that they set on it. Both parents were grieved by Esau's heathen marriages (26. 35). She did not directly suggest to Isaac Jacob's departure for Haran. Perhaps there was an agreement between them that Jacob should be instructed to take a wife from the members of her family. At any rate she has but to mention the possibility of Jacob's following Esau's example, as she probably knew, to cause Isaac to send Jacob away. This clever woman was thus able to conceal from her husband the existence of Esau's murderous designs, and from Esau the fact that she knew of his intentions or that Jacob's departure had any con-

cern with them. Rebekah could scheme, but her schemes succeeded only where they set forward God's great purpose, and no further. God uses and ignores at will the scheming of a clever woman. *The daughters of Heth.* Rebekah probably did not like her daughters-in-law, but she has chiefly in view the fact that Jacob as much as Esau came in contact with many Hittite women in the course of business and the daily routine. All or any of these women she regards as having designs on Jacob.

If Jacob take a wife of the daughters of Heth. Such an eventuality would have frustrated God's purpose, and Rebekah was right to guard against it. It would have been equivalent to being unequally yoked with unbelievers (2 Cor. 6. 14). In the same way it is essential for us as the people of God to guard our separation from the world. Compromise with the world and action in concert with it are fatal.

CHAPTER 28

IN this chapter there are three sections. The first describes the departure of Jacob with his father's blessing (1-5). In the second we find the effect of Jacob's going upon Esau, who tried an ineffectual reform (6-9). The last section tells the important and well-known story of Jacob's vision at Bethel (10-22). The chief lesson of the chapter lies in the description of God's guiding Hand on Jacob

VERSE 1. *Blessed him.* Isaac was now reconciled to God's purpose as regards the blessing. ' By faith Isaac blessed Jacob ' (Heb. 11. 20). Dr. E. W. Bullinger thought that the Epistle to the Hebrews was referring to the blessing of chapter 27. 27-29. The circumstances however of that blessing, intended wrongly by Isaac for Esau, make it almost impossible to believe that it was given in faith. It is more likely that the events of chapter 27 opened Isaac's eyes to the purpose of God and the proper direction of the blessing. A blessing given by faith was not only Isaac's blessing but also God's.

Charged him. No blessing can be given without responsibility attached. In blessing us in Christ God has given us also a charge and a commandment. It is to go and make disciples of all nations (Mt. 28. 19). Every man at his conversion, when he first obtains the blessing, is called into the service of God, as the apostles Simon and Andrew (Mt. 4. 19), and later the apostle Paul (Acts 26. 15-18).

Thou shalt not take a wife of the daughters of Canaan. Isaac faithfully passes on to Jacob the instructions that his father Abraham had given him (24. 3). When God called Abraham and entered into covenant relationship with him, He put a barrier between his family and the heathen. He called it into separation and holiness. The same call is given to us, when we enter in Christ into a peculiar relationship with God. We are not to be unequally yoked with unbelievers, but are to come out and be separate and touch not the unclean thing (2 Cor. 6. 14, 17).

VERSE 2. *Arise, go.* The spiritual principle behind these words has two implications. Jacob's journey was not like the journeyings of Abraham and Isaac, in themselves alone a parable of the pilgrim life. His whole lifetime was that (47. 9). (1) It was rather the journey to the place of service appointed by God. It corresponds to the ' go ' of Mt. 28. 19. (2) Since Jacob now becomes the bridegroom charged with seeking a wife, the command to go corresponds to the sending of Christ by the Father into the world (Jo. 3. 17; 10. 36).

Padan-Aram. Aram is Syria. This was a district of Syria which lay around Haran (verse 10), where Abraham had sojourned during his father's lifetime (11. 31, 32).

Bethuel. See 22. 22.

Laban. See 24. 29. Laban was at least forty years older than Jacob, and must by now have been a man of 110 or over. On the scale of life at

the present day he would be a man of about 60, an age that closely fits the narrative and the events. Jacob was to take a wife of his own kin, as Isaac had done. In the same way the heavenly Bridegroom wins a bride of his own kin, a great assembly of redeemed humanity, whose nature He took (Heb. 2. 16).

VERSE 3. *God Almighty.* The use of this title (Heb. El-Shaddai) established a connection with Abraham, who habitually used it.

Bless thee. The blessing of God derives from His grace and favour and results in fruitfulness. All the people of God are blessed in Christ (Eph. 1. 3), Whose offering of Himself to God on our behalf supplies the channel through which God's grace can reach us. His blessing results in fruitful service and the inheritance of the kingdom of God (Mt. 25. 34).

Make thee fruitful, and multiply thee. These go closely with blessing, and are its immediate results. God intends us also to bring forth fruit to His glory, whether the fruit of the Spirit (Gal. 5. 22), or the fruit of souls won for Christ.

That thou mayest be a multitude of people. This was fulfilled (1) in the twelve tribes of Old Testament Israel especially in the days of David and Solomon, when the people held an empire over several surrounding nations. (2) It is fulfilled in the Christian church, gathered from every tribe and people and nation and tongue, and one day to appear before the throne of God as a great multitude that no man can number (Rev. 7. 9).

VERSE 4. *The blessing of Abraham.* At last Isaac fell in with the purpose of God and realised by faith that the redemptive promises made to Abraham were to descend to Jacob and his line, and not to Esau. *To thee.* Isaac prayed that Jacob himself might have personal blessing, as Abraham had it, and as he himself had known it. Perhaps as he uttered this prayer, a revival of spiritual life took place in his heart. The blessing of Abraham included, and indeed was based upon, a right standing with God received by faith and made possible by the coming death of Abraham's great descendant, Jesus Christ (Gen. 15. 6). Jacob was therefore led by his father to expect from God personal justification, if he did not possess it already. *To thy seed with thee.* The seed of Jacob was (1) Christ, on Whom the blessing of God was concentrated and in Whom it all meets. He is the only Man Who has perfectly pleased God (Mt. 3. 17; 17. 5), and He has been given the Name that is above every name and exalted to the right hand of God (Phil. 2. 9; Eph. 1. 20, 21). The seed is (2) all the people of Christ, that is to say, the whole Israel of God, which will be saved with an everlasting salvation (Gal. 3. 29; Isa. 45. 17; Heb. 5. 9).

That thou mayest inherit. God's blessings and rewards are consistently spoken of throughout the Bible as inheritance. Eternal life is inherited. Inheritance does not depend upon merit, nor upon personal prowess, talents or gifts, but upon family relationship. A man inherits life and all other blessing if he is a child of God, and because he is such. *The land.* The inheritance was (1) Palestine, which was a type and picture of the ' new earth ' or new land, which is eternal and belongs to the world to come. Jacob himself never possessed Palestine, doing so only in the persons of his natural descendants. The land is (2) the new earth, for which we Christians look (2 Pet. 3. 13). Abraham also looked for this heavenly country (Heb. 11. 16). The new earth, which is regarded in the Bible as having continuity with the typical Palestine, will be possessed by Jacob personally with Abraham and Isaac (Mt. 8. 11).

Wherein thou art a stranger. Jacob was a stranger in Palestine, just as the elect are strangers on earth (1 Chron. 29. 15). He will inherit the antitypical land in the world to come, just as the meek will inherit the earth (Ps. 37. 11). They are strangers and sojourners, often rejected and hated, on the present earth. They will inherit the new created earth in eternal glory.

Which God gave unto Abraham. See 13. 17; 15. 18. This statement was another link between Jacob and the blessing of Abraham, and it must have encouraged him in his knowledge that he was the heir of the promises. His father's words would also assure him of a safe return from Syria. Notice the use of the Divine Name Elohim. Though the immediate context deals with the blessing of Abraham and is therefore redemptive, the emphasis on God as Creator is proper in view of Jacob's departure to Syria. God would work upon and among those with whom he would be, even though they were outside the covenant.

VERSE 5. *Isaac sent away Jacob.* So the family was broken up in consequence of the low plane of spiritual life on which it had been living. Isaac's attempt to get behind the purpose of God, Rebekah's schemes and Jacob's act of deception all contributed to this end. But Jacob's departure was part of God's purpose for him. Evidently He intended to take him out of the atmosphere and surroundings that seem to have held him back spiritually and to train his character. A long and hard training ensued.

Padan-Aram . . . Laban . . . Bethuel. See on verse 2.

VERSE 6. In this and the following three verses we find a half-hearted attempt of Esau to reform. *Esau.* He was nursing a murderous hatred against his brother, and he now had an earnest desire to obtain the blessing of which he thought he had been wrongly deprived, though he had despised it before. We can therefore understand his interest in what was taking place and his watchfulness to seize any opportunity of reversing his father's decision that might present itself.

Blessed Jacob. Esau saw this with rage and grief. Carnal sinners and the people of the world resent the blessing, peace and happiness of the elect. *Sent him away to Padan-Aram, to take him a wife.* Esau noticed the connection between the blessing and the wife. It seems clear that he did not understand the spiritual reason for the connection. He had no sense of the need of separation. He may have thought the charge the result of a whim of his parents.

Thou shalt not take a wife of the daughters of Canaan. This was just what Esau had done. He accordingly thought that he had found the reason why the blessing had been withheld from him. He did not at all understand that God had an elective purpose. Yet he was right in supposing that his heathen wives were a bar to blessing.

VERSE 7. *And that Jacob obeyed his father and his mother and was gone.* Notice that Jacob's obedience and the sacrifice that he made in order to comply with his father's wishes and to obtain the blessing of Abraham, which he so greatly valued, are the first facts mentioned to have a serious effect upon Esau. He got the impression that something serious and real was taking place. In the same way obedience and sacrifice on the part of the people of God will impress and move the unconverted.

VERSE 8. *The daughters of Canaan pleased not Isaac his father.* He must have known this ever since his first marriage (26. 34, 35), but no doubt he had made every effort to put the knowledge out of his head and to pretend that the situation was different. Now his interest in the blessing and the shock of disappointment that he had received made him realise the significance of his father's attitude.

VERSE 9. *Then went Esau unto Ishmael.* Notice that Esau showed no sign of repentance. He attempted by going to Ishmael to make himself respectable in his father's estimation, and perhaps fit himself to receive a blessing. He understood that there was a connection between the blessing

and marriage with kinsfolk.

Daughter of Ishmael. Mahalath is likely to have been Ishmael's daughter in the second or third generation, grand-daughter, or great-grand-daughter, as we should say. If she were the child of a brother of Nebajoth, she might well be called in Hebrew his sister.

VERSE 10. This verse opens the account of Jacob's dream, which continues to the end of the chapter.

Jacob went out from Beer-sheba. Beer-sheba was in the extreme south of Palestine. Jacob had therefore to traverse the whole length of the country from south to north before reaching Syria. This would give him an opportunity of seeing the land that had been promised to his descendants. His journey was also a picture of the journey of the Son of God from the bosom of the Father to the cross of Calvary in order to seek and win His bride. This journey was the farthest that it was possible to go. It was in fact of infinite length by reason of its starting-point. It reached also to infinite unplumbed depths.

Went toward Haran. Just as Jacob knew clearly from the beginning where he was going and set his thoughts on his journey's end, so the Son of God fixed His mind and heart on Calvary, the end of His journey, from the moment that he set forth. At the age of twelve He must be about His Father's business (Lk. 2. 49). Again and again He foretold the end (e.g. Mt. 16. 21) and explained the reason for His coming (Mt. 20. 28; Jo. 3. 14, 15; 6. 50, 51, 53). He knew the end from the beginning. To say that the possibility of the cross dawned upon Jesus is to contradict His own words; and to suppose that a kingdom was offered to the Jews, which, if accepted, might have averted the cross, is to misunderstand the whole basis of the Gospel. The Lord Jesus Christ came into the world to die.

VERSE 11. *He lighted upon a certain place.* So it seemed to Jacob, and so undoubtedly it was. But the hand of God brought him to the place.

Tarried there all night. As we read this account, we gather a deep sense of the loneliness of Jacob. We see him as a solitary figure, leaving the home of his parents and setting out quite alone into the unknown. In actual fact it may well be that Jacob was accompanied by one or more of his father's servants (compare 22. 3), but the personal experiences through which he passed that night emphasised the sense of solitariness to Jacob. The story also emphasises it. If there were personal servants with Jacob, they remain unmentioned in order to heighten the picture of the lonely Son of God, unique in the world, the secrets of His Being and mission locked within His heart, misunderstood, rejected, hated, hounded to death and dishonour. 'I have trodden the winepress, alone, and of the people there was none with me' (Isa. 63. 3.) 'Oh wondrous love, that Jesus there alone, On Calvarys' cross for sinners should atone.'

Because the sun was set. It was because the sun of life and hope was set over the world, that Jesus came to it to restore light and life. *The stones of that place.* These were hard pillows, but they were at least pillows. 'The Son of man hath not where to lay his head' (Mt. 8. 20). So again in this detail Jacob becomes a picture of his great Descendant, Who, though He was rich, yet for our sakes became poor, that we through His poverty might become rich (2 Cor. 8. 9).

Lay down in that place to sleep. It was in his sleep that blessing came to him by the renewal of the promise and through him to all his descendants. Sleep is a picture of death, and it was in death that the victory of the Lord Jesus Christ came to Him and through Him to all His people.

VERSE 12. *He dreamed.* In the Bible we find that God often speaks to men in dreams. The same method is sometimes used today in the case of Chinese and other oriental Christians. *A ladder.* The ladder is the Lord Jesus Christ, as He Himself made clear in His allusion to this passage in Jo. 1. 51. He is the way by which man reaches God. No man comes to the Father except by Him (Jo. 14. 6).

Set up on the earth. The ladder reaches down to meet the vilest sinner's deepest need. The Lord came down to earth and took human nature in order to set it up, and suffered and died in order that it might be firmly based and set on the ground and never moved. He remains a man for ever in His glorified nature (1 Tim. 2. 5). *The top of it reached to heaven.* It carries the sinner who steps on to its lowest rung into the holiest of all, the very presence of God Himself, and gives him access there for ever. Perhaps the ladder acts in the same way as what in the twentieth century we call an escalator.

The angels of God ascending and descending on it. The presence of the angels on the ladder freely passing to and fro proves that heaven and earth are brought together in one world. Now they are separate because of the holiness of God and the sin of man. In the world to come there will be a new heaven and a new earth which will interpenetrate each other. The tabernacle of God will be with men (Rev. 21. 3). The reconciliation and reunion of God with men is what Jesus died to accomplish.

VERSE 13. *The Lord stood above it.* The angels were called the angels of Elohim, because they have no part in redemption. They speak of the new creation. The promise that is about to be made to Jacob is a redemptive promise, fulfilling a part of the great redemptive purpose. Therefore we have the Name Jahweh. Throughout this chapter the titles Elohim and Jahweh are frequently interchanged. This is clean contrary to the critical composite theories, but fits the needs of the context very well. By standing above the ladder Jahweh makes plain to Jacob that it is by means of the ladder that He intends to bless him. Jahweh Himself is at the upper end of the ladder. 'God was in Christ, reconciling the world unto Himself' (2 Cor. 5. 19). He Himself is the goal of faith.

I am the Lord God of Abraham thy father, and the God of Isaac. These words again bring Jacob into the line of the patriarchal promises. His blessing is rooted in the past, and the circumstances in which it was given to him prove its connection with the new heaven and earth. He was gathered up into God's great purpose, which led on to the coming of Christ and is to be consummated in the glory to come.

The land whereon thou liest, to thee will I give it. This is the first of four promises which are here taken from the blessing of Abraham and made over to Jacob. They are followed by three further promises of an immediate and personal nature, and these again by an assurance. We have (1) the gift of the land. The land was given to Jacob in the persons of his natural descendants, Old Testament Israel, who conquered it under Joshua and remained in it till part of them were carried captive by Nebuchadnezzar. A small number returned and remained in it till their final destruction by the Romans. Jacob himself never possessed the land. He will possess however the far better land, 'the new land', of which Palestine was a type and picture. He and all his faithful descendants, the true seed of Israel, with all believers in Christ, will possess Palestine for ever in the sense that it was the scene of the Saviour's atoning death and resurrection.

VERSE 14. *Thy seed shall be as the dust of the earth.* This is (2) the second of the four promises made to Jacob on this occasion. It is fulfilled (a) in the large increase of Old Testament Israel (Ex. 1. 7) and (b) in the great multitude of the redeemed, or true Israelites, the spiritual descendants of Abraham, Isaac and Jacob.

Thou shalt spread abroad. We can scarcely say that this was fulfilled in the dispersion of the Jews, which took place in judgment rather than in mercy, although it was over-ruled for blessing and turned out for the furtherance of the Gospel. The promise is fulfilled in the spread of the Gospel among Jew and Gentile in all parts of the world, so that many will come from the east and the west, from the north and from the south, and sit down with Abraham, Isaac and Jacob in the kingdom of God (Isa. 49. 12; Mt. 8. 11). All believers, whether Jew or Gentile by race, are the spiritual seed of Jacob, as they are of Abraham (Gal. 3. 29).

In thee and in thy seed shall all the families of the earth be blessed. This is a repetition and confirmation of the promise given to Abraham in 12. 3 and 22. 18. Jacob himself becomes a blessing to all families of the earth because he is the ancestor of Christ through Whom the blessing comes. The seed is Christ (Gal. 3. 16). The blessing consists of the privileges of the Gospel and the benefits of Christ's passion, conversion from iniquity and justification by faith (Acts 3. 25, 26; Gal. 3. 8). It extends to all those Gentiles who believe as well as to believing Jews.

VERSE 15. The application to Jacob of the Abrahamic blessings and covenant is followed by three personal promises, which may be described as (1) the presence of God, (2) preservation, and (3) perseverance. They are promises which apply to every believer.

I am with thee. The same words had been spoken to Isaac (26. 24). The assurance of God's presence is the solution of all problems, the destruction of all doubts and the certainty of final victory and of everlasting life, for God's presence can be with no one (except in the general sense of His omnipresence as Creator, which applies to all creation, animal, vegetable and inanimate) who has not been justified by His grace and received in Christ a perfect standing that gives him access to God and enables God to dwell with him without derogation to His own holiness and righteousness. Furthermore no enemy can finally stand in the presence of God, neither Satan, nor sin, nor death. We too may be assured of the presence of God with us by reliance upon the promises of His Word and by the witness of the Holy Spirit dwelling in our hearts as much as Jacob who in his dream had a direct statement of it made to him.

I will keep thee in all places whither thou goest. The second promise was of preservation. Jacob's journey might be dangerous. He might meet with dangers in the country to which he was going. He furthermore needed spiritual keeping. We need the same and may also possess it. The promise was given at the threshold of a journey and at the beginning of a long absence from home. The believer lives on earth in similar circumstances. His whole life is a journey. It often consists of a series of expeditions or journeys undertaken to seek the lost in the service of God, and it is spent in absence from his Father's home in heaven, to which he hopes to come. He is surrounded with dangers, known and unknown, and confronted with difficulties and problems among which a false step might be fatal. Like Jacob he needs and has the assurance of God's keeping.

Will bring thee again into this land. Thirdly comes the promise of perseverance. Jacob's journey will not be in vain. Should he fail to return, God's promise to Abraham would fall to the ground. He now has an assured hope for the future. He will return safe home. We have a similar but a better promise. We shall be brought safe through, not to Palestine a land of sojourning, but to the permanent possession of our home in glory, from which we shall never go out again, but live in eternal security. The promises of God's Word, to be embraced by faith, provide us with an assurance of the realisation of this hope in our own personal case as definite as that which was given to Jacob, and we may equally as much rely on it for our comfort.

I will not leave thee. In these words we have the foundation of the promises and assurances given to Jacob. He would never be left to himself. He would never be at the mercy of circumstances, or of his enemies, human or spiritual. Nothing would happen to him by chance. He could assure himself that the whole of his life, step by step, would be the outworking of God's sovereign purpose and decree for him. If weakness or sin temporarily overcame him, he was in the hands of a God Who was well able to deal with it. The promise of God never to leave him implied victory over sin and deliverance from it, so that Jacob would never be left in its power. In the course of the story we shall find Jacob sometimes afraid, we shall find his faith sometimes weak, but his fears are always groundless. Exactly the same promise has been left to us. God has said, ' I will never leave thee nor forsake thee, so that we may boldly say, The Lord is my helper, I will not fear ' (Heb. 13. 5, 6).

Until I have done that which I have spoken to thee of. Here we go deeper still into the foundations of of the promises and assurances of God. God's. acts of grace towards us rest upon what He has said in His Word. He made certain decrees in eternity past (Rom. 8. 29, 30). He has made known to us much of His purpose in the promises He has given us in the Scriptures. ' What He hath promised He is able also to perform ' (Rom. 4. 21). He has promised us eternal life (Jo. 10. 28) and entire sanctification (1 Thess. 5. 23, 24), assuring us again and again that He will never let us go, but will keep His promises and bring them to completion and perfection. We may rest our faith for time and eternity upon God's Word. Not to do so is foolish and presumptuous.

VERSE 16. *Jacob awaked out of his sleep.* He found himself in his everyday surroundings. This is the experience that comes to all of us. No saint remains always on the mountain top. He comes down into the practical life of every day. There he must find the promises of God to avail and hold good. Jacob came down, as we ought each day to come down, with the vision that he had seen bright in his memory and the words that he had heard sounding in his ears. It was in the life of every-day that the promises of God were to work out.

Surely the Lord is in this place. Notice that the redemptive title Jahweh is used. Jacob was right. Jahweh was in that place. He was wrong however in thinking that God might be in certain places and not in others. His mind was not emancipated from the heathenism around him.

And I knew it not. These words imply (1) that Jacob would not have ventured to the place, had he known that he was going to meet the Lord there. He was not anxious to meet Him, being evidently afraid of Him. This fear arose, as it does in all sinners, as the result of a guilty conscience. There are men who refuse to go where they might hear the Gospel for fear of being brought into touch with God. (2) The words imply that Jacob felt that he ought to have made some preparation or brought some offering, before meeting with God. He had no idea that God in His grace longs to meet the sinner just as he is, and never waits for him to accomplish the impossible task of making himself fit. (3) The words express the experience of many a saint and many a sinner, who find God seeking them, meeting with them, unexpectedly blessing through the medium of some experience in which they never suspected that He had some direct part.

VERSE 17. *He was afraid.* His awe and sense of guilt were so strong, that the memory of the promises made to him and the blessings granted him in his dream failed to reassure him. Jacob had greatly desired the blessing. He had lowered his character in order to obtain it. Yet he was not ready to come into personal contact with God. Like many a sinner, he

wanted blessing, but did not want God. When he found that the blessing was bound up with the personal presence of God, he feared it instead of welcoming it.

How dreadful is this place. His ignorance and the weakness of his faith are revealed by these words. He connected the presence of God with a particular place. It is true that typically and for purposes of illustration God localised Himself in the Jewish church, but the idea is heathen and magical. It is prevalent in Romanism and Anglo-Romanism, in which God is localised in churches, on altars, in aumbries and even in a little piece of biscuit. ' But the Most High dwelleth not in temples made with hands ' (Acts 7. 48). Not only did Jacob connect the presence of God with a particular place. He dreaded the place and was afraid to be in it. *The House of God.* The Hebrew is Bethel. The only true house of God is the whole company of faithful people in which He will dwell for ever (Eph. 2. 22). He also dwells in each of His people's individual hearts (1 Cor. 3. 16; 6. 19).

The gate of heaven. It is extraordinary that the gate of heaven should be considered by Jacob to be dreadful. Though his fear may have arisen partly through ignorance and guilt, we should do well to catch something of his spirit. We sometimes forget that heaven is the abode of God's holiness, and that nothing that defiles can ever enter in (Rev. 21. 27). We think too easily of all and sundry being one day in heaven without their having any claim whatever to be there. Without holiness no man shall see the Lord (Heb. 12. 14). If the house of God and the gate of heaven are one and the same, then our hearts, in which the Spirit dwells, are the gate of heaven. In ourselves we know this to be so. May they be gates through which many a needy sinner may enter in Christ the presence of God.

VERSE 18. *Rose up early in the morning.* He did wisely since he wanted to meet with God. Abraham used to rise early in the morning (19. 27; 22. 3). Joshua also did so (Jos. 3. 1). Above all the Lord Himself rose very early to pray (Mk. 1. 35). We also shall generally find that the early morning is the best time for meeting with God and reading His Word. *The stone that he had put for his pillows.* The stone is a symbol of Christ (Isa. 28. 16; Ps. 118. 22; 1 Pet. 2. 4). On this stone Jacob had rested his head, making himself unwittingly the picture of the believer trusting to Christ, resting on Him and relying on Him.

Set it up for a pillar. Jacob made the stone, as it were, his representative before God. The stone was intended also as a sign that Jacob dedicated his life to God, intending to lead a new life and walk thenceforward in God's holy ways. It was his response to the promise that God had given to him and to the manifestation of His presence. Thus Jacob first committed himself to the stone and then dedicated his life to God.

Poured oil upon the top of it. Oil is the symbol of the Holy Ghost. In Jacob's action we may see (1) a further picture in the stone of the anointed Messiah, and (2) an intimation that the life lived in dedication to God is lived under the power and leading of the Holy Spirit.

VERSE 19. *Bethel.* This means the house of God. The place that previously had been a heathen city now becomes the house of God. This did not happen on Jacob's initiative, but by a manifestation of God's grace. So our own hearts and bodies are changed from being centres of heathen activity to being dwelling-places of God, when God in Christ manifests Himself to us in grace (1 Cor. 6. 19; Eph. 3. 17).

The name of that city was called Luz at the first. The place was thus a Canaanite city, although there is no hint of it in the foregoing verses. Evidently Jacob did not enter the city to spend the night in it. He wisely and rightly kept himself separate from

the company of the Canaanites, preferring to remain outside on the bare ground where he could meet with God than enjoy what comfort the heathen city could offer him. The Christian often finds a similar choice occurring to him. Notice that the name is glossed as it were in reverse. The mention of the early Canaanite name shows the narrative to be early. If it had been composed during the Israelite kingdom period, there would have been no object in mentioning the early name, which would have been long disused and lost. The name disappeared during the conquest of Canaan soon after the death of Joshua (Jud. 1. 23-26).

VERSE 20. *Vowed a vow.* This was a dedication of himself by Jacob. So far as we know, it was the first that he had made in his life. Certainly the occasion was a turning-point in Jacob's spiritual experience. Every man's conversion is his vow. A true conversion involves a dedication of oneself to the service of God and entrance into a new relationship with God. As Christian men do we realise that we are dedicated to God's service, and have we made the vow, an open confession of Christ before men, whether by the normal God-given method of baptism, or by confirmation, or by uniting ourselves publicly with a local church or group of Christians?

If God will be with me. Jacob is usually criticised for prefixing these conditions to his vow, and is regarded as manifesting a very low stage of spiritual experience. The terms of the vow certainly seem to be those of a man who is only at the beginning of his spiritual life. At the same time it is perhaps doubtful, if weakness of faith is demonstrated by the four conditions. A careful consideration of them, as they are set out in this verse and in the first sentence of the next, seems to show that they are indispensable conditions for the fulfilment of the vow. The crux of the vow appears in the next verse. Meanwhile it is open to us to feel that

Jacob should have attached no condition to his vow, but rather have shown the spirit manifested by Job when he said, ' Though he slay me, yet will I trust him ' (Job 13. 15). Yet it is also open to us to regard these apparent conditions in the light of a heartfelt prayer — ' if only God will be with me, if only He will keep me '. At least the four conditions show Jacob's sense of dependence on God. He had a sense of his need of God's presence and a sense of dependence upon God for preservation and provision. In all this he was right. In wanting God to be with him he wanted the best. Such a desire involved the meeting of all his needs. The words of the request are the simplest possible, but the meaning is inexhaustibly profound.

Will keep me in this way that I go. Jacob recognised that the possibility of a life of service to God depended on God's preservation of him. Notice that his sense of need and his prayer (if we may regard these conditions as expressions of prayer) were definite. He declared his need of keeping on the actual journey on which he was at the moment going. This is another instance of the practical and definite nature of scriptural prayers. We too may pray the same. Our journey is the way through life and the end of the journey is the promised heavenly land. We could not reach the journey's end without God's keeping power. The way is full of enemies and dangers. The devil seeks to devour us (1 Pet. 5. 8), the world to allure us and sin to entrap us. We need the Christ Who saved us also to keep us.

Bread to eat. Jacob realised his dependence on God for the supply of his physical needs. Ours is no less great, though concealed by the complex economic system under which we live. Greater still is our need of spiritual food. Of this we have no lack, God having provided the bread from heaven for us (Jo. 6. 50). Christ is that bread. We feed on Him in a spiritual and not in a material sense by partaking of Holy Communion. Such is the awful doctrine of the Mass. He has gone up to heaven where He was before, and His body has never been present on earth since His ascension. We feed on Him spiritually when we read the Bible. His words are our food (Jo. 6. 62, 63). They mediate Christ to us. Man lives not only on material bread but on every word that comes out of the mouth of God (Deut. 8. 3; Mt. 4. 4; Lk. 4. 4),

Raiment to put on. Man's second basic need after his food is for clothing. Christ has promised the supply of food and clothing to all who put Him and His interests first in their lives (Mt. 6. 31-33), but a far greater need is that of spiritual raiment. Without it we must appear before God naked in all our guilt and shame (Rev. 3. 18). God has provided for us the white robe of Christ's righteousness, which we shall wear for ever in heaven, in which alone we are able to have access to God here in our sinful state (Rev. 7. 14; 19. 8). He has also provided the beautiful garments of salvation and holiness (Isa. 52. 1). In the glory and beauty of these God-given garments, provided at the cost of the blood of the Lamb, we may have access to God's presence when we will. Our clothing is of wrought gold. We are brought unto the king in raiment of needlework, and we shall stand upon His right hand in gold of Ophir (Ps. 45. 9, 13, 14).

VERSE 21. *So that I come again to my father's house in peace.* Like the rest of his petitions Jacob's desire to return safe home is a parable of spiritual things. The same is desired by every one of the people of God. Jacob had seen his father's home. We have not. The word ' again ' applies to us only in the sense that God foreknew us and predestinated us in eternity past (Rom. 8. 29, 30; Eph. 1. 4). Yet though we were born in exile, we know instinctively that we belong to the Father's home. So does many an unconverted man in the depths of his heart. The prodigal son knew (Lk. 15. 18). In order to come to our Father's home we need just the four things that have been mentioned in the previous verse. We need (1) God to be with us. This He can only be in Christ. Apart from Christ He is against us, and His wrath abides on us (Jo. 3. 36). Our first need therefore is to have Christ as our Saviour. (2) We need God's keeping power to preserve us in the way to the end (Col. 1. 23). He alone can supply us with the grace to persevere. (3) We need the heavenly food, Christ as the bread of God (Jo. 6. 54). (4) We need the robe of Christ's righteousness, that marriage garment without which we shall be cast out of the heavenly baunqueting hall into outer darkness (Mt. 22. 11-13). If we have these four things, we shall be found of Him on the great day in peace (2 Pet. 3. 14), we shall be gathered by the angels into the heavenly home (Mt. 24. 31), and we shall there possess and enjoy eternal peace and security (Ps. 37. 11).

Then shall the Lord be my God. If these words are the correct rendering of the Hebrew, we cannot acquit Jacob of an almost intolerable air of patronage in his dealings with God. In any case the bargaining spirit, so congenial to his nature, is present, but in this sentence Jacob speaks as if he were conferring a favour on Jahweh by permitting Him, if He fulfilled certain conditions, to be his God. Unbearable as this appears to us, Jacob is not alone in patronising God. Many have done it in every age, and many do it today. They carry out religious duties in a spirit of conferring a favour on God. The words thus provide a practical warning. But is it certain that our version represents correctly what Jacob said? In the margin of the R.V. we shall find a rendering which reads ' if ' for ' then ' and ' then ' for ' and ' as the opening word for verse 22. The sentence would then read, ' And if the Lord will be my God '. This is much more in accordance with truth. It prevents Jacob from thinking that he could make Jahweh his God or not at will. No man can do this. He can indeed decide whether Christ shall

be his Saviour or not in the sense of an appropriation of Him. In this sense it may to a certain extent be true that one can make the Lord one's God or not at will. If our version is correct, this is the meaning we must put upon the words. But if we take the reading of the R.V. margin, we find that it depends on Jahweh, not upon Jacob, whether or not He is or becomes Jacob's God. This is at any rate true to fact.

VERSE 22. *This stone, which I have set for a pillar, shall be God's house.* Jacob means that when he comes safely home to Palestine, he will make a sanctuary, or centre of worship, at Bethel as a reminder of God's appearance to him. In the statement that the stone would be God's house we are reminded of two things. (1) The stone represents Christ. Christ is the perfect and eternal house of God in which the Father dwells in all His fulness for ever (Col. 2. 9). (2) The stone, being that which Jacob dedicated to God, represents his own heart and life, one of the living stones which are built into God's dwelling-place upon the foundation of Christ (1 Pet. 2. 4, 5). This stone was (a) set for a pillar, that is to say, openly dedicated to God and left standing for all to see. So must our own lives be dedicated openly to God at our conversion and left openly standing in worship and service before Him. (b) The stone was to be God's house. Even so our hearts are Christ's dwelling-place (Eph. 3. 17), and in them we are to set up a sanctuary to the Lord Christ (1 Pet. 3. 15).

Of all that thou shalt give me. Jacob recognised that he was dependent upon God for the necessities of life and that all were gifts of God. So it is with us. Everything we possess or enjoy, physical or spiritual, is a gift from the Creator and loving heavenly Father. So is the capacity for enjoyment. Even the faith by which we apprehend Christ is a gift of God (Eph. 2. 8).

I will surely give the tenth unto thee. Jacob is again criticised for niggardliness in making this vow. It is supposed that he ought to have said that he would give back everything. This may be so. We must not look for spiritual maturity in Jacob at this stage of his career. He was only at the beginning of his spiritual experience. At the same time Jacob may be intending to give a practical and definite amount of his income for the maintenance of the Bethel sanctuary. He chose the proportion which was known to Abraham (14. 20) and was afterwards embodied in the levitical law (Lev. 27. 30; Num. 18. 21, 24). Under the Gospel God invites us to set aside a certain proportion of our income for the direct support of His people or His work (1 Cor. 16. 2). The natural amount is the proportion definitely laid down under the levitical law. Whatever be the proportion, no Christian is using his money properly, unless he sets aside a definite amount from it for the work of God abroad or at home. Those who have not been accustomed to do this would scarcely credit the blessing that the practice brings. Those who regularly give their tenth often experience a God-given financial prosperity.

CHAPTER 29

IN this chapter we have the story of Jacob's arrival in Syria, of his meeting with Rachel and Laban, of his service for Rachel, his deception by Laban and the births of his four eldest sons. The general impression obtained from the chapter is that of the sovereign providence of God carrying out His purposes for Jacob and fulfilling the promises made to him at Bethel. Jacob becomes a type of Christ the heavenly Bridegroom, and there are evangelical lessons in the names of his four sons.

VERSE 1. *Went on his journey.* Jacob's journey is a picture of that of the heavenly Bridegroom, Who journeyed from the bosom of the Father (Jo. 1. 18) to the manger of Bethlehem (Lk. 2. 16) and finally to the cross of Calvary (Mk. 15. 24).

The land of the people of the east. Jacob arrived where he had set out to go, as did the Saviour, never faltering till the end.

VERSE 2. *A well in the field.* The well represents the source of the water of life (Jo. 4. 14). The water is the Holy Ghost (Jo. 7. 38, 39). The well in which He is contained, through which He is mediated, is the Scripture (Jo. 6. 63). The well was in the field, that is to say, it was in the world (Mt. 13. 38), available for the people of the world. *Three flocks of sheep lying by it.* Here is a picture of the thirsty exhausted peoples of the world lying around the water of life. If there is any significance in the number three, we may perhaps see in it an indication of the children of Shem, Ham and Japheth. In contrast to the multitudinous peoples the Lord has but one flock (Jo. 10. 16).

Out of that well. There is no other well but that of the water of life to be found in Jesus alone. ' There is no other name under heaven given among men whereby we must be saved ' (Acts 4. 12). There is nothing else but the broken cisterns of the world, hewn out by men, which can hold no water (Jer. 2. 13).

A great stone was upon the well's mouth. In the same way there is a great barrier of sin and unbelief between the people of the world and the water of life.

VERSE 3. This verse explains why the water was denied to the thirsty flocks. The people of the country appear to have been in bondage to a custom. We may therefore learn from this verse (1) how unnecessary custom and vain habit are often instrumental in keeping men back from the water of life. Convention is a great enemy of the Gospel. As illustrations of Gospel truth we may also see from this verse (2) that all the flocks obtain their water together. There is only one well for them all. One group of people ought not to suppose that it has priority of interest in the Gospel. ' There is no respect of persons with

God ' (Acts 10. 34). (3) We learn that there is only one opportunity for the flocks of access to the well of life. This opportunity extends in general to the natural life-time in this world and never under any circumstances beyond it, and it extends in particular to the one or more moments of decision at which the Gospel faces and challenges the individual. ' Behold, now is the accepted time, behold, now is the day of salvation ' (2 Cor. 6. 2).

VERSE 4. Jacob now starts particular enquiries directed towards the definite end that he had in view. *Whence be ye?* This question is asked in effect by the heavenly Bridegroom of those whom He comes to seek. When the question reaches them, His sheep know His voice (Jo. 10. 4). ' He that doeth the truth cometh to the light ' (Jo. 3. 21). The Gospel distinguishes those who are of light from those who are of darkness.

VERSE 5. *Laban the son of Nahor.* Jacob was searching for his own, just as the heavenly Bridegroom came to search for His own sheep, knowing and loving each individual among them.

VERSE 6. *Is he well?* The Saviour seeks the welfare and peace of His own.

Rachel his daughter cometh with the sheep. Rachel is here the picture of the bride, just as Rebekah was in chapter 24. Here we see another characteristic of the bride. She is with the sheep. In actual spiritual fact the bride and the sheep are identical, but it is easy to see in this picture the church thought of as a whole caring for the individual sheep of the flock of God. In Rebekah and Rachel we have this double picture of the church. She cares for the camels, and she tends the sheep.

VERSE 7. *It is yet high day.* This is just the time when the sheep need the water, yet it was impossible for them to get it.

Neither is it time that the cattle

should be gathered together. While the day of this world lasts, the flock of God is not gathered together. The gathering will come at the end of the world, when the Son of man will send His angels and gather together His elect from the four winds (Mt. 24. 31). At present the heat of the sun lights on them. The sun burns them by day and the moon by night. As soon as they are safely gathered before the throne of God, these conditions will cease (Rev. 7. 16).

Water ye the sheep and go and feed them. This is a command of the heavenly Bridegroom to the undershepherds, and it comes to us today. Any who have any position of responsibility in the church are commanded to distribute to the sheep the living water and the spiritual food from the Scriptures. This involves *going*. The sheep will not seek the fold or the shepherd. The shepherd must seek the sheep. This may involve going along the streets of a home town or going to spend a life-time in a distant country.

VERSE 8. *We cannot.* This is too often the answer that the Lord Jesus receives from weakness of faith, or from unbelief. The shepherds in this story seem to have been hidebound by custom. We are often in the same case. We cannot leave the ordinary routine of life to strike out on the revolutionary ways of soul-winning. We cannot break convention for fear of what others will say.

Until. Yet a spiritual truth lies behind the impossibility expressed by the shepherds. It is certainly impossible to water the sheep until the two conditions mentioned in this verse are fulfilled. (1) The flocks must be gathered together to Christ, the well of life. Before the Gospel came, it was impossible to water the thirsty waiting flocks. The final gathering at the last day (Mt. 24. 31) will introduce the flocks to the eternal pasturage (Rev. 7. 17). (2) There is no living water available till the stone is rolled from the well's mouth and the barrier of sin and death taken away.

271

This was accomplished by the Saviour's death and resurrection and was sealed and demonstrated by the rolling away of the stone from the door of the Saviour's tomb.

Then we water the sheep. When these things have happened, the water of life becomes available to the thirsty (Rev. 21. 6; 22. 17).

VERSE 9. *While he yet spake with them.* No delay occurs in the carrying out of God's purposes. All moves forward at the right time pre-determined by His sovereign wisdom.

Rachel came. Rachel is a picture of ' the bride, the Lamb's wife ' (Rev. 21. 9), as Rebekah had been before her.

With her father's sheep: for she kept them. This is exactly the occupation and work of the Lamb's bride. Her father is God Himself. All who make up the bride are children of God by faith in Christ Jesus (Gal. 3. 26). The task of the bride, while she is in this world, is to tend and keep God's sheep. This she can only do by the grace of Christ and the power of the Holy Ghost. She is not the source of their blessing, but its channel.

VERSE 10. *When Jacob saw Rachel.* The heavenly Bridegroom saw the bride in eternity past (Eph. 1. 4). He saw her with omniscience and faith as He died for her on the cross (Eph. 5. 25), and one day He will present her to Himself without spot or wrinkle or any such thing (Eph. 5. 27).

The daughter of Laban his mother's brother. The Bridegroom recognises the bride as belonging to His own kith and kin. She is the child of Adam whom He loved, whose nature He took (Heb. 2. 15, 16). *The sheep of Laban his mother's brother.* He knew His sheep from eternity past and went after that which was lost till He found it (Jo. 10. 14, 15; Lk. 15. 4). *Jacob went near.* The heavenly bridegroom did the same. He came down to us and near to us in our need and misery and lost condition. He came unto His own (Jo.

1. 11).

Rolled the stone from the well's mouth. This is what the heavenly Bridegroom did. He exhausted Himself in rolling away the barrier of sin and death that stood between the sheep and the water of life. He gave His life to remove it. He took the sin of the world on Himself, and the rolling of the stone from the door of His tomb was the proof that sin and death were overcome for ever (Mt. 28. 2).

Watered the flock. The Saviour has provided the water of life for all believers.

VERSE 11. *Jacob kissed Rachel.* Having loved His own which were in the world Jesus loved them unto the end (Jo. 13. 1).

Lifted up his voice, and wept. He was moved to tears and tender affection, his emotions stirred by the poignancy of the scene and the memory of the mother whom he had left behind. In the same way the Lord Jesus was moved with compassion when He saw the pitiable condition of the crowds (Mt. 9. 36) and wept at the grave of Lazarus (Jo. 11. 35).

VERSE 12. *That he was her father's brother.* Our High Priest is in all points like as we are (Heb. 2. 17; 4. 15).

Rebekah's son. The heavenly Bridegroom is in His human nature the son of the bride, just as in His Divine nature He is her Bridegroom (Rev. 12. 5).

She ran and told her father. In the same way the bride runs to tell the good tidings that the Bridegroom has come into the world. Rachel went naturally first to her own father, just as Andrew first found his own brother Simon (Jo. 1. 41).

VERSE 13. *He ran to meet him, and embraced him, and kissed him.* The affectionate and enthusiastic welcome turned out afterwards to be hypocritical and false. The same was true to a large extent in the case of our Lord. ' The common people heard him gladly ' (Mk. 12. 37), but the same people were soon asking for His crucifixion (Mk. 15. 11). In the same way many receive the Gospel with joy, but have no root in themselves (Mt. 13. 20, 21). It is the same to-day. Not a mission passes but there are spurious conversions among the real. Many appear to welcome the Gospel who afterwards become indifferent or even bitter opponents. We all need to search our own hearts (2 Cor. 13. 5).

He told Laban all these things. In the same way the Lord Jesus kept nothing back from men, but told them the whole counsel of God and explained exactly why He had been sent into the world (Jo. 3. 14-18; 6. 37-40, 50, 51, 58).

VERSE 14. *Surely thou art my bone and my flesh.* Laban's recognition of Jacob's close relationship put his subsequent behaviour in an even worse light. As his kinsman he had obligations to him which he did not honour. How much greater is the believer's obligation to Christ seeing he is a member of His body, of His flesh and of His bones (Eph. 5. 30).

He abode with him the space of a month. It was not long before their mutual relationship changed and was placed on a more formal basis. When the Lord comes to abide in our heart, He comes not for a month, nor for a year, nor even for a lifetime, but for ever (Jo. 14. 16, 17).

VERSE 15. Because thou art my *brother.* Christ is our brother and is not ashamed to call us brethren (Heb. 2. 11, 12).

Shouldest thou therefore serve me for nought? Christ's graciousness and condescension in making Himself one of ourselves and serving God on our behalf to the bitter end does not excuse us from being under an obligation to Him. Rather it puts us under infinite obligation.

What shall thy wages be? What shall I render unto the Lord for all His benefits toward me? (Ps. 116. 12). The astonishing answer in the follow-

ing verse of the Psalm is that He wants us to take more.

VERSE 16. *Two daughters.* These perhaps represent the old and new covenants, somewhat like Hagar and Sarah. The beloved and true bride was the younger.

Leah. The meaning of the name is not rightly known.

Rachel. The name means Ewe, and emphasises Rachel's connection with the flocks. Neither of the sisters could have been very young at this time. Perhaps it had been difficult to find a husband for Leah, and perhaps Rachel had for this reason been prevented from marrying (see verse 26). Perhaps they were women whose ages corresponded to about thirty-five and thirty respectively on the modern scale of life.

VERSE 17. *Tender eyed.* The old Israel was like this. She could not see Christ in her types and ceremonies, nor in the messages of her prophets, because of the weakness of her faith.

Rachel was beautiful and well favoured. The heavenly bride will be the same, glorious and without spot or wrinkle (Eph. 5. 27). She is well favoured by the abundant grace of God.

VERSE 18. *Jacob loved Rachel.* Christ also loved the church (Eph. 5. 25), and has told us that He has loved us with an everlasting love (Jer. 31. 3).

I will serve thee seven years for Rachel. Christ also served and toiled for the church that He loved so dearly during the long years of the incarnation, culminating in the public ministry which led direct to the cross. *Thy younger daughter.* It was the younger daughter, the new Israel, on whom Christ's love was set from all eternity.

VERSE 19. *It is better that I should give her to thee.* It is indeed. No parent could say a wiser word about their child. It is better to belong to Christ than to have the best that the world can give. It means victory and happiness in the present world in spite of persecutions and in the world to come everlasting life. Happy is the child who is dedicated to Christ in infancy, prayed for by parents so that his heart is turned towards God in Christ, and brought up for the service of the Lord.

Abide with me. These are familiar words. They are words that the Lord loves to hear from the sinner. They are words that every sinner uses in effect at his conversion when he opens the door of his heart to invite the Saviour in (Rev. 3. 20). Such a request is never refused by the Saviour, and its fulfilment brings more to the sinner than anything of which he could have ever dreamed.

' In life, in death, O Lord, abide with me.'

VERSE 20. *Jacob served seven years for Rachel.* So the Lord served for His bride, emptying Himself to take upon Him the form of a servant and humbling Himself to be obedient unto death, and that the death of the cross (Phil. 2. 6-8).

They seemed unto him but a few days. In the same way the Lord endured the cross and despised the shame for the joy that was set before Him (Heb. 12. 2).

For the love he had to her. Having loved His own which were in the world Jesus loved them unto the end (Jo. 13. 1).

VERSE 21. *Give me my wife.* The bride of Christ has been given to Him by the Father (Jo. 6. 37; 17. 6).

My days are fulfilled. The days of Christ's serving were fulfilled when He rose from the dead and was exalted to the right hand of the Father, but the days of waiting will continue till the end of the world. If an even greater fulness of joy is to come then to Christ as well as to His people, do we by our dilatoriness in His service and slackness in evangelisation help to put it off?

That I may go in unto her. The time will be when the marriage of the

Lamb will come and Christ will be united to His people for ever (Rev. 19. 7). ' As the bridegroom rejoiceth over the bride, so shall thy God rejoice over thee ' (Isa. 62. 5).

VERSE 22. *Laban gathered together all the men of the place,* just as the heavenly Father sends out His servants into the highways and by-ways to gather together all whom they find, in order to furnish His Son's wedding feast with guests (Mt. 22. 10).

Made a feast. There has never been such a feast as that which will take place on the great day, when Christ and His people are united for ever, but it may be anticipated now in the heart of any sinner, when he opens the door to let Christ in to dwell with him and to sup with him (Rev. 3. 20).

VERSE 23. Here is the first act of deception practised upon Jacob by Laban. It was the first of a series, in which he was going to find himself the victim of the same sort of conduct that he had practised on his father. The story of Jacob's sojourn in Syria is the outworking of the principle that with what measure we mete, it shall be meted out to us again (Mt. 7. 2). Perhaps we may see in the marriage of Leah a hint of the fact that the old covenant preceded the new, and that the old Israel first became the people of the Lord, though His heart was set from all eternity upon the bride whom He loved, for whom He gave Himself (Eph. 5. 25).

VERSE 24. The slave-girl is given to the bride. This was so under the old covenant. The history of the world, particularly of those nations in the neighbourhood of Palestine, revolved round that of Israel and was made subservient to it (Deut. 32. 8). The Egyptian oppressor was used to weld Israel into a nation and provide a picture in history of the meaning of redemption. Pharaoh's heart was hardened (Rom. 9. 17, 18). The Assyrian and Babylonian empires were raised up in order to be the instruments of God's chastisement. Alexander the Great without knowing what he was doing prepared by his conquests for the spread of the Greek language, the translation of the Scriptures and the spread of the Gospel. The dangerous world situation today is as much in the hands of God. It is serving the purpose of the Gospel and working out to the glory of God and the good of His church.

Verse 25. *What is this thou hast done unto me?* How often must the Lord to Whom we owe all have occasion to say this to us? Our failure, half-heartedness and hypocrisy grieve Him. The question was asked in effect of ancient Israel.

Did not I serve with thee for Rachel? Where the Lord expects beauty and grace He finds weakness of faith and dimness of spiritual vision.

Wherefore then hast thou beguiled me? Jacob could be beguiled. Thank God, it is impossible to beguile the Lord, although we sometimes behave as if we thought we could do so.

Verse 26. This may be the reason why it seems to have been difficult for the sisters to find husbands. If Rachel had been the elder, both might have been married long ago. This reverence, or supposed reverence, for the elder of the two may have struck a chord in Jacob's heart and reminded him of the deceptions that he had practised on his elder brother in order to obtain his birthright and step into his place.

Verse 27. *Fulfil her week,* that is to say, serve another seven years. Laban tricked Jacob into giving him unpaid service for fourteen years. Notice the use of the word ' week ' to express years, not days. This explains for us the meaning of Daniel 9. 24-27. A day is put for a year also in Num. 14. 33, 34 and Ezek. 4. 6.

We will give thee this also. Jacob got Rachel, but he had to have Leah as well. So in possessing us and

dwelling in our hearts the Lord finds the old evil corrupt nature in us as well as the new.

Verse 28. *Jacob did so.* Nothing would deter him, so great was his love for Rachel. In the same way nothing would deter the Saviour, though all seemed against Him, from going to the bitter end, so great was His love for His people.

Fulfilled her week. So the Lord fulfilled all that was necessary in order to bring us to Himself.

He gave him Rachel. It is usually thought that Jacob served the second seven years after his marriage to Leah, but before his marriage to Rachel The narrative and the ages of his sons however seem to make it more probable that Rachel was given to him at the same time as Leah on the pledge that he would subsequently serve a second seven years. He would be bound to keep his pledge by the likely refusal of Leah and Rachel to leave their father's house with him, if he decided to go. The mention in verse 30 of ' yet seven other years ' can scarcely be a third seven (see 31. 41), but must refer to the second period. The language of verse 30 gives at least an impression that the period followed, not preceded, Rachel's marriage.

Verse 29. See on verse 24. If history moved round the purposes of God for the old Israel, it serves still more the advance of the Gospel. The Roman Empire had been brought into existence to create conditions for the spread of the Gospel at the beginning. To a less extent the British Empire served missionary effort in the nineteenth century. Printing was invented in time for the Reformation, which could . scarcely have succeeded without it. In the present age the invention of means of transport of incredible speed greatly facilitates the evangelisation of the world.

Verse 30. *He went in also unto Rachel.* The marriage of the Lamb will one day come (Rev. 19. 7).

275

He loved also Rachel more than Leah, just as God loved the world (Jo. 3 16), but God in Christ loved His own which were in the world (Jo. 13. 1).

Served with him yet seven other years. See on verse 27.

VERSE 31. *When the Lord saw that Leah was hated, he opened her womb.* In these sentences there is a variety of points to notice: (1) the Divine Name Jahweh. This is the redemptive Name. It occurs here because the building of Jacob's family is part of the inner redemptive Messianic purpose, which was being worked out in the family of the patriarchs. (2) the figure of speech by which Jahweh is said to perceive a thing and to act in consequence of what He sees. These expressions reveal condescending grace. God comes down to man and takes him on his own ground. He knew from eternity past what Jacob's attitude would be, but we could not learn the lessons that God desires to teach us except by His acting, or appearing to act, as part of the series of events which we initiate and take part in or appear to. (3) The expression 'hated'. This is a Hebraism for 'not preferred'. Jacob was in fact fond of Leah (49. 31). He loved her, though he loved Rachel more (verse 30). The expression occurs again in Deut. 21. 15 and in Lk. 14. 26, where its meaning is clear by comparison with Mt. 10. 37. (4) the revelation of the character of Jahweh that is given in this incident by His special care for the sad and oppressed. He deliberately acts out of pure compassion, and we get a foretaste of the compassion and pity of Jesus. (5) the sovereign power of God in the matter of procreation. Children and the fruit of the womb are an heritage of the Lord (Ps. 127. 3).

Rachel was barren. The situation of Hagar and Sarah is repeated. Similarly the new Jerusalem was barren till the coming of the Gospel (Gal. 4. 26, 27).

VERSE 32. In the last four verses of this chapter we read of the birth of Jacob's four eldest sons. Each of his sons has a name which illustrates Gospel truth.

Reuben. This is the beginning of the Gospel. The name means, ' See a son '. It was the Jewish nation living under the old covenant that brought God's Son into the world as to His human nature. At His birth the Lord looked indeed upon the nation and pointed them to His Son (Lk. 2. 11; Mt. 3. 17; 17. 5). The first movement of the sinner in response to the Gospel must be to see God's Son as his own personal Saviour and realise that Jesus is the Son of God. Every sinner, as he sees God's Son for the first time, says in his heart, ' Surely the Lord hath looked upon my affliction '. He realises God's eternal interest in him and His intervention in his life to deliver him from the bondage of guilt and sin. Similarly the Jewish nation, to whom we may perhaps liken Leah, realised the Lord's intervention. ' He hath visited and redeemed His people ' (Lk. 1. 68).

Now therefore my husband will love me. As he sees God's Son, the sinner realises that he enters into a new relationship of love to God. Whereas he was under God's wrath, he steps at conversion into the unhindered rays of the love of God. Not that God does not love and long for every sinner, but sin sets up a barrier which prevents God's love from effectually reaching the sinner. Faith in Christ removes the barrier.

VERSE 33. *Because the Lord hath heard that I was hated.* The next thing the sinner realises on conversion is that God has heard his prayer. If he prayed at all in his unconverted days, his prayers were ineffectual and appeared to receive no answer. Now he is able to pray. If he has been truly convicted and converted, he has poured out his misery and guilt into his Saviour's ear, and he realises that he has been heard. This fact governs all his Christian life.

GENESIS

Simeon means ' Hearing '.

VERSE 34. *Will my husband be joined unto me.* The next thing that the converted sinner realises is that Christ is joined to him. He becomes a member of His body (Eph. 1. 23; 5. 30), and he is joined in spirit to Christ (1 Cor. 6. 17). He abides in Christ, and Christ in him (Jo. 15. 3). This is the truth illustrated by the name of Leah's third son. The attitude of her mind and the direction of her desire were overruled by the Holy Spirit, so that the name should be given which would produce with the others a sequence of Gospel truth.

Levi means ' joined.'

VERSE 35. *Now will I praise the Lord.* The saved sinner after first seeing in Christ the Son of God appointed to be his Saviour, then realising that he is heard by God and joined to Christ, breaks out into praise to the Lord and sets out on a life which consists in His praise. In Christ we are to the praise of the glory of God's grace (Eph. 1. 6, 12, 14).

Judah means ' Praise.'

Left bearing, thus leaving these four names standing in a section by themselves as a complete indication of evangelical experience. Notice that they are the names of the children of Leah, who rather represents the old Israel. The realities of which the names speak are experiences to which the Jew is invited, experiences which the godly Jew was the first to share. There is thus a special emphasis on the name Judah with which the series ends, and a moving reminder that God's purpose for the Jew has always been to show forth His praise.

CHAPTER 30

THIS chapter gives us the further story of the increase of Jacob's family and of his sojourn with Laban. Rachel's maid Bilhah bears Jacob two sons (1-8). Leah then gives Zilpah to Jacob, and she also bears two sons (9-13). Leah then lures her husband from Rachel with the mandrakes found by Reuben and becomes the mother of two more sons and a daughter (14-21). Finally Rachel bears Joseph (22-24). Jacob then seeks to depart, but is detained by Laban, who accepts an arrangement made by Jacob that he should retain a certain proportion of the cattle (25-36). Laban tries to deprive Jacob of his hire, and Jacob tries by superstitious means to increase it (37-43). The chapter shows us the sovereign over-ruling hand of God and the faithless superstition of both Rachel and Jacob as well as the deceitful conduct of both uncle and nephew towards each other.

VERSE 1. *She bare Jacob no children.* Worse than Rachel's condition is spiritual barrenness. The Christian who is not winning others for Christ, whether directly or indirectly, is not fulfilling the purpose for which he has been taken into Christ's service. The purpose of our belonging to the One Who was raised from the dead is that we may bear fruit to God (Rom. 7. 4).

Rachel envied her sister. Consciousness of the lack of spiritual blessing or power is a source of envy against those who possess them. Before the coming of the Gospel the Gentile hated and oppressed the Jew, the unconverted man sometimes secretly envies the joy and victory of the converted, and the barren Christian shuns the company of those whose chief interest is that of winning others for Christ.

Said unto Jacob. She applied in the wrong place. In this she is followed by many an unconverted man and professing Christian. Many seek to remedy spiritual barrenness of which they are conscious by seeking to a priest or even to a psychiatrist or doctor, or undertaking religious exercise or burying themselves in work, or plunging into amusement.

Give me children. or else I die. In the intensity of her desire Rachel sets a good example to the people of God. She felt that motherhood was the only thing worth living for. If more

277

Christians felt the same about winning souls, it would not be long before revival broke out.

VERSE 2. *Jacob's anger was kindled.* He was angry because he felt helpless. The fervour of her desire had deprived her of common sense.

Am I in God's stead. Though he was angry, Jacob said the right thing and referred Rachel to God, to Whom she should have applied in the beginning. Believing prayer would have solved Rachel's problem. She would have obtained from God what she wanted, or else would have discovered the reason why it was best that it should not be granted, and would have been content. The secret of spiritual fruitfulness also lies in God alone.

Who hath withheld from thee the fruit of the womb? God gives and withholds according to His sovereign pleasure. He alone gives to the believer the grace of fruitfulness. Notice the use in this verse of the Divine title Elohim, not Jahweh. The reason is that a natural function is being dealt with, not anything that is peculiar to the redemptive purpose.

VERSE 3. *My maid Bilhah.* Rachel took the same step as Sarah had done (16. 1-3).

She shall bear upon my knees. This means in Rachel's stead and as her representative. The child would be reckoned as Rachel's, as if she had borne it. For the knees in connection with parturition see Job 3. 12.

That I may also have children by her. The Hebrew says, ' be built by her '. Parenthood was thought of among the Syrians and Hebrews as building a house or household. The ' house ' was a living house, and the idea is the basis of that of the living church, which is the house or household of Christ (Heb. 3-6). Every servant of the Lord is a fellow-builder with Christ of that house. Rachel seems to have meant here that she would obtain a family by Bilhah, and does not appear to be thinking of

subsequently having children herself. Yet modern psychology and experience seem to show that her instinct, as well as that of Sarah and subsequently of Leah (verse 9), was not wholly misplaced. The adoption of a child by an apparently barren woman sometimes results in her having one of her own.

VERSE 4. *She gave him Bilhah.* This appears to have been done at some sacrifice, real or apparent. In the same way it is the privilege of parents to give their children to the service of the Saviour, or for anyone to do the same in the case of those over whom they have any influence.

VERSE 5. This was the whole purpose of the union and of her mistress's dedication of her. The same is God's spiritual purpose for all who are united to Christ (Rom. 7. 4).

VERSE 6. In Rachel's description of what had occurred we find the threefold experience of the converted sinner.

God hath judged me. ' Judged ' here means ' vindicated ', so that we have (1) the fact of justification. Every believer is vindicated before God because the full claims of the Divine law are met in his case by the suffering and death of Christ. From the moment he believes he has a perfect standing with God. Judgment has been passed upon him, and he will not come into condemnation, but is passed from death to life (Jo. 5. 24).

Hath also heard my voice. (2) This is the second fact that the converted sinner realises. His cry for mercy and forgiveness has been heard and accepted. His need was anticipated by the Saviour's incarnation and death, and the ear of God is open to his prayer. *Hath given me a son.* (3) The point of this statement is that barrenness has been turned into fruitfulness. This is true also of every converted sinner. He is now in a position to please God, which he could not do before (Rom. 8. 8).

The righteousness of the law is fulfilled in him (Rom. 8. 4), and he is ready to bring forth fruit unto God (Rom. 7. 4). It is true that Rachel was not directly the mother of the child, but this is true of the believer also. All his works are wrought in him by Christ (Isa. 26. 12; Jo. 3 21; 15. 5; Phil. 2. 13).

Dan means judging. Rachel rightly selected as the name of her child the first of the three experiences which she mentions. It is the fundamental and most important of the three.

VERSE 7. *Bilhah Rachel's maid conceived again.* The despised slave-girl became fruitful. In the same way the Gentiles, who were utterly separated from God and distant from Him, have received the Gospel that has been preached to them and borne fruit to the glory of His Name (Gal. 3. 8; Eph. 2. 11-13).

VERSE 8. *With great wrestlings have I wrestled with my sister.* In naming Bilhah's elder son Rachel described the initial experiences of the Christian life. In the case of the younger she passes to the Christian's day-by-day post-conversion experience. We have already seen (29. 27) that in certain respects we may compare Leah to the old nature and Rachel to the new. The same aspect comes out here. In the Christian's heart the new nature wrestles with the old, locked in a deadly and life-long struggle (Rom. 7. 23; Gal. 5. 17). The Hebrew for ' great wrestlings ' is ' wrestlings of God '. This is a literal description of the wrestlings that go on in the heart of the believer. It is God's indwelling Spirit that lusteth against the flesh and is contrary to it.

I have prevailed. Wherever the Spirit and the flesh are locked in combat, the Spirit always has the victory in the end. Notice that the victory is expressed in fruitfulness.

Naphtali means ' My wrestling '

VERSE 9. *When Leah saw that she had left bearing.* The effect upon Leah of the birth of Bilhah's sons was the same as that which God intends the conversion of the Gentiles to have upon the Jews (Rom. 11. 11, 14).

She took Zilpah her maid, and gave her to Jacob to wife. Leah followed the example of Rachel. It will be a good day for the cause of Christ when the Jew follows the example of the Gentile in believing on the Saviour (Rom. 11. 15).

VERSE 10. *Zilpah Leah's maid bare Jacob a son.* Again the despised slave-girl proves fruitful where the married wife is barren (Gal. 4. 27).

VERSE 11. *A troop cometh.* This translation seems to be right in grammar but wrong in the meaning of the noun. The word ' Gad ' appears to mean ' Fortune ', not ' A troop '. The translation ' Fortune cometh ' appears in the Hebrew margin, the Targum of Onkelos, followed by the Syriac Peshitto version, and the Jerusalum targum. The Hebrew text, the Greek Septuagint version, and the Latin Vulgate version have ' With Fortune ', meaning, ' Fortunate am I '. It is not easy to catch Leah's meaning when she made this remark. The conception of ' fortune ' or ' chance ' was, and still is, superstitious and is derogatory to one who professes to worship the true God. In Isaiah 65. 11, where the same word Gad occurs, it is condemned. Leah may therefore be showing that she had not lost all her heathen ideas. This was very true of Old Testament Israel, and is true of many of the children of God. At the same time, if this is the meaning of the name Gad, the sequence of spiritual meanings associated with the names of the rest of Jacob's sons is broken. Perhaps Leah was using the word ' fortune ' in the sense of prosperity. If so, as she names her slave-girl's child, she expressed what is true of every believer on conversion. ' Prosperity cometh '. See Mt. 19. 29.

VERSE 12. See on verse 10.

VERSE 13. *Happy am I.* This again is true of the believer, not only at his conversion, but throughout his life, not only in this world but in that to come.

The daughters will call me blessed. All the people of God will congratulate the believer through the ages of eternity. He is to be an everlasting demonstration of the kindness and grace of God (Eph. 2. 7).

Asher means 'Happy'.

VERSE 14. In verses 14-21 we have the account of the births of Leah's last three children with the story of the incident that led up to this.

Reuben. At this time he might have been a child of any age between eight and thirteen.

The days of wheat harvest. Perhaps the boy went to help in the harvest or watch the work.

Mandrakes. These were plants resembling potatoes in their manner of growth with mauve flowers and yellow fruit. The fruit was generally and popularly believed to promote conception. The belief was superstitious and unscientific.

In the field. The field is the world (Mt. 13. 38), just the place where superstitions grow in abundance.

Brought them unto his mother Leah. The child may have done this as any child brings to his mother something new that takes his fancy, or he may have been old enough to appreciate the supposed function of the mandrakes.

Rachel said to Leah, Give me. She asked directly of the sister whom she envied out of an overbearing sense of need. Instead of resorting to the living God in prevailing prayer Rachel resorted to magic.

VERSE 15. *Taken my husband.* Just as Rachel was envious of Leah, so Leah was jealous of Rachel. What a miserable family life they had. No wonder the majority of Jacob's sons grew up to be men of bad character. The Bible never says in so many words that polygamy is contrary to God's mind. It does what is wiser

and better. It shows us pictures such as this of polygamous family life.

Wouldst thou take away my son's mandrakes also? Leah's anger shows the value that she set on the mandrakes. Both sisters were full of heathen superstition.

Therefore he shall lie with thee tonight for thy son's mandrakes. Rachel gave up the husband who loved her for a superstitious fruit. Many in the world make a similar choice. They lightly reject the Saviour Who loves them and gave Himself for them in order to possess instead some empty advantage which they ignorantly suppose is going to satisfy their deepest needs. Rachel seems to have known nothing of prayer and faith. She is more likely to have obtained what she longed for so desperately by having her husband with her that night than by ignorantly eating a fruit about which she had completely foolish ideas. If only men could be brought to see that Christ, and Christ alone, can satisfy their deepest needs. Instead of Him they will take any prescription that a devil-driven world can offer.

VERSE 16. Leah made the wise choice and had the best of the bargain. She was willing to let the mandrakes go if she could have her husband to herself. So to the believing Christian nothing in the world, its religions, its superstitions or its follies can be compared with the Lord Jesus Christ, Who is the chiefest among ten thousand (Cant. 5. 10, 16).

VERSE 17. *God hearkened unto Leah.* She had therefore been praying. Perhaps she had not prayed intelligibly. Perhaps what God heard was no more than a sigh in her heart. But it seems to have been in the right direction. She does not pray to Jahweh, the Lord of the redemptive purpose, but to Elohim, the God of nature. She is not thinking — naturally enough — of promises made to Abraham, but of her own material longings and her desire to capture her husband's heart.

She conceived. The answer to her prayer was to make her fruitful. The answers to our prayers will tend in the same direction.

VERSE 18. The Holy Spirit guides Leah in naming her three youngest children to lay the emphasis on the last day and the world to come.

God hath given me my hire. The hire or reward of every child of God is everlasting life (Mt. 19. 29). When the Lord comes, His reward will be with Him (Rev. 22. 12). Even in this life the believer receives an immense reward. Salvation and everlasting life are his already, and the Holy Spirit is in his heart.

Because I have given my maiden to my husband. Apart from her children who belonged to her husband already, her maiden was perhaps her most valuable possession. The sinner has nothing to give to Christ but himself. If he gives himself, he obtains the reward.

Issachar means ' Hire '. Leah's connection with the birth of her son of her giving Zilpah to Jacob may be not altogether ill-founded according to modern psychological ideas.

VERSE 19. *Leah conceived again.* She continued fruitful. The Lord has promised continual fruitfulness to all who abide in Him (Jo. 15. 5).

VERSE 20. *God hath endued me with a good dowry.* She meant that her six sons were a rich present with which to attract her husband's affection. We too, if we win others to Christ, are sure to get blessing from Him.

Now will my husband dwell with me. The central blessing of salvation and the ultimate aim of God in saving us are that He may dwell in our hearts for ever. This He does by His Holy Spirit from the moment of our conversion (Eph. 3. 17), but the fulness of His dwelling will be in the world to come (Rev. 21. 3).

Because I have born him six sons. When the trumpet sounds and the eternal world is set up, the time for evangelisation and the increase of the body will be over.

Zebulun means ' Dwelling '.

VERSE 21. *Afterwards she bare a daughter.* This was her youngest child.

Dinah means ' Judgment '. Thus the names of Leah's seven children take us right through the believer's spiritual life. They begin with the evangelist's finger pointing the sinner to the Son of God. They show us the sinner hearing the Gospel and joining himself to the Saviour to live a life of praise to Him. After an interval the end of all comes. The servant of Christ obtains his reward and enters into life where the Saviour dwells with him for ever, this taking place on the day of judgment at the end of the world. Notice that Leah says nothing at Dinah's birth as she had done at the birth of all her other children. This fact is also true to spiritual reality. On the day of judgment every mouth will be stopped (Rom. 3. 19). The guilty sinner will have nothing to say, neither will the saint be able to find words with which to express the love, mercy and grace of God.

VERSE 22. *God remembered Rachel.* Not that He had ever forgotten her. The expression which is often used in the Bible (e.g. Gen. 8. 1; 1 Sam. 1. 19; Rev. 16. 19) means that after a long delay, during which it might appear that God had forgotten, He suddenly acts. The expression also implies the attention, care and compassion of God.

God hearkened to her. This means that Rachel had at last been praying. At first she had turned in petulance to her husband (verse 1). This had only made him angry, and she had found the help of man to fail. Next she had turned to magic and superstition, supposing that the mandrakes would solve the problem (verse 14). Now at last she had begun to pray. It is not clear how long she had to wait before obtaining the answer. It may not have been long. In any case she obtained it, and found, as so many others have found, that prayer succeeded where human aid had failed.

Opened her womb. A prayer for fruitfulness is always after the mind of God.

VERSE 23. *She conceived, and bare a son.* Why had this natural fruitfulness not found its outlet before? It seems clear that her mind had been roving and anxious. She had such an intense desire for motherhood that it dominated her mind and defeated its own purpose. This corresponds spiritually to self-effort, that intense activity in the flesh which brings defeat to so many Christian lives. From this it seems that she turned to put her trust in God, if not to rest wholly in His will. *God hath taken away my reproach.* Just as barrenness was regarded as a reproach by women in the ancient east, so is spiritual barrenness a real spiritual loss and reproach. If we are neither bringing forth the fruit of the Spirit (Gal. 5. 22), nor winning souls for Christ, something is wrong with our spiritual lives.

VERSE 24. *Joseph* means 'Adding'. Here in one word is described the secret of a successful Christian life of service. Rachel's word was prophetic. She was looking to the future. She was not content with what had been achieved. She made Joseph all his life a monument of blessing and fruitfulness.

The Lord shall add to me another son. Notice the change in two sentences from Elohim to Jahweh. The theories of Wellhausen and similar critics can only be sustained here by those who are blinded by prejudice or obsessed with doctrinaire theory. In the matter of the birth itself and of her bodily powers she called on the Creator, the God of nature. She had come to know something however of her husband's God and of His great redemptive purposes and promises, and she realises that in building up her husband's family Jahweh is fulfilling them. So she enters by faith into the Redeemer's plan.

VERSE 25. In this verse and the following we find the account of Jacob's desire to go home, which was frustrated by Laban, and of the deceitful interplay between uncle and nephew, each trying fraudulently to make what he could out of the other.

When Rachel had born Joseph. The time seems to have coincided with the end of the fourteen years which Jacob served for the two sisters. Perhaps he felt that with the eleven sons and at least one daughter his family was now complete. He was accustomed to think of Joseph as ' the son of his old age ' (37. 3). When the great family of the church is complete and the Gospel has finished its work of gathering all in, it will be time to return home. *Laban* was turning into a taskmaster. He is becoming a picture of the world.

Send me away. This is a fruitless appeal. The world does not want from one point of view to get rid of the church. It is too much conscious of the social benefits that she has conferred upon it as by-products of the Gospel to wish to let her go altogether.

Unto mine own place, and to my country. This world is not the home of the people of God. They have a place of their own and a heavenly country (Heb. 11. 14-16).

VERSE 26. The devil, the world, sin and the flesh are all hard taskmasters. They will never let a man go unless compelled.

VERSE 27. *I pray thee, if I have found favour in thine eyes.* Laban veils his evil intentions beneath a cloak of politeness, as the world so often does.

I have learned by experience that the Lord hath blessed me for thy sake. This is a revealing remark. It would be true of every employer that employs a Christian man, or of anyone in the world that stands in any sort of social relationship with a believer. God blessed His servant and in blessing him blessed also those for whom he worked. In the same way those countries that have recognised the Gospel have been greatly blessed for the Gospel's sake. Notice that Laban uses the name Jahweh, or some equivalent Aramaic name which then or later could be properly rendered as Jahweh. He himself was heathen. He did not worship Jahweh, but the blessing that he had experienced taught him that Jahweh was real, and he acknowledges Him, intentionally or not, as the God of nature. The purpose of the blessing that God gives as a by-product of the Gospel always has as its aim the bringing of men to acknowledge the true God.

VERSE 28. Both the request and the statement in this verse were hypocritical. Laban did not mean to give Jacob anything but to get back from him what he could, as the sequel shows. The child of God often appears to be at the mercy of the hypocrisy of the world, but the blessing and protection of God counteracts its effect, as the rest of this narrative shows to have been the case with Jacob.

VERSE 29. *Thou knowest how I have served thee.* Jacob was with Laban as a servant. The Lord Jesus Himself was in the world as one who served (Mt. 20. 28; Lk. 22. 27), and it is our place also to be the same (Gal. 5. 13).

How thy cattle was with me. Jacob had a position of trust. We also should show ourselves by grace to be such men that we are instinctively given similar positions.

VERSE 30. *It was little which thou hadst before I came.* These words might be spoken by the Gospel to any country, family or group of men. They are true of our own country before the coming of the Gospel at the Reformation. It was little which she had before, no science, little culture, no sanitation, no political freedom, little knowledge of the way to God.

It is now increased unto a multitude. This was also true of our own country and of other Protestant nations. As a result of the coming of the Gospel at the Reformation the country obtained political freedom, more social justice, greatly widened culture, immense economic wealth, and increasing amenities due to the advance of scientific knowledge.

The Lord hath blessed thee since my coming. Blessing means prosperity and fruitfulness. These words are also profoundly true in the case of those countries to which the Gospel has come. The words ' since my coming ' are literally in Hebrew ' at my foot '. They might be translated, ' wherever I went '. Whichever translation be correct, the statement remains profoundly true of the Gospel.

When shall I provide for mine own house. The time will come when the temporal blessings that the Gospel bestows upon the nations which accept it will fail, and eternal provision will be made for the household of faith. Time will give place to eternity, this present evil world to the new heavens and earth, wherein dwelleth righteousness (2 Pet. 3. 13). The true church of Christ will enter her eternal home.

VERSE 31. *What shall I give thee?* The world wants to bribe the Gospel or to patronise Christ.

Thou shalt not give me anything. Christ and His church refuse to take anything from the world.

If thou wilt do this thing for me. The Gospel seeks from the world freedom to do what it wants and have its way with the flock.

I will again feed and keep thy flock. Jacob's interest was in the flock, as is that of the Good Shepherd in His sheep. ' And ye, my flock, the flock of my pasture, are men, and I am your Lord God ' (Ezek. 34. 31).

VERSE 32. *I will pass through all thy flock,* just as the Gospel passes through all the world.

Today. The Gospel is preached in time, not in eternity. ' Today is the day of salvation ' (2 Cor. 6. 2). ' The Holy Ghost saith, Today ' (Heb. 3. 7). *Removing from thence.* It is the function of the Gospel to remove and separate believers from this present evil world (Gal. 1. 4) and to set them apart as belonging to Christ.

Speckled and spotted among the cattle, that is to say, those that are stained by sin and unfit either for service or for sacrifice. Christ is ever the friend of sinners and seeks for them throughout the world, saying to them, ' Only acknowledge thine iniquity ' (Jer. 3. 13). Notice that the speckled and spotted are accepted just as they are. No attempt is made to change them — indeed to do so would be impossible — before they become the property of the Good Shepherd.

The brown cattle among the sheep, that is, those who are the colour of earth, of the earth, earthy. Christ's Gospel goes out to the unheavenly-minded.

The spotted and speckled among the goats, that is, stained with sin and unfit for sacrifice. *Of such shall be my hire.* The weary sin-stained worldling, whom the Saviour loves so deeply, becomes His in recompense for His sufferings on the cross.

VERSE 33. *So shall my righteousness answer for me in time to come.* The cattle would be a proof of Jacob's righteousness. In the same way the Good Shepherd's flock will be a proof of their Shepherd's righteousness in saving consistently with the Divine holiness. In the end His righteousness will be openly showed (Ps. 98. 2).

When it shall come for my hire before thy face. This means, when the question of Jacob's hire is brought before Laban. It will be found that Jacob possesses nothing but what he has a right to. It will be the same with Christ. He will be found to possess those whom He has bought for His own with His life-blood.

Every one that is not speckled and spotted. Christ did not come to call the righteous (Mt. 9. 13).

That shall be counted stolen. These words, even though they are hypothetical, could never be referred to Christ to Whom all men belong by right, but their force is that Jacob made no claim to any but the speckled and spotted. In the same way the Saviour gives no call to the self-righteous.

VERSE 34. Laban, who had now become envious and antagonistic to Jacob, readily agrees because he means to deceive him and prevent him from getting what he claimed. From this verse we learn the danger of the world's smile. If it professes to agree with us, its concealed purpose is to do the Gospel harm. It has some scheme to defraud us by putting us off with fair words.

VERSE 35. *He removed that day.* Laban took immediate steps to see that Jacob did not get what he himself had professed to agree was due to him. In the same way the devil and the world do all in their power to remove the sinner out of the reach of the Gospel. Like Laban they are quick and energetic in their work and sometimes put Christ's servants to shame.

Every one that had some white in it. Notice the difference in Laban's viewpoint from that of Jacob. Jacob does not mention white (verse 32). To him nothing is white that is not wholly white. Laban sees in the same sheep ' some white '. This is the viewpoint of the world and of most sinners about themselves. They realise that they are not entirely white— ' no one of course can be perfect ' — but the confused complex sinful heart appears to them to have ' some white ' in it — ' I have lived a good life '. Only the Holy Spirit can convince a man how great is the darkness within him, if the light that is in him be darkness (Mt. 6. 23). ' They that are in the flesh cannot please God ' (Rom. 8. 8). *Gave them into the hand of his sons.* This is exactly what the world and the devil do to those who need the Gospel, if they can keep them from hearing it. They are given into the hand of false religious teachers, or of communism, or of evil literature, or the influence of the radio, and of many other absorbing attractions and occupations, which guard them from all evangelical approach and keep them from hearing God's Word.

Verse 36. *He set three days' journey betwixt himself and Jacob*. This corresponds to the distance of the world from Christ. It is three days' distance from Him, the days of crucifixion, burial and resurrection. It is on the wrong side of the cross, separated by a great gulf from Christ. The believer on the other is crucified with Christ (Gal. 2. 19), buried with Him in baptism (Col. 2. 12), and raised together with Him (Eph. 2. 6).

Jacob fed the rest of Laban's flocks. Thank God that those who were once Laban's and have escaped the clutches of the world, the flesh and the devil, are fed by the Good Shepherd.

Verse 37. This and the following six verses tell us the means by which Jacob won his possessions and increased his flock. On Jacob's part they seem to have been clever, deceitful, superstitious and unscientific. In the following chapter we find it revealed to him that his success was not due to these means, but to the power and grace of his God (31. 10-12). This is not the first time in Jacob's life that God had allowed him to make use of low methods to bring about what proved to be the Divine purpose (see chapter 27), and just as we found in the former case that the methods concealed some illustration of spiritual truth, so it is in this case also.

Of green poplar, and of the hazel and chesnut tree. The tree in the Bible points to the cross (1 Pet. 2. 24). In the three kinds of tree here mentioned we may perhaps find three aspects of the cross. The poplar speaks of its abomination (Hos. 4. 13, the only other place of its occurrence), the hazel (occurring no where else in the Bible) speaks of its uniqueness, the chesnut (occurring elsewhere only in Ezek. 31. 8) speaks of its

beauty. First therefore Jacob set the cross in all its aspects before his flocks. He showed them that it was the scene of the judgment and curse of God, he showed them it was the only way by which God is reconciled to man, and he showed them that it was the revelation of God's love in all its glory and beauty.

Made the white appear. Next Jacob showed his flocks that the cross was the way to righteousness and holiness. He made the white appear. He showed them that they are justified through the redemption that is in Christ Jesus (Rom. 3. 24).

Verse 38. *He set the rods which he had pilled before the flocks in the gutters in the watering troughs when the flocks came to drink*. In this he was like a faithful preacher and evangelist, who lifts up the cross before the eyes of his thirsty people when they come to slake their spiritual thirst with the water of life which the Spirit gives them in the Word. Such preaching is as rare today as it is successful.

Conceive when they came to drink. A draught of the water of life is the way to make a sinner or a believer bring forth fruit to God (Rom. 7. 4), fruit which is unto holiness (Rom. 6. 22).

Verse 39. *The flocks conceived before the rods*. The way to become fruitful for God is to stand before the cross of Jesus.

Cattle ringstraked, speckled and spotted. Those who are begotten of the seed of the Word (1 Pet. 1. 23) and brought forth by the servants of Christ are by nature children of wrath as are the others (Eph. 2. 3). The corruption of their nature remains within them as children of God so long as they are in this world (1 Jo. 1. 8; Gal. 5. 17). Their safety and assurance lies in the fact that they belong to the Good Shepherd.

Verse 40. This verse tells us three things that Jacob did which showed his wisdom as a shepherd and pastor.

(1) *Jacob did separate the lambs*. This is most wise and far seeing. It is the work of the godly Sunday school teacher. To keep the lambs from defilement and evil association is one of the most deep-seated works for the kingdom of God. It is sometimes neglected today. If it were taken in hand more seriously, perhaps a more careful choice of school would be made, and at least the insidious convent schools would be avoided like the plague and seen to be what they are.

(2) *And set the faces of the flocks toward the ringstraked*. The wise pastor trains his flock to be soul-winners. He sets their faces towards the sinners and the earth-bound, who still belong to Laban, who are still in the grip of the devil and the world.

(3) *He put his own flock by themselves*. This is what the Good Shepherd does with His own, and the under-shepherds are wise to follow Him. ' Wherefore come ye out from among them, and be ye separate ', saith the Lord (2 Cor. 6. 17).

Put them not unto Laban's cattle. ' And touch not the unclean thing ' (2 Cor. 6. 17). Laban has plenty of religious cattle as well as worldly and vicious. There is a great deal of mixture of Christ's flock with worldly flocks today.

VERSE 41. We may regard this and the following verse as setting a standard for personal work in distinction from that of public preaching, which we may see in verses 37-39. There the cross was set before the eyes of all the cattle without distinction. Here a difference is made. We may regard the stronger cattle mentioned in this verse as corresponding to the elect, those to whom the Holy Spirit guides the evangelist. Alternatively we may regard the stronger cattle as being only those who conceived. In this case the verse would tell us that the cross of Jesus, appropriated by the believer, is the only way to holy fruitfulness. We must not forget also that the verse describes a literal act of what we might term ' sharp practice ' on the part of Jacob in order to get the better of his uncle Laban.

VERSE 42. *When the cattle were feeble*. No mention is made of conception here, though the narrative implies that it took place. These feeble cattle are a picture of the unconverted whom the apostle describes as being ' without strength ' (Rom. 5. 6).

VERSE 43. *The man increased exceedingly*. Jacob is again here a type of the Good Shepherd, of the increase of Whose government there shall be no end (Isa. 9. 7). John the Baptist knew of this increase and proclaimed it, although it meant his own decrease (Jo. 3. 30).

Notice the five things in which the increase was made. They typify the Saviour's increase. (1) *Much cattle*. These are the oxen, suitable both for patient service and for sacrifice. They represent the Christian worker (1 Cor. 9. 9, 10; 1 Tim. 5. 17, 18). While it remains true today as at the first that the labourers are few (Mt. 9. 37), yet the enormous increase in their numbers throughout the world today might astonish the apostles. (2) *Maidservants*. These are like the faithful women who in every age have served the Master so well. They were there in the beginning (see Phil. 4. 2, 3 and many of their names in Rom. 16. 3-16). Today women are the first to volunteer for the mission field, and the part that they play in the work of Christ as a whole proportionately exceeds that taken by men. (3) *Menservants*. These are spiritually much the same as the cattle. The reference to them here emphasises the need for them equally with the maidservants. What a privilege to be among these cattle or these menservants. The Lord Who could do all by the breath of His mouth deigns to use our service, and we are apt to forget that having done what is commanded us, we are still unprofitable servants. (4) *Camels*. The camel in the Bible is the picture of the rich man of the world. It is an obstinate, unclean, rather stupid and rather vicious animal. It is a comforting assurance that the camels belong to the Lord. Though they do not know it, yet He uses their services to set forward the Gospel. Their money and their influence provide channels for it in many ways. Their industries provide transport for the missionary and evangelist, paper for the printing of Bibles and tracts, food and houses for the Lord's servants, and many other things of which Christian people may take advantage. (5) *Asses*. As opposed to the camels, these are the ordinary patient working people of the world. They are not clean animals. Their intelligence is limited, and their behaviour is sometimes unrestrained and not always predictable. But the Lord uses them in countless ways in the work of the Gospel. Their contribution is unintelligent, and their only hope is to undergo by the Gospel a transformation of nature. All of us were born asses. The Holy Spirit has turned those of us who believe into Christ's sheep, but we have many reminders of the original assinine nature within.

CHAPTER 31

THIS chapter gives us the story of Jacob's flight from Laban and his departure for his own country. Its two chief lessons are (1) the sovereign power and providence of God, and (2) the deceitfulness of sinful human nature, seen at work in Laban and Rachel, if not again in Jacob himself.

VERSE 1. *The words of Laban's sons*. The devil speaks through his sons who are in the world (Jo. 8. 44; 1 Jo. 3. 8, 12).

Jacob hath taken away all that was our father's. In the same way Jesus Christ was manifested to undo the works of the devil (1 Jo. 3. 8). He has spoiled principalities and powers and made a show of them openly (Col. 2. 15). He has led captive and given gifts to men (Eph. 4. 2). In the end the devil will be left destitute, defeated and destroyed, thank God (Rom. 16. 20; Rev. 20. 10).

Of that which was our father's hath he gotten all this glory. The glory of the Lord Jesus comes to Him from His people (Rev. 5. 13; 7. 10), all of whom were born in Satan's kingdom, children of wrath (Eph. 2. 3) and in bondage to sin (Rom. 6. 17). Once they walked according to the prince of the power of the air (Eph. 2. 2), but they have been won from the devil by the Saviour's meritorious life of obedience and substitutionary blood-shedding.

VERSE 2. *It was not toward him*. The world may welcome the Gospel as long as it thinks it may hold some advantages for it. The crowds welcomed Christ when they found they could be healed of physical disease. But when the world realises that Christ has come by the Gospel to despoil it, it becomes hostile. The world is jealous of the Christian's blessing, though it will not submit to the conditions necessary for obtaining it.

VERSE 3. *The Lord said unto Jacob*. Notice the name Jahweh. God spoke to Jacob as the God of the covenant, intending to fulfil in him the promises and pledges of the redemptive purpose. He spoke either in a dream or vision, or by an impression in Jacob's mind.

Return. This is a favourite word with God. He calls the sinner to return to Himself and the wandering saint to return to the right way. Jacob had been in the land of his fathers and among his kindred before. The people of God have only been so in eternity past in the mind of God, and not in actual experience. What a day that will be when they see the land for the first time (2 Pet. 3. 13) and are each found among their kindred (Gal. 3. 26, 28; Eph. 4. 6; Heb. 2. 11).

I will be with thee. This promise covers every need and meets every eventuality. To have the presence of God is to have His favour, His protection, His wisdom, His strength, His guidance and His blessing. It is fulfilled in every believer (1 Cor. 6. 19; Eph. 3. 17).

VERSE 4. This verse gives us the picture of the heavenly Bridegroom calling the bride into the world to the flock. She is called to ' follow the Lamb whithersoever He goeth ' (Rev. 14. 4). His interests are in the world with the flock that needs His care. The same call comes to us His people. We are not to linger at home. We are to go to the world unto His flock. There we shall find Him. We shall find too that it is by this way that He is calling us to accompany Him to His own country.

VERSE 5. *It is not toward me as before.* The world is hostile to Christ and His Gospel. It may at first be curious and interested, it may feel that some advantage is to be got out of the Gospel, but when it discovers its true nature, it quickly turns against it.

The God of my father hath been with me. The hostile intentions of Laban were frustrated at every step by the care and protection of God. So it is with us. God watches over His people in the world and guards His Gospel. They may suffer hardship and adversity at the hands of those who are ill-disposed towards them, but they can never be ultimately harmed. The presence of God and the knowledge of doing His will compensate for all that a hostile world can do.

VERSE 6. If the statement of this verse is true of Jacob and Laban, it is also true of Christ and mankind. With all His power the Saviour ministered to the world, and in giving His life for sin almost outstripped the power of His human nature, as may be seen from His agony in Gethsemane. If He did so, it is our duty as His people to serve mankind with all our power, to seek by the Gospel to draw them to Christ in the face of their indifference and misunderstanding, and faithfully to denounce the wickedness of sin.

VERSE 7. *Your father hath deceived me.* The devil was a liar from the beginning (Jo. 8. 44), and the essence of sin is deceit. The believer should never be deceived by false prophets (Mt. 24. 4), but he is sometimes deceived by the changeableness of those who hear the Gospel, not knowing whether they intend to believe, or merely pretend to do so.

My wages. The only wages that the servant of Christ expects to receive in respect of the Gospel are precious souls won from sin to the Saviour. *God suffered him not to hurt me.* The title Elohim (God) is here proper in place of Jahweh for two reasons: (1) Jacob is speaking to his wives who were brought up heathen, and therefore knew nothing of the covenant Name Jahweh, although they were beginning to learn its meaning; (2) the action of God of which Jacob was speaking was in the realm of nature. How many times in countless ways is this statement true of the believer. He is protected from permanent spiritual harm. The devil may rage, but God frustrates all his evil purposes.

VERSE 8. Notice how God took Laban at his word and caused his schemes to work out for the great advantage of Jacob (Rom. 8. 28).

VERSE 9. Cattle are clean beasts, fit for service and sacrifice. They represent the servants of Christ (1 Cor. 9. 9; 1 Tim. 5. 18). At first they belong to Laban, slaves of sin (Jo. 8. 34) and children of wrath (Eph. 2. 3), but by the action of the Holy Spirit through the Gospel they are taken away from the devil and the world and given to Christ. All that come to Christ have been given to Him by the Father (Jo. 5. 37; 17. 6-8).

VERSE 10. This and the two verses following provide the secret of the apparent success of Jacob's scheme described in 30. 37-42. Jacob's action was not the cause of his success but the working of God. Jacob saw in a dream what he could not see with his eyes. Perhaps the cattle, or some of them, were outwardly white. Perhaps what Jacob saw was something of the hidden mechanism of heredity, the production of ring-straked cattle through the tranmission of features that did not appear in the generation immediately preceding. Perhaps he witnessed a supernatural act of God. In any case, whether by natural or supernatural means, God was at work for him.

VERSE 11. *The angel of God.* This is the pre-incarnate Christ, the second Person of the Holy Trinity. The word ' angel ' appears to be used here and in other similar passages, not in the sense of ' messenger ', but in that of ' replica ', or ' exact representative '. It is exactly in this sense that Christ is the Angel of God (Heb. 1. 3).

Spake unto me in a dream. If Jacob is referring to the communication spoken of in verse 3, we have here the method by which it was made.

Jacob. God knows each one of His servants, and calls each one by his name.

Here am I. Note the ready response and the personal address.

VERSE 12. *All the rams which leap upon the cattle.* In this dream God assured Jacob that the effects which he had made such efforts to create were being brought about, not by the superstitious methods that he had put into operation, but by the sovereign action of the God of nature. From this fact we learn (1) that we ought not to rely on our own methods and contraptions, and that effects which we may believe due to them may have no connection with them at all. (2) We learn that God acts on our behalf in spite of our foolish self-effort and does for us what we vainly suppose we have done for ourselves.

I have seen all that Laban doeth unto thee. God sees all that our enemies do to us. He knows the extent to which we are exposed to the rage of the devil, the contempt of the world and the depredations of the flesh. He watches over us, taking steps behind the veil to make His blessing effective and to counteract the steps taken by our enemies.

VERSE 13. *I am the God of Bethel.* God means that He is the same God as appeared to Jacob at Bethel, and that He is prepared to fulfil the promises that He made to him there. He takes Jacob back to his first personal spiritual experience, at any rate the first that is recorded. It is good to be reminded as we read God's Word that our spiritual life and blessing are built upon the foundation of the great transaction that took place at our first meeting with God, which contained the potentialities of all that follows.

Where thou anointedst the pillar. The pillar set up by Jacob at Bethel was a picture of Christ standing in the house of God, our surety and advocate perpetually in the presence of God. The pillar is anointed just as the Holy Ghost anoints Christ as prophet, priest and king. Jacob's anointing of the pillar means that he recognises and appropriates Christ as his prophet, priest and king. *Where thou vowedst a vow unto me.* At the same time as Jacob appropriated Christ he dedicated his life to God, so that his transaction at Bethel becomes a picture of every true conversion.

Arise, get thee out from this land. This is the call that comes from God both to every sinner and everyone of His children. He calls us to be saved from this crooked generation (Acts 2. 40) and to come out from among them and be separate (2 Cor. 6. 17), and He says that the purpose of the Lord Jesus Christ in giving Himself for our sins was to deliver us from this present evil world (Gal. 1. 4).

Return unto the land of thy kindred. This also is part of God's call to His lost ones. To separate oneself from this present evil world is to return to God. The prodigal son came to himself and said that he would return to his father (Lk. 15. 18). ' Return, thou backsliding Israel, saith the Lord ' (Jer. 3. 12). The turning of conversion is a return to the Lord.

VERSE 14. *Rachel and Leah*. The bride throws in her lot with the Bridegroom. This is what all the people of God are called upon to do. *Is there yet any portion or inheritance for us in our father's house?* There is none. The father they speak of is their natural father, not their heavenly Father. The devil and the world can give the sinner nothing in the end. The world is passing away (1 Jo. 2. 17; 1 Cor. 7. 31). Even if he gains the whole of it, the sinner profits nothing if he loses his own soul (Lk. 9. 25). ' Hearken, O daughter, and consider, and incline thine ear: forget also thine own people, and thy father's house: so shall the king greatly desire thy beauty ' (Ps. 45. 10, 11). The bride of Christ finds that God is her portion for ever (Ps. 73. 26), and that she has an inheritance, incorruptible and undefiled and that fadeth not away, reserved in heaven for her (1 Pet. 1. 4).

VERSE 15. *Are we not counted of him strangers?* The world always counts the members of the true church as strangers. The Lord Jesus Christ told us not to marvel if the world hate us (Jo. 15. 18; 1 Jo. 3. 13). The world does not understand or appreciate Christian principles or standards. *He hath sold us.* The world sells all its children into slavery to sin.

Devoured also our money. The child of the world who is sold into sin obtains no advantage from the price that is paid for him. That price is consumed, spent and thrown away by the world on the vain things that go to make up its life. Alternatively (though not so easily with the context) we may regard the expression ' our money ' as referring to the inheritance which the children expected to receive from their father. Neither from this do they obtain any advantage. It is squandered and gone. On the day of judgment each will find that he has nothing. The children of God like Rachel and Leah discover this fact in time, and throwing in

their lot with the heavenly Bridegroom, find the heavenly inheritance to be theirs.

VERSE 16. *All the riches which God hath taken from our father, that is ours, and our children's.* Throughout the Gospel dispensation the resources of the world are taken from it by God and used for the advancement of His glory, the good of His church, and the progress of the Gospel. Roman rule and Roman roads contributed to these, and in modern days the beneficial results of scientific knowledge have played their part in the spread of the Gospel. Even the murderous bombs have created a psychological atmosphere that has proved favourable to the preaching of the Word. Similarly the Kingdom of God was taken from the Jews and given to the true Israel (Mt. 21. 43; 1 Pet. 2. 9). On the day of judgment the belongings of the world will be finally taken away and given to those who have turned their possessions to the advantage of their Lord (Mt. 25. 28, 29).

Now then, whatsoever God hath said unto thee, do. This is advice that fits every man, sinner or saint, under every conceivable circumstance. It is one of the broad fundamental principles of the Bible, spoken originally by Rachel and Leah with reference to the particular occasion, but introduced by the Holy Spirit into the sacred text with the intention of striking the reader and opening his eyes to the fact that the words fit his own circumstances. This is a text for ' Daily Light ', suitable at any time and in any context. God generally speaks to us by His Word. The text is therefore a challenge to us to know the commands of Scripture and to see that we are obeying them. God may speak equally clearly through circumstances, or He may give us *ad hoc* guidance by an impression in our mind. In all these cases also this text holds good. It is perhaps particularly applicable when we are urging a sinner to escape from the corruptions of the world and find a refuge in Christ.

VERSE 17. *Then Jacob rose up.* So the heavenly Bridegroom rises up to the help of His people (Dan. 12. 1). He did so when He rose victorious from the grave. He did so in fact when He was born in Bethlehem and as He died upon the cross. He did so when He sent the Holy Spirit from heaven, and He does so again and again as occasions of need continually arise.

His sons. This is a proper name for Christ's people (see Heb. 2. 13).

His wives. This is a picture, though a poor one, of the one spotless bride of Christ (Eph. 5. 25-32; Rev. 19. 7, 8).

Upon camels. The resources of the rich and influential men of the world are used in spite of themselves and often without their knowledge to advance the Gospel and so to carry God's people away safe to heaven. The camel is a picture in the Bible of the rich man.

VERSE 18. *He carried away.* The Lord Jesus Christ carries safely away all who belong to Him out of this world. Dying with Christ from the rudiments of the world (Col. 2. 20), raised with Him (Col. 3. 1) and seated with Him in the heavenly places (Eph. 2. 6), His people find that their life is hid with Him in God (Col. 3. 3). Of all that the Father has given Him He will not lose one, but will raise it up at the last day (Jo. 6. 39), bearing it safe in resurrection glory to His Father's home.

All his cattle. These are His faithful servants who have worked for Him in the world and have been ready to lay their lives on the altar as living sacrifices.

All his goods which he had gotten. These are the spoil from among mankind, won by the Saviour's toil and suffering and death, precious souls, whom He gathers out of every nation under heaven (Rom. 15. 16). Once they were Laban's, but they have been gotten by Jacob for himself.

The cattle of his getting. These are the faithful servants and the sacrificed

lives that His cross had won and inspired.

In Padan-Aram. Here in exile in this world, away from the Father's bosom and far from His heavenly home the Saviour won His subjects and servants to Himself by His suffering and death.

For to go to Isaac his father in the land of Canaan. The Saviour has returned in triumph and glory to the Father's throne, but He has not returned empty-handed. He is the forerunner (Heb. 6. 20) of a great multitude that no man can number out of every nation and people and tribe and tongue (Rev. 7. 9), who are His for ever.

VERSE 19. *Laban went.* A better translation would be ' had gone '. He was away looking after his own interests.

To shear his sheep. Laban was engaged in depriving his own people of all that belonged to them for his own advantage.

Rachel had stolen the images that were her father's. The images were teraphim (see margin), or household gods, figurines made of clay, or perhaps metal to which incense might be burned. They were supposed to possess and exercise potent influence. They were to be found probably in every heathen household. We are not told what Rachel's motive was in stealing them. It is scarcely conceivable that she did so from a spiritual point of view in a desire to deprive her father of means of heathen worship. The use of the word ' stolen ' and our knowledge of Rachel's outlook and background make it reasonably certain that she believed in their power, and that she took them supposing that their possession would bring her help and good fortune, and that her father might be deprived of the power of harming her husband. Rachel, like the visible church, had not left her heathenism behind her. She started on the journey to the promised land, but she took with her the symbols of heathenism and all that they stood for.

VERSE 20. Laban was quite taken by surprise. In the same way the devil and the world were taken by surprise by the victorious outcome of the Saviour's death and by His resurrection. The Man-child was caught safely up to the Father's throne out of reach of the devil (Rev. 12. 5).

VERSE 21. *He fled with all that he had.* In the same way the Saviour escaped by resurrection from the power of all His enemies. He that sitteth in the heavens laughed them to scorn, and in spite of all that they could do, set His king upon His holy hill of Sion (Ps. 2. 4, 6). But Christ not only escaped Himself from the power of the devil and death, He brings with Him all His people. *He rose up.* This was the very way by which the Saviour escaped. He rose the third day according to the Scriptures (1 Cor. 15. 4). The actions of Jacob, as they are here described by the Holy Ghost, become types of the great redemptive acts of Christ.

Passed over the river. The river was not the Jordan, which throughout the Bible is typical of death, but the Euphrates, which is the boundary of the promised land (15. 18). After His resurrection Christ entered in Person the world to come, or heavenly land, where He now is at God's right hand as our forerunner (Heb. 6. 20) and advocate (1 Jo. 2. 1). We also are seated there with Him in spirit by faith (Eph. 2. 6).

Set his face toward the mount Gilead. So the great journey of the church, with her Bridegroom at her head, through the Gospel age began. It remains unfinished, but seems to be near its end.

VERSE 22. *On the third day.* This was the moment at which the world became aware that the Lord had escaped death and could be reached or touched by the devil no more (1 Cor. 15. 4).

VERSE 23. *He took his brethren with him.* Laban's brethren were his relatives and the members of his household. The devil associates with him those who belong to him in the world in his persecution of the church.

Pursued after him seven days' journey. The devil pursues Christ by persecuting His people (Acts 9. 5; Rev. 12. 13, 15).

Overtook him in the mount Gilead. The devil finds the company of Christian people safe indeed beyond the Euphrates within the compass of the land, but in a place where they are still exposed to his attacks. This is exactly the position of the true church in this world.

VERSE 24. *God came to Laban.* God intervened to protect His people, as He always does when necessary, restraining Laban as He restrains Satan (Job 1. 12; 2. 6).

Either good or bad. The Hebrew says literally, ' from good to bad ' This means *either* that he was to say nothing to Jacob at all, nothing, that is to say, decisive that related to his flight and departure, *or* that, having once been good to him, he was not now to turn and do him harm. On either interpretation the effect is substantially the same.

VERSE 25. *Laban overtook Jacob.* In the providence of God the devil can overtake and approach the people of God while they are still on their journey in this world, but cannot do them harm.

Jacob had pitched his tent. He was on a journey and had no permanent dwelling-place. So are the people of God as they escape from their bondage to sin and make their way to the heavenly land. They are also pilgrims and dwell in tents.

In the mount. It is good to pitch on the mountain of prayer, adoration and communion with God. Here we are safe from all the evil intentions of the devil.

Pitched in the mount of Gilead. The devil and the world can intrude into the very place of prayer and communion. We ought not to think that we can certainly be rid of their presence there. Thoughts may wander and evil may enter the mind.

CHAPTER 31 (CONTINUED)

VERSE 26. Laban has the temerity to reproach Jacob, as if he had wronged him. In the same way the world sometimes supposes that it has been wronged by Christ and the Gospel.

Stolen away unawares to me. No wrong was done to the Jews and other enemies of Christ by their not being aware of the purpose of God to raise Christ from the dead, although as a matter of fact they were amply warned of it, feared that the resurrection would take place and took vain steps to prevent it (Mt. 27. 62-66).

Carried away my daughters. Laban conveniently forgot that his daughters were now Jacob's wives, and that Jacob had the right to them. In the same way the world refuses to recognise that those who have been converted no longer belong to it, but have been purchased by Christ (Jo. 17. 16; 1 Cor. 6. 20).

Captives taken with the sword. Christ has spoiled principalities and powers (Col. 2. 15), led captivity captive (Eph. 4. 8), and delivered us from the power of darkness (Col. 1. 13).

VERSE 27. *Flee away secretly.* Laban repeats and emphasises his reproach, but Jacob's action was due to Laban's own treatment of him. *Steal away from me '.* The Hebrew says, ' Hast stolen me '. Laban seems to have felt that he had suffered in his whole state and position by Jacob's departure. This is certainly true of the devil and the world in relation to the resurrection of Christ and His going into heaven. He is defeated and spoiled.

That I might have sent thee away. Laban pretends that he would have given Jacob a great send-off. Similarly the world sometimes asserts its friendship to the Gospel and complains that it is regarded with suspicion. The world knows no true mirth, songs or music.

VERSE 28. *Hast not suffered me to kiss my sons and my daughters.* This is the last thing that was desirable. The kiss of the world is dangerous and poisonous. ' The kisses of an enemy are deceitful ' (Prov. 27. 6). Laban persists in regarding Leah and Rachel and their children as his, disregarding the fact that they now belong to Jacob. The attitude of the world towards the people of God is the same.

Thou hast now done foolishly. The world always thinks that the Gospel is foolishness and the believer a fool (1 Cor. 1. 21; 2. 14).

VERSE 29. *It is in the power of my hand to do you hurt.* The world is always in this position apart from the restraining hand of God. It often tries to do us hurt by persecution and by other means. It does not realise that it cannot essentially touch us (Mt. 10. 28; Heb. 13. 6).

But the God of your father. The intervention of God makes the essential difference. The hand of God is always outstretched to protect and save His people and His eyes run to and fro throughout the whole earth to show Himself strong on their behalf (2 Chron. 16. 9). Sometimes, perhaps usually, God restrains by the force of circumstances. Here He spoke definitely to Laban.

VERSE 30. *Though thou wouldest needs be gone.* Laban, perhaps grudgingly, recognises the necessity for Jacob's departure. So the world, if it realises that the hand of God is over the church, understands and agrees that it does not belong to it.

Because thou sore longedst after thy father's house. This is the longing that should be in the heart of every child of God as he looks for the blessed hope (Tit. 2. 13) and for the time when he will be a pillar in his Father's house and never go out any more (Rev. 3. 12).

Wherefore hast thou stolen my gods? The world always objects to interference with its religion. It has a comfortable smooth worldly respectable religion with no cross, that makes, if any, only congenial demands.

VERSE 31. *Because I was afraid*. This is not intended, nor was it understood, as an answer to the question of verse 30, but to those of verses 26-28. The heavenly Bridegroom is never afraid of the devil, but He takes steps to draw His people away from the world and protect them from the devil's power.

Thou wouldest take by force thy daughters from me. The devil longs to get back into his power those who were once in his prisons, but have been set free and purchased by Christ. The extent of his desire to do so may be measured by the importunity and success with which he wooes those who have made a profession of Christ's Name without a real work of regeneration having been done in their hearts. Yet neither by force, nor by fraud, nor by subtlety, can the devil ever tear away from the Saviour those who belong to Him. Their life is hid with Christ in God (Col. 3. 3). They shall never perish, and no one can pluck them out of their Shepherd's hand (Jo. 10. 28). Nothing can separate them from the love of God that is in Christ Jesus their Lord (Rom. 8. 38, 39).

VERSE 32. *Let him not live*. Jacob had no idea that he was in effect sentencing his beloved Rachel to death. Yet he was right. He was thinking not so much perhaps of the theft as of the defilement of idolatry among his people. Idolatry is a great sin. The Bible makes clear that nothing can be more dangerous than religion. It is like fire, a valuable servant but a deadly master. There are Christian churches today that are false in name and heathen in doctrine and practice. Some, even among the sound and true, fail to realise the danger of compromise with heathenism and apostasy. Lack of vision and fear of man have deprived us of the courage and clear-sightedness of our Puritan fathers.

Ritualism, sensuousness, the doctrine of personal merit, are the marks of the unconverted. They will bring a soul to final condemnation, and they will damage the spiritual lives of true Christians who may be caught in their toils. Indulgence in them will bring a church to its death and cause its candlestick to be removed out of its place (Rev. 2. 5).

Before our brethren. Laban is openly challenged. So Christ has thrown down the gauntlet to the devil and the world.

What is thine with me. Christ desires nor takes nothing from the world. It may keep its rags, its pride and filth and corrupt religion.

Take it to thee. Laban may have his own idols. They have no value for Jacob. Let us leave to the world what belongs to it, make a clean separation from all and follow our Redeemer on the road to the heavenly land.

Jacob knew not. There is nothing that Christ does not know, but the point of this statement is that Jacob had no responsibility for the theft of the teraphim. It was altogether Rachel's. Christ has no part in the mingling of heathenism with the worship of His church. The weak, wayward faithless church has introduced it herself without consulting Him.

VERSE 33. Notice the separate tents, comprising together a single company. During the days of the journey Jacob had a separate tent. In the same way in this Gospel age, while the church is on the march, the Bridegroom has, as it were, a separate tent in heaven. In fact He dwells already in the eternal home. The existence of the other tents in the case of Jacob's family was not ideal. They demonstrated his polygamy. They illustrate the division of the church into a variety of denominations, a fact that is clearly contrary to the will of God (and could be quickly rectified by the exhibition of a modicum of patience, vision and give-and-take). Yet notice that Jacob was lord of all the tents.

They may have entertained feelings of jealousy and bitterness against each other, but they all looked to him as their lord and bridegroom. However much they may have been divided among themselves, they were yet one company, because they were united under the lordship of Jacob. They were one because of him and in him and under him. So it is with the feeble divided church. The relationship of all to Christ makes them one in a unity which can never be broken. It cannot be made, or established, by so-called oecumenical movements, which ignore the truth and the Scriptures, or by any other equally empty means. It exists in Christ. It is to be kept, not made (Eph. 4. 3). The order in which Laban entered the tents is that which would be natural were they standing in a circle There were altogether five tents. Leah's was next to Jacob's on one side. Those of the maidservants were farthest from Jacob's, beyond Leah's and between hers and Rachel's. Passing round the circle he came to Rachel's, which was again next to Jacob's. The description of the tents carries a further implication in its wording. In the last two sentences of the verse the omission of the maidservants implies that they are grouped with Leah. There was a longer space between the maidservants and Rachel than between them and Leah. Leah was closer to the maidservants than she was to Jacob. This implies that Rachel was conspicuously close to Jacob. It is true that he did not know that she had betrayed him in the matter of the idols. Yet this could hardly have been an isolated act. He had had twenty years in which to observe the fickleness of her character. Yet he loved her, and loved her best of all. What a picture of the Saviour!

Verse 34. *Rachel had taken the images.* She was clearly aware of the sentence pronounced by Jacob. She had not left her tent, but had heard the argument between Laban and Jacob being carried on hotly and loudly in the clear air outside. She did two things with the images which went far to counteract the superstitious belief in their efficacy which had induced her to steal them. (1) She *put them in the camel's furniture.* This means either the harness or the fodder. She hid them away. What gods to be hidden away out of sight. In putting them moreover in the camel's furniture she associated them with an unclean beast. By contact with the camel's furniture they perhaps became unclean. She gave them their right place. (2) She *sat upon them.* What gods to be sat upon. She must have killed any belief in them that she might have entertained. Instinctively she knew that they could not protect her, and she put them to humiliation.

Laban searched all the tent. For 'searched' the Hebrew has 'felt'. What anxious moments as the merciless hands of Laban, probing and poking, moved stealthily over all that was in the tent.

But found them not. No, nor can the devil find anything of his in the tent of a believer's heart and life, though he accuse us before our God day and night (Rev. 12. 10). The prince of this world came and found nothing in the Saviour (Jo. 14. 30), nor can he find anything in the elect, for who can bring any charge against them (Rom. 8. 33)? His evil hands may probe and search and poke and feel, but all is whiter than snow, washed white in the blood of the Lamb. And if we feel or find them searching, it is good to remember that the search will prove vain and can only demonstrate the completion of the Saviour's perfect work and Satan's defeat and discomfiture.

Verse 35. *Let it not displease my lord that I cannot rise up before thee.* Notice the courtesy and respect that Rachel showed to Laban. Christians should always take care to do the same. No unconverted person is won by rudeness. Many are repelled by it. *The custom of women is upon me.*

She meant that she was passing through her menstrual period. In the east women remain at such times resting in their tents. Under Jewish law the woman was at this time ceremonially unclean, and this is the association that readers after the time of Moses (if not before it) would give to the passage . If Rachel's statement were true, the situation would not only point to providential protection on God's part, but would have forced Rachel to put the idols in their proper place and demonstrate their uncleanness. Objects associated with her in such circumstances became unclean. Thus the complete humiliation of these heathen idols took place. If Rachel's statement were false and merely a device for escaping her father's search, it means that in effect she made and declared herself unclean owing to her association with the idols. Such is the actual result of all association with heathen religion, whether in the case of ancient Israel or in that of the Christian church.

He searched, but found not. See on verse 34. The corrupt nature of the elect persisting in them after justification is covered and hid by the robe of Christ's righteousness until the day of resurrection, when it will disappear for ever. This robe is the gift of God's love, which covers a multitude of sins (1 Pet. 4. 8).

Verse 36. *Jacob was wroth, and chode with Laban.* Christ's just anger falls upon the devil, His people's accuser and enemy. Satan will shortly be beaten down under our feet (Rom. 16. 20). He will be cast into the lake of fire (Rev. 20. 10) and put out of existence for ever (Ezek. 28. 19).

What is my trespass? What is my sin? The Saviour spoke similar words which carried a wider, more substantial and an absolute meaning. 'Which of you convinceth me of sin?' (Jo. 8. 46). He was found sinless by the Jews, pronounced faultless by Pilate (Jo. 18. 38), declared righteous by the Roman centurion (Lk. 23. 47), and proclaimed by inspired apostles as the Sinless One (1 Pet. 2. 22; 1 Jo. 3. 5; 2 Cor. 5. 21).

Hotly pursued after me. Christ does nothing to deserve the world's hatred and persecution. His presence in it was the proof of God's love to it (Jo. 3. 16). Yet the world hates Him and seeks to destroy His people. Jacob had done Laban nothing but good, yet he pursued, and could have had no other object in doing so but to destroy him.

Verse 37. *Thou hast searched.* (See on verse 34).

What hast thou found? See on verse 34.

Set it here before my brethren and thy brethren. On the day of judgment the devil will be challenged to show what fault he can find in the children of God. There will be two similar companies, ' my brethren ' and ' thy brethren ', present then (Mt. 25. 40).

Verse 38. *This twenty years.* The Saviour was even longer in the world (Jo. 16. 28) in the form of a servant (Phil. 2. 7).

Thy ewes and thy she goats. Jacob's service had been faithful. Even more so was the Lord's. Ours should be the same in all earthly matters.

Have I not eaten. Jacob obtained no personal advantage out of Laban. The Saviour certainly obtained none out of the world, and we should be the same in this respect. Jacob's principles did not prevent him from accepting his agreed wages, nor need ours.

Verse 39. *I bare the loss of it.* The Saviour restored to God on the cross that which He took not away (Ps. 69. 4). There were demanded of Him all that were torn of the beasts of sin, or stolen openly or secretly by the devil.

Verse 40. This verse might be a description of the Lord's toil and sorrow. He was ' a man of sorrows, and acqauinted with grief' (Isa. 53. 3).

VERSE 41. *Twenty years*. The Lord Jesus Christ was for over thirty-three years in the inhospitable house of the world.

Thy two daughters. Christ's service and suffering won Him a bride (Eph. 5. 25-27).

Thy cattle. Christ's service and suffering also won Him a company of faithful servants, whom the cattle portray (1 Cor. 9. 9), who will serve Him for ever and see His face (Rev. 22. 3).

Thou hast changed my wages. Laban behaved all the time with dishonesty and shabbiness. In the providence of God this happened in order that Jacob might realise the meaning of his own deceitful conduct towards his father. He found himself the victim of what he had practised.

Ten times. This appears to be a Hebraism for many times, and is not necessarily literal.

VERSE 42. *Except the God of my father*. In these words two important statements of faith are made by Jacob. (1) He attributes his blessing to God *alone*. This is implicit in the word 'Except'. Jacob was right. All blessing and all deliverance, whether for him, for us, or for any generation of saints, depends upon God and upon nothing else. In all other circumstances, except God had been with him, Jacob would have been sent away destitute. His success did not depend upon his own hard toil, though his wives and others who knew only the outward circumstances might have thought so. His success did not depend upon his integrity, complete as that appears to have been. None of these things would have prevented his destitution. Are we ever tempted to suppose that our own labours or our own good character have contributed to our salvation? The thought is false and devilish. We are saved, blessed and delivered from spiritual destitution only because the sovereign will of

God decreed our blessing, and because we have been the objects of His love, care and wisdom. (2) In speaking of 'the God of my father', Jacob asserted that he had not been blessed and delivered primarily for his own sake, but because of promises made to another. It is the same with us. We are saved in fulfilment of such promises made by the Father to the Lord Jesus Christ as we find in Isa. 53. 11, 12, or Psa. 2. 8. We are saved entirely because of the merits and deserts of the Lord Jesus Christ.

The God of Abraham, and the fear of Isaac. Jacob connects the circumstances of his prosperity and protection with the redemptive promises made to Abraham and renewed to Isaac. In fact he realises that the grace that is given to him is part of a large purpose. So it is with us. The blessing we receive is a part of the great plan of God to bring all things to a head in Christ (Eph. 1. 10). This does not take away from our own enjoyment of it, but adds to the significance of our receiving of it.

Had been with me. To have God with us is to have everything in and with Him.

Thou hadst sent me away now empty. The world has much to offer but nothing to give. It always sends away empty those who have not God with them. It is certain they can carry nothing out of the world (1 Tim. 6. 7), and they go to face a righteous God on the day of judgment without a single plea. *God hath seen mine affliction*. He has seen not Jacob's only, but that of every one of His people. Not a sigh escapes the lips of one of His children, but God sees it and marks it, and He has revealed His intention to wipe away all tears from off all faces (Isa. 25. 8; Rev. 7. 17). Jacob's affliction was caused by the craft and hostility of Laban. That of the children of God is caused in the same way by the craft and hostility of the world.

The labour of my hands. The implication is that the labour, or some of it, was unnecessary. No work for God is ever unnecessary, but undoubtedly superfluous toil is caused by the carelessness, selfishness, or antagonism of the world. If so, God sees and marks it all.

Rebuked thee yesternight. So God rebukes the devil (Zech. 3. 2), restrains his wrath (Job 1. 12; 2. 6), and protects His people.

VERSE 43. *All that thou seest is mine.* Laban is restrained by ties of relationship, just as the world is sometimes restrained by the bonds of common humanity. Often, like Laban, it wrongly claims proprietorship in what belongs to Christ.

VERSE 44. *Come thou.* Like the elder Abimelech (chap. 20; 21. 27) and the younger Abimelech (26. 31) Laban now desired a covenant with Jacob. He had undergone this change of attitude on three grounds. (1) He had had a revelation from God (ver. 24), which had clearly revealed the Divine will that enmity to Jacob was wrong. (2) He had been rebuked by Jacob (verses 36-42). (3) He recognised his kinship with the people of Christ. In the same way the Holy Ghost makes the truth of the Gospel real to the sinner's heart, convicts him of sin and unbelief, and binds him in spirit to the people of the Lord.

A covenant. In the same way we Gentiles, who were strangers from the commonwealth of Israel (Eph. 2. 12), have been brought nigh by the blood of Christ (Eph. 2. 13) to share the promised blessings and the covenant mercies.

A witness. The covenant in the blood of Jesus is a witness that the middle wall of partition between Jew and Gentile, as well as between God and man, has been broken down (Eph. 2. 14) and the enmity abolished (ibid).

VERSE 45. *Jacob took a stone,* just as he had at Bethel (28. 18). The stone is Christ (Mt. 21. 42; 1 Pet. 2. 6-8).

Set it up for a pillar. In the same way the Son of Man was lifted up (Jo. 3. 14; 8. 28; 12. 32) to be the pillar that stands for all to see and believe.

VERSE 46. *Jacob said unto his brethren, Gather stones.* This is a Gospel command, and is the very command given by Christ to us His brethren. We ourselves have been gathered as living stones (1 Pet. 2. 5) to Christ, and our work for Christ consists in gathering others.

Made an heap. The heap of stones, gathered round the central pillar, represents the true church of Christ, which consists of living stones brought to Him and built upon Him (1 Pet. 2. 5).

They did eat there upon the heap. The true church is the place of fellowship, where the people of God may feed together upon Christ the living bread and true paschal Lamb. All this goes to show that those with whom the covenant is made in Christ's blood become members of the true church, built upon the foundation of the apostles and prophets (Eph. 2. 20), enjoy fellowship one with another (1 Jo. 1. 3) and are nourished on Christ Himself (Jo. 6. 48-56).

VERSE 47. *Jegar-sahadutha.* This means ' Heap of witness ' in Aramaic, the language of Syria, which Laban spoke.

Galeed. This means ' Heap of witness ' in Hebrew, the language of Palestine, which Jacob spoke and had never forgotten during the twenty years in Syria, when he must have been accustomed to speaking Aramaic to Laban and his people, and even at first to his own wives. May we never forget the language of heaven during our sojourn on earth. In this verse we find a difference of language, which is superficial, combined with a unity of thought and fellowship, which is substantial. This is a little picture of the unity of the many languages of earth among the redeemed in Christ (Rev. 7. 9).

VERSE 48. *This heap is a witness between me and thee this day.* The existence of the church is a witness to the reality of the covenant. The members of the true church are witnesses unto Christ in the sense that they proclaim the facts of redemption in preaching the Gospel (Acts 1. 8), but also living witnesses of the fulfilment of God's Word and the reality of His grace. In controversy with the idols God points to His people to prove by the transformation of their lives the truth of His claim to be the only true and living God (Isa. 43. 10; 44. 8). The existence of the true church is a proof that the enmity between God and man has been broken down and that the distinction between Jew and Gentile exists no more.

Therefore was the name of it called Galeed. The name is repeated, a fact that shows the emphasis that should be laid upon it. The purpose of the heap was above all else for witness. Likewise is the purpose of the church. God has placed His people in the world as a witness to men, and to all eternity they will be a witness to angels (Eph. 2. 7; 3. 10).

VERSE 49. *Mizpah.* This means a 'watch-tower'. The true church consists of a praying people to whom the word is given to watch and pray (Lk. 21. 36). From the watch-tower of the church, gathered always round the central pillar, which is Christ Himself, the army of the enemy may be overlooked and circumvented.

The Lord watch between me and thee, when we are absent one from another. This passage is generally taken in isolation to mean that absent friends may safely entrust each other to the Lord's protecting care. This idea is undoubtedly true, but it does not seem to be the primary

meaning of the passage. Laban's prayer rather is that when he and Jacob are out of each other's sight the Lord may keep a mutual watch against any preparations for hostile action that the one might take against the other. In actual practice Jacob was unlikely to take such action, and the words therefore applied to Laban alone. The spiritual lesson seems to be that through the prayers of His people God will guard them against the machinations of their enemies.

VERSE 50. *If thou shalt afflict my daughters.* Satan may well boast that if Christ should afflict His people, he is justified in his enmity and malice. Nothing of the sort can ever happen. Even the yoke that the Saviour puts on His people's necks is light (Mt. 11. 30), and His commandments are not grievous (1 Jo. 5. 3). It is He that delivers them from all the afflictions of sin and Satan and gives unto them eternal life (Jo. 10. 28) and pleasures at His right hand for evermore (Ps. 16. 11).

Other wives beside my daughters. The bride of Christ, to whom He is eternally faithful, is the company of redeemed humanity. He will take no other, whether from among different created beings, such as angels, or among those descendants of Adam who refuse to believe.

No man is with us. The general sense of this observation is clear. It means that in the circumstances named by Laban the covenant of friendship would become void. Its particular sense however is rather difficult. Laban may mean (1) that if the particular circumstances which he mentioned should arise, he and Jacob would be found in such irreconcilably hostile camps that no man could be a friend to them both at the same time. Alternatively and more probably (2) the emphatic word is *man*. If a breach of the covenant takes place, it will not be a man who will judge between them, but God. This is a solemn truth. Sin and unfaithfulness are not judged by man but by Christ at the last day. We believe that He will come to be our judge. ' It is a fearful thing to fall into the hands of the living God ' (Heb. 10. 31).

God is witness betwixt me and thee. God is the witness of every profession of faith and of every dedicatory vow. He is the witness of every move on the part of the enemies of the truth, and His hand is outstretched to protect His people.

Verse 51. *Behold this heap.* The heap represents the true church, which is like a city set on a hill, the light of which cannot be hid (Mt. 5. 14). *Behold this pillar.* The pillar represents the Lord Jesus Christ, the facts of Whose earthly life, death and resurrection cannot be hid.

Which I have cast betwixt me and thee. These words are lies. Laban had not cast the heap or the pillar at all. Jacob had done both (verses 45, 46). Every assertion and every thought that we ourselves have done anything to establish a covenant with Christ or to set ourselves right with God are false. He has done all in grace, and we are helpless without Him.

Verse 52. The heap and the pillar were not only (1) a witness and (2) a watch-tower, but also (3) a boundary mark. Within Christ and His true church are life, outside Him is death, judgment and destruction (1 Jo. 5. 12). Christ is the door of the sheepfold (Jo. 10. 9) and the entrance into the kingdom of heaven. By receiving Him, entering into Him and possessing Him the sinner passes from death to life (Jo. 5. 24).

Verse 53. *The God of Abraham, and the God of Nahor, the God of their father.* The father of Abraham and Nahor was Terah. Jacob was a descendant of Abraham and Laban of Nahor. In speaking of the God of Abraham and the God of Nahor as one, Laban may have had in his mind reminiscent echoes of the fact

that the family of Terah was of Semitic stock and went back to remote ancestors who knew the true God. He was right in the sense that there is only one God, Who is the God of all men. If God was Abraham's Redeemer, He was Nahor's Creator. But this was not what Laban meant. Like so many today and in all generations who cling to false religions, he implied the identification of the true and the false. He had no sense of the exclusiveness of true religion. He would have said that all religion was the same at heart, though possibly expressed in different ways and under different forms; that what one believed did not matter, so long as it was sincerely held. He was a good picture of the worldly religious man. *Judge betwixt us.* His prayer was vain and his plea ineffectual because he did not properly know to whom it was directed.

Jacob sware. He entered in God's Name into a most solemn obligation. Oaths are forbidden to us under the Gospel (Mt. 5. 34; Jas. 5. 12), because the evil in human nature to which they pay deference, which makes them necessary (Mt. 5. 37), is dealt with by Christ. But obligations remain. As the people of God we are debtors to all men (Rom. 1. 14). At the end of our lives how much of that debt will alas! remain unpaid.

The fear of his father Isaac. Notice (1) in contrast to Laban Jacob sware by the true and living God only. He did not identify Him with the God of Nahor or of Terah, who worshipped idols (Josh. 24. 2). He realised that the only living God had revealed Himself to Abraham and Isaac and formed them into a peculiar people in a special relationship to Himself. He rightly held and believed the exclusive nature of special revelation, and he did not identify it with natural religion. (2) He still thinks of God as his father's God. He dare not yet call Him his own. A sense of his own unworthiness, which breaks forth in the next chapter (32. 10), begins to steal over him. He realised however that he could claim the protection of his father's God, and that he had been blessed because of promises made to another, and that he had a part in the redemptive purpose in which his family was involved.

VERSE 54. In this verse we find three things which accompanied the covenant and made it effectual. (1) *Jacob offered sacrifice.* The margin says ' killed beasts ', the very language demonstrating that sacrifice and death are inseparable. Thus the new covenant that has been made with us in Jesus' blood was inaugurated by His sacrifice, in which as priest and victim He offered His life to God for us. ' By one offering He hath perfected for ever them that are sanctified ' (Heb. 10. 14).

Upon the mount. The sacrifice was offered in the open in a prominent place visibly and evidently. In the same way the offering of Christ was made openly before the eyes of men, in this world and in the flesh, not in any hidden world behind the scenes. ' The Word became flesh, and we beheld His glory ' (Jo. 1. 14). It was made on a hill against the sky-line at a time when the city at which it took place was crowded and overcrowded with persons who had travelled from many parts of the known world. It took place at an open point in history, which has never passed out of sight and never will, but marks the turning-point of time today, as it has done ever since.

(2) *Jacob called his brethren to eat bread.* So Christ calls His people to feed on Himself, the heavenly manna, Who has been offered in sacrifice for their sins. This feeding is all by faith. It means appropriation of Christ by the reception of the Gospel and the building up and nourishing of the spiritual life by reading God's Word and seeing Christ in every part of it. The Lord's

Supper signifies this feeding, but does not actually consist of it, as the Romanist and Anglo-Romanist with other unreformed churches foolishly believe and blasphemously teach.

They did eat bread. They accepted the call and obeyed the invitation, as do all the people of God, the Holy Spirit bringing them to the Word and dividing it out to them according to their several needs. This common meal denotes not only nourishment but fellowship. Christ invites His people to fellowship with Himself and each other (1 Jo. 1, 3, 4).

(3) They *tarried all night in the mount.* The covenant when effective in the lives of the people of God begets prayer. This tarrying in the mount is a picture of a night of prayer. Most of us are too weak to keep awake for such an occasion, but when the Holy Spirit has called and empowered to it, a night of prayer has sometimes been the means of setting revival in motion.

VERSE 55. In this verse we note five things about Laban, which are typical of the Christian who professes but does not possess. (1) *Early in the morning Laban rose up.* He showed an eagerness, which might well be mistaken for that of a true Christian. The Lord's work might well prosper more if more of His people rose up early in the morning to pray. But the sequel showed that the real object of Laban's eagerness was to get back as quickly as possible to the world. He therefore showed a misdirected eagerness, which might at first have been mistaken for Christian zeal. (2) *He kissed his sons and his daughters.* He showed affection and friendship to the people of God in such a way as to hint, imply or whisper that he regarded them all the time as belonging to himself. The worldly man, if well disposed towards the church, looks on it as an activity of the world.

(3) *He blessed them.* He wished the church well, and spoke fair to

it. He patronised it with a blessing, for which it was no better off. The only blessing that could prosper Leah and Rachel was Jacob's blessing, or God's blessing.

(4) *Laban departed.* He never had had any thought or intention of throwing in his lot with Jacob and his family, or of joining them in their pilgrim life, or of seeking a share in the inheritance of the promised land. Such desires were uncongenial to him. When Jacob and his company moved on towards home, Laban left them and departed. He had come far enough, and he did not mean to go farther.

(5) *He returned unto his place.* He went back to settle down again in the world from which he had come. He was drawn back again to the place where his heart and his home were. In the same way every child of the devil, however zealously he may profess to be well affected towards the people of Christ, however warmly he may kiss them, however loudly he may bless them, goes sooner or later back to his own place in the world, there to enjoy the pleasures of sin for a season, or suffer the griefs which grow out of the perversities of the world, and to find in the end that he has lost his own soul.

CHAPTER 32

THIS remarkable chapter provides us with an inspired insight into the character and conduct of Jacob, and we see his spiritual life developing with many hesitations. First he is met by angels (1, 2). Next he sends in trepidation to Esau to tell him of his return (3-5). He is told that Esau is coming to meet him with a band of men and is thrown into consternation (6-8). Rightly he resorts to prayer and reliance on God's promises (9-12). In returning weakness he sends an elaborate present to Esau (13-21), sends his family over the Jabbok and remains alone (22, 23). The chapter culminates in the impressive and significant incident of Jacob's wrestle with the angel (24-32).

VERSE 1. *Jacob went on his way.* Christ went on His way triumphantly from the bosom of the Father to the throne of creation through Bethlehem, Calvary, resurrection and ascension. The church also goes on her way. Laban may delay her, but he cannot stop her, and she sets out on another stage of her journey to the promised land. In the pursuit of Laban we have seen the opposition of the devil and the world. In this and the following chapter we shall see the opposition of the flesh.

The angels of God met him. Here was a blessed provision by God. The angels are ministering spirits, sent forth to minister unto them which shall be heirs of salvation (Heb. 1. 14). Their presence here with Jacob thus proves him to have been an heir of salvation. The same angels are sent forth to minister to us, but we do not as a rule see them, as Jacob appears to have done. Their ministry is not spiritual, and we ought never to fall into the error, freely indulged in by the unreformed churches, of supposing that it is. We do not need angels to carry our prayers or to give us access to the Father (Rom. 5. 2; Heb. 4. 16). It is by Christ, and by Him alone, that we can come to the Father (Heb. 7. 25). Their ministry is to protect from physical dangers (2 Ki. 6. 17). Though they disappeared from Jacob's sight, we may safely infer that their presence remained with him, and a remembrance of this fact might have saved him from all his subsequent fears. It is interesting to notice that the blessed, ministering, friendly angels met Jacob at the border of the promised land, as if sent to welcome him on his return. In the same way there is joy in the presence of the angels of God over every sinner that repenteth (Lk. 15. 10), and on the day of resurrection the angels will meet the elect at the border of the land and attend them into it (Mt. 24. 31).

VERSE 2. *When Jacob saw them*. His eyes were opened to see the angels, as were those of Elisha's servant (2 Ki. 6. 17). In modern days such a sight is still very occasionally granted. Jacob needed special grace and special encouragement, and he was graciously granted them by God. The sight of the angels should have kept him from the fears that subsequently distracted him.

This is God's host. He knew that the angels were the army used by God to protect His own and to make war against the devil. ' The chariots of God are twenty thousand, even thousands of angels ' (Ps. 68. 17). In Rev. 12. 7-9 we see this host at war with the devil, led by the archangel, whom we should probably identify with the Lord Jesus Christ, the Angel of the Lord. The Lord is among His angels (Ps. 68. 17). The sight of the angels was therefore an additional confirmation to Jacob that the presence of the Lord of hosts was with him.

He called the name of that place. He marked it in his own memory and mind as a noticeable step in his spiritual experience, and by giving a name to the place which endured among his descendants (Josh. 13. 26; 2 Sam. 17. 24) he testified to what God had done for him. We ought to do the same. *Mahanaim*. This means ' two hosts ' or ' two camps '. Which were the two? Does Jacob mean that he saw two separate armies of angels, one on each side of him? This may be so, but he did not say so. He mentions only one host, and this he probably saw ranged right round him, as the horses and chariots of fire were ' round about Elisha ' (2 Ki. 6. 17). It is more likely that he means by the two camps that of the angels in addition to *his own*. God was in either, and the camp of the angels lent its strength to the weakness of his own. Jacob was not alone in his weakness. There were two camps. The strength of the unseen forces was brought to his aid and united with his feeble resources. We are in just the same position as we journey through the dangers of the world.

VERSE 3. *Jacob sent messengers before him to Esau his brother*. Esau is a type of the flesh, and the despatch of the messengers seems to have been an unnecessary act. Jacob might have done better to have ignored Esau and left God to deal with him. Fear seems to have been his motive in sending the messengers. He was trying to placate the flesh, and in so doing he was perhaps wrongly making ' provision ' for it (Rom. 13. 14).

The land of Seir. Esau did not live in the promised land. It had no attraction for him, and he had turned his back on it. The same is true of the flesh.

The country of Edom. The Hebrew word translated ' country ' means ' field '. ' The field is the world ' (Mt. 13. 38). It is in the world that the flesh is at home.

VERSE 4. In his message to Esau Jacob made six mistakes. (1) He addressed Esau as ' my lord '. He thus implied the dominion of the flesh. (2) He calls himself Esau's servant. He who thinks himself or calls himself the servant of the flesh is likely to serve it in earnest. (3) He told Esau the facts of his life, the story of the past years, and how God had dealt with him. This did not concern Esau.

VERSE 5. (4) Jacob's fourth mistake was that he told Esau what he possessed. This would expose them to Esau's jealous desires and place them at Esau's disposal. (5) He was probably wrong in sending a message to Esau at all. (6) He wanted to find grace in Esau's sight. But it is not likely that he could please God and please Esau at the same time.

VERSE 6. *We came to thy brother*

Esau. If they had never been sent, and had never come to him, Jacob might have had nothing to fear.

He cometh to meet thee, and four hundred men with him. Esau took full advantage of Jacob's conciliatory attitude. This is the usual result of compromise with the flesh. Esau's object in bringing the four hundred men is not told us. It may have been in order to be ready for all eventualities. It may have been in order to make a display. It may have been with the intention of capturing and destroying Jacob. The last is what Jacob obviously supposed. Each of these motives is consistent with the desires of the flesh.

VERSE 7. *Jacob was greatly afraid and distressed.* He forgot the host of angels which he had seen at Mahanaim, which still encamped around him, though now invisible. He could not say, ' I will trust and not be afraid ' (Isa. 12. 2). He could scarcely say, " What time I am afraid, I will trust in thee ' (Ps. 56. 3). His fears seem to have been mostly for his wives and children, but he could have committed them all to the Lord. Jacob was not strong enough in the spiritual life to know the peace of God that passeth all understanding (Phil. 4. 7).

He divided the people that was with him, thus dissipating their strength and breaking their unity. Compromise with the flesh often leads to weakness. *The flocks.* He divided and weakened his ability to sacrifice.

Herds. He divided and weakened his ability for service.

The camels. He divided and weakened his financial resources.

Two bands. He may have supposed that the two bands would give a deceptive appearance of double strength, but his real reason for the division appears in the following verse.

VERSE 8. His motive in dividing his resources was fear for their safety.

His reasoning seems to have been unsound. If Esau could smite one band, he could easily smite the other, if he were so minded. We see in him here the picture of a weak, frightened man. Not that the danger from Esau was unreal. The danger from the flesh is not unreal. It comes with its four hundred envyings, jealousies, murders, sorceries and lusts, advancing in terrifying strength to destroy the pilgrim on his way. Jacob was right to recognise his weakness. He was wrong to forget his strength, the unseen host of angels, just as the Christian is apt to forget the unseen strength which he possesses in the Lord and the power of His might (Eph. 6. 10).

VERSE 9. *Jacob said.* Though he was weak and frightened, he rightly turned to prayer. Prayer alone would have been the better course, but in all the circumstances we can see the over-ruling hand of God. This is a very genuine prayer. If we compare it with the prayer which Jacob offered at Bethel (28. 20-22), we shall not fail to see the extent to which his spiritual life had advanced. His experiences at Padan-Aram had taught him much, but this is the prayer of a man who felt himself in a critical situation. It was his great fear and distress that called forth this prayer, and they were therefore brought upon him and used by God for this very purpose. We may sometimes experience such fear and distress. If we do, we may be certain that God has allowed them for a purpose to our spiritual advantage, and it may well be that that purpose is to drive us to prayer. The prayer that follows in this and the following three verses is a very proper model for all who pray. It contains six parts: (1) reliance on the promises of God; (2) a statement of unworthiness; (3) a reminder of God's mercies; (4) a definite petition; (5) a simple opening of the heart; (6) a re-repeated reliance on God's promises.

O God of my father Abraham, and

God of my father Isaac. Jacob begins his prayer by placing his faith in the God Who had made promises to his fathers, and was blessing him for their sake. We too must pray to the God and Father of our Lord Jesus Christ, Who blesses us for Christ's sake (Eph. 1. 3). *The Lord.* This is the name Jahweh, occurring here in a chapter where otherwise we find Elohim, exactly in the place and context that we should expect. Jacob refers to the Redeemer in Whose covenant purpose he realises himself to be playing a part.

Which saidst unto me, Return unto thy country, and to thy kindred. Jacob relies for the answer to his prayer upon the promise and instruction of God. He believes that what He had promised He was able also to perform (Rom. 4. 21). He rightly sees (1) that if Jahweh had told him to return, He would bring him safely the whole length of the journey, (2) that He would never have commanded him to return merely to fall into the hands of Esau. He thus instinctively realises that it was God's will that Esau should not harm him. He is therefore able to pray for protection from Esau in line with what he knew to be God's will (1 Jo. 5. 14).

I will deal well with thee. This was a gracious promise which went to strengthen Jacob's conviction and prayer. This plea and this promise are continually made by God. He calls to the sinner, 'Return, and I will deal well with thee'.

VERSE 10. *I am not worthy of the least of all the mercies.* The Hebrew says, 'I am less than all the mercies.' The meaning is brilliantly caught in the beautiful English translation of the A.V. Jacob's fear and distress were factors used by the Holy Ghost in bringing him to this humble confession. We too must have the same spirit, if we are to obtain blessing from God. Jacob began to see that God's goodness and mercy had followed him all the days of his life (Ps. 23. 6). It was easy to see the gracious revelation at Bethel as a mercy, or his meeting with Rachel, the birth of his children, and the building up of his family. These are probably what Jacob had chiefly in mind, but did he not begin to see the whole course of his life, the lonely departure from home, the hard servitude with Laban, even the antagonism and bitterness that drove him to return, all as a course of merciful discipline? Perhaps he looked back further still to the oracle given to his mother before his birth, to the providential over-ruling that through all and in spite of all brought him the birthright and the blessing. His complaints and sadness were turned into humble thanksgiving, as he faced new dangers and realised the hand of God in all that was past.

And of all the truth. Jacob saw that God had been not only merciful to him, but also *faithful.* In showing mercy God had been faithful to His own nature. Above all He had been faithful in His dealings with Jacob to His promises and declared purpose. He had been faithful all the time to the oracle given to Rebekah before Jacob's birth (25. 23). Jacob felt that his own unworthiness might well have forfeited the promises and given God good reason for altering His purpose and not fulfilling it. Jacob's case here is exactly our own. We too are followed by God's mercies, but His dealings with us rest on His faithfulness to His own nature, seen conspicuously in the sufferings and death of the Saviour. God is faithful to us for Christ's sake. We do not merit His mercy or His faithfulness. He has had every reason in our case to abandon His promises in righteousness indignation, but He has not done so. We are not worthy of the least of all His mercies and of all His truth.

Which thou hast shewed unto thy servant. To show the mercies and the truth is more than to practise them. Through the mercies and truth God was showing, or revealing, to Jacob what He Himself was like, and it is the same with us. By His dealing with us, which always partakes of the two qualities of mercy and faithfulness, we get to know more what He is like. In referring to himself as God's servant Jacob professes that he stands in a particular relationship with God, and implies that He takes on its obligations. *With my staff.* Jacob means that he was alone but for his staff and had no property beside it. *I passed over this Jordan.* Jordan is the river of death. Every man passes through it alone. He passes alone also through the spiritual experience of dying with Christ to sin, which takes place at every true conversion.

Now I am become two bands. This is the proper experience of the servant of God. He passes alone from death to life, but he bears fruit as his life of service goes on, and he should arrive in heaven surrounded by the bands of those whom he has led into a like experience to his own. The two bands to which Jacob referred were those into which he had himself divided his people and animals (verse 7).

VERSE 11. *Deliver me.* Here is a simple, primitive, definite prayer, of which none of us in this life gets beyond the need. It implies dependence upon God for security. ' Deliver us from evil ' (Mt. 6. 13). Apart from God's deliverance we should become a prey to evil, just as Jacob might have become a prey to Esau.

From the hand of my brother. Esau was very close to Jacob. He was in fact a twin with him. So in each one of us the old nature, though utterly different in character and destiny, is very close to the new.

From the hand of Esau. Esau is the type of the flesh. He was a profane, that is to say, a worldly-minded man and a fornicator (Heb. 12. 16). Every servant of God needs continual deliverance from Esau,

who lurks within ready to destroy the spiritual life and to turn the grace of God into lasciviousness (Jude 4). God has shown us the way of deliverance from him. ' Walk in the Spirit, and ye shall not fulfil the lust of the flesh ' (Gal. 5. 16).

I fear him. Jacob's fear was due to wavering faith. There is no need for the servant of God to fear Esau.

Lest he will come and smite me. This Esau can never do. He may intrude and frighten and roar and fuss, but God's Word says that he will never have dominion (Rom. 6. 14).

And the mother with the children. Jacob was right, if he feared at all, in fearing for those who belonged to him. A successful destructive effort on the part of the flesh has wide repercussions and destroys the spiritual life and happiness of those in touch with the one primarily affected.

VERSE 12. *And thou saidst.* Jacob ends his prayer with another act of faith, taking his stand on the only ground that is firm, the rock of God's promises.

I will surely do thee good. What can God do to anyone that trusts Him but good? He longs to do good to all (1 Tim. 2. 4). Like Jacob we may trust to God's expressed purpose to bless us in Christ, which will override all temptation and danger.

And make thy seed as the sand of the sea. Jacob could rely not only on a promise to himself personally, but also upon one made to his seed. This promise had actually been made to Abraham (22. 17), and in claiming it Jacob testified that he knew himself to be in the line of Abraham's true seed, heir to Abraham's promises, and partaker in the great Divine purpose of redemption which manifested itself in the call of Abraham. This was an even firmer ground on which to rest his faith and assurance of deliverance. We have firmer ground still. We have seen the purpose fulfilled in Christ. We have historical proof that what God has promised He is able also to perform. We rest on the finished work of Christ, and we know that it cannot fail.

Which cannot be numbered for multitude. This promise began to be fulfilled in the large increase of Israel after the flesh (Ex. 1. 7), but will have its final fulfilment in the numberless multitude of the redeemed (Rev. 7. 9), who are the true seed of Abraham, for whom the promises are intended (Gal. 3. 29). This promise is quoted from this passage, much in the form in which Jacob here claims it, by the writer to the Hebrews (11. 12), who refers it to Abraham.

VERSE 13. *He lodged there that same night.* If he did not advance, he had the faith to stand his ground. Whether he laid him down and slept in peace or not, we do not know. There was every reason for him to do so. We too are to take our stand and remain standing (Eph. 6. 13).

Took of that which came to his hand. His faith fails him again, and he turns as we so often do, from trust to expediency. He appears to have acted hastily without prayer or deliberation. He took the first thing he could lay hands on.

A present for Esau. It was a sop, an unnecessary concession, inspired by fear and put together in prayerless haste. We ought not to give presents to the flesh, but instead to make no provision for it (Rom. 13. 14). Let it starve rather than allow it the opportunity of enjoying the luxuries in which it delights.

VERSE 14. This and the following verse describe the present, which was ostentatious in its munificence and seems to have been intended as much to impress Esau with the greatness and affluence of Jacob as to appease him. In the account of the present we may see something of what Jacob gave away and lost to the flesh as a result of his fear and the weakness of his faith, which led him to make this concession to Esau. The she goats and ewes as well as the he goats and rams are part of the flock of God. They were sacrificed in this unnecessary manner. In parallel circumstances in the spiritual sphere large numbers of the Lord's flock are likely to suffer. There were so many less opportunities for increasing the flock and so many less for sacrificial offerings. These are just the two activities that compromise with the flesh always interferes with.

VERSE 15. *Thirty milch camels with their colts.* The camel is the scriptural type of the rich man of the world. It is an unclean but useful beast. It cannot be used for food or for sacrifice, but its activities help the kingdom of God. These activities are here given away by Jacob and turned to the use of the flesh.

Forty kine, and ten bulls. Oxen are types of the servants of God (1 Cor. 9. 9, 10). By Jacob's concession to the flesh so many servants of God were turned into wrong channels. In similar circumstances this is always the case.

Twenty she asses, and ten foals. These are pictures of the ordinary people of the world. By Jacob's concession and compromise, by which they were detached from Jacob and handed over to Esau, they were humanly speaking lost.

VERSE 16. *He delivered them into the hands of his servants.* He associated his servants with him in what he was doing. When he made a mistake, others were involved in it.

Every drove by themselves. The animals were kept separate, making five droves in all.

Put a space betwixt drove and drove. Jacob took elaborate precautions. He had quite forgotten the angels of Mahanaim.

VERSE 17. Jacob expected and anticipated many questions from Esau.

VERSE 18. This verse provides a

good version of the evangelist's message, though if used in this sense it must be taken in isolation from the context. Thus there are three statements made: (1) These blessings are not our property, they do not derive from us, but from the unseen Christ, Who stands behind us (Acts 3. 12, 13). (2) These blessings are not for sale, but all are free gifts (Rom. 6. 23; Rev. 21. 6). (3) The Christ Who offers them through us comes behind us desiring to meet you Himself and to become your reconciled friend and brother.

VERSE 19. *The second, and the third, and all that followed.* Many opportunities for reconciliation were provided for Esau, just as one Gospel message after another is so often given to the lost.

When ye find him. It is the duty of the evangelist to seek as well as to speak, though we often forget it. The Saviour came to seek and to save. Esau must be found before the message is given to him.

VERSE 20. *Thy servant Jacob is behind us.* The special emphasis of the message was to be upon Jacob himself, as is always the case with the Gospel. If the word ' servant ' seems inappropriate, we must remember that Christ Himself told us that He came to minister (Mt. 20. 28). He left us an example by washing His disciple's feet (Jo. 13. 13-15), and when He came into the world, He took on Him the form of a servant (Phil. 2. 7). The evangelist thus preaches the Christ Who came to save and to give His life a ransom for many.

I will appease him with the present. The remaining section of this verse is enough to show us that the context is not evangelistic. These words of Jacob could not in any sense be typical of any words of Christ. The Saviour does not need to appease anyone.

Afterward I will see his face. Even this may have been unneces-

sary. Jacob himself had provoked the meeting. (Verse 3).

Peradventure he will accept of me. It made no real difference whether Jacob was accepted by Esau or not. All that matters is whether present or absent to be well-pleasing to the Lord (2 Cor. 5. 9).

VERSE 21. *So went the present over before him.* The context seems to make the whole incident of the present an example of an unnecessary concession to the flesh. It is also possible to see in it — though it seems less likely — an illustration of prudence and practical common sense. In addition to prayer Jacob took such active steps as were open to him to bring about the answer to his prayer. This is the view taken by Matthew Henry (*loc. cit.*). There are circumstances in which such co-operation is taught and demanded in the Bible, but it does not seem easy to see that we are taught it in these verses.

Himself lodged that night in the company. It is not clear whether this was the same night as that referred to in verse 13, or the following one. If it was the same night, the present must have been hastily got together late in the evening and despatched by night. More probably the morning was occupied with the assembly of the present, which would have been sent away by noon. The night here referred to would thus be the following night to that mentioned in verse 13. If so, suspense and anxiety would increase during the day, especially as the day would be an inactive one. Jacob however still stood his ground. He did not retreat.

VERSE 22. *He rose up that night.* He was up in the small hours because he wanted to have time alone with God at this crisis, as the sequel shows.

Took his two wives, and his two women servants, and his eleven sons. He sent his family on because he must be alone with God. He intended to rejoin them before the danger arose, and in fact he did so.

The ford Jabbok. The Jabbok is a tributary of the Jordan, which comes down from the mountains of Ammon. It flows west into the Jordan, and Jacob crossed it from north to south. Esau was coming northwards east of the Jordan from Mount Seir in Edom, where he lived.

VERSE 23. Jacob sent away all that he had. He must meet God without even his nearest and dearest. Evidently he took his wives and children over the brook by the ford and returned himself to the northern bank.

VERSE 24. With this verse begins the account of the great crisis in the life of Jacob. He was expecting a crisis of another sort, but God showed him that the real crisis was in his own spiritual life. Thus the approach of Esau and the fear and distress into which Jacob was thrown appear in their right setting. They were the means by which Jacob was brought face to face with God, incidents ordained by God as the vehicle of spiritual activities and spiritual reality. We may confidently expect that if incidents that cause us fear and distress confront us, they are but the tools of God, used by Him to bring us in closer touch with Himself. We need never fear them. The incident described in these verses is one of four (possibly only three) used by the prophet Hosea (12. 3, 4) to sketch the life of Jacob. The first is his catching hold of Esau at his birth (25. 26). The prophet evidently regards this as a shadow of things that were to come. The second is the present incident, in which the emphatic points are the power and victory of Jacob. The third (unless as some think, it belongs here) is his weeping and supplication. It probably refers to the prayer of verses 9-12 of this chapter. The last is God's finding of Jacob at Bethel (28. 10-22).

Jacob was left alone. This is

clearly what he had intended. He had sent his family onward and returned himself across the brook in order to be alone with God. This passage is one of the most important of those in the Bible which deal with the subject of prayer, and the first point that it makes is prayer's individual aspect. ' The faith that thou hast, have it to thyself before God ' (Rom. 14. 22). Public prayer, prayer in fellowship with other Christians, has an essential and important place, but it is not the foundation of the spiritual life. Church life never can be. The foundation is laid in the individual's secret contact with God, which alone makes him able to take part in the fellowship of the church. Those who teach that the foundation of spiritual life is ecclesiastical teach what is contrary to the Bible, and do so because they are ignorant of the real spiritual life and must find some religious substitute for it. The Lord Jesus Christ Himself teaches in emphatic terms the necessity and responsibility of private individual prayer (Mt. 6. 6).

There wrestled a man with him. We notice that though Jacob rightly took steps to get himself alone, evidently intending to meet with God, he did not initiate the wrestling. The supernatural visitor took the initiative. This suggests that God had the initiative all the time, and not only the initiative, but the whole operation and the accomplishment. His intention was to bring about the effect in Jacob's life that was in fact brought about by this encounter. He used the approach of Esau as a means to this end, and implanted in Jacob's heart the urge to be alone with God, which led him to send away his family. The nature of this encounter is mysterious, and the description of it gives an impression almost of weirdness. This fact teaches us that we should expect an element of mystery in God's dealings with us. We must not suppose we can understand all His purposes or all His methods. Wrestling is the picture of a certain aspect of prayer. But of which aspect? From one point of view prayer is a struggle with powers of evil, as we may see from the delay imposed upon the answer to Daniel's prayer by spiritual forces of evil (Dan. 10. 12, 13). But this is not the aspect. The struggle was not with powers of evil but with God. Two important aspects of the spiritual life appear to be illustrated: (1) the ultimate victory of Jacob in the struggle typifies what we rightly call prevailing prayer. The victory appears to lie in the power to persevere, a side to prayer which the Lord emphasises as being of the utmost importance (Lk. 18. 1-8). Here appears to lie, at least in part, the meaning of the prophet Hosea, when he says that Jacob had power with God, had power over the angel, and prevailed (Hos. 12. 3, 4). (2) But there is a second significance which we can hardly neglect in considering this mysterious episode. It seems to typify and gather into itself the whole of God's attitude towards Jacob, and His dealing with Him, during the whole of his life. God wrestles with the stubborn Jacob, as He wrestles with us, seeking to sanctify him, to refine him, to destroy his carnal nature and make him a new man. Jacob resists and appears to prevail, until God, as we shall see, has recourse to the touch which cripples him. This is the aspect that seems nearest to the meaning of Hosea in the passage referred to. The prophet connects this power and prevailing of Jacob with the act by which he supplanted his brother at birth, which was an act of the carnal nature. He thus means to emphasise the strength and obstinacy of Jacob the sinner, which was remedied by prayer and by the revelation made to him at Bethel. The wrestler is referred to as ' a man '. Later He is called God by Jacob himself (verse 30), and He is called God by the prophet Hosea (12. 3), who also calls Him ' the angel ' (12. 4). There can be little doubt of His identity. He

was the Angel of the Lord, the preincarnate Christ, the second Person of the Blessed Trinity, Who is the exact image of the Father's Person (Heb. 1. 3), Michael our prince (Dan. 10. 13, 21; 12. 1), Lord and chief of angels, one day to take human flesh of the virgin for our sakes, and rejoicing before that to appear as a man among the sons of men whom He loves.

Until the breaking of the day. The Hebrew says ' the ascending of the morning '. As the bout began in darkness, this seems a long time to wrestle. Today the same God in the Person of the Holy Ghost does not shrink from wrestling with us and our stubborn natures, and will go on wrestling till the resurrection morning dawns.

VERSE 25. `When he saw that he prevailed not against him,* that is, when the Man saw that He was not prevailing against Jacob, as He must often see with us, our stubborn natures being prone to resist Him to the last. How gracious and condescending of Him to wrestle at all.

He touched the hollow of his thigh. It would have been easy for the Divine wrestler to have done this at any point in the course of the struggle. His aim had been to overcome Jacob without causing him any pain or distress. Jacob's stubborn resistance obliged Him to abandon that aim and to assert His power and mastery at a stroke. Our experience is often the same.

The hollow of Jacob's thigh was out of joint. This would make him weak and lame, and would be likely to be painful. It would effectually prevent Jacob continuing the struggle.

VERSE 26. *He said,* that is, the Man said.

Let me go. Jacob could no longer wrestle, but he could cling. So long as he wrestled, he got no blessing. Now faith takes the place of struggle and self-effort. This is the second sense in which Jacob prevailed. The old nature prevailed in stubborn resistance until it was disabled. Now faith prevails in persevering prayer. The believer learns that the road to blessing is to cling, and only the hands of faith can do that.

For the day breaketh. It made no difference to the Divine wrestler whether it were night or day. ' Darkness and light are both alike to ' Him (Ps. 139. 12). The significance of this sentence seems to be that time is running on. Jacob must attend to his business.

I will not let thee go, except thou bless me. Jacob was not deterred any more than is the man who has learnt to pray. This is the attitude, and this is the prayer that is dear to God's heart. He is bound to bless a faith that will not be gainsaid.

VERSE 27. Now the two aspects of the struggle combine to effect the blessing. The Man wrestled with Jacob to change his nature, Jacob wrestled in prayer to obtain a blessing. *What is thy name?* The name was the expression of the personality and character. The question therefore meant, Who are you? What are you really like?

He said, Jacob. Jacob answered rightly. The name means ' supplanter '. As he ceases to be able to wrestle and learns to cling, he is convicted of being what he is and confesses it in the single word ' Jacob '. He knows he has been supplanting and deceiving others for his own advantage, even striving by such means to obtain the blessing which he knew God had promised him. He thinks of Esau and the advantage taken of his hunger, his old father Isaac and the trick played upon him to obtain the blessing, the deceitful methods used to enrich himself at Laban's expense. Perhaps he reflected that all had brought him trouble and sorrow, Esau's hatred, exile from home, Laban's antagonism. Yet God had blessed him through all, given him what he had sought to win by crooked means, and never withdrawn

His favour from him.

VERSE 28. *Thy name shall be called no more Jacob.* The same thing had happened in the case of Abraham (7. 5). The change of name signifies a change of nature by regeneration. Yet we ought not to think of the present crisis in Jacob's life as the moment of his conversion. The new name signified regeneration, but did not confer it, exactly as circumcision had done in the case of Abraham. The crisis of Jacob's conversion had been at Bethel (28. 11-22), where God had shown him the ladder, that is to say, Jesus Christ as the way to heaven (28. 12; Jo. 1. 51). The wrestling was a crisis of sanctification. Perhaps the prophet Hosea means to imply this by inverting the order of events and placing Bethel after the wrestling.

Israel. This means ' a prince of God '.

As a prince hast thou power with God and with men, and hast prevailed. This wonderful name Israel would remind Jacob for the rest of his life of both aspects of the spiritual struggle. He would remember his old nature's obstinate struggle, how it was subdued only by the disabling touch. He would remember too the prevailing power of faith, the persistent clinging that obtained the blessing. The same name Israel would speak of the same things to those among the thousands of his descendants in the flesh who were enlightened by the Spirit to look into these things, and it speaks to us who are still called by it (Gal. 6. 16). God has the same struggle with each one of us, and if we are truly His, we also have been taught to cling in faith and prevail in prayer.

VERSE 29. *Jacob asked him.* In the circumstances the question was natural.

Tell me, I pray thee, thy name. Though his opponent was in human form, Jacob must have known from the beginning that He was a supernatural being. He at least suspected that he was in contact with God Himself, or he would not have asked for a blessing, but remembering the angels at Mahanaim, he may well have thought that the One who wrestled with him was an angel, sent as God's representative. Jacob was right, but his opponent was no created being. He was the Angel of the Lord. In asking for the name Jacob may have been seeking to find out this very point. *Wherefore is it that thou dost ask after my name?* This question at once revealed to Jacob the identity of the One whom he was addressing. He had the ineffable Name. God's Name, that is to say, His Being, Substance, Person and Character, can never be known by man, except in so far as He chooses to reveal it, and it can never be but partially revealed, for there is nothing with which God's infinite majesty, which is the foundation of all things, can be compared. He revealed His Name to Moses as ' I am that I am ' (Ex. 3. 14). This tells us nothing of what God is like, because He is like nothing. It tells us that God is unique, alone, absolute, and self-sufficient. To Jacob God says, ' Wherefore dost thou ask?' No man can know. God is unknowable. We cannot tell what He is like. All derives from Him. *He blessed him there.* It is wonderful to realise that the infinite, unknowable, mysterious and Almighty God, then as now and always, comes for the purpose of blessing. God's infinite remoteness and God's love are the two foundations of the revelation of the Bible. ' O give thanks unto the Lord; for he is good: for his mercy endureth for ever ' (Ps. 136. 1). God gave to Jacob His favour, His help and His smile with assurance of happiness for the future. All these things are comprised in the blessing of God. He blessed him ' there ', at that moment and at that spot, at the time of his need, in the midst of a crisis of circumstances. God always comes to us in Christ to the spot where we need

Him to bless us there.

VERSE 30. *Peniel.* This means ' the face of God '. The question about the Name and the blessing had convinced Jacob that he had been wrestling with God Himself.

I have seen God face to face, and my life is preserved. This is the great problem of the approach by a sinner to the holy God, which is answered by the Gospel of the substitutionary death of Christ on the cross, and by that alone. Christ is the mediator between God and man (1 Tim. 2. 5). Christ is the daysman, of whom Job in his distress did not know (Job 9. 33). It is only in Christ that we can see God's face without forfeiting our life. But He has made perfect atonement and has brought us to God (1 Pet. 3. 18), and we are to see His face for ever (Rev. 22. 4). Jacob did not know fully how the problem of the sinner's access to God would be solved, but his experience at Peniel proved to him that God had solved it.

VERSE 31. *As he passed over Peniel,* that is to say, over the ford of the brook Jabbok to rejoin his wives and children.

The sun rose upon him. The day with its dangers had begun. There was need of haste.

He halted upon his thigh. He could not make haste. He was reminded that he had no more strength, but that his life thenceforward must be lived in dependence upon God, in the spirit of clinging, not of struggling.

VERSE 32. It is evident that the story of Peniel must have come from Jacob, for he was alone when he passed through its experiences. Perhaps it was passed down by word of mouth until it reached Moses. Perhaps there was a collection of the stories of the events of Jacob's life in writing by the time of his death. This verse however evidently could not have come from Jacob. It is a gloss to the story, added probably by Moses, if he did not write it all. The verse tells us that there was a permanent reminder of Jacob's experiences. Every such experience in the case of any child of God leaves a permanent effect. Thus from generation to generation Jacob's descendants were reminded that the touch of God shrinks or withers the old corrupt sinful nature, and that that which so shrinks is permanently useless as a means of nourishment to the people of God. Our spirits can only be fed on that which comes from God in His Word, ministered to us by His Spirit. The ideas and opinions of unregenerate man are only poison to our souls.

CHAPTER 33

THE principal subject of this chapter is the meeting of Jacob with Esau, which occupies verses 1-16. Next we have Jacob's arrival at Succoth (17), and lastly his purchase of land and erection of an altar (18-20).

VERSE 1. *Jacob lifted up his eyes and looked.* We do not know what his mood was now. Some of his actions seem evidence of weakness. On the other hand he concludes the meeting with Esau by a decision made with dignity and firmness. His conscience still troubles him over his conduct towards Esau so many years before. Apart from that he seems to be confident and to have learnt better how to trust in God. *Esau came, and with him four hundred men.* The moment of the meeting, which he had himself provoked, had arrived.

He divided the children. This seems to have been an act of fear. The troubles of an evil conscience persisted through the great spiritual experiences through which Jacob had passed. So sin and selfishness have a mastery over a man's life that can dominate and trouble its whole course.

VERSE 2. This is the familiar order in which he loved and valued his wives. The camp on Gilead showed the same order (see on 31. 33). If anything must fall into the hands of the flesh, he will make it easiest for the least valuable to do so. He was quite right.

VERSE 3. This elaborate ceremonial of submission seems to be due to more than courtesy. Fear, springing from a bad conscience, lay behind it. A bad conscience is a powerful agent in leading a man to submit to the flesh.

VERSE 4. In a moment the crisis is resolved. Doubt and anxiety, though latterly tempered by faith in God, had mounted in Jacob's heart until now. There had been no need for them. Whatever had been Esau's intentions in setting out with the four hundred men, his mind is so disposed that he receives his brother with tender affection. This was the answer to Jacob's prayer. He learnt, as he had already learnt in the case of Laban, that God disposes of the hearts of all men. The hearts of kings are in His rule and governance. 'When a man's ways please the Lord, he maketh even his enemies to be at peace with him' (Prov. 16. 7). Now there is no teaching in the Bible that God changes the old carnal corrupt nature. It remains the same to the end, brings the mortal body to the grave, and is not obliterated until the day of resurrection. It continues during the whole of the believer's life on earth to be his stubborn enemy. God does however so dispose of the mortal *body* that it becomes a willing servant of the new nature, although at the beginning it served the old (Rom. 6. 19). The change in Esau recorded in this chapter may therefore perhaps remind us of that fact.

VERSE 5. *Who are those with thee?* The carnal nature is always barren. Those engaged in the fierce struggling activities of the world, undertaken in the flesh and never moving a single member of the human race an inch nearer to God, express surprise when they stop to see the fruitfulness of the Spirit at work in gathering men and women to Christ. The child of God is never alone. There are always those with him. Here there is a company of like-minded believers, and there there will be thousands upon thousands making up the great company of the redeemed.

The children which God hath graciously given thy servant. Jacob here rightly recognises and testifies that the ordinary forces of human increase are subject to the providence of God. Children are God's gift. So are spiritual children. Probably there is no healthy believer who has not been used by God, directly or indirectly, in the increase of the church. The process is not confined to direct evangelism. The building up of Christians to make them successful workers in the evangelistic field is part of it.

Verse 6. The handmaidens and their children are presented to Esau as a witness to the power and goodness of God.

Verse 7. Leah and her children are also presented, followed by Rachel and her child, an ascending order that showed more and more of God's goodness.

Verse 8. *All this drove.* Esau is referring to the present (32. 13-21).

These are to find grace in the sight of my Lord. Perhaps we may think of the present as the assignation of resources to the needs of the body, in order to make it amenable to the tasks of the spiritual life.

Verse 9. *I have enough.* Esau showed no greed or covetousness. His behaviour was a model of courtesy. He was now behaving towards Jacob better than Jacob had behaved towards Laban. To our shame it sometimes happens that the conduct of the carnal is on a higher plane than that of Christians. In quite another sense the statement is one which those who are in the flesh sometimes wrongly make. They think they have enough, all that they need, in the things of this world, when they really have nothing. If a man does not possess Christ, he possesses nothing at all.

Keep that thou hast unto thyself. Again this remark shows consideration and lack of rapacity on the part of Esau. At the same time it is a remark that is too often made in substance by the man of the world to the evangelist, and through him to the Lord Jesus Christ, when he is approached with the Gospel. He does not want to be disturbed by the claims of Christ. He does not feel that the Gospel is for him. He has no sense of need, and politely or otherwise he suggests that the Christian should keep his religion to himself and not seek gratuitously to give it away to those who have enough for their needs without it.

Verse 10. *Jacob said, Nay, I pray thee.* His answer was that of a good evangelist, who refuses to take no for an answer. He may have been wrong in preparing the present, but having offered it, he was determined that it should be accepted.

If now I have found grace in thy sight. Jacob made the acceptance of his present a demonstration of Esau's friendship. So does God declare that acceptance of the gift of His Son is the proof and evidence of friendship with Himself. Christ declares the same over the acceptance of salvation, and the evangelist over the acceptance of the Gospel, though the evangelist of course may and should maintain a personal friendship with those who refuse acceptance.

Then receive my present at my hand. Jacob thought that the acceptance of the present would put Esau on his honour not to harm him, and would remove all danger from him.

No doubt he was right. The evangelist also knows that the acceptance of the Gospel will turn the sinner into a friend. All that we can render to the Lord for all His benefits to us is to take the cup of salvation (Ps. 116. 12, 13).

Therefore I have seen thy face. Though it does not seem clear how truthfully Jacob's words exactly met the situation, what he appears to have wished Esau to think is that his whole purpose in seeking a meeting with him was to get him to accept a present. Jacob may have felt that he would be exposed to danger from Esau for the rest of his life, unless he could find means of rendering Esau harmless. The acceptance of a present from Jacob might well have bound Esau to friendship with Jacob by some rough code of honour, such as for instance the Albanian tribesmen use. Whatever may have been the situation between the two brothers, the statement represents exactly the attitude of the evangelist. His reason for seeing the sinner's face is to persuade him to accept the present that he has to offer, which is nothing less than the Lord Jesus Christ Himself and the righteousness and salvation that He has won for him.

As though I had seen the face of God. We may well believe that Jacob's use of this expression was determined by his recent experience at Penuel, but it is not easy to see what he means. He may mean (1) that in seeing Esau's face and meeting with him he could see the face of God in the arrangement and overruling of the circumstances. In this case he was giving praise to God for disposing of the heart of Esau and averting danger from himself and his family. (2) He may mean that the kindness, brotherly affection and friendship, which he found in the face, that is to say in the presence, of Esau, appeared to him to be a reflection and resemblance to the favour, grace and loving-kindness which he had seen at Penuel in the

face of God. (3) He may be using extremely flattering language towards Esau, carried almost to a blasphemous extent, by comparing the effect of Esau's presence and condescension to that caused by the presence and condescension of God, which he had just experienced at Penuel. We may say of these three alternatives that (1) was perfectly true and proper, (2) is true up to a point, but an unnecessary thing to say, (3) is irreverent to the point of blasphemy, and while certainly not true, yet in the context appears to be the most natural construction to put upon Jacob's remark. If this is what he meant, his fear once again gained the upper hand.

Thou wast pleased with me. Jacob appears to mean (1) that in the fact of being pleased with him Esau was like God. This is a roundabout confession of the goodness and grace of God to him. The experience of Penuel had proved to Jacob that it was possible for God to be pleased with a sinner, though he did not know the marvel of the manner in which the problem that was involved could be solved. (2) Jacob reverts to the idea that the acceptance of the present would be the proof of Esau's pleasure. The same is true of the evangelist and the sinner. The sinner may speak the Gospel fair, he may not wish to appear in the position of refusing it, but the only proof of his favour towards it is his wholehearted acceptance of it.

Verse 11. *Take, I pray thee.* Jacob continues to urge acceptance, and so ought the evangelist.

My blessing. The present is now called a blessing. It was a tangible blessing. It was a proof in kind of Jacob's good will. It is exactly the same with the Gospel. The Gospel is a present, a free gift (Rom. 6. 23; Rev. 21. 6). It is undoubtedly and emphatically a blessing. It is a demonstration of God's good will to the sinner.

That is brought to thee. The

Gospel is brought to the sinner from heaven at infinite cost. It was purchased for him at the price of the life-blood of the Son of God and conveyed to the sinner's door by the travail of the church.

Because God hath dealt graciously with me. Jacob means that he can well spare what he is offering to Esau. God having been gracious to him, he wishes to be gracious himself. He wishes to give because God has given so much to him. This is the spirit in which God wants His children to live. If they have nothing material to give, they have themselves, their prayers and their ministry (1 Thess. 2. 8).

Because I have enough. The Hebrew word translated 'enough' means 'all things'. By translating it in this way the translators show that they took it — rightly enough — in a relative sense. They took it to mean, 'I have all things that I need'. Jacob felt that since he belonged to God, all his needs were supplied. This is quite right. It is the experience of every child of God. But there is also an absolute sense in which the Hebrew words are true. 'All things are yours', says the apostle, 'and ye are Christ's, and Christ is God's' (1 Cor. 3. 21, 22). He describes himself as 'possessing all things' (2 Cor. 6. 10). Thus when the servant of God offers the Gospel to the sinner, he asks him to be a partaker of infinite abundance.

He urged him, and he took it. More urgency on our part might result in more sinners taking the Gospel. Jacob was now reasonably safe from all danger arising from Esau.

VERSE 12. *He said,* that is to say, Esau said. The acceptance of the blessing had not brought about any real change of heart on the part of Esau. He and his descendants never became part of the Israel of God (except in so far as any of them who might have been alive after the opening of the Gospel age have

accepted the Gospel).

Let us take our journey, and let us go. Esau now wanted to join Jacob's pilgrimage and to journey in his company, but not to go to the right place. He intended going to Seir (verse 14), which was the land of Edom, the country of the flesh. This is exactly what many carnally-minded people want to do. They are glad to journey with the church, if all may go together to some earthly paradise, some Jerusalem built in England's green and pleasant fields, or elsewhere, some Kingdom of God on earth, which is intended to make the world a more comfortable place for sinners to go on sinning in. They will go anywhere but to the promised land. Like Esau they already have their home outside it.

I will go before thee. Esau not only wanted to journey in Jacob's company, he wanted Jacob to submit to his leadership and guidance. This is typical of the world and the flesh. Like Jacob, we must never submit to it. We do so at the peril of our spiritual lives.

VERSE 13. Jacob rightly saw that it would never do to journey in Esau's company. Apparently he dared not say so straight out. He gives a reason for his refusal which appears to have been perfectly correct so far as it went, and Esau does not seem to have noticed that the true reason was not mentioned. The brothers were dealing with each other on the basis of politeness. Jacob's reason was a good one. He said that he must consider the weak. Those young in the faith must not be over-driven. Those whose minds are pregnant with great decisions must be tenderly cared for and not driven beyond their strength. They must especially be kept from contact with the world and the flesh.

VERSE 14. *Let my lord, I pray thee, pass over before his servant.* The flesh is to run ahead of the spirit, as it often does, in a fever of activity and haste. It is to make better headway, point to its better staying-powers, and invite admiration of its success. Perhaps it would not call attention to the fact that it was not journeying to the promised land but to Seir, the land of Edom or Idumea, which will one day be turned into burning pitch and not be quenched for ever (Isa. 34. 9, 10). *I will lead on softly.* The church moves in gentle and humble dependence on her Master.

According as the cattle that goeth before me and the children be able to endure. The Hebrew says, ' According to the foot of the work . . . and according to the foot of the children.' Here we have the two measures which should determine the pace and activity of each Christian church and of every believer. The first criterion is the work. Christ has work for all His people, and He alone can rightly determine its nature. The Christian's life should centre round the work that the Master has given him to do. Secondly, the believer's activity should be governed by the needs of the weak and young in Christ. He does not live to himself but to them, and they will instinctively follow his example.

Until I come unto my Lord unto Seir. In saying this Jacob may (1) have deliberately directed Esau's attention to Seir so as to make sure that he would make his way there, while intending himself to go in another direction. This would be deceitful, but consistent with the character of Jacob as he was when a young man. (2) Jacob may have subtly used the word ' until ', meaning that it should never be fulfilled. He could say that he never promised to come. (3) He may have intended to pay a personal visit to his brother in Seir after he had brought his family over Jordan. He may in fact have done so, though if he did, we have no record of the fact. In any case the mention of Seir in this connection seems to have been unnecessary.

VERSE 15. *Let me now leave with thee some of the folk that are with me.* Jacob wanted to separate from Esau altogether, which was the wise thing to do, but if Esau could not stay himself, he wanted to leave some of his entourage hanging about Jacob. Thus when the flesh at conversion is told to depart, it seeks to leave some of the things that accompany it and belong to it to go with the pilgrim on his journey. It usually succeeds in doing so.

What needeth it? This was a very suitable question for Jacob to ask. He had with him the angels whom he had seen at Mahanaim, indeed, as he well knew, he had with him the presence of God Himself. He certainly had no need of Esau's men to protect him. In the same way the Christian pilgrim, as he journeys through the world, has no need of the world's arms to protect him. *Let me find grace in the sight of my lord.* This was a polite formula for making a request.

VERSE 16. Esau found that none of his suggestions were complied with. If only we and all the people of God could say the same about the suggestions of the carnal nature. He therefore returned to Seir. He went back to the world. He never intended coming to the promised land, any more than had Laban.

VERSE 17. *Jacob journeyed to Succoth.* Succoth means ' booths ', and this emphasises the pilgrim life. We live in tents (2 Pet. 1. 13, 14), and have here no abiding city (Heb. 13. 14).

Built him an house. This seems a strange thing to do at Succoth, but it has parallels in the spiritual sphere. (1) Christ is building of living stones a house in which to live for ever (Eph. 2. 21, 22), now in this present age while His church is dwelling in tents. (2) The believer may build a house for himself in Christ by faith, abiding and dwelling in Him (Jo. 15. 4), while he is still here in his tent on earth journeying to the heavenly city.

Made booths for his cattle. The cattle represent the Christian worker (1 Cor. 9. 9). The booths were perhaps constructed of branches and leafy boughs and intended to shelter the cattle from the heat of the sun, which would be intense if the place were situated in the Jordan valley. Christ's workers are always sheltered and refreshed by His protecting care as they labour for Him on earth.

Therefore the name of the place is called Succoth. When the toil is forgotten, the restful refreshing booths will be remembered as evidence of the heavenly Herdsman's love and care. In heaven the redeemed will always sing and praise the Saviour's goodness which was over them all the time they were on earth.

VERSE 18. *Jacob came to Shalem.* This name is said to mean ' safety ' or ' perfection '. Jacob had passed over Jordan now and come safe into the promised land, having completed his journey. Jacob did not yet possess the land, but was only a sojourner in it like his fathers. But when the people of God complete their journey and reach the safety of the heavenly land, it will be to possess it for ever.

Shechem was an important city in the central tableland of Palestine near Mounts Ebal and Gerizim.

The land of Canaan, not yet the land of Israel. The Canaanite was still there, just as the forces of evil are still in the heavenly places (Eph. 6. 12).

When he came from Padan-Aram. Padan-Aram was the place of his exile and servitude. He had left that behind and come safe back to Canaan, though he was still a sojourner.

Pitched his tent. This proves that Jacob was still a pilgrim.

VERSE 19. *He bought a parcel of a field.* Jacob had no possession in the land of promise. What he needed he had to buy, just as Abraham had to

buy a burying-place for Sarah (chap. 23). In the same way Christ Himself had to buy the world which He had been promised, which in fact He had created, at the cost of His own life-blood. There is a sense too in which the believer must buy the world for Christ at the cost of his toil and time (Eph. 5. 16; Col. 4. 5). Notice that it is not the whole field that is bought, as in Abraham's case (chap. 23). There the whole was bought for the sake of the cave that was in it. Thus Christ bought the whole world for the sake of the treasure hidden in it (Mt. 13. 44). Here only a parcel of the field is bought. This represents the actual purchase, as it will be when the transaction is completed. A part of mankind — all who believe — will have been bought for Christ.

Where he had spread his tent. The pilgrim's basic needs must be met by purchase from those who at present own the land. Thus the Christian is subject to the economic system of the world. He possesses all things and has a right to all, yet he must earn his living, buy his bread, and pay taxes to the authorities (Rom. 13. 6, 7).

The children of Hamor, Shechem's father. This may mean that Hamor was the founder of the city of Shechem, but as the next chapter tells the story of a young man called Shechem who was the son of Hamor, it is possible that he is referred to. In any case the identity of name between place and person shows that the family was closely connected with the town. No wonder they regarded it as their own and would only part with it by purchase.

One hundred pieces of money. The margin gives the alternative rendering ' lambs '. The money contrasts with Christ. We were not redeemed with corruptible things such as silver and gold, but with the precious blood of Christ (1 Pet. 1. 18, 19). The lambs illustrate Him. He is the Lamb of God that taketh away the sin of the world (Jo. 1. 29), but of such infinite worth that not only cannot a hundred lambs approach Him in value, but not even all the millions put together that have ever been born. It was in this parcel of ground that Joseph was buried (Josh. 24. 32) and the eleven other sons of Jacob (Acts 7. 15, 16), though not Jacob himself (49. 29-32; 50. 13). The purchase by Jacob of this land in Shechem is mentioned by Stephen in his speech before the Council (Acts 7. 16). The fact that he says that the purchase was made by Abraham has been seized on by the destructive critics and liberal theologians who wait like vultures round the Scripture waiting to snatch at anything that can be mangled into the appearance of a contradiction. They delight in pointing to Stephen's 'mistake' in saying 'Abraham' when he ought to have said 'Jacob'. Their triumph is not so easily won. The name Abraham is used by Stephen in the sense in which Israel is used frequently in the Bible, that is to say as the name of a group, tribe, or race of the personal Israel's descendants. So here the name Abraham is used in the collective sense of the tribe or clan of Abraham, which had entered Palestine in the days of its founder and may well have been known to the inhabitants of that country by its founder's name.

VERSE 20. *He erected there an altar.* Having acquired some ground of his own, Jacob immediately made it the centre of the worship of the true God. Material altars passed away with the old law. The use of the word altar in conection with Christian worship is an anomaly and a misnomer, and has been introduced from heathenism. The Christian erects his altar (1) when he believes in, and proclaims his belief in, the atoning death of Christ as the ground of his salvation, (2) when he presents his body as a living sacrifice (Rom. 12. 1), (3) when he offers the sacrifice of praise continually (Heb. 13. 15), (4) when he does good and shares with others (Heb. 13. 16). (5) when he

offers the incense of prayer (Rev. 8. 3, 4). Jacob set a good example to every child of God. Wherever the believer settles, his first duty is to erect his altar to His God by establishing habits of worship and prayer.

Called it El-elohe-Israel. This means that he called it the altar of El-elohe-Israel and dedicated his house and family to Him. The name means God, the God of Israel. The usual plural term Elohim is not used here, but two rarer forms, intended to strike the memory and mark Jacob's act. In calling God the God of Israel, Jacob meant (1) that he dedicated his life and family to the worship and service of God. He has advanced far beyond the bargain that he tried to make with God at Bethel (28. 20, 21). (2) Jacob meant that the eternal God and Creator was in a special sense the God of Israel, that is to say of Jacob and his descendants, the covenant people. This is not to deny that God is not the God of all men, but Jacob here recognised the special relationship of God with those within the covenant. This is a principle which is one of the foundations of the Gospel. In the Old Testament the special relationship with Israel was in a sense arbitrary. It was typical, illustrative and symbolical. Under the Gospel the special relationship is real. The believer enters by regeneration into a new relationship with his God in Christ, which makes him a child of God (Jo. 1. 12) and endures eternally. God is the God and Creator of all men, He is the God and Father of His people. Notice that Jacob uses the name Israel which had been conferred upon him at Penuel (32. 31), thus emphasising his new nature and new relationship with Christ.

CHAPTER 34

THIS chapter is occupied with the story of the rape of Dinah. Its chief lessons are (1) the danger of compromise with the world, (2) the far-reaching effects of sin, worldliness leading to lust, that to treachery and cruelty, and those putting the covenant people in danger, (3) the impossibility of trying to enter God's covenant when not called by Him and the fatal result of such an attempt, (4) the over-ruling protecting providence of God.

VERSE 1. *Dinah the daughter of Leah.* It may not be without significance that she is called the daughter of Leah rather than the daughter of Jacob. Perhaps she did not know her father's God. Perhaps she was a true child of Laban, having something of her mother's heathen upbringing in her character.

Went out to see the daughters of the land. She made friends with the people of the world and sought their companionship, not in order to win them, but to engage in their pursuits and enjoy their company. She did what both Lot (see chapter 19) and Esau (26. 34) had done before her. Her example is followed by many who profess to be within the covenant.

VERSE 2. *Shechem the son of Hamor the Hivite.* The Hivites were among the seven nations who inhabited Canaan. The two names appear to be Canaanite, but some have identified the Hivites with the Achæans (A-chaiw-oi), in which case they would be akin to the Greeks.

Saw her. The lust of the eyes was in operation (1 Jo. 2. 16).

He took her. Here we have the pride of life (1 Jo. 2. 16). Shechem imperiously carried out his own will, irrespective of the will of others. Dinah herself seems not to have been consulted, certainly not Jacob.

Lay with her. Here is the lust of the flesh in operation (1 Jo. 2 . 16).

Defiled her. The Hebrew says ' humbled her '. By this act of Shechem Dinah's womanhood was humbled according to the standards of the Gospel. Perhaps that would not be thought so much of in Jacob's day, nor even in Moses'. The mean-

ing seems to be that she was defiled or humbled as an Israelite. Contact with the uncircumcised Gentile broke her position in the covenant and was therefore an offence against Jahweh, the God of the covenant. This was all the result of Dinah's desire for the companionship of the Canaanite women. The incident ought to be a grave warning to us against friendship with the world.

VERSE 3. In this verse we have a description of natural affection at its highest and best. Though it was here manifested by a heathen and Gentile, he was yet a man made in the image of God, and we need not be afraid to see in this threefold description of affection a picture of the love of Christ for His people and something of what their love to Him ought to be in return.

(1) *His soul clave unto Dinah.* Thus Christ would dwell in the hearts of His people (Eph. 3. 17), and has told them to abide in Him (Jo. 15. 3). Christ is ever faithful to His people. He cleaves to them and never fails or forsakes them (Heb. 13. 5).

(2) *He loved the damsel.* Christ's love is practical, never merely sentimental. Shechem's love resulted in action. He made efforts to get Dinah for his wife. Christ went to the lowest depths in order to win His people for Himself for all eternity. This fact we all know, believe and rejoice in, yet so great is the corruption of sin remaining in our nature, that we are very slow to make any sacrifice in His service.

(3) *Spake kindly unto the damsel.* This is the translation of the beautiful Hebrew phrase, ' Spake to the heart of the damsel.' This is a true expression of love. In the same way the voice of Christ is heard by His people, speaking to them from His Word great blessings and promises and whispering to their hearts words of comfort by the Holy Ghost in power and tender support. In all this we see the expression of a right

instinct in Shechem but in wrong circumstances. He was using the powers and emotions that God had planted in his heart for wrong ends. This is the essence of sin.

VERSE 4. *Shechem spake unto his father Hamor.* Hamor was the prince, who had the authority and power. As he had no power over Jacob, it is difficult to see that he could do more than his son unaided. What a contrast to our Father, Who is sovereign Lord of all. We do right to follow Shechem's example and look to our Father to supply our needs, and we may do so with confidence and assurance that He is able to do so according to His riches in glory (Phil. 4. 19).

Get me this damsel to wife. Notice how definite and detailed is the request. Our requests to the heavenly Father should be the same. This very request may literally be made by many a young Christian man. It is in type a request that we may say with reverence was made by the Lord Jesus Christ to the Father in eternity past as He looked forward to the salvation of the elect, and at creation when His delights were with the sons of men (Prov. 8. 31).

VERSE 5. *Jacob heard that he had defiled Dinah his daughter.* Some fathers might have thought a union with a prince to be a matter of congratulation. Not so Jacob. His heart was now so much set on the things of God, and he had such a sense of the purpose of God for himself and his family, that the standards of the world meant nothing to him and he thought what had happened to his daughter humbling and defiling. If by her ways Dinah was the daughter of Leah, as a child of the covenant she was the daughter of Jacob.

His sons were with his cattle in the field. This is exactly where God's sons are. They are on service for Him in the world (Mt. 13. 38; Col.

1. 6). *Jacob held his peace until they were come.* He did not want to act without them. Perhaps he felt he wanted their advice. In something of the same way God is holding His peace and not acting against the enemies of His people till His sons come home from their work on the day of resurrection. Then He will associate them with Him in judgment (Isa. 42. 14; Mt. 19. 28; 1 Cor. 6. 2).

VERSE 6. In this verse is described the frequent device of the heathen world, in which it is too often successful. It comes out to commune with us, and we are often persuaded by its suggestions.

VERSE 7. *The sons of Jacob came out of the field when they heard of it.* They left their work in order to deal with the humiliation and defilement that had befallen Dinah and in her had befallen them all as a covenant people. In giving precedence to this we may reckon them right. With a broken covenant their work would have been of little value.

The men were grieved, and they were very wroth. This reaction was right. Sin ought to produce it in us. In the days of the judgment of Jerusalem a mark was set on the foreheads of those who sighed and cried for the abominations therein (Ezek. 9. 4). Anger is not wrong for the child of God so long as it is not associated with sin. In Eph. 4. 26 we are told, 'Be ye angry, and sin not,' a verse, as Philip Henry, the commentator's father, says, in which the easiest of all instructions in the Bible is followed by the hardest of all prohibitions. The Lord showed anger during His ministry, although it is only recorded of Him once (Mk. 3. 5).

He had wrought folly in Israel. They rightly regarded the whole covenant people as outraged by Shechem's act. It was not done against Dinah alone. The whole people of God are one, and a sin against one of them is a sin against all and a sin against Christ (1 Cor. 8. 12).

Which thing ought not to be done. The law of Moses had not yet been given, but the family of Jacob had inherited standards of conduct from Abraham and beyond him from their godly Semitic forefathers.

VERSE 8. *Hamor communed with them.* Notice that it was Hamor who took the initiative. The wise Christian avoids communing with the world, but the world sometimes seeks fellowship with the church, if it thinks it can derive any advantage from it. *The soul of my son Shechem.* This is an intensive expression for Shechem himself. We sometimes say, ' His whole soul '.

Longeth for your daughter. This is sometimes the case with a worldly man and a Christian girl. If pursued, it brings disaster.

I pray you give her him to wife. This was a suggestion which might have brought some worldly advantage, if acceded to. It would however have frustrated God's purpose for the family of Jacob and thus have destroyed God's plan of redemption for the world. Jacob and his sons can scarcely be expected to have foreseen all this, but they had enough light to know which of the ways opening out immediately before them was right. We too need to remember that greater issues than we may be aware of depend upon our walking step by step in the line of God's revealed will.

VERSE 9. In this and the following verse a fourfold invitation, accompanied by a promise of assurance, was given by Hamor to the family of Jacob. It contains four enticements which in the spiritual sphere have often been made by the world to the church. (1) *Make ye marriages with us.* The most subtle and dangerous suggestion came first. It amounts to complete identification, the absorption of the church into the world. Pressure to accede to this suggestion is always present among unconverted professing Christians, and the visible church has often succumbed to it. The world dislikes peculiarity and exclusiveness in Christian things. Being unable to discern the spiritual (1 Cor. 2. 14), it can only regard the church as the religious activity of the world, an attitude that is reciprocated by worldly Christians. They sometimes suppose that amalgamation with the world will bring a ' Christian spirit ' or Christian morality into worldly affairs. In fact it invariably kills Gospel witness and floods the church with the spirit of the world.

VERSE 10. (2) *Ye shall dwell with us.* The Christian is invited to forsake his pilgrim life and his hope of the heavenly country and to settle down in the world and make it his home. To those who do this Gospel activity soon appears superfluous.

The land shall be before you. The seductive promise is made by the world that the Christian need no longer submit to the restraints and restrictions of the pilgrim life. There is plenty of room for him in the world. All his wants can be supplied and all his desires indulged.

(3) *Dwell and trade ye therein.* The third suggestion is to bargain with the world. Jacob possessed little but flocks and herds, intended under the covenant to supply his needs and to be offered in sacrifice to God. Now these sacred things are to be bartered in exchange for the whims and follies of the world, and the things of God are to become the subject of sale and purchase. The true church can never offer the things of God for sale.

(4) *Get you possessions therein.* The fourth suggestion made is to heap up treasures on earth rather than in heaven (Mt. 6. 19-21), to live for the material things of this world, to accumulate wealth and spend care and time upon it. All these four things the professing church has frequently done, and it succumbs to

this day to these four suggestions.

VERSE 11. Shechem made a special plea of his own. *Let me find grace in your eyes*. This expression means, 'Grant my request'. To the seductive temptations to worldly advantage is added the moving plea of an honourable and probably charming young man, made with genuineness and in integrity of spirit. Such a personal appeal is difficult to refuse.

What ye shall say unto me I will give. Shechem naturally thought in terms of worldly advantage and was quite prepared for a large demand. This fact added further strength to this temptation, as Jacob and his family could have asked for as much as they wanted.

VERSE 12. *Ask me never so much dowry and gift*. He so valued Dinah that he was ready to give anything for her. In spite of the wrong circumstances he resembled in this the heavenly Bridegroom, Who so loved His bride that He did not withhold His own life-blood for her.

I will give according as ye shall say unto me. He was ready to measure his gift by the scale of the inexorable demands of the Divine holiness.

Give me the damsel to wife. Shechem had one supreme desire and one definite request. In the same way the sinner's one desire should be to possess Christ and to abide in Him.

VERSE 13. *The sons of Jacob answered*. The young men took the whole matter in hand. We do not therefore know what Jacob would have done. Probably he would have been less precipitative and would have waited on God.

Deceitfully. Their attitude and motive seems to have been right, but their method was wrong. Jacob dissociated himself from it (verse 30; 49. 5-7). Both their cruelty and their deceit were unworthy of the cause for which they were acting.

Right ends may be carried out by wrong means, a fact that we need to consider when engaged in God's work.

Because he had defiled Dinah their sister. They seem to have been bent upon personal revenge as much as upon the vindication of the covenant. Thus not only was their method wrong, but their motive seems to have been mixed. This is often true with us.

VERSE 14. *We cannot do this thing*. This was a true and right answer. The sons of Jacob, rough and cruel though they were, evidently had a strong sense of their covenant position and of the separation that sprang out of their peculiar relationship with God. The principle remains true of us today. We cannot amalgamate with the world, nor compromise with sin. 'He that is born of God cannot sin' (1 Jo. 3. 9).

To give our sister to one that is uncircumcised. This would mean to be unequally yoked with unbelievers (2 Cor. 6. 14).

That were a reproach unto us. This means that it would give them cause for shame. All compromise with the world or the flesh is a cause of shame to the believer and to the whole Christian community. If the sons of Jacob had stopped at these words and said no more to Hamor and Shechem, they would have been quite right and might have expected the blessing and protection of God. It is true that the situation was complicated for them by the fait accompli of the rape of Dinah. Their family was already suffering reproach.

VERSE 15. *In this will we consent unto you*. The sons of Jacob had no right to say this. If they had meant it, it would have been wrong. As they did not mean it, it was doubly wrong. The Israel of God may never, then or now, consent to compromise with the uncircumcised.

If ye will be as we be. The sons of Jacob either supposed themselves or deliberately led Hamor to think (as he naturally would), that circumcision of the flesh would make him and his people Israelites. They forgot, or withheld the fact, that circumcision is a sign and seal of a reality possessed beforehand. Circumcision did not confer membership of Israel, it signified it (Rom. 4. 11). Under the old covenant, which was in force in those days, natural birth with descent from Abraham, Isaac and Jacob conferred membership of Israel. Circumcision signified that descent. What the sons of Jacob suggested to Hamor in regard to circumcision many unscriptural religious teachers repeat today with regard to baptism. They declare that by submitting to baptism — and that generally as infants — the unsaved can be as the saved. But as in the old Israel with circumcision, so in the new Israel with baptism. It does not confer regeneration, it signifies it. Membership of the Israel of God is conferred only by the new birth, a secret operation of the Holy Spirit in the heart in response to faith. Many are deceived today, as the sons of Jacob sought then to deceive the Shechemites.

That every male of you be circumcised. There was a deceitful purpose in this suggestion, as the sequel shows.

VERSE 16. Here are three results which the sons of Jacob suggested would arise from the circumcision of the Shechemites. Notice that nothing is said of any call of God or of Divine revelation. All three things were to be lines of action on the part of Jacob's sons. There was to be amalgamation or absorption through intermarriage, identity of habitation, and finally complete identification. In local churches and in various denominations this fatal result often takes place today and has done so in almost every age of the church's life. If it is brought about, it does not spring from the will of God, but from deliberate human action, as the sons

of Jacob suggested here. But in their case the sense and the language begin to imply, and the sequel shows, that they never intended to put these propositions into action.

VERSE 17. *If ye will not hearken unto us, to be circumcised.* Their language still betrays them. It was their own suggestion, not God's.

Then will we take our daughter, and we will be gone. How did they propose to take her? Perhaps there was a code of honour which would have obliged her return if no agreement had been reached. If so, there was no need for the subsequent conduct of Jacob's sons, unless they felt that nothing but the death of Shechem could restore Dinah's respect. Perhaps they implied that they would take her by force if her return was resisted. Perhaps they spoke only vaguely. As their words were not true, they may have intended no more but to play upon Shechem's feelings. This seems the most likely.

VERSE 18. *Their words pleased Hamor, and Shechem, Hamor's son.* Each was pleased for a different reason, as the sequel shows.

VERSE 19. *The young man deferred not to do the thing.* As opposed to his father he had a genuine definite desire.

Because he had delight in Jacob's daughter. He had no ulterior motives. No doubt he believed what Jacob's sons had said. He is like those who sincerely seek the truth, but are deceived into believing that they can become Christians through baptism, or ecclesiastical association, or some outward act or ritual.

He was more honourable than all the house of his father. This is an illuminating judgment of the Holy Ghost's. It is not entirely such as we might expect, because Shechem was the one who did the wrong in the first place, and the whole situation arose from his act. He was more honourable, because he sought a genuine friendship with the people of God. He did not want to steal Dinah from them, but to treat honourably for her marriage, and he was willing to become one with the people of God.

Verse 20. *Hamor and Shechem his son.* Shechem is associated with his father in this parley with the citizens, but we may imagine that the ideas and words were Hamor's.

Communed with the men of their city. Notice how a widening circle is drawn into the net. Dinah's compromise with the world led to Shechem's lustful act. This in turn led to Jacob's sons' deceit, and this to the destruction of a whole city.

Verse 21. *These men are peaceable with us.* There was harmony, as it were, between Christ and Belial (2 Cor. 6. 15).

Let them dwell in the land. The Hivites thought it condescending on their part to grant Jacob permission to dwell in the land which God had promised him. We do wrong if we take anything on sufferance from the world.

And trade therein. We must never seek to barter spiritual things with the people of the world.

Large enough for them. Alas! The world is large enough for the Christian if he wants to live there. Satan sees that there is plenty of room.

Let us take their daughters to us for wives. This is sometimes the actual wish in a literal sense of the people of the world. If put into effect, it brings disaster to the Christian. In a wider sense the world constantly seeks to entice the believer to become one with it.

Let us give them our daughters. The world often seeks to place its members in Christian churches and in Christian fellowship. It has no more deadly way of doing this than by persuading a Christian man to marry an unconverted woman.

Verse 22. Hamor knew nothing of the promises to Abraham, the purpose of redemption, the relationship of Israel to God, or the meaning of circumcision. He thought the condition made by Jacob's sons a foolish whim, which could be easily complied with. He had no idea of the deceptive purpose that was in their minds.

Verse 23. *Shall not their cattle and their substance and every beast of theirs be ours?* Here is Hamor's real purpose revealed. The world's purpose is the same. It seeks to get the church and what belongs to it into its clutches, and is quite ready to pay the simple price of a meaningless baptism and of conformity to other religious rites in order to obtain this end. In its relationship with the visible church it has in general obtained it.

Only let us consent unto them. The condition if complied with would be temporarily troublesome, but would pay heavy dividends. In the same way to worldly people attendance at church is wearisome but brings many advantages in the way of ecclesiastical respectability.

They will dwell with us. Again and again it has happened in the history of the church that in response to some external religious concession the visible church has been content to dwell with the world and employ her strength in the attainment of worldly aspirations.

Verse 24. *Hearkened all that went out of the gate of his city.* They were all eager to get the worldly advantages which they thought were being placed within their reach.

Every male was circumcised. This was an act (1) of selfishness and greed, carried out in the hope of its being a means to exploit the strangers and acquire control of their property. The same spirit has often been displayed by worldly people in their profession of Christianity and adherence to some ecclesiastical body. (2)

C

It was an act of blasphemy, although this aspect of it was concealed from those who took part in it. It amounted to an attempt to attain membership of Israel by unreal and carnal means. The Hivites had never been called to membership of Israel. They could not be one with Israel apart from a Divine call and a Divine revelation. Yet by undergoing circumcision, which was the seal of the covenant, they assumed the sign without possessing the reality and presumed to thrust themselves, unfit and unbidden, into the temple of God. This is what was done by thousands who underwent baptism in the days of Constantine the Great, has been done by thousands ever since, and is still being done today. Baptism effects no change in a man's condition spiritually, and if it has any effect at all upon those who receive it unworthily, it can only be to consign them to the wrath of God. (3) It was an act of ignorance and folly. The Hivites were unaware of God's covenant with Abraham and had no sense of its meaning. This did not make their action less irreverent in the sight of God, but they cannot be said to be responsible for the blasphemy. Those who suggested their circumcision would be guilty in that respect, though in the greatly complicated circumstances of this narrative the sons of Jacob had not made the suggestion in order to bring the Hivites by false means into the covenant. In their ignorance the Hivites placed themselves at the mercy of their enemies. So do those who make an outward profession of Christianity without possessing the spiritual reality in their heart place themselves in the power of the devil.

When they were sore. An unreal spiritual life brings trouble and irritating annoyance. All true Christianity is irksome to the unconverted. *Dinah's brethren.* They were greatly incensed and had a fierce desire for revenge.

Sword. This is like the Word of God in the mouths of His prophets, which hews and slays the wicked and the false professors (Hos. 6. 5).

Slew all the males. This would have been quite unnecessary in connection with the wrong done by Shechem to Dinah. The men of the city were not guilty. Jacob dissociated himself from this act. He might have thought and prayed out a plan whereby he could have effected the rescue of Dinah and perhaps the death of Shechem. Once they had been circumcised, however, their death may well have been morally necessary. They had done something of the same sort as Uzzah did in touching the ark (2 Sam. 6. 6, 7). As the sons of Jacob had suggested their circumcision, they were guilty of their death.

VERSE 26. *They slew Hamor.* This greedy schemer, who thought to take advantage of sin and get possession of the covenant people and their property, suffered speedy retribution. His plans brought him no advantage, but only a violent death. This is a warning to every age. All who scheme against the people of God, even if it be half ignorantly, as seemed to be the case with Hamor, will suffer God's judgment, if not in this world, yet on the great day.

Shechem his son. Shechem's rash act probably made his death inevitable in God's sight. As long as he lived, Dinah belonged to him and could rightly belong to no other (see 2. 24). There thus existed an evil association between the covenant people and the heathen, which might have frustrated the redemptive purpose of God. The moral necessity for the death of Shechem is unaffected by the wrongness of the method used to bring it about, from which Jacob dissociated himself (verse 30), which was also condemned by the Holy Ghost speaking through Jacob at the blessing of his sons on his deathbed (49. 5-7).

Took Dinah out of Shechem's house. She belonged there no more and the defilement could be rectified.

The integrity of the covenant people was restored. Yet notice the train of events set in motion by Dinah's initial compromise. How subtly the devil took advantage of it. As soon as she became involved with Shechem, a situation arose which could only be resolved by Shechem's death. This it was almost impossible for Jacob's family to accomplish without being themselves involved in great dangers and the risk of almost certain destruction. The dilemma in which Satan seemed to have placed them was only solved by an act of deceit and cruelty. Thus one sin led to another. Yet whatever the method Dinah was restored. In the same way a child of God may be restored after falling into compromise and sin, although such sin can scarcely fail to bring trouble and distress upon all who are involved in it.

Went out. They had accomplished their purpose, which was the restoration of Dinah and of the integrity of the covenant and the honour of the family.

VERSE 27. *The sons of Jacob.* This may mean (1) the remaining sons of Jacob, or some of them, besides Simeon and Levi, who can be thought of as flying upon the spoil, after Simeon and Levi had cleared the way. More probably (2) Simeon and Levi are referred to, verses 27 to 29 giving a more detailed description of the expedition and describing what the two brothers did at the same time as they killed the Shechemites and rescued Dinah.

Came upon the slain. Slain men are helpless. Thus those dead in trespasses and sins are helpless, thank God, in the face of the Gospel, and will be helpless on the great day of wrath, when all they have will be taken from them. Again those dead in Christ should be as slain men, unresisting to the assaults and persecutions of evil men, inattentive to their scorn or flattery, and unresponsive to the temptations of the devil.

Spoiled the city, because they had defiled their sister. Their reason was not really logical. It was natural, however, to follow the slaying with the spoiling. However much they resented Dinah's humiliation, they saw to it that their material wealth was increased, and they may be said to have fallen into the same sin of greed as that of which the Hivites had been guilty.

VERSE 28. This and the following verse tell us of six things which were taken by the sons of Jacob. However cruel and violent their method, it remains true that these six things represent heathen property which was taken by the covenant people. They thus represent spoil taken from the Gentiles for Christ (Isa. 66. 20; Rom. 15. 16). Our own methods of evangelism are not always perfect. Thus the sons of Jacob took (1) their *sheep,* that is to say, those among the heathen who would be given grace to offer their bodies a living sacrifice (Rom. 12. 1). (2) They took their *oxen,* those among the heathen who would patiently serve and work for Christ, and perhaps give their lives as a sacrifice in the end. (3) They took their *asses,* unclean animals, unfit for sacrifice, but in taking such from the world the Gospel transforms their nature, doing what the sons of Jacob could not. We all once had the nature of asses, being children of wrath as others (Eph. 2. 3). (4) They took what was *in the city.* Thank God that spoil can be taken, and often is, from professing Christians, those who are or imagine themselves to be, already in the city of the church. (5) They took what was *in the field,* raw heathen taken direct from the jungle of the world, outside all contact with visible Christianity.

VERSE 29. (6) They took *all their wealth.* So Christ takes from among men all that is valuable to Him, all that will turn from sin and recognise His claims. Christ sets an infinite value on the precious souls for whom

He died. When He wins them, He wins great wealth.

All their little ones, and their wives took they captive, just as Christ took captivity captive (Eph. 4. 8). We may thank God that so many little ones are, literally speaking, taken captive for Christ. *Spoiled even all that was in the house.* Not only what was in the field of the world (Mt. 13. 38), or in the city of the visible church, but also what is in the house of close association with true believers, perhaps members of their families, perhaps unconverted members of true, sound and keen evangelical churches (2 Tim. 2. 20), may be taken as spoil for Christ.

VERSE 30. *Jacob said to Simeon and Levi.* He does not seem to have dissociated himself from his sons' action on moral or spiritual grounds, but on the grounds of fear. His old weakness of faith reasserted itself. He never forgot the incident, and when blessing his sons under the inspiration of the Spirit on his dying bed, he condemned the action of Simeon and Levi on more solid grounds (49. 5-7).

Ye have troubled me to make me stink. This is strong, even crude, language, but it is true. All inconsistent action on the part of the people of God has this effect. Members of a church can bring a whole church into disrepute, and inconsistency of life on the part of Christian people is often made an excuse by unbelievers to refuse the Gospel.

The Canaanites and the Perizzites. These were not Hivites, but however much these nations differed among themselves, all were united against the people of God.

I being few in number. Notice how Jacob by using the singular word 'I' identifies himself with his whole family and household. This strong sense of community persisted in the ancient east. It is in this sense that Abraham and Jacob were both promised possession of Palestine. Neither possessed any of it, except

very small areas which they bought, and never will. But their descendants possessed it. In the same way the martyr Stephen speaks of a purchase by Abraham of land in Shechem (Acts 7. 16). In the same way the Lord Jesus Christ does not shrink from identifying Himself with His people: 'Saul, Saul, why persecutest thou me?' (Acts 9. 4). That identification will be maintained on the day of judgment (Mt. 25. 40, 45). Jacob realised that he was few in number in comparison with the inhabitants of the land in which he sojourned. This has been the case in every generation with the people of God in comparison with the people of the world. They have always been a 'little flock' (Lk. 12. 32).

They shall gather themselves together against me and slay me. Jacob had either once again forgotten Mahanaim, or perhaps he thought that his sons' action had forfeited God's protection. He was wrong. If God purposes to bless, He blesses. If He makes promises, He is able to perform them. In spite of all our weaknesses, failures and inconsistencies, He will never fail nor forsake His people, but will protect them to the end, keep them through all dangers and temptations, raise them up at the last day (Heb. 13. 5; Jo. 6. 39), and present them faultless at the end (Jude 24).

I shall be destroyed, I and my house. The people of God may at times fear that this will happen, but it will never be.

CHAPTER 35

THIS chapter completes the story of Jacob's return home to his father. A new revelation is given to Jacob at Bethel (1-15), where Rebekah's nurse dies (8). Next follow the birth of Benjamin and death of Rachel (16-20). The mention of Reuben's adultery with Bilhah (21, 22) is followed by a list of Jacob's sons (27-29). The chief lesson of the chapter is the goodness and faithful ness of God.

VERSE 1. *God said unto Jacob*. We note that God takes the initiative. Jacob is directed and empowered in his relations with God. In all our salvation from the beginning God takes the initiative. He chose us in Christ before the foundation of the world (Eph. 1. 4), gave us to His Son (Jo. 6. 37; 10. 29), gave us the gift of salvation (Eph. 2. 8) and saved us by grace (*ibid.*).

Arise. Though the initiative comes from God, an effort of co-operation must be made by Jacob.

Go up to Bethel. He was to go to Bethel (1) because it was the place where God first appeared to him. A man's first real religious experience sets the tone of his whole spiritual life. We can never go back on our conversion. There we potentially receive all. If we wander away, as Jacob had done, we must come back. (2) He was to go because it was Beth-El, the house of God. As a child of God Jacob was welcome in that house.

Dwell there. There is no better place to dwell. One day we shall dwell in the house of the Lord for ever (Ps. 23. 6). Here on earth we may dwell by faith in the heavenly sanctuary and find our place as living stones in the eternal temple.

Make there an altar unto God. There is no approach to God without an altar. Yet no Christian altar exists on earth. Christ is the living Altar in the living temple. On that Altar as Priest He offered Himself as Victim once and for all at Calvary. When the sinner makes Christ's soul an offering for sin, he becomes a child of God (Isa. 53. 10) and welcome in the Father's home. Thus every true believer makes Christ and Christ alone his altar. He may also offer to God his own self in the body as a living sacrifice (Rom. 12. 1), he may offer continually a sacrifice of praise (Heb. 13. 15), and he may set up an altar of incense, which is the type of prayer (Rev. 8. 4). All this

he does in his heart, where he sanctifies the Lord Christ (1 Pet. 3. 15), and never externally.

That appeared unto thee. The altar can only be made because God has appeared and revealed Himself. He intervened to redeem man by sending His Son, and we cannot offer Him our lives until He has revealed Himself to us in Christ through the Gospel.

When thou fleddest. It was when Jacob was in trouble and distress that God appeared to him. He was fleeing from the face of Esau, who represents the flesh. In the same way it is when the lost and helpless sinner is fleeing before the power of the flesh, unable to stand against it, turned out of his home and country, an exile from his God and the heritage that he was created to enjoy, that God reveals Himself to him in his need. It was to sinners in this hopeless condition that God sent His Son, Who did not shrink from giving His life for them (Mt. 9. 13; 1 Tim. 1. 15).

VERSE 2. This verse shows that Jacob now knew enough of God to be aware instinctively that he must separate himself from sin before meeting Him. Notice that there were two sets of people to whom Jacob issued these instructions, *his household*, whom we might call members of Israel, and *all that were with him*, whom we might call associates. As they were to go up to Bethel as a community, the attitude of both these groups was important. We may learn from this the importance of the attitude towards sin of all members of a church or group of Christians, professors as well as possessors, if that church as a whole is to obtain blessing from God. Notice the three things that the community was to do: (1) *Put away the strange gods that are among you*. The captive Shechemite women may have had strange gods (34. 29), but we know that Rachel had (31. 29, 34, 35). We do not know whether or not Jacob was aware of this yet, but in any case the strange gods were as near to Jacob as they could be, possessed and treasured by the most honoured member of the community. This is a picture of a frequent situation. The strange god of many churches today is called Finance, and his needs are attended to before any and every spiritual requirement. Time and energy that might be spent in the Lord's service are wasted upon him. The individual also treasures strange gods. He can set up idols in his heart (Ezek. 14. 3). Lust and covetousness are idolatry (Eph. 5. 5). If a church or an individual are to obtain the blessing which God longs to give, at least obtain it fully, these strange gods must be put away.

(2) *Be clean*. The blood and water necessary for cleansing both flow from the Saviour's wounded side (Jo. 19. 34). The blood of Jesus Christ cleanses from all sin in the sight of God (1 Jo. 1. 7) and gives a clean heart (Ps. 51. 10). The believing sinner is also cleansed by the Word of God in which he receives the washing of regeneration (Eph. 5. 26; Tit. 3. 5). When once he is regenerate the believer can never be bathed again, but needs only the occasional washing of his feet (Jo. 13. 10). To meet with God and obtain any blessing from Him we must be clean in heart by the blood of Jesus, and in order, to enjoy and use the blessing our feet must be washed in the water of the Word. The feet stand for the walk or conduct of the believer.

(3) *Change your garments*. The filthy garments of sin (Zech. 3. 3) must be exchanged for the robe of Christ's righteousness (Isa. 61. 10) and the beautiful garments of sanctification (Isa. 52. 1). In fact the robes must be washed and made white in the blood of the Lamb (Rev. 7. 14), and we must put on Jesus Christ (Rom. 13. 14).

VERSE 3. *Let us arise*. Being prepared and equipped by Divine instruction and in the Divine way to

meet God in His house the Christian must co-operate with God by a deliberate act and effort. He will not meet God if he stays silent and motionless. He must awake and arise from the dead (Eph. 5. 14).

And go up to Bethel. Bethel means the house of God. We also must go up, coming with boldness to the throne of grace (Heb. 4. 16), where we may meet God and find grace to help in time of need.

I will make there an altar unto God. We may do the same. We may re-appropriate by faith our Saviour and the virtue of His death for us, trusting ever deeper in His mercy, love and power. We may offer and present ourselves, our souls and bodies, as a reasonable, true and lively sacrifice. We may offer to Him the sacrifice of praise and thanksgiving, and gifts that are well-pleasing to Him.

Who answered me in the day of my distress. If Jacob was correct in using the word 'answered' in a strictly accurate sense, he must have called to God to help him on the day that he left home, a lonely exile in fear of Esau's anger. Perhaps he uttered no prayer, but looked up half consciously in his heart to God. Whatever the form of his cry to God, he is conscious that God's appearance to him at Bethel was the answer to it.

And was with me in the way which I went. Perhaps Jacob did not realise God's presence at the time, but as he looks back he becomes aware that God was always at his side. The way to which he refers evidently extends beyond the actual journey to Padan-aram. He means that God was with him through all his way of life, through the hard toil and unfriendly atmosphere of Padan-aram, through the hazards of the journey home, through the encounter with Esau and back again to the promised land. Thus God was to Jacob what He is and has been to all His people. They all know Him as the One to Whom they can turn with unfailing assurance in distress, Who answers their plaints and cries by the revelation of Himself, Who never leaves them but accompanies them through every step on the way of life and is about their path and their bed.

VERSE 4. *They gave unto Jacob.* They would not have been likely to do so, if God the Holy Spirit were not moving powerfully in their midst. Perhaps they had been impressed by Dinah's humiliation, or by the danger that they might well have been in from the Hivites and Canaanites, or by the consideration that they were about to meet with the true and living God and see the place where He had manifested Himself so long ago. Whatever it was that moved their minds, a kind of revival seemed to break out among them, and they handed over to Jacob all the false gods. We too shall get blessing when we give all the idols up to Christ.

All the strange gods which were in their hand. We have not read of anyone in the company possessing strange gods except Rachel. What secrets were revealed on that day! Jacob must have suspected the presence of strange gods, even if he had no evidence of it, or he would never have asked that they should be given up. Was he shocked on that day to find that Rachel had Laban's teraphim, which he had denied having ever brought away from Padan-aram? But it mattered no more. The idols were being given up. If secrets were revealed, the revelation meant the putting right of what had been wrong. A great confession and clearance of sin was made.

And all their earrings which were in their ears. They showed the reality of their repentance by giving up more than they had been asked for. It is not clear why they gave up their earrings. They must have felt them to be in some way a hindrance to holiness. Perhaps it was no more than that they were ostentatious and the wearing of them worldly. Perhaps there was in their shape something

directly sinful. Perhaps they had come to be regarded as charms and become objects of superstition. Whatever the reason, the Holy Ghost moved them to see instinctively that there was something in the earrings inconsistent with witness to the true God. If the idols were sin, the earrings were at least weights (Heb. 12. 1).

Jacob hid them under the oak. All sins are buried under the tree. Christ ' bare our sins in His own body on the tree ' (1 Pet. 2. 24). There beneath the tree, as soon as they are confessed, sins are hidden away for ever.

Which was in Shechem. The tree was in Shechem, the dwelling-place of the heathen, who knew nothing of the true God. This is exactly where the cross was. It was set up in this wicked world among sinners in their need, and its efficacy is available for all who will receive it.

VERSE 5. *They journeyed.* So long as they are in this world the people of God are continually journeying. Here we have no abiding city, but we seek one to come (Heb. 13. 14). ' We are travelling home to God '.

The terror of God. This is one of many instances of the protection given by God to His own. He can strike terror into any number of human hearts as He wills.

They did not pursue. After the incident at Shechem they naturally would have pursued them, and this is what Jacob feared they would do (34. 30). Notice that the protection of God is not withdrawn from His people even though they commit an act of reckless folly which exposed them to danger.

VERSE 6. *Luz, which is in the land of Canaan.* The place was a Canaanite city in a wicked land. It became Bethel only because God made it so. In the same way we shall find that it is in this life among the evil surroundings in which we live that God reveals Himself to our hearts. We must not expect the place or the people to be changed. It is to us alone that Luz becomes Bethel. To those who live there it remains Luz.

That is, Bethel. To the Canaanite the city was just Luz, as it always had been. To Jacob it was henceforth Bethel. The name Bethel meant nothing to the inhabitant of the land. To one who has met with God the meaning of life, even the character of the cities of the world, are changed. What a difference there is between the meaning of the name Keswick and its meaning to the holiday-maker and its meaning to the Christian.

He and all the people that were with him. Jacob's personal religion and his leadership brought his family and household to meet with God at Bethel, as he himself had met with Him. Thus Jacob, once blessed himself, became a channel of blessing to others. This is normally the case with all the people of God.

VERSE 7. *He built there an altar.* He built it at the place where God had appeared to him, to which God had told him to return. Since the coming of the Gospel that place is Calvary. There we must go, no longer to build an altar ourselves, but to find it built and already standing. Nor can we offer any sacrifice for sin upon it. That was done by the great High Priest when He offered His body once for all. A burnt-offering we may offer, ourselves, our souls and our bodies, and a peace-offering, the fruit of our lips, giving praise to His Name (Rom. 12. 1; Heb. 13. 15).

El-beth-el. This means the God of the house of God. By Jacob's second visit Bethel became doubly sacred to him. He found God a second time and added His Name a second time to the name of the place. This name emphasises to us that it is not the house of God that matters, but the God of the house. The church is of no value apart from the God Who is Lord of it. Our Christian fellowship may come to mean

more to us than the Saviour to Whom we belong.

There God appeared to him. It is only ' there ' at Calvary that God appears to us. He is revealed to us only in and through Jesus Christ. He appears only at the place of His choosing. But in Christ He appears, so that the one to whom He is revealed enters into a higher plane of life, he comes to know what others have no conception of, he passes into light from darkness into the presence and knowledge of God from blindness, ignorance and sin.

When he fled from the face of his brother. Jacob never forgot that God appeared to him just when he needed Him, in the time of his distress and fear. ' Just when I need Him most, Jesus is near to comfort and cheer, Just when I need Him most.'

VERSE 8. This verse interrupts the narrative to tell us of the death of Deborah. We must ask two questions with regard to it: (1) Why does this verse come at exactly this spot in the narrative? (2) Why does the Holy Spirit tell us of the death of Deborah at all? (1) Does the occurrence of this verse at this point in the narrative mean that it was at this point of time that Deborah died? Deborah came originally with Rebekah from Padan-aram (24. 59). Now we must remember that at this time Jacob was a man of about a hundred years old. His mother had been married for twenty years before he was born (25. 20, 26). She was therefore about or nearly a hundred-and-forty years old if she was still alive. Deborah was Rebekah's nurse. She was therefore at least about or nearly twenty years older than Rebekah. A hundred-and-sixty years was quite a possible age (25. 7; 35. 28), but it is the least that Deborah could be. Then if she died at this point, what was she doing in Jacob's company? Had she retraced her steps a second time from Padan-aram? That she went there and returned again seems unlikely. Did she come from Isaac to meet Jacob at Bethel? This again seems very unlikely. If Isaac wished to send a messenger to Jacob, he would hardly send a woman of at least a hundred-and-sixty who was on the point of death. It is far more probable that Deborah had died at Bethel at some time in the past, and that her death is mentioned here because at this point in the narrative Jacob arrives at Bethel. But why and when did she die at Bethel? There is no record of Isaac and Rebekah having been at Bethel, and even if they had sojourned there during some time that Jacob was away, it is evident that the death of Deborah was something known to Jacob, which affected him greatly. Is it not likely that Deborah accompanied Jacob on his journey to Padan-aram twenty years previously and died at Bethel on the way? She would have a double reason for accompanying him. Jacob was the favourite of Rebekah (25. 28), and as such probably adored and spoilt by Rebekah's old nurse. He was also the sort of character that would return her a deep affection. When Jacob left home on a visit that it was expected would last a few days for the home of Deborah, how natural that Rebekah should suggest her accompanying him to ' show him the ropes ' in Laban's household at Padan-aram. In addition Deborah would welcome the opportunity to visit her own people. So she set out with Jacob, but died at Bethel on the way, a fact that contributed to Jacob's feeling of loneliness there. (2) We can now more easily see why we are given this information. It tells us (a) that God broke the last tie that bound Jacob to his old life at the moment that He revealed Himself to him. (b) The spiritual meaning that the incident has for us Christians holds good, whatever be the time and circumstances under which Deborah died at Bethel. We saw when Deborah was first mentioned (24. 59) that she may well have been as Rebekah's nurse the picture of the law. There we

had the picture of the fulfilment of the law in the bridal train of the Gospel. Here we have the other side. On becoming joined to Christ, a man is found to be dead to the law through the body of Christ (Rom. 7. 4). The part of the law has been fulfilled and ends when the Gospel comes in (Rom. 10. 4). So when Christ is revealed to Jacob as the way to heaven, the ladder set up on earth and reaching to heaven (28. 12), the law with its sanctions and claims dies, and Jacob becomes the example of a man no longer under law, but under grace.

VERSE 9. *God appeared unto Jacob again.* This shows that we ought not to expect only one experience of meeting with God and no more. After His first revelation to Jacob at Bethel (28. 17), God spoke to him in Padan-aram (31. 11-13), at Penuel (32. 24-31), and now again at Bethel. Our conversion is a beginning, and we ought to expect further revelations of God to us as He wills and as we need.

When he came out of Padan-aram. God had appeared to him at the time of his need when he was leaving home in his loneliness, but He also appeared on the day of happiness on his return. In need or in joy God makes Himself known. Jacob was to start another phase of his life. So often we do the same, and we may expect God to make Himself known to us in a special way when we set out on it.

Blessed him. God when He appears always blesses us, seeks, and contrives our good, and makes plain that His purpose is to lead us on to the highest and happiest possible condition. Blessing implies fruitfulness, so that God's blessing enabled Jacob and his family to be prosperous and fruitful, and enables us to bring forth fruit to the glory of God, whether the fruit of the Spirit (Gal. 5. 22), or an increase of souls won to Christ.

VERSE 10. *Thy name is Jacob*. This means 'supplanter' or 'deceiver'. It signified Jacob's nature, which was always seeking to obtain for itself something to which it had no right. It is good for us to be reminded of what we are by nature. A revelation from God always begins with conviction and the manifestation of need.

Thy name shall not be called any more Jacob. Thank God, He taketh away the old, that He may establish the new (Heb. 10. 9). The old name, the old nature, the old character cease to be, here in this life progressively and imperfectly, on the day of resurrection completely, absorbed in eternal likeness to Christ (1 Co. 15. 54).

Israel shall be thy name. In place of the old deceitful acquisitive nature Jacob receives a new name denoting victory and power. He becomes a prince with God and men, able to prevail in prayer and able to lead others to the true God. Every child of God in varying measure becomes an Israel in this way, when transformed by the will and Word of God through the indwelling Spirit.

He called his name Israel. God repeats what He had done at Penuel (32. 28), in order to give Jacob double assurance. Indeed He does more. He again promises the change, as He had done at Penuel. But now at Bethel He not only promises the change of name, but actually calls Jacob by the new name, that is to say, acts on the assumption of its accomplishment. God does the same with all of us. He looks upon us in Christ as perfect Israel's. Indeed we have now and for ever an unassailable perfect standing before Him. ' Now are we the children of God, and it doth not yet appear what we shall be. But we know that if He appear, we shall be like Him, for we shall see Him as He is ' (1 Jo. 3. 2).

VERSE 11. *I am God Almighty*. God bases His promises to Jacob, as He did with Abraham (17. 1), on the fact of what He Himself is. El Shaddai, as the Name is here in Hebrew, means ' the bountiful God.' Shaddai means something very like *alma*. God's promises and blessings are all based on what he Himself is, that is to say, on His sovereign will and on His grace and goodness. There would be no blessing, if God did not take the initiative and determine to give it.

Be fruitful and multiply. This was the command given to Adam (1. 28) and to Noah (9. 1). Its repetition here is significant. The line of Jacob is connected with those of Adam and Noah, from whom it descends, and thus the family through which the redeemed humanity would come into being is indicated. This is God's command to all His children. He demands and confers fruitfulness. He intends that we should all be channels of blessing to others and appear in heaven not alone, but accompanied by many others whom we shall have led, or helped to lead, to Christ.

A nation and a company of nations. Under the law this promise was fulfilled typically in Israel after the flesh, which was a nation itself and composed of a number of tribes, which were regarded in Scripture as themselves nations (48. 19). Its final fulfilment under the Gospel is in the holy nation (1 Pet. 2. 9) which is the Christian church, itself composed of a fulness of nations (Rom. 11. 25; Rev. 21. 24).

Kings shall come out of thy loins. This is fulfilled in King Saul, King David and his line and in the various dynasties that ruled the northern kingdom of Israel, but they were all typical of the ultimate fulfilment in the royal priesthood (1 Pet. 2. 9) of the new Israel. Every servant of God is a king and will reign for ever and ever (Rev. 22. 5), and everyone who is Christ's looks to Jacob as his father (Gal. 3. 29).

VERSE 12. *The land which I gave Abraham and Isaac*. This land in type was Palestine. It had been promised three times to Abraham (12. 7; 13. 15; 17. 8), once to Isaac (26. 3), and once previously to Jacob (28. 13). Not one of them personally ever possessed a square foot of it. They possessed it in their natural seed. They will also possess it for ever as the scene of the great redemptive acts, where the Lord was crucified and rose again, from the soil of which He ascended into heaven. Thus Palestine plays an eternal part in the redemptive purposes of God. Yet Abraham never looked for Palestine. He understood the promise as making him heir of the world (Rom. 4. 13), and he looked for the heavenly country, which is better than Palestine (Heb. 11. 15, 16). We cannot doubt that Jacob did the same. *To thee will I give it.* This promise associates Jacob with the great redemptive blessings given to Abraham and Isaac. He is made an heir of the promises.

To thy seed after thee. The natural seed inherited Palestine, and the spiritual seed inherits the heavenly country.

VERSE 13. *God went up from him.* This is the same expression as is used when God spoke to Abraham at the time of the covenant of circumcision (17. 22). It implies that God had revealed Himself visibly to Jacob, and that when He had finished speaking to him He visibly ascended into heaven. This was to give the impression (1) that God lives elsewhere than on the earth among men. Even the old days when He walked in Eden were gone. The barrier of sin had separated Him from men. (2) The impression was given that God is higher than man. He dwells in the high and holy place (Isa. 57. 15). If God made Himself visible when He spoke to Jacob, the speaker was the second Person of the Holy Trinity, the Angel of the Lord and pre-incarnate Christ. No man has seen the Father at any time (Jo.

1. 18; 1 Tim. 6. 16).

VERSE 14. *Jacob set up a pillar.* The pillar represents Christ.

In the place where he talked with him. The pillar set up at that very place signified that it is in Christ that we have access to God. Christ is the link between God and ourselves, the one Mediator between God and man (1 Tim. 2. 5).

Even a pillar of stone. Christ is the foundation stone, elect and precious (1 Pet. 2. 4).

He poured a drink offering thereon. The drink offering was supplementary to the burnt offering (Num. 15. 5). It accompanied and emphasised the blood sacrifice, though it involved no blood-shedding itself. The offering was of wine, which symbolised both the blood of the sacrifice and the Holy Spirit. Jacob in making this offering made a sign that he devoted his life to the service of God. The believer today does the same in the much clearer light of the Gospel. He pours out his life on the great sacrifice that Christ has made for him, and sees in spirit also the great pillar on which his salvation is founded stained with the blood of Calvary.

He poured oil thereon. Oil in the Bible is one of the pictures of the Holy Ghost. By pouring oil on the pillar Jacob signified the fact that Christ was anointed with the Holy Ghost, and also that the life poured out in His service must be one that is led by the Holy Ghost.

VERSE 15. Jacob had done the same thing more than twenty years previously. Here again he confirms the name that he had given before. He found God the same God and His gracious promises the same, and it may be that Jacob's spiritual facilities had been so awakened by the Holy Spirit, that he felt as if this was the first time that he had known God. He felt that a revelation as great as that at the beginning had been made to him. Our Bethel is in heaven where our great Anointed Pillar stands, and we approach it in the depths of our hearts by faith (1 Pet. 3. 15).

VERSE 16. This and the following four verses give an account of the birth of Benjamin and the death of Rachel.

They journeyed from Bethel. Not even at the meeting-place with God is there any permanent resting-place for the people of God in this world. They are pilgrims and are always journeying.

There was but a little way to come to Ephrath. Ephrath is Bethlehem (verse 19). Notice where this son of Jacob was born. All his other sons were born in exile. So all the sons of God are born in the exile of this world, lost in Adam, except One. He was begotten in eternity past, ' before all worlds ' (Col. 1. 15), not in exile, but in the Father's home, but He was begotten on the way to Ephrath. That way to Bethlehem, and through it to Calvary, began in eternity past. His goings forth were of old, from everlasting, yet He came out of Bethlehem (Mic. 5. 2). This is the first characteristic in which Benjamin typifies Christ.

Rachel travailed. What travail was necessary in order to bring Christ into the world, the bondage in Egypt and the whole sacrificial system of the Old Testament lasting for hundreds of years (Rev. 12. 2). *She had hard labour.* What sorrow and toil were necessary to bring Christ into the world. The faithful remnant and heroic prophets risked their lives to foretell His coming and maintain the truth. There is as much need for travail and hard labour today on the part of the church in gathering in the lost sheep that are scattered abroad.

VERSE 17. *When she was in hard labour, that the midwife said unto her.* In all her toil and tribulation and tumult of her war, in the agony of prayer and of conflict with the devil, amid the attacks of Satan and

the hatred of men, in the hardships and deprivations of her missionary efforts, the church hears the gentle voice of the Holy Spirit, the heavenly midwife, Who is responsible for the safe delivery of souls into spiritual life.

Fear not. The words spoken were words of comfort, encouragement and peace. The Lord Jesus said the same words: ' Fear not them which kill the body ', ' Fear ye not therefore ' (Mt. 10. 28, 31), and we in reply may boldly say, ' The Lord is my helper, I will not fear ' (Heb. 13. 6).

Thou shalt have this son also. The work of winning souls is sometimes hard and discouraging, and we need the assurance of the Holy Spirit that the Gospel is the power of God unto salvation.

VERSE 18. *As her soul was in departing.* This does not mean that her soul was leaving her body in the sense that her personality broke up into two elements, one of which carried consciousness and went on living. The Bible never teaches such a conception. Her soul means her whole conscious natural life, and the expression means that this was coming to an end, being explained as such by the following phrase, set in our version between brackets.

She died. When Christ was born, the old covenant and the old Israel died, being replaced by the new covenant of the Gospel and the new Israel of the redeemed. In the same way no believer can win a soul for Christ without first becoming dead to sin (Rom. 6. 11) and dead with Christ to the elements of the world (Col. 2. 20).

Ben-oni. This means ' son of my sorrow '. Perhaps this points to Christ in His human nature. He was ' a man of sorrows and acquainted with grief ' (Isa. 53. 3). This is also perhaps the view which the travailing church inclines to take of the sons whom she wins.

Benjamin. This means ' son of the

336

right hand '. Benjamin is the beloved of the Lord, that dwells in safety by Him (Deut. 33. 12). 'There' also 'is little Benjamin their ruler' (Ps. 68. 27). Here are pictures of the Lord Jesus Christ in His Divine nature. He is the Father's beloved Son (Mt. 3. 17; 17. 5; Col. 1. 13), and He will 'reign over the house of Jacob for ever' (Lk. 1. 33).

VERSE 19. *Rachel died.* See on verse 18. This was a sad blow to Jacob, who was watching by her bedside (48. 7).

Was buried. It is good and proper for the dead to be buried out of sight. Thus it is good for the believer who is dead with Christ (Col. 2. 20) to be buried with Him in baptism (Col. 2. 12).

In the way to Ephrath, which is Bethlehem. Where Rachel was buried Benjamin was born. So where a heart becomes dead to self, Christ is formed within (Gal. 4. 19).

VERSE 20. *A pillar.* We may think of the pillar as representing either Christ Himself or a life dedicated to His service. In either case we find this pillar raised upon a grave. The glory of Christ rests on the fact of His suffering and death, and the dedicated life rests not only on Christ's death but also on participation in that death by the believer. Many a pillar in the form of a life converted to God and sent out into fruitful service for Christ may be seen raised over the grave of some self.

Unto this day. Such a memorial is permanent, and will endure for ever in heaven (1 Thess. 2. 19, 20).

VERSE 21. *Israel journeyed.* Notice that it was Jacob who set up the pillar over Rachel's grave. The name emphasises the human or natural side and points us to the bereaved husband. But here it is Israel who journeyed. He journeyed as the believer in God and God's servant, knowing that he was in line with

God's will and carrying out God's great purposes in fulfilment of the promises made to his family.

Spread his tent. Israel pursued the pilgrim life to the end, just as we must, if we are to pass safely through the journey of life and reach the heavenly country.

Beyond the tower of Edar. Edar means the flock. The tower of the flock is the Lord Himself (Ps. 18. 2). 'The name of the Lord is a strong tower; the righteous runneth into it, and is safe' (Prov. 18. 10). The Lord's flock takes refuge from wolves and thieves in the high tower. There abiding in Him by the exercise of simple faith is our refuge today. Now Israel pitched his tent beyond the tower. He went to the right place. The Hebrew word translated 'beyond' is *halah* and means 'forward of', 'in front of'. Israel passed by the tower and pitched safe on the inner side of it, so as to enjoy whatever protection it might afford. So must we. We must pitch, if we may may say so with reverence, on the heavenward side of Jesus.

VERSE 22. Notice that we are still dealing with Israel, not with Jacob. The incident mentioned in this verse affected the covenant life of the family and its relationship with the God of the covenant. It is recorded to show that the three eldest sons of Israel were set aside by God from being ancestors of Christ. The deceit and cruelty of Simeon and Levi are described in chapter 34. This verse tells us of the lust of Reuben, who committed incestuous adultery. Israel never forgot these things. They affected the destiny of his sons (49. 3-7). The fourth son Judah seems to have had no better a character, as we may gather from the narrative about him in chapter 38. But through the sordid story of his conduct there told us we see the over-ruling hand of God at work to make him the ancestor of the Redeemer to come.

Israel heard of it. Obviously neither Reuben nor Bilhah told him. He heard of it from the spiteful brothers or the gossip of the women. How this incident, which arose out of his polygamy, must have troubled him. He recognised it as a defilement of the covenant, something that ought not to be done in Israel. Whether or not he took it to God in prayer, he never forgot it, and rightly allowed it to affect his dying blessing of his son (49. 4).

The sons of Jacob were twelve. They were the ancestors of the twelve tribes (Acts 26. 7). Their number probably set the number of the Lord's apostles, and their names will be on gates of the heavenly Jerusalem (Rev. 22. 12).

VERSE 23. In this and the next three verses we find one of several lists of Jacob's sons that occur in the Bible. Their order here is not that of birth, nor that into which Jacob divided them when he was confronted by Esau, which order was determined by his affection for their mothers. Here they are given in an order which is determined by their mothers' identity.

The sons of Leah. Leah comes first (1) because she was married first, and (2) because she was through Judah she was the ancestress of Christ. Thus, as so often, God chose the despised, not the beloved, for that inestimable honour.

Reuben. Here we have a different arrangement of the names of the sons than the first one in chapters 29 and 30, but they yield equally rich fruit, Reuben means 'See, a son', so that first of all the sinner is pointed to the Son of God.

Jacob's firstborn. This fact is emphasised, perhaps to imply that the foundation of all spiritual experience is to be pointed to Jesus Christ.

Simeon. This means 'Hearing'. The next step to blessing is to hear and obey Christ.

Levi. This means 'Joined'. In faith and obedience the believer becomes joined to Christ, Who abides in him, and he in Him.

Judah. This means 'Praise'. A thankful heart and a life of praise follow.

Issachar means 'Hire'. At the end of his life of obedience and praise the believer meets the Lord, Who comes with His reward with Him (Rev. 22. 12). The reward is Christ's gift of eternal life, and it is great in heaven (Mt. 5. 12).

Zebulun means 'Dwelling'. At the last the believer dwells with Christ for ever.

VERSE 24. *The sons of Rachel.* Rachel comes next as she was married next, though her children were not born till after those of the handmaids. She would naturally be mentioned before them.

Joseph. The name means 'Adding'. Thus Christ is continually adding to His church.

Benjamin means 'Son of my old age' with the emphasis on the father's love (see 37. 3). Christ is the Father's beloved Son (Col. 1. 13).

VERSE 25. *The sons of Bilhah, Rachel's handmaid.* They were older than Rachel's sons and older than Issachar and Zebulun, but Bilhah is in her right place behind Leah and Rachel and before Zilpah as the first of the two handmaids to be married. The names of her sons point to the two great activities of Christ.

Dan. This means 'Judge'. Christ will judge the world at the last day, the Father having committed all judgment to Him (Jo. 5. 22, 27).

Naphtali means 'Wrestling'. So on the cross Christ wrestled with the devil with great wrestlings and, as Rachel said of herself, prevailed (1 Jo. 3. 8).

VERSE 26. *Gad and Asher.* These names mean 'Fortunate' and 'Happy'. They present a true picture of the 'people saved by the Lord' (Deut. 33. 29).

The sons of Jacob. It was good to be a son of Jacob, born within the covenant. It is far better still to be a son of God, born under the new covenant by faith and the operation of the Holy Ghost.

In Padan-aram. Benjamin was not born there, though he was born before Jacob actually arrived home in Hebron where his father was. The birth of Benjamin having been described a few verses previously, it is evident that the statement is a general one. It applies to eleven of the twelve sons. A modern writer might have inserted the words ' Except Benjamin ' in a footnote. An ancient writer would regard this as quite unnecessary.

VERSE 27. *Jacob came unto Isaac his father.* So Christ came to His (Jo. 17. 11), and like Jacob, though He went out alone into long and bitter exile, which began in the virgin's womb and ended in the grave, He returned with a large potential family, born in exile, the great multitude of the redeemed.

Mamre. This is where Abraham had lived (13. 18). The family had been in Beersheba in the extreme south, when Jacob had left home (28. 10). Meanwhile Rebekah was presumably dead, and Isaac had returned to the place where his father and mother lay buried (23. 19; 25. 9).

The city of Arbah, which is Hebron. Notice the gloss. The ancient name is explained by a more recent one, as we might say, ' the city of Eboracum, which is York '. This is one of the incidental proofs of the antiquity of Genesis.

Sojourned. Abraham and Isaac were strangers and sojourners all their lives, which were typical of the lives of the people of God in every age of the world.

VERSE 28. *The days of Isaac.* ' So teach us to number our days, that we may apply our hearts unto wisdom ' (Ps. 90. 12).

VERSE 29. *Isaac gave up the ghost.* His spirit returned to God Who gave it (Eccl. 12. 7). God took back from him the life principle, which fell back, as it were, into God's reservoir.

Died. His death was not the end. Though he still sleeps today in Machpelah, he is assured of a glorious resurrection, because God, Who is the God of the living, is his God (Mt. 22. 32).

Was gathered unto his people. This was not as a wraith, but in the cave where Abraham and Sarah lay, and in the grave where his ancestors were. As his remote ancestors were idolators (Josh. 24. 2), he could not have met them in some other world. See 15. 15 and 25. 8.

Old and full of days. Thus Isaac's life was a type of the life of the redeemed, which will last for ever and ever (Rev. 22. 5). In that life however there will be no old age in the sense of decay, but only in that of blessedness and honour.

His sons Esau and Jacob. These two brothers, hostile and suspicious, with differing outlooks, differing natures and differing destinies, are yet brought together by their common bereavement. Death can bring together as well as divide. This verse does not tell us the place of Isaac's burial, but Jacob tells us later that it was with Abraham and Sarah at Machpelah. There these grand and faithful patriarchs sleep, while the centuries pass over their heads in an instant of time to bring them without conscious break to a glorious resurrection.

CHAPTER 36

THE eighth of the eleven divisions of the book of Genesis ended with chapter 35. It was the ' generations of Isaac ', which began with 25. 19. The present chapter contains in itself the ninth and tenth divisions, the generations of Esau (36. 1-8), and the generations of Esau as father of the Edomites (36. 9-43). Verses 1-8 tell us the names of Esau's wives and sons, and describe his migration to Mount Seir. In the tenth division we find (1) the names of Esau's sons and descendants (9-14), the list of dukes or chieftains among Esau's sons (15-19), the sons of Seir the Horite (20-28), the dukes of Horite origin (29-30), the kings of Edom (31-39), and finally a further list of Edomite dukes (40-43). The chapter consists of little more than names. This is intended to be a contrast to the full narratives about the sons of Israel.

VERSE 1. *The generations of Esau.* No doubt these are inserted because of the contact maintained between Israel and Edom during their history. Esau is a type of the flesh, and during the whole history of the Christian church as well as during the earthly life-time of the individual believer the flesh maintains itself in contact with the spirit. It is possible for it, as Isaac foretold (27. 40), to have the dominion and break the yoke of Israel.

Who is Edom. There is no need to suppose that this is a late note. Edom was well known to Israel in the time of Moses (Num. 20. 14-21).

VERSE 2. *The daughters of Canaan.* Esau could not resist women (Heb. 12. 16). He therefore became unequally yoked with unbelievers (2 Cor. 6. 14). He broke the spirit of God's covenant by so doing, offended God and grieved his parents (26. 35). He is for all time the type of the man who throws away eternal realities for the passing pleasures of the world and the flesh.

Adah the daughter of Elon the Hittite. In 26. 34 she is called Bashemath. All three wives of Esau have different names in this verse from those by which they are called in 26. 34 and 28. 9. This is a delight to the liberal critics and theologians, who point eagerly to a discrepancy, which they hasten to teach is due to there being independent and contradictory origins to the two passages. A moment spent however in consideration and comparison of

the names will show the reasonable probability that the names given in the present verse are those borne by the women in their fathers' homes before they were married, while those which they have in the two previous passages were given them by their husband on marriage. This seems evident in the case of Aholibamah, who is mentioned second in this verse, but first in 26. 34 under the name of Judith. Aholibamah is a heathen name with evil associations. The name Adah, which may have meant 'ornament', may also have had heathen associations in the minds of the covenant family. They knew of an Adah in the remote past who was one of the wives of Lamech, a wicked descendant of Cain (4. 19). Even if the name Adah itself was quite innocent, we can well imagine Isaac and Rebekah wishing for its change, in order to conceal the Hittite connection. Perhaps they brought pressure to bear on Esau, who humoured them in this by changing his wife's name from Adah to Bashemath (26. 34). This name was a sort of compromise. It was in use in Ishmael's family (verse 3), who was a son of Abraham. There may have been a second reason in the minds of Esau and his parents for changing these women's names. They may have felt that the alteration was to some extent a connection with the change of Abram's name by God to Abraham (17. 5). This change was made at the time of the establishment of the covenant. It would be typical of the natural man if Esau thought that by artificially changing his wives' names he could bring them within the covenant, just as so many unconverted religious people today suppose that baptism can bring a person into covenant relationship with God, irrespective of a regenerating work in the heart by the Holy Ghost. Adah's name was thus changed by her husband to Bashemath, the meaning of which does not seem to be clearly known. In spite of her change of name she remained a heathen Hittite in heart and habit.

Aholibamah, the daughter of Anah. The name Aholibamah means ' tent of the high place ', and thus has definitely evil associations connected with heathen worship. It may not be too speculative to suggest that she had been a temple prostitute, and it is not inconceivable that Esau met her in that capacity. In any case the name must obviously be changed, and so it was to Judith (26. 34), which is a very respectable Hebrew name, connected etymologically with that of Judah. But what about Aholibamah's father? In 36. 24 he is called Beeri. We might suppose that Beeri was her father and Anah her mother. But the R.V. margin suggests that Anah may not have been a woman after all, but that he was the son, not the daughter, of Zibeon. This agrees with verse 24, where we find that Anah was a man. There also we are told that he found the mules in the wilderness, but if we turn again to the R.V., we shall see that what he found were not mules, but hot springs. After the discovery he called himself Beeri, which means ' my well '. Thus Anah was his original name; and Beeri that by which he commemorated his discovery. It is thus easy to see that Aholibamah the daughter of Anah was identical with Judith the daughter of Beeri (26. 34).

The daughter. The Samaritan recension, the Septuagint Greek version and the Syriac Peshitto all read 'son' here for the 'daughter' of the Hebrew text. We may take it that they are right in view of verse 24. A copyist mistakenly repeated the word 'daughter' in the text that lay behind the Massoretic.

Zibeon the Hivite. His son Anah, or Beeri, is called a Hittite in 26. 34. In verse 20 Zibeon is called a Horite, or Hurrian. There is no reason to suspect inaccuracy, and there may be more than one explanation of the difference. Racial distinction may have been hard to maintain, when a small land such as Palestine was peopled

by so many races and nations. In origin Hurrian, Zibeon may have become a member of a Hivite community and his son of a Hittite one.

VERSE 3. *Bashemath Ishmael's daughter.* This was her original name, but Esau changed it to Mahalath (28. 9). The reason for his doing so was probably that he already had a wife called Bashemath, which was the more respectable name that he had given to Adah, Elon's daughter (26. 34; 36. 2). He was therefore obliged to change this lady's name, though we do not know why he selected the name Mahalath. On Mahalath's relationship to Ishmael and Nebajoth see on 28. 9.

VERSE 4. *Eliphaz* was the ancestor of Eliphaz, the friend of Job (Job 2. 11).

VERSE 5. *Jeush, and Jaalam, and Korah.* The fact that Aholibamah was the mother of three sons in contrast to the one each of the other wives tends to show that she was the favourite. If we are right in our suggestion as to the meaning of her name and the circumstances under which Esau met her (see verse 2), this is perhaps what was to be expected.

Born unto him in the land of Canaan. All Jacob's sons except one were born outside the land. Esau's on the contrary were born inside it. Here is an ironical situation. Jacob's family came from exile and entered into the inheritance. Esau's family, though born inside it, rejected it and let it go. Thus Esau shows himself again the type of the flesh, which in Adam rejected and lost what God had bestowed upon it, while Jacob like the repenting sinner returned from exile to claim it.

VERSE 6. Notice the seven classes of persons and things affected by Esau's rejection of the promised inheritance. (1) *His wives,* that is, those closest to him and his fellow-companions in the sins of the flesh. These missed the inheritance, almost as a matter of course by their association with Esau. (2) *His sons.* They are a picture of all those who are in the flesh, serve it and live for it (Rom. 8. 7, 8, 13). They all lose the inheritance. (3) *His daughters.* These are born in the family of Esau, but go out from it in marriage and leave it. Is it fanciful to see in them a picture of those who go out from the flesh in death perhaps in childhood or youth? They too, if come to years of responsibility, lose the inheritance. (4) *All the persons of his house.* All those whom a sinner influences, who become entangled with him, lose the birthright and inheritance to which they were potentially born. ' Persons ' is the correct translation of the Hebrew *nephesh,* which means 'soul'. It always means 'soul' in the sense of ' person '. (5) *His cattle.* The flesh, the world and sin drag from the inheritance for which they were created all those who toil so hard in their interests. (6) *All his beasts.* These are those who might have been devoted in sacrifice to the Lord. They too lost their opportunity and their inheritance. (7) *All his substance.* The whole world of material things is put to wrong uses by the flesh and the world.

Which he had got in the land of Canaan. Everything that the sinner possesses and enjoys is a gift to him from God.

Went into the country. Like the prodigal son he went into a far country (Lk. 15. 13).

From the face of his brother Jacob. Esau had moved to Seir before Jacob's return from Padan-aram (32. 3), but this verse tells us the reason for his going. The incident of the blessing (chap. 27) had convinced him in his heart that Jacob would inherit the land of promise and not himself. Perhaps he felt that Jacob would one day overspread it and that he must therefore make a home for his children, while there

were time and room. In any case he felt that he could not live with his brother Jacob. Their interests were clean contrary. The one hated what the other loved. In the same way the flesh is antagonistic to the spirit (Gal. 5. 17), and the people of the world seek to get as far as they can from the spiritual atmosphere of the true church.

VERSE 7. *Their riches were more than that they might dwell together.* There is no room in the same heart for the riches of the flesh and the riches of the spirit. Whoever wants to become rich in spirit must be ready to be poor in the things of the flesh.

The land wherein they were strangers. This is the scene of the pilgrim life.

Could not bear them. The heart that is looking for the heavenly country and living on earth as a stranger cannot endure the presence of the flesh as well as that of the spirit, but must drive it out, just as Ishmael was driven out of the house of Abraham (21. 8-21).

Because of their cattle. The cattle are the animals of service and work. It is the works of the flesh and the work of the Spirit that are mutually incompatible and cannot exist side by side.

VERSE 8. *Thus dwelt Esau in mount Seir.* He went to live among the Horites, one of the nations of the land which represent the powers of evil (Eph. 6. 12). They are congenial to the flesh, which always goes to live in their company. In mount Seir Esau found himself no stranger. He had not to live a pilgrim life, but could settle down. The flesh always seeks to settle down in the world.

Esau is Edom. He was not only his brother's enemy personally, but he grew into a nation, which opposed Israel during much of its history. Many carnal men do something like the same. The godless decision of one man may extend its influence and exercise immense power for evil throughout the course of history upon many generations of men. Such were the decisions made by such men as Constantine the Great, or King James I, or Charles II, or E. B. Pusey.

VERSE 9. *These are the generations of Esau*. These words begin the tenth division of the book of Genesis. This section consists mostly of nothing but names. Its presence here teaches us two things: (1) Its brevity and lack of narrative set it in contrast with the sections that deal with the people who are in the line of the redemptive purpose. The whole emphasis of the Bible is on this purpose. It is intended to claim and hold our interest just as it holds the interest and energy of God Himself. (2) The fact that these people's names are listed and brought before us in God's Word shows that the Holy Spirit takes an interest in them. To us these people are nothing but names, but He knew them and cared for each one. If they are carnal and lost, God knows and is grieved. God shows by including such sections as these that His purpose was one day to include the Gentiles and that His love reached out to them (1 Jo. 2. 2; Eph. 3. 6).

In mount Seir. Esau's immediate children were born in the land of promise and moved out of it with him. Now he becomes fruitful in the congenial surroundings of the wicked world. The second generation of his descendants is born there. This often happens in the case of an unregenerate man who is brought up as a professing Christian and is the child of Christian parents. His children are born in the land. They know something by hearsay, or at second-hand, of the Gospel, though they do not accept it. Their own children do not call themselves Christians at all.

VERSE 10. The names of Esau's sons are repeated in this verse (see verse

4) (1) for the sake of completeness. The generations which follow could not easily be given without the intervening link. (2) The repetition of the names emphasises their importance to God and speaks once again of His care for the lost. (3) The repetition tends to prove that verses 9-43 are not contemporary with verses 1-8, but added later. It is evident that no more than verses 1-8 could have been recorded in Jacob's time. It is likely that the present section was added by Moses, or possibly later (see verse 31).

VERSE 11. *Eliphaz*. He was half Edomite and half Hittite. What a combination! But it is a sadly true picture of the unconverted heart.

Teman. He was the ancestor of Eliphaz, Job's friend (Job 2. 11).

VERSE 12. *Concubine to Eliphaz*. We do not know what Timna's parentage was. She is probably mentioned as a concubine as opposed to the principal wife or wives, in order to emphasise the unworthy origin of her son Amalek, whose descendants were bitter enemies of Israel.

VERSE 13. *Reuel* had a less alien maternal ancestry. His mother descended from Ishmael, Abraham's son by Hagar. She was nevertheless outside the chosen family.

VERSE 14. *The daughter of Zibeon*. Again in this verse the Samaritan recension, the Septuagint Greek version and the Peshitto Syriac version all read ' son ', as in verse 2. It is reasonably certain that ' son ' is the correct reading, and that the reading ' daughter ' arose from the mistake of a pre-Massorite copyist, who repeated it from the preceding phrase either here or in verse 2. Once established in one of these two places, the reading was repeated from it in the other. The mistake in transcription must have occurred after the Greek translation had been made in the third century B.C., unless that translation was taken from a family of MSS not followed by the Massoretes.

VERSE 15. *Dukes.* This means chieftains of clans, or sheikhs.

VERSE 16. *In the land of Edom.* They all became chieftains and important in their own sphere. But all the time they were in the land of Edom, living in and after the flesh (Rom. 8. 12, 13). What profit is there in being a duke in the land of Edom? *The sons of Adah.* They were all akin to the Hittites, just as the Lord told the Jews, ' Ye are of your father the devil ' (Jo. 8. 44).

VERSE 17. Notice how each of the sons became the chieftain of a tribe of his own. This is how the nation grew. The members of the tribe consisted of the slaves, servants and those who made up the household, of whom Esau, who could muster four hundred men (32. 6; 33. 1), had plenty in his lifetime.

VERSE 18. *The dukes that came of Aholibamah.* They were of mixed race, partly Horite, partly Hivite, and partly Hittite (see on verse 2). Notice the difference of expression used to describe the children of Aholibamah from those of Adah and Bashemath (verses 16, 17). This all goes to show that she was the favourite wife, perhaps an attractive and wicked woman, plunged into sin in early youth or childhood by her parents for the sake of gain.

VERSE 19. This verse is a colophon that closes the list. We may well suppose it to have been originally a separate document, gathered by Moses from Edomite sources, or from lists available in Egypt, under the inspiration of the Holy Spirit.

VERSE 20. Verses 20-30 give us another list, this time of the original inhabitants of Seir when Esau moved there. He inter-married with them, and this list gives us the origin of Timna, Eliphaz's concubine, and

especially of Aholibamah. Moses might have found the material in Egypt. We may also imagine that it may have been preserved among the Edomites, wrongly proud of their maternal ancestry. It is possible that the custom of matriarchy may have obtained at some time among the Horites or Hurrians. This was a degrading way of life involving polyandry. The emphasis upon descent through women that we find, even to a small extent, in this table is totally foreign to Semite custom. The purpose of the inclusion of the list here seems to be to establish the mixed semi-heathen origin of the Edomites. They were really Horites, not children of Abraham and Isaac. How typical of families once professedly Christian, but unrenewed in heart, who leave the Christian fellowship and take pride in their worldly connections.

The sons. This probably means ' descendants '. *Seir the Horite, who inhabited the land.* The land belonged to heathen people, yet Esau was no sojourner in it. He settled down among the heathen, became absorbed among them, made himself one with them and adopted their ways.

VERSE 21. *Dukes.* Again this means chieftains or sheikhs. When Esau went to Seir, there were seven Hurrian tribes in the country.

VERSE 22. *Hori.* This is a racial name. It shows that others beside the Hurrian tribes lived, or were coming to live, in the land, and it probably marks the entrance of Esau. *Timna.* She was concubine to Eliphaz and the mother of Amalek (verse 12). Though we do not know her exact parentage, this verse tells us that she was a Hurrian. As the generations are not carried further back than Lotan, Timna's brother, who was head of his clan at the time that Esau entered the land, it seems that these records were begun and kept by the Edomites.

VERSE 23. *The children of Shobal.* This was the second of the seven Horite tribes mentioned in verse 20. The five children of Shobal were not ' dukes ', that is to say, they did not form separate tribes. They lived within the tribe of their father. There seem to have been no more than the seven tribes.

VERSE 24. *Zibeon.* He was the chieftain of the third tribe (verse 20). Though chief of a Hurrian tribe, he was in some sense, whether in origin, by occupation, or by association, a Hivite (verse 2). *Anah.* He was the father of Aholibamah (ver. 2, 14), and the only one of the Horites of whom we know more than his name. The incident that is told of him appears to have created a deep impression throughout the country.

The mules. Undoubtedly the R.V. gives the correct meaning as ' hot springs '. It was because of this discovery that Anah assumed the name of Beeri, ' my well ', by which he is called in 26. 34. We may notice four things about this discovery: (1) the object of the discovery was hot springs, not the cooling streams of the water of life, but the hot springs of carnal passion and worldy excitement, or anger and envy, or battle and murder. The discovery typified the gratification of the carnal nature. (2) The place of the discovery was *in the wilderness*, exactly as we should expect. There are no hot springs in Zion, but there are plenty in the wilderness of this world, where Anah would naturally be found. (3) Notice the occupation of the finder: *as he fed the asses of Zibeon his father*. He was not feeding Christ's sheep but the devil's asses. The ass is an unclean, though useful, animal, unfit for food or sacrifice. It is a picture in the Bible of the unconverted man. It is fed through the press and the wireless and the cinema, and by an innumerable quantity of books, which are all carnal, if not generally so in a gross sense. It rejects the good food of the Gospel and

the Word of God. Many thousands of people are engaged on feeding the asses in the wilderness, and they often discover hot springs, though in finding them do no more than tap the same vein which flows from hell. (4) As a result of his discovery Anah changed his name to Beeri, that is to say, he boasted about it for the rest of his life. This is the usual way of many in the world who find hot springs for the asses to drink.

VERSE 25. *The children of Anah.* Anah was the son of Zibeon, though mentioned by his side as a chieftain in verse 20. He headed a clan of his own, which broke off from that of his father, probably being invited or encouraged to do so as a result of his discovery of the hot springs, which brought him fame.

Dishon. This is likely to be the same Dishon as is mentioned after Anah in verse 21. In this case we have three generations of chieftains, each head of a clan of his own. This proves this family to have been active and enterprising. It seems in fact to have been a family of great worldly renown and repute. *Aholibamah the daughter of Anah.* This was the notorious favourite wife of Esau, through whom these records must have come, of whom so much is said in this chapter.

VERSE 27. *Ezer* follows Dishon in verse 21.

VERSE 28. *Dishan* follows Ezer in verse 21.

Uz, and Aran. Compare 22. 21. This may indicate that the varied peoples living east and south-east of Palestine were of mixed origin like Sheba and Dedan (10. 11; 25. 3).

VERSE 29. *The dukes.* This means chieftains. The list is the same as that given in verses 20 and 21. Esau is careful to repeat and emphasise that his wife came of a good family.

Of the Horites. It did not disturb him that her origin was heathen. It was her social position that pleased him. The word ' duke ' occurs ten times in this single verse.

Of Hori. The descent of his wife from Hori may have been specially pleasing to Esau, but the Holy Spirit intends this information to be a serious warning to us.

The land of Seir. This is ' a thirsty land where no water is ' (Ps. 63. 1). How different from the land of promise!

VERSE 31. *The kings that reigned in the land of Edom.* The king was evidently a super-chieftain, who combined all the clans and their heads under his rule. Edom is a picture of the flesh. Many kings reign there, King Pride, King Folly, King Envy, King Malice, King Lust, King Deceit, King Dishonesty, or King Finance.

Before there reigned any king over the children of Israel. This passage is a favourite hunting-ground of the liberal critics and rationalistic theologians. The mention of Israelite kings leads them to assume that the whole book of Genesis dates from the time of the kingdoms of Israel and Judah. This conclusion however in no way rightly follows. (1) Moses himself anticipated kings in Israel (Deut. 17. 14-20), an anticipation which may well have been based on the promises made to Abraham (Gen. 17. 16). In verses 32-39 of the present chapter we have a list of eight kings, which would well fill less than the period between Esau and Moses. (2) If we insist that the mention of kings of Israel here implies a period during or subsequent to the kingdoms of Israel and Judah, a sense of proportion will show us that the date of Genesis is not affected. A very small addition has been made in this case to the text at an appropriate point. In a modern work this would be an editor's footnote, which no one would suppose dated the work as a whole or its author. It might have been written on the margin of the original skin roll. At the same time if we insist on the later date

and treat the list of kings as an insertion, we must answer the difficult question why only eight kings are found in the list.

VERSE 32. *Beor.* He was perhaps the same as the ancestor of Balaam (Num. 22. 5).

City. Life became settled, no longer nomadic. As Cain built a city (4. 17), so did Esau's descendants. It was symbolic of the repudiation of the pilgrim life.

VERSE 33. *Bela died.* Contrast the unshakeable kingdom, which the saints possess (Heb. 12. 28).

VERSE 34. *Temani.* These were descendants of Eliphaz (verse 15).

VERSE 35. *Who smote Midian.* This is the only exploit of the Edomite kings mentioned in these verses. Contrast the work of the Prince of Peace.

VERSE 37. *The river.* This means the Euphrates. King Saul seems to have been a foreign conqueror who had come a long way.

VERSE 39. *Hadar.* A variant of his name is Hadad, the letters r and d being very much alike in Hebrew.

Mehetabel, the daughter of Matred, the daughter of Mezahab. This descent through the mother implies the possibility that there were remnants of a matriarchate system among the peoples of this region. Such a system was known among the people of the Adriatic coast and in central Europe. It was scandalously immoral and involved polyandry.

VERSE 40. *Dukes.* See on verse 15. The fourteen chiefs among Esau's immediate descendants (verses 15-19) and the seven Hurrian chiefs (verses 20, 29) are now replaced by eleven chiefs, who appear to comprise a mixture of the two. In view of the hints that have already appeared in the chapter of a Hurrian matriarchate system it is significant that two women are named among them, Timnah and Aholibamah.

Duke Timnah. The R.V. calls her Timna, as she is called in verse 12. She was concubine to Esau's son Eliphaz and ancestress of the Amalekites. She is thus typical of those whom the world and the flesh promote to honour.

VERSE 41. *Duke Aholibamah.* This was the notorious favourite wife of Esau. She probably succeeded with her husband's consent to the chieftainship of her father's clan, perhaps also her grandfather's (verses 20, 29). The last we hear of her is that she was chief of an Edomite clan. Thus we can trace something of the history of this wicked woman, who may have been an able and powerful personality. She seems to have begun life as a temple prostitute, a capacity in which she may well first have met Esau. He took her to be his wife, changing her name out of deference to his parents' outlook and religion. She exercised a paramount influence over him, and we finally find her governing one of the tribes of the country. She was quite a little Jezebel, and not unlike the great evil church of which Jezebel is the declared type.

VERSE 42. *Duke Kenaz, Duke Teman.* See verse 15. Both these clans remained in the hands of Esau's descendants.

VERSE 43. *According to their habitations.* In verse 40 we are told that the chiefs are classified by three categories, their family, their place or habitation, and their name. These are just the three ways in which the child of God is classified. We may ask what our family is. If the answer is that we are children of God, we are happy indeed. We may also ask where we dwell, and if the answer is that we abide in Christ, we have nothing to fear. If we ask what name we bear, we may boldly answer that our name is that of Christ our Lord.

In the land of their possession. Esau had moved to it of his own accord, but it was a poor land. It had the fatness of the earth (27. 39), but this is something to perish with the using (Col. 2. 22). It cannot be compared with the land of Israel, that new earth wherein dwelleth righteousness (2 Pet. 3. 13).

The father of the Edomites. Esau, who is a type of the flesh, always begets sons like himself. Since Adam's fall the brood of Edomites has been fast increasing.

CHAPTER 37

WITH this chapter we begin the last section of the book of Genesis, which consists of the generations of Jacob (37. 2). The section gives us the story of Joseph, interrupted near its beginning by the narrative of the birth of Judah's sons. This is included because Judah and his son Phares were direct ancestors of the Lord Jesus Christ. The atmosphere of the story of Joseph is one of godliness and purity and contrasts strongly with the preceding chapter about Esau as well as with that dealing with Judah. Joseph is the first Old Testament character whose whole life is seen to be typical of the Saviour's life and work. Perhaps the only other such character is David, many others being types of Christ is one or more incidents only in their lives. Joseph's career falls into three parts, the early years in his father's home, then his betrayal by his brethren, humiliation and suffering, and finally his exaltation and glory. In this last condition he receives his old father and his family in Egypt, where Jacob dies. Genesis ends with the death of Joseph. Joseph is the most innocent and purest of all in the Bible with the exception of the Lord Himself, and it is difficult to put one's finger upon any fault in his character. There was however at least one recorded, and it is possible that another may be implied in the present chapter. In the whole section of the generations of Jacob we see in Joseph a clear image and foreshadowing of Christ, and we see in the story of Judah's family the development of Christ's genealogy. In the present chapter we have the story of Jacob's special love for Joseph, of Joseph's dreams, of his mission to his brethren, followed by their conspiracy against him and his betrayal and sale. The great lesson of the chapter is seen in the foreshadowing of the work of Christ.

Verse 1. *Jacob dwelt in the land wherein his father was a stranger.* This means that he maintained the pilgrim life in contrast to Esau who left it and settled down in Seir. If we want to remain within the bounds of God's redemptive purpose, we too must maintain the pilgrim life. *In the land of Canaan.* If we do so, we shall find ourselves among enemies as yet not dispossessed. The devil is still the prince of this world (Jo. 14. 30) and the god of this age (2 Cor. 4. 4). He opposes the Gospel, snatches the seed from hearts in which it has been sown (Mt. 13. 19) and seeks to devour the children of God (1 Pet. 5. 8). So long as the world remains in the possession of the Canaanites, the people of God can never settle down in it.

Verse 2. *The generations of Jacob.* It is obvious that this phrase cannot refer to what has gone before. If it did, its place would have been at the end of chapter 35. What follows is the history of Jacob's family and his personal biography till his death. This means that the influence of Jacob reaches forward, a fact that provides both promise and warning for us. The evangelical movement of today might in the same way perhaps be referred to as part of 'the generations of Wesley', and the work here in the University of Cambridge might be called the generations of Simeon.

Seventeen years old. This was very young, and would correspond with us to about twelve or thirteen.

Feeding the flock. He started very young in a very blessed and useful work. Lack of experience is no bar to the operation of the Holy Spirit's gifts (1 Tim. 4. 12). A boy or young man can do valuable pastoral work among those who are younger than himself, and so can those who are young in the faith.

With his brethren. He was too young to be entrusted with responsibility alone, but he was not too young to help his brethren. There are many things in Christian work that a boy can do. *With the sons of Bilhah, and with the sons of Zilpah.* These were Dan and Naphthali, Gad and Asher. The status of their mothers would make it likely that they would be the least satisfactory morally of all the brothers.

Brought unto his father their evil report. There is no need to suppose that this was done maliciously or in the character of a tale-bearer. It may be imagined that it could be perfectly natural. At the same time we cannot completely dismiss the idea that Joseph told tales. If so, it was one of the faults of his character, one or two, or at most three points, in which he was unlike the Saviour Whom he typified so naturally.

Verse 3. *Israel loved Joseph more than all his children.* This is the first point in which Joseph was like Christ. He was the beloved of his father, just as Christ was the Father's well-beloved and the Son of His love (Mt. 3. 17; Mk. 12. 6; Col. 1. 13).

The son of his old age. There is both comparison and contrast between this statement and the fact that Christ was the eternal Son, ' begotten of His Father before all worlds ', the firstborn of all creation (Col. 1. 15). Christ is the only Son of the ancient of days (Dan. 7. 9).

A coat of many colours. The R.V. margin probably translates this correctly as ' a long garment with sleeves'. It was the dress of the heir and the proof that Jacob treated Joseph as his eldest son and intended him to be his heir. In the same way Christ has been appointed by God the heir of all things (Rom. 8. 17; Heb. 1. 2). We who belong to Him share His inheritance.

VERSE 4. *When his brethren saw.* The brethren refused to accept their father's will or to acquiesce in it. They thought it was unjust and supposed they thought more truly than their father. This is a reflection of every sinner in his relationship with God. *They hated him,* exactly as Christ's brethren after the flesh, the Jewish nation as a whole and their religious leaders, hated Him (Jo. 15. 23-25).

Could not speak peaceably unto him. Notice that they 'could' not speak peaceably. Here is an example of the sinner's moral impotence. Doubtless they did not want to speak peaceably to him, but whether they did or did not, their sinful nature made them powerless in the matter (Rom. 8. 8). In the same way the Jews could not speak peaceably to Christ. Instead He endured a contradiction of sinners against Himself (Heb. 12. 3).

VERSE 5. *Joseph dreamed a dream.* Joseph's dreams are a type and illustration of the predictions made by the Spirit of Christ through the Old Testament prophets of Christ's glory to come (1 Pet. 1. 11). They make him in yet one further respect a picture of the Lord Jesus.

He told it his brethren. In the same way the purpose of God in glorifying Christ was told and made known through the Old Testament prophets. *They hated him yet the more.* The claims of Christ roused the bitter antagonism of the Jews.

VERSE 6. *Hear, I pray you, this dream which I have dreamed.* In the same way the Lord Jesus Christ pleaded with the Jews to hear and receive and appreciate the purpose of God, which was centred in Himself.

VERSE 7. The imagery of the dream concerned sheaves of corn. The relevance of this in Joseph's case seems to be that the fulfilment took place at and because of a search by the brethren for corn, which Joseph was dealing out and selling at the time (42. 3, 6). In so far as the dream foreshadows Christ, the sheaves point to harvest, and the harvest is the end of the world (Mt. 13. 40). It will be then at the end on the day of judgment that every knee will bow to Him (Phil. 2. 10).

VERSE 8. *Shalt thou indeed reign over us?* Again Joseph is closely like the Saviour. 'His citizens hated him, and sent an embassage after him saying, We will not have this man to reign over us ' (Lk. 19. 14).

Shalt thou indeed have dominion over us? In spite of opposition from Jew or Gentile, devil or man, the Lord Jesus Christ will have the dominion. ' He shall have dominion also from sea to sea, and from the river unto the ends of the earth ' (Ps. 72. 8).

They hated him yet the more for his dreams. The claims of the Lord Jesus Christ, based on the will of God as revealed in the Old Testament Scriptures, infuriated the Jews.

And for his words. They knew that He was speaking of them and in consequence they sought to lay hands on Him (Mt. 21. 46).

VERSE 9. The imagery of the second dream is that of the heavenly bodies. It is possible that this might suggest to Joseph the environment of a kingdom and ordered government. The fulfilment in Egypt might add point to the dream. The dream also shows Joseph as a type of Christ. The imagery of the heavenly bodies suggests a fulfilment in heaven, as is actually the case. The Lord Jesus Christ has been exalted to His Father's throne in heaven, and there every knee will bow to Him, of things in heaven as well as things on earth (Phil. 2. 10). A curious feature of the dream is the obeisance of the sun, which is naturally thought of as supreme among the heavenly bodies. Joseph probably thought of himself as (a) the twelfth of the twelve stars. In this case we see a picture of the humiliation of Christ (Phil. 2. 5-8). Though He was humbled on earth in the flesh, like one star of many as it were, yet all heaven bows down to Him. Again Joseph may have thought of himself as (b) separate from sun, moon and stars together. In this case he is revealed in the dream as a picture of the unique Christ, the Son of God.

Verse 10. *He told it to his father*. He appears to have told his father the second dream immediately and directly, but not the first. The reason was that nothing but eleven sheaves, representing the brothers, appeared in the first dream, while the sun and moon in addition to the eleven stars appeared in the second.

His father rebuked him. It is not clear whether Joseph deserved the rebuke or not. If he did, we have here one of only two or three faults in his character that appear in his story. It is however very natural for the boy to tell the dream, which was strange enough to set up a reaction in his father similar to that of his brothers, but without their fierce malice. If this is the right interpretation, we may see in the rebuke the first step in the innocent suffering which Joseph was to undergo as the type and picture of the Messiah. *Thy mother*. Joseph's mother was dead (35. 19, 20). Jacob may mean (1) that he foresees a fulfilment in the world to come. We know from the New Testament that the patriarchs looked for the resurrection of the dead and the life of the world to come. If this is what Jacob meant, he must have looked beyond Joseph to Christ, the antitype, as like Abraham he might quite well have done (Jo. 8. 56). (2) Jacob may have been

referring to Leah. In the circumstances it would not have been unnatural to refer to Leah as the boy's mother. Leah appears to have been dead before Jacob went down into Egypt (49. 31). If the moon in the dream signifies Leah, the fulfilment might perhaps be sought in 43. 11-14. (3) Jacob may have wrongly interpreted the dream and sought to place a specific meaning on every detail, although the Holy Spirit may not have intended more by the dream than a general picture of obeisance. There is no record of Jacob himself ever making obeisance to Joseph. The practice of forcing an interpretation upon every detail of a parable is a common one, and it is interesting, if not encouraging, to know that it may be as old as Jacob.

Verse 11. *His brethren envied him*. This is the first of two points from this chapter mentioned by Stephen in his speech before the council (Acts 7. 9). Since Stephen's purpose was to prove that the Jews' rejection of Jesus Christ was the culmination of their conduct throughout their history, it is probable that he meant to compare the envy of Joseph's brethren with the attitude of the religious leaders and people towards the Saviour. The Jews were envious of Christ because, much like Joseph, He claimed to be the rejected stone which would one day become the head of the corner (Mt. 21. 42-46; 27. 18).

His father observed the saying. Notice the difference in attitude. The wicked brothers were moved to blind envy and hatred. The godly father in spite of a mild rebuke treasured up what his son had said to see whether or not some purpose of God was revealed in it. The dream was in fact a word of God, a revelation by the Spirit, and in this way we have an example of the opposite effects created by the Word upon the two classes of men. The one observes it, the other is moved by it to hatred and envy.

350

VERSE 12. *His brethren went to feed their father's flock.* This was a proper and natural occupation. It is the very thing that God desires His sons to be doing. Are we as children of God engaged in feeding our Father's flock? His flock consists of men (Ezek. 34. 31). We ought to be busy in feeding those who are safely in the fold or on the pasture, or, perhaps still more important, seeking those who have gone astray or have never yet been found.

Shechem was on the hill-country in the centre of Palestine in what was later the territory of the tribe of Ephraim. It had been the scene of the rape of Dinah (33. 18-34. 31).

VERSE 13. *In Shechem.* Jacob was perhaps afraid that his sons might be in danger in the neighbourhood of Shechem owing to hostility aroused among the inhabitants by their action over Dinah (34. 30).

Come, and I will send thee unto them. Here is another important respect in which Joseph typified the Lord Jesus Christ. His Father purposed to send Him into the world.

Here am I. Joseph was ready and willing to go, just as the Saviour was ready and willing to come. ' Then said I, Lo, I come: In the volume of the book it is written of me, I delight to do thy will, O my God ' (Ps. 40. 7, 8).

VERSE 14. *See whether it be well with thy brethren.* The Hebrew says, ' See the peace of thy brethren '. Jacob perhaps thought his sons were in danger from the enmity of the people of the land. Those to whom the Lord Jesus Christ was sent by the Father was certainly in danger from the wrath of God on the day of judgment, from the dominion and power of sin, and from eternal death. Jesus Christ was sent into the world to deal with the peace of mankind. His mission was to bring them peace with God through the blood of the cross (Col. 1. 20).

Well with the flocks. Notice that there were two classes to whom Joseph was sent. (1) his brethren and (2) the flocks. We may perhaps see in these two (1) the people of God, who are actually redeemed, and (2) the rest, who are potentially redeemed. Christ came to bring a message from His Father for the shepherds and to give His life for the sheep.

Bring me word again. The Father in heaven takes the liveliest interest in the mission of His Son.

So he sent him. ' Having therefore yet one son, his well-beloved, he sent him ' (Mk. 12. 6). ' God so loved the world, that he gave his only begotten Son ' (Jo. 3. 16). ' He spared not his own Son, but delivered him up for us all ' (Rom. 8. 32).

Out of the vale of Hebron. Hebron was in southern Palestine, south of Jerusalem and west of the Dead Sea, in what was later the territory of Judah, so that Joseph had a long way to go. The Lord Jesus Christ came, not from the vale of Hebron, but from the bosom of the Father (Jo. 1. 18). *He came to Shechem,* just as Jesus Christ came into the world.

VERSE 15. *A certain man found him.* If we are to see any spiritual antitype to this unknown man, we can only see in him the Holy Spirit. No one could direct Christ but the Spirit, Who came upon Him to supply all the wisdom, understanding, counsel, might and knowledge that He needed for His spotless life and ministry (Isa. 11. 2).

He was wandering in the field. The field is the world (Mt. 13. 38). Christ never wandered aimlessly in the world, but we may perhaps compare Joseph's wandering with that long period in Jesus Christ's life before the Spirit came upon Him at His baptism to equip Him for His ministry.

What seekest thou? Was it at the time of the temptation in the wilderness that the Spirit asked Christ, ' What seekest thou?'

VERSE 16. *I seek my brethren.* A
true answer. In the same way the
Son of man came to seek and to save
that which is lost (Lk. 19. 10). Christ
is always seeking, and seeks till He
finds. He sought Adam in Eden (3.
9), and today He seeks the lost in
the world through the Gospel. As
He is Himself a man, those whom He
is seeking are His brother men.

Tell me, I pray thee, where. Thus
we may think of our Lord Jesus
Christ seeking direction for His life
and ministry from the Spirit. It was
to Calvary that He was led.

VERSE 17. *They are departed hence.*
Joseph's brethren were not in the
place where their father expected
them to be. In the same way mankind has left the place of honour in
which God set them at their creation
(Ps. 49. 12).

I heard them say, Let us go. Man
fell into sin of his own free will.

*Joseph went after his brethren, and
found them.* So the Saviour goes
after that which is lost until He finds
it (Lk. 15. 4).

VERSE 18. *When they saw him afar
off.* Their attitude was hostile from
the beginning. In the same way the
Jews were hostile to Christ from the
beginning. In the Old Testament
days they persecuted and murdered
the prophets sent by God to foretell
His coming (Mt. 21. 35, 36; 23. 37;
1 Thess. 2. 15), and before He was
two years old His death was attempted by Herod (Mt. 2. 13, 16-18).

*They conspired against him to slay
him.* As the object of this conspiracy
Joseph was again like the Lord Jesus
Christ (see Mt. 26. 3-5).

VERSE 19. *This dreamer.* They were
particularly angry at the revelation
which had been given to Joseph of
his future glory. In the same way
the fury of the Jewish religious
leaders was roused by the Lord's
declaration of His future glory (Mt.
26. 64). This they rightly connected
with His claim to be Christ the Son

of God. Joseph's brothers perhaps
connected the matter of his dreams
with his being his father's appointed
heir, though in this they were wrong.

VERSE 20. *Let us slay him.* God
prevented their design from taking
effect in Joseph's case, but did not
restrain the plot of the Jews against
His own Son. 'He spared not his
own Son, but delivered him up for
us all ' (Rom. 8. 32).

Cast him into some pit. Their
purpose was to conceal their crime.

Some evil beast hath devoured him.
The Jews were ready to put the responsibility for the Saviour's death
upon the Romans.

*We shall see what will become of
his dreams.* The brethren tried to
frustrate God's purpose for Joseph,
just as the Jews tried to frustrate
God's purpose for Christ. Both attempts miserably failed (Ps. 2. 4).

VERSE 21. There is a lesson in the
fact that Reuben's merciful plans
failed because they were not in line
with the purpose of God, while those
of the wicked brothers succeeded because they conformed to God's purpose (45. 8). This may be the solution to many a puzzle that arises
out of the circumstances of life. We
can see the same principle at work in
the failure of Pilate's efforts to release the Lord (Lk. 23. 16, 22; Jo.
19. 12).

VERSE 22. Reuben did not disclose
his real purpose to his brothers. He
implied to them that Joseph should
be left to die in the pit. He perhaps
played upon their superstition by
suggesting that no blood be shed.
They may have shared a heathen idea
that murder consisted of blood-shedding in a literal sense, and that to
leave someone to starve or die was
less guilty, perhaps not murder at all.
He intended however from the beginning to rescue Joseph and restore him
to his father. Reuben thus seems to
have been without envy, especially in
view of the fact that he was actually

the eldest son, and without the cruelty that appeared in the nature of Simeon and Levi (34. 30; 49. 5-7). There was a generous trait in his nature in spite of his failure through lust (35. 22).

Verse 23. *When Joseph was come unto his brethren.* He had come a long journey to them, had sought them diligently and found them with difficulty and brought them a message of affection and solicitude from his father. In all this he was just like Jesus, Who came from heaven to seek and save what was lost, bringing a message of tender love and of care for their welfare from His heavenly Father. ' He came unto his own, and his own received him not ' (Jo. 1. 11).

They stript Joseph out of his coat, that is to say, they refused to recognise his position as heir and tried to deprive him of it, like the wicked husbandmen in the parable who said, ' This is the heir, come let us kill him, and the inheritance shall be ours ' (Mt. 21. 38).

Verse 24. *They took him, and cast him into a pit.* So the Saviour was taken and cast into the pit of death and the grave, the Jews and Romans, nor the devil either, not knowing what they were doing, but thinking that they would silence and destroy Him for ever. They killed the Prince of life (Acts 3. 15).

The pit was empty, there was no water in it. The pit was a disused stone cistern, constructed after the custom of the country to hold water for irrigation and other purposes. The purpose of these two statements about the pit is to show that Joseph did not drown in it, but simply lay a helpless captive. In the same way the grave was not the end of the Saviour, as Satan and the Jews hoped it would be. The pit was empty because at the moment of His death on the cross He had exhausted the last drop of the ocean of the wrath of God. The grave could neither

hold nor destroy Him. Yet He was not helpless as Joseph was. He had power to lay down His life and power to take it again (Jo. 10. 18).

Verse 25. *They sat down to eat bread* in callous indifference to Joseph's sufferings, as he starved in the pit. In the same way the world carries on its vain everyday business, quite indifferent to the sufferings and death of Christ which were undergone on its behalf.

They lifted up their eyes and looked. They had no difficulty in seeing and attending to what was likely to further their schemes and bring them material advantage. In this they were typical of all the world.

A company of Ishmeelites. Notice five things about this company: (1) who they were. They were Ishmeelites, descendants of Abraham (16. 15), that is to say, people with a respectable religious ' Christian ' background, but outside the covenant, because they were children of the flesh and not of the promise (21. 10). Notice (2) where they came from. It was from Gilead, which was east of Jordan, that is to say, on the wrong side of it. They lived outside resurrection ground. (3) They were accompanied by camels. The camel in the Bible is the picture of the rich man of the world. This company was dealing in the mammon of unrighteousness. (4) Notice what they were carrying: *spicery and balm and myrrh.* These were luxuries and the products of Gilead. (5) They were bound for Egypt, always in the Bible the type of the world. These were the people who co-operated with Joseph's brethren in their crime against him, being probably little aware of the circumstances and perhaps ignorant of Joseph's true relationship to his brothers. These respectable worldly people always co-operate in the crucifixion of Christ.

Verse 26. *Judah.* If the sin of

Reuben was lust, and the sin of Simeon and Levi cruelty, that of Judah seems to have been avarice.

What profit. Even if he had gained the whole world by this wicked transaction, he would have profited nothing (Mt. 16. 26).

If we slay our brother. Judah does not seem to have given a thought to the wickedness of this proposal, but only to the question whether or not advantage could be got out of it. Like Esau and like every sinner he had a completely reversed sense of values.

VERSE 27. *Come, and let us sell him.* Judah was like his namesake, Judas Iscariot, whom he here typified. Judas sold the Lord for thirty pieces of silver (Mt. 26. 14-16). In all this there is a warning to all of us. Whenever Christ is not supreme in our hearts, our thoughts, our actions and our whole lives, our sense of values is at fault. There are subtler and less open ways of selling and betraying the Master than those used by Judas in the case of Christ or Judah in the case of Joseph. *Let not our hand be upon him.* Judah shrank from murdering his brother when it came to the actual deed. In this he was unlike the Jews, who gladly took Christ's blood upon themselves (Mt. 27. 25).

He is our brother and our flesh. This was the relationship of Christ to the Jews (Rom. 9. 5), but it carried no weight with them.

Were content. The Hebrew says ' hearkened '. They listened to their brother rather than to their conscience. It is a dreadful thing to be content with sin. Only if a sinner is restless does the Holy Spirit work on his heart to convict him.

VERSE 28. *Midianites.* The Midianites were Ishmeelites (Jud. 8. 3, 5, 12, 22, 24). The names stand in much the same relationship to each other as do the names English and British. Midian was a son of Abraham (25. 2), by Keturah. Midianites and Ishmeelites lived to the east or south-east of Palestine, and evidently by this time their tribes were confused. Ignorance of Judges 8. 24 has led liberal critics to deduce a discrepancy in this passage, and they commonly teach the foolish theory of the assimilation of two separate original ' strata '.

They drew, that is, the brethren, not the Midianites.

Sold Joseph, just as Judas sold the Lord for thirty pieces of silver, and the Jews, as it were, sold Him into the hands of the Romans. This verse, which speaks of the selling of Joseph into Egypt, is the second of the two selected by the Holy Ghost in His comment on the Genesis narrative made by the martyr Stephen before the Jewish Sanhedrin (Acts 7. 9). The first reference was to the envy of verse 11. Thus the outstanding points in this chapter are the envy and the sale, both emphasised by Stephen in order to bring home to the Jews their sin in hating and selling the Saviour.

They brought Joseph into Egypt. Like Joseph the Saviour took on Him the form of a slave (Phil. 2. 7), but unlike him He came voluntarily of His own accord into the world. Joseph came from his father's home into the slavery of Egypt, just as the Lord came from the Father's bosom into the world.

VERSE 29. Reuben's merciful intention was frustrated by the providence of God, Who had another purpose (45. 7, 8), which necessitated anguish and suffering on the part of Joseph.

VERSE 30. Reuben showed genuine distress.

VERSE 31. *They took Joseph's coat.* Both Reuben and the other brothers misunderstood the purpose that God was working out in and for Joseph. Reuben desired that he should not suffer at all. In this he was like Peter, who rebuked the Lord (Mt. 16. 22), and like many today who cannot understand the necessity for Christ's sufferings. The attitude of the other brothers was quite different. They took the coat which was the evidence of their guilt. They had stripped Joseph out of it. They sought at once to mislead their father and conceal their sin.

And killed a kid of the goats, and dipped the coat in the blood. They thought that by dipping the coat in the blood of a kid they could cover their sin, just as the Jews who rejected and murdered the Lord thought that the continuance of their temple sacrifices would take away sin. The idea that blood other than the blood of Christ can atone for sin is not altogether unknown today. During the first world war a well-known bishop in the Church of England remarked that Europe was again being redeemed by precious blood. Every instructed Christian who read these words shrank in horror from their blasphemy, but the conception that inspired them hangs even about evangelical churches on the day in November known as ' Remembrance Sunday ', and many people who are ignorant of the Gospel suppose that a soldier who dies in battle in what is thought to be a good cause goes to heaven. Joseph's brothers sought to cover their sin by blood which had no atoning efficacy.

Verse 32. They added deceit to their hatred and murder in thus trying to mislead their father. The heavenly Father can never be deceived, though many people act as if they supposed that He could.

Verse 33. *An evil beast hath devoured him.* The poor old man was mistaken. This had not happened to Joseph, but in the very sight of His Father the Lord Jesus Christ was devoured by the evil beast of sin and death, the cruelty of man and the rage of His enemies.

Joseph is without doubt rent in pieces. Again the old man's conclusion was wrong. Notice how easy it

is to be deceived when deceit is unsuspected. We are only safe by expecting the practices of deceit and watching against it. Joseph was not rent in pieces, but the Saviour was broken and crushed on the cross.

Verse 34. The human interest and pathos of the story break out in this verse. The purpose of God for the ultimate saving of life (45. 7) involved suffering for Jacob as well as for Joseph, the chief factor in it. We may reverently compare Jacob's grief with that of the Father in heaven, as He watched the suffering and murder of His Son.

Verse 35. *All his sons and all his daughters.* Perhaps the grief of their father may have brought about a first step to repentance in the wicked sons. There are hints later in the narrative that his overwhelming sorrow affected them with some sense of the enormity of what they had done. Thus even Jacob's grief bore fruit, though it was not at first apparent. As to Jacob's daughters, we hear of none but Dinah the daughter of Leah. It may be (1) that Leah, or even Rachel, or the handmaids, had daughters who are not mentioned, the particular allusions to Dinah being due to the part she played in the incident of Shechem (chapter 34). (2) The daughters may include grand-daughters, children of Reuben or the other elder sons. (3) The expression could well refer in Hebrew usage to women members of the household or settlement.

He refused to be comforted. The loss of Joseph was to affect Jacob for the rest of his life. In the same way, speaking with great reverence and care, we may say that the Godhead is eternally affected by the incarnation, death and resurrection of the Lord Jesus Christ. It has been said with reason that the redemption of man shook the Godhead to its foundations.

The grave. This represents the Hebrew *sheol*. It is the first occurrence in the Bible of the Hebrew word, and it is very properly and rightly translated ' the grave '. Jacob expressed in the usual vivid pictorial oriental language that he would join his son among the dead, life being not worth living without him. The underlying conception is one of sorrow, gloom and despair. If Jacob had thought of being consciously reunited to his son at death in another world, he is likely to have said that he would have gone rejoicing, not mourning.

His father wept for him. May we reverently think that this is a picture of something that took place in the heart of God at the time of Calvary?

VERSE 36. *Sold him.* Thus Joseph came into Egypt in the form of a slave (compare Phil. 2. 7). *Into Egypt.* Egypt represents the world, which the Saviour entered at His incarnation, and it is in the world of men that He later receives His kingdom and glory.

Officer. The Hebrew says 'eunuch'. It is possible that the word may have been used in a derived sense to denote a court officer, or chamberlain, as the translators of the A.V. evidently thought. Language provides many parallels to such a usage. Perhaps the majority of the words that we use do not carry their original literal sense. If however the word means literally a eunuch, an explanation of the conduct of Potiphar's wife towards Joseph (chap. 39) begins to come into view.

Captain of the guard. This means ' chief of the executioners '. Joseph's sadness and homesickness must have been increased by the atmosphere in the household of a master whose work was so grim and sinister.

As we reach the end of this chapter it might be useful to list the respects in which Joseph appears in it as typical of the Lord Jesus Christ: (1) He was the beloved of his Father (ver. 3); (2) He was his father's heir (ver. 3); (3) He was hated by his brethren (ver. 4); (5) He was sent

after his brethren (ver. 13, 14); (6) He sought his brethren when they were lost (ver. 16); (7) A conspiracy was made against him (ver. 18); (8) He was cast into a pit and left for dead (ver. 24); (9) He was sold by his own people for twenty pieces of silver (ver. 28); (10) He entered Egypt in the form of a slave (ver. 36). As Joseph was like the Saviour in his sufferings, so was he later like Him in his glory, as the story goes on to tell. We too, if we are united to Christ in the likeness of His death, shall be also in the likeness of His resurrection (Rom. 6. 5).

CHAPTER 38

IN this chapter the story of Joseph is interrupted, in order that an account may be given of the birth of Pharez, the son of Judah and ancestor of the Lord Jesus Christ. The contrast in atmosphere between the story told here and that of the story of Joseph is striking. We pass for a moment out of an environment of faith, godliness and purity to one of lust and conspiracy. Yet it was into the family of Judah, not that of Joseph, that the Friend of sinners was born. Judah marries a Canaanitish woman, who bears him three sons. He takes a Canaanitish wife for the eldest, who dies because of his wickedness. She is married to the second but again becomes a widow. Finding that her marriage to the third son is delayed, she pretends to become a prostitute and becomes the mother of twin boys by Judah himself. The main lessons of the chapter are the over-ruling providence of God and the reward of persistency in pressing one's way into the covenant.

VERSE 1. *At that time,* that is, at the time of the betrayal and sale of Joseph. At the very time of this wicked deed Judah could go about his business with indifference. In this he was a true man of the world. The world today cares nothing for the suffering of Jesus Christ. Its conscience is seared with a hot iron (1 Tim. 4. 2). It can carry on its business and indulge its sinful pleasures as if no Saviour had ever died for it.

Went down from his brethren. Judah separated from the company of those who were within the covenant. This is a step into sin. The professed Christian who finds his heart is not in line with the family of God is in a dangerous position.

Turned in to a certain Adullamite. He went to live, or at least to stay, with a Canaanite, with whom he must have had interests in common, *Whose name was Hirah.* The appearance of this detail is natural in a true story. It would be pointless in a fictitious one.

VERSE 2. *Judah saw there.* The lust of the eyes (1 Jo. 2. 16) was at work. By going to the wrong place and making the wrong friends Judah laid himself open to temptation. So shall we in similar circumstances.

A daughter of a certain Canaanite. Judah was repeating the sin of Esau (26. 34, 35), against which Abraham had so solemnly warned his family (24. 3). He was becoming yoked with an unbeliever (2 Cor. 6. 14).

Whose name was Shuah. See on verse 1.

He took her, and went in unto her. The lust of the eye leads regularly to the lust of the flesh (1 Jo. 2. 16).

VERSE 3. *She conceived, and bare a son.* The lust of the eye and the lust of the flesh bear shameful fruit (Rom. 6. 21). Judah now had a semi-Canaanite son. What hope or promise could there be for a child in such circumstances to grow up to serve God? *Er* means ' watchful '. He turned out to be watchful for opportunities of evil.

VERSE 4. *She conceived again.* Sin goes on bearing shameful fruit (Rom. 6. 21).

Onan means ' strong '. He turned out to be strong in sin.

VERSE 5. *She yet again conceived.* Sin cannot be prevented from bearing more and more fruit. It is always prolific.

Shelah means ' petition '. What Judah meant by the name we cannot tell. Shelah was later the object of a sad, if unexpressed, petition by Tamar, which went unanswered. Unanswered prayer is always connected with sin.

Chezib means ' false '. Thus like every sinner Judah was in a false position when the fruit of his sin appeared. It was false in respect both of God and of himself.

VERSE 6. *Tamar* means ' palm tree ', the picture of the righteous (Ps. 92. 12). In the end she turned out to be righteous (ver. 26). Judah seems to have found the right wife, but he made her pass through much insult and suffering by yoking her with his sons. Righteousness always suffers when in company with sinners.

VERSE 7. *Wicked.* We are not told the nature of Er's wickedness. By comparing with this verse what is said in 13. 13, and considering what we are subsequently told of the conduct of Onan, with whom Er is regularly coupled, we can make a reasonable guess. Whatever the nature of the wickedness, what else could Judah expect in the offspring of a Canaanite marriage? If a Christian marries outside the family of God and brings children into the world, he must expect his children to be children of hell.

The Lord slew him. Here we find a dramatic demonstration of the fact that the wages of sin is death (Rom. 6. 23), but we may ask why this fundamental principle was put in operation in this case in so signal a way. Millions of men are wicked in the sight of the Lord, but they live out their normal span and do not appear to perish as an open and direct consequence of their wickedness. The answer seems to be that Er stood very near to the redemptive purpose of God. Judah was to be the ancestor of Christ. His family must therefore be preserved, and the genealogical line kept clear. With high privilege goes great responsibility. Er failed to discharge his responsibility, and the privilege was taken from him, but it could only be taken with his life. The use of the Divine Name Jahweh in verses 7 and 10 of this chapter shows that we are dealing with the Divine purpose of redemption. If Er had been in the position of an ordinary man, perhaps he would have lived on and found opportunities (whether or not he would have availed himself of them) for repentance. His nearness to the Divine purpose cut him off. What a warning to all who possess spiritual privilege.

Verse 8. In this verse we have the custom known as levirate marriage, by which a younger brother married his elder brother's widow, his children by her being reckoned legally as the deceased elder brother's. The principle was formulated in the law of Moses (Deut. 25. 5-10), but was evidently an ancient Semitic custom like so much else in the Mosaic enactments. The custom was appealed to by the Sadducees in their controversy with the Lord over the resurrection (Mt. 22. 24; Mk. 12. 19; Lk. 20. 28).

Raise up seed to thy brother. This is a picture of the duty and privilege of the believer in the world. He is entrusted with the seed of the Word, which he is to sow by proclaiming the Gospel in the hearts of men and thus raise up seed to Christ his elder brother, Who has left this world. The seed thus begotten is Christ's, not the believer's.

Verse 9. *Knew that the seed should not be his.* This was his reason for refusing his duty. He cared only for his own personal selfish interests. He had no family feeling and had not his elder brother's interests at heart. These words are like a piercing glance into the heart and motive of the man who refuses to give himself to the service of Christ. He knows that to do so will bring no glory to himself. All that is won will be his Master's.

He spilled it on the ground, lest that he should give seed to his brother. The selfish man will waste his life and powers rather than allow them to serve the interests of Christ.

Verse 10. *The thing which he did.* What Onan did had nothing to do with the practice to which his name became wrongly attached. It was premature withdrawal. It was not done for purposes of physical gratification, but in order to avoid his duty to his brother. It was grossly insulting to Tamar.

Displeased the Lord. All sin displeases the Lord, but this is specially mentioned because it was a sin against the covenant and destructive of the purpose of redemption. The use of the Divine Name Jahweh emphasises this aspect.

Wherefore he slew him also. His sin was a sin against the light tantamount to trampling under foot the redemptive covenant. It was typical of deliberate rejection of the Gospel. This leads to judgment and death.

Verse 11. *Remain a widow.* Tamar was in the position of any member of the fallen human race. She had lost her former status and was desolate, but she was given hope for the future.

Till Shelah my son be grown. So the Christian believer is dead to the law, that he might be married to another (Rom. 7. 4).

For he said. It is not clear whether Shelah was grown up already. In any case it seems that Judah had already made up his mind that he would not marry Tamar to his surviving son. He seems to have thought that in her father's house she would be out of touch with what was happening, and perhaps he hoped that she would forget Shelah. He therefore sent her back to a Canaanite environment. He tried to exclude her from the covenant and from relationship to Christ.

Lest peradventure he die also. Judah was afraid of losing his last surviving son. From whatever point of view he made this remark, he seems to have misconstrued what had happened. Either (1) he did not know the reason for his sons' deaths. Perhaps he attributed them, or pretended to attribute them, to the influence of Tamar, and therefore wished to keep his surviving son from her. Or (2) he knew the reason for their deaths, particularly for that of Onan, and feared that Shelah might follow their example. If this was the case, he showed that his sons were completely out of his control. Yet it was through all these tangled circumstances that God was working in sovereign power to bring Christ into the world.

Dwelt in her father's house. Tamar thus lived outside the covenant and alienated from the family of Israel. This is the position of the sinner. (Eph. 2. 12).

Verse 12. *In process of time.* Joseph was absent in Egypt for twenty-two years before his father and brothers rejoined him. Most of this period may well be covered by this chapter. At the end of it Judah was a man of about forty-eight.

Judah's wife died. Notice the hand of God in these events: (1) openly seen in the deaths of Er and Onan; (2) less conspicuous in the death of Judah's wife; (3) unnoticed in the ordinary fact of Judah's going up to his sheep-shearers, yet in all these circumstances working His purpose out in sovereign power. No one could properly interpret these events, or understand their full significance, until the lapse of hundreds of years with the coming of Christ and the Gospel. In the same way today and always God is working His purpose out. We may seldom be able to understand what He is doing, but we

may be assured that nothing deflects His purpose so much as by a hair's breadth. Here in this chapter we see God clearing the way for the birth of Pharez and Zarah and through Pharez for the coming of Christ.

Judah was comforted. This perhaps means that he brought his period of mourning to an end, and resumed ordinary life.

Went up unto his sheep-shearers. There was nothing extraordinary in his doing this, but Jahweh made this ordinary incident into Tamar's opportunity. Thus God works both by extraordinary judgments such as the deaths of Er and Onan, or through everyday happenings. *His friend Hirah.* Hirah is mentioned because he had a small but necessary part to play in the story (ver. 20-23).

Verse 13. *It was told Tamar.* She was evidently awaiting her opportunity, and she is the picture of one who by persistence and perseverance presses his way into the kingdom of God. We shall see what steps she took.

To shear his sheep. Judah as a shepherd was concerned with his flock, just as the Good Shepherd is concerned with His. Judah was going to take the wool from his flock, something that they could give him which would bring reward and profit. In the same way Christ's flock can bring Him pleasure and glory.

Verse 14. Notice the four steps that Tamar took. They represent four steps that must be taken by the repentant sinner. (1) *She put her widow's garments off from her,* that is to say, she discarded all her rights and claims. She did not come to Judah as the wronged widow, seeking to make good a claim to his favour. In the same way the seeker after Christ has no claim, and makes no claim, upon Him.

(2) *She covered her with a vail.* She hid and extinguished all that was of herself. She was prepared to die to herself and its claims. In the

same way the true seeker must be prepared to cover himself.

(3) She *wrapped herself*. This turned her into a harlot (verse 15). She thus came to Judah as a sinner, and this is the only guise in which anyone can come with acceptance to Christ.

(4) She *sat in an open place, which is by the way to Timnath*, that is to say, she put herself in the way in which Judah was likely to pass. So the true seeker, if he would find Christ, must put himself in the way of the Gospel and go where he has reason to believe it will be preached. The Hebrew words translated ' an open place ' mean literally, ' the door of eyes '. She sat where she could be seen at the door of the kingdom of heaven. So the seeker must make himself known as a seeker to the servants of Christ and ministers of the Gospel.

She saw that Shelah was grown, and she was not given unto him to wife. She saw that in the old life, in which she had rights and claims, there was no hope for her. Its promises had deceived her. The law, which gave her the right to become Shelah's wife, had disappointed her and brought her nothing. She therefore determined in desperation to risk all. Thus she was like a resolute seeker.

VERSE 15. In the same way Christ takes notice of one whom He knows to be a self-abhorring and self-effacing sinner.

VERSE 16. *He turned unto her by the way*, just as Jesus turned to Zacchæus (Lk. 19. 5), and as He turns today to every needy suppliant and wistful sinner.

Let me come in unto thee. The Saviour knocks at the door of the sinner's heart and longs to come into his life (Rev. 3. 20).

He knew not. These words are a necessary explanation of Judah's request. There is nothing that the Saviour does not know about the sinner's heart, life, or identity.

What wilt thou give me. This is quite a proper question for the seeker to ask, because he that cometh to God must believe that He is a rewarder of them that diligently seek Him (Heb. 11. 6).

VERSE 17. *A kid from the flock*. We may see in the kid a picture of the Lamb slain, Who will be the believer's eternal reward. Once having fed on Him, he will never again be hungry (Jo. 6. 35).

Wilt thou give me a pledge. The believer has in his heart the pledge or earnest of the Spirit Who is the guarantee of the eternal inheritance (Eph. 1. 13, 14).

VERSE 18. *Thy signet, and thy bracelets, and thy staff that is in thine hand*. These three things are all pictures of the believer's great pledge, God the Holy Spirit, in some aspect or other of His present work in the believer's heart. The signet typifies the Spirit in His aspect of seal, by Whom the believer is sealed until the day of redemption (Eph. 1. 13; Rev. 7. 2, 3). The Hebrew word translated ' bracelets ' is better rendered ' cord ', as in the R.V. It was the cord by which the signet was attached to Judah's person, perhaps hanging round his neck, possibly round his wrist. It represents the Spirit as the Love of God shed abroad in the believer's heart (Rom. 5. 5), which attaches Christ to his heart and his heart to Christ, and is the pledge that his hope will never make him ashamed (ibid.) The staff represents the Spirit as guide (Rom. 8. 14) and support (Rom. 8. 26).

He gave it her. God has given us of His Spirit.

Came in unto her, like Christ the Friend of sinners, Who gave Himself for us.

She conceived by him. In the same way the believer bears fruit unto God, when united to the One Who was raised from the dead (Rom. 7. 4).

VERSE 19. *Laid by her vail from her.* On coming to the Saviour the believer casts off sin and becomes dead to it (Rom. 6. 11).

Put on the garments of her widowhood. The righteousness of the law is fulfilled in us (Rom. 8. 4).

VERSE 20. *He found her not.* Tamar had disappeared, just as the believer dies when he comes to Christ (Col. 3. 3).

VERSE 21. *Harlot.* The Hebrew is *kedeshah,* which means a temple prostitute.

There was no harlot. Tamar's acquaintances had known her only as a respectable widow. Many a man or woman appears outwardly respectable.

VERSE 22. *I cannot find her.* Tamar was so changed and transformed that nobody knew her.

VERSE 23. *Lest we be ashamed.* The hope that Christ gives to the believer never puts him to shame (Rom. 5. 5).

VERSE 24. Tamar is accused and is in danger of her life. Thus every sinner stands guilty at the bar of God.

Let her be burnt. This does not necessarily mean that she would be burnt alive. She might be stoned first.

VERSE 25. On the day of judgment, when about to perish, Tamar produced the pledge. In the same way the presence of the Holy Spirit in the believer's heart will be the sign on that day that he is justified.

VERSE 26. *Judah acknowledged* them. So Christ will acknowledge His own Spirit and will raise from the dead all those in whom the Spirit has dwelt (Rom. 8. 11).

She hath been more righteous than I. Judah generously acknowledged that Tamar had been right. Tamar had taken a risk and made a coura-

geous act of faith. It is only by staking all in faith on Christ that a sinner can obtain righteousness.

VERSE 27. *Twins were in her womb.* She was in the same position as Rebekah had been (25. 22, 23). In the case of Rebekah however the twins represented the flesh and the spirit. Esau passed outside the covenant altogether. Here both children grew up as Israelites, and we may perhaps see in the circumstances of their birth a picture of the Law and the Gospel.

VERSE 28. *The one put out his hand.* This is like the hand of faith which Abraham and the fathers put out from one world into another, saluting and grasping the promises from far off (Heb. 11. 13).

The midwife. The heavenly midwife is the Holy Spirit, attending upon the spiritual birth of thousands of souls and safely delivering them from sin and darkness into the world of life and light. *A scarlet thread.* If we compare this with Rahab's scarlet thread (Josh. 2. 18), we may conclude that it is a picture and sign of faith.

This came out first. In one sense the midwife was proved in the event to be wrong. In another she was right. Faith and the promises came first before the law (Gal. 3. 17), but they were not realised until the Gospel.

VERSE 29. *As he drew back his hand.* Israel in Egypt and at the time of the exodus failed to exercise a saving faith (Ps. 95. 10), so that the law was given because of transgressions (Rom. 5. 20; Gal. 3. 19).

His brother came out. The law unexpectedly came first.

How hast thou broken forth? The law came in in addition, making a breach as it were, in the sequence of the promises. Yet it was from Pharez that Christ was descended, which agrees with the figure, as He was made under the law (Gal. 4. 4).

Pharez. This means 'breach'.

VERSE 30. *Afterward came out his brother.* The Gospel with the scarlet thread of promise attached to the hand of faith came after the law.

Zarah. This means 'sunrise', a name that well fits the Gospel. The Law with its curses and sanctions, unaccompanied by power, came like a breach in the redemptive purposes revealed by Abraham. The Gospel came like sunrise to the believing sinner. Thus buried away in the story of the birth of Judah's sons we see not only the actual preparations for the Saviour's coming, but something of the meaning and sequence of the plan of redemption, hidden by the Holy Spirit in a narrative which gives a vivid illustration of it to our minds.

CHAPTER 39

WITH this chapter we resume the story of Joseph, which continues to the end of the book. The background of blessing and prosperity which he brought to his master's house (1-6) was broken by the wicked woman's temptation (7-12), followed by her malice when he failed. Joseph is then thrown into prison for no fault of his own, but even there prospers because of the presence and help of the Lord (20-23). The narrative of the chapter is simple. We see God's sovereign hand bringing about all the circumstances of Joseph's suffering in order to effect His purpose, for Joseph's glorification and the saving of life. We also see Joseph resembling Christ in (1) the blessing of God which attended him, (2) in experiencing acute temptation but remaining sinless, (3) in suffering innocently for the sin of another.

VERSE 1. *Joseph was brought down to Egypt.* The narrative is resumed from the end of chapter 37. Egypt is a picture in the Bible of the world, so that we see in this fact a type of the Saviour's coming into the

world, which was to be the scene of His suffering. The martyr Stephen emphasises this point in his great speech (Acts 7-9).

Potiphar, an officer of Pharaoh, captain of the guard. See on 37. 36.

An Egyptian. The point of this description probably lies in the fact that the reigning dynasty was Semite, known to Egyptian history as the Hyksos. They were hated by their Egyptian subjects, whom they seldom employed in positions of responsibility. Potiphar was an exception to this rule. In the case of Joseph his sale to an Egyptian rather than, as might have been possible, to a member of his own race, perhaps made his condition even sadder and more difficult.

Bought him. Joseph was sold and bought as a slave. So the Saviour took on Him the form of a servant (Greek, *doulos,* meaning 'slave' (Phil. 2. 7).

The Ishmaelites. These are the same as the Midianites of 37. 36 (see on 37. 28).

VERSE 2. *The Lord was with Joseph.* This was the whole secret of Joseph's blessing and success, his consolation in his suffering and misery, and his strength and support in all the difficult circumstances through which he passed. He was called to suffer. He could not escape it, but in his suffering he had the conscious presence of his and his father's God. Joseph recognised that it was Jahweh Who was with him, the God of Israel, the God of Abraham and the God of the covenant. He must have guessed that Jahweh would deliver him and bring him safe through and out of all at the end. Perhaps his knowledge and love of Jahweh were such that the presence of Jahweh made his sad, homeless and friendless condition seem light. Notice the use of the Name Jahweh, showing that in thus being with Joseph God was at work on His redemptive purpose, as indeed the sequel shows also. This fact of God's presence with Joseph is the second point recorded in this chapter emphasised and repeated by Stephen (Acts 7. 9).

He was a prosperous man. This was a natural result of the presence of Jahweh with him. His prosperity did not involve escape from suffering, but success in all that he undertook. In this he was like the Saviour, Who went about doing good, attended by blessing and prosperity wherever He went, because of God's continual indwelling presence with Him. The presence of God with us also will bring about the same result, so far as the Spirit of God has play in our lives. *He was in the house of his master.* He did not have to be in special circumstances in order to enjoy the presence of God, certainly not in any religious community, or any hallowed place. He was in the everyday environment of his ordinary domestic work. His routine, perhaps of menial tasks, was lit by the Divine presence. So it may be, and should be, with us. It is in our ordinary affairs that we may look for the presence and companionship of God. We may be in Christ Jesus and yet in Philippi (Phil. 1. 1). We may be saints in Caesar's household (Phil. 4. 22).

VERSE 3. *His master saw.* What advantage would the Divine presence have been to Joseph, if his master had not seen? Of course a witness was given. If others, and especially those with whom and for whom we work every day, do not see that God's presence is with us, we may doubt whether we have it. His master saw.

(1) *That the Lord was with him,* that is to say, he saw a difference in Joseph's personal life from the lives of others, and he realised that this was due to the presence of God. He could scarcely have realised this, if Joseph had not dropped a tactful word to explain it from time to time, as the difficult circumstances permitted.

(2) *That the Lord made all that he did to prosper in his hand.* He

saw also that the presence of the Lord made a difference to Joseph's outward circumstances. This also would have needed a word of explanation in case the prosperity should be attributed to Joseph's personal wisdom and skill. We also shall find that, if the Lord is with us, our occupation prospers.

VERSE 4. *Joseph found grace in his sight.* The beauty of Joseph's character and conduct attracted Potiphar, who consequently showed him confidence, affection and kindness. We too, like Noah (6. 8) and Lot (19. 19), find grace in the eyes of the Lord, and we are accustomed very properly to recollect that there is no beauty or desert of any sort whatever in us to attract God's grace. Joseph's case was so far similar to ours, that he was a slave entirely at Potiphar's discretion, and that whatever may have been the exciting cause, Potiphar's favour was not given of right because Joseph had no claim upon him. In Joseph's case however the context shows that Potiphar's grace, or favour, was called forth by the beauty and attractiveness of Joseph's spirit. Is there anything to correspond to this in our case? There is. The Father's smile and favour are called forth by the beauty of Christ which He sees as He looks at us. Christ is our substitute and representative, Who has condescended to identify us with Himself, so that when the Father looks upon the beauty of Christ His grace is extended to all those who are united to Him and belong to Him. See Ps. 84. 9.

He served him. This seems to have been personal service. Whatever the service may have been, Joseph's position corresponds in this respect exactly to ours. We and all those who are the objects of God's grace are called to His service, which is found in some aspect of witness or ministry.

He made him overseer over his house. Joseph was placed in a position of responsibility because his master saw that his character and conduct warranted it, and his character and conduct were what they were because of the presence of God with him. Thus his sufferings, though not removed, were relieved. God has positions of responsibility in His service in which He desires to place us.

All that he had he put into his hand. Joseph was also placed in a position of trust, just as God longs and plans to place us. He did not know that he was being trained for his future great position under Pharaoh. Perhaps the same thing happens also with us.

VERSE 5. *From the time that.* It was clear from the time that it began that the blessing was to be attributed to God's presence with Joseph.

Blessed the Egyptian's house for Joseph's sake. In the same way God blesses us and all His people for Christ's sake and extends the by-products of the blessings of the Gospel to the lives and houses of the people of the world.

Upon all that he had. If God blesses, He blesses entirely. He makes no exception.

In the house. God's blessing is upon all that we do within the household of His church. He blesses us for Christ's sake, so that our service for Him prospers.

And in the field. God's blessing also falls for Christ's sake upon our ordinary worldly occupations, so that they succeed and prosper.

VERSE 6. *He left all that he had in Joseph's hand.* In this position of trust and responsibility Joseph typified the Lord Jesus Christ, to Whom the Father has committed all judgment (Jo. 5. 22, 27). All that is the Father's is also His Son's (Jo. 17. 10).

Save the bread which he did eat. The heavenly Father reserves to Himself His knowledge of His own Son, the bread of God (Jo. 6. 33; Mt. 11. 27).

Joseph was a goodly person, and well favoured. In this respect he was

unlike his great Antitype in the literal sense, because in Him there was no beauty that we should desire Him (Isa. 53. 2), but an exact type of Him in the spiritual and moral sense, Christ's whole life on earth being one of excellent grace and beauty.

VERSE 7. *Cast her eyes upon Joseph.* This is the lust of the eyes (1 Jo. 2. 16).

VERSE 8. *He refused.* In this he was like the Lord Jesus Christ, Who was subjected to temptation, but refused its suggestions (Mt. 4. 1-11). There was an essential difference in the kind of temptation. Every man is tempted when he is drawn aside of his own lust and enticed (Jas. 1. 14). Joseph, being a member of our fallen race, had indwelling sin and that within him to which Potiphar's wife's temptation could make an appeal. The Saviour had no indwelling sin and could not be tempted in such a way (2 Cor. 5. 21; Heb. 4. 15), because there was nothing in Him that could respond to such temptation. If we study carefully what is recorded of His temptations, we shall perhaps conclude that they were all temptations to substitute the good for the best. Joseph rightly made the responsibility which he had been given and the trust in which he was held reasons for not wronging his master.

VERSE 9. Joseph gave the importance of his position as a third reason for refusing the evil suggestion.

Thou art his wife. The principle of the seventh commandment was known and practised long before it was embodied in the law at Sinai.

How then can I do this great wickedness, and sin against God? This is one of the great sentences of the Bible. It is in this sense (perhaps in addition to others) that he that is begotten of God cannot sin (1 Jo. 3. 9). Joseph realises that what would be a sin against himself, against Potiphar's wife, and against Potiphar was primarily a sin against God. David realised the same fact in similar though sadder circumstances (2 Sam. 12, 13). Notice the use by Joseph of the Divine Name Elohim. Elsewhere in the chapter the Name used is Jahweh (verses 2, 3, 5, 21, 23). The context in this verse demands ' Elohim ', as the name Jahweh would have been meaningless to Potiphar's wife. She knew only ' God ' or ' the gods '. The context thus accounts naturally for the use of the names, and those who insist on the foolish theory that the difference of Name indicates difference of source are put to strange shifts to explain this passage.

VERSE 10. Notice the insistence of the woman and the persistence of the temptation. Joseph's integrity was astonishing and must have been wrought in him by the Holy Ghost.

VERSE 11. In working out His purpose for Joseph and through him for others by means of suffering God saw to it that there was no witness available to exonerate Joseph.

VERSE 12. *Fled.* This was the right thing to do (2 Tim. 2. 22).

VERSE 13. *Left his garments in her hand.* Here was a witness whose silence could give an impression opposite to the truth.

VERSE 14. Notice the drama and human interest of these verses. The wicked woman was a good liar.

VERSE 16. Her passion on being frustrated turned to hatred and malice. She may have feared that if she did not forestall him, Joseph would tell her husband what had occurred.

VERSE 19. The effect on Potiphar was to be expected. He naturally believed his wife.

VERSE 20. *Put him into the prison.* Joseph now becomes like Christ in the most important point of all.

Though innocent himself, he suffers the penalty for another's sin. The analogy is not exact, because Christ's suffering and death are unique events, which cannot be perfectly illustrated or typified, but it is sufficiently clear. God made Christ to be sin for us, Who knew no sin, that we might be made the righteousness of God in Him (2 Cor. 5. 21). Christ was put in the prison of death.

A place where the king's prisoners were bound. This is a good description of death. In it God's prisoners are bound waiting for the day when they will be brought up before Him for judgment. The believing dead are called prisoners by the prophet Zechariah (Zech. 9. 11, 12).

He was there in the prison. Joseph's fortunes now reached their lowest ebb. So much sorrow and misery might have overwhelmed this young and innocent man. Many troubles shall be to the righteous, but the Lord delivereth him out of them all (Ps. 34. 19). The Lord also was three days in the tomb in the prison of death.

VERSE 21. *The Lord was with Joseph.* As He had been with him when he was brought as a slave to Potiphar's house, so He was with him in the prison. Misunderstood, deserted and falsely accused by man, Joseph was never forsaken by his God. This fact was the secret of the endurance which he must have shown. Having the Divine presence, comfort and support, he had all. See Acts 7. 9.

Shewed him mercy. The Hebrew says ' extended kindness unto him.' Where men were unkind, the Lord was kind. The kindness seems to have chiefly consisted in moving the hearts of Joseph's enemies and those who had to do with him to pity and help him. If a man's ways please the Lord, He maketh even his enemies to be at peace with him (Prov. 16. 7).

Gave him favour. Just as he had found grace with Potiphar, so he found favour with the keeper of the prison. In this he was like the Lord Jesus, Who increased in favour with God and man (Lk. 2. 52). This is the third and last point from this chapter referred to by Stephen in his speech (Acts 7. 10), though under the inspiration of the Holy Spirit he transfers the reference to Joseph's relationship with Pharaoh (41. 38-45), of which of course it is undoubtedly true.

Verse 22. In this verse we see in Joseph a very clear type of the Saviour. *Committed to Joseph's hand all the prisoners that were in the prison.* All the believing dead, the prisoners of hope (Zech. 9. 12), are committed to Christ. He is Lord of the dead as well as of the living (Rom. 14. 9), and He has promised to raise them all up at the last day (Jo. 6. 39). *Whatsoever they did there, he was the doer of it.* In a different connection this is true of Christ. He is the doer of all that His people do in His service. Their works are wrought in God (Jo. 3. 21), and it is God that works in them both to will and to do after His good pleasure (Phil. 2. 13).

Verse 23. *Looked not to anything that was under his hand.* Joseph found himself in the same position of trust and responsibility in the prison as he had in Potiphar's house.

Because the Lord was with him. Success in positions of trust and responsibility depends upon relationship with God. Conversely such a relationship with God as was enjoyed by Joseph and belongs to all His people leads to responsibility.

That which he did, the Lord made it to prosper. Our life and actions are in the Lord's hands. We may sow and water, but it is only God Who gives the increase (1 Cor. 3. 6). We could not be in a safer, happier situation. Our actions without Him are of no avail. He gives the meaning, direction and force to them. He did this for Joseph (1) out of pure love and mercy to His child, (2) as

a preparation for the great responsibilities that He was leading Joseph to assume in the future. Both these motives hold good in our own case. We may be assured that if we work in His service and commit our actions to Him in faith, He will assure their successful result.

CHAPTER 40

THIS chapter gives us the story of the dreams of Pharaoh's butler and chief baker, interpreted by Joseph in the prison. The passage is an important link in the story of Joseph, as it was through his contact with the chief butler that he came in touch later with Pharaoh. The spiritual lesson of the chapter lies in the two dreams, which illustrate the double destiny of the human race.

Verse 1. *After these things.* The passage gives a picture of the application of the Gospel. It therefore comes properly after that part of the story which illustrates the suffering of Christ.

Butler. This means cupbearer.

The King of Egypt. In this passage the King of Egypt represents the heavenly King.

Had offended, just as every sinner has offended God and provoked most justly His wrath and indignation against him.

Verse 2. *Pharaoh was wroth,* just as God is angry with the sinner every day (Ps. 7. 11). The wrath of God abides on everyone who disbelieves and disobeys His Son (Jo. 3. 36), and the impenitent treasure up for themselves wrath in the day of wrath (Rom. 2. 5).

Against two of his officers. Notice that both these men had offended and were both under the wrath of the king. There was no difference. Both were in the same place. We were all by nature children of wrath, even as others (Eph. 2. 3).

VERSE 3. *He put them in ward.* In the same way God has concluded all under unbelief (Rom. 11. 32). While we are in the flesh, we are shut up in sin and death and separated from God. *Into the house of the captain of the guard.* This seems to have been Potiphar's house (39. 1), which was perhaps attached to the prison, so that Joseph was not far from the scene of his former labours and of his temptation.

The place where Joseph was bound. What blessing and significance this had for the two imprisoned officers. In the same way we sinners find ourselves in the same place where the Lord Jesus Christ was. He lived in the flesh in this world of sin and death. He was a prisoner as we are, though innocent and undeserving.

VERSE 4. *The captain of the guard.* Unless this officer had been changed, this was Potiphar himself. If it was Potiphar, it is clear that he had come to disbelieve his wife's charges against Joseph, but was perhaps afraid to release him.

Charged Joseph with them. Thank God that the Lord Jesus Christ has been charged with the interests of us sinners.

He served them. It was wonderful that the innocent Joseph should be found in an Egyptian prison serving two prisoners. It is more wonderful that the Son of Man came into our world not to be ministered unto, but to minister (Mt. 20. 28). He came among us as one that served (Lk. 22. 27).

They continued a season in ward. Thus every man born into the world continues for the season of his lifetime in the prison of the flesh. The believer in another sense continues until his conversion in the prison of sin. The Jews continued from Moses to Christ in the prison of the law, and all men continue from death till judgment in the prison of the tomb.

VERSE 5. *They dreamed a dream.* A revelation was given to each of these offenders alike. Thus the Gospel is preached to all sinners alike.

Each man his dream in one night. Neither has precedence over the other. The revelation is given equally to either. Thus the Gospel is preached to all with equal emphasis.

Each man according to the interpretation of his dream. The dream of one told him exactly the opposite to the dream of the other. Thus the Gospel speaks of life to the penitent and of death to the unbeliever.

Which were bound in the prison. The Gospel comes to those who are bound in the prison of the flesh, of sin, or the law, and speaks to them of freedom and the intentions of the King to bring them out.

VERSE 6. *Joseph came in unto them in the morning.* The Saviour comes to us as the Friend of sinners.

Looked upon them. ' Jesus looking upon him loved him ' (Mt. 10. 21). He looks into the hearts of all men and knows them all.

They were sad. The Gospel with its proclamation of the fact of judgment and the need of repentance often makes men sad when it first comes to them. They need a friend to interpret to them, and this place is supplied by the Holy Spirit.

VERSE 7. *Pharaoh's officers.* This description can be applied spiritually to all men, who were created to serve God in positions of responsibility. *With him in the ward of his lord's house.* Jesus was here in the world with us.

Wherefore look ye so sadly? The Lord always sought to interpret men's hearts to them.

VERSE 8. *We have dreamed a dream.* A revelation is made to sinners either through their conscience, or through the law or through the Gospel.

There is no interpreter of it. This is the sad condition of most people in the world. Generation after generation passes ignorant of God's love and the facts of redemption. Man is a moral being. His conscience troubles him, yet there is no one to tell him how it can be set at rest in Christ. How can they hear without a preacher? (Rom. 10. 14).

Do not interpretations belong to God? Only the Holy Spirit can interpret to man the longings of his troubled conscience.

Tell me them. Yet the Spirit does not, and may not, speak direct to the sinner's heart. The barrier raised against God by sin prevents this. The rare cases in which it seems to take place (such as that of John Berridge) are probably to be regarded as a call to remembrance of words read or heard through a human intermediary. It is through a human intermediary that the Spirit speaks to those who are dead in trespasses and sins. Thus Joseph in the same breath as that in which he says that interpretations belong to God asks to be told the dream. He knew himself to be an instrument of God.

Verse 9. *A vine was before me.* Christ is the true vine (Jo. 15. 1).

Verse 10. *Three branches.* These had a special relevance to the chief butler's situation (see verse 12). *It budded and her blossoms shot forth; and the clusters thereof brought forth ripe grapes.* By His death and resurrection Christ became fruitful, bringing forth fruit for the salvation of many.

Verse 11. *Pharaoh's cup was in my hand.* The chief butler found himself in a position to offer something to Pharaoh. So the Gospel puts the sinner in the position to offer something to God. *I took the grapes.* With the hand of faith the believing sinner takes Christ.

And pressed them into Pharaoh's cup, so that in the cup was found wine juice, or 'the blood of grapes' (49. 11). This is an apt picture of the blood of Christ which is offered by the sinner to God at the call of the Gospel.

' Nothing in my hand I bring,
Simply to Thy cross I cling.'
' When thou shalt make His soul an offering for sin, He shall see His seed ' (Isa. 53. 10).

I gave the cup into Pharaoh's hand. So the repenting sinner brings to God the very soul and blood of Jesus Christ, Who died for him once for all on Calvary, declaring that he puts his whole trust and confidence in Christ's sacrifice for him.

Verse 12. *Three days.* There were three days to wait between the dream and the deliverance. So the believer must wait three days, the day of his life in the flesh, the day of death, and the day of judgment.

Verse 13. *Lift up thine head.* The head of the sinner who is accepted by grace for the sake of Christ will be lifted up on the last day in resurrection.

Restore thee unto thy place. The elect will receive back in the world to come all that they lost in Adam.

Thou shalt deliver Pharaoh's cup into his hand. ' His servants shall serve Him ' (Rev. 22. 3).

After the former manner. In the way that was God's intention when He created man.

Verse 14. *Think of me.* The saved sinner is asked to remember his Saviour, especially as He appears to him in the guise of those who need salvation.

When it shall be well with thee. It is the duty of one who is himself rejoicing in salvation to think of those who are still in the prison of sin.

Show kindness, I pray thee, unto me. All kindness shown to the least of Christ's brethren is shown unto Him (Mt. 25. 40).

Make mention of me unto Pharaoh. This is a call to prayer. We are to mention the lost to God.

Bring me out of this house. The incoherent cry of the prisoner of sin is brought by the Holy Ghost to the ear of the praying saint, who has audience with God the sovereign Father.

VERSE 15. *I was stolen away out of the land of the Hebrews.* The desperate plight of man pulled at the heartstrings of the Son of God and stole Him from the bosom of the Father.

Here also have I done nothing that they should put me into the dungeon. The blameless Christ challenged His enemies to convince Him of sin (Jo. 8. 46). Pontius Pilate found Him faultless (Jo. 18. 38). The centurion at His crucifixion pronounced Him righteous (Lk. 23. 47). The apostles testify that He did no sin and knew no sin (1 Pet. 2. 22; 2 Cor. 5. 21).

VERSE 16. *Saw that the interpretation was good.* He attributed nothing but personal advantage to the Gospel. He might have concealed his dream, if the interpretation of the former dream had not been good. He was not willing to receive God's Word whatever it had to say to him, but only if it fitted in with what he wanted.

I had three white baskets on my head. Instead of one cup in his hand he had three baskets on his head. Instead of the hand of faith reaching out to God and offering for His acceptance the one sacrifice once offered he had a variety of works to offer devised out of his own head. The baskets were white with self-righteousness. We might call them the basket of good deeds, the basket of religious observance and the basket of proud respectability.

VERSE 17. *In the uppermost basket,* the one which he thought was nearest to God.

All manner of bakemeats for Pharaoh. Not the fruit of the vine, but the work of a baker. Not the fruit of the Spirit, but the works of the flesh.

The birds did eat them out of the basket upon my head. These fine man-made confections were devoured by the birds, that is to say, by the devil (Mt. 13. 4, 19). He nourishes himself upon them and through them he strengthens his hold upon the hearts of men. No good work can ever win anything from God, and whoever tries to please God in any other way but by faith in Christ plays into the hands of Satan.

VERSE 18. *This is the interpretation thereof.* The Gospel contains the wrath of God as well as His righteousness (Rom. 1. 17, 18). It proclaims condemnation to the unbeliever and salvation to the believer. The same sun melts the wax and hardens the clay.

Three days. The sinner waits also three days for condemnation, the day of his life in the flesh, the day of death, and the day of judgment.

VERSE 19. *Lift up thy head from off thee.* The unrepentant sinner will be finally severed on the day of judgment from life and peace.

Shall hang thee on a tree. ' He that is hanged is accursed of God ' (Deut. 21. 23). This is therefore a picture of the curse of God which will finally fall on the sinner on the day of judgment.

The birds shall eat thy flesh from off thee. The birds represent the devil (Mt. 13. 4, 19). The unrepentant sinner is finally cast unto everlasting fire, prepared for the devil and his angels (Mt. 25. 41).

VERSE 20. *The third day* represents the day of judgment.

Pharaoh's birthday. That great day will be like a birthday. It will be the day of the creation of the new heavens and the new earth, and the day when God becomes all in all. For the first time the whole church of God of every age and generation will be together, and the day of resurrection and redemption of our bodies will be the day in which a nation is born in one day (Isa. 66. 8).

He made a feast unto all his servants. The Lord will do the same on that day (Mt. 22. 2; Lk. 13. 29; 22. 30).

He lifted up the head of the chief butler and of the chief baker. There will be a resurrection both of the just and of the unjust (Acts 24. 15).

VERSE 21. *He restored the chief butler.* On that day the broken image of God will be fully and finally restored on all the people of God (Eph. 4. 24; Col. 3. 10).

He gave the cup into Pharaoh's hand. 'His servants shall serve Him' (Rev. 22. 3).

VERSE 22. *He hanged the chief baker.* Everyone who is not found written in the book of life is cast into the lake of fire (Rev. 20. 15). Notice that the destiny of these two men, types of the saved and the unsaved, was entirely at the king's disposal. When we face a man with the challenge of the Gospel, we may rightly tell him that his destiny depends on his decision. This however is not the same thing as saying that his destiny depends on him himself. God is not a puppet, helpless in the hands of His puny creatures, His purposes for them frustrated by their sinful wills, when they cannot even properly understand the issues. He Himself knows what He will do (Jo. 6. 6). In the ultimate sense every man's destiny depends upon the holy will of God, working out His unfailing purpose in righteousness and knowing all His works from the beginning (Acts 15. 18).

As Joseph had interpreted. The Word of God interpreted to men by His faithful evangelists and prophets will be unerringly fulfilled.

VERSE 23. *Did not the chief butler remember Joseph, but forgat him.* How like ourselves! How often in the enjoyment of forgiveness, freedom and salvation we forget the Saviour Who died for us and the need of the perishing world.

CHAPTER 41

THE thread of the story of Joseph is continued in this chapter. Pharaoh has a dream which troubles him. The chief butler remembers Joseph, who is summoned before Pharaoh and interprets the dream, which was a warning of seven years of plenty to be followed by seven years of famine. To deal with this situation Joseph is put in charge of the whole land, and gathers stores of food. When the famine begins, the surrounding lands sent into Egypt to buy food from Joseph. The spiritual lessons of the chapter are to be found (1) in the meaning of Pharaoh's dreams. The temporary plenty of this world will be followed for those who are unprepared by an eternal famine. (2) The greatest lesson is the change in Joseph's fortunes. His suffering gives place suddenly to glory. The analogy with Christ is obvious. (3) In Joseph alone are to be found safety and provision against the years of famine.

VERSE 1. *Two full years.* During this time Joseph was still waiting in innocent suffering. How often does the Saviour have to wait for us until we trust Him!

Pharaoh dreamed. His dream was a warning of the future, as those of the butler and baker had been. The Gospel is also a revelation from God, which warns of future destiny.

He stood by the river. The river was the Nile, the great river on which the life and traffic of Egypt depended. Egypt in the Bible represents the world. In the Nile we may see, as it were, the stream of this world's life. We may contrast it with the river of God, the Holy Spirit Himself.

VERSE 2. *There came up out of the river,* that is to say, out of the life and history of this present evil world (Gal. 1. 4).

Seven well favoured kine and fatfleshed. These represented the coming seven years of plenty (verse 26). They are like the years of those who are prosperous and comfortable in this world (Ps. 73. 3-12).

They fed in a meadow. For 'meadow' the R.V. has 'reed-grass'. Their pasture was close to the river and depended on it. The lives of the worldly are nourished on the spirit of the world.

VERSE 3. *Seven other kine came up after them*. These represent by contrast the eternal famine of the future.

Out of the river. Loss in the world to come springs from the sinful spirit of this world. It arises as a result of sins committed here. 'The wages of sin is death' (Rom. 6. 23).

Ill favoured and leanfleshed. Sorrow and loss in the world to come inevitably follow selfish prosperity in this.

Stood by the other kine. The miserable future is the certain companion of the selfish present. *Upon the brink of the river*, that is to say, in this present world. It is during this time when the two are together, before the one devours the other, that escape can be found.

VERSE 4. *Did eat up*. The eternal future absorbs and devours the present world and its life, just as the seven years of famine devoured the preceding years of plenty, so that the plenty was forgotten (ver. 30).

Pharaoh awoke. Many never awake after hearing the Gospel warning and perish in their dreams. 'Awake thou that sleepest, and arise from the dead, and Christ shall give thee light' (Eph. 5. 14).

VERSE 5. *He slept and dreamed the second time*. Pharaoh had not rejected the message and warning of his first dream. He had not understood it. God graciously determined to confirm it to him. In similar circumstances God often challenges a man with the Gospel twice and more than twice, never leaving him till he comes to an intelligent decision to accept or reject it.

Seven ears of corn came up upon one stalk, rank and good. They correspond to the seven fat kine. They represent the plenty and satisfaction of a prosperous and selfish life in this world. The one stalk emphasises the fact that we live this life only once, and that we can never go back on it.

VERSE 6. These seven ears correspond to the lean cattle. To Pharaoh they were a warning of the seven years of famine to come. These years represent the eternity of loss that follows a selfish life of plenty in the world. They are thin because they can provide no satisfaction, and they are blasted with the east wind of destruction and the curse of God.

VERSE 7. *The seven thin ears devoured the seven rank and full ears*. Thus life in this world will be made away with, so that nothing of it is left of it or counts for anything. Its pleasures will be forgotten.

Pharaoh awoke, like the sinner who wakes at the Gospel call.

It was a dream. This did not mean to Pharaoh, as it might to us, that it was empty and nothing, altogether unreal, but that it was a revelation from God. The awaking sinner realises that the Gospel is God's call to him.

VERSE 8. *His spirit was troubled*. It was troubled in a right sense. He realised that God had spoken to him, but he did not understand the meaning of what He had said. What a good thing it would be if more were troubled in this way when they hear the Gospel.

He sent and called for all the magicians of Egypt. When a man is aroused by the Gospel, he will often call for the priests or clergy to whose ministrations he is accustomed and ask them to explain it to him.

All the wise men thereof. When his conscience is aroused, a man may sometimes seek the views of scholarship on his difficulty.

Pharaoh told them his dreams. So perhaps the seeker will faithfully recount what has been revealed to him in the Gospel.

There was none that could interpret them. The Holy Spirit alone can interpret His own Word to the troubled seeker.

VERSE 9. *The chief butler.* He represents one who knew the Gospel by experience.

I do remember my faults this day. When confronted with another's need, he remembers that he had forgotten the one who brought him comfort and assurance for the future and had failed to witness to him or speak about him.

VERSE 10. He begins to tell his own experiences from the beginning. *Pharaoh was wroth with his servants.* He remembers his consciousness of being under the wrath of God.

Put me in ward. He remembers that he was the devil's prisoner and the slave of sin.

Me and the chief baker. He goes on to explain that this is the lot of others as well as himself, indeed of all men.

VERSE 11. *We dreamed a dream in one night.* A revelation from God had been made to him by the Gospel, as it has just been made to Pharaoh.

According to the interpretation of his dream. What God said had proved in his experience to be true.

VERSE 12. *There was there with us a young man.* The Lord Jesus came as a man into our world, and He is still here with us whenever we need Him. *An Hebrew.* This refers to Joseph's origin. So the Lord Jesus Christ did not originate in our world, but came down from heaven. He was very God of very God.

Servant to the captain of the guard. In the same way the Lord Jesus took upon Him the form of a servant, and was found in fashion as a man (Phil. 2. 7).

We told him. In the same way we may and ought to tell the Lord Jesus all our troubles and questions. *He interpreted to us our dreams.* Jesus Christ by the Holy Spirit interprets the Gospel to the troubled seeker.

To each man according to his dream. The believer is given peace and assurance. The unbeliever is confirmed in his fear of judgment to come (Heb. 10. 27).

VERSE 13. *As he interpreted to us, so it was.* This is always so. God's Word never returns to Him void (Isa. 55. 11). What He has promised He is able also to perform (Rom. 4. 21). He cannot deny Himself (2 Tim. 2. 13).

Me he restored into mine office. The opportunity and power to serve God, for which man was created, lost in Adam, is restored to the believer.

Him he hanged. The unbeliever passes to destruction with the curse of God upon him.

CHAPTER 41 (CONTINUED)

VERSE 14. *Pharaoh sent and called Joseph.* So the Lord Jesus Christ was called by the Father from the tomb.

They brought him hastily out of the dungeon. In a moment of time the Lord Jesus rose from the dead and passed into a glorified life. The angels welcomed and attended Him.

He shaved himself. As a Hebrew Joseph wore a beard. The Egyptians habitually shaved. When He rose, the Lord rid Himself of the carnal nature which He had taken as a child of Adam.

And changed his raiment. He put off the carnal nature and put on a glorified human body. Not but what it was the same body as He took from Mary, but its nature was changed.

Came in unto Pharaoh. One like the Son of Man came with the clouds of heaven, and came unto the ancient of days, and they brought Him near before Him (Dan. 7. 13). The Lord Jesus ascended up on high far above all heavens (Eph. 4. 10), into the very presence of the Father in the holiest of all, where He is today as our representative and advocate.

VERSE 15. *I have dreamed a dream, and there is none that can interpret it.* Notice (1) that Pharaoh on his throne is in just the same position as his butler and baker when it comes to a revelation from God to him. (2) Notice that if we think of Pharaoh as representing God the heavenly King and Joseph as representing Christ, we are reminded that none but Christ can unseal the book of the purpose of God and insure its being carried into effect.

I have heard say of thee. The seeking sinner is told of the Christian evangelist or minister. May we become known as those who are able to help and explain in such circumstances.

Thou canst understand a dream to interpret it. The Word of Christ should dwell richly in each one of us, so that we can interpret a man's need and interpret the Gospel to him (Col. 3. 16).

VERSE 16. *It is not in me.* This is the proper answer. We can do nothing by our own power or godliness (Acts 3. 12).

God shall give Pharaoh an answer of peace. The Gospel is God's answer to the need of sinful man. It is an answer of peace with God through our Lord Jesus Christ, through Whom we have received access by faith into this grace in which we stand (Rom. 5. 1, 2).

VERSE 17. *The repetition of Pharaoh's* dreams in this and the following verses, in which they are given in a slightly fuller form, shows the important part they play as illustrations of the Gospel.

I stood upon the bank of the river. Pharaoh stood by the Nile, watching the life and history of the world flow by. So the Gospel brings before a man's eyes the great and pompous but corrupted stream of the world.

VERSE 18. *There came up out of the river.* The Gospel shows us the origin of the life of the world in the elements of the world (1 Jo. 2. 16; Gal. 4. 3; Col. 2. 20).

Seven kine, fatfleshed and well favoured. These represented the seven years of plenty (vv. 26, 29). The seven years themselves represent a life of selfish pleasure and prosperity in this present world.

They fed in a meadow. The meadow was the reed-grass beside the Nile. A life of pleasure in this world takes its nourishment and inspiration from the things of the world.

VERSE 19. *Seven other kine came up after them.* These represented the seven years of famine (vv. 27, 30). The years of famine represent the eternity of loss that follows the selfish plenty of this present life.

Poor and very ill favoured and leanfleshed. These represent the misery and eternal destruction of the

A

lost (Mt. 8. 12; Lk. 12. 20).

Such as I never saw in all the land of Egypt for badness. No sorrow or disappointment that has ever been experienced in the world can be compared with that which will be experienced by the wicked on the day of judgment.

VERSE 20. The life of this world, which is only vanity (Eccl. 1. 2), will count for nothing and will be absorbed and forgotten in the realities of eternity.

VERSE 21. *It could not be known that they had eaten them.* The life of this world is as nothing compared with eternity, and its amenities will not affect or alter it to any degree.

So I awoke. Pharaoh was like a man aroused and startled by the preaching of the Gospel and the faithful revelation of judgment to come.

VERSE 22. *Seven ears came up.* They represent the seven years of plenty (verses 26, 29). The years of plenty represent a lifetime spent in the enjoyment of the things of the world.

In one stalk. Together the years make up a single lifetime, which is lived once and can never be repeated.

Full and good, like the rich man who was clothed in purple and scarlet and fed sumptuously every day (Lk. 16. 19).

VERSE 23. *Seven ears.* These represent the eternity that follows life in this world.

Withered, thin, and blasted with the east wind. There will be no satisfaction for the wicked in the world to come.

VERSE 24. *Devoured.* Time and this world will be absorbed in the eternity to come.

I told this unto the magicians. The seeker, troubled on hearing the Gospel, goes to the clergy and religious leaders.

There was none that could declare it to me. The fact of coming judgment is strange and unpalatable to religious leaders of all ages.

VERSE 25. *The dream of Pharaoh is one.* In whatever way it be presented, there is only one Gospel. *God hath shewed Pharaoh what He is about to do.* So in the Gospel God makes clearly known what He will do with the believer, and what with the unbeliever on the day of judgment. Notice throughout this chapter the use of the Divine Name Elohim, demanded by the context, as Joseph was conversing all the time with Egyptians, who would never have heard or understood the Name Jahweh.

VERSE 26. *Seven years.* These years are typical of the present lifetime.

The dream is one. Joseph repeats this. To us it emphasises the fact that there is only one Gospel, one faith once for all delivered to the saints (Jude 3), one hope and one baptism (Eph. 4. 4, 5).

VERSE 27. *Seven years of famine,* the lean time, when on the day of judgment the man who has lived for this world will find that he has nothing left.

VERSE 28. *This is the thing which I have spoken unto Pharaoh.* The point of the dream and the purpose of God for the future are found in these two series of years. So the foundation of the Gospel lies in the fact that an eternal world follows the present transient life.

What God is about to do he showeth unto Pharaoh. God in mercy reveals His purpose to men in the Gospel.

VERSE 29. The present life is by no means a life of plenty to many who live it, but it is so to those in similar positions to Pharaoh, and it is to people in such positions that warnings are often given by the Lord Jesus

(Mt. 19. 23, 24; Lk. 6. 24, 25; 12. 16;
16. 1, 19). Compare Jas. 5. 1-6.

VERSE 30. *After them*. There are a
judgment and an eternity after this
life.

All the plenty shall be forgotten.
Silver and gold will stand no man in
stead on that day.

The famine shall consume the land.
God's judgment will destroy and eat
up the world.

VERSE 31. *The plenty shall not be
known*. It will be nothing on the day
of judgment.

It shall be very grievous. ' There
shall be weeping and gnashing of
teeth ' (Mt. 8. 12).

VERSE 32. *Doubled unto Pharaoh
twice*. Thus a man may be challenged
twice or more with the Gospel. Or
we may think of the double witness
of the Word and the Spirit, or the
Gospel and the conscience, or the
Scripture and reason. These two
agree together in such a way that the
truth of the Gospel is inescapable.

The thing is established by God.
God has made known to us the immutability of His counsel (Heb. 6.
17). Heaven and earth will pass
away, but the words of the Lord
Jesus will not pass away (Mt. 24.
35).

God will shortly bring it to pass.
The present age is like a moment, and
the Lord is coming quickly to judgment (Rev. 22. 20). In the actual
situation confronting Pharaoh Joseph
meant that the seven years of plenty
would quickly begin. In fact they
began at once with the very next year.
This throws light upon the phrase
used in Rev. 1. 1, where we are told
that the things prophesied in the book
of Revelation must shortly come to
pass. It means that they were to begin to happen at once, as in fact they
did.

VERSE 33. Thank God, the Gospel
not only warns of judgment to come,
but also explains the way of escape.

Let Pharaoh look out a man. God
looked out a man, the only man that
could deal with the situation, the
Lord Jesus Christ.

Discreet and wise. The Spirit of
wisdom, understanding, counsel and
knowledge rested upon Christ (Isa.
11. 2), and in Him are hid all the
treasures of wisdom and knowledge
(Col. 2. 3).

Set him over the land of Egypt.
In the same way Christ has been
given all power in heaven and on
earth (Mt. 28. 18).

VERSE 34. *Let Pharaoh do this*. It
is important not only to think about
it and intend it, but do it. *Appoint
officers over the land*. They were to
work under the discreet and wise
man, and they correspond to the
faithful servants of Christ who work
under Him here for the furtherance
of the Gospel and will reign with
Him for ever and ever (Rev. 22. 5).

*Take up the fifth part of the land
of Egypt in the seven plenteous years*.
These men were to be engaged in
making provision for the future. In
the same way the servants of Christ
by believing and preaching the Gospel during the continuance of this
present world store up spiritual provision against the future. The resources of this world are used in this
work.

VERSE 35. *Let them gather all the
food of those good years that come*.
Our Lord said the same thing when
He told us to make to ourselves
friends out of the mammon of unrighteousness (Lk. 16. 9).

*Lay up corn under the hand of
Pharaoh*. In the same way we are
to lay up for ourselves treasures in
heaven (Mt. 6. 20).

Let them keep food in the cities.
Christ Himself is our heavenly food
(Jo. 6. 51, 54). We keep Him by
continuing in faith in Him to our
lives' end, so that the heavenly food
will avail us on the day of judgment.

VERSE 36. *That food shall be for*

store to the land. If Jesus Christ is our Saviour now, He will be our Saviour and Advocate on the day of judgment. *That the land perish not.* He that hath the Son hath life, and he that hath not the Son of God hath not life (1 Jo. 5. 12).

VERSE 37. *The thing was good in the eyes of Pharaoh.* The purpose of redemption in and through Christ was pleasing to God.
And in the eyes of all his servants. All who love and fear God approve His wonderful salvation.

VERSE 38. *Can we find such a one as this is.* The Lord Jesus Christ is the chiefest among ten thousand and altogether lovely (Cant. 5. 10, 16).
A man in whom the Spirit of God is. So the Spirit of the Lord rested upon Christ (Isa. 11. 2).

VERSE 39. *Forasmuch as God hath shewed thee all this.* The heavenly Joseph was in the counsel of the Father from eternity past and knew all His purpose.
There is none so discreet and wise as thou art. In Christ are hid all the treasures of wisdom and knowledge (Col. 2. 3), and He knows what is in man (Jo. 2. 25).

VERSE 40. *Thou shalt be over my house.* Christ as a Son is over the house of God (Heb. 3. 6).
According unto thy word shall all my people be ruled. All power is given unto Christ in heaven and on earth (Mt. 28. 18).
Only in the throne will I be greater than thou. In the same way the Lord Jesus said, ' My Father is greater than I ' (Jo. 14. 28). He Himself reigns and rules with the Father's authority till all His enemies are destroyed (1 Cor. 15. 25).

VERSE 41. *I have set thee over all the land of Egypt.* In the same way Christ is now head over all things to the church (Eph. 1. 22), and the Prince of the kings of the earth (Rev.

1. 5). He is administering the world.

VERSE 42. *Took off his ring from his hand, and put it upon Joseph's hand.* This was Pharaoh's signet ring, as the Revised Version makes clear. In the same way the Son of man had the seal of God the Father (Jo. 6. 27).
Vestures of fine linen. This represents the righteousness of Christ.
A gold chain about his neck. This is symbolic of glory and represents the glory of the Lord Jesus after His resurrection.

VERSE 43. *He made him to ride in the second chariot which he had.* The chariots of God are twenty thousand, even thousands of angels (Ps. 68. 17). So the holy angels accompany Christ in His glory (Mt. 16. 27).
Bow the knee. This is an Egyptian word, in the original probably meaning, ' Make way '.
Ruler over all the land of Egypt. After His resurrection Christ was given all power in heaven and earth (Mt. 28. 18).

VERSE 44. *I am Pharaoh.* Joseph's authority was ultimately derived from Pharaoh's decree. In the same way Jesus Christ derived His authority from the Father, Who raised Him from the dead and gave Him glory (1 Pet. 1. 21).
Without thee shall no man lift up his hand or foot in all the land of Egypt. Joseph was given absolute authority. In the same way Christ has absolute authority in the world. Nothing can happen without His permission.

VERSE 45. *Zaphnath-paaneah.* This means ' revealer of secrets '. So Christ is the revealer of God's secrets to men (Mt. 11. 27).
He gave him to wife Asenath. Christ's church is His bride (Eph. 5. 25, 29, 32).
Joseph went out over all the land of Egypt. In the same way Christ goes out over all the world by the Spirit in the Gospel.

VERSE 46. *Thirty years old*. He was still a young man. His troubles had lasted thirteen years, a long and miserable period for one of his age, but it was a small proportion of his life, which was to last eighty years longer (50. 22).

Stood before Pharaoh. On the day of His ascension the Saviour returned to the Father and stood before Him victorious over Satan and death.

Went out from the presence of Pharaoh. By the Spirit Christ returns, as it were, into the world, though we ought never to confuse the coming of the Holy Ghost with Christ's final bodily return in glory.

Went throughout all the land of Egypt. By the Spirit the heavenly Joseph goes in triumphant progress winning evangelical victories over Satan and sin.

VERSE 47. *In the seven plenteous years*. These represent the life of this present world.

The earth brought forth by handfuls. Abundant provision is made by God in Christ through the Gospel for the needs of the sinner on the day of judgment and in the world to come. This provision is made in handfuls, which can be easily grasped by the hand of faith. The provision is made during the plenteous years only, and never on any account at any later time. During this life only is it possible to prepare for eternity (Prov. 11. 7).

VERSE 48. *He gathered up all the food of the seven years*. We too should use this world in the service of Christ and make to ourselves friends of the mammon of unrighteousness (Lk. 16. 9).

Which were in the land of Egypt. Egypt in the Bible is the picture of the world. The resources of this world are to be used to save life and set forward the Gospel.

Laid up the food in the cities. In the same way we are to lay up treasure in heaven, the city of God (Mt. 6. 20).

The food of the field. The field is the world (Mt. 13. 38).

Laid he up in the same. We too are to lay up treasure in the city of God by committing our all to Christ, so that our life is hid with God in Him (Col. 3. 3).

VERSE 49. *As the sand of the sea, very much*. The resources that we have in Christ are immense and amply sufficient for all our needs. *It was without number*. The provision of Christ for us is boundless.

VERSE 50. *Two sons before the years of famine came*. So Christ's people bear fruit to Him in this world through the Gospel (Rom. 7. 4). The two sons represent two aspects of the Christian church.

VERSE 51. *Manasseh*. The name means ' forgetting '. The names of Joseph's sons illustrate spiritual truth, as did those of Jacob (see 29. 31-30.23). Thus the church of Christ is called upon to forget her own people and her father's house (Ps. 45. 10). We are to forget our old life and walk in newness of life.

For God, said he, hath made me forget all my toil. In the joy that is set before Him the Lord Himself forgets all His toil and suffering in the world, and His people the toil of their former unhappy sinful life.

All my father's house. In so far as this refers to Christ, the father that He forgets is Adam and the house that He forgets is His life in the flesh. His people forget their former life which was lived without Him.

VERSE 52. *Ephraim*. This means ' fruitful '. The name is an illustration of the true and proper spiritual life, which brings forth the fruit of the Spirit (Gal. 5. 22). and wins others for Christ.

God hath caused me to be fruitful in the land of my affliction. Egypt was the land of Joseph's affliction. This world is the land of Christ's affliction, and it is in this world that He is fruitful, winning thousands to His Father and Himself by the Gospel, made possible only by His suffering. The people of God are also fruitful in Him in the world where they suffer for Him.

VERSE 53. Life in this world with the pleasures and comforts that it brings to so many will come to an end.

VERSE 54. *The seven years of dearth began to come.* The years of dearth represent (1) for the unbeliever the day of judgment and eternity of loss that follow life lived for this world and for self, (2) for the convicted sinner, eventually to become a believer, the time when he realises his need and helplessness, as the prodigal son did (Lk. 15. 14-16).

According as Joseph had said. The Gospel warns men of the hopelessness of their condition apart from Christ.

The dearth was in all lands. It is inescapable. Wherever the sinner is, his hopelessness and despair are with him, whether it be in this present life under the conviction of the Spirit, or on the day of judgment.

In all the land of Egypt there was bread. There was bread there because Joseph was there and had stored it up. In the same way there is bread available in all the world because Christ may be found there by all who seek Him and ask for Him.

VERSE 55. *When all the land of Egypt was famished.* It is only in the realisation of need that men will look to the future and call upon God. The temporal judgments which God is always carrying out in the world are intended to assist this realisation. The goodness of God leads men to repentance (Rom. 2. 4). *The people cried to Pharaoh for bread.* Many will pray to God in times of need or extremity. *Go unto*

Joseph. The Holy Spirit through the Word continually points men to Jesus Christ. *What he saith to you do.* The teaching of Christ in the Gospels, expanded and expounded by the apostles in the rest of the New Testament, explains the way of salvation.

VERSE 56. *The famine was over all the face of the earth.* Wherever sin and death reign, there are spiritual hunger, need and despair.

Joseph opened all the storehouses. The Lord Jesus Christ opens to us all the storehouses of God's grace to supply the need of us sinners for righteousness, sanctification and redemption.

Sold unto the Egyptians. Pharaoh and Joseph made the Egyptians buy the food they needed. The Lord sells without money and without price (Isa. 55. 1). Our spiritual needs are filled by the gifts of God's grace. *The famine waxed sore in the land of Egypt.* The way of transgressors is hard, and the world may become a place in which men and women starve spiritually, though surrounded by material luxury.

VERSE 57. *All countries came.* The Gospel is open to all the world, and we Gentiles have been invited to come.

To Joseph. It was the heavenly Joseph Who said, ' Come unto Me, all ye that labour and are heavy laden ' (Mt. 11. 28).

For to buy corn. Those who came were asked for money. We have none to give, nor are we asked for any. The water of life is given to us freely (Rev. 21. 6). The Lord Jesus Himself is the bread of life, Who came down from heaven to give Himself for the life of the world (Jo. 6. 51).

The famine was so sore in all lands. Thank God for the famine and the sense of need which drive those that feel them to Christ in order to satisfy their spiritual hunger.

CHAPTER 42

THIS chapter connects closely with the last and continues step by step the story of Joseph and his brethren. The famine drives Jacob to send his sons to Egypt to buy corn. Joseph recognises his brothers and seeks at once to bring them to repentance. He pretends to take them for spies, keeps Simeon in prison, and sends them back home to fetch and bring Benjamin, whom they had mentioned to him, as proof that they were true. The chapter provides an illustration of the means by which the Saviour works upon sinners to bring them to repentance.

VERSE 1. *When Jacob saw that there was corn in Egypt.* Notice that it does not say ' When he *heard,*' but ' When he *saw.*' That he had heard we know from the following verse, but before he took action he needed evidence. He no doubt saw corn actually brought back from Egypt by those who had gone there to obtain it. In the same way the sinner who is conscious of his need requires evidence that it can be supplied in Christ, and he can only find this evidence in the transformed lives of Christ's people. Holiness will never secure for the man who possesses it a place in heaven. Unless he has that place already by faith in Christ, he cannot have any holiness at all. But holiness can and does lead others to put their faith in Christ because it is evidence of Christ's saving power.

Why do ye look one upon another? There is no need for the sinner to despair. There is life and salvation awaiting him in Christ.

VERSE 2. *I have heard that there is corn in Egypt.* Jacob had not only seen the corn being brought back to Canaan. He had also been told where it came from. The evidence of a Christian life will lead no man to Christ, unless the source of the life is clearly explained. If no ex-

planation is made, the glory will go to the Christian instead of to his Master.

Get you down thither. We always have to go down to Christ. Any vestige of pride, self-satisfaction, or self-sufficiency will prevent our reaching Him. Thus our Lord said to Zacchæus, ' Make haste and come down ' (Lk. 19. 5). *Buy for us from thence.* The sinner always instinctively thinks that salvation must be bought. The sequel shows that Joseph took no money from his brethren. It is certainly true that Christ takes nothing from sinners in return for salvation. Indeed they have nothing to give. If they had, they could not buy salvation with it, if only because it was fully paid for by the Saviour Himself when He died on the cross.

That we may live, and not die. Jacob recognised that it was a matter of life and death. To obtain Christ, the living bread from heaven, is to find eternal life. Without Him the sinner will perish for ever (1 Jo. 5. 12).

VERSE 3. They not only realised their need and the tremendous issues at stake, and they not only believed what they heard as to where the need could be supplied, but they rightly took action and went down to Egypt. This meant for them a journey at considerable trouble and expense. How much more important it is for the sinner to come to Christ, when the issue is infinitely greater, and when he can come to Christ there and then in his heart by prayer.

VERSE 4. *Benjamin, Joseph's brother, Jacob sent not.* He did not send him because he did not know who Joseph was. He knew there was corn in Egypt, but he did not know that all depended on Joseph. Many feel there is satisfaction to be found in Christianity, but have no idea that all depends upon their personal relationship with a living, loving Christ. Thus Jacob kept Benjamin back, and refused to let him go. The sequel will show that this had to be remedied before recognition could take place.

Lest peradventure mischief befall him. Jacob feared he might lose by sending Benjamin, just as the sinner so often fears he will lose by surrendering all to Christ. Not that in the circumstances Jacob's fear was not reasonable. He had before him the brothers' treatment of Joseph, which it is likely by now he had discovered or at least suspected. He hints that something of the same sort might happen to Benjamin, whom he was afraid to entrust to them. Thus the bad characters and reputations of the brothers prevented Benjamin from meeting Joseph sooner than he did.

Verse 5. *Among those that came.* They could hardly have expected any privilege in Egypt because they were sons of Israel, but if they did, they were mistaken. All that came were on the same level and were treated alike. It is the same with those who come to Christ. Jew or Gentile, bond or free, all receive the same consideration and the same gift.

The famine. Their need drove them to Joseph, as the sinner's need drives him to Christ.

Verse 6. *Joseph was the governor*. He was the picture of Christ, Who is the Governor of heaven and earth.

He it was that sold to all the people of the land. It is the Lord Jesus Who gives freely from the inexhaustible resources of His grace to all who seek the satisfaction of their need.

Joseph's brethren came. They are those who rejected, betrayed and sold him. They are typical of all sinners in the world, but perhaps in a special and moving sense of the Jewish nation.

Bowed down themselves before him. So the dream which they had so resented was fulfilled (37. 7, 9, 10). In the same way He has decreed that to Him every knee should bow in the Name of Jesus (Isa. 45.

23; Phil. 2. 10).

Verse 7. *Joseph saw his brethren, and he knew them*. In the same way the Saviour sees, knows and loves all who come to Him.

Made himself strange unto them. He at once began dealing with them in a way intended to lead them to recognition, repentance and reconciliation. In the same way and perhaps for the same reason the Saviour strictly charged His disciples to tell no man that He was the Christ (Mt. 16. 20). *Spake roughly unto them*, rather in the same way as Christ sometimes appeared to make it seem a hard thing to become His disciple. The eventual purpose in each case was to test sincerity. *Whence come ye?* This is the first question that needs to be brought to the mind of sinners. We must look back to see and admit that we are strangers and foreigners and that we come from a far country.

From the land of Canaan to buy food. This answer was correct. It admitted their distant and foreign origin and it admitted their need.

Verse 8. Long before we know the Saviour He knows us. He knew us as His sheep before the foundation of the world (Eph. 1. 4). In this world He knows us from the womb (Gal. 1. 15), and in all His dealings with us, however contrary we may suppose them to be, He seeks to bring us to reconciliation.

Verse 9. *Remembered the dreams*, just as the Lord knows clearly and carries out faultlessly the purpose that God has for Him in relation to our redemption.

Ye are spies. Joseph suggests that their motive was hypocritical. In the same way the Holy Spirit searches our hearts and seeks to reveal them to us.

Verse 10. The brethren maintain that their only purpose is the satisfaction of their need. This they could not finally get till they recognised Joseph and were reconciled to him.

VERSE 11. The brethren maintain that they had a single purpose, and they begin to open up to him something of their situation. In the same way the Saviour moves the sinner to open his heart more and more.

VERSE 12. Joseph does not accept their answer, but skilfully goes on to oblige them to mention Benjamin, whom Jacob had kept at home.

VERSE 13. Here the brethren open their hearts more plainly still and mention the point which Joseph desired. So the Holy Spirit probes in our hearts more and more deeply.

VERSE 14. Joseph still maintains his suggestion that they were hypocrites.

VERSE 15. *Hereby ye shall be proved.* The proof of their sincerity was whether they would bring their youngest brother. So the proof of ours is whether we will bring all to Christ and keep nothing back.

VERSE 16. *Ye shall be kept in prison.* No one is spiritually free until he is ready to give all to Christ.

VERSE 17. Joseph's method is an illustration of the severity of God, by which He seeks to work upon and soften the hearts of men.

VERSE 18. *The third day.* The expression reminds us instinctively of the Lord's resurrection. Joseph speaks to his brothers as a type of the risen Lord.

This do, and live. The heavenly Joseph offers eternal life to all who will receive it of Him.

I fear God. Notice in these words (1) Joseph's testimony to his personal faith, (2) the implication that those who fear God will show mercy and kindness, (3) the obvious implication that God desires men to live. ' I

have no pleasure in the death of him that dieth, saith the Lord God; wherefore turn yourselves, and live ye ' (Ezek. 18. 32).

VERSE 19. *If ye be true men, let one of your brethren be bound.* The pledge of sincerity was acquiescence in loss and suffering, of which the minimum consistent with the existence of the pledge was inflicted.

Go ye, carry corn for the famine of your houses. This was the first of two conditions on which the life mentioned in verse 18 depends. The first and fundamental condition is the reception of the bread of life to supply spiritual famine.

VERSE 20. *But bring your youngest brother unto me.* This is the second condition. It is tantamount to surrendering all to Christ and holding nothing back from Him. It is not so much a condition of life — as indeed is clear from this passage, as it was the corn received and carried away which supplied and sustained life — but it was a proof that the life and intentions were true.

So shall your words be verified. Professions of faith are proved true by actions. Good works are the pledge of living faith.

Ye shall not die. No man who believes in his heart as well as confessing with his mouth will ever perish.

They did so. Their agreement and obedience already proved them to be genuine.

VERSE 21. *We are verily guilty concerning our brother.* Here is the true repentance beginning, towards which Joseph's treatment of his brethren was directed. All these years they had a guilty conscience, which broke out into activity when they were touched by trouble. Joseph's way with them was already justified. This is what the heavenly Joseph waits for. He seeks to bring sinners to the point at which they say, ' We are verily guilty,' and not only so, but

add also, ' Concerning our brother.'
Before he can be saved, the sinner
must be brought to the place where
he realises he is guilty of rejecting
and betraying Christ. *We saw the
anguish of his soul.* No one can
measure the anguish of Christ when
He poured out His soul unto death
(Isa. 53. 11, 12).

When he besought us. Christ in
His suffering made an appeal to all
sinners.

We would not hear. This is true
of all the unbelieving world.

*Therefore is this distress come
upon us.* The brothers were right,
and every sinner who acknowledges
the same fact in regard to Christ is
right. Every unrepentant man will
acknowledge it on the day of judgment.

Verse 22. *Do not sin against the
child.* Reuben had advised against
downright rejection and betrayal and
murder. He had intended to restore
Joseph to his father (37. 22). He
was rather like Pontius Pilate. Like
him, he went with the stream. He
never enlightened Jacob as to what
had happened, so far as we know.
In any case Jacob believed that
Joseph was dead. Reuben never set
on foot any enquiries which might
have led to the recovery of Joseph
from Egypt. He was shocked by
extremes, but he took no trouble to
do the right.

His blood is required. The blood
of Christ will be required of a guilty
world on the day of judgment.

Verse 23. *They knew not that
Joseph understood them.* While the
sinner is pondering over his rejection
of Christ, or discussing his guilt with
others, he little knows that Jesus
Christ Himself is at his side, not only
listening to his words, but penetrating
his very thoughts.

*He spake unto them by an inter-
preter.* The Holy Spirit is the interpreter of the mind of Christ to men,
but in this case the interpreter points
rather to the evangelist or Christian

witness.

Verse 24. *Wept.* The heart of Christ
is moved over the repenting sinner
with all the compassion that He
showed when He was on earth. He
is the same yesterday, today and for
ever (Heb. 13. 8).

Returned to them again. Christ
cannot leave the sinner in his distress.

Communed with them. Through
His servants, who are His witnesses
in the world, Christ continues to
speak with the sinner.

Simeon. If Reuben had not dis-
closed that he had been against the
outrage committed against Joseph,
Joseph might have selected him as the
eldest. Simeon came next to Reuben
in age, and was also noted for his
cruelty (49. 5, 7). We may well suppose that he played a leading part
in the betrayal of Joseph.

Verse 25. Notice in this verse the
illustration of three things which the
Saviour does for the sinner who applies to Him. *Joseph commanded*:
(1) *to fill their sacks with corn.* He
provides him with the bread of life
which he needs, so that coming to
Christ he never hungers (Jo. 6, 35).
(2) *To restore every man's money
into his sack.* All that the sinner
seeks to give in exchange for the
bread of life the Saviour returns to
him. Any sacrifice that he seeks to
make for Christ is restored to him
with interest. (3) *To give them provision for the way.* Not only are the
sinner's fundamental spiritual needs
supplied, but the material things
which he needs for his journey
through the world are promised him
(Mt. 6. 31-33).

Thus did he unto them. Joseph's
commands were obeyed. We should
be happy, if we were as quick and
faithful in obeying the commands of
our heavenly Joseph.

Verse 26. *They laded their asses
with the corn.* The ass in the Bible
is the picture of the unregenerate
man. Many of them are unwittingly

used in the spread of the Gospel and the sustenance of the believer, for example, the world's printers. The ass's interests are limited to his own narrow outlook, and he knows nothing of the meaning of that which he is indispensably helping to set forward.

VERSE 27. *He espied his money.* The seeking sinner becomes conscious, through faithful preaching or through the conviction of the Spirit, that his self-effort is not accepted, and that he cannot purchase salvation. He sees his money restored.

VERSE 28. *Their heart failed them, and they were afraid.* They were completely puzzled by the way that they were being treated. They feared that the restoration of their money was a trick to facilitate their being accused of stealing. We who have been Christians for longer do not always realise the fear that arises in a man's heart when he first comes in contact with the Gospel. The root cause is the same with the sinner today as it was with the brethren of Joseph — a guilty conscience. It is evident that their conscience had been burdened all down the years by their sin against their brother.

What is this that God hath done unto us? Their evil conscience continually expected a judgment of God, but they were at least right in attributing what was happening to them to the hand of God.

VERSE 29. *They came unto Jacob their father unto the land of Canaan, and told him.* They rightly reported their experiences. It is a mistake to be too reserved in the things of the Gospel. We Christians may also take this verse in isolation and learn from it the duty of coming to our heavenly Father and telling Him all that befalls us.

VERSE 30. *The man who is the lord of the land.* They little knew his identity. Joseph was still a stranger

to them. They were in the place of the sinner who has begun to come into contact with Christ, but does not yet personally know Him. They were afraid and confused.

Spake roughly to us. The Hebrew says, ' Spake with us hard things.' Joseph was a faithful type of the Saviour, Who did just the same thing (Jo. 6. 60). *Took us for spies of the country.* Joseph really knew them and was dealing in this way with them in order to win them. The Saviour sets going a search in the sinner's heart whether he is genuine or hypocritical.

VERSE 31. The brothers maintained that they were truly seeking the satisfaction of their need.

VERSE 32. *One is not.* This was an awkward understatement.

The youngest is this day with our father. This was the next point of issue. Benjamin had been held back and reserved for Jacob. He would not let him go.

VERSE 33. *Hereby shall I know.* Tests are always imposed upon faith.

True men. True faith and true seeking will pass all tests.

Leave one of your brethren here with me. This gave them a tie with Joseph and gave Joseph a stake in them. Once a man has heard the Gospel and come in contact with Christ, he enters into a responsibility and gets into a position from which he can never entirely retreat. *Take food for the famine of your households.* Joseph did not allow those in need to suffer through the stratagem that he was adopting. In the same way Christ demonstrates His mercy in the very tests.

VERSE 34. *Bring your youngest brother unto me.* Christ demands that everything be laid at His feet and nothing be held back.

Then shall I know. Christ knows that we are true when we bring all to Him. Compare 22. 12. Notice the two consequences that were to follow their surrendering all. (1) *So will I deliver you your brother.* The first result is complete freedom. (2) *Ye shall traffick in the land.* The second result is access to transact business in the heavenly land.

VERSE 35. *Every man's bundle of money was in his sack.* This fact may have emphasised to them the implication in the words of Joseph which they had last quoted. The return of the money may have been intended to convey to them that they had no right to traffic in the land. Their transactions there were entirely at Joseph's disposal, that is to say, they were of grace, not of right.

They were afraid. The brothers' fear arose through their guilty conscience, Jacob's through weakness of faith.

VERSE 36. In this verse we meet with the old vacillating Jacob, whose faith forsook him for fear of Esau. His fears were groundless. Joseph was safe and prospering. Simeon was safe in Joseph's keeping, though for the time being a prisoner. No harm would come to Benjamin. Jacob had not the vision to see any purpose of God being worked out in the events that were happening.

All these things are against me. These forlorn words show a strange weakness of faith. In fact none of these things were against him. They were all factors in God's purpose to save his life, establish his family and redeem the world. He was walking by sight instead of by faith. We may well be tempted to do the same, but we have the great promise, which had not been given in so many words to Jacob, that all things work together for good to them that love God (Rom. 8. 28). Faith may rest its weight on this.

VERSE 37. Reuben's sense of need and eagerness to persuade his father outran his prudence. He was tempting his father to trust in him rather

than in God. The uncertainties and mysteriousness of their relationship with Joseph should have warned him not to speak so rashly.

VERSE 38. *My son shall not go down with you.* Notice that Jacob still holds back from giving all. Joseph required the presence of Benjamin. In the same way the Saviour rightly claims all that we have and are.

His brother is dead. Notice that Jacob's refusal to give all was based, as it so often is in our case, on a complete misapprehension of the facts. Jacob felt sure of his facts. He had no doubt that Joseph was dead, but he was wrong. On this wrong view of the facts he held back what Joseph demanded.

He is left alone. If this had been true, it would have been no good reason for holding Benjamin back. If we possess one thing in which our heart is wrapped up, it still belongs to Christ. God Himself spared not His *only* Son, but delivered Him up for us all (Jo. 3. 16; Rom. 8. 32).

If mischief befall him. He had the precedent of Joseph before him. He little knew that he was sending Benjamin to the one who above all loved him dearly.

The grave. This is Hebrew '*sheol*', often translated ' hell '. ' The grave ' is the best translation.

CHAPTER 43

THE story of Joseph and his brethren is continued in detail in this chapter. It is one of the most dramatic and closely told of all stories in the Bible. Driven by need Jacob urges his sons to go down to Egypt again and buy food. They refuse to go unless they are accompanied by Benjamin. Jacob gives way and sends him with a present for Joseph. When they arrive, they are invited to Joseph's house, where they dine with him. All Joseph's dealings with them are directed towards bringing them to repentance. The chapter is an illusstration of Christ's working towards the sinner.

VERSE 1. The need of these men continued. When the Holy Spirit is seeking a lost soul for Christ and is bringing him under conviction, He often brings him almost to despair through a sense of spiritual need. Notice that the famine was felt in the whole land. Though God had a purpose through this famine for the one family, large numbers of people were affected by it. God may set on foot currents that move a world in order to accomplish His purposes for His own.

VERSE 2. They had been in contact with Joseph, and they had had a foretaste, as it were, of the blessing that he could give. They did not yet know him. So what they had had they had eaten up, and they needed to replenish their supplies. He that cometh to Jesus shall never hunger (Jo. 6. 35).

Buy us a little food. Notice that Jacob expected (1) to have to buy what he needed, and (2) that he expected to obtain only 'a little'. He did not know that Joseph the forerunner was waiting to nourish him and his family in the place where he himself lived.

VERSE 3. *The man did solemnly protest.* This was like the Lord Jesus, Who used to say, 'Verily, verily I say unto you.'

Ye shall not see my face, except your brother be with you. In the same way we shall not see Christ's face unless we are prepared to bring everything to Him and lay it at His feet (Lk. 14. 33).

VERSE 4. The handing over of everything to Christ is the ultimate means of obtaining spiritual satisfaction.

VERSE 5. Refusal to hand over all to Christ prevents our finding spiritual satisfaction, which can only be obtained in the presence of Christ and

by personal knowledge of Him and access to Him. This knowledge and access He refuses except on condition of total surrender (Lk. 14. 33). True faith involves total surrender. Unless we believe that our needs can be supplied in Christ alone, we shall never get them supplied.

VERSE 6. *Israel.* The new name bestowed in connection with the covenant is used in this chapter (see ver. 8, 11) no doubt to emphasise the importance of these events for the furtherance of the plan of redemption.

As to tell the man whether ye had yet a brother. The issue which he was afraid to face he wanted concealed altogether. In the same way we sometimes seek vainly to conceal some issue from Christ.

VERSE 7. *The man asked us straitly of our state.* This is exactly what Jesus Christ does to all those who seek Him. He demands that every issue should be brought to light.

Of our kindred. Our home and family life are also the concern of Christ, if we want to come to Him.

We told him. They did not try to conceal anything, but answered truthfully what they were asked, not knowing that the questioner knew whether they were doing so or not. This was a step in the way of their finding ultimate blessing. We too should tell Christ everything that He asks us in our hearts.

Could we certainly know. The seeker is seldom aware of the demands that Christ will make of him.

VERSE 8. *Send the lad with me.* Judah persuades his father to comply. The Judah who offered to protect Benjamin was a different man from the one who had suggested selling Joseph (37. 26, 27).

That we may live, and not die. Judah realised that the issue was one of life and death. So is the issue of acceptance or rejection of Christ. No man can live eternally without the bread that Christ gives him.

VERSE 9. Judah is here really pledging Joseph, and we can do the same for our Saviour and Master. We may pledge Him to give freedom and safety.

VERSE 10. *Except we had lingered.* It is foolish to linger in a matter of life and death. Yet many sinners do so when urged to flee to Christ.

VERSE 11. *If it must be so now.* Israel resigned himself to what he found to be unavoidable. The spirit in which he did so does not seem to have been free or happy, but he was right to recognise that Joseph's demands were imperative. The sinner is happy who recognises the same of the claims of Christ.

Take of the best fruits in the land. Our best is nothing to Christ. He does not need it. We need what He has to give us. We can give nothing to Him. There is a hymn, which is unfortunately rather popular, which says,

' Just a I am, young, strong and free,
To be the best that I can be.'

We have no best. Indeed we have no good. The hymn is a parody of a good Gospel one by Charlotte Eliott, which says,

' Just as I am without one plea
But that Thy blood was shed for me.'

If we come to Christ with our best, we may never find Him. If we come to Him with nothing, without one plea, we are certain of acceptance. *Carry down the man a present.* The present was not a symbol of dedication like those of the wise men (Mt. 2. 11). It was intended as an appeasement. It made no difference whatever to Joseph's plans for the reclamation of his brethren, which had been formed long since and were already in process of being carried into effect. None of the six ingredients in the present was needed by Joseph. He had more than enough of them

all in his glory in Egypt. They reflected the instinctive needs of Jacob.

A little. Israel was right in this estimation.

Balm. We need the balm of the Holy Spirit's consolation. Christ does not. He is the source of it.

Honey. We need the honey of the Word of God (Ps. 19. 9, 10; 119. 103).

Spices. We have no spices to offer to Christ. We need the fragrant spices of His own Divine beauty (Cant. 4. 16).

Myrrh. We need the tender myrrh of the heart of Christ. As sinners we have none to give Him.

Nuts, and almonds. We need the nourishment and the delights of His presence in our hearts.

VERSE 12. *Take double money.* The sinner and the seeker constantly think that they have got to pay for salvation, and they are always thinking that they don't pay enough.

Peradventure it was an oversight. This was a strange estimate. Nothing is an oversight with Christ.

VERSE 13. *Take also your brother.* This is what mattered. The present did not matter at all. Like so many sinners Jacob was eager to give what was needless and unnecessary, and reluctant to yield what was demanded and claimed.

VERSE 14. *God Almighty.* The Hebrew is El Shaddai, the Name by which God revealed Himself to Abraham (see 17. 1).

Give you mercy before the man. Israel was right to believe that God disposes the hearts of rulers and of all men. He prayed that God would make Joseph merciful.

That he may send away. Jacob feared that Simeon and Benjamin would come to permanent harm at the hands of Joseph. The sinner thinks often the same of himself and those he surrenders at the hands of Christ.

If I be bereaved of my children,

I am bereaved. This note of sad resignation is different from that of happy faith, but it is one that we often hear.

Verse 15. *Took that present.* They need not have done so. It was not going to affect Joseph's plans in the slightest.

Took double money. This too was quite needless. They were not being asked for money.

Benjamin. This is what mattered. Joseph had asked for him as a test of their sincerity. Their taking of Benjamin symbolised that they were ready to surrender all.

Stood before Joseph. Every man sooner or later must stand before Christ. He must present himself before Him now in this life as His subject, or else stand before Him condemned on the day of judgment.

Verse 16. *When Joseph saw Benjamin.* He did not look at the present or ask for the money. He wished to see the one on whom his affections were set, being enabled to see him because Jacob had been driven by famine to the point at which he was prepared to surrender him. What a parable of the spiritual life.

Bring these men home. In these words of Joseph to the ruler of his house we hear an echo of the words of the Lord Jesus Christ to us His servants and witnesses as He looks out on the unsaved millions of a lost world.

Slay. Before they could dine with Joseph the death of an animal must take place. So before we can feast with Christ in the heavenly home, the Saviour Himself was slain.

Make ready. This we cannot do, nor can any man. The Saviour Himself is doing it (Jo. 14. 2).

These men shall dine with me at noon. We too shall feast with Christ in the eternal noonday of the heavenly home (Mt. 26. 29).

Verse 17. *The man did as Joseph bade.* Here is a good motto for us.

We do not always promptly obey our Master in the matter of evangelisation. *The man brought the men into Joseph's house.* This is exactly what we are to do. We are to bring those who have been invited into Joseph's house. We are to go out into the highways and byeways and compel them to come in (Mt. 22. 9; Lk. 4. 21-23).

Verse 18. *The men were afraid,* just as the sinner is so often afraid when he is brought into the Christian fellowship, or first brought into touch with Christ.

They were brought into Joseph's house. At this stage of the brethren's experience we must think of this as equivalent to the sinner's being brought into Christian fellowship, to services or meetings. *Because of the money.* They were wrong in their estimate of the reason. They were wrong also in their conclusion about the money being given back. Their fear was due, though they did not know it, to a guilty conscience. The sinner often fears Christ till the sin question has been dealt with. *That he may seek occasion against us, and fall upon us.* The Hebrew for ' seek occasion ' is the very expressive ' roll himself upon us '. The sinner fears that Christ is going to crush him and suffocate him, keep him under and suppress his personality. The opposite is the case. The sinner misjudges Christ, just as the brethren misjudged Joseph.

Take us for bondmen. The sinner often fears that in yielding to Christ he will lose his freedom and happiness. The opposite is the case. It is true that when he comes to Christ, he becomes His bondman, but Christ's service is perfect freedom. *And our asses.* These are surprising and suggestive words. If the men themselves became bondmen, it would not much matter about the asses. Their anxiety about their asses betray a certain covetousness. They did not want their property to become Joseph's, even if they did so themselves. They felt that the appropriation of their property as well as their persons must add to their misery. The sinner often feels, perhaps vaguely, the same. He does not want his money to be used in Christ's service, nor his unconverted friends to be troubled by Him.

VERSE 19. *They came near to the steward of Joseph's house.* They did the right thing. If only the sinner and the man who is afraid would come more often to the evangelist or minister!

At the door of the house. How important are these conversations on the threshold of the house of Christ. Here the witness and the servant of Christ may stand and seek to explain the purpose and claims of Christ to those who stand at the door afraid to come in.

VERSE 20. In their bewilderment they knew one thing for certain, the reality of their need. They only knew how to satisfy it temporarily by buying. They had no idea that Joseph was waiting to satisfy it permanently without any payment on their part.

VERSE 21. *Every man's money.* Joseph could not take money from his brethren any more than the Lord Jesus Christ can regard merit in His own, but until they knew him and were reconciled to him he could not tell them why he had given it back.

VERSE 22. *Other money have we brought.* They still thought they must buy what they needed.

VERSE 23. *Peace be to you, fear not.* The steward reassures and comforts the bewildered and frightened men. We as servants of Christ ought to do the same. There is peace with God by the blood of the cross available for them, and the trust in Christ into which we invite them will rule out fear.

Your God, and the God of your father. The steward, who was probably an Egyptian, seems to be careful not to associate himself with the God of Israel. It is however obvious that he knows of Him and knows of His power. He knows that Joseph has a God, or if he had not guessed the relationship of these men to Joseph, he knows that there is a great God Whom the Semites worship. This was due to Joseph's witness. The steward must have heard him speak of his father's God, and his proximity to Joseph cannot fail to have shown him the reality of God to his master.

Hath given you treasure. The steward recognised that though it was by Joseph's order and his own act that the money had been returned to the sacks, yet it was the gift of God. He thus recognised God as the disposer of all. The word 'treasure' seems to be more than a description of the money. The money was treasure because it was the symbol of grace and kindness. There is no greater treasure than the grace of Christ.

I had your money. This statement was intended to reassure them. Joseph and the steward knew what they were doing when they returned the money. There was a purpose in it. Thus we are encouraged to believe that though God's ways may for the time being be mysterious to us, a purpose of grace lies behind them.

He brought Simeon out unto them. The grace of God brings freedom out of bondage.

VERSE 24. *The man brought the men into Joseph's house.* So we are to bring sinners and seekers into Christian fellowship. This hospitality was the second of three steps taken by Joseph to bring his brothers to repentance, recognition and reconciliation. The first had been his rough speech to them. This had alarmed and puzzled them and brought them to a remembrance of their sin and a sense of shame. The second step was this kindness and hospitality which bewildered them. In the same way we are to show to sinners and seekers the kindness of Christ.

Gave them water, and they washed their feet. Notice that this was not the water of life, as it were, for them to drink. Nor was it the washing of regeneration in which it is necessary to bathe (Jo. 13. 10; Eph. 5. 26; Tit. 3. 5). It was merely water to wash their feet. They had not yet come to repentance or to the true knowledge of Joseph. The purpose of the water was for the ordinary decent practice of hospitality on entering the house. So the sinner and the seeker, when brought into the Christian fellowship, find a standard of conduct there to which it is necessary to conform. *He gave their asses provender.* Asses in the Bible are a picture of the unconverted. When the sinner or the seeker are brought into the Christian fellowship preparatory to being introduced to the personal knowledge of Christ, the members of their families and those who belong to them benefit by it.

VERSE 25. *They made ready the present.* What Joseph wanted was themselves and their love, not their present. In the same way the heavenly Joseph desires our hearts, not anything that we can bring Him.

They heard that they should eat bread there. The steward had told them. So we should tell sinners and seekers that a feast awaits them in the house of Christ.

VERSE 26. *Bowed themselves to him to the earth.* They did not know yet who he was, but they knew that he was the one that could supply their need, and they knew that he had all power. Notice how many things they knew about Joseph and how close they were brought to him, actually dining with him in his house, before they knew who he was or knew him personally. How easy it is to profess a knowledge of Christ and to know much about Him without actually knowing Him. As these men supposed they knew a great deal

about Joseph, so do many suppose they know much about Christ without knowing His identity and the essential transforming facts about Him.

VERSE 27. *He asked them of their welfare.* The Hebrew word translated ' welfare ' means ' peace '. Christ is interested in our peace. Are we at peace with God? Have we the peace of Christ in our hearts? *The old man of whom ye spake.* This is one of the most moving moments in this drama of family affection. Joseph's story is the most beautiful and intimate story of family life in the Bible. It speaks to every human heart, being inspired by the God Who created the family and seeks to gather the redeemed into the most loving and intimately holy family in existence.

VERSE 28. *Thy servant our father is in good health.* These words meant much more to Joseph than they imagined. *They bowed down their heads, and made obeisance,* exactly as Joseph had foreseen in his dream.

VERSE 29. *His brother Benjamin, his mother's son.* In the same way Christ sees in the seeker a brother man, whom He graciously regards as near to Himself.

God be gracious unto thee, my son. These were not empty words, but a heartfelt prayer. It is a prayer that we ought to be ready to pray for every sinner, introducing him to the grace of God.

VERSE 30. *His bowels did yearn upon his brother.* In this he was like the Lord Jesus Christ, Who was moved with compassion when He saw the multitudes like sheep without a shepherd (Mt. 9. 36). Jesus Christ is the same yesterday, today and for ever (Heb. 13. 8), and we may be sure that He has the same tender feelings towards us today in our distresses.

He entered into his chamber, and wept there. These tender feelings must be concealed from the sinner till the moment that he knows Christ.

Verse 31. *Refrained himself.* The heart of Christ longs to go out to the sinner, but awaits the time when he comes to Him in repentance and faith.

Verse 32. Notice the three classes of people who dined separately. First there was Joseph by himself. He corresponds to the Lord Jesus Christ Who is and always has been unique, whether in His Father's glory before the world began, or as the sinless Man on earth, or now in heaven on the Father's throne. He is and always will be *by Himself.* Secondly we find the brethren, still ignorant and still only seekers, but potentially those who know Joseph, and are in family relationship with him. Thus the people of God are separate from Christ in His uniqueness on the one side and from the people of the world on the other. Thirdly we see the Egyptians, who represent the people of the world, outwardly appearing to know Joseph better than the brethren. Worldly people often profess or appear to be better Christians than the true, or than the seeker who is coming to Christ oppressed with his guilt.

The Egyptians might not eat bread with the Hebrews. Notice that the objection came from the Egyptians. They were like those people of the world who despise Christians and refuse to associate with them.

An abomination unto the Egyptians. They felt they would be contaminated. Their objection to associating with Hebrews was religious, as is the objection of many worldly people today to associating with Christians.

Verse 33. *The firstborn according to his birthright, and the youngest according to his youth.* The purpose of this arrangement was to show that Joseph knew them and knew

all about them. The sinner or seeker, when brought into Christ's house, finds this out sooner or later. He finds that the Scripture speaks to his heart and that the Gospel suits his case. The sinner discovers that he is known by Christ.

The men marvelled. The discovery is always a wonderful thing. The brothers could not understand it at the time, but afterwards when Joseph declared himself, the incident became intelligible, and helped to demonstrate the truth of what he said.

Verse 34. *He took and sent messes.* This was a mark of favour. When the seeker is brought in contact with Christ, His kindness and favour soon become known to him.

Benjamin's mess was five times so much. This was not due to partiality, but nearness of kin. Those who are near to Christ reap more of His favour than those who stand farther away. Five is a number sometimes associated in the Bible with grace. Such an association is appropriate here.

They drank, and were merry with him. This was a foretaste of what they would enjoy when they came to know Joseph. The exhilaration that they felt is a picture of the joy of the Holy Ghost (Eph. 5. 18), and this may be anticipated to a certain extent by the seeker as he is brought into the Christian fellowship. Not that it comes from within him, but he may be conscious of its glow around him.

CHAPTER 44

In this chapter we have the detailed account of the last of three steps taken by Joseph for his brothers' reclamation. He brings them as represented by Judah to repentance. Judah, who sold Joseph, is brought to the place where he is willing to remain as a slave in Egypt in Benjamin's stead. Joseph's silver cup is placed at his order by his steward in Benjamin's sack without his or his brethren's knowledge. The steward pursues them, accuses them of stealing it and claims the one in whose sack it is found as his master's slave. They all return in great trouble and distraction to Joseph, where Judah makes his offer. This leads up to Joseph's fourth and final step, recounted in the following chapter, his disclosure to them of his identity. The spiritual lesson of this chapter is the need and importance of repentance.

VERSE 1. *He commanded the steward of his house.* The steward was the one through whom Joseph's purposes for his brethren were carried out. It is through us that the heavenly Joseph seeks to win the sinner.

Fill the men's sacks with food. It was not food which had yet been prepared for eating. It was provision for the future. So we as Christ's stewards are to fill men's minds with the food of the Word of God, which will one day nourish them when they come to Christ.

As much as they can carry. Christ gives to all as much as they need and as much as they have capacity for.

Put every man's money. Once again the men are shown that Christ's gifts cannot be bought. They interpreted the return of the money as meaning that they were not accepted and would ultimately get nothing. It really meant that all their needs would be satisfied freely.

VERSE 2. *Put my cup.* The cup was a special and particularly prized possession of great value to Joseph. Christ's cup is the cup of suffering, curse and death that He drank for us to the full.

The silver cup. Silver is the same word as is used for money. It speaks of cost and price, and so of redemption. The cup was the cup of redemption, which belongs to Christ alone.

In the sack's mouth of the youngest. This was to give the impression that he had stolen the cup. Every

man who rejects Christ steals as it were His redemptive sufferings and the price that He paid, making them vain in his own case.

And his corn money. No man can pay anything for spiritual food. It is given freely.

He did according to the word that Joseph had spoken. As servants of Christ it is our business to obey Him and to explain to men that in rejecting Christ they take advantage of His sufferings for them and that they can never obtain eternal life except as a free gift (Rom. 6. 23).

VERSE 3. These men wanted to go home still not knowing who Joseph was, but Joseph took steps to prevent them.

VERSE 4. *Not yet far off.* If we let the sinner or the seeker stray too far from the influence of the Christian fellowship, he may reach a place where it is not possible to recover him.

Up, follow after the men. These might be the very words of our Lord Jesus Christ to His servants and ministers. We are to follow the sinner as he goes his own way wandering farther and farther from God back to his own haunts and pursuits.

Wherefore have ye rewarded evil for good? This is what every sinner has done and we ought certainly to charge them all with it. The love of God has been met with indifference, the demands of God with rebellion, the suffering and death of Christ with hostility and misunderstanding.

VERSE 5. *Whereby indeed he divineth.* Divining is sorcery and sinful. If Joseph practised it, he did wrong. At the same time, if he did not, it was scarcely right to pretend to do so. So far as the steward meant to imply that Joseph knew all about the men, he was right.

VERSE 6. May we too overtake many sinners and speak our Master's words to them.

VERSE 7. The men denied the charge brought against them, and did so quite sincerely. Till he is convicted of the Holy Ghost the sinner does the same.

VERSE 8. As the sinner so often does, they protested their sincerity and self-righteousness.

VERSE 9. These rash suggestions were not intended to be taken at their face value. They were an emphatic declaration of innocence. They were more just than the speakers imagined.

VERSE 10. *Let it be according unto your words.* They were taken at their word, but the harshness of their vow was very mercifully modified. Christ does not desire or purpose any man's death. He wants us to enter His service, and He wants us to be blameless. He alone can make us this.

VERSE 11. They were confident of the result, just as the sinner is so often confident that no fault can be found with him.

VERSE 12. *He searched.* As servants of Christ we also are to search men's hearts under the guidance of the Spirit through the Word.
Began at the eldest, and left at the youngest. This was another demonstration of the knowledge that Joseph had of their state and circumstances. Christ has perfect knowledge of every sinner.
The cup was found in Benjamin's sack. It was found with the one who seemed the most innocent. The Holy Spirit intends to show us that the simplest and most apparently innocent of men are guilty sinners in God's sight.

VERSE 13. *They rent their clothes.* Bitter distress came upon them as they found they could not escape the charge.
Returned to the city. They did the right thing. Indeed there was noth-

ing else they could do, unless they let Benjamin go. In their anxiety and conviction they went back to Joseph.

VERSE 14. *Judah and his brethren.* Judah led them because he was the one who had been entrusted by Jacob with Benjamin. He had also been the prime mover in the sale of Joseph (37. 26, 27). The expression may also be a hint of the distinction between Jew and Gentile, both under sin and in need of Christ (Rom. 3. 9).
Came to Joseph's house. They came to the Christian fellowship.
He was yet there. There was still time to meet him in repentance. Time is urgent for every sinner, and only a few years will set him beyond the possibility of repentance and conversion. *They fell before him on the ground.* This was a right step. They realised that they were utterly in Joseph's power. It is good when the sinner understands that he is completely at Christ's disposal.

VERSE 15. *What deed is this that ye have done?* The question went deeper than the incident of the cup and recalled to their guilty consciences the great sin of their lives when they sold their brother into slavery.
Divine. Either Joseph actually practised sorcery, which would be sinful, or he pretended that he did so, which was at least unfortunate. In these words we may perhaps find one of the rare flaws in his character, as it is presented to us in the narrative. In any case Joseph means to imply that he can search and know their hearts, and in doing so he was like the Lord Jesus Christ.

VERSE 16. *What shall we say unto my lord?* On the day of judgment every mouth will be stopped (Rom. 3. 19). So the sinner when convicted of his guilt realises that he has nothing to say.
God hath found out the iniquity of thy servants. They could not have been referring to the incident of the

cup. They speak for themselves as a whole, not Benjamin only. Besides they could hardly have believed that Benjamin had actually stolen it. They were referring to their sinful hearts and particularly to their crime against Joseph committed twenty-two years previously. They felt that it had come back upon them and that Joseph's apparently cantankerous behaviour towards them was God's way of retribution. Joseph had won his point. In the same way the changes and chances of this present life, its mysteries and apparent injustices, are God's means of leading sinners to conviction and repentance.

We are my lord's servants. Their raging consciences led them to offer themselves to a life of slavery. They consented to just judgment coming upon them. This means repentance.

VERSE 17. Joseph here reaches the last step in his test. Would the brothers accept this offer, and leave for home letting Benjamin stay behind in slavery? It is evident that Benjamin, though he did not know it at the moment, was in no real danger. If they had taken that course, Joseph could have immediately made himself known to Benjamin and perhaps sent him up for his father without including the brothers in the invitation. Would they on the other hand sacrifice themselves for Benjamin's safety, as in fact they did? If so, he would have gained his brothers. It is noteworthy that from the moment that he saw them at the time of their first visit Joseph concentrated all his efforts on leading them to repentance. In this he was exactly like the Saviour.

VERSE 18. With this verse begins Judah's address to Joseph, which occupies the rest of the chapter. It falls into four sections: (a) the humble request not to incur anger (18); (b) the statement of the facts (19-29); (c) the fact of Judah's own suretyship (30-32); (d) his offer of himself (33-34). Judah is like the

returning and repenting sinner, who is under the conviction of the Holy Ghost.

Let thy servant, I pray thee, speak a word. The convicted sinner realises that he has no right to speak. He scarcely dares to pray.

Let not thine anger burn against thy servant. So the sinner seeks escape from the wrath to come (1 Thess. 1. 10).

Thou art even as Pharaoh. The convicted sinner is brought to realise that Christ is Lord of all and the supreme judge and disposer of men. He does not yet know that He is his brother and Saviour.

VERSE 19. *My lord asked his servants.* The sinner understands that Christ has been searching his heart and enquiring after his state.

VERSE 20. The answer given was simple and true.

VERSE 21. The sinner relates the demand made upon him by Christ. All must be brought to Him.

VERSE 22. Before he comes to know Christ the sinner expostulates against His claims. He thinks it would mean death, or at any rate the end of all that makes life worth living, to meet them and accept them.

VERSE 23. Christ reiterates to the sinner His demand for full surrender, making compliance the condition of entering His presence (Lk. 14. 33).

VERSE 24. The brethren faithfully reported Joseph's words to their father. So the sinner recounts the words and claims of Christ, as it were, to his own heart.

VERSE 25. Spiritual dearth drives the sinner back to Christ Whose claims he had tried to avoid.

VERSE 26. The sinner realises that he cannot seek for the satisfaction of his need from Christ, unless he is prepared to fulfil His demands.

VERSE 27. The old father declares the value and preciousness of the one who is the subject of Joseph's demands. So the sinner in his blindness and ignorance struggles within himself, as he is faced with the alternatives of spiritual death or surrender to Christ.

VERSE 28. Notice that Jacob, though he did not know it, was wrong in his estimate of what had happened to Joseph. In the same way in seeking to excuse himself from meeting Christ's claims the sinner often draws a false comparison.

VERSE 29. *Mischief befall him.* The sinner who is confronted with the claims of Christ often supposes that mischief will befall him, or that he will suffer loss if he accepts them. Indeed as Jacob believed that he would be brought down to the grave by the loss of Benjamin, so the sinner believes that to yield to Christ will be the end of all happiness.

VERSE 30. *His life is bound up in the lad's life.* Here is a vivid and true Hebrew expression, which strikes to the root of human nature. The life of each one of us is bound up with something. If it is something, or indeed someone, that will perish with this world, our life will perish with it. True happiness belongs only to the man whose life is bound up with the life and interests of Christ, and the Saviour graciously invites the sinners for whom He died to wrap up their lives with His own.

VERSE 31. Judah realises that this is a matter of life and death. So is our relationship to Christ in the case of each one of us.
The grave. Here and in verse 29 above the Hebrew is *Sheol,* often ambiguously translated ' hell ', but here rightly translated ' the grave '.

VERSE 32. *Became surety.* This was an act of faith. In effect Judah pledged Joseph to return Benjamin safely. In practice therefore in becoming surety for him Judah put his trust in Joseph.

I shall bear the blame to my father for ever. If Joseph failed him and retained Benjamin, Judah would be guilty for ever. If Christ were to fail us sinners (which is impossible), we should be lost and guilty for ever.

VERSE 33. *Let thy servant abide instead of the lad.* Judah was ready to act and stake all on the pledge of faith that he had given. Thus he came to the place where he surrendered himself and gave what amounted to his life for the sake of his brother. This is a picture of faith that works by love (Gal. 5. 6). It is a sketch in miniature of the Christian life as God intends it to be lived.

Let the lad go up with his brethren. These remarkable words show that Joseph had succeeded in gaining his point. Judah was repentant and changed. The same man who had sold one brother for a paltry sum, had been deaf to his anguished entreaties and contemptuously indifferent to his suffering, now offers himself into lifelong slavery in order that the other brother might return in safety to his father. Joseph's wise treatment, working upon an angry conscience, had effected this transformation. So Christ by the Holy Spirit convicts the sinner of his guilt, brings him to repentance and transforms his spirit.

VERSE 34. The man who could once deceive his father over the death of Joseph, quite indifferent to the old man's moving and heartbroken sorrow, now offers himself as a slave in order to keep his father from further suffering. Here is a picture on a small scale of the transformation wrought in the sinner's heart by the grace of God in Christ.

CHAPTER 45

THE subject of this chapter is the reconciliation of Joseph and his brethren and the consequences that flowed from it. With great emotion Joseph makes himself known and declares the providence of God in all the events of his life. He tells them to go up and fetch Jacob into Egypt. Pharaoh is pleased at what has happened and confirms the invitation to Jacob. Joseph sends wagons for his father and his household and a present, and the brothers return quickly to Jacob. At first Jacob cannot believe them, but the sight of the wagons convinces him, and he decides to go down to Egypt to see him. Joseph is revealed in this chapter as the Saviour and Forerunner of his people, and the events of his remarkable life appear as a prediction in fact and in narrative of Christ's great redemptive acts. The martyr Stephen in his speech before the Council (Acts 7) selects four points from this passage. They are (1) Joseph's disclosure of his identity (ver. 3; Acts 7. 13); (2) the sale of Joseph (ver. 4; Acts 7. 9); (3) Joseph's summons to his father (ver. 9-11; Acts 7. 14); (4) Pharaoh's pleasure in the reconciliation (ver. 16; Acts 7. 13). These four points illustrate (1) the entry by the sinner into personal relationship with Christ; (2) the rejection and suffering of Christ; (3) Christ's call to His people to follow Him to the heavenly land; (4) the joy in heaven over repenting sinners. The importance of the passage lies in its illustration of these things.

VERSE 1. *Joseph could not refrain himself.* In this he was like the Saviour Who can never refrain Himself at the sight of sinners in their need. He did not refrain Himself from leaving the bosom of the Father and entering a world of sin. He did not spare His strength in the service of the unworthy, and He did not hold back from the cross. All this He did because He could not hold back His love for sinners.

Cause every man to go out from me. The Saviour came into the world alone, and He trod the winepress alone (Isa. 63. 3). He was utterly alone on the cross, cut off from all intercourse with human friends (Ps. 88. 18) and with His Father in heaven (Mt. 27. 46).

There stood no man with him, while Joseph made himself known unto his brethren. Notice that the brethren could never have got to know Joseph, if he had not made himself known to them. They knew much about him. They knew that he was lord of the country, but they did not know that he was their own brother and loved them, until the moment came when he chose to reveal it. It was a moment towards which he had been working ever since they came in touch with him. As soon as he had proved their repentance and change of heart, the moment came. In the same way no one can get to know Christ as his Saviour, till He makes Himself known to him. Men may know of Christ as the Lord and Sovereign of the world, but only His self-revelation can make known the fact that He is a loving Saviour and Brother. This revelation takes place in the heart of the repenting sinner at the moment of his conversion. It is a transaction that takes place between Jesus Christ and the sinner alone in the secret depths of the heart. No one can witness it, though many may witness its effects.

VERSE 2. *He wept aloud.* If we could see the heart of Christ as He finds His lost sheep and welcomes it home, we should see it moved with strong emotion. Jesus Christ is the same yesterday, today and for ever (Heb. 13. 8). If He was moved with compassion when on earth (Mt. 9. 36), He is moved with compassion now. If He wept when on earth (Jo. 11. 35), He may weep now.

The Egyptians and the house of

Pharaoh heard. No one on earth can hear or know what goes on in the secret of the heart when the sinner meets with Jesus, but the angels that surround the throne hear and know something of it (Lk. 15. 7, 10).

VERSE 3. *I am Joseph.* We are reminded of the words of the heavenly Joseph to the apostle, ' I am Jesus ' (Acts 9. 5).

Doth my father yet live? Joseph's first words are of tender affection.

Could not answer him. Who has anything to say to the Saviour's wonderful love, especially as it is seen against the background of the sinner's mean unworthiness? (Rom. 8. 31).

They were troubled at his presence. For ' troubled ' the margin has ' terrified '. A surge of guilt and shame and fear swept through their hearts, as they realised that they were face to face with the one whom they had wronged and sold. So at the moment when Christ's love is revealed to him, the sinner is often overwhelmed by the thought of the selfishness and indifference of his previous life, much more if it has been a life of hostility to Christ, as was the case with the apostle.

VERSE 4. *Come near to me, I pray you.* The Saviour graciously issues a similar invitation (Mt. 11. 28; Rev. 22. 17).

They came near. They could not do this before. There was a great barrier between them and Joseph. They could only stand at a distance and prostrate themselves and answer questions and fear and submit. Now they may come near. So on his repentance the sinner finds that the barrier of sin has been broken down and he may come near to the Saviour Who has loved and sought him all the time. This near approach to the Saviour to be with Him for ever is the beginning of real happiness.

I am Joseph your brother. In the same way Jesus Christ reveals Himself to the sinner as his Brother and fellow-man, understanding his temptations (Heb. 4. 15), and establishing Himself as his eternal friend.

Whom ye sold into Egypt. Not only the Jews, but every sinner in the world is guilty of selling and rejecting Christ. Conversion in its deepest meaning is a change of attitude towards Christ and of relationship with Him. It is this relationship that is brought fundamentally into account on the day of judgment (Mt. 25. 35, 36, 42, 43).

VERSE 5. *Be not grieved, nor angry with yourselves.* The generous affectionate heart of Joseph was a shadow of that of the Lord Jesus Christ. On the cross He prayed for the forgiveness of His murderers (Lk. 23. 34), and the Holy Spirit told them through the apostle Peter that He knew that they had done it in ignorance (Acts 3. 17). He says the same words to every repenting sinner, ' Be not grieved, nor angry with yourselves.'

God did send me before you. Joseph shows by these words that he understood the fundamental truth of the sovereignty of God. The brethren's envy and wickedness were but instruments in the Divine purpose. This is a close picture of the forces which were at work in the crucifixion of Christ. It was by wicked hands that He was crucified and slain (Acts 2. 23), and yet it was by the determinate counsel and foreknowledge of God (ibid). Joseph accepted all that had happened to him from the hands of God, and we may and ought to do the same.

To preserve life. God's purpose in sending Joseph down to Egypt and bringing him through a furnace of affliction and sorrow, necessary for his training, was in order to preserve the lives of Jacob and the covenant family during the drought. His far greater purpose in bringing Jesus Christ through the suffering and death of the cross was to preserve the lives of the redeemed through the dangers of this world, the darkness of the tomb, and the righteous condemnation of the day of judgment. All who seek to Christ for spiritual sustenance, as the brethren did, and come to know Him as personal Saviour and brother, as the brethren did Joseph, are preserved in spiritual famine and brought safe to the country where Joseph reigns.

VERSE 6. When the sinner comes to know Christ as his Saviour through the Gospel, his need is not all in the past. There are still five years of famine. He has the remainder of his life in this world to pass through before he reaches the harvest of the resurrection. During this time the heavenly Joseph sustains and nourishes him with the spiritual food of the Word in which he feeds on Christ Himself. This depends upon Christ's sovereign power in heaven, and this again upon the suffering through which He passed, having its climax and culmination in His glorious resurrection.

VERSE 7. *God sent me before you.* In the same way God sent Jesus Christ through death and resurrection to heaven as the forerunner of His people (Heb. 6. 20), and they will one day follow Him to the same country to be with Him and serve Him for ever.

To preserve you a posterity in the earth. These words apply directly to the death of Christ. By His death we are delivered from judgment to come, from the power of Satan and sin in this world, and from the darkness of the grave.

VERSE 8. *It was not you that sent me hither.* Neither the devil nor man had power to touch Christ without the permission of God. He was immortal till His hour came (Jo. 2. 4; 7. 6; 12. 27), and even the Roman governor could do nothing against Him apart from permission from above (Jo. 19. 11).

But God. God sent His Son into the world to die for the sins of mankind, and in His determinate counsel

brought about all the events of the passion (Jo. 18. 11; Acts 2. 23).

He hath made me a father to Pharaoh. In the same way Christ is the everlasting Father (Isa. 9. 6). He is seated on the Father's throne (Rev. 3. 21), and will there reign until all His enemies become subject to Him (Ps. 110. 1).

Lord of all his house. Christ as the Son is over all God's house (Heb. 3. 6), and has been made Head over all things to the church (Eph. 1. 22).

Ruler throughout all the land of Egypt. Christ is the Prince of the kings of the earth (Rev. 1. 5).

VERSE 9. *Haste ye.* These are the words of Christ to all His servants from the moment that they enter His service. The King's business requireth haste (Esther 3. 15; 8. 14). The proclamation of the Gospel is urgent. Men are perishing and starving. A Chinese man and his wife, converted some twenty years ago almost as soon as they heard the Gospel, lamented that their parents, who had been seeking the light, had died just previously without hearing it. A Burmese lad, who had once heard the Gospel without properly understanding it, died after a long, lingering illness, during which he constantly exclaimed, ' Why don't the Jesus people come?' And there are many such cases.

Go up to my father. Jacob is not here the picture of the heavenly Father, but rather of Christ's father Adam and of the whole race represented by Adam and lost in him.

Thus saith thy son Joseph. The invitation comes from the Son of man, Who is on the throne of God. *God hath made me lord of all Egypt.* There is a Man on the throne of the world.

Come down unto me. Jesus Christ's gracious invitation to come to Him goes out to all that have ears to hear, but if we want to reach Him, we must like Zacchæus come down (Lk. 19. 5) from the pedestal of our own pride, wisdom and self-conceit.

Tarry not. This should be the

message to every man who is confronted with the Gospel. Time and again a man has put off acceptance of Christ until it is too late.

VERSE 10. *Thou shalt dwell in the land of Goshen.* This was the best and most fruitful part of Egypt. Those who belong to Christ always dwell in the best part of the land, whether in this world, or in the world to come. *Thou shalt be near unto me.* This is better still. In this life the Lord is near (Phil. 4. 5). In the life to come we shall be where He is (Jo. 14. 3).

Thy children, and thy children's children. The children of the child of God are those whom he brings to Christ. In the nature of the case no direct promise can be given to any man in respect of his natural children, as the Gospel must be accepted individually, but they should have great privilege of opportunity, and a parent may rely on answer to his prayers.

Thy flocks, and thy herds. The sheep and cattle are the animals appointed for sacrifice. All those who offer their lives as living sacrifices to Christ dwell in the best of the land and are near to Christ. *All that thou hast.* A man's relatives, friends, servants, and even his animals, are all affected by his personal relationship to Christ.

VERSE 11. *There will I nourish thee.* The child of God is nourished from heaven in a world of spiritual famine by the heavenly manna, Christ Himself (Jo. 6. 35, 48, 50, 51), on Whom he feeds in the Scriptures (Jo. 6. 63).

Yet there are five years of famine. There is an interval between the sinner's conversion and the moment of his resurrection and final rest. He must pass through the world, in which he will find no spiritual food, except what is provided for him from above.

Come to poverty. This is the certain fate of all who do not share the riches of Christ. This world has nothing to give. We brought nothing into this world, and it is certain we can carry nothing out (1 Tim. 6. 7). The wicked are reduced to abject poverty, standing naked before God on the day of judgment, and losing even life itself. Nor need the spiritual life of the child of God be a poor one. Infinite riches are available for him in Christ.

VERSE 12. The repenting sinner who comes near to Christ has the certain assurance in his own experience of the identity of Jesus Christ and the witness of the Spirit in his heart that Christ is his Saviour and God his Father (Rom. 8. 16). In addition to this the Spirit throws such light upon the Word that Christ becomes alive to the regenerate man in the Scriptures, and he is able with perfect conviction to identify the Christ of the Scriptures with the Christ Who dwells in his heart.

VERSE 13. *Ye shall tell.* It is always the business of the man who has found Christ to tell. Let the redeemed of the Lord say so (Ps. 107. 2).

All my glory in Egypt. Our message is to be of Jesus Christ exalted to God's right hand and given all power in heaven and earth. We are to tell men of a glorified risen Saviour.

Of all that ye have seen. Personal experience must always enter into the Christian message (1 Jo. 1. 1-3). We cannot convince others of what we do not know firsthand ourselves.

Ye shall haste. We are often so slow to obey the Master. We let many perish before we make up our minds to go.

Bring down my father hither. We must bring to Christ those who are lost in Adam, so that they may be born again and renewed.

VERSE 14. Benjamin had taken no direct part in selling Joseph. He was not like one of the Jews who murdered their Messiah. He was more

like one of the ignorant heathen who
knows nothing of Christ. But he had
the same need as the rest, and was
faced with the same spiritual poverty
and starvation. The tender love of
Joseph went out to him. Notice
again that Joseph took the initiative.
Benjamin responded. This is always
the case with Christ and the sinner.

VERSE 15. The display of Christ's
love is first made to the sinner, who
is brought to realise it by the work
of the Holy Spirit in his heart pointing him to Calvary and showering
upon him spiritual blessings. The
warming influence begins to evaporate
the sinner's shyness, and he starts a
life of converse with his Saviour. It
is the duty and privilege of each one
of us to take full advantage of these
opportunities for converse day by
day.

VERSE 16. In the same way there is
joy in the presence of the angels of
God over one sinner that repenteth
(Lk. 15. 7, 10). The Father Himself
runs to welcome the returning sinner
(Lk. 15. 20).

VERSE 17. *Pharaoh said unto Joseph.*
Just as Pharaoh stood behind Joseph
in his welcome of his father and his
brethren, so the heavenly Father co-
operates with the Son in the welcoming home of repenting sinners.

Say unto thy brethren. Notice that
the command is given by Pharaoh to
Joseph to pass on to his brethren,
who are the instruments in carrying it
out. Thus we as the human brethren
(Mt. 25. 40) and servants of Christ
carry out the will of the Father
through the Gospel.

This do ye. Activity and energy
are needed in the service of Christ.

Lade your beasts. The beasts were
the asses, which the brethren had
been so afraid would be taken from
them by Joseph (43. 18), so that all
possibility of returning home would
be taken away. Now they are willingly and spontaneously used by their
owners in the service of Joseph to

carry out Pharaoh's command. How
often the same situation arises in the
case of the man who is afraid to surrender all his possessions to Christ.
He finds that they are returned to
him for profitable use in the Master's
happy service. The asses are the
picture of the unconverted people of
the world. Just as the brethren were
to lade their asses, so are we to make
use of the people and products of the
world for the advancement of the
Gospel.

*Go, get you unto the land of
Canaan.* In the same way we are to
go into all the world and make disciples of all nations (Mt. 28. 19).

VERSE 18. *Take your father, and
your households, and come unto me.*
We are to come to Christ at our conversion, we are to come to Him every
day in prayer, and finally on the day
of resurrection we shall come to Him
to be with Him for ever. But we are
not to come to Him empty or alone.
We are to bring others who are
starving and have the same needs as
ourselves.

*I will give you the good of the land
of Egypt.* Our Father in heaven daily
loads us with benefits (Ps. 68. 19). He
pours upon us the riches of His grace,
and supplies our material needs in addition. In the world to come He will
add glory to grace, and there will be
pleasures at His right hand for evermore (Ps. 16. 11).

Ye shall eat the fat of the land.
When Christ comes into a man's
heart, He comes to sup with him, and
the subsequent life of such a man is
a continual feast (Rev. 3. 20).

VERSE 19. *Now thou art commanded.*
These words of Pharaoh are addressed to Joseph. In the same way
we may think of the Gospel, and indeed the whole process of redemption, as the subject of a command
given by the Father to the Son, no
less for that reason joyfully received
and obeyed. The Father sent the Son
to be the Saviour of the world (1 Jo.
4. 14).

This do ye. Pharaoh himself repeats to the brethren what he had told Joseph to say to them. Thus we are the servants of God being servants of Christ. Christ's commands are the Father's commands. Our duty to God is fulfilled in our activity in the service of Christ.

Take you wagons. The wagons were sent to help and support the weak. They were a practical expression of consideration and kindness, such as the Saviour repeatedly shows and calls upon us to show in His Name.

Come. The Spirit and the bride say, Come, and let him that is athirst come, and whosoever will let him take of the water of life freely (Rev. 22. 17).

VERSE 20. *Regard not your stuff.* This means that they need not trouble to bring it and need not mind if it had to be left behind. They must not wait for it. The all-important thing was to come with all speed and leave everything behind that could not be brought, or that might delay their coming. It is the same with us when we are invited to come to Christ. We must not let interest or property delay us. Too often we regard our stuff, and allow our solicitude for it to keep us back from blessing.

The good of all the land of Egypt is yours. As children of God we possess the riches of the glory of our inheritance in Christ (Eph. 1. 18). All things are ours, and we are Christ's, and He is God's (1 Cor. 3. 23). In comparison with these infinite riches anything that we may have to leave in order to come to Christ counts for nothing.

VERSE 21. *The children of Israel did so.* They saw where their interests lay and took the right steps towards appropriating what they had been offered. What happiness there would be in the world if more did the same in regard to their spiritual interests!

Joseph gave them wagons. The means of helping the weak are entrusted by Christ to His representatives in the world.

According to the commandment of Pharaoh. The Father Himself loveth you (Jo. 14. 21, 23, 31).

Gave them provision for the way. Their immediate needs were not forgotten, nor are ours. We have the Word of God on which to feed continually during our journey through life from this world to the next. We have the earnest of the Spirit in our hearts (Eph. 1. 14) and His witness within (Rom. 8. 16). We have the supply of all our bodily needs promised and assured (Mt. 6. 33).

VERSE 22. *Changes of raiment.* These represent the transformation of life and character that comes to the regenerate. When we are born again, we are to put on the Lord Jesus Christ (Rom. 13. 14).

To Benjamin. Benjamin represents the beloved of the Lord (Deut. 33. 12), and thus those who are chosen from the beginning unto salvation by sanctification of the Spirit and belief of the truth (2 Thess. 2. 13).

Three hundred pieces of silver, and five changes of raiment. If we may see without fancifulness any significance in these numbers, we have in this gift a picture of four spiritual realities. The number three hundred may perhaps point to heavenly glory. Silver, being the same word as is used for money, points to cost, and so to redemption. Five is a number sometimes associated in the Bible with grace. We may thus see in the gifts given to Benjamin a reminder of the fact that the beloved of the Lord are brought to glory by redemption and are transformed in character by grace.

VERSE 23. The present sent by Joseph to his father is yet another picture of the gifts of God's redemptive grace to those who belong to Christ.

Ten asses laden with the good things of Egypt. The good things of Egypt represent the heavenly blessings which come from God to the believer as he journeys through life to the world to come. They come in response to faith through the medium of the Word of God and are not obtained through any other channel. They are brought on asses. The ass in the Bible is a picture of the unconverted. Thus the people of the world are used by God to bring the Gospel to those who believe. The Roman governors and road builders were so used, the printers of the fifteenth century and since, and the engineers today who construct the means of transport by which the evangelist, the missionary and the preacher carry the Gospel over the world.

Ten she asses laden with corn and bread and meat for his father by the way. The mention of she asses indicates the lesser value of this part of the gift. It was for a temporary purpose only. The pilgrim needs spiritual sustenance as he makes his journey through the world. He feeds on Christ, the living Bread, in and through the Word. He also requires provision for his bodily needs, and these are supplied to him by God through a multitude of unconverted people in the world.

VERSE 24. *He sent his brethren away.* As soon as we become personally reconciled to Christ, we too are sent away into the world to carry the Gospel to those who are still starving, as we once were.

They departed. It was very reasonable that they should, seeing that their father, their wives and their children were in desperate need and facing ultimate death. It is even more reasonable that we should depart to take food and assurance to those who are perishing, but we are slow to do so. We prefer to linger where Joseph is, enjoying the plenty of Egypt, and we hope that perhaps one or two of the others might be sufficient to go back and bring our kinsfolk, or that Benjamin might go alone, or even some of the Egyptians be sent. But we are all needed. We are all sent, and we ought all to depart.

See that ye fall not out by the way.

They were instructed to remain united, just as the Lord prayed that we all might be one (Jo. 17. 21). But alas! we have fallen out on a variety of trivial questions, whether we ought to have bishops, or only presbyters, or no regular ministry at all, whether we should use water at an infant's initiatory dedication or when he becomes a full member of the church, whether we grow gradually in holiness or experience a sudden crisis of sanctification, on the meaning of the promises of the Lord's return, and on countless questions dealing with the Jews and the millennium. We have done exactly what the heavenly Joseph warned us not to do, and it is to be feared that in consequence many of the starving have had to wait so long that they have perished before being able to reach the land of plenty at all.

VERSE 25. They undertook the journey on which they were sent and reached those to whom they were sent. As servants of Christ can we all be sure that we have done the same?

VERSE 26. *Joseph is yet alive, and he is the governor over all the land of Egypt.* Notice three points about this message, which prefigures the Gospel. (1) It concerns Joseph personally. They did not speak — or at least first speak — about the glories of Egypt, its plenty, or the abundance of corn to be found there. They spoke of Joseph. In the same way the chief message of the Gospel is not about the glories of heaven, nor even about the victory and power which God's grace can bring to the believer. It is not about salvation from death or assurance of freedom from poverty and loss. The sinner's need does not come first in the message, though maybe we often put these things first. The message of the Gospel is supremely about Jesus (Rom. 1. 1-3). (2) The message consisted of news that Joseph was alive. The brethren did not first explain the providence of

God in the sale of Joseph into Egypt, nor the incalculable consequences for the preservation of life which flowed from it. That came later. They brought the joyful and startling news that Joseph was alive. So the message of the Gospel is supremely the message of the resurrection. Jesus lives. It was the resurrection of Jesus that was emphasised by the primitive preachers of the Gospel (Acts 2. 24, 32; 3. 15; 17. 18). The sinner needs to know that the sinner's Friend is alive today to carry on in a higher sphere the works of love and mercy which He performed when in the flesh, and that He is near him and desires to be his friend today. (3) Lastly the message was concerned with the power and glory of Joseph. Their own Joseph was in supreme power and in a position to supply all their need. In the same way the Gospel tells us that Jesus is on the Father's throne (Rev. 3. 21) and exalted to God's right hand (Phil. 2. 9). A Man, the Friend of sinners, is on the throne of God.

Jacob's heart fainted. The shock overwhelmed the old man.

He believed them not. This was no wilful unbelief. Jacob was like the disciples who believed not for joy (Lk. 24. 41). It was too good to be true. And so it might well have been. Jacob might have rejected the story, if he had not had the foreshadowing of this very situation in Joseph's dreams so many years before, which he had not forgotten but carefully preserved in his mind (37. 11). In the same way the first disciples had the Lord's prophecies of His resurrection.

VERSE 27. *They told him all the words of Joseph.* In the same way in the preaching of the Gospel the message of the resurrection is accompanied by repetition of the teaching of Jesus Christ (Mt. 28. 20). The words of Joseph which they repeated to their father would include (1) his revelation of his identity, (2) his explanation of his sale, rejection and

sufferings as due to the providence of God with the purpose of saving life, (3) his promise to maintain and nourish them, (4) his advice to them not to quarrel on the journey. All these things may easily be seen as typical of the Gospel message.

When he saw the wagons. The words were insufficient to convince him. He believed when he saw the practical acts of kindness done to the weak and needy. In the same way it is when men see our good works that they will glorify our Father in heaven (Mt. 5. 16). *The spirit of Jacob their father revived.* In the same way the message of the Gospel revives the hearts of those who believe it by bringing them hope for despair, joy for sorrow, light for darkness, and life from the dead. The name Jacob is used because the verse describes Jacob in his weakness, and littleness of faith. He is still more like the old Jacob than the new Israel.

VERSE 28. *Israel said.* By striking contrast the name Israel is used, because Israel is seen believing and falling in with the promises of God. The resolution that he makes is to carry out a purpose which was in the mind of God and was a step in the redemptive plan of which the family were instruments and channels. As Jacob he acts in weakness outside of God's plan. As Israel he falls in with it. The same two natures as are typified in these two names are in every believer.

It is enough. He may have meant that he needed no more argument to convince him. Thus the Gospel, as evidenced in the lives and characters of those who believe it, is sufficient to convince men of the truth of Christ's religion. They need nothing more. This was the case even under the old dispensation (Lk. 16. 31). Secondly Israel may have meant that the desire of his heart was satisfied by this news. For years he had mourned over Joseph. The wound had never been healed. Now he found in this message new life and new hope, which completely satisfied him. This also is true in the case of everyone that hears and believes in the Gospel. His deepest longings are satisfied. The Gospel is enough and more than enough to make the heart of every sinner rejoice.

Joseph my son is yet alive. So the believer who understands and embraces the Gospel exclaims, ' Jesus lives '.

I will go and see him. In the same way the sinner in his need says, ' I will arise and go unto my father ' (Lk. 15. 18). On believing the Gospel the sinner is led by the Spirit to arise in his heart and go to Jesus, so that he may see Him by the eye of faith. *Before I die.* If the sinner does not enter into personal relationship with Jesus before he dies, and when he is still in this life, he will die eternally and be lost for ever. All talk about ' a second chance in the life to come ' introduces an element which cannot be true in the nature of things and arises from misunderstanding of the Gospel. ' When a wicked man dieth, his expectation shall perish ' (Prov. 11. 7).

CHAPTER 46

THIS chapter divides naturally into four sections. First we have Jacob's departure for Egypt, encouraged by a special vision from God (1-7). This is followed by the list and enumeration of Jacob's family (8-27). Next comes the meeting of Jacob with Joseph (28-30), and lastly Joseph's proposal to present his brothers to Pharaoh and instructions to them what to say.

VERSE 1. *Israel took his journey.* To the end of his days Israel was a pilgrim. Born in a country in which his family were strangers, he sojourned twenty years in another, returned to live in tents, and now towards the close of his life leaves the land of his birth for a third country, where he is to die. We also are pilgrims and strangers. We are to move about

the world as God sends us, privileged to have a higher vocation than Israel ever knew and bearing greater tidings than were revealed in his day.

With all that he had. He left nothing behind, but determined to throw everything into the service of God.

Came to Beer-sheba. This was the frontier place. Israel stood on the threshold of a new stage in his pilgrimage which he knew must be the last. He was never to see Canaan again. Here at the well of the oath, whence he had started for Haran (28. 10), where a covenant had originally been made (21. 33), a place of many memories, he makes the final decision and takes the irrevocable step.

Offered sacrifices unto the God of his father Isaac. At the moment of his important decision Israel rightly offers sacrifices. He re-dedicated himself to the God Whom he had been brought up from childhood's days to serve. At a similar moment of decision and at the beginning of a new stage in our lives we too should offer our bodies as a reasonable, holy and lively sacrifice to God (Rom. 12. 1). As we survey the past, we should offer again the sacrifice of praise to God, the fruit of our lips giving thanks to His Name (Heb. 13. 15), and all must be based on the sin-offering made once for all by Christ on the cross, which we can never too often appropriate.

VERSE 2. *God spake unto Israel.* This is a striking phrase. We should expect ' Jahweh spake unto Israel '. The name Elohim recalls its use in chapter 32, the description of Jacob's wrestling with God, but its use also emphasises the fact that Israel is leaving the promised land and going down into Egypt. He had the support and presence of the Creator God of Egypt and of all the nations of the world. Yet it is Israel who is going down to Egypt in furtherance of the great redemptive purpose. *In the visions of the night.* Here one of the ways in which God communicated with men is defined. Dreams are regarded by eastern people as important and serious, and have often been used by God as means of speaking to His people or of convicting sinners.

Jacob, Jacob. God speaks to the old Jacob, reminding him of what he had been and emphasising His love and care for Jacob exactly as he was in his weakness. His love for us is of just the same nature.

Here am I. These simple words express Jacob's response. They may mean much. They can express a desire to put oneself entirely at God's disposal. They can demonstrate the fact that we have nothing to give to God but ourselves as we are, which is all that God desires. In Jacob's case they may have expressed a note of expectancy. He stood at a crisis in his life. He might expect God to speak to him, and he was ready to obey Him, whether He told him to proceed or turn back. In all this we see example and instruction for ourselves.

VERSE 3. *I am God.* The Name here is in Hebrew El, not the common form. It connects with the Name El-Shaddai, translated God Almighty. The root meaning seems to be ' the Strong One ', and the Name seems to have been in use among Semitic peoples from primitive times.

The God of thy father. This fact was a call upon Jacob's allegiance and an intimation of his responsibility towards God. There is no stronger call upon any man today than to be reminded of the God Whom his parents worshipped in the home of his childhood.

Fear not to go down into Egypt. God gave Jacob guidance just when he needed it, as He had done when he left home for Padan-aram (28. 15) and again when he left Padan-aram for home (31. 13). We may expect unmistakable guidance at times of crisis in our lives. On the previous occasion at Padan-aram God simply gave a command to go home. Now He not only does so, but encourages Jacob not to fear. He was now old

and getting weaker. Besides, in going down to Egypt he was doing what had proved disastrous in the case of Abraham (12. 10-20). He might well doubt whether it was God's will that he should go.

I will there make of thee a great nation. Further details in the purpose of God were revealed to Jacob. The tribes of Israel were to pass in Egypt through an experience which they would never forget during the whole of their national history. They were to be welded into a nation in the furnace of affliction, and they would look back to God's great deliverance of them as the foundation of their life as a people. Similarly in the afflictions of the world, indeed in its great tribulation, the redeemed are welded together into a numberless people, the one eternal church of Christ (Rev. 7. 9-17).

VERSE 4. *I will go down with thee into Egypt.* If Jacob had the assurance of God's presence he could go safely into Egypt. He could go in fact to the ends of the earth, and even to hell itself. And so might we. God was with Jacob and his family in all the experiences of Egypt, and in every experience He is also with us.

I will also surely bring thee up again. Jacob himself would be brought up only in his coffin (50. 4-13), but he is here, as is so often the case in the language of the Bible, identified with his descendants. They would be brought up at the great exodus, led by Moses under the blood of the Passover Lamb. God here repeats in different terms to Jacob what He had already told Abraham (15. 13-16). The sojourn in Egypt, the bondage and the exodus were part of God's plan for the covenant family from the beginning. They did for Israel after the flesh what the eternal redemption in Christ has done for the new Israel which the old Israel typified.

Joseph shall put his hand upon thine eyes. This means that he will meet and greet him. Joseph is pictured as tenderly caressing the old man's cheek with his hand, or putting his hand on his forehead and looking into his eyes. Alternatively and perhaps more probably it means that Joseph would close his father's eyes at the time of his death. Joseph would be with him when he died. Notice the personal promise graciously made to Jacob, which would compensate him for the long years of sorrow and mourning for Joseph. God cares and provides for the personal needs of His servants (1 Pet. 5. 7).

VERSE 5. *Jacob rose up from Beersheba.* He could go on his journey assured and happy, knowing that he was in line with the Divine Will and that his most precious wishes were about to be fulfilled.

Carried Jacob their father. Special provision was made on this journey for the weak. In the same way the Saviour carries the lambs in His bosom (Isa. 40. 11), and we who are strong ought to bear the burdens of the weak (Rom. 15. 1).

VERSE 6. *They took their cattle.* They brought with them opportunities for work and for sacrifice, which are the two functions of cattle.

Their goods, which they had gotten in the land of Canaan. They brought with them what their skill and industry had won, to use in God's service and help in setting forward His redemptive purpose. We may compare Eph. 4. 28.

Came into Egypt. Egypt in this immediate passage is not the picture of the world, though it soon reverts to being so again. It was the land where Joseph lived and reigned. To the land where Jesus reigns all the faithful come now in spirit in their hearts by faith and will one day be gathered on the day of resurrection.

Jacob, and all his seed with him. This small family was the picture of the whole company of the redeemed, who are one family in Christ and are called to be with Him where He is

(Jo. 14. 3).

VERSE 7. Just as Jacob brought all who belonged to him into Egypt, so does Christ bring all who are His safe through to the land of His glory (Jo. 6. 39).

VERSE 8. From this verse on to the end of verse 27 we have the names and enumeration of Jacob's family. In chapters 29 and 30 we saw that the names given to his children had an evangelical significance and were illustrative of the spiritual life. They are repeated here in a partially different order. A few of the names of the second generation are doubtful in meaning, and the meaning of a few appears to be unknown or lost. Most however seem to carry on the illustrations.

The children of Israel which came into Egypt. The opening sentence of the prediction made to Abraham (15. 13) was thus fulfilled. Notice that true to the principle of prophecy the prediction did not mention Egypt by name. It simply spoke of ' a land that is not theirs '. The fulfilment revealed that the land meant was Egypt. Remembrance of this principle might have prevented much dogmatism about the future.

Jacob and his sons. Contrary to the case of Abraham the Holy Spirit continually reverts to the name Jacob. In doing so He reminds us (1) what Jacob had been, (2) that much of the old nature remained in him. (3) that God is not ashamed to own the old Jacob, one time sinner and supplanter, as His friend. In all these things Jacob is like ourselves.

Reuben. This means ' See, a son '. The name points men first of all to the Son of God and reminds them to fix their eyes on Him.

VERSE 9. *The sons of Reuben.* Their names will tell us what follows on from a sight of the Saviour. *Hanoch* means ' Dedication '. The one whose eyes are fixed on the Son of God dedicates himself to His service. This

c

is followed by a life of separation from sin and the world, indicated by the name *Phallu*, which means ' Distinguished ' in the sense of different or separated. Such a life is lived by ' Dwelling ' in Christ. ' Dwelling ' being the possible meaning of the name *Hezron*. Finally one whose eyes are fixed on the Saviour becomes a *Carmi*, or ' Vine-dresser '. He works in the Saviour's vineyard.

VERSE 10. *The sons of Simeon*. The name Simeon means ' Hearing ', and points to listening to and obeying Christ. His sons are *Jemuel*, the meaning of which does not seem to be known. There is a variant reading ' Nemuel '. We can see the syllable ' el ', which means God, at the end of the word, and we can tell at least that in some way or other God comes into the life of the obedient man. Jamin means ' Right Hand '. Thus there follows from obedience a powerful, practical skill, typified by the right hand, in God's service. Next comes *Ohad*, which perhaps means ' Might '. It is certain that power follows obedience. *Jachin* means ' He will establish '. This was afterwards one of the names of the two pillars that stood in front of Solomon's temple (1 Ki. 7. 21). The one who obeys Christ is rooted and established by God. *Zohar* means ' Light '. The obedient may expect to enjoy the light of God in their hearts. Finally we have *Shaul the son of a Canaanitish woman*. He was a mixture, half Canaanite, the result of compromise with the devil. His name means ' Asked for ', and he stands as an example of the fact that the answer to prayer depends on faith. Simeon, as it were, obtained what he wanted at the level at which he asked.

VERSE 11. *The sons of Levi*. Levi ' Joined '. The names of his second and third sons give a miniature picture of the life of the man who is joined to Christ. The meaning of the name *Gershon* does not seem to be known. *Kohath* means ' Assembly '.

Anyone joined to Christ will be found in the assembly of His people and at the last in the assembly and church of the first-born (Heb. 12. 23). *Merari* means ' Bitter '. To be joined to Christ means sometimes bitter persecution in this world (Mk. 10. 30; Rev. 10. 9, 10), just as the Lord Himself suffered the bitter cross and shame.

VERSE 12. *Judah* means ' Praise '. His name represents the man who lives to the praise of the glory of God's grace (Eph. 1. 6). *Er* and *Onan* died because of sin (see chap. 38). It is noteworthy that in Judah's family only have we this story of premature death. So it was in Judah's line that the Saviour came to die for sin, and suffered bearing guilt and shame, the centre and butt of every sin committed throughout the whole history of the world, all of which were made to meet on His head (Isa. 53. 6). *Shelah* means ' Petition '. The man of praise is also the man of prayer. *Pharez* means ' Breach '. His praises break forth, and he also breaks forth in the power and grace of Christ from the death of sin to the life of righteousness. *Zarah* means ' Sunrise '. The man of praise lives in resurrection power and looks forward to the resurrection morning. The two sons of Pharez replace Er and Onan to make up the number of Judah's descendants, as it were. Thus it was in Christ, Who came in Judah's line, that the redeemed humanity took the place of the race that perished in Adam. The names of the two are *Hezron* and *Hamul*. Hezron perhaps means ' Dwelling '. Those who break through in Christ from death to life dwell with Him for ever. Hamul means ' Spared '. Those who possess new life and stand on resurrection ground are spared on the great day of judgment (Jo. 5. 24) in contrast to their Saviour, who was not spared (Rom. 8. 32). It is interesting to note that the sons of Pharez could scarcely have been born at the time that Jacob and Judah went down to Egypt. Joseph was thirty-nine or forty at the time, Judah about forty-seven or forty-eight. Shelah, who was Judah's third son, would be thirty at the very most, and probably not that. Pharez was not born till Shelah was grown (38. 14). Pharez would be fourteen at the very most, and it is conceivable that he might have had twin infant sons. It is more probable that the unborn sons were reckoned in the record as compensatory for Er and Onan. If they were still unborn, the spiritual truths brought out by the presence of their names would appear in sharper outline.

VERSE 13. *Issachar* means ' Hire ' or ' Reward '. His name points to the man who receives Christ as his reward (see 15. 1). His sons have strange names. *Tola* means ' Worm '. The man who sees in Christ his exceeding great reward sees himself as a worm, the very condition to which Christ was reduced on the cross (Ps. 22. 6). *Phuvah* means ' Mouth '. Such a man speaks for Christ. *Job* perhaps means ' Persecuted ', but it is noteworthy that the Samaritan recension reads *Jashub*, the form which is found in the parallel list in 1 Chron. 7. 1. Jashub means ' He returns ', and reminds us of the coming of the Lord with His reward (Rev. 22. 12). On textual grounds Jashub is more likely to have been the original form, and the spiritual meaning fits well. *Shimron* means ' Watchful '. We thus are reminded of the man who watches for Christ's return and looks for his reward there.

VERSE 14. *Zebulun* means ' Dwelling '. *Sered* strangely enough means ' Fear '. This is what the man who abides in Christ is free from, but he shows and exercises the right fear of the Lord. *Elon* means ' Terebinth Tree ', and like all trees points to the cross (1 Pet. 2. 24). The man who abides in Christ dwells under the shadow of the cross. *Jahleel* means ' Wait for God '. This is the very attitude of one who abides in Christ under the shadow of the cross (Isa. 25. 9; 1 Thess. 1. 10).

VERSE 15. *Dinah* means ' Judgment '. No names accompany this. God's judgment is final.

His sons and his daughters. Dinah seems to have been his only daughter. No other daughters are mentioned in verses 18, 22 or 25. The plural is used as a formality in the enumeration.

Thirty and three. This number (as may be seen by simple addition) includes Jacob himself. It leaves out Er and Onan, but puts in Hezron and Hamul (ver. 12), not yet born at the time of the migration, to make up for them. It was compiled or extracted from the records by Moses. It may represent the family as it was seventeen years later at the time of Jacob's death (47. 28). The words in verse 8, ' which came into Egypt ', need not mean that everyone named in the list came personally into Egypt. They are no more than a statement that the family as a whole came there.

VERSE 16. *Gad* means ' Fortunate ', perhaps in the sense of ' successful ' or ' prosperous '. The names of the sons, so far as their meanings are known, describe the attitude of the man who is spiritually prosperous or successful. *Ziphion* means ' Looking out ', indicating perhaps an attitude of looking out over the world to bring help to the many needs of those in it. *Haggi* and *Shuni* mean respectively ' Festive ' and ' Quiet '. These words speak for themselves in this connection. The former reminds us of Rev. 3. 20. The meaning of the name *Ezbon* does not seem to be known. *Eri* means ' Watchful '. The meanings of *Arodi* and *Areli* both seem doubtful.

VERSE 17. *Asher* means ' Happy '. The names of his children, so far as their meanings are known, illustrate this condition. *Jimnah* perhaps means

' Good Fortune '. *Ishuah* and *Isui* both mean ' Peaceful '. Here is a double emphasis on peace, one of the essentials of happiness. Peace with God comes by the blood of the cross (Col. 1. 20), and the peace of God reigns in the believer's heart (Col. 3. 15). The meaning of *Beriah* is not known. *Serah* means ' Abundance '. This is what God gives the believer. *Heber* means ' Fellowship '. The Christian enjoys happy fellowship with God and other believers. *Malchiel* means ' My king is God '. This is a great secret of happiness, which comes from the surrender of the life to God's control.

VERSE 18. *Sixteen souls*. Added to the thirty-three of verse 15 this comes to forty-nine.

VERSE 19. *Joseph* means ' Adding '. *Benjamin* means ' Son of my right hand ', that is to say, ' specially beloved ' (see Deut. 33. 12).

VERSE 20. *Manasseh* means ' One who causes to forget '. One who is engaged in adding to the numbers of the church of Christ by missionary or evangelistic work must be content to forget his old life, his possessions, and even his family.

Ephraim means ' Fruitful '. In connection with Joseph, which means ' Adding ', this speaks for itself. Forgetfulness of the old life and fruitfulness in the new always go together.

VERSE 21. Benjamin's ten sons may have been born over a period of eighteen years. Marriage generally took place at a very young age. The meanings of their names are not easy to interpret and seem to lead us through a wide range of spiritual experience. The first is *Belah,* which means ' Destruction '. Here is the condition of the sinner before he comes to Christ. He is in the jaws of death and doomed to eternal destruction. The next is *Becher*. This means ' Young Camel '. The camel is an unclean animal and is often used in the Bible as a picture of the rich man of this world. It is another picture of the unconverted sinner. The meaning of *Ashbel* seems not to be known. *Gera* means ' Grain ', and we are reminded at once of the corn of wheat falling into the ground and dying (Jo. 12. 24). True first of Jesus Himself, this principle applies also to His people. When the sinner comes to Christ, he dies with Him (Rom. 6. 3), and rises with Him to newness of life (Rom. 6. 4). The name Gera thus speaks to us of the sinner's conversion. *Naaman,* the next name, means ' Pleasantness '. This is the experience of the sinner who was previously on the way to destruction, as soon as he is converted. *Ehi* means ' My Brother is Lofty '. Christ is the Brother of all believers, and He is in ' the highest place that heaven affords '. The believer has a Kinsman on the throne of God making intercession for him there. *Rosh* means ' Head '. The believer is the member of a body of which Christ is the Head (Eph. 1. 22, 23). For *Muppim* the parallel list in 1 Chron. 7. 12, which is almost certainly taken from this one, reads *Shuppim,* the initial letters being very alike in Hebrew, and the one having been mistaken by a copyist for the other. In partial agreement with the latter the name in Num. 26. 39 reads *Shupham.* If we take this as the original form, we get the possible meaning ' Serpent '. The believer is to be as wise as a serpent (Mt. 10. 16), but he is also liable to be attacked by the serpent, the great enemy of God and of mankind, and if he is, he will find *Huppim,* or ' Coverings ', that is to say, shelter in the Rock of Ages and at the throne of grace. The meaning of the name *Ard* is not known.

VERSE 22. *All the souls were fourteen.* This added to the previous forty-nine makes sixty-three.

VERSE 23. *Dan* means ' Judge '. *Hushim* means ' Those who make haste '. So in these two names we have the pictures (1) of a world hastening to meet its Judge, unaware of its doom and destiny, and (2) of convicted sinners hastening, as they should do, to flee from the wrath to come.

VERSE 24. *Naphthali.* This means ' Wrestling '. We think of the Saviour wrestling in His temptations and His passion with the devil, and of the Christian wrestling in prayer. The result of this wrestling is (1) *Jahzeel,* which means ' God allots '. Christ's wrestling won for the believer an inheritance, incorruptible and undefiled and that fadeth not away (1 Pet. 1. 4), reserved for him in heaven and bestowed on him by God. (2) *Guni* means ' Painted with Colours '. This speaks of the glory of the inheritance to come (Isa. 54. 11). (3) *Jezer* means ' Form '. In this name we see the beauty of holiness with which the bride of Christ is adorned. Finally, (4) we have *Shillem,* which means ' Requital '. When the church shines forth in all her glory in the world to come, she will find that all her suffering will be requited. Satan will be beaten down beneath her feet and destroyed for ever. Thus after passing through various aspects of the Gospel and the Christian life we end with the sons of Dan and Napththali, which point to judgment and the world to come. Only the inspiration of the Holy Spirit could have brought about this sequence, and behind that we see the sovereign providence of God at work in the actual bestowal of the names. For of Him and through Him are all things. To Him be glory for ever. Amen (Rom. 11. 36).

VERSE 25. *All the souls were seven.* Added to the sixty-three already reckoned, this makes seventy souls.

All the souls were three score and six. These sixty-six (1) accompanied Jacob into Egypt, (2) consisted of his children or grandchildren, (3) excluded his sons' wives. From the

seventy, to which the enumeration in verses 8 to 25 adds up, there are omitted in this verse Jacob himself and also Joseph and his two sons, who did not accompany Jacob. By subtracting these four the number sixty-six is arrived at.

VERSE 27. *All the souls of the house of Jacob, which came into Egypt, were threescore and ten.* In this verse Joseph, his two sons, and Jacob himself, all of whom belonged to the ' house ', are reckoned in, so that by adding these four to the sixty-six the complete number of seventy is reached. Notice that the verse does not state that every person mentioned actually ' came into Egypt '. The two sons of Joseph were born there. It was the house as a whole, which ' came into Egypt '. The statement is perfectly accurate. In place of the number seventy the Septuagint Greek version has seventy-five. It makes up this number by adding at the appropriate place in verse 20 five descendants of Joseph, not born till later. There is no means of knowing what led the translators to insert these names. The Septuagint rendering is however made important because it is followed by Stephen in his speech (Acts 7. 14). That verse says that Joseph sent for Jacob his father and all his kindred. The number seventy-five includes Jacob and Joseph and therefore belongs not only to the ' kindred ', but to the whole verse. It is preceded in Greek by the preposition *en,* which can well be translated, 'consisting of ', but might be rendered ' reckoned as '. If the preposition will bear the latter meaning, the Holy Spirit has inspired the writer of Acts, and doubtless behind him Stephen himself, to use an accurate expression even while quoting from the Greek version which he knew and read. But discussion of this point belongs to a commentary on Acts rather than on Genesis.

VERSE 28. *He sent Judah before him unto Goshen,* just as Old Testament Israel, commonly known as the Jews, was sent before, as it were, to direct men's faces to Christ. The preparation of Israel under the Old Covenant was essential for the accomplishment of Christ's redemptive mission. *The land of Goshen,* that is, the good land where Joseph lived and reigned.

VERSE 29. This moving meeting reminds us of the meeting of the father and the prodigal son (Lk. 15. 20). In the same way Christ comes up to meet every returning sinner and presents Himself to him in great love and tenderness.

VERSE 30. *Now let me die, since I have seen thy face, because thou art yet alive.* The old man meant that he could now die happy because he had attained more than his dearest wish on earth and life could hold nothing better for him. The words express in three senses what the sinner feels when he finds the Saviour. (1) The saved sinner is ready to die. He fears death no longer. Instead of its leading him to judgment and condemnation it leads him in an instant to resurrection glory and his Saviour's presence. By it he can magnify Christ as much as by life (Phil. 1. 20-23). (2) The one who has truly believed in Christ, appropriated Him and appreciated Him as the chiefest among ten thousand and altogether lovely (Cant. 5. 10) and knows Him to be alive from the dead can think, like Jacob, of nothing better that life can hold than this knowledge of the Saviour (Phil. 3. 10). (3) In a sense quite unknown to Jacob he can say, ' Now let me die '. Let me die with Christ to sin and rise with my living Saviour to the life of righteousness. As many of us as were baptised into Christ Jesus were baptised into His death (Rom. 6. 3).

VERSE 31. *I will go up, and shew Pharaoh.* In the same way Christ has gone up to the Majesty on high to show Him by His very presence as

alive from the dead in the body, albeit glorified, that He took from Mary, and by the prints of the nails in His hands and feet, that redemption is accomplished, and that His brethren and His Father's house are come. A lost and hopeless humanity, whose nature the Saviour took, has come back to God, the barrier between them being quite broken down.

My brethren, and my father's house. Though the father knows us and made us and loves us all, there is still a sense in which Christ will present us before Him with exceeding joy, rejoicing to own us as His brethren (Jude 24. 25). *Which were in the land of Canaan,* once away in a strange land, unable to see Pharaoh's face, and even ignorant that Joseph was alive. *Are come unto me.* No one gives a thought to the need that first drove the brethren to go down into Egypt nor to the expectation of its permanent satisfaction there. That was thrown in and taken in the stride. The supreme thing was that the family was reunited with Joseph himself. The same is true with Christ and the sinner. He answers His invitation to ' come unto Me ' (Mt. 11. 28). Jesus matters far more than heaven. Indeed the presence of Jesus makes heaven.

VERSE 32. *The men are shepherds.* It is the business of all the people of Christ to be shepherds and to go after the lost sheep.

Their trade hath been to feed cattle. May this be said of us when we are brought into the Father's presence on the last day. Till then may we occupy till the Lord comes (Lk. 19. 13), and may we be found feeding His sheep and lambs (Jo. 21. 15-17).

They have brought their flocks, and their herds, and all that they have. Doubtless we shall do the same, and may we have much to bring, so that we find an abundant entrance into the heavenly kingdom accompanied by many whom we have been the means of bringing there.

VERSE 33. *What is your occupation?*
This is a question that will be asked
on the day of judgment, as seems
clear from Mt. 25. 34-46, Rev. 20. 12.
It is a question that as professed
servants of Christ we should do well
to ask ourselves from time to time.

VERSE 34. *Thy servants' trade hath
been about cattle.* This is the answer
that Pharaoh wanted to hear. It will
be the answer that the great King will
wish to hear on that day. Shall we
have been concerned with tending
Christ's flock and seeking the lost
among them, or shall we be found
to have amused ourselves with the
unclean animals of the world? Notice
that Joseph put these words in his
brothers' mouths. The words were no
less true for that reason, but it was
Joseph who encouraged them to speak
and told them what to say. So our
heavenly Joseph speaks for us in the
presence of the Father and will make
us stand in that day (Rom. 14. 4).

*That ye may dwell in the land of
Goshen.* The children of Israel were
to be utterly separate from the Egyptians. We too are to dwell in the
land of Goshen, in Egypt but not of
it. As the people of God we are a
separate community, which ought to
be an example to the world of the
working of the principle of love. We
are holy to the Lord. We live where
we can carry on our occupation. The
separation to which we are called is
difficult and costly, and each of us
finds it easy to make some adjustment or compromise with the world.

*Every shepherd is an abomination
unto the Egyptians.* This remains
true in the spiritual sense. The work
of tending the flock of God is misunderstood and disliked by the world.
It thinks it unproductive or anti-
social. The Egyptians had their
sacred bulls, their cats and their
crocodiles. They had no use for
sheep. So in the world today Christ's
sheep and their shepherds are hated
and despised.

Note on the number 70 in verse 27

of this chapter contrasted with the
number 75 in Acts 7. 14. So little
is known about the building up of
the text of the Greek Septuagint
version, and it seems so certain that
the text as we have it has been influenced by versions made after the New
Testament was written, that it may
not be impossible that the Septuagint
text as we have it today has been
affected by that of the New Testament. It is therefore conceivable that
the number 75 appeared first in
Stephen's speech and was incorporated thence into the Septuagint text,
the names of Joseph's grandsons being added at the same time to account
for the number. If this were the case,
the number in Acts 7. 14 would be
made up as follows: the total number
excluding Jacob, Joseph, Manasseh
and Ephraim, appears in Gen. 46. 26
as 66. From these Stephen deducted
Er and Onan who were dead and did
not put the two sons of Pharez in
their places because they were not
born at the time of the migration.
This would leave him with 64. To
this he added the wives of the eleven
brothers, expressly excluded in Gen.
46. 26, which would give him his 75.
While we know that Judah's Canaanite wife was dead (38. 12), it is probable that he took another after the
incident with Tamar, whom he did
not make his wife (38. 26). Indeed
the statement in 46. 26 suggests that
all the sons including Judah had
wives. If this be the explanation of
the appearance as the number in Acts
7. 14, the phrase containing the
number applies to the ' kindred ' only
and means ' consisting of seventy-five
souls '.

CHAPTER 47

THIS chapter falls into three
sections. In verses 1-12 we
have the introduction of Joseph's
family to Pharaoh and their settlement in the land of Goshen, in verses
13-26 the settlement of the land of
Egypt and the concentration of
property in Pharaoh's hands, and in

verses 27-31 Jacob's wishes about his burial. We see in the chapter the nourishment of God's people with the bread of life, the conditions on which sinners may be received and sustained, and lastly Jacob's faith in God's promises and reverence for His purpose.

VERSE 1. *Joseph came and told Pharaoh.* In the same way the Saviour at His ascension came with the clouds of heaven and was brought near to the Ancient of Days (Dan. 7. 13). He came to announce His victory over Satan, sin and death, and that He had brought His people safely through them to the land of plenty.

My father and my brethren. These typify the human kinsmen of Christ, Adam and his children.

Their flocks, and their herds. These represent the same people under a different figure and aspect. The flocks are the people of God, nourished by Christ and fed and tended by the under-shepherds. The herds are the cattle which do the work and are capable of sacrifice. So we have a threefold picture of the church. It consists of kinsmen of Christ, heirs of God and joint-heirs with Christ (Rom. 8. 17), of people in varying stages of spiritual growth and experience who need feeding, tending, teaching and guarding (Acts 20. 28; 1 Pet. 5. 2). Lastly the same people are all actual or potential workers in the service of Christ (1 Thess. 1. 3), called upon to present their bodies a living sacrifice (Rom. 12. 1).

All that they have. We too must bring all that we have and lay it at the feet of Christ.

Are come out of the land of Canaan. Canaan is the type of the devil. All that are Christ's come safely out of the possession and power of the devil. *They are in the land of Goshen.* The people of Christ are settled in the land where Christ has placed them, near to Himself, separate from the world and enjoying the best of God's gifts to

them in Christ.

VERSE 2. *He took some of his brethren,* as one day Christ will take us.

Even five men. Five is a number often associated in the Bible with grace. If we make the association here, we shall be reminded of the fact that by grace and grace alone are we saved by Christ and presented to the Father.

Presented them unto Pharaoh. So Christ presents His whole church unto His Father, a glorious church without spot or wrinkle, or any such thing.

VERSE 3. *What is your occupation?* This question will be asked on the day of judgment. It is one that we may well ask ourselves (see on 46. 33). *Thy servants are shepherds.* The business of the people of God is to look after the flock of God. *Also our fathers.* We are the children of those who were likewise shepherds from the days of the beginning of the church.

VERSE 4. *For to sojourn in the land are we come.* They still rightly regarded themselves as sojourners. They may have thought that when the famine was over they would return to Canaan. They may have known the promises made to Abraham and have realised that they would always be sojourners till they took possession of the land of promise.

Thy servants have no pasture for their flocks. There is nothing in this world on which to feed the flock of God. *The famine is sore in the land of Canaan.* Wherever the devil lives and reigns, there is spiritual dearth. *Let thy servants dwell in the land of Goshen.* Joseph had told them to ask this. So any petition made to God in Christ's Name cannot be denied.

VERSE 5. *Thy father and thy brethren are come unto thee.* Again the emphasis is not that they had come to Goshen, nor to plenty, nor to safety, but to Joseph. In the same way by the Gospel it is to Christ that we come (Mt. 11. 28).

Verse 6. *The land of Egypt is before thee.* Pharaoh's generosity is but a faint shadow of the grace and goodness of God.

In the best of the land. God always gives the best and most enjoyable and most satisfying. He gave His only Son for us all, and He daily loads us with benefits.

In the land of Goshen let them dwell. This was not only the best, but it was a land in which they could live separate from the Egyptians. It is a picture of the spiritual condition of the true believer in the present world.

If thou knowest any men of activity among them. Notice that all were to dwell in Goshen and enjoy the best of the land. This was given them for Joseph's sake. In addition to this any suitable among them were to have positions of responsibility. In the same way not all of God's people are called to responsibility in the church or the world. All enjoy the benefits of grace, but God looks out His men of activity and assigns places to them, where they can feed the flock.

Make them rulers over my cattle. This probably means that they were to be rulers over those that looked after the cattle. At any rate they were to oversee the work that was done in the fields and provide for the care of the workers. God needs such in the great work for Christ that continually goes on in the world. We may well ask our own hearts and seek the will of God to see if the place that He has for us may not be one of responsibility. But are we men of activity?

Verse 7. This was a unique and moving meeting when the old pilgrim and man of God met the great king. It is evident that Jacob possessed a dignity, due no doubt to his spiritual experience and long walk with God, which was recognised by Pharaoh, who asked for Jacob's blessing, or at least consented to his giving it. It is the greater who blesses the less (Heb. 7. 7). A lifelong walk with God gives a man a dignity which even the great people of the world respect and recognise.

Verse 8. *How old art thou?* This was a polite question asked out of interest and respect. Pharaoh was impressed with the old man's age and experience. If there is any parallel question that the heavenly Father and King will ever ask of us, it may be to enquire when we were born again.

Verse 9. *My pilgrimage.* The old man looked back on his whole life as a journey and pilgrimage, a sojourning, as the Hebrew literally says. Here he had no abiding city, but he looked for one to come (Heb. 13. 14). He looked like Abraham for the city which hath foundations, whose maker and builder is God (Heb. 11. 10). His life, like those of Abraham and Isaac, was a type of the spiritual pilgrimage undertaken by every believer in Christ as he follows his Master through the world to the country which is to come.

An hundred and thirty years. The number was exact, as verse 28 makes clear. It makes a useful point of time from which we can trace back Jacob's age at the time of the various events in his life. We know that Joseph was now thirty-nine or forty. Jacob was therefore ninety at the time of his birth, which coincided with the departure from Padan-aram (30. 25). As he was there twenty years (31. 38), he must have been seventy when he went there at the time of his experience at Bethel. All the great spiritual events and crises of Jacob's life thus took place in the second half of it. Let no man think that God will not speak to him because he has passed the days of his youth. In Jacob's case God waited to do so until he was well in middle life. On the other hand the most dangerous thing that a young man can do is to postpone his reckoning with God. No one that does so has any right to feel that God will speak to him later. The opposite is more likely to be the case.

Few and evil. The context forbids us to suppose that Jacob was blaming God, or even that he was speaking peevishly. He was comparing his life with those of Abraham and Isaac, and in such a comparison he was right. Abraham had lived to 175 and Isaac to 180 (25. 7; 35. 28). Jacob's life had been one of disappointments, difficulties and sorrows. Perhaps he felt that he had served God badly, and he may have thought that his days were being shortened because of this. A study of his life seems to show that he never reached the depths and spiritual maturity that Abraham attained and that he did not enjoy the long quiet uneventful years which the unadventurous Isaac had passed through. The beginning of his life was crooked and the end was storm-tossed. Yet at least he meant to convey to Pharaoh that he had the hope of rest and stability to come. Like Abraham he looked for the city and with Abraham he will enter it at last, the short sad pilgrimage over and the eternal security before him (Mt. 8. 11).

VERSE 10. *Jacob blessed Pharaoh*. Evidently the dignity of the presence of God shined through the old man who thought his life so short and unsatisfactory. Perhaps he meant to convey to Pharaoh that he would have done better to have met Abraham or Isaac, and that he might have seen better from one of them what God can do with a life that sets out on pilgrimage at His call.

Went out from before Pharaoh, whom perhaps he did not see again. He will however spend eternity in the presence of an even greater king.

VERSE 11. *Joseph placed his father and his brethren*. This is exactly what Christ seeks to do for us. He has a place in His plan for us. If we are disciples of His, are we certain that we are in that place?

Gave them a possession in the land of Egypt. In the same way Christ gives a possession and an inheritance to all His people. He Himself is our inheritance. He gives us grace, mercy and peace in this world with happy service and work for Him and abundant joy even in persecutions (Mt. 5. 12), and in the world to come life everlasting.

In the best of the land. Christ's people always have the best.

As Pharaoh had commanded. Christ's care for His people comes ultimately from the Father with Whom He is one. In His mediatorial and redemptive work Christ is but carrying out the will of the Father.

VERSE 12. *Nourished his father, and his brethren, and all his father's household, with bread*. So the heavenly Joseph nourishes us with the living Bread from heaven, which is Himself, found by us when we feed upon Him in our hearts by faith in the Scriptures.

According to their families. The Hebrew says ' according to the little ones '. This may be interpreted (1) as our version has it. In this case it means that the food was proportioned to the needs of each family, having special respect to the number of children in it. In the same way Christ, the heavenly Bread, exactly fulfils the needs of all who partake of Him and satisfies them perfectly. Alternatively (2) the meaning of this phrase may be as the margin suggests, ' as a little child is nourished '. This interpretation emphasises the dependence of the whole family on Joseph and our complete dependence on Christ. We can no more find our own spiritual food than a helpless babe. Happy is the man who relies for the establishment of his spiritual life entirely on the grace of God and the activity of His Spirit appropriated by faith.

VERSE 13. *There was no bread in all the land.* The verses dealing with the Egyptian famine and its effect upon the people are introduced by an easy transition of ideas. These words imply a strong contrast with the preceding verse. Joseph's own people were nourished with bread, but the Egyptians had none. This is true spiritually in the world today. The people of Christ are nourished from heaven, but the people of the world have nothing to live on and are indeed dead in trespasses and sins (Eph. 2. 1).

The famine was very sore. This is the spiritual condition of all members of the fallen human race. We are reminded of the prodigal son in the far country (Lk. 15. 14). It may be that the famine is not immediately felt, but it arises to some extent or other in the course of every sinner's life. *The land of Egypt and all the land of Canaan fainted by reason of the famine.* Egypt represents the world and Canaan represents the devil. The people of the world, who are in the power of Satan, faint spiritually and morally, indeed they are dead, and need to be woken and to rise from the dead if they are to come to God (Eph. 5. 14).

VERSE 14. In this and the following verse we are told two things about the money of Egypt and Canaan. (1) It was all gathered up by Joseph. Money is that which buys and is given in exchange. It represents merit in the spiritual sphere. Now Joseph gathered up all this money. In the same way the heavenly Joseph gathers up into Himself all the merit of the human race. No one else has any merit at all. Jesus alone has meritorious standing before God. Joseph brought this money into Pharaoh's house. In the same way all the merit of the human race, which is concentrated on Jesus alone, is brought by Him into the Father's house and

there presented before Him. Jesus' merit avails for all the fallen race.

VERSE 15. (2) The second thing told us about the money of Egypt was that it failed. Here the whole matter of merit is regarded from a different angle, but the illustration is equally true. Human merit and desert completely fail before God. Anyone who seeks to buy the bread of life (as many do) cannot but fail to obtain it. We may think of those who sought to give money for it as being like those who live before God under conscience. They may think that for a time they are obtaining supplies, but their money inevitably fails.

Give us bread; for why should we die in thy presence? These are the very words that the famished soul cries to God as soon as it realises by grace that it is at the end of its own resources. The sinner realises that the spiritual bread, which alone sustains everlasting life, is a gift (Rom. 6. 23) and that without it he must die.

VERSE 16. *Give your cattle.* When merit is found to fail, the next thing to try is hard work and sacrifice. These are the two things which the cattle represent. Joseph was bringing the people step by step to the end of their resources. This is just how God deals with men.

VERSE 17. *They brought their cattle unto Joseph.* This was an advance upon the money, but it only proved to be another temporary palliative. We might liken the people who brought their cattle to those living under the law of Moses. A sacrificial system was there added to the principle of merit. *For horses, and for the flocks, and for the cattle of the herds, and for the asses.* Horses and asses were both unclean animals, useful for work, but unfit for sacrifice. Their addition here to flocks and herds warns us that uncleanness is present in any approach to God that is made on any other ground but His free grace in Christ. *He fed them with bread for all their cattle for that year.* The surrender of their cattle provided them temporarily with food, just as we might say that the sacrifices of the law temporarily sustained the spiritual life of Old Testament Israel.

VERSE 18. *When that year was ended.* The period during which the law was in force came to an end.

We will not hide it from my lord. The way to blessing is to confess one's needs to the Saviour.

Our money is spent. All attempts to buy salvation fail us.

My lord also hath our herds of cattle. Toil and sacrifice can never give permanent satisfaction.

There is not ought left in the sight of my lord. The sinner is brought by grace to realise that he has nothing that he can offer to God in exchange for eternal life.

' Nothing in my hand I bring,
Simply to Thy cross I cling.'

But our bodies, and our lands. That is to say, ourselves. The lands are the picture of the ground of the heart, which can bring forth thorns and thistles (Heb. 6. 8), or be sown with the good seed of the Word of life (Mt. 13. 19-23). Christ wants nothing from us, but requires us to surrender ourselves into His hands, so that He can take the control from our incompetent grasp and bring us safe to eternal life.

' Just as I am, without one plea
But that Thy blood was shed for me,
And that Thou bidd'st me come to Thee,
O Lamb of God, I come.'

VERSE 19. *Wherefore shall we die.* There is no answer to this question. God Himself asks it, and implies that it has no answer (Ezek. 18. 31).

Buy us and our land for bread. This is exactly what the Lord Jesus has done. We are not our own, we are bought with a price (1 Cor. 6. 20). The price was the life blood of the

Son of God (1 Pet. 18. 19). Having bought us He at once gives us the Bread that comes down from heaven which feeds us with life everlasting.

We and our land will be servants unto Pharaoh. Every man who is brought by regeneration to receive the bread of life becomes at the same time a servant of God. No man can be justified by faith without entering the service of Christ (Acts 26. 15-18). Pharaoh thenceforth took responsibility for the people. Many of them continued to till the same land as before, but now they did it for Pharaoh with the assurance of being maintained. Uncertainty and anxiety gave place to security. *Give us seed.* The heavenly Joseph provides us with the seed of the Word of life which we may sow in our hearts (Mt. 13. 3).

That we may live and not die. The Egyptians realised that life and death were at stake. Many sinners close their eyes and hearts to the far greater issue of eternal life and eternal death which confronts them all.

That the land be not desolate. Nothing is more desolate than the heart that is dead in trespasses and sins, having no hope and without God in the world (Eph. 2. 1, 12).

VERSE 20. *Joseph bought all the land of Egypt for Pharaoh.* The Lord Jesus Christ bought the whole world back into the possession of the Father for the sake of the treasure of the elect which was hidden in it (Mt. 13. 44).

Sold every man his field. They gave their land to Pharaoh in order to obtain food and preserve their lives. In the same way the repenting sinner hands his life over to Christ in order that he may preserve it and obtain the Bread of life (Lk. 17. 33). *The famine prevailed over them,* just as it prevailed over the prodigal son (Lk. 15. 14-18). Every sinner starves spiritually, but he does not become aware of what is wrong until he is convicted of sin by the Holy Ghost. *The land became Pharaoh's.* In the same way the heart and life of the sinner, being redeemed by Christ, return on repentance and faith to the possession of his Sovereign and Creator.

VERSE 21. *He removed them to cities.* He made them secure. Thus Christ gives security and assurance to the believer and makes him a member of the new Jerusalem, the city of God (Eph. 2. 19; Rev. 21. 2). There is another reading in the Septuagint Greek version, the Samaritan recension and the Vulgate Latin. They all say, ' Made slaves of them '. Every man is a slave. He is either the servant of sin or he is set free from sin and enslaved to righteousness (Rom. 6. 16-18). The Egyptians, though made slaves to Pharaoh, were made free from their own anxieties and cares.

From one end of the borders of Egypt even to the other thereof. The believer is as far as it is possible to be from his former unbelieving state. He is alive from the dead (Eph. 5. 14), and a new creature in Christ Jesus (2 Cor. 5. 17; Gal. 6. 15).

VERSE 22. This verse gives us a small picture within a picture. The priests were heathen and the exception of their land from the sale shows their privilege and power. Egypt was priest-ridden, as is so often the case in a country where priests form a class or order. Yet in this verse they may well be intended by the Holy Spirit to be a picture of the priesthood of all believers. We believers have a goodly portion assigned us of our heavenly Pharaoh and Sovereign. Our portion is Jesus Himself, Whom God delivered up for us all (Rom. 8. 32). God gave us His only begotten Son (Jo. 3. 16), and we feed on Him in our hearts by faith with thanksgiving. We do not sell our lands nor anything else. God takes nothing from us, but gives us all.

VERSE 23. The main narrative about the people as a whole is resumed in this verse.

I have bought you this day and your land for Pharaoh. These might be the words of Christ to His people. ' I have redeemed thee, thou art Mine ' (Isa. 43. 1). Christ has bought us, not with corruptible things such as silver and gold, but with His own precious blood (1 Pet. 1. 18). We have been brought back to God, that He may take the pleasure in us which He intended when we were created.

Lo, here is seed for you. The seed of the Word is entrusted by Christ to all that He has bought, so that they may go out and sow it by the Gospel in men's hearts.

VERSE 24. Here is a picture of our bountiful God, Who gives back to His people four-fifths of what He has redeemed to be His own. The increase of the seed of the Word is seen in our own spiritual lives. Notice the five sections into which this increase is divided. (1) The fifth part goes to Pharaoh. This is the first charge and has priority over everything. Our first duty in life is to give God Himself His due in worship, praise and prayer. (2) The second of the five parts is ' for seed of the field ', that is to say, for evangelisation and the spread of the Gospel. This is our next duty. If the first may be expressed in the words, ' Hallowed be Thy Name,' this is equivalent to ' Thy Kingdom come, Thy will be done '. (3) After this the increase is *for your food.* ' Give us this day our daily bread.' After the duty of evangelisation our next is to feed upon Christ in His Word and build ourselves up in our most holy faith (Jude 20). (4) When we are sufficiently built up ourselves, our next duty is to feed those who are of the household of faith, *them of your households.* (5) Lastly are mentioned *your little ones,* though they are not to be thought of as the least important. They represent both actual children and those who are young in the faith.

VERSE 25. *Thou hast saved our lives.* Every believer looks gratefully to

Christ Who has done this very thing. He has redeemed us from the curse of the law (Gal. 3. 13) and from eternal destruction (Mt. 25. 41).

Let us find grace in the sight of my lord. By grace are we saved through faith, and that not of ourselves, it is the gift of God (Eph. 2. 8). We need constantly more grace for the life of faith day by day, and we may find it by coming boldly to the throne of grace to find grace to help in time of need (Heb. 4. 16).

We will be Pharaoh's servants. All those who find and enjoy the grace of God become thereby His servants. No one can be saved without entering His service. When the Lord Jesus said, ' Come unto Me ', He also said, ' Take My yoke upon you ', but the yoke is easy and the burden light (Mt. 11. 28-30).

VERSE 26. *Joseph made it a law over the land of Egypt unto this day, that Pharaoh should have the fifth part.* In the same way the heavenly Joseph makes it a law under the Gospel that God should have His part and tells us that the first and great commandment is that we should love God with all our heart.

Except the land of the priests only. This phrase reminds us that there is a company of priests in the world who are separate from all others. This is the Christian church, which is a royal priesthood (1 Pet. 2. 9), sanctified and separated to the service of God. Their hearts and possessions are God's from the moment of their conversion.

VERSE 27. *Israel.* This means the people of Israel, and this seems to be the first place in the Bible in which the name is used in this sense. *In the land of Egypt.* The Israel of God in this Gospel age is living in the world.

In the country of Goshen. At the same time Israel lives in a spiritual country of its own, unknown to the unconverted, where it enjoys fellowship with God by faith.

They had possessions therein. In the land of Goshen the Israel of God possesses the riches of His grace, the hope of the world to come and the indwelling Spirit of God.

Grew, and multiplied exceedingly. It is here in the land of Goshen in the heart of Egypt, before it moves out in resurrection to possess the world to come, that Israel grows and multiplies. The church has grown from the initial few into a company of millions. When all the separate generations of Christian people are brought together on the day of resurrection, they will comprise a great multitude that no man can number (Rev. 7. 9). On that day the number of the elect will be filled up and the church consummated, and there will be no more growth and multiplication.

VERSE 28. *Seventeen years.* This was only a small portion of Jacob's life, but it was long enough to enable him to look back over the whole of it and realise that God was bringing His purpose to pass. These seventeen years were a kind of crown to Jacob's life. During them he enjoyed the presence of Joseph and their peace and restfulness must have been a very suitable preparation for his falling asleep and passing in less than an instant of time to a blaze of resurrection glory.

An hundred forty and seven years. This was thirty-three years fewer than Isaac and twenty-eight fewer than Abraham (25. 7; 35. 28), but it is a satisfying number. It is 7 x 7 x 3, factors that speak of perfection of spiritual life and of God's quickening creative power. The figures seem to tell us that the Holy Spirit had completed His work in Jacob's life.

VERSE 29. *Israel must die.* Since Adam's disobedience this imperative has applied to all men (Rom. 5. 12). Two only have escaped it by the intervention of God (Gen. 5. 24; 2 Ki. 2. 11). Believers living at the end of the world will also escape it (1 Cor. 15. 51, 52; 1 Thess. 4. 17). Till then it comes alike to saint and sinner.

*Put, I pray thee, thy hand under
my thigh.* See on 24. 2.

Deal kindly and truly with me.
Jacob would not know whether this
were done or not, but he had a great
interest in the doing of it. Notice
that a man's honour and interest are
independent of what he himself feels
or is aware of. A man may be dis-
graced in the eyes of God and man
after his death without knowing it.

Bury me not, I pray thee, in Egypt.
This is a different attitude from the
modern one, which claims that their
place of burial makes no difference to
the dead.

VERSE 30. This is what it means to
be gathered to one's fathers. Notice
how burial is thought of as naturally
following death. It may be that some
who have died with Christ (Col. 2.
20) have never been buried with Him
by baptism (Rom. 6. 4; Col. 2. 12).

VERSE 31. *Israel bowed himself upon
the bed's head.* ' Bowed himself '
means ' worshipped '. In the Septuagint Greek version this statement appears as, ' He worshipped upon the
end of his staff ', and it is in this form
that it is carried over from the Septuagint into the Epistle to the Hebrews
(Heb. 11. 21). The reason for the
difference is as follows: no vowels are
written in Hebrew, but consonants
only, and the consonants of the words
for ' bed ' and ' staff ' are identical.
The unwritten vowels are different in
either word, but the sense and context alone can tell the reader which
meaning is correct. When the Massoretes came to add vowel-points to
the text, they inserted those which
make the word mean ' bed ', while the
Septuagint translators had rendered it
as ' staff '. As the consonants only
are inspired, the word can be given
either meaning without affecting inspiration. A moment's thought will
show us that both meanings are correct. The old man was in bed, probably on a mattress on the ground.
In order to kneel in worship, he drew
himself up at the head of the bed on

to his knees with the help of his staff,
which we can think of as having been
resting beside him. With his failing
strength Israel acknowledges the God
Who had led him his life through.

CHAPTER 48

THIS chapter gives us the story of
the blessing by Jacob of Ephraim
and Manasseh, the two sons of Joseph.
We find in it another illustration and
confirmation of the principle which
appeared in the case of Isaac and
Ishmael, and again of Jacob and Esau,
and again of Pharez and Zarah. The
younger was in each case preferred
before the elder. These are examples
of the principle that ' many that are
first shall be last; and the last shall
be first ' (Mt. 19. 30). Values in God's
sight are reversed from what they are
in the world (see 1 Sam. 2. 4-8; Lk.
1. 52, 53; 1 Cor. 1. 27-29).

VERSE 1. *Thy father is sick.* This is
a euphemism for ' dying '. The message obviously meant that he was
mortally sick.

He took with him his two sons.
Joseph intended that his father should
bless them. Two quite separate suggestions are made to our minds by
these words. (1) The heavenly Joseph
brings us His children (Heb. 2. 13) to
His Father for His blessing, which is
readily given us for Christ's sake. (2)
Joseph sought for his sons the blessing
of a dying man. The efficacy of the
blessing was connected in his mind
with his father's approaching death.
In the same way all true blessing is
bound up with the death of the Lord
Jesus Christ.

VERSE 2. *One told Jacob.* No one
needs to tell God our heavenly Father
when we come to Him seeking a blessing.

Israel strengthened himself. Our
heavenly Father has no need to do
this. His strength is always perfect
and all His resources are at our disposal. *Sat upon the bed.* This does
not mean that he sat, in the sense in

which we moderns should use the expression, on the side of a raised bed with his feet on the ground, but that he drew himself up from a lying to a sitting posture on the mattress which acted as bed.

Verse 3. Jacob begins by recalling God's goodness and blessing to him in the past. This is the proper place on which to base all service to others. *God Almighty appeared unto me.* This was the beginning of Jacob's spiritual experience, as it is the beginning of every man's. Until God appears to us, we are dead in trespasses and sins, and we have neither the will nor the power to rise to a life of righteousness and enter the service of God. The initiative is always with God. Now He appears to us in Christ through the Gospel by the convicting power of the Holy Spirit.

At Luz. Jacob does not say ' At Bethel '. Luz was the old Canaanite name of the place. It only became Bethel at the time of, and because of, God's appearance to Jacob there. God did not wait to appear till Jacob had made the place into a Bethel. He came to Jacob when he was still a sinner in the old life. While we were yet sinners, Christ died for the ungodly (Rom. 5. 6-8). He came to call sinners to repentance (Mt. 9. 13), and He comes to us just as we are, Himself to effect the change which we are powerless even to begin.

In the land of Canaan. God not only appeared to Jacob at Luz when he was still living the old death-life of sin, but He came to him ' in the land of Canaan ', that is to say, He broke into the course of his ordinary every-day life in the world. He came to meet him just as he was. In the same way He comes to us in Christ right into the course of our life in this world, that He may bless us and save us.

Blessed me. God never appears to us without blessing us, that is to say, He not only bestows life upon us, but makes us fruitful and gives us the power to multiply and be means and channels of blessing to others. If a man is blessed, his life is turned outwards towards the service of others.

Verse 4. Jacob recalls four promises made to him by God not only at Bethel, where perhaps they were all implied, but during the whole course of his life. They show that he was conscious of being the heir of Abraham and Isaac and that the promises made to them applied also to him.

I will make thee fruitful. This is the first promise. It was fulfilled first in the birth of Jacob's twelve sons and of the growing family which had reached seventy by the time of the migration into Egypt, afterwards in the increase of the nation, the birth of Christ and the ingathering of the Church. God has promised to make us fruitful also, the fruit being found in Gal. 5. 22, 23.

Multiply thee. This is the second promise. It was fulfilled in the largeness of Israel's increase (Ex. 1. 7) and in the enormous numberless multitude of the redeemed (Rev. 7. 9), who are children of Jacob because they are Christ's (Gal. 3. 29). God promises to multiply us also, so that many may come to believe through our testimony.

A multitude of people. ' People ' means ' peoples ' or ' nations '. The promise was fulfilled typically in the twelve tribes of Israel and will be finally fulfilled in the nations of them which are saved (Rev. 21. 24), who will comprise the numberless multitude of the redeemed.

Will give this land to thy seed after thee. On the meaning of the gift of the land and its manner of fulfilment see on 13. 15. The natural descendants of Jacob possessed the land from the time of Joshua till that of the Assyrian and Babylonian captivities and later they inhabited it in subjection to Gentile nations up till the destruction of Jerusalem in A.D. 70. A nucleus of them has recently taken possession of part of it in independence. The land is the possession of the spiritual seed in the sense that the great events of redemption on which their salvation depends took place there.

An everlasting possession. See on 13. 15. This cannot be taken literally because Palestine will perish when the earth is destroyed by fire (2 Pet. 3. 10-12). It is everlasting because of the everlasting redemption that was accomplished in it and because it is the type of the new earth, or new land (Isa. 65. 17; 66. 2; 2 Pet. 3. 13), which will be the everlasting possession and dwelling-place of the true Israel. This new land is described by the prophets in the geography of the old.

VERSE 5. *And now thy two sons.* The The result of receiving blessing oneself is to pass it on to others. *Are mine.* Jacob means that Ephraim and Manasseh would receive inheritance as if they were his own sons. Thus there was no tribe of Joseph, but there were tribes of Ephraim and Manasseh respectively.

As Reuben and Simeon. Ephraim and Manasseh were not only to count as sons of Jacob, they were to be his eldest sons. Thus we too, though born in Egypt (which typifies the sinful world), receive the Spirit of adoption and become sons of God for Christ's sake (Rom. 8. 15; Gal. 4. 5, 6; Eph. 1. 5).

VERSE 6. Jacob means that Joseph's own name would be perpetuated in those of his sons, and that the descendants of Ephraim and Manasseh would be known by those two names in their tribal life, not by that of Joseph. This arrangement ensured a double portion to Joseph. He sank his name in order to obtain the portion, just as the Lord Jesus lost all in order that He might enjoy for ever the inheritance of those who are given to Him by the Father.

VERSE 7. This moving reference to Rachel and her death is introduced by Jacob to supply the reason why he adopted Joseph's sons and appointed Joseph a double portion. His affection

was so strongly set upon Joseph because he was the son of his beloved Rachel, whom he had lost in such tragic circumstances. In something of the same way God's love is set on us the more dearly and especially as He remembers the death of His beloved Son, Who did not like Rachel come a little short of Bethlehem, but passed on through it to Calvary.

VERSE 8. *Who are these?* We are not to suppose that Jacob did not know who they were, or that he had never seen them during the seventeen years that he passed in Egypt. He probably saw them frequently. The question was (a) formal, a preliminary to the blessing, and (b) an expression of wonder and joy on the lines of verse 11.

VERSE 9. This verse typifies the transaction that will take place on the day of resurrection and glory. On that day the Saviour will bring near to His Father all the children (Heb. 2. 13) whom He will have acquired in the world, and the Father will give them His eternal blessing. ' Come, ye blessed of my Father ' (Mt. 25. 34). This is anticipated, as it were, in the case of every child of God at his conversion when he is brought near by Christ to the Father and receives His blessing.

VERSE 10. *The eyes of Israel were dim for age.* His natural powers had been taken from him. He relies upon wisdom in his acts of blessing. We too must rely upon the wisdom of God (Prov. 3. 5). *He brought them near unto him.* So Christ has brought us near unto God (Eph. 2. 13). *He kissed them, and embraced them.* These were tokens of his love. In the same way the father runs to meet the returning prodigal, falls on his neck and kisses him (Lk. 15. 20).

VERSE 11. The apparently irreparable loss was turned into a double gain. Thus in a sense we may reverently say that the total abandonment by God

D

of His beloved Son on the cross has not only brought Him back Himself in resurrection but a countless number with Him, begotten to life as a result of His sorrow and travail. It is certainly true that humanity, having lost all in Adam and never able of its own effort to recover it, has received back double in Christ for all it lost.

VERSE 12. *Joseph brought them out from between his knees.* They were young men of over twenty. They had evidently been standing in front of their father, whose hands perhaps had been on their shoulders or on their breasts.

He bowed himself with his face to the earth. This is the attitude that we must take if we desire God's blessing.

VERSE 13. Notice the great care that Joseph took to obtain the blessing in the manner that he wanted and the order in which he thought it ought to be given. We are sometimes like him.

Brought them near unto him. The Lord Jesus Christ has brought us near to God so that we can obtain His blessing. We also can bring others near in prayer and lift them up, as it were, before God.

VERSE 14. Israel showed great wisdom. As he was blind, or nearly so, he must have guessed that Joseph would place his sons in the position in which as a matter of fact he did. He must also have been closely in touch with God in prayer, so that the Spirit could reveal to him the will of God in the matter of the blessing. Once again, as in the case of Ishmael and Isaac and in that of Esau and Jacob, the natural order was reversed. Once again God teaches us plainly that in spiritual things the order and values of the world are reversed.

Manasseh was the firstborn. He and his father both expected the better blessing on the grounds of his birth. They were relying on nature instead of on grace. If it had been possible for Manasseh to have grace not to expect

greater blessing than his brother, who knows whether he would not have obtained it?

VERSE 15. *He blessed Joseph.* He blessed him in the persons of his sons, with whom he was considered to be one. Thus we are all one in Christ Jesus (Gal. 3. 28), and the blessing which belongs to Christ, infinite and abundant as it is, is ours because we belong to Him. His blessing was not His own. It was an invocation of God's blessing upon the two lads. We ourselves have no power to bless, though language is sometimes used which suggests that there are human beings who possess such power. All we can rightly say is, ' *The Lord* bless you and keep you,' or ' To *God's* gracious mercy and protection we commit you.'

God. Israel names three past manifestations of God's grace, which were (a) proofs of His power and willingness to bless the young men, and (b) illustrations of the forms which His blessing would take.

(1) *Before whom my fathers Abraham and Isaac did walk.* The first encouragement to expect God's blessing lay in the fact that God had called the family and gave to Abraham and Isaac His fellowship and His blessing. Anyone who loves and clings to the God of his parents may confidently expect a continuance of blessing.

(2) *The God which fed me all my life long unto this day.* Here was a testimony to God's keeping power. In the early barren years at home, in the hard toil of Padan-aram, in the sorrows and dangers of the family life in Canaan, and in the last restful years in Goshen God had never failed to provide. Dangers might threaten and famines deprive of the ordinary means of sustenance, but God's care never failed. Israel said this to show the young men that all their lives through, whatever happens, they could rely on their faithful God.

VERSE 16. (3) *The Angel which redeemed me from all evil.* Notice first that God and the Angel are identical, just as they were at Penuel (32. 30; Hos. 12. 4). The Angel is the second Person of the Holy Trinity, the pre-incarnate Christ. The Angel is rightly named as the Redeemer. Jacob may have been thinking of protection from the wrath of Esau or the craftiness of Laban, or preservation from destruction at the hands of the Canaanites, but the Holy Spirit by introducing the word ' redeemed ' calls attention to the redemption which is in Christ Jesus (Rom. 3. 24), Who on the cross delivered His people from the power of Satan, sin and death at the cost of His own blood.

Bless the lads. The three facts which Israel has mentioned imply the nature of the blessing which he wished the lads to have. All is illustrative of Gospel blessing. Our blessing in Christ consists (1) of walking before God in holiness and righteousness all the days of our life (Lk. 1. 75), an experience, that is to say, of regeneration and sanctification. This is based upon (2) God's provision of spiritual nourishment all our lives through, as He feeds us with the heavenly manna in His Word. This provision again is made possible by (3) the redemption which is in Christ Jesus, by which we were brought from Satan and sin to be God's people. We may contrast this blessing of Ephraim and Manasseh with the blessing of Pharaoh described in 47. 7-10. There we have Jacob, the man of weak faith, here we have Israel, the man with a new nature. There he gave the blessing himself, and it had no effect beyond a momentary impression. Here he commends the young men to God's blessing, which finds its fulfilment down many generations. There Jacob says that his days were few and evil. Here Israel says that he has been fed all his life long and redeemed from all evil. We can have no clearer contrast between the viewpoints and acts of nature on the one side and grace on the other.

Let my name be named on them. Here we have another important principle in connection with the blessing. The young men were given the name of Israel, Abraham and Isaac. They were blessed for the sake of another and were incorporated into another. In the same way the Name of the Lord Jesus Christ is named upon all His people. This means that we share His blessing, His glory and His inheritance, that we enter the presence of God in His Name and on His authority, and that we belong to Him and are bound to His service.

Let them grow into a multitude. Increase is the fundamental feature of blessing.

In the midst of the earth. This means in the midst of the land. To us the expression would mean the planet, but no such conception existed in those days. Ephraim and Manasseh occupied inheritances in the centre of Palestine.

Verse 17. Joseph wanted God's blessing to be given on natural grounds. This is never the case. It is always given on grounds of grace. We too are apt to misunderstand God's ways and to be displeased when we see the hand of God descend in blessing on what we suppose to be the wrong head. In such cases it is always we who are wrong and God Who is right.

Verse 18. *Not so, my father.* How often in effect do we say this to God. Joseph did not wish to dispute his father's expressed will, but he thought he was making a mistake due to his blindness. We express our belief in God's almighty power and wisdom, but we do not always trust Him as if He possessed them.

This is the firstborn. Joseph thought that blessing ought to be given on the ground of natural birth, but those who receive Christ and believe on His Name are not born of blood, but of God (Jo. 1. 13).

Put thy right hand on his head. Joseph in effect tried to dictate to his father who should receive the greater blessing. Are we not sometimes also surprised when God does not bless those whom we expect in the way that we expect?

VERSE 19. *His father refused.* What a good thing that God sometimes refuses our requests, so often made in ignorance.

He also shall become a people. This was fulfilled in the development and history of the tribe of Manasseh.

He also shall be great. The tribe of Manasseh became in fact so great that it was divided into two halves and obtained a double inheritance, part west and part east of Jordan (Josh. 17. 5).

His younger brother shall be greater than he. In this fact we see (1) the working of the principle of the reversal of values in the spiritual sphere, and (2) the type of Israel's seed. The elder brother was Israel after the flesh (1 Cor. 10. 18), the natural and typical Israel of the Old Testament. He became a people, and he became great. No single people has exercised such an immense influence on the history and life of the world as have the Jews. They were called of God to a special covenant relationship with Himself, and their history was a preparation for the coming of Christ. But the younger brother, the new and true Israel of God (Gal. 6. 16), the Christian church, is far greater than the old Israel. The relationship of all its members with God is spiritual and eternal, it is the bride of Christ, the new and heavenly Jerusalem, the subject of the prophets' promises and predictions, known of God from eternity past, and destined to show forth His kindness and glorify His Name throughout a triumphant eternity.

His seed shall become a multitude of nations. For ' multitude ' the Hebrew says ' fulness ', as we see in the margins of our Bibles. This is a most important phrase. The expression occurs no where else in the Old Testament, but it is taken up by the apostle Paul and used of the true Israel in Rom. 11. 25. If we can determine its meaning here as used of Ephraim, we shall understand the reference in Rom. 11. 25. Now in the later history of Israel the nation becomes divided on the death of Solomon into two kingdoms. The southern consisted of the tribes of Judah, Simeon and Benjamin and was known as Judah. Often in the prophets however this northern section was known as Ephraim. See for instance Hos. 4. 17-14. 9, where Ephraim is often identified with Israel and contrasted with Judah. This means that Ephraim was the outstanding tribe in the northern section, the nucleus and basis of the whole, with which the other tribes came to be identified and into which they were gathered. Thus the whole northern kingdom could be spoken of as Ephraim. In the same way in Rom. 11. 25 the apostle means that Israel is the nucleus and basis of the Christian church, Gentile believers becoming identified with her and gathered into her, indeed grafted into her (Rom. 11. 24), so that the whole church, though predominantly Gentile, is called the Israel of God, just as the whole northern kingdom was called Ephraim. Thus in the development of the fulness of nations the type of the older Israel and the younger Israel, which we have already noticed in this verse, is continued. Manasseh is the type of the Old Testament Israel, Jahweh's firstborn (Ex. 4. 22), and Ephraim is the type of the younger Israel of God, the Christian church, which is greater than the elder and becomes the fulness of nations.

VERSE 20. *He blessed them that day.* That day of blessing made a difference to their lives and to those of their children ever afterwards. A similar difference is made in our own lives when God blesses us on the day of our conversion. This is the manifestation in time of His blessing given to us in Christ Jesus before the world began (Eph. 1. 3, 4).

In thee shall Israel bless. Ephraim and Manasseh were to be so blessed, that others would take them as the example of blessing. No greater wish could be entertained and no greater prayer offered than that a people or an individual should be like the one or the other. Happy are we if we are so blessed by God that others can think of nothing better than to share our blessing.

God make thee as Ephraim and as Manasseh. The ultimate pattern is Jesus Himself. Our likeness to Him is not only the subject of a pious wish or prayer, but will become an eternal reality (Rom. 8. 29).

He set Ephraim before Manasseh, just as God brings down the mighty from their seat and exalts the humble and meek (Lk. 1. 52), and just as He has set the new Israel before the old.

VERSE 21. *Behold, I die.* He had served his generation and was to rest in peace until the last day when he will rise again in glory.

God shall be with you. Israel does not mean that his own death would cut him off from his eternal fellowship with God, or break his relationship with Him. God is his God and is the God of the living, not the God of the dead (Mt. 22. 32). He means that notwithstanding his own death God will continue to be with Joseph and the whole family.

Bring you again into the land of your fathers. Joseph himself only reached it in his coffin (Ex. 13. 19; Josh. 24. 32), nor did Ephraim and Manasseh ever get there in person. But their children reached it. Even so God will be with us. Indeed He is with us, dwelling in our hearts by faith (Eph. 3. 17). He will bring us again to the land of our fathers, the new heaven and the new land wherein dwelleth righteousness (2 Pet. 3. 13), promised to us in Christ, for which our fathers looked. We shall indeed be fully restored to God and receive back more than we ever lost in Adam.

VERSE 22. *One portion above thy brethren.* In the same way the heavenly Joseph is anointed with the oil of gladness above His fellows (Ps. 45. 7;

Heb. 1. 9). Jesus Christ is supreme, and has been given the Name which is above every name (Phil. 2. 9).

Which I took out of the hand of the Amorite with my sword and with my bow. The Amorite typifies Satan. In Christ God won the victory over Satan, despoiled him of his prey and bestowed it on the victorious Saviour Himself. We believers are that portion. 'The Lord's portion is His people' (Deut. 32. 9), and we have been given as God's gift to Christ (Jo. 6. 37).

CHAPTER 49

IN this important chapter we have Jacob's blessing of his sons followed by his death. The blessing of Judah is Messianic in character. Joseph's blessing maintains the typical character in which Joseph has appeared in the narrative. It uses language of Joseph which points to Christ. The remainder of the blessings have a literal fulfilment in the history of Old Testament Israel in Palestine but in addition they are often typical of spiritual truths.

VERSE 1. *Jacob called unto his sons.* The occasion and contents of the message show that he was charged by God with it for his sons. They did not ask for a blessing. Jacob took the initiative. In the same way we are charged with a message from God to the people of the world, and ought to call to them to hear it.

Gather yourselves together. Jacob's message was to the whole family considered as a unit.

That which shall befall you in the last days. The message did not consist entirely of blessing. There was disappointment and even cursing in some of it. Like the sons of Jacob mankind has a double destiny (Mt. 25. 34, 41). The expression 'the last days' in the Bible is usually equivalent to 'in the Messianic age'. The chief part of Jacob's message has to do with the coming of Christ.

Verse 2. *Gather yourselves together*. We also are not to forsake the assembling of ourselves together (Heb. 10. 25).

And hear. We too should have a ready listening ear to all that God has to say to us in His Word.

Hearken unto Israel your father. We too must listen to our heavenly Father. Indeed all mankind ought to listen to God, and it would be to their happiness if they did so.

Verse 3. This verse tells us what Reuben at first was and might have remained. In the five characteristics mentioned in this verse he was a picture of the Lord Jesus Christ.

My firstborn. Christ is made God's firstborn, higher than the kings of the earth (Ps. 89. 27). This means that He is God's heir (Heb. 1. 2), and that all sovereignty is concentrated in His hands. It is God's purpose that we should honour the Son as we honour the Father (Jo. 5. 23).

My might. Jacob meant that the birth of Reuben was the manifestation or evidence of his might. In the same way the resurrection of Christ was the manifestation of God's mighty strength, the exceeding greatness of His power available for believers (Eph. 1. 19).

The beginning of my strength. Jacob implies that his strength consists in his family of children. In the same way the power of God is seen first in creation, but particularly in resurrection. Christ is the firstborn from the dead (Rev. 1. 5), and we who are Christ's at His coming will also be the objects of God's great power in resurrection (1 Cor. 15. 23).

The excellency of dignity. The meaning of the Hebrew word here translated ' dignity ' seems to be pre-eminence. Thus Christ has the excellency of pre-eminence. He is before all things, and the purpose of His resurrection was that in all things He might have the pre-eminence (Col. 1. 17, 18).

The excellency of power. In this fifth and last characteristic Reuben is also a picture of Christ, for all power is given unto Christ in heaven and on earth (Mt. 28. 18). He now sits on His Father's throne (Rev. 3. 21) at the right hand of God (Ps. 110. 1) exercising His conquering power.

Verse 4. This verse tells us of Reuben's failure, and we see him as utterly unlike the Lord Jesus Christ as the last verse showed him to be like Him.

Unstable as water. Reuben proved unreliable. He could not be trusted. His moral principles melted and flowed away like a stream of water. In contrast to this we are to be grounded and firm and rooted in Christ (Col. 1. 23; 2. 7).

Thou shalt not excel. Instability brings at least mediocrity and at worst failure. If we are of a double mind, we must expect nothing from Christ (Jas. 1. 7, 8).

Thou wentest up to thy father's bed. Reuben harboured an evil design and quite deliberately put himself in the way of temptation. If he had kept out of Bilhah's tent and refused to entertain the thought of going there, he might have had an honoured place in the family and nation. If Joseph knew what was right (39. 9), Reuben must also have known.

Then defiledst thou it. Reuben not only put himself in the way of temptation, but yielded to it. He gave way to lust and carried through his design to the end (35. 22). He was carried away of his own lust and enticed (Jas. 1. 14). Notice the word ' defile ' used to express adultery. Sin of this sort is regarded throughout the Bible as being unclean, and the apostle Paul uses the word ' uncleanness ' to describe it, contrasting it with holiness (Rom. 6. 19; 1 Thess. 4. 3-5). *He went up to my couch*. This may be an emphatic summing up and conclusion of the last two clauses, but the marginal reading seems to make the better sense. It is ' My couch is gone '. Read thus, the sentence is a powerful climax. It expresses the appalling result of Reuben's act, a permanent loss and damage, the severing of his father's marriage relationship with Bilhah. Thus inherent instability of character led Reuben to commit sin which resulted in permanent damage to an innocent party. Here in this verse the inspiring Spirit with consummate skill and creative power has pictured fallen human nature as it reveals itself in every member of Adam's race.

VERSE 5. *Simeon and Levi are brethren.* This means that they were united in the act of murder and cruelty to which Jacob refers. As so often happens, there was a conspiracy of like-minded wicked men.

Instruments of cruelty are in their habitations. The instruments were their swords. These were in their habitations, ready to hand, habitually used. They did not have to go out to buy or borrow swords. They kept them close at hand, cruelty being a regular practice with them. Thus their action against Shechem (34. 25-27) was an expression of their habitual nature, as is usually the case with sinners. Thus where Reuben failed through lust, Simeon and Levi failed through violence and cruelty.

VERSE 6. *O my soul, come not thou into their secret.* This means, 'I will not come into their secret'. 'My soul' (Heb. *nephesh*) means 'I myself'. Jacob here speaks for all righteous men when he refuses to join the secret designs of the wicked. The whole sentence gives the impression of the darkness in which a sinful design is conceived. It is kept secret in the recesses of a dark heart from all eyes but those of God. Simeon and Levi plotted the murder of the inhabitants of Shechem. No doubt they felt insulted over Dinah, but they may well have thought it a good opportunity to seize the Shechemites' property. *Unto their assembly.* A sinful action may come from a whole group.

Mine honour. The poetical address by Jacob to his honour means that to join the assembly of sinners is inconsistent with honour. True honour lies in faith and righteousness.

Be not thou united. To join with sinners in their wicked schemes means to be one with them. *In their anger.* Anger here is equivalent to self-will. There is a righteous anger, which is properly exercised by believers on proper occasions. The Lord is spoken of as being angry once only during His life in the flesh (Mk. 3. 5). This shows how sparingly anger should be felt and resorted to, though sin and wickedness ought on occasion to arouse it. At the same time we have the warning, 'Be ye angry and sin not' (Eph. 4. 26). Anger and sin are too close together in those who still possess a fallen nature for the utmost caution not to be used. With us anger is usually equivalent to self-will, as it was with Simeon and Levi.

They slew a man. The anger resulted in murder, as it so often does if unrestrained. Indeed our Lord tells us that anger and murder are identical. The expression 'a man' may be put for many men. If it refers to only one, the man meant must be Shechem (34. 26).

They digged down a wall. Their self-will resulted in the destruction of property. This same rule of violence prevails in the world today.

VERSE 7. *Cursed be their anger.* Sin brings the curse of God. The smallest disobedience to the law of God inevitably calls down God's curse (Deut. 27. 15-26), and God's curse leads equally inevitably to everlasting fire (Mt. 25. 41). There would be no hope for sinners if God had not intervened, but Christ has redeemed us from the curse of the law, being made a curse for us (Gal. 3. 13).

Their wrath, for it was cruel. Fierce anger and cruel wrath are frequent products of the fallen human heart. They dominate the world today.

I will divide them in Jacob, and scatter them in Israel. Notice that the sin of Simeon and Levi affected their descendants for many generations. The effects of sin can never be confined to the individual sinner. Probably every sin committed brings suffering on many who are not responsible for it. The curse which fell on the two cruel brothers was passed on to their descendants, just as Adam's curse came down to the whole race. In Simeon's case there seems to have been no relief. We hear little of this tribe after the account of their obtaining their inheritance (Josh. 19. 1-9). This inheritance was entirely confined within that of Judah, so that the tribe became absorbed in Judah and apparently lost as a separate entity. Possibly the inheritance of Simeon was not continuous. They may have been allotted separate towns and areas at various points within the inheritance of Judah. It will be noticed that in Josh. 19. 1-9 there is no account of any boundaries. Thus Simeon was divided. The Levites also had no inheritance of their own, but they were scattered in cities throughout all the tribes of Israel. The effect of the curse remained, but it was turned into a blessing. The Levites were given the privilege of priesthood and of service about the sacred things. The place that they occupied in Israel is an illustration of the principle expressed in Rom. 8. 28.

VERSE 8. In this and the following four verses we find the blessing of Judah, which is Messianic in character, Judah being the ancestor of Jesus Christ. In this verse we have three predictions about Judah, which are all fulfilled in our Lord Jesus Christ. We might call them (1) glory, (2) victory, and (3) sovereignty.

Thou art he whom thy brethren shall praise. The name Judah means 'praise'. Jesus Christ is the eternal object of His people's praise. Those whom He redeems are His brethren (Heb. 2. 12), and they praise Him for ever for His love, mercy, power and victory, for His willingness to redeem and the cost of redemption. Worthy is the Lamb which was slain to receive power and riches and wisdom and might and honour and glory and blessing (Rev. 5. 12).

Thy hand shall be in the neck of thine enemies. This is a vivid expression for the complete defeat and utter subjugation of the enemies of Christ. Jesus Christ of the tribe of Judah is the eternal conqueror. He won the victory on the cross, not by might, nor by power, but by God's Spirit (Zech. 4. 6). No act of violence could be a victory to God, any more than the crushing of a fly could be accounted a victory for us. The victory was won by love, humility and obedience. He gave Himself to the death, that the people of God might be justified and redeemed and the demands of God's holiness satisfied on their behalf. Now He sits exalted at God's right hand waiting for the victory to be applied in its fulness and the enemies to be made the footstool of His feet (Heb. 10. 13).

Thy father's children shall bow down before thee. This was fulfilled in type when David and his line occupied the throne. Its real and final fulfilment is in the worship of Jesus Christ by the whole company of the redeemed. This takes place imperfectly in this world generation by generation in the heart by faith. In the world to come it will take place fully and eternally. ' Thy father's children ' is an expression that means Israel after the flesh during Old Testament times. In the case of Jesus Christ it means the redeemed church, whose members are all children of God by faith in Him (Gal. 3. 26). In the three statements of this verse we may thus see (1) Christ in His relationship to the church on earth, (2) Christ in His relationship to the world, (3) Christ in His relationship to the church in heaven.

VERSE 9. In this verse we have the description of the Lion of the tribe of Judah (Rev. 5. 5). *Judah is a lion's whelp,* that is to say, young, fierce and irresistible. The Saviour has almighty strength and conquering power. The first of the four Gospels is the one that shows Him most clearly in this royal aspect.

From the prey, my son, thou art gone up. Here we have not only Jacob speaking to his son Judah, but the Father of heaven speaking to His eternal Son, and speaking on the day of His ascension to heaven in glory to take His seat at His Father's right hand. This is the scene depicted in the fifth chapter of the Apocalypse, where Christ appears as the Lion (Rev. 5. 5). Christ returned in triumph from His capture of the prey, having put off from Him principalities and powers, triumphing over them by the cross (Col. 2. 15), leading captivity captive (Eph. 4. 8), and delivering the elect people of God, who had become lost and estranged in Adam.

He stooped down. In this and the following words there is drawn for us the picture of the lion stooping ready to spring on its prey. In the same way the Saviour stooped from heaven, taking upon Him the form of a servant, and being found in fashion as a man (Phil. 2. 7).

He couched as a lion. He bowed down to the ground beneath the load of sin which was laid upon Him by the Father, Who laid on Him the transgressions of us all (Isa. 53. 6). ' O Christ, what burdens bowed Thy head!' He was weighed down and bowed into the dust of death and brought right down to the death, but, though His enemies never knew it and His friends at the time failed to realise it, this bowing down to the depths was only the couching of the lion in the act of springing on the prey. The subjection and couching were the very means of eternal victory.

And as an old lion. It was as the Ancient of Days (Dan. 7. 9) with the wisdom and experience of eternity that Christ undertook the redemption of His people. The strong and eternal Son of God came to our help, stooped to earth, couched beneath the burden and sprang on the prey.

Who shall rouse him up? This means, Who shall raise Him from the couching position when once He had

stooped to spring on the prey? No one could do so, glory to His Name. The devil tried again and again, in the wilderness (Mt. 4. 1-11), through the apostle Peter (Mt. 16. 22, 23) and in the garden of Gethsemane (Mt. 26. 39), but he failed completely. The lion couched to the lowest depths and sprang upon the prey.

VERSE 10. This verse gives us the prediction of the royalty of the tribe of Judah.

The sceptre shall not depart from Judah. The sceptre means the ruling power. The sceptre of Israel first came to Benjamin in the person of Saul the son of Kish, but he forfeited it by disobedience, and it was given to David of Bethlehem, a member of the tribe of Judah, in whose house it remained until the nation was taken captive and lost its independence altogether. After that no king reigned till Christ came. The prophecy therefore means to say that from the time that royalty was vested in David no other tribe would receive it. During all the time that the various dynasties reigned in northern Israel the house of David reigned in Jerusalem, and during the years of exile and subjection the line of the royal house continued in being till it reached Christ.

Nor a lawgiver from between his feet. This statement is parallel to the last. Between the time of Zedekiah and that of Christ there was a line of lawgivers, who did not however exercise their functions because of the condition of the nation. This prophecy has to be taken alongside those which predicted the captivity of the people conditional on disobedience and came true in history because the conditions were fulfilled. The expression ' from between his feet ' means ' from his descendants '.

Until Shiloh come. The meaning of the word Shiloh is not known. It has generally been taken as, and most probably is, a name for the Messiah. The interpretation which we have just given of the two preceding sentences

depends on the view that Shiloh is a
name of Christ. The meaning of the
name however cannot be told for certain. The generality of commentators
from patristic days onwards through
the Reformers have assumed its connection with the root that means
' peace '. Shiloh would thus mean the
Prince of peace. This is a very good
and proper conception (Isa. 9. 6), but
we cannot be certain that it is original.
The Septuagint Greek version read
the Hebrew as if it was differently
pointed and translated ' shelloh ' instead of ' Shiloh '. This means ' he
to whom it belongs ' and is a very
proper name for Christ (Ezek. 21. 27).
The passage would then mean that
royalty would be held in trust by the
tribe of Judah until Christ to Whom
it belonged came to assume it. This
fits the facts of the case and covers
the period of captivity and subjection
more easily. Alternatively it seems to
be possible that the name Shiloh is
not a name of Christ Himself, but the
name for the eternal state — perhaps
emphasising peace — when His final
victory would be won. In this case
the passage means that Christ the
great Lawgiver, the Lion of the tribe
of Judah, after assuming royal power
at His ascension (Mt. 28. 18) would
never relinquish it till He brings forth
judgment unto victory (Mt. 12. 20).
Whatever the exact interpretation of
this difficult word, we need not have
the slightest uncertainty that in this
verse we have a prophecy of Jesus
Christ and His Kingdom.

*Unto him shall the gathering of the
people be.* The word ' him ' refers to
Judah as represented by his great descendant Christ. When the Lord was
on earth, the crowds continually gathered round Him to be healed and to
hear His teaching. Now as one generation succeeds another the Gospel is
gathering in the lost from all the
peoples of the world. On the last day
He will send His angels and gather
together His elect from the four winds
from the uttermost part of the earth
to the uttermost part of heaven (Mt.
24. 31), and His wheat will be gath-

ered into His garner (Mt. 13. 30).

Verse 11. In this and the following
verse we are directed away from Christ
Himself to His people, the true descendants of Judah and the only people
to whom the name Jew in God's sight
rightly belongs (Rom. 2. 28, 29).

Binding his foal unto the vine. This
and the parallel sentence which follows are intended to express the great
richness, fertility and fruitfulness of
the vines which will belong to Judah.
The vine will be so common that it
will be commonly used to tether asses
to. Now Jesus Christ is the true vine
and His people are its branches (Jo.
15. 5). This means that for the people
of God Christ and His riches will be
ever available and always near. ' Of
His fulness have all we received ' (Jo.
1. 16). Indeed it is the Spirit's purpose that we should be filled unto all
the fulness of God (Eph. 3. 19).
Abundance and plenty characterise the
Saviour's gifts to us. We notice that
the foal and the ass's colt will be
bound to the choice vine. The ass
represents the ordinary toiling unconverted person of the world, an unclean
but useful animal. It was to be
Judah's function to bind this foal to
the vine. So it is our joy and responsibility to bind the people of the
world to Christ with the cords of love,
so that they become His and come
themselves to enjoy the riches and
fulness which are ours already.

He washed his garments in wine.
The immediate sense of these phrases
is again to express abundance. There
will be so much wine, that garments
and clothes will be washed in it instead of in water. In both these verses
we thus find emphasis laid on the
riches and abundance available in
Christ for all who believe. Every
need is satisfied many times over. In
the New Testament this is brought out
more in the Epistle to the Ephesians,
chapters 1-3, than anywhere else. But
there is more than this in these sentences. They are quoted in Rev. 7.
14, where we find the great multitude
of the redeemed who have washed

their robes and made them white in the blood of the Lamb. The filthy garments, stained with sin, foul with stench, tattered and unfit for view, plunged into the fountain filled with blood drawn from Emmanuel's veins, emerge spotless, glittering, pure and perfectly whole. The child of God stands now here in this world clothed in the white robe of Christ's righteousness, having a perfect and irrevocable standing with God. When he takes his place among the great company of the redeemed on the day of resurrection, he will still be wearing this robe. In addition he will be clothed with the white robes of a perfectly sanctified character, all of them whitened by the blood of the Lamb applied to him by the Spirit in the new wine of the Gospel. Christ came to turn the old dirty water of Judaism into the choice wine of the Gospel (Jo. 2. 1-11).

VERSE 12. In this verse we have the last two statements about the spiritual condition of the true descendants of Judah, the people of Christ.

His eyes shall be red with wine. This means that he will have drunk of it abundantly. The child of God drinks the spiritual wine of the Gospel as the Spirit pours it out for him in the Word of God. He may drink as fully as he will. This reddens his eyes, that is to say, his sight is purified by the precious blood of Christ, the eyes of his understanding are opened (Eph. 1. 18), and he is able to perceive the things of the Spirit of God (1 Cor. 2. 13-15).

His teeth white with milk. The milk is the sincere milk of the Word (1 Pet. 2. 2). This whitens the teeth of the child of God and gives him health and beauty.

VERSE 13. The blessing of Zebulun is not Messianic in the direct sense. It concerns the then future of the tribe in Palestine, but it is typical of spiritual things.

Zebulun shall dwell at the haven of the sea. According to Joshua 19.

11 the border of Zebulun went toward the sea. It apparently reached it at a single point where Asher and Manasseh also met (Josh. 17. 7) near the town of Dor. The name Zebulun means ' dwelling '. The tribe was like the Christian church, which dwells at the haven of the sea of peoples, that troubled sea, which rages in the hearts of the wicked (Isa. 57. 20). The spiritual Zebulun lives at the haven, where it may welcome the stormtossed traveller and bring him safe to land.

He shall be for an haven of ships. Zebulun not only dwells at the haven, he is placed there for the very purpose of providing shelter. So we today stand between the raging sea of sin and the security of the heavenly land.

His border shall be unto Zidon. This does not mean that the territory of Zebulun marched with either the city or territory of Zidon, which was not the case. The word translated ' border ' means literally side. The The sentence means that the northern side of the territory of Zebulun faced Sidon, as a glance at a map of the tribes shows to have been the case. We may interpret this to mean that the aim of Zebulun was directed towards Zidon. The Zidonians were Canaanites and are thus pictures of the spiritual powers of wickedness (Eph. 6. 12). Thus those who abide in Christ and dwell at the haven of the sea, engaged in the work of rescuing and welcoming the travellers who come from it, must always be facing the devil and ready to fight him.

VERSE 14. Issachar as depicted in this and the following verse is a type of the worldly, compromising professing Christian, not like Lot one who is justified but very imperfectly sanctified, but one who is a member of the visible Christian church without having ever received the saving grace of God in his heart.

Issachar is a strong ass. He is not one of Christ's sheep, but one of the devil's asses. The ass is an unclean animal and represents the unregenerate man.

Couching down between two burdens. In the case of the tribe of Issachar in Palestine this probably means that it was situated between two groups of unconquered Canaanites. How true this is spiritually of the strong unregenerate ass, who like Issachar has a place outwardly and by profession within the covenant relationship with God. He couches down between the burden of his sin on the one hand and that of his religion on the other. He has no power to rid himself of the former and no courage to cast off the latter.

VERSE 15. *He saw that rest was good.* He was unprepared to enter the fight against the Lord's enemies. He sought ease and comfort.

The land that it was pleasant. He is prepared to enjoy a comfortable churchmanship, so long as it does not make demands upon his energy or require of him enthusiasm or the loss of respectability. He gladly conforms to a polite and worldly religious society.

Bowed his shoulder to bear. In order to obtain an easy life he submits to what Satan lays on him. A comfortable set of beliefs in conformity with modern thought go with a decent standard of citizenship. The voice of conscience is scarcely ever heard, being stilled by evenings of bridge at the club, the church whist drives, or the beauties of the sea coast and countryside when seen on Sunday afternoon car trips, which provide relief from the dull morning service in church.

Became a servant unto tribute. Issachar's friends are not told about the tribute. ' He that committeth sin is the servant of sin ' (Jo. 8. 34). Issachar does not care to think of death and the life to come, and he is enraged or at least uncomfortable if he is brought in touch with a true Christian.

VERSE 16. *Dan shall judge his people.*

The name Dan means ' judge '. The reference may be to Samson, the most conspicuous of the judges (Jud. 13-16). The great Judge Who will judge all His people is the Lord Jesus Christ.

As one of the tribes of Israel. This seems to mean that the tribe of Dan will produce a judge, as it did in Samson, as much as any other of the tribes. The tribe of Dan was a true Israelite tribe. These words, if this be their proper emphasis, form a background for what follows.

VERSE 17. *Dan shall be a serpent by the way.* The reference seems to be to the introduction of idolatry by the tribe of Dan. An idolatrous worship became the recognised religion of the settlement which they acquired at Laish not long after the death of Joshua (Jud. 18), and it was here that Jeroboam, the first king of northern Israel, set up one of the two golden calves that he made (1 Ki. 12. 26-30). In all this we see a picture of the introduction of heathen idolatry into the Christian church in the time of Constantine the Great and later by Christians who compromised with the world and set themselves up in league with the state as judges of their own people.

That biteth the horse heels. The horse and his rider are no picture of true spiritual things. The type points rather to the pomp and glory of the world, and from this we may learn that it is the world and the unconverted who suffer from apostasy in the church. During the centuries-long mediæval apostasy, which was only broken by the Reformation, perishing heathen waited in vain for generation after generation for the Gospel to be brought to them.

VERSE 18. *I have waited for thy salvation, O Lord.* Jacob here echoes and makes his own the cry of the saints down all the generations, as they see wickedness apparently in power, sin rampant, apostasy deepening, and the truth appearing to prevail little. How long, O Lord, dost Thou not judge? (Rev. 6. 10). Not that believers have not assurance of salvation. They enjoy unhindered peace with God, and they find the Holy Spirit at work in their hearts in sanctifying power. But they all groan within themselves, looking for the redemption of their body (Rom. 8. 23) on the glorious day of resurrection, when Satan will be bruised under their feet (Rom. 16. 20). So as he sees the horse heels bitten and the rider falling backward, the believer waits patiently but longingly for the salvation ready to be revealed in the last time (1 Pet. 1. 5).

The above interpretation of the blessing of Dan seems to be the natural one, because it accounts for the known history of the tribe of Dan in Palestine in Old Testament times. It is however possible to see an alternative, which makes Dan in these verses a type of Christ. As judge of his people Dan is the picture of Christ the final judge. The serpent and adder may also be pictures of Christ made sin on the cross (Jo. 3. 14), and the horse and rider may be sin and Satan bitten and made to fall by the Divine serpent in dying victory. In that case this fall of the rider would be the very salvation that Jacob mentions, to the accomplishment of which he looks forward.

Verse 19. The bleessing of God in this verse is a description of the redemptive acts of Christ and likewise of the destiny of His people. A troop of devils and wicked sinners overcame Christ (or appeared to do so) when His hour was come and He was handed over by His Father to the power of darkness. But Christ will overcome at the last. His victory is already won and His triumph apparent. He is seated at God's right hand waiting for the final subjugation of His enemies. In the same way Gad, the troop of God's people, is overcome by the troop of Satan, sin and death, lost in Adam, subjugated to sin and under the power of the grave. This powerful troop overcame the people of God. But they will overcome in the end by the merits of Christ and through His power. Satan is overcome by the blood of the Lamb, sin in others (as often also in themselves) is overcome by the word of their testimony, and death is overcome, when they love not their lives, in a glorious resurrection at the end.

Verse 20. Out of Asher. This means ' out of the inheritance occupied by Asher.' Asher's land provides him with bread that is fat. So does the inheritance of the people of the Lord. That inheritance is the Lord Himself, and He feeds them on the fat of the land. They feast on Christ in His Word. Like Asher's their land yields them royal dainties, food fit for kings, distributed to His people by Christ from His Word. The people of the world cannot stomach it.

Verse 21. Two statements are made in this verse about Naphtali. As they stand, there seems no connection between them, but in fact both seem rooted in the name ' Naphtali ', which means ' wrestling '. In Naphtali we have the picture of the one who wrestles in prayer, strives against sin and struggles with the devil for the souls of men (Col. 2. 1; Heb. 12. 4). Such a one may expect the two blessings mentioned here, which spring from the wrestle in prayer.

Naphtali is a hind let loose, that is to say, he enjoys perfect freedom, ranging the parks and mountains, running and leaping with unsurpassed swiftness, without care and happy, going from pasture to pasture at will, free to breed and shelter and move. This is the privilege of the child of God who enjoys deep fellowship with Him. It is fulfilled by faith and in spirit only while he is in this world, but it is a striking picture of the joys and freedom of the world to come.

He giveth goodly words. This is another consequence of wrestling in prayer and struggling for souls. What the child of God learns in his

Father's presence he instinctively passes on, and his words are therefore always goodly. Thus in the blessing of Naphtali we have an inspired threefold picture of the Christian's spiritual life. (1) He is a wrestler in prayer and a struggler with the devil, (2) He enjoys wide freedom and fleetness of foot to pass from one delightful pasture to another. (3) He has a message of freedom and power that brings life from the dead and does good to the souls of men.

VERSE 22. This and the four following verses give us the blessing of Joseph. It is Messianic in character, but not in the same sense as that of Judah (vv. 8-12). Judah's blessing was a direct Messianic prophecy, Judah being the ancestor of Christ. The blessing of Joseph is also a description of the victories of Christ, cast in a form as if it related to Joseph himself or his descendants. It does so in the sense that Joseph was a definite type and picture of Christ. The blessing refers to the heavenly Joseph. Parts of it are adapted to the situation of the two Joseph tribes later in Palestine.

Joseph is a fruitful bough. So is Christ. He is the Branch, grown from the roots of Jesse (Isa. 11. 1; Jer. 23. 5), and He bears fruit by the Gospel throughout the world. This fruit is seen in the increase of the church, which began at Pentecost (Acts 2. 41) and will continue till the redeemed appear as an innumerable multitude (Rev. 7. 9). It is seen in the sanctified lives of His people also (Jo. 15. 5, 8, 16).

A fruitful bough by a well. The well is the source of the fruitfulness. It represents the water of life, the Holy Spirit Himself (Jo. 7. 38). The Lord Jesus Himself was filled with the Spirit (Isa. 11. 2), and the same Spirit is a well of water springing up in the hearts of God's people to eternal life (Jo. 4. 14).

Whose branches run over the wall. There may be a reference here to the extension of the tribe of Manasseh

over to the east of Jordan, one half living in Gilead and one half in Canaan proper (Josh. 13. 29-31). The descendants of Joseph were so fruitful that they overstepped the bounds of the inheritance originally intended for them. But the real reference is to the fruitfulness of Christ. His branches passed over the wall of sin and death that separates fallen man from God and carried the life-giving fruit safe on to resurrection ground in the eternal land of glory. He Himself with all His branches passed safe over Jordan. We may compare 2 Sam. 22. 30.

VERSE 23. The statements in this verse refer in the first place to the afflictions of Joseph, his sale into Egypt and his unjust imprisonment there. This however was all typical of the sufferings of the Lord Jesus Christ.

The archers have sorely grieved him. The archers are Satan, the Jews, the Romans and all the enemies of Christ. They sorely grieved Him by their attacks upon Him during His life and ministry, making Him a Man of sorrows and acquainted with grief (Isa. 53. 3).

And shot at him. When the Lord's hour was come, the arrows found their mark. He was betrayed by one of His own, arrested by His enemies, deserted by His friends, subjected to a trial that was nothing but a mockery, inhumanly treated and finally crucified. His dead body was, as it were, thrown back to His friends. All this was the action of the power of darkness (Lk. 22. 53), and yet carried out by the determinate counsel and foreknowledge of God (Acts 2. 23), Who handed His Son over to His enemies (Rom. 8. 32; 1 Cor. 11. 23). (Note the word translated ' delivered up ' in the former of these passages is the same as that translated ' betrayed ' in the latter). *And hated him.* This hatred of the world for the Son of God, manifested during His life on earth and ever since against the Gospel and those who preach it, is one of the strongest possible indications of the utter corruption of the fallen nature of man. God so loved the world that He gave His Son and sent Him into the world to save it, and the reply of the world was to murder Him (Jo. 15. 23-25). The utmost that God could do in love and mercy was met by a wild unreasoning hatred.

VERSE 24. *But his bow abode in strength.* The bow is an aggressive weapon, not one of defence, and the meaning of the passage is that in spite of the worst that His enemies could do, in spite of His death and burial in the silence of the grave, His complete cutting off out of the land of the living, yet He retained His power to attack and destroy His enemies. Indeed these very events were the means of His victory. The bow of Christ is His covenant with His people, and His arrows are the people of the covenant shot out as His witnesses into the hearts of His enemies. This covenant with all its strength and power to save remained as strong as ever through all the suffering and rejection of Christ.

The arms of his hands. This peculiar expression seems to indicate that the figure is of the hands of the mighty One of Jacob being placed on the arms or wrists of the shooter behind the hands which actually held the bow, in order to steady and strengthen them.

Were made strong. The strength of Christ during His incarnation and suffering lay in His dependence upon the Father. We shall find that ours lies in the same place. He constantly dwelt on, and spoke of, the fact that He was carrying out His Father's will.

The mighty God of Jacob. There is no noun for the Divine Name in the original. The Hebrew says 'the Mighty One of Jacob'. The expression implies that the might or strength is used especially, if not exclusively, for the advantage or protection of Jacob. Our God is a God of strength, not of weakness, and the exceeding greatness of His power is available for us who believe in accordance with the energising activity of His mighty strength (Eph. 1. 19). He is the mighty One of Jacob. His strength is at the disposal of His people.

From thence. These are important and difficult words. They are a correct translation of Hebrew *mshan.* (1) They cannot mean 'from Joseph', or 'from the tribe of Joseph'. Christ, Who is undoubtedly referred to under the titles Shepherd and Stone, did not spring from either of the tribes of Joseph, but from that of Judah (Heb. 7. 14). (2) They are very generally taken to mean 'from the mighty One of Jacob'. In this sense they are true. Christ sprang from God, was the Son of God, was sent into the world by God, and derived His work and mission from God. It may also be truly said that He was appointed the Shepherd of His people by God and laid in Sion as the Stone by God. Yet taken in this sense the sentence introduced by these words seems little more than a truism. We may try to add to its force by emphasising the titles Shepherd and Stone. We may say that it means that the particular functions and capacities of being Shepherd and Stone were marked out for Christ by God. Even so the sentence has no context. Why should there suddenly be a statement in the midst of the blessing of Joseph that Christ comes from God? (3) Is not the sentence given both force and appropriateness, if we take the words 'from thence' in the sense of 'from these things' (that is, from the fruitfulness of Joseph, the grief of Joseph, the hatred against Joseph, the strengthening of Joseph by the mighty One of Jacob) — 'from these things' we may derive a picture or type of the Shepherd and Stone of Israel, the heavenly Joseph, Jesus Himself? (4) Again we may take 'from thence' to mean 'as a result of these things', and we may refer the whole sentence to Joseph. As a result of these things Joseph has become the Shepherd and

Stone of Israel. The Bible student must seek the guidance of the Holy Spirit in selecting which alternative he considers right.

The Shepherd. Whether we take this sentence, or not, as referring in any typical sense to Joseph, it certainly refers to Christ. Jesus is the Good Shepherd (Jo. 10. 11). He feeds and cares for His flock. We men are the flock of His pasture (Ezek. 34: 23, 31). We may see from the Providence that overruled the life of Joseph what the nature of His care for His flock is. Joseph provided food for his people, nourished and sustained them, and placed them in a good land. He could not have done this, unless he had first suffered humiliation and injustice. In the same way the suffering of the Saviour lies at the root of His power to shepherd His people.

The stone of Israel. Joseph was like a rock on which the survival of Israel was founded and built. It was laid under the ground like a foundation stone when he sank into slavery and imprisonment. The heavenly Joseph is the corner stone of His people (Mt. 21. 42). He is the Rock on which His church is built (Mt. 16. 18; Eph. 2. 20), the Stone laid in Sion, elect and precious (1 Pet. 2. 6). On Him rest all His people's hopes for salvation. He carries the weight of His whole church. He is the Rock from which the living waters flow (Ex. 17. 6; 1 Cor. 10. 4), but they flow only when the Rock is cleft as the Saviour was on Calvary. He is the Rock beneath which His people shelter from the fierce heat which beats down in its implacable fulness upon Him.

VERSE 25. The statements of this verse expand that about being strengthened by the mighty One of Jacob, which we have in the previous verse.

Even by the God of thy father. Joseph was strengthened by the God Who had made promises to Jacob, strengthened in order to be the minister and shepherd of the whole family

and thus be instrumental in fulfilling the blessings and promises. In the same way Christ became a minister of the circumcision in order to confirm the promises made to the fathers (Rom. 15. 8).

Who shall help thee. While we need more than help, yet the Bible often speaks of God helping us. His help is included in His salvation. It involves support and shelter, but it implies co-operation in the spheres in which it operates. The help of God can never be given to unbelievers. One of the chief spheres of God's help is in prayer. Thus the Spirit helps our infirmities, because we do not know what to pray for as we ought (Rom. 8. 26).

The Almighty. This is the third title of God in these two verses. He is the mighty One of Jacob, that is to say, the bestower of power on His people. He is the God of our father, that is to say, the One Who has pledged His word to us. He is also the Almighty, Shaddai, that is to say, the God of all grace.

Who shall bless thee. God's blessing gives prosperity and increase. Notice the threefold blessing: (1) *blessings of heaven above.* All the blessings of heaven are Christ's. He came with the clouds of heaven and was brought near to the Ancient of Days (Dan. 7. 13). He has entered into heaven itself, now to appear before the presence of God for us (Heb. 9. 24). His throne is established for ever in heaven (Ps. 89. 36, 37). He is blessed for ever by the angels in heaven (Rev. 5. 12). (2) *blessings of the deep that lieth under.* In the Name of Jesus every knee shall bow of those that are under the earth (Phil. 2. 10). The dead in Christ will rise to bless Him and glorify Him for ever. (3) *blessings of the breasts, and of the womb.* This means a great increase of descendants. As the Gospel spreads, the people of Christ increase until they become a great multitude that no man can number (Rev. 7. 9). In the case of the tribes of Joseph in Palestine the blessings refer to (1) the sunshine and rain from heaven, (2) the fertility of the earth in which the seed lies hidden, (3) abundant human fertility.

VERSE 26. *The blessings of thy father have prevailed above the blessings of my progenitors.* Notice the increase in Jacob's faith and his growth in grace which took place during the last seventeen peaceful years of his life when he was in Egypt, his troubles over and his brightest hopes for this present life fulfilled. When he comes into Egypt he says that his days had been few and evil (47. 9). Towards the end he says that God had fed him all his life long and the Angel of God had redeemed him from all evil (48. 16). Now right at the end he says that he has been blessed infinitely more than his forbears. Thus his complaints were turned to contentment, and finally to a realisation that he had been loaded lavishly with benefits. The precise meaning of Jacob's statement here depends on whom he is referring to when he speaks of ' my progenitors '. (1) If he means Abraham and Isaac, we can scarcely think of him as saying that his spiritual blessings were much greater than theirs. If he means this, he can only be meaning it in the sense that he had been infinitely more unworthy than they to receive God's blessing. The story of his life shows that there is truth in such an estimate. (2) Again he may be referring to temporal blessings consisting of the numbers of his family, which contrasts with the one son of Abraham and the two sons of Isaac, and of the peaceful sojourn in Egypt in his old age, where he was kept in plenty while the world was starving. Such blessings however could scarcely be said to prevail *unto the utmost bound of the everlasting hills,* and it is difficult to see how they could be passed on to Joseph. They cannot be messianic. (3) If he means by his progenitors his heathen ancestors in Mesopotamia, he is associating himself with Abraham and Isaac as the recipient of covenant blessings. Of the three alternatives, Nos. 1 and 3 are the most probable, and No. 3 perhaps the more satisfactory.

Unto the utmost bound of the everlasting hills. Into eternity and the world to come.

They shall be on the head of Joseph. Joseph is here the type of the heavenly Joseph, the Shepherd and Stone of Israel. The covenant blessings and promises are all concentrated on the head of the Lord Jesus Christ, the promised seed in Whom they are all fulfilled.

On the crown of the head of him that was separate from his brethren. Joseph was separate from his brethren. In childhood he was given a special place in his father's affections and marked out to be his heir. He was sold away from his family as a slave and passed over twenty years in Egypt apart from his father and brothers. After they rejoined him he was still separate, being the shepherd and sustainer of them all. But in all these things he was a picture of Jesus, to Whom the words apply much more suitably. The Lord Jesus is separate from His brethren as being the Son of God from all eternity, Who came down from heaven and was made man. He was separate from sinners, the spotless Son of God (Heb. 7. 26). He was separate from His brethren as He hung dying for them on the cross. ' Jesus there alone for sinners did atone ' . He was separate in resurrection of which He is the firstfruits (1 Cor. 15. 23). He is separate from them today as He sits in exaltation on the throne of God, their forerunner in the Holy Presence (Heb. 6. 20). However much He is one with His people, He will always be personally unique.

VERSE 27. The predictions about Benjamin in this verse may refer (1) to the Benjamite wars recorded in Jud. 20 and 21. Benjamin here certainly ravined as a wolf. In the two battles that he won he devoured the prey. Later he divided the spoil when he captured the women of Jabesh-Gilead. (2) The prophecy may also refer to King Saul, the first King of Israel, who was a Benjamite. This warrior king devoured the prey and divided the spoil. Yet he proved a wolf all the time, devouring the flock of God. (3) The prediction is often taken to refer to the greatest of all members of the tribe of Benjamin, the apostle Paul. Before his conversion he ravined as a wolf against the people of God and devoured them like prey (Acts 9. 1, 2; 26. 9-11), but after his conversion he took much spoil for Christ. (4) In this last sense the prophecy is fulfilled in every child of God, who, whether he actually persecutes or not, is like Paul a wolf by nature, raging against and devouring the people of God and the Gospel by selfishness and sin, but when brought to Christ begins a life of victorious witness and with all Christ's people divides the spoil.

VERSE 28. *All these are the twelve tribes of Israel.* This is intended as a proper literary conclusion to the blessing. This statement also implies that the recipients of the blessing are definitely limited in number and character. The blessing is for the tribes of Israel. In the same way the spiritual blessings of the Gospel are for the believing people of Christ, the new Israel, and quite definitely for them alone.

This is it that their father spake unto them, and blessed them. As the recipients are limited, so the blessing is definite. It was decreed by God, known to God, revealed by God, and spoken to them by their father in his capacity of a prophet. Our heavenly Father has also blessed us with all spiritual blessings in Christ before the world began (Eph. 1, 3, 4). These blessings were brought to us by Christ and applied to us through the Gospel. They comprise a perfect standing with God, a close personal relationship with Christ, the indwelling of the Holy Spirit, grace, repentance, faith, dominion over sin, everlasting life and

glory.

Every one according to his blessing he blessed them. Notice (1) that all the predictions made by Jacob and recorded in the verses above are called blessings. Hard things are said of some of the tribes, but yet they are all blessings. Sorrow and grief are sometimes blessings, and chastening judgments are always so. (2) The particular blessing fitted the particular tribe. It is the same with us. God blesses each one of us in the way He knows in His perfect knowledge and inscrutable wisdom to be best for us.

VERSE 29. *He charged them.* The giving and reception of this charge reveals the unity and loyalty of the family and the reverence felt for the father.

I am to be gathered unto my people. Compare 25. 8. The expression is ancient and probably referred at first to burial in a common grave. By the time of the patriarchs it meant to join one's ancestors in death in a quite general sense. It did not convey the idea of a conscious reunion in a world of ghosts. The words express the solemnity, sadness and inevitability of death, which since Adam's sin no one can escape (Rom. 5. 12), except by the miraculous intervention of God, which has occurred in only two cases (Gen. 5. 24; 2 Ki. 2. 11).

Bury me with my fathers. Notice how important it was to Jacob to be buried with his own people. The conception so prevalent today, that it does not matter what happens to the dead, is absent from the Bible. Burning, even if called by the high-sounding name of cremation, a technical term invented to mask the reality and give a false impression of reverence, was a disgrace (Am. 2. 1). Knowledge of irreverent treatment after death might bring fear and shame during life (Jer. 22. 18, 19). Not that we should suppose that the preservation or any other treatment of a body affects its resurrection (Rev. 20. 13). But man is made in the image of God, and his dead body is entitled to reverent treatment and decent burial. *In the cave.* It was a natural burying-place, not an artificial one.

The field of Ephron, the Hittite, from whom it had been bought. The family possessed no ground, even for burying. They were a pilgrim family. So the family of God possesses nothing in the world but what it must buy from the inhabitants.

VERSE 30. *In the land of Canaan,* that is, in the land of promise, in which the family had been strangers and pilgrims.

Which Abraham bought. Jacob himself had not bought it. The head of the family had done so. In the same way all that we possess has been bought for us by Christ.

For a possession of a burying-place. All that we need from the world while we are strangers and pilgrims in it is somewhere to lie dead in. We are dead in Christ and crucified to the world (Gal. 6. 14).

VERSE 31. *Sarah his wife.* She was the first to be buried there, and it was on her death that the field was purchased (23. 19). For Abraham's burial see 25. 9.

There they buried Isaac. See 35. 29.

Rebekah his wife. This is the first time we hear of Rebekah's death and burial. We are not told when or in what circumstances it took place.

There I buried Leah. She had died before the migration into Egypt. Though Rachel was the wife whom he loved, Jacob here shows an affectionate remembrance of Leah. The cave of Machpelah was the scene of a sad, yet hopeful, family gathering. It is said that the sarcophagi are still visible in the cave beneath the mosque that has been built on the site. There the faithful family sleeps awaiting the day of glorious resurrection (Mt. 8. 11; 22. 32).

VERSE 32. The purpose of these words is to make doubly sure the exact place of burial. They may have been added by Moses rather than spoken by Jacob. They emphasise the fact of the purchase and that the family were strangers and pilgrims still.

VERSE 33. *When Jacob had made an end.* He did not die until he had finished what he intended to do. In a greater sense the Saviour could say, ' I have finished the work that Thou gavest me to do ' (Jo. 17. 4), and the apostle could say, ' I have finished my course ' (2 Tim. 4. 7).

He gathered up his feet into the bed. This perhaps means that he drew up his knees in the act of dying. Notice three things that are said of Jacob in this verse. (1) This is the first. So when a man comes in Christ to die to sin in order to live to righteousness, he gathers up the feet that had run in the devil's ways and been so swift to shed blood and never puts them to the ground again. His old walk in sin and the flesh is brought to an end.

(2) *Yielded up the ghost.* Jacob's spirit returned to God Who gave it (Eccl. 12. 7). The life principle which God had given him fell back into God's reservoir, leaving the vessel which had contained it empty. So when a man dies to sin, he yields up the spirit of sin and of the world which had previously animated him and becomes spiritually minded (Rom. 8. 6).

Was gathered unto his people. He joined Abraham and Isaac in the land of darkness and silence. In the same way, but in a much happier sense, the man who dies in Christ to sin is gathered into the great family of God, which he finds to consist of his own people thenceforward, an innumerable band of brothers and sisters, with whom in Christ he is for ever bound up in the bundle of life.

CHAPTER 50

THIS last chapter of the book, which brings the story of the patriarchs to an end, falls into three distinct sections. Verses 1-13 tell of the burial of Jacob, verses 14-21 of Joseph's brothers' fear of him and his kindness to them, and verses 22-26 of the death of Joseph. The public burial of Jacob is a picture of the baptism of one who is dead with Christ (Col. 2. 12). The relationship of Joseph with his brethren is a picture of the relationship of Christ with the sinners He saves. The circumstances of Joseph's death are an example of faith (Heb. 11. 22).

VERSE 1. Notice (1) that Joseph's family affection was more to him than all his glory in Egypt. His dignity and greatness did not prevent him paying his tribute to his father. So our relationship with our heavenly Father and His family in Christ should be more to us than all our worldly circumstances or whatever position we have in this life. (2) Notice the grief and sorrow that accompany death. The sorrow of the Christian ought to be much lighter than that of the people of the world. They have no hope for the future, and no justification for having any. We have a sure and certain hope of the resurrection of the dead (1 Thess. 4. 13). (3) Notice the expression of reverence and affection which Joseph gave in kissing his father. This and the carrying out of his wishes for burial were the only ways left open to him in which to honour his father.

VERSE 2. *His servants the physicians.* They were Egyptians, outside the covenant, the type of men of the world.

To embalm his father. The Egyptians were adepts at this. To be embalmed was an honour, entailed great expense, and was usually reserved for the great. Joseph may have given the order for two reasons: (1) he may have intended to bestow special honour on his father. (2) Embalming may have been necessary, or at least very desirable, in view of the time that must elapse before Jacob's burial could take place.

The physicians embalmed Israel. In this they acted like typical men of the world. When a man becomes dead with Christ to the elements of the world by repentance and faith (Col. 2. 20), his worldly friends and acquaintances sometimes seek to embalm him, that is to say, they seek (1) to conceal the fact of death and corruption and retain him as much as possible like a man still living in the world. Embalming preserves a corpse. The physicians could not prevent death. That is a natural event which comes from the hand of God and at best can only be postponed by man. In the same way a man's worldly acquaintances may postpone his conversion or modify the circumstances of it. They can never prevent the effectual call of the elect of God. But when this call has taken place and the man has been gathered into the family of Christ's people, they can seek to dress him up like a worldling, and they sometimes succeed. Conversion reveals the corruption of sin and the rottenness of the world. Sinners try to prevent this revelation and hinder its effects. (2) Embalming is a long process. It postpones burial. Spiritual burial is baptism, the open confession of Christ before men, and if sinners cannot prevent a man's conversion, they can postpone his final break with the world, and they often succeed in doing so. Let the young Christian who has just been converted resist the process of embalming and insist on being buried quickly.

VERSE 3. *Forty days.* This was probably the time taken to complete the process of embalming. *So are fulfilled.* It was an Egyptian custom. There was a smell of the world about the circumstances of Israel's burial. There can sometimes be a worldly flavour about baptism.

The Egyptians mourned. It is a good thing when a child of God becomes so much honoured in the world that the unconverted feel his loss and mourn for him. So it was with Jacob in Egypt. Joseph was the link between them. The Egyptians were paying honour to the father of their great benefactor. We may be reminded of the funeral of Charles Simeon in the Cambridge of 1836.

Threescore and ten days. The number speaks of the Spirit of glory (1 Pet. 4. 14). This spirit had rested upon Israel.

VERSE 4. *When the days of his mourning were past.* The dead man could be kept from burial no longer. *Joseph spake unto the house of Pharaoh.* Residing in Egypt he was tied up with the Egyptians. He could make no move without their consent. This is a warning to us not to live there, but to remain in tents in the land of Canaan.

If now I have found grace in your eyes. Joseph knew that they rightly regarded him as their benefactor and friend.

Speak, I pray you, in the ears of Pharaoh. It seems that it may not have been thought proper for Joseph to enter Pharaoh's presence himself before the burial of his father.

VERSE 5. Jacob had stipulated that if he died he was not to be left in Egypt, but was to be taken up to the land of promise. It is a good thing for a man to decide at his conversion to make a complete break with the world.

VERSE 6. A foreshadowing of the servitude is seen in the fact that the King's permission had to be obtained for the burial. But God is sovereign and disposes of the hearts of kings as seems best to His Divine Majesty.

VERSE 7. *Joseph went up.* This was Joseph's first and only visit to Canaan since he had left it as a slave boy about thirty-nine years previously.

With him went up. A funeral usually attracts a varied crowd and may prove a good opportunity for witness to the Gospel. Spiritual burial is public also and a God-given opportunity for confession of Christ. Notice the six groups of people that went up with Joseph to the burial of

Jacob. (1) *All the servants of Pharaoh.* These represent the people of the world. They usually come to a funeral, and they will often come to a baptism. It is all important that the meaning of baptism be explained to them, so that they can see the Word in action and the Gospel symbolised by descent into the waters of death and the wrath of God and the rising from them to newness of life.

(2) *The elders of his house.* These perhaps represent the religious leaders, who are usually (though, thank God, not always) unconverted, even if they belong to a professing Christian Church. They will generally come to a funeral, though they might never come to a baptism. They badly need the witness.

(3) *All the elders of the land of Egypt.* These perhaps represent the officials of the government and state. A funeral or a baptism are perhaps the best opportunities to bring them within the sound of the Gospel.

VERSE 8. (4) *All the house of Joseph.* Next we come to those within the covenant. Where Gospel witness is concerned, the unconverted are the more important and are rightly placed first. This fourth group is a picture of the true church of Christ, who form the house of God (Heb. 3. 6). They went up because they had a deep personal interest in the one who was being buried.

(5) *His brethren.* This is another picture of the church (Heb. 2. 12).

(6) *His father's house.* These represent those who had a particular personal interest in the one who was being buried. They are like those who have led the one being baptised to the Lord, taught him, prayed for him, and led him on.

Their little ones. Funerals and baptisms are no more suitable occasions for little ones than they are for flocks and herds.

VERSE 9. The occasion was rightly made a great one. A great witness was given.

VERSE 10. *The threshing-floor of Atad.* This is a great place of purging. A threshing-floor is where the wheat is purged from the chaff (Mt. 3. 12), and the name Atad, though said by some to mean cactus, has usually been regarded as meaning buckthorn. A powerful purgative is obtained from it. Notice that the threshing-floor was *beyond Jordan,* which is always in the Bible the picture of death. Thus death itself, or a burial so closely associated with death, or a baptism, which is the spiritual counterpart of burial, are represented here as being purging agents. Death and destruction purge God's creation of evil. The second death will be the final purging. The Saviour's death purged our sins (Heb. 1. 3). The baptism of the Holy Ghost, which occurs to every believer at his conversion and engrafts him into Christ (Mt. 3. 11; Rom. 6. 3; 1 Cor. 12. 13; Eph. 4. 5), applies the purging of sins to the individual. Even a funeral has the effect of purging away earthly thoughts and tends to concentrate the mind on death and judgment.

They mourned. Mourning in those days was greater than it need be under the Gospel, by which life and immortality have been brought to light (2 Tim. 1. 10). It was however a proper sign of reverence for the dead, and it may perhaps be thought of as a dim instinctive recognition of God's judgment on sin. The sinner ought to mourn in repentance, so that he is saved from mourning on the day of judgment.

VERSE 11. *When the inhabitants of the land, the Canaanites, saw.* A witness was given, as is sometimes done by a funeral and always by a baptism.

A grievous mourning of the Egyptians. Egyptians are the proper people to mourn grievously. They represent the people of the world. It is sad that the Canaanites appear to have been unable to distinguish between Israelites and Egyptians. They called them all Egyptians. This was no fault of Joseph and his brethren in the circumstances of the time. They were rightly in Egypt at the command of God. The fact however is no less a warning to us that it is possible for the Christian believer to be so much wrapped up in the world that the unconverted cannot distinguish him from the worldling. *Abel-mizraim.* This means ' mourning of the Egyptians '.

Which is beyond Jordan. It is difficult to know which side of Jordan is meant. If the viewpoint is Egyptian, the expression might mean within Canaan, though there is no need to cross the Jordan to enter Canaan from Egypt. If the viewpoint is Palestinian, the expression would mean east of Jordan, that is outside the promised land. In this case it is difficult to understand what the company was doing there, as Jacob was buried in Hebron. The narrator does not give us enough detail to make this clear. The expression has a spiritual meaning however. If the mourning took place inside the promised land, we may compare it to godly sorrow (2 Cor. 7. 10). If it took place outside the land, we may compare it to the sorrow of the world (ibid). Perhaps the meaning of the words ' beyond Jordan ' is left purposely indistinct to emphasise the fact that they mean the opposite for Egyptians to what they mean for Israelites. The people of the world are on the wrong side of death. The believer is safe in Christ on resurrection ground.

VERSE 12. If only this could be said of us and of all the sons of the heavenly Father.

VERSE 13. *Carried him into the land of Canaan.* We too are carried into the land of promise by the eternal decrees of God, the propitiatory death of Christ and the work of the Holy Spirit. We cannot move one step towards it of our own accord.

Buried him. The believer is not buried with Christ in baptism (Rom. 6. 4) until he has reached the promised land.

In the cave of the field. The field is the world (Mt. 13. 38). This also is an appropriate figure. When the believer is buried with Christ in baptism to enter upon a life of service and devotion, he is in the promised land by faith (though not yet openly enjoying it) and at the same time in the world.

Which Abraham bought with the field. Thus Christ bought the world by His death, not because He needed the world (see Jo. 18. 36), but because he needed in it for the time being a burying-place for His elect, who are hidden in it till the last day.

Ephron the Hittite. He was an inhabitant of the land and thus represents the world-rulers of this darkness (Eph. 6. 12). Christ redeemed the world from the power of the devil.

VERSE 14. *Returned into Egypt.* This is what every child of God must do as long as he is in the body. From every mountain top of prayer, from every time of meditation in the heavenlies, from all communion with God and re-invigorating study of His Word we must return into Egypt.

After he had buried his father. Perhaps no other occasion would produce a greater reaction than this. So worldly reaction may appear in our own lives, and we need constantly to rely on the keeping power of God.

VERSE 15. In this and the following six verses we have a touching account of the relationship of Joseph and his brethren, which is full of moral and spiritual lessons.

When Joseph's brethren saw that their father was dead. Their faith had been set in the wrong place. They were relying for peace and assurance upon a temporal factor, which was now taken away from them. Many Christians do the same. Sometimes trust is placed, for example, in the fellowship of a particular group, or in an individual minister or particular ministry.

Joseph will peradventure hate us. They cruelly misjudged their Shepherd and Rock. We too find it hard not to believe that His wrath will break out on us and to fear the day of judgment.

Will certainly requite us all the evil which we did unto him. These words speak to us clearly of the strength and persistence of an evil conscience. The brethren had had many proofs of Joseph's goodwill towards them, but their guilt, speaking to them across the long years of the past, persuaded them that he would take vengeance upon them. They were quite mistaken and wrong. They were like the Christian who had received grace but lacks assurance. We may notice that their guilty fears did not alter the actual situation. Joseph had no vengeful intentions against them. We may thank God that our hearts are sprinkled from an evil conscience (Heb. 10. 22), and that if our heart condemn us, God is greater than our heart (1 Jo. 3. 20).

VERSE 16. *They sent a messenger unto Joseph.* They were afraid to go to him themselves. The Christian who lacks assurance sometimes fears and fails to pray. He seeks for an intermediary between himself and his Saviour and is prone to fall into the hands of those who call themselves priests and profess to be able to act as such.

Thy father did command before he died. There is no evidence for the truth of this statement. They seem to have made it up. They tried to move the mind of Joseph with other considerations than those of his mere grace. Many people try to approach God in such ways.

VERSE 17. *Forgive, I pray thee, now.* They were right to ask for forgiveness, although they were only moved by fear. The first step in approaching Christ must be to ask for forgiveness.

The trespass of thy brethren, and their sin. Notice the twofold definition of their wicked act. Their trespass was their conduct towards Joseph which overstepped the proper bounds of brotherly affection and right behaviour. Their sin was their failure to show the kindness which they ought to have shown. When we are dealing with trespass and sin against God, we may see in the former the evil actions which are the fruit of the latter, the sinful fallen nature.

They did unto thee evil. If Jacob had never actually said this, he must have known and felt it. So every sinner in the world has done evil to Christ by causing His crucifixion, neglecting His Gospel, opposing His servants and rejecting His love.

Now, we pray thee, forgive. They were right to ask. Their fears showed that their wicked treatment of their innocent brother had been the outstanding event of their lives, eating like a canker into their hearts and peace of mind. They were reminded immediately of it when trouble first came to them on their journey into Egypt to buy corn (42. 21). Even after their reconciliation to Joseph, the consciousness of it never left them. Their father's death brought it again to the surface, and guilty consciences continued to trouble them. Here is a shadow and faint picture of the fear and guilt of the unconverted on the day of judgment. There they will realise their sin against Christ, and the rejection and crucifixion of God's Son will be brought home to them.

The servants of the God of thy father. If they meant that they were within the covenant, their plea was a right one. They confessed the true God. Whether they did so sincerely or insincerely we cannot tell. They showed at least that they knew that there was a difference between their God and those of the Egyptians.

Joseph wept. This shows his mercy, tenderness and love. His heart was a picture of that of the Saviour, which goes out in compassion to all His people, and especially perhaps to the sinner who comes to Him for the first time to ask for forgiveness.

VERSE 18. *His brethren also went.* After sending the messenger they took courage to go themselves. The sinner must never be satisfied with the prayers of a child of God on his behalf. If he wants forgiveness and reconciliation, he must go himself to Christ.

Fell down before his face. So the one who needs forgiveness from Christ must come in humility and lowly worship, acknowledging Him to be Sovereign and Lord.

We be thy servants. Everyone who asks and obtains forgiveness is thereby called to the service of Christ. He invites us to take His yoke upon us at the same time as we find rest to our souls (Mt. 11. 29).

VERSE 19. *Fear not.* These happy comforting words are spoken by the Saviour to every repenting sinner. ' Fear not, only believe ' (Mk. 5. 36), and they are spoken again and again to the weak, doubting, trembling saint throughout his life in the flesh.

Am I in the place of God? Joseph seems to mean that he has no right to condemn them, but being their fellow-sinner can only forgive them. If this is his meaning, we have another proof of the wonderful extent to which he had been led and taught by the Holy Ghost.

VERSE 20. *Ye thought evil against me.* In the same way Christ by wicked hands was crucified and slain (Acts 2. 23). The Jews thought evil against Him and delivered Him up to be slain.

God meant it unto good. In the same way it was by the crucifixion and resurrection of Christ that God fulfilled the promises made through the prophets and to the fathers (Acts 13. 32, 33). The sale of Joseph was only fulfilling the purpose of God for the covenant family. In the same way the infinitely greater redemptive purpose of God was fulfilled through wicked men who rejected and crucified Christ.

To save much people alive. All who

believe are saved from eternal death by the death of the Saviour. Without it they would have perished.

Verse 21. *Now therefore fear ye not.* Joseph's recognition of the hand of God in all that had happened was the basis of his attitude towards his brothers. In the same way our faith in what God has done for us in Christ should govern our attitude to our fellow-men. We also need not fear. If when we were enemies we were rconciled to God by the death of His Son, how much more shall we be saved from wrath by His life (Rom. 5. 9, 10). *I will nourish you.* So Christ feeds us through His Word with the living Bread from heaven.

Your little ones. Those led to Christ by believers are also nourished and fed.

He comforted them. So the Holy Spirit comes to live in the heart of each believer to comfort and assure his heart.

Spake kindly unto them. The Holy Spirit does this to each believer throughout his life on earth, opening up to him great and precious promises from God's Word and assuring his heart of God's favour and love.

Verse 22. In the last five verses of the chapter the whole book of Genesis draws to a quiet close with the account of Joseph's death in Egypt.

Joseph dwelt in Egypt. This every believer must do so long as he is in the flesh. He dwells in the world, though if he is truly Christ's, he is never of it. Here he has no abiding city (Heb. 13. 14), but he awaits the redemption of his body (Rom. 8. 23), just as the Israelites in Egypt waited for the great exodus to fulfil the promises made to the fathers.

An hundred and ten years. This was a shorter life than that of the three great patriarchs. The length of human life was gradually approximating to what is now normal. The number emphasises the number eleven, which is often associated in the Bible

with disintegration and death.

Verse 23. *Ephraim's children of the third generation.* They were Joseph's great-grandchildren. Joseph was allowed to see the purpose of God for the increase of the family into a nation going on towards fulfilment. He had proof enough given him of the final fulfilment of all the blessings and promises. And so have we as we see the hand of God at work in the spread of the Gospel in the world.

Verse 24. *I die.* These are words that each of us must one day say, unless the coming of the Lord in glory and the end of the world supervene. Joseph's time had come, as the time of each one of us will. But there is no more for the believer to fear in death than in going to sleep each night.

God will surely visit you. Joseph was referring to the exodus. This was to be a great typical redemptive act, delivering the people from Egyptian bondage and bringing them safe to the promised land. So in an infinitely greater way God in Christ has visited and redeemed His people (Lk. 1. 68). We also look for the last glorious visitation to bring us resurrection at the end of the world.

Bring you out of this land. God has brought us already out of the power of Satan and sin (1 Jo. 5. 18; Rom. 6. 14). On the day of resurrection He will bring us safe out of this world altogether and deliver us finally from the power of death.

Unto the land which he sware to Abraham, to Isaac, and to Jacob. God will bring us in to the heavenly land that He has promised us in Christ, the new heaven and earth wherein dwelleth righteousness. Just as the promises were made to the ancestors of the Israelites before they were born, so were God's promises made to Christ in eternity past, and we benefit from them because we are one with Christ.

VERSE 25. *Joseph took an oath of the children of Israel.* Because of this the Holy Ghost in the Epistle to the Hebrews includes Joseph among the heroes of faith and says that it was by faith that he gave this commandment (Heb. 11. 22). He trusted in, rested on, and acted on the promises of God.

God will surely visit you. He repeats his certainty of the intervention of God to carry out His purpose and fulfil His promises.

Ye shall carry up my bones. So they did (Ex. 13. 19; Josh. 24. 32). Preserved through the centuries of bondage and the perils of the wilderness journey, the bones found their resting place at last in the place of Joseph's choice. If God could preserve the bones of Joseph through all these vicissitudes, how much more will He preserve us and bring us finally safe to our inheritance reserved for us in the promised land (1 Pet. 1. 4).

VERSE 26. *Joseph died.* The patriarchal age was finished. That of the nation had begun.

An hundred and ten years old. See on verse 22.

They embalmed him. The Egyptians did this. They wished to honour him for all the service that he had given to them. Notice that their action made no difference to Joseph either good or bad. If we too are dead with Christ from the elements of the world (Col. 2. 20), the honours of the world will affect us no more than the reproaches and persecutions of the world, and as little as they affected Joseph.

He was put in a coffin in Egypt. This is a dramatic ending to the book of Genesis. It speaks to us vividly of the power of sin and death and the extent of man's fall. The book which begins, ' In the beginning God created the heavens and earth ', ends ' in a coffin in Egypt.' All seems lost, finished, reduced to dust and ashes, futility and vanity. This would be the story of man apart from Christ. We may thank God that it is not the end of the story.

NOTES

NOTES

NOTES

NOTES